W9-BMU-699

Teacher Edition

fusion [FYOO • zhuhn] a combination of two or more things that releases energy

HOLT McDOUGAL

HOUGHTON MIFFLIN HARCOURT

Professional Development

Houghton Mifflin Harcourt and NSTA, the National Science Teacher's Association, have partnered to provide customized professional and development resources for teachers using *ScienceFusion*.

The Professional Development Resources in the NSTA Learning Center include:

—do-it-yourself resources, where you can study at your own pace.

—live and archived online seminars.

—journal articles, many of which include lesson plans.

—fee-based eBooks, eBook chapters, online short courses, symposia, and conferences.

Access to the NSTA Learning Center is provided in the *ScienceFusion* Online Resources.

Acknowledgments for Covers

Volcanic eruption (bg) ©Photo Researchers, Inc.; *viscous lava* (l) ©Bruce Omori/epa/Corbis; *Mars Rover* (cl) ©Mark Garlick/Photo Researchers, Inc.; *mushroom rock* (cr) ©John Elk III/Alamy; *anemometer* (r) ©Ryan McGinnis/Flickr/Getty Images.

Interior, digital screens: *giraffes* ©Corbis.

Printed in the U.S.A.

ISBN 978-0-547-59387-6

7 8 9 10 2266 20 19 18 17 16 15 14

4500503962 C D E F G

Contents in Brief

About the Program

Teaching Tools

Units at a Glance

Resources

Consulting Authors

Michael A. DiSpezio

Global Educator
North Falmouth, Massachusetts

Michael DiSpezio is a renaissance educator who moved from the research laboratory of a Nobel Prize winner to the K–12 science classroom. He has authored or coauthored numerous textbooks and written more than 25 trade books. For nearly a decade, he worked with the JASON Project under the auspices of the National Geographic Society, where he designed curriculum, wrote lessons, and hosted dozens of studio and location broadcasts. Over the past two decades, he has developed supplementary material for organizations and shows that include PBS's *Scientific American Frontiers, Discover* magazine, and the Discovery Channel. He has extended his reach outside the United States and into topics of crucial importance today. To all his projects, he brings his extensive background in science and his expertise in classroom teaching at the elementary, middle, and high school levels.

Marjorie Frank

Science Writer and
Content-Area Reading Specialist
Brooklyn, New York

An educator and linguist by training, a writer and poet by nature, Marjorie Frank has authored and designed a generation of instructional materials in all subject areas, including past HMH Science programs. Her other credits include authoring science issues of an award-winning children's magazine; writing game-based digital assessments in math, reading, and language arts; and serving as instructional designer and coauthor of pioneering school-to-work software for Classroom Inc., a nonprofit organization dedicated to improving reading and math skills for middle and high school learners. She wrote lyrics and music for *SCIENCE SONGS*, which was an American Library Association nominee for notable recording. In addition, she has served on the adjunct faculty of Hunter, Manhattan, and Brooklyn Colleges, teaching courses in science methods, literacy, and writing.

Michael R. Heithaus

Director, School of Environment and Society
Associate Professor, Department of Biological Sciences
Florida International University
North Miami, Florida

Mike Heithaus joined the Florida International University Biology Department in 2003. He has served as Director of the Marine Sciences Program and is now Director of the School of Environment and Society, which brings together the natural and social sciences and humanities to develop solutions to today's environmental challenges. While earning his doctorate, he began the research that grew into the Shark Bay Ecosystem Project in Western Australia, with which he still works. Back in the United States, he served as a Research Fellow with National Geographic, using remote imaging in his research and hosting a 13-part *Crittercam* television series on the National Geographic Channel. His current research centers on predator-prey interactions among vertebrates, such as tiger sharks, dolphins, dugongs, sea turtles, and cormorants.

Donna M. Ogle

Professor of Reading and Language
National-Louis University
Chicago, Illinois

Creator of the well-known KWL strategy, Donna Ogle has directed many staff development projects translating theory and research into school practice in middle and secondary schools throughout the United States. She is a past president of the International Reading Association and has served as a consultant on literacy projects worldwide. Her extensive international experience includes coordinating the Reading and Writing for Critical Thinking Project in Eastern Europe, developing an integrated curriculum for a USAID Afghan Education Project, and speaking and consulting on projects in several Latin American countries and in Asia. Her books include *Coming Together as Readers; Reading Comprehension: Strategies for Independent Learners; All Children Read;* and *Literacy for a Democratic Society.*

Program Reviewers

Content Reviewers

Paul D. Asimow, PhD
Professor of Geology and Geochemistry
Division of Geological and Planetary Sciences
California Institute of Technology
Pasadena, CA

Laura K. Baumgartner, PhD
Postdoctoral Researcher
Molecular, Cellular, and Developmental Biology
University of Colorado
Boulder, CO

Eileen Cashman, PhD
Professor
Department of Environmental Resources Engineering
Humboldt State University
Arcata, CA

Hilary Clement Olson, PhD
Research Scientist Associate V
Institute for Geophysics, Jackson School of Geosciences
The University of Texas at Austin
Austin, TX

Joe W. Crim, PhD
Professor Emeritus
Department of Cellular Biology
The University of Georgia
Athens, GA

Elizabeth A. De Stasio, PhD
Raymond H. Herzog Professor of Science
Professor of Biology
Department of Biology
Lawrence University
Appleton, WI

Dan Franck, PhD
Botany Education Consultant
Chatham, NY

Julia R. Greer, PhD
Assistant Professor of Materials Science and Mechanics
Division of Engineering and Applied Science
California Institute of Technology
Pasadena, CA

John E. Hoover, PhD
Professor
Department of Biology
Millersville University
Millersville, PA

William H. Ingham, PhD
Professor (Emeritus)
Department of Physics and Astronomy
James Madison University
Harrisonburg, VA

Charles W. Johnson, PhD
Chairman, Division of Natural Sciences, Mathematics, and Physical Education
Associate Professor of Physics
South Georgia College
Douglas, GA

Tatiana A. Krivosheev, PhD
Associate Professor of Physics
Department of Natural Sciences
Clayton State University
Morrow, GA

Joseph A. McClure, PhD
Associate Professor Emeritus
Department of Physics
Georgetown University
Washington, DC

Mark Moldwin, PhD
Professor of Space Sciences
Atmospheric, Oceanic, and Space Sciences
University of Michigan
Ann Arbor, MI

Russell Patrick, PhD
Professor of Physics
Department of Biology, Chemistry, and Physics
Southern Polytechnic State University
Marietta, GA

Patricia M. Pauley, PhD
Meteorologist, Data Assimilation Group
Naval Research Laboratory
Monterey, CA

Stephen F. Pavkovic, PhD
Professor Emeritus
Department of Chemistry
Loyola University of Chicago
Chicago, IL

L. Jeanne Perry, PhD
Director (Retired)
Protein Expression Technology Center
Institute for Genomics and Proteomics
University of California, Los Angeles
Los Angeles, CA

Kenneth H. Rubin, PhD
Professor
Department of Geology and Geophysics
University of Hawaii
Honolulu, HI

Brandon E. Schwab, PhD
Associate Professor
Department of Geology
Humboldt State University
Arcata, CA

Marllin L. Simon, Ph.D.
Associate Professor
Department of Physics
Auburn University
Auburn, AL

Larry Stookey, PE
Upper Iowa University
Wausau, WI

Kim Withers, PhD
Associate Research Scientist
Center for Coastal Studies
Texas A&M University-Corpus Christi
Corpus Christi, TX

Matthew A. Wood, PhD
Professor
Department of Physics & Space Sciences
Florida Institute of Technology
Melbourne, FL

Adam D. Woods, PhD
Associate Professor
Department of Geological Sciences
California State University, Fullerton
Fullerton, CA

Natalie Zayas, MS, EdD
Lecturer
Division of Science and Environmental Policy
California State University, Monterey Bay
Seaside, CA

Teacher Reviewers

Ann Barrette, MST
Whitman Middle School
Wauwatosa, WI

Barbara Brege
Crestwood Middle School
Kentwood, MI

Katherine Eaton Campbell, M Ed
Chicago Public Schools-Area 2 Office
Chicago, IL

Karen Cavalluzzi, M Ed, NBCT
Sunny Vale Middle School
Blue Springs, MO

Katie Demorest, MA Ed Tech
Marshall Middle School
Marshall, MI

Jennifer Eddy, M Ed
Lindale Middle School
Linthicum, MD

Tully Fenner
George Fox Middle School
Pasadena, MD

Dave Grabski, MS Ed
PJ Jacobs Junior High School
Stevens Point, WI

Amelia C. Holm, M Ed
McKinley Middle School
Kenosha, WI

Ben Hondorp
Creekside Middle School
Zeeland, MI

George E. Hunkele, M Ed
Harborside Middle School
Milford, CT

Jude Kesl
Science Teaching Specialist 6–8
Milwaukee Public Schools
Milwaukee, WI

Joe Kubasta, M Ed
Rockwood Valley Middle School
St. Louis, MO

Mary Larsen
Science Instructional Coach
Helena Public Schools
Helena, MT

Angie Larson
Bernard Campbell Middle School
Lee's Summit, MO

Christy Leier
Horizon Middle School
Moorhead, MN

Helen Mihm, NBCT
Crofton Middle School
Crofton, MDL

Jeff Moravec, Sr., MS Ed
Teaching Specialist
Milwaukee Public Schools
Milwaukee, WI

Nancy Kawecki Nega, MST, NBCT, PAESMT
Churchville Middle School
Elmhurst, IL

Mark E. Poggensee, MS Ed
Elkhorn Middle School
Elkhorn, WI

Sherry Rich
Bernard Campbell Middle School
Lee's Summit, MO

Mike Szydlowski, M Ed
Science Coordinator
Columbia Public Schools
Columbia, MO

Nichole Trzasko, M Ed
Clarkston Junior High School
Clarkston, MI

Heather Wares, M Ed
Traverse City West Middle School
Traverse City, MI

Power up with SCIENCE FUSION

Print

The **Write-in Student Edition** teaches science content through constant **interaction** with the text.

Labs and Activities

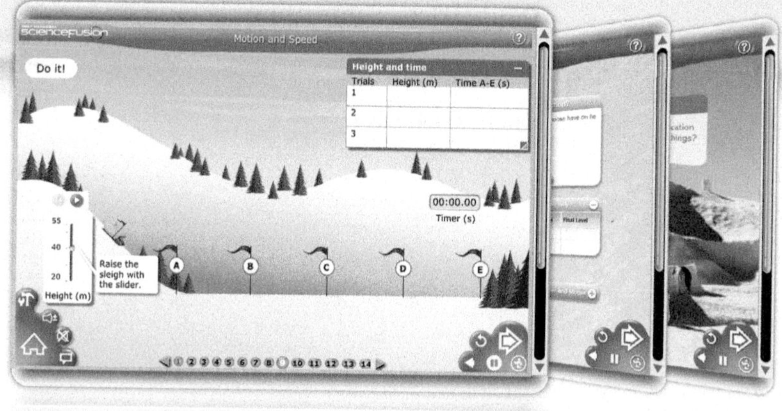

Digital

The parallel **Digital Curriculum** provides **e-learning digital lessons and virtual labs** for every print lesson of the program.

Energize your students through a multimodal blend of Print, Inquiry, and Digital experiences.

The Hands-on Labs and Virtual Labs

provide meaningful and exciting inquiry experiences.

Unit Assessment

Formative Assessment

Strategies RTI
Throughout TE

Lesson Reviews SE

Unit PreTest

Summative Assessment

Alternative Assessment
(1 per lesson) RTI

Lesson Quizzes

Unit Tests A and B

Unit Review RTI
(with answer remediation)

Practice Tests
(end of module)

Project-Based Assessment

See the Assessment Guide for quizzes and tests.

Go Online to edit and create quizzes and tests.

See RTI teacher support materials.

Print

The **Write-in Student Edition** teaches science content through constant **interaction** with the text.

360° of Inquiry

Write-in Student Edition

The *ScienceFusion* write-in student edition promotes a student-centered approach for

- learning and applying inquiry skills in the student edition
- building STEM and 21st Century skills
- keeping digital natives engaged and interactive

Research shows that an interactive text teaches students how to relate to content in a personal, meaningful way. They learn how to be attentive, energetic readers who reach a deep level of comprehension.

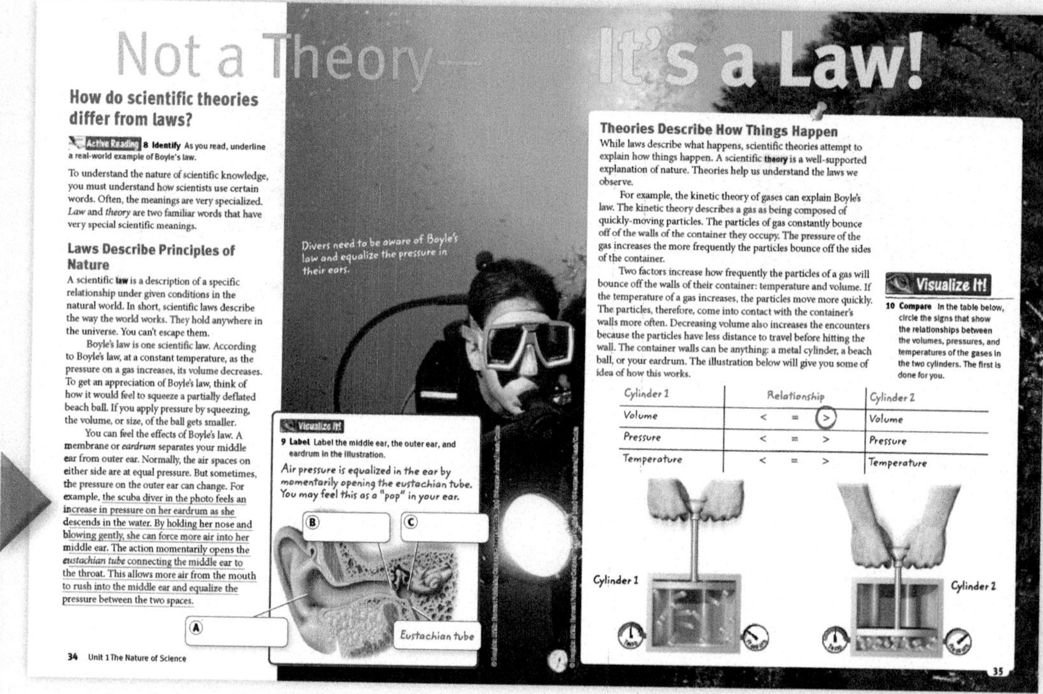

Not a Theory—It's a Law!

How do scientific theories differ from laws?

Active Reading **8 Identify** As you read, underline a real-world example of Boyle's law.

To understand the nature of scientific knowledge, you must understand how scientists use certain words. Often, the meanings are very specialized. *Law* and *theory* are two familiar words that have very special scientific meanings.

Laws Describe Principles of Nature

A scientific **law** is a description of a specific relationship under given conditions in the natural world. In short, scientific laws describe the way the world works. They hold anywhere in the universe. You can't escape them.

Boyle's law is one scientific law. According to Boyle's law, at a constant temperature, as the pressure on a gas increases, its volume decreases. To get an appreciation of Boyle's law, think of how it would feel to squeeze a partially deflated beach ball. If you apply pressure by squeezing, the volume, or size, of the ball gets smaller.

You can feel the effects of Boyle's law. A membrane or *eardrum* separates your middle ear from outer ear. Normally, the air spaces on either side are at equal pressure. But sometimes, the pressure on the outer ear can change. For example, the scuba diver in the photo feels an increase in pressure on her eardrum as she descends in the water. By holding her nose and blowing gently, she can force more air into her middle ear. The action momentarily opens the *eustachian tube* connecting the middle ear to the throat. This allows more air from the mouth to rush into the middle ear and equalize the pressure between the two spaces.

Divers need to be aware of Boyle's law and equalize the pressure in their ears.

Visualize It!

9 Label Label the middle ear, the outer ear, and eardrum in the illustration.

Air pressure is equalized in the ear by momentarily opening the eustachian tube. You may feel this as a "pop" in your ear.

A
B
C
Eustachian tube

34 Unit 1 The Nature of Science

Theories Describe How Things Happen

While laws describe what happens, scientific theories attempt to explain how things happen. A scientific **theory** is a well-supported explanation of nature. Theories help us understand the laws we observe.

For example, the kinetic theory of gases can explain Boyle's law. The kinetic theory describes a gas as being composed of quickly-moving particles. The particles of gas constantly bounce off of the walls of the container they occupy. The pressure of the gas increases the more frequently the particles bounce off the sides of the container.

Two factors increase how frequently the particles of a gas will bounce off the walls of their container: temperature and volume. If the temperature of a gas increases, the particles move more quickly. The particles, therefore, come into contact with the container's walls more often. Decreasing volume also increases the encounters because the particles have less distance to travel before hitting the wall. The container walls can be anything: a metal cylinder, a beach ball, or your eardrum. The illustration below will give you some of idea of how this works.

Visualize It!

10 Compare In the table below, circle the signs that show the relationships between the volumes, pressures, and temperatures of the gases in the two cylinders. The first is done for you.

Cylinder 1	Relationship	Cylinder 2
Volume	< = >	Volume
Pressure	< = >	Pressure
Temperature	< = >	Temperature

Cylinder 1

Cylinder 2

35

Big Ideas & Essential Questions

Each unit is designed to focus on a Big Idea and supporting lesson-level Essential Questions.

S.T.E.M.

STEM activities in every unit ask students to apply engineering and technology solutions in scenario-based learning situations.

Connect Essential Questions

At the close of every unit, students build enduring understandings through synthesizing connections between different Essential Questions.

Think Outside the Book

Students may wish to keep a Science Notebook to record illustrations and written work assignments. Blank pages at the end of each unit can also be used for this purpose.

Active Reading

Annotation prompts and questions throughout the text teach students how to analyze and interact with content.

Visualize It!

As concepts become more abstract, Visualize It! provides additional support for conceptual understanding.

The **Hands-on Labs** and **Virtual Labs** provide meaningful and exciting inquiry experiences.

360° of Inquiry

Labs and Activities

S.T.E.M. Engineering & Technology

STEM activities in every unit focus on

- **engineering and technology**
- **developing critical thinking and problem solving skills**
- **building inquiry, STEM, and 21st Century skills**

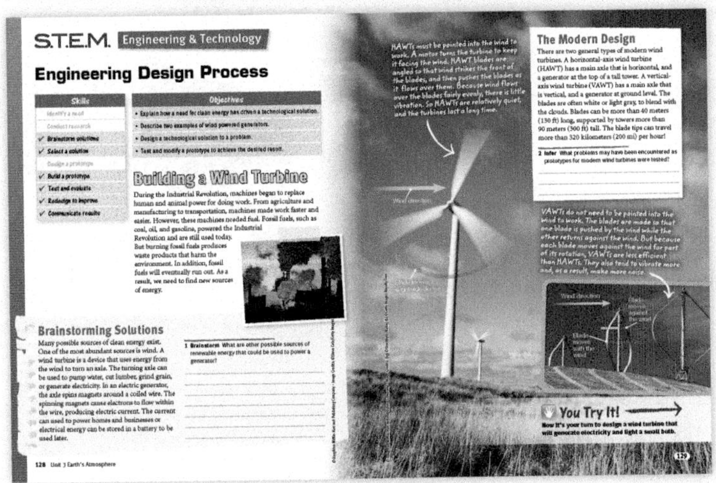

Scenario-Based STEM Activity

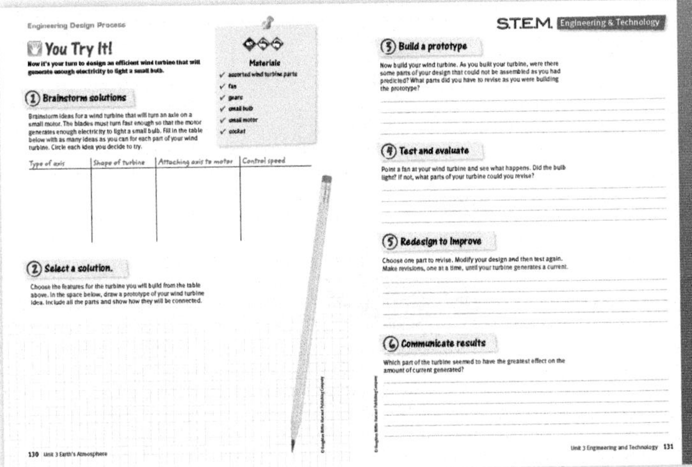

You Try It!

Hands-On and Virtual

Three levels—directed, guided, and independent—of labs and activities plus lesson level Virtual Labs give students wall-to-wall options for exploring science concepts and building inquiry skills.

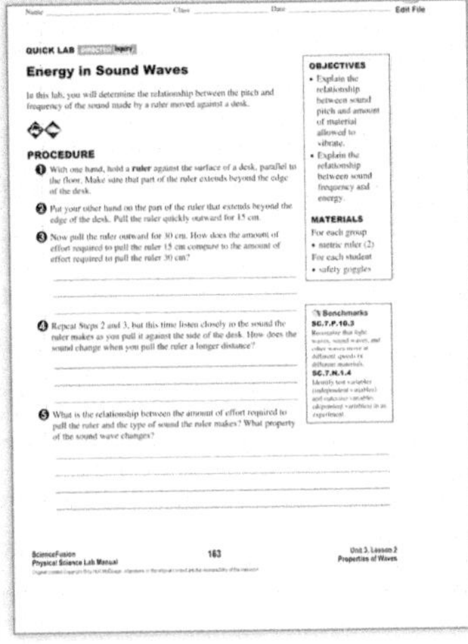

Hands-On Labs and Activities

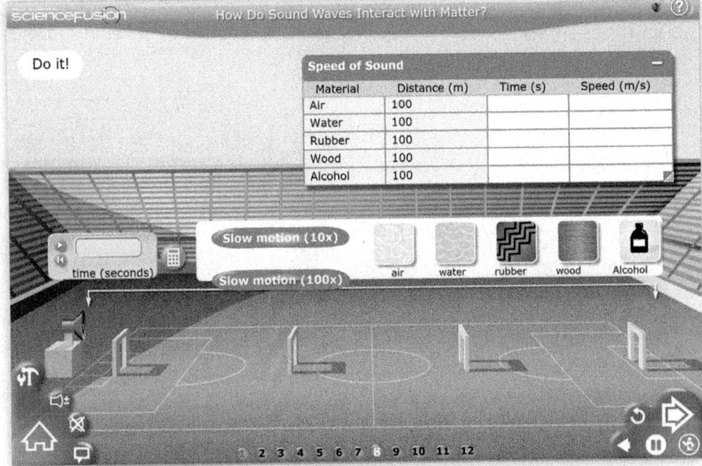

Material	Distance (m)	Time (s)	Speed (m/s)
Air	100		
Water	100		
Rubber	100		
Wood	100		
Alcohol	100		

Virtual Lab

The parallel-to-print **Digital Curriculum** provides **e-learning digital lessons and virtual labs** for every print lesson of the program.

360° of Inquiry

Digital Lessons and Virtual Labs

Digital Lessons and Virtual Labs provide an e-Learning environment of interactivity, videos, simulations, animations, and assessment designed for the way digital natives learn. An online Student Edition provides students anytime access to their student book.

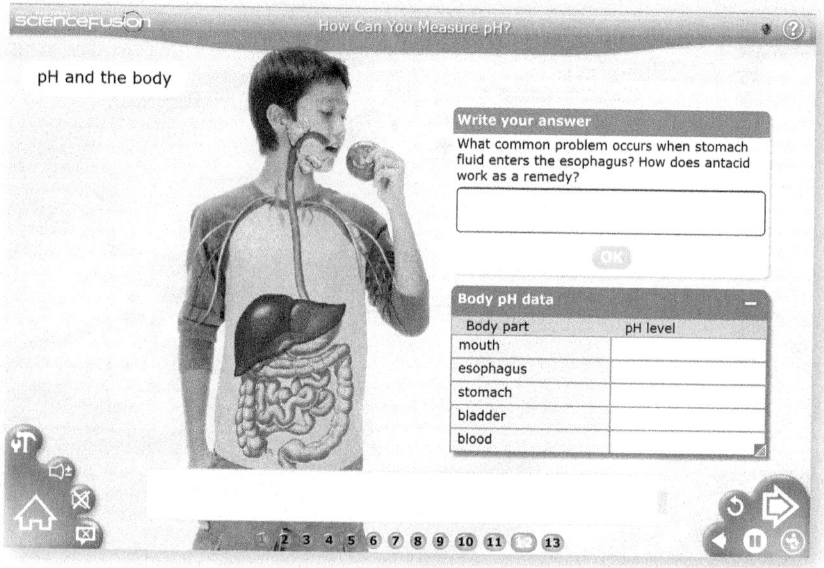

Digital Lessons

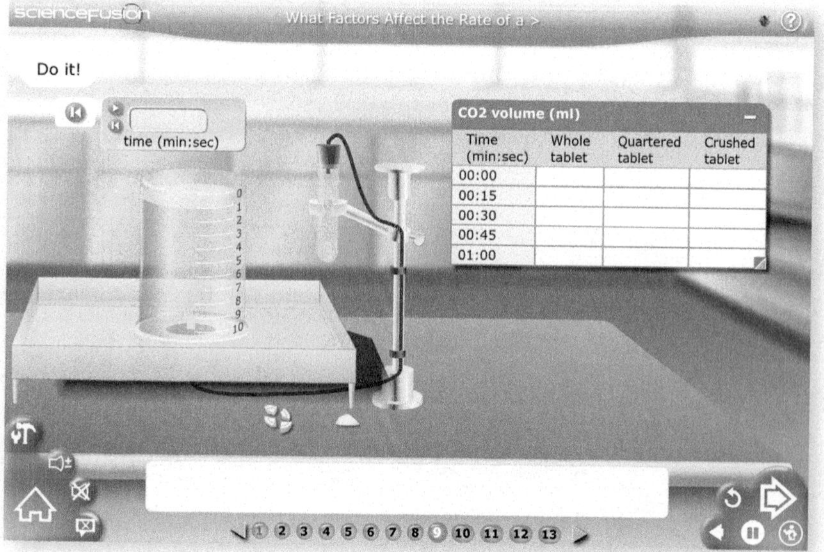

Virtual Labs

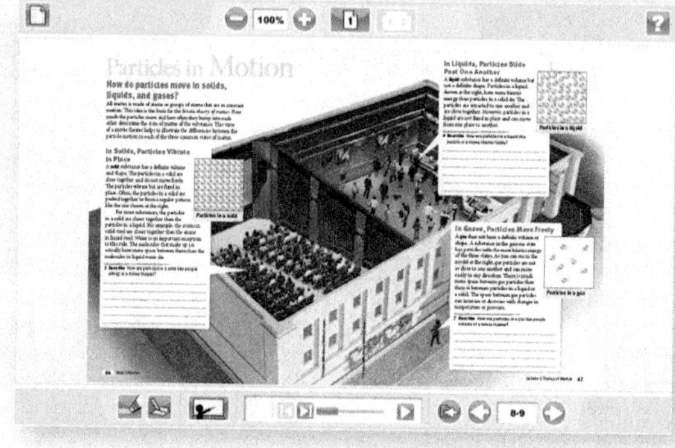

Online Student Edition

Video-Based Projects

Also available online:

- NSTA *SciLinks*
- Digital Lesson Progress Sheets
- Video-Based Projects
- Virtual Lab Datasheets
- People in Science Gallery
- Media Gallery
- Extra Support for Vocabulary and Concepts

All paths lead to a full suite of print and online **Assessment Options** right at your fingertips.

Classroom Management
Integrated Assessment Options

The *ScienceFusion* assessment options give you maximum flexibility in assessing what your students know and what they can do. Both the print and digital paths include formative and summative assessment. See the **Assessment Guide** for a comprehensive overview of your assessment options.

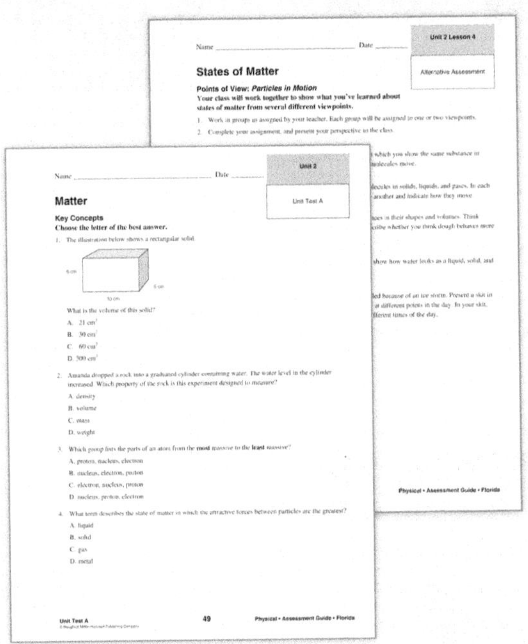
Unit 2 Lesson 4

Alternative Assessment

States of Matter

Points of View: *Particles in Motion*

Unit 2

Unit Test A

Matter

Key Concepts

Choose the letter of the best answer.

Print Assessment

The print **Assessment Guide** includes

- **Lesson Quizzes**
- **Unit Tests**
- **Unit Performance Assessments**

Teacher Online Management Center

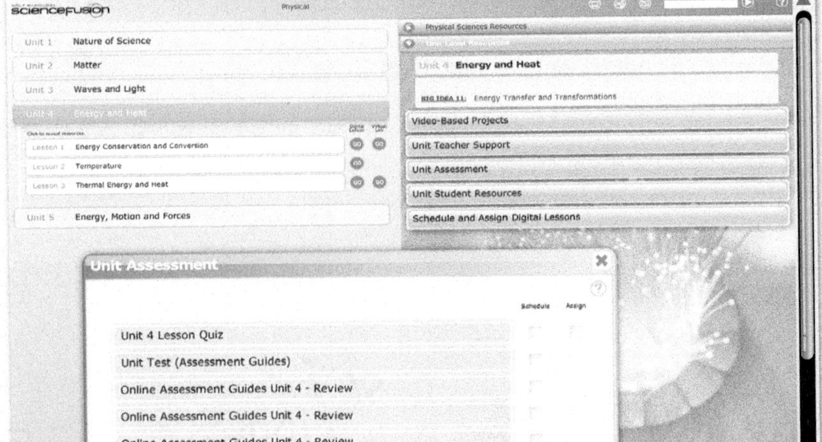

Online Assessment

The **Digital Assessment** includes

- **assignable leveled assessments for individuals**
- **customizable lesson quizzes and unit tests**
- **individual and whole class reporting**

Customizing Assessment for Your Classroom

Editable quizzes and tests are available in ExamView and online at **thinkcentral.com.** You can customize a quiz or test by adding or deleting items, revising difficulty levels, changing formats, revising sequence, and editing items. Students can also take quizzes and tests directly online.

Choose Your Options

with two powerful teaching tools— a comprehensive **Teacher Edition** and the **Teacher Online Management Center.**

Classroom Management Teacher Edition

Lesson level teaching support, includes activities, probing questions, misconception alerts, differentiated instruction, and interpreting visuals.

- **Lessons organized around a 5E lesson format**
- **Comprehensive support—print, digital, or hands-on—to match all teaching styles.**
- **Extension strategies for every lesson give teacher more tools to review and reinforce.**

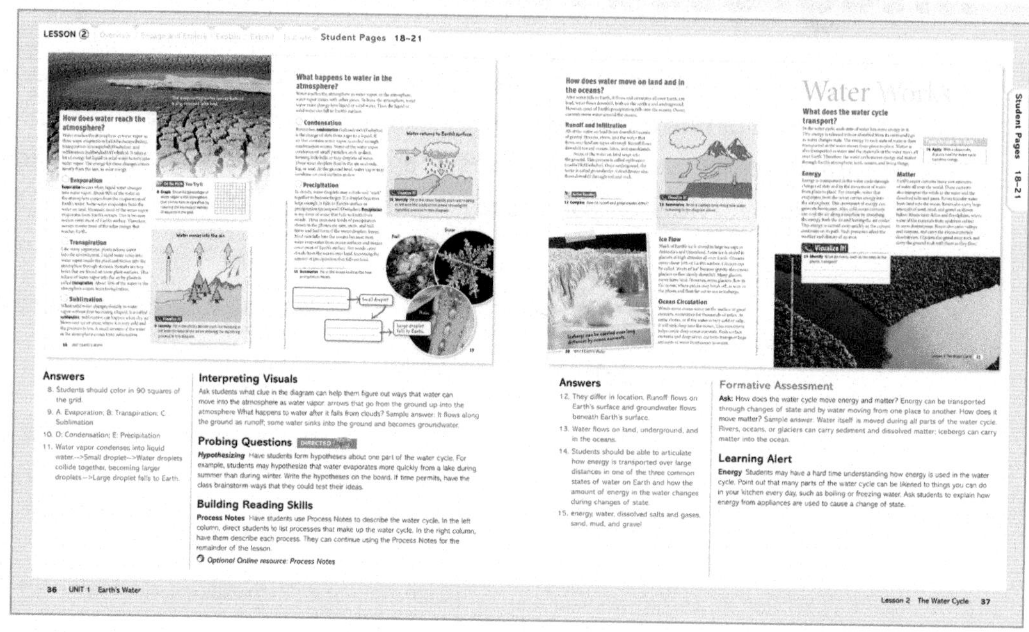

LESSON 2 Student Pages 18–21

Answers

8. Students should color in 90 squares of the grid.
9. A: Evaporation; B: Transpiration; C: Sublimation
10. D: Condensation; E: Precipitation
11. Water vapor condenses into liquid water.-->Small droplet-->Water droplets collide together, becoming larger droplets-->Large droplet falls to Earth.

Interpreting Visuals

Ask students what clue in the diagram can help them figure out ways that water can move into the atmosphere as water vapor. arrows that go from the ground up into the atmosphere What happens to water after it falls from clouds? Sample answer: It flows along the ground as runoff; some water sinks into the ground and becomes groundwater.

Probing Questions DIRECTED

Hypothesizing Have students form hypotheses about one part of the water cycle. For example, students may hypothesize that water evaporates more quickly from a lake during summer than during winter. Write the hypotheses on the board. If time permits, have the class brainstorm ways that they could test their ideas.

Building Reading Skills

Process Notes Have students use Process Notes to describe the water cycle. In the left column, direct students to list processes that make up the water cycle. In the right column, have them describe each process. They can continue using the Process Notes for the remainder of the lesson.

Optional Online resource: Process Notes

36 UNIT 1 Earth's Water

Answers

12. They differ in location. Runoff flows on Earth's surface and groundwater flows beneath Earth's surface.
13. Water flows on land, underground, and in the oceans.
14. Students should be able to articulate how energy is transported over large distances in one of the three common states of water on Earth and how the amount of energy in the water changes during changes of state.
15. energy, water, dissolved salts and gases, sand, mud, and gravel

Formative Assessment

Ask: How does the water cycle move energy and matter? Energy can be transported through changes of state and by water moving from one place to another. How does it move matter? Sample answer: Water itself is moved during all parts of the water cycle. Rivers, oceans, or glaciers can carry sediment and dissolved matter; icebergs can carry matter into the ocean.

Learning Alert

Energy Students may have a hard time understanding how energy is used in the water cycle. Point out that many parts of the water cycle can be likened to things you can do in your kitchen every day, such as boiling or freezing water. Ask students to explain how energy from appliances are used to cause a change of state.

Lesson 2 The Water Cycle 37

- Easy access to NSTA's e-professional development center, *The Learning Center*
- SciLinks provide students and teachers content-specific online support.

21st Century SKILLS

Additional support for STEM activities focuses on 21st century skills and helping students master the multi-dimensional abilities required of them in the 21st century.

RTI Response to Intervention

Response to Intervention is a process for identifying and supporting students who are not making expected progress toward essential learning goals.

Probing Questions

Lesson level questions and suggestions provide teachers with options for getting students to think more deeply and critically about a science concept.

Professional Development

Unit and lesson level professional development focuses on supporting teachers and building educator capacity in key areas of academic achievement.

Learning Alert MISCONCEPTION

The Learning Alert section previews Inquiry Activities and Lessons to gather and manage the materials needed for each lesson.

Classroom Management

Online teaching and planning

ScienceFusion is a comprehensive, multimodal science program that provides all the digital tools teachers need to engage students in inquiry-based learning. *The Teacher Online Management Center,* at thinkcentral.com, is designed to make it easier for teachers to access program resources to plan, teach, assess, and track.

- Program resources can be easily previewed in PDF format and downloaded for editing.
- Assign and schedule resources online, and they will appear in your students' inboxes.
- All quizzes and tests can be taken and automatically scored online.
- Easily monitor and track student progress.

Teaching with Technology Made Easy

ScienceFusion's 3,000+ animations, simulations, videos, & interactivities are organized to provide

- flexible options for delivering exciting and engaging digital lessons
- Teacher Resource Questions, for every lesson, to ensure that the important information is learned
- multimodal learning options that connect online learning to concepts learned from reading, writing, and hands-on inquiry

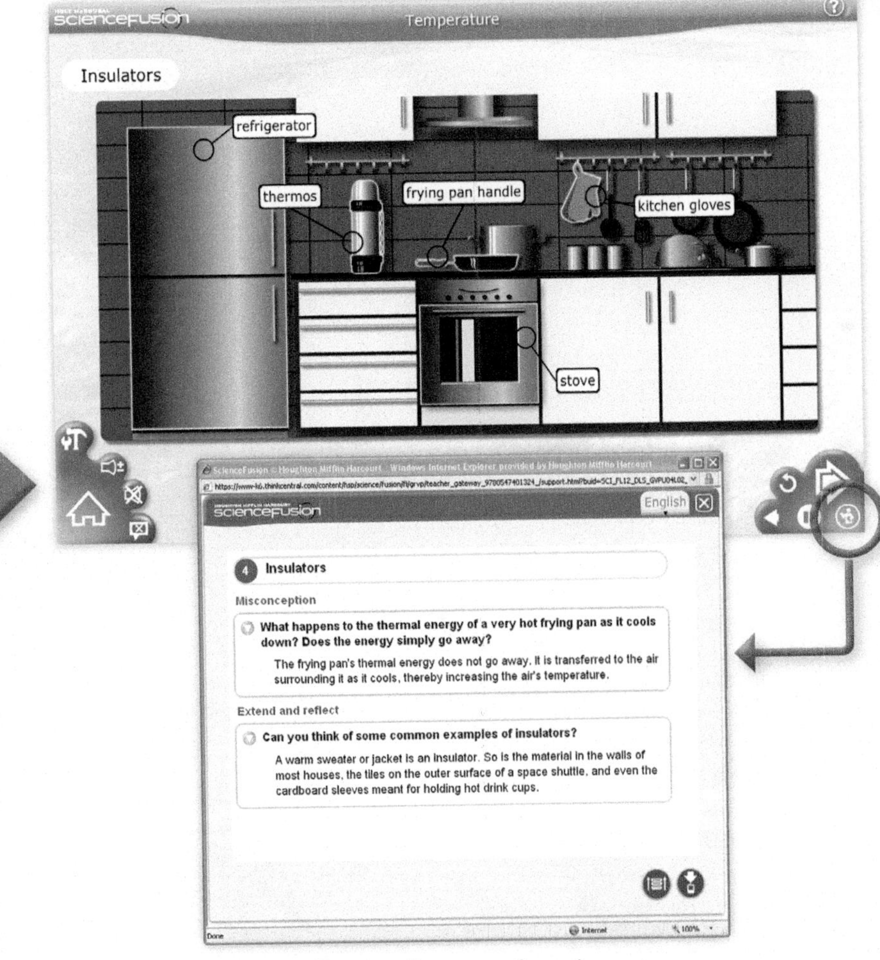

Teacher Resource Questions

Student Edition Contents

Although most of Earth's water is found in the oceans and in ice, a large amount of water is also part of the atmosphere.

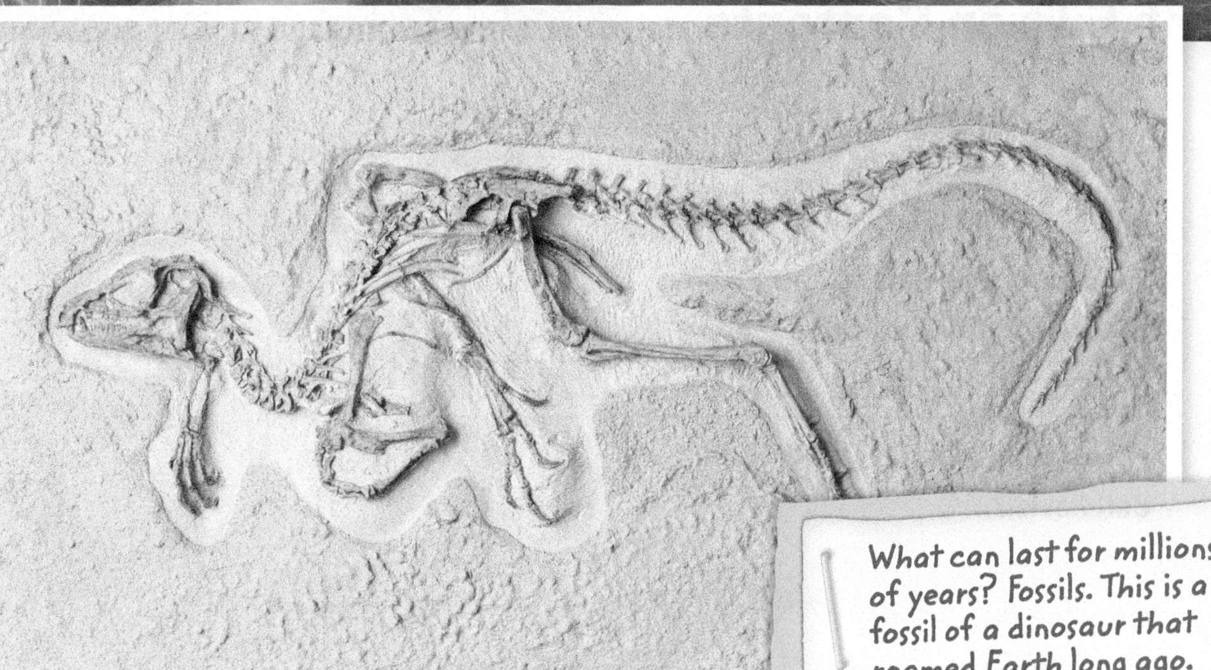

What can last for millions of years? Fossils. This is a fossil of a dinosaur that roamed Earth long ago.

The trilobite was a marine organism.

Assignments:

Student Edition Contents

The huge White Cliffs of Dover were formed from the skeletons of organisms like the microscopic marine algae shown here.

Assignments:

Imagine how hot it must be for rock to melt and flow like water! That's lava for you.

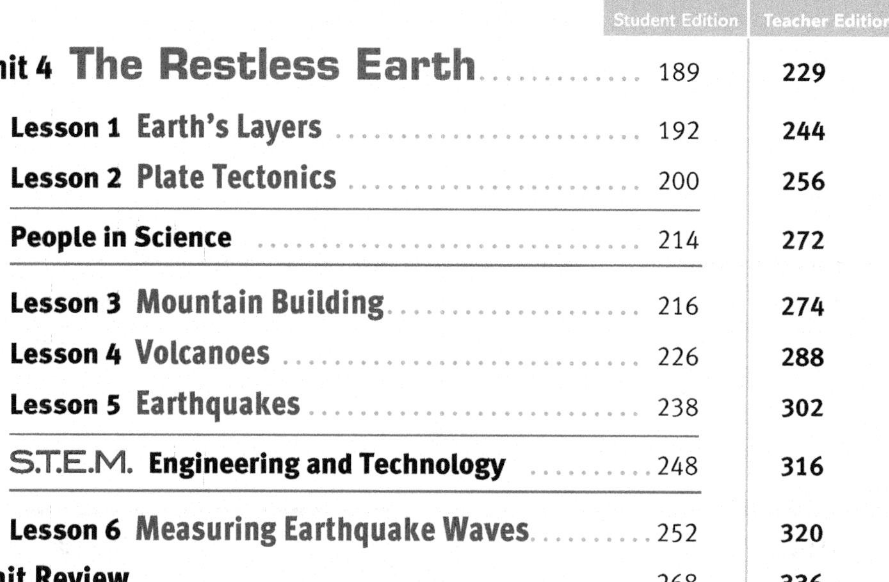

Movement in Earth's crust releases tremendous amounts of energy, which can cause a lot of damage.

Program Scope and Sequence

ScienceFusion is organized by five major strands of science. Each strand includes Big Ideas that flow throughout all grade levels and build in rigor as students move to higher grades.

ScienceFusion Grade Levels and Units

	GRADE K	GRADE 1	GRADE 2	GRADE 3
Nature of Science	**Unit 1** Doing Science	**Unit 1** How Scientists Work	**Unit 1** Work Like a Scientist	**Unit 1** Investigating Questions
STEM		**Unit 2** Technology All Around Us	**Unit 2** Technology and Our World	**Unit 2** The Engineering Process
Life Science	**Unit 2** Animals **Unit 3** Plants **Unit 4** Habitats	**Unit 3** Animals **Unit 4** Plants **Unit 5** Environments	**Unit 3** All About Animals **Unit 4** All About Plants **Unit 5** Environments for Living Things	**Unit 3** Plants and Animals **Unit 4** Ecosystems and Interactions

GRADE 4	GRADE 5	GRADES 6-8
Unit 1 Studying Science	**Unit 1** How Scientists Work	**Module K** Introduction to Science and Technology **Unit 1** The Nature of Science **Unit 2** Measurement and Data
Unit 2 The Engineering Process	**Unit 2** The Engineering Process	**Module K** Introduction to Science and Technology **Unit 3** Engineering, Technology, and Society
Unit 3 Plants and Animals **Unit 4** Energy and Ecosystems	**Unit 3** Cells to Body Systems **Unit 4** Living Things Grow and Reproduce **Unit 5** Ecosystems **Unit 6** Energy and Ecosystems	**Module A** Cells and Heredity **Unit 1** Cells **Unit 2** Reproduction and Heredity **Module B** The Diversity of Living Things **Unit 1** Life over Time **Unit 2** Earth's Organisms **Module C** The Human Body **Unit 1** Human Body Systems **Unit 2** Human Health **Module D** Ecology and the Environment **Unit 1** Interactions of Living Things **Unit 2** Earth's Biomes and Ecosystems **Unit 3** Earth's Resources **Unit 4** Human Impact on the Environment

ScienceFusion Grade Levels and Units

	GRADE K	GRADE 1	GRADE 2	GRADE 3
Earth Science	**Unit 5** Day and Night **Unit 6** Earth's Resources **Unit 7** Weather and the Seasons	**Unit 6** Earth's Resources **Unit 7** Weather and Seasons **Unit 8** Objects in the Sky	**Unit 6** Earth and Its Resources **Unit 7** All About Weather **Unit 8** The Solar System	**Unit 5** Changes to Earth's Surface **Unit 6** People and Resources **Unit 7** Water and Weather **Unit 8** Earth and Its Moon
Physical Science	**Unit 8** Matter **Unit 9** Energy **Unit 10** Motion	**Unit 9** All About Matter **Unit 10** Forces and Energy	**Unit 9** Changes in Matter **Unit 10** Energy and Magnets	**Unit 9** Matter **Unit 10** Simple and Compound Machines

GRADE 4	GRADE 5	GRADES 6-8
Unit 5 Weather **Unit 6** Earth and Space	**Unit 7** Natural Resources **Unit 8** Changes to Earth's Surface **Unit 9** The Rock Cycle **Unit 10** Fossils **Unit 11** Earth's Oceans **Unit 12** The Solar System and the Universe	**Module E** The Dynamic Earth **Unit 1** Earth's Surface **Unit 2** Earth's History **Unit 3** Minerals and Rocks **Unit 4** The Restless Earth **Module F** Earth's Water and Atmosphere **Unit 1** Earth's Water **Unit 2** Oceanography **Unit 3** Earth's Atmosphere **Unit 4** Weather and Climate **Module G** Space Science **Unit 1** The Universe **Unit 2** The Solar System **Unit 3** The Earth-Moon-Sun System **Unit 4** Exploring Space
Unit 7 Properties of Matter **Unit 8** Changes in Matter **Unit 9** Energy **Unit 10** Electricity **Unit 11** Motion	**Unit 13** Matter **Unit 14** Light and Sound **Unit 15** Forces and Motion	**Module H** Matter and Energy **Unit 1** Matter **Unit 2** Energy **Unit 3** Atoms and the Periodic Table **Unit 4** Interactions of Matter **Unit 5** Solutions, Acids, and Bases **Module I** Motion, Forces, and Energy **Unit 1** Motion and Forces **Unit 2** Work, Energy, and Machines **Unit 3** Electricity and Magnetism **Module J** Sound and Light **Unit 1** Introduction to Waves **Unit 2** Sound **Unit 3** Light

ScienceFusion

Video-Based Projects

Available in Online Resources

This video series, hosted by program authors Michael Heithaus and Michael DiSpezio, develops science learning through real-world science and engineering challenges.

Ecology

Leave your lab coat at home! Not all science research takes place in a lab. Host Michael Heithaus takes you around the globe to see ecology field research, including tagging sharks and tracking sea turtles. Students research, graph, and analyze results to complete the project worksheets.

Module	Video Title
A	Photosynthesis
B	Expedition Evolution Animal Behavior
D	A Trip Down Shark River The Producers of Florida Bay
E	Transforming Earth
I	Animals in Motion
J	Animals and Sound
K	Invaders in the Everglades Data from Space

S.T.E.M. Science, Technology, Engineering, and Math

Host Michael DiSpezio poses a series of design problems that challenge students' ingenuity. Each video follows the engineering process. Worksheets guide students through the process and help them document their results.

Module	Video Title
A	An Inside View**
C	Prosthetics Robotic Assist**
D	Got Water?
E	Seismic Monitoring
F	When the Wind Blows Tornado Warning
G	Soft Landing
H	Just Add Heat
I	Take the Long Way

** In partnership with Children's Hospital Of Boston

Enduring Understandings

Big Ideas, Essential Questions

by Marjorie Frank

It goes without saying that a primary goal for your students is to develop understandings of science concepts that endure well past the next test. The question is, what is the best way to achieve that goal?

Research and learning experts suggest that students learn most effectively through a constructivist approach in which they build concepts through active involvement in their own learning. While constructivism may lead to superior learning on a lesson-by-lesson basis, the approach does not address how to organize lessons into a program of instruction. Schema theory, from cognitive science, suggests that knowledge is organized into units and that information is stored in these units, much as files are stored in a digital or paper folder. Informed by our understanding of schema theory, we set about organizing *ScienceFusion*. We began by identifying the Big Ideas of science.

Big Ideas are generalizations—broad, powerful concepts that connect facts and events that may otherwise seem unrelated. Big Ideas are implicit understandings that help the world make sense. Big Ideas define the "folders," or units, of *ScienceFusion*. Each is a statement that articulates the overarching teaching and learning goals of a unit.

Essential Questions define the "files," or information, in a unit. Each Essential Question identifies the conceptual focus of a lesson that contributes to your students' growing understanding of the associated Big Idea. As such, Essential Questions give your students a sense of direction and purpose.

With *ScienceFusion*, our goal is to provide you with a tool that helps you help your students develop Enduring Understandings in science. Our strategy for achieving that goal has been to provide lesson plans with 5E-based learning experiences organized in a framework informed by schema theory.

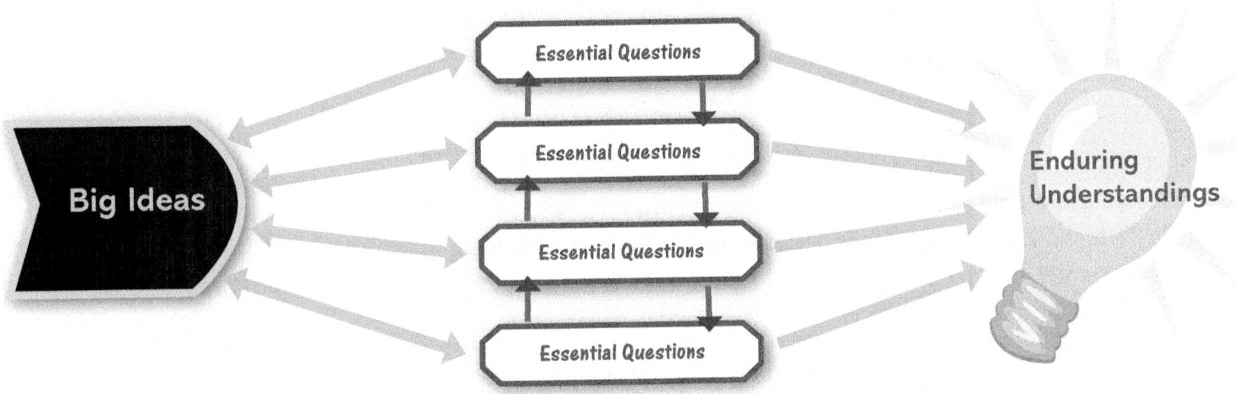

21st Century Skills/STEM

Skills Redefined

by Michael A. DiSpezio

Our world has changed. Globalization and the digital revolution have redefined the skill set that is essential for student success in the classroom and beyond. Known collectively as 21st Century Skills, these areas of competence and aptitude go beyond the three Rs of reading, writing, and arithmetic. 21st Century Skills incorporate a battery of high-level thinking skills and technological capabilities.

21st Century SKILLS A Sample List

Learning and Innovation Skills

- Creativity and Innovation
- Critical Thinking and Problem Solving
- Communication and Collaboration

Information, Media, and Technology Skills

- Information Literacy
- Media Literacy
- ICT (Information, Communications, and Technology) Literacy

Life and Career Skills

- Flexibility and Adaptability
- Initiative and Self-Direction
- Productivity and Accountability
- Leadership and Responsibility

S.T.E.M.

Curriculum that integrates Science, Technology, Engineering, and Mathematics

21st Century Skills are best taught in the context of the core subject areas. Science makes an ideal subject for integrating these important skills because it involves many skills, including inquiry, collaboration, and problem solving. An even deeper level of incorporating these skills can be found with Science, Technology, Engineering, and Mathematics (STEM) lessons and activities. Hands-on STEM lessons that provide students with engineering design challenges are ideal for developing Learning and Innovation Skills. Students develop creativity and innovation as they engineer novel solutions to posed problems. They communicate and collaborate as they engage higher-level thinking skills to help shape their inquiry experience. Students assume ownership of the learning. From this emerges increased self-motivation and personal accountability.

With STEM lessons and activities, related disciplines are seamlessly integrated into a rich experience that becomes far more than the sum of its parts. Students explore real-world scenarios using their understanding of core science concepts, ability for higher level analysis, technological know-how, and communication skills essential for collaboration. From this experience, the learner constructs not only a response to the STEM challenge, but the elements of 21st Century Skills.

ScienceFusion provides deep science content and STEM lessons, activities, and Video-Based Projects that incorporate and develop 21st Century Skills. This provides an effective learning landscape that will prepare students for success in the workplace—and in life.

Professional Development

Differentiated Instruction

Reaching All Learners

by Marjorie Frank

Your students learn in different ways, at different speeds, and through different means. Channeling the energy and richness of that diversity is part of the beauty of teaching. A classroom atmosphere that encourages academic risk-taking encourages learning. This is especially true in science, where learning involves making predictions (which could turn out to be inaccurate), offering explanations (which could turn out to be incomplete), and doing things (which could result in observable mistakes).

Like most people, students are more likely to take risks in a low-stress environment. Science, with its emphasis on exploring through hands-on activities and interactive reading, provides a natural vehicle for low-stress learning. Low stress, however, may mean different things to different people. For students with learning challenges, low stress may mean being encouraged to respond at the level they are able. Another factor in meeting the needs of diverse students is the instructional tools. Are they flexible? Inviting? *ScienceFusion* addresses the needs of diverse students at every step in the instructional process.

As You Plan

Select from these resources to meet individual needs.

- For each unit, the Differentiated Instruction page in the Teacher Edition identifies program resources specifically geared to diverse learners.
- Leveled activities in the Lesson Planning pages of the Teacher Edition provide additional learning opportunities for students with beginning, intermediate, or advanced proficiency.
- A bibliography contains notable trade books with in-depth information on content. Many of the books are recommendations of the National Science Teachers Association and the Children's Book Council.
- Online Resources: Alternative Assessment worksheets for each lesson provide varied strategies for learning content.
- Online Resources: Digital lessons, virtual labs, and video-based projects appeal to all students, especially struggling readers and visual learners.
- Student Edition with Audio is online as PDF files with audio readings for use with students who have vision impairments or learning difficulties.
- Student Edition reading strategies focus on vocabulary, concept development, and inquiry skills.

As You Teach

Take advantage of these point-of-use features.

- A mix of Directed Inquiry and Independent Inquiry prompts suitable for different kinds of learners
- Short-cut codes to specific interactive digital lessons

Take It Home

As you reach out to families, look for these school-home connections.

- Take It Home activities found at the beginning of many units in the Student Edition
- Additional Take It Home worksheets are available in the Online Resources
- School-Home Connection Letters for every unit, available online as files you can download and print as-is or customize

The 5E Model and Levels of Inquiry

How do students best learn science? Extensive research and data show that the most effective learning emerges from situations in which one builds understanding based upon personal experiences. Learning is not transmitted from instructor to passive receiver; instead, understanding is constructed through the experience.

by Michael A. DiSpezio

The 5E Model for Effective Science Lessons

In the 1960s, Robert Karplus and his colleagues developed a three-step instructional model that became known as the Learning Cycle. This model was expanded into what is today referred to as the 5E Model. To emulate the elements of how an actual scientist works, this model is broken down into five components for an effective lesson: Engage, Explore, Explain, Extend (or Elaborate), and Evaluate.

Engage—The engagement sets the scene for learning. It is a warm-up during which students are introduced to the learning experience. Prior knowledge is assessed and its analysis used to develop an effective plan to meet stated objectives. Typically, an essential question is then posed; the question leads the now motivated and engaged students into the exploration.

Explore—This is the stage where the students become actively involved in hands-on process. They communicate and collaborate to develop a strategy that addresses the posed problem. Emphasis is placed on inquiry and hands-on investigation. The hands-on experience may be highly prescribed or open-ended in nature.

Explain—Students answer the initial question by using their findings and information they may be reading about, discussing with classmates, or experiencing through digital media. Their experience and understanding of concepts, processes, and hands-on skills is strengthened at this point. New vocabulary may be introduced.

Extend (or Elaborate)—The explanation is now extended to other situations, questions, or problems. During this stage the learner more closely examines findings in terms of context and transferable application. In short, extension reveals the application and implication of the internalized explanation. Extension may involve connections to other curriculum areas.

Evaluate—Although evaluation is an ongoing process, this is the stage in which a final assessment is most often performed. The instructor evaluates lesson effectiveness by using a variety of formal and informal assessment tools to measure student performance.

The 5E lesson format is used in all the *ScienceFusion* Teacher Edition lessons.

Levels of Inquiry

It wasn't that long ago that science was taught mostly through demonstration and lecture. Today, however, most instructional strategies integrate an inquiry-based approach to learning science. This methodology is founded in higher-level thinking and facilitates the students' construction of understanding from experience. When offered opportunities to ask questions, design investigations, collect and analyze data, and communicate their findings, each student assumes the role of an active participant in shaping his or her own learning process.

The degree to which any activity engages the inquiry process is variable, from highly prescribed steps to a completely learner-generated design. Researchers have established three distinct levels of inquiry: directed (or structured) inquiry, guided inquiry, and independent (or open) inquiry. These levels are distinguished by the amount of guidance offered by the instructor.

DIRECTED inquiry

In this level of inquiry, the instructor poses a question or suggests an investigation, and students follow a prescribed set of instructions. The outcome may be unknown to the students, but it is known to the instructor. Students follow the structured outline to uncover an outcome that supports the construction of lesson concepts.

GUIDED inquiry

As in Directed Inquiry, the instructor poses to the students a question to investigate. While students are conducting the investigation, the instruction focuses on developing one or more inquiry skills. Focus may also be provided for students to learn to use methods or tools of science. In *ScienceFusion*, the Teacher Edition provides scaffolding for developing inquiry skills, science methods, or tools. Student pages accompany these lessons and provide prompts for writing hypotheses, recording data, and drawing conclusions.

INDEPENDENT inquiry

This is the most complex level of inquiry experience. A prompt is provided, but students must design their own investigation in response to the prompt. In some cases, students will write their own questions and then plan and perform scientific investigations that will answer those questions. This level of inquiry is often used for science fair projects. Independent Inquiry does not necessarily mean individual inquiry. Investigations can be conducted by individual students or by pairs or teams of students.

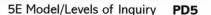

Response to Intervention

by Marjorie Frank

In a traditional model, assessment marks the end of an instructional cycle. Students work through a unit, take a test, and move on, regardless of their performance. However, current research suggests that assessment should be part of the instructional cycle, that it should be ongoing, and that it should be used to identify students needing intervention. This may sound like a tall order—who wants to give tests all the time?—but it may not be as difficult as it seems. In some ways, you are probably doing it already.

Assessment

Every student interaction has the potential to be an assessment. It all depends on how you perceive and use the interaction.

- Suppose you ask a question. You can just listen to your student's response, or you can assess it. Does the response indicate comprehension of the concept? If not, intervention may be needed.
- Suppose a student offers an explanation of a phenomenon depicted in a photo. You can assess the explanation. Does it show accurate factual knowledge? Does it reveal a misconception? If so, intervention may be needed.
- Suppose a student draws a diagram to illustrate a concept. You can assess the diagram. Is it accurate? If not, intervention may be needed.

As the examples indicate, assessing students' understandings can—and should—be an integral part of the instructional cycle and be used to make decisions about the next steps of instruction. For students making good progress, next steps might be exploring a related concept, a new lesson, or an additional challenge. For students who are not making adequate progress, intervention may be needed.

Assessment and intervention are tightly linked. Assessment leads to intervention—fresh approaches, different groupings, new materials—which, in turn, leads to assessment. Response to Intervention (RTI) gives shape and substance to this linkage.

RTI Response to Intervention

Response to Intervention is a process for identifying and supporting students who are not making expected progress toward essential learning goals.

RTI is a three-tiered approach based on an ongoing cycle of superior instruction, frequent monitoring of students' learning (assessments), and appropriate interventions. Students who are found not to be making expected progress in one Tier move to the next higher Tier, where they receive more intense instruction.

- **Tier I:** Students receive whole-class, core instruction.
- **Tier II:** Students work in small groups that supplement and reinforce core instruction.
- **Tier III:** Students receive individualized instruction.

How RTI and *ScienceFusion* Work

ScienceFusion provides many opportunities to assess students' understanding and many components appropriate for students in all Tiers.

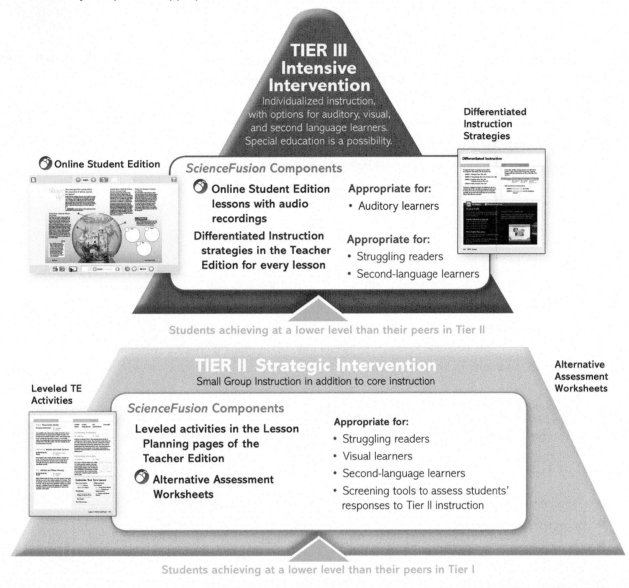

TIER III Intensive Intervention

Individualized instruction, with options for auditory, visual, and second language learners. Special education is a possibility.

Online Student Edition

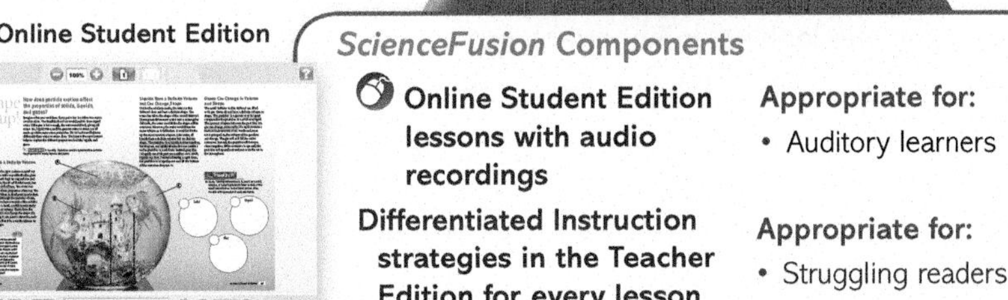

Differentiated Instruction Strategies

ScienceFusion Components

Online Student Edition lessons with audio recordings

Appropriate for:
- Auditory learners

Differentiated Instruction strategies in the Teacher Edition for every lesson

Appropriate for:
- Struggling readers
- Second-language learners

Students achieving at a lower level than their peers in Tier II

TIER II Strategic Intervention

Small Group Instruction in addition to core instruction

Leveled TE Activities

Alternative Assessment Worksheets

ScienceFusion Components

Leveled activities in the Lesson Planning pages of the Teacher Edition

Alternative Assessment Worksheets

Appropriate for:
- Struggling readers
- Visual learners
- Second-language learners
- Screening tools to assess students' responses to Tier II instruction

Students achieving at a lower level than their peers in Tier I

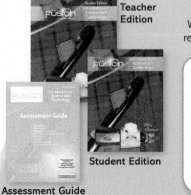

TIER I Core Classroom Instruction

With the help of extensive point-of-use strategies that support superior teaching, students receive whole-class instruction and engage productively in small-group work as appropriate.

Teacher Edition

Student Edition

Assessment Guide

ScienceFusion Components

Student Edition

Differentiated Instruction strategies in the TE for every lesson

Teacher Edition

Assessment Guide

Online Digital Curriculum

Appropriate for:
- Screening tools to assess students' responses to Tier I instruction
- Tier I intervention for students unable to complete the activity independently

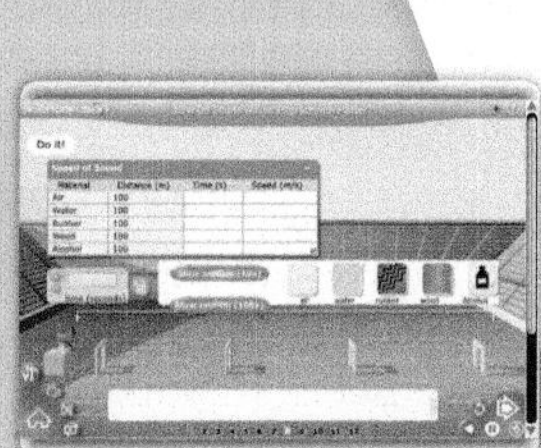

Digital Curriculum

Active Reading

Reading is a complex process in which readers use their knowledge and experience to make meaning from text. Though rarely accompanied by obvious large-muscle movement, reading is very much an active endeavor.

by Marjorie Frank

Think back to your days as a college student when you pored over your textbooks to prepare for class or for an exam—or, more recently, concentrated on an article or book with information you wanted to remember.

- You probably paid close attention to the text.
- Perhaps you paused to ask yourself questions.
- You might have broken off temporarily to look up an important, but unfamiliar, word.
- You may have stopped to reread a challenging passage or to "catch up" if your mind wandered for a moment.

If you owned the reading material, you also may have used a pencil or marker to interact with the text right there on the page (or in a digital file).

In short, you were having a conversation with yourself about the text. You were engaged. You were thinking critically.

These are the characteristics of active readers. This is precisely the kind of reader you want your students to be, because research suggests that active reading enables readers to understand and remember more information.

Active Reading involves interacting with text cognitively, metacognitively, and quite literally. You can actually see active readers at work. They are not sitting quietly as they read; they're underlining, marking, boxing, bracketing, drawing arrows, numbering, and writing comments. Here is what they may be noting:

- key terms and main ideas
- connections between ideas
- questions they have, opinions, agreements, and disagreements
- important facts and details
- sequences of events
- words, such as *because, before,* and *but,* that signal connections between ideas
- problems/solutions
- definitions and examples
- characteristics

The very process of interacting actively with text helps keep readers focused, thinking, comprehending, and remembering. But interacting in this way means readers are marking up the text. This is exactly why *ScienceFusion* Student Editions are consumable. They are meant to be marked up.

Active Reading and *ScienceFusion*

ScienceFusion includes Active Reading prompts throughout the Student Editions. The prompts appear as part of the lesson opener and on most two-page spreads.

Students are often given an Active Reading prompt before reading a section or paragraph. These prompts ask students to underline certain words or number the steps in a process. Marking the text in this way is called *annotating*, and the students' marks are called *annotations*. Annotating the text can help students identify important concepts while reading. Other ways of annotating the text include placing an asterisk by vocabulary terms, marking unfamiliar or confusing terms and information with a question mark, and underlining main ideas. Students can even invent their own systems for annotating the text. An example of an annotation prompt is shown at right.

Active Reading **5 Identify** As you read, underline sources of energy for living things.

In addition, there are Active Reading questions throughout each lesson. These questions have write-on lines accompanying them, so students can answer right on the page. Students will be asked to **describe** what they've just read about, **apply** concepts, **compare** concepts, **summarize** processes, and **identify cause-and-effect** relationships. By answering these Active Reading questions while reading the text, students will be strengthening those and other critical thinking skills that are used so often in science.

Active Reading **16 Compare** What is the difference between the pulmonary and systemic circulations?

Students' Responses to Active Reading Prompts

Active Reading has benefits for you as well as for your students. You can use students' responses to Active Reading prompts and the other interactive prompts in *ScienceFusion* as ongoing assessments. A quick review of students' responses provides a great deal of information about their learning.

- Are students comprehending the text?
- How deeply do they understand the concepts developed?
- Did they get the main idea? the cause? the order in which things happen?
- Which part of a lesson needs more attention? for whom?

Answers to these questions are available in students' responses to Active Learning prompts throughout a lesson—long before you might see poor results on an end-of-lesson or end-of-unit assessment. If you are following Response to Intervention (RTI) protocols, these frequent and regular assessments, no matter how informal, are integral parts of an effective intervention program.

The Active Reading prompts in *ScienceFusion* help make everyone a winner.

Project-Based Learning

For a list of the *ScienceFusion* Video-Based Projects, see page xxiv.

by
Michael R. Heithaus

When asked why I decided to become a biologist, the answer is pretty simple. I was inspired by spending almost every day outdoors, exploring under every rock, getting muddy in creeks and streams, and fishing in farm ponds, rivers, and—when I was really lucky—the oceans. Combine that with the spectacular stories of amazing animals and adventure that I saw on TV and I was hooked. As I've progressed in my career as a biologist, that same excitement and curiosity that I had as a ten-year-old looking for a salamander is still driving me.

But today's kids live in a very different world. Cable and satellite TV, Twitter, MP3 players, cell phones, and video games all compete with the outdoors for kids' time and attention. Education budget cuts, legal issues, and the pressures of standardized testing have also limited the opportunities for students to explore outdoors with their teachers.

How do we overcome these challenges so as to inspire kids' curiosity, help them connect with the natural world, and get them to engage in science and math? This is a critical issue. Not only do we need to ensure our national competitiveness and the conservation of our natural resources by training the next generation of scientists, we also need to ensure that every kid grows up to understand how scientists work and why their work is important.

To overcome these challenges, there is no question that we need to grab students' attention and get them to actively engage in the learning process. Research shows that students who are active and engaged participants in their learning have greater gains in concept and skills development than students who are passive in the classroom.

Project-based learning is one way to engage students. And when the stimulus for the project is exciting video content, engaged and active learning is almost guaranteed. Nothing captures a student's attention faster than exciting video. I have noticed that when my university students have video to accompany a lesson, they learn and retain the material better. It's no different for younger students! Videos need to do more than just "talk at" students to have a real impact. Videos need to engage students and require participation.

Teachers and students who use *ScienceFusion* video-based projects have noticed the following:

- The videos use captivating imagery, dynamic scientists, and cool stories to inspire kids to be curious about the world around them.
- Students connect to the projects by having the videos present interesting problems for them to solve.
- The videos engage students with projects woven into the story of the video so students are doing the work of real scientists!

The start-to-finish nature of the video projects, where students do background research and develop their own hypotheses, should lead to students' personal investment in solving the challenges that are presented. By seeing real scientists who are excellent role models gather data that they have to graph and interpret, students will not only learn the science standards being addressed, they will see that they can apply the scientific method to their lives. One day, they too could be a scientist!

Based on my experiences teaching in the university classroom, leading field trips for middle school students, and taking the first project-based videos into the classroom, project-based learning has considerable benefits. The video-based projects generate enthusiasm and curiosity. They also help students develop a deeper understanding of science content as well as how to go about a scientific investigation. If we inspire students to ask questions and seek answers for themselves, we will go a long way toward closing achievement gaps in science and math and facilitate the development of the next generation of scientists and scientifically literate citizens.

Developing Visual Literacy

Science teachers can build the bridges between students' general literacy and their scientific literacy by focusing attention on the particular kinds of reading strategies students need to be successful. One such strategy is that of knowing how to read and interpret the various visual displays used in science.

by Donna M. Ogle

Many young readers receive little instruction in reading charts, tables, diagrams, photographs, or illustrations in their language arts/reading classes. Science is where these skills can and must be developed. Science provides a meaningful context where students can learn to read visually presented forms of information and to create their own visual representations. Research studies have shown that students take longer to read science materials containing combinations of visual displays and narrative texts than they do to read narrative text alone. The process of reading the combination materials is slower and more difficult because the reader must relate the visual displays to the narrative text and build a meaning that is based on information from both.

We also know that students benefit when teachers take time to explain how each visual form is constructed and to guide students in the thinking needed to make sense of these forms. Even the seemingly simple act of interpreting a photograph needs to be taught to most students. Here are some ways to help students develop the ability to think more critically about what they view:

- Model for students how to look carefully at a photograph and list what they notice.
- Divide the photograph into quadrants and have students think more deeply about what the photographer has used as the focus of the image and what context is provided.
- Have students use language such as *zoom, close-up, foreground, background*, or *panorama views* to describe photographs.

The ability to interpret a photograph is clearly a part of the scientific skill of engaging in careful observation. This skill helps students when they are using print materials, observing nature, and making their own photographs of aspects of their experiments.

Attention to the other forms of visual displays frequently used in science is also important to students' learning of scientific concepts and processes. For example, students in grades 4 through 8 need to learn to interpret and then construct each of the types of graphs, from circle graphs and bar graphs to more complex line graphs.

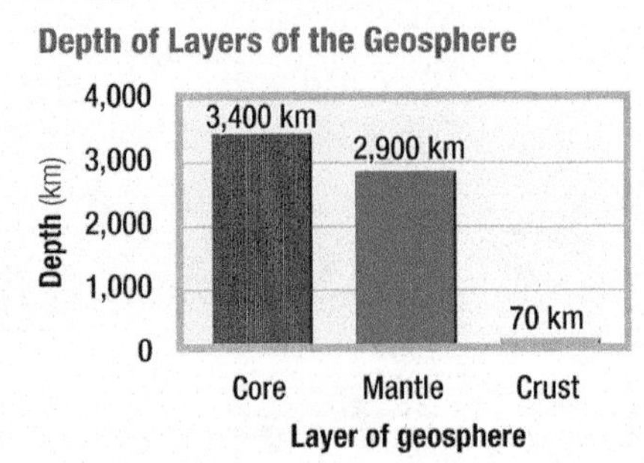

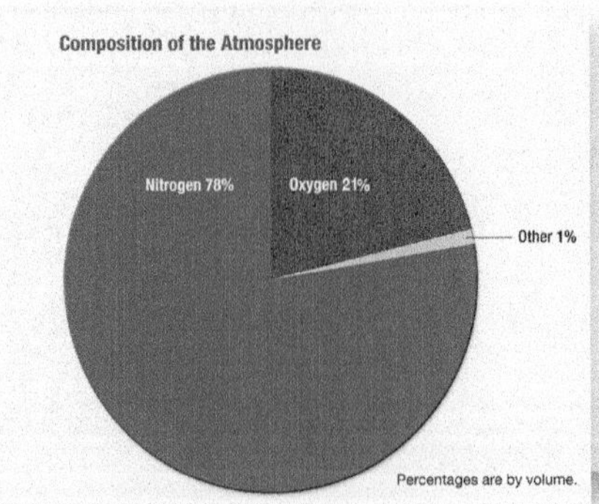

Science Notebooks and *ScienceFusion*

In many ways, the *ScienceFusion* worktexts are Science Notebooks in themselves. Students are encouraged to write answers directly in the text and to annotate the text for better understanding. However, a separate Science Notebook can still be an invaluable part of your student's learning experience with *ScienceFusion*. Student uses for a Science Notebook along with the worktext include:

- writing answers for the Unit Review
- writing responses to the Think Outside the Book features in each lesson
- planning for and writing answers to the Citizen Science feature in each unit
- working through answers before writing them in the worktext
- writing all answers if you choose not to have students work directly in the worktext
- taking notes on additional materials you present outside of the worktext
- making observations and recording data from Daily Demos and additional activities provided in the Teacher Edition
- collecting data and writing notes for labs performed from the Lab Manual
- making notes and writing answers for Digital Lessons and Virtual Labs
- collecting data and writing answers for the Project-Based Videos

The Benefits (for You and Your Students) of Science Notebooking

No doubt, it takes time and effort to help students set up and maintain Science Notebooks, not to mention the time it takes you to review them and provide meaningful feedback. The payoff is well worth it. Here's why:

Keeping a Science Notebook:

- leads each learner to engage with ideas
- engages students in writing—an active, thinking, analytical process
- causes students to organize their thinking
- provides students with multiple opportunities and modes to process new information
- makes learning experiences more personal
- provides students with a record of their own progress and accomplishments
- doubles as a study guide for formal assessments
- creates an additional vehicle for students to improve their reading and writing skills

As you and your students embrace Science Notebooking, you will surely find it to be an engaging, enriching, and very valuable endeavor.

Using the *ScienceFusion* Worktext

Research shows that an interactive text teaches students how to relate to content in a personal, meaningful way. They learn how to be attentive, energetic readers who reach a deep level of comprehension. Still, the worktext format may be new to you and your students. Below are some answers to questions—both pedagogical and practical—you may have about *ScienceFusion's* worktext format.

How does the worktext format help my students learn?

- In this format, your students will interact with the text and visuals on every page. This will teach them to read expertly, to think critically, and to communicate effectively—all skills that are crucial for success in the 21st century.
- The use of images and text on every page of the *ScienceFusion* worktext accommodates both visual and verbal learners. Students are engaged by the less formal, magazine-like presentation of the content.
- By the end of the school year, the worktexts become a record of the knowledge and skills your students learned in class. Students can use their books as a study guide to prepare for tests.

What are some features that make the *ScienceFusion* worktext different from a regular textbook?

Some of the special features of the *ScienceFusion* worktext include these prompts for writing directly in the worktext:

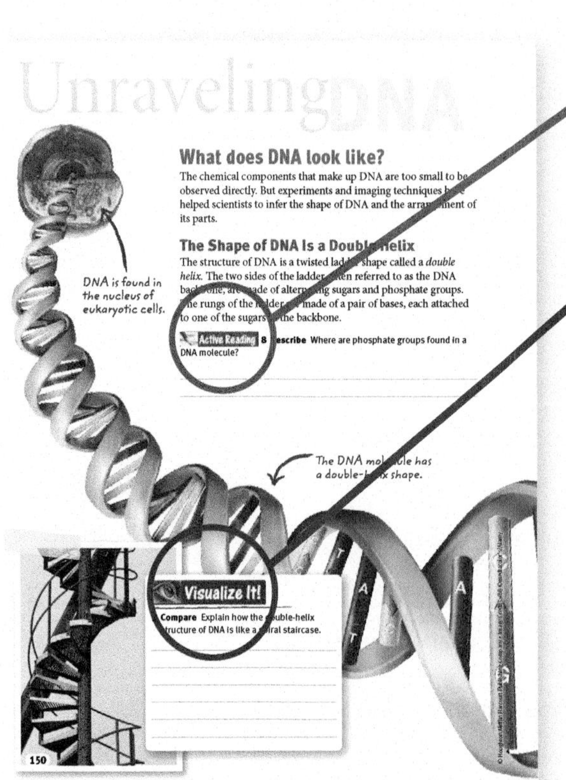

Active Reading
Annotation prompts and questions throughout the worktext teach students how to analyze and interact with content as they read.

Visualize It!
Questions and completion prompts that accompany images help develop visual literacy.

Engage Your Brain
Math problems, with on-page guidance, allow students to understand the relationships between math and science and to practice their math skills.

Do the Math
Interesting questions and activities on the lesson opener pages help prepare students for the lesson content.

Are my students really supposed to write directly in the book?

Yes! Write-on lines are provided for students to answer questions on-page, while the student is reading. Additional prompts are given for students to annotate the pages. You can even encourage your students to experiment with their own systems of annotation. More information can be found in "A How-To Manual for Active Reading" in the Look It Up! Section at the end of the Student Edition and Teacher Edition.

You might wish to encourage your students to write in the worktexts using pencils so that they can more easily revise their answers and notes as needed.

We will have to use the same set of worktexts for several years. How can students use the worktexts if they can't write in them?

Though *ScienceFusion* is set up in a worktext format, the books can still be used in a more traditional fashion. Simply tell your students that they cannot write in the textbooks but should instead use their Science Notebooks for taking notes and answering questions. (See the article titled "Science Notebooking" for more information about using Notebooks with *ScienceFusion*.)

How do I grade my students' answers in the worktext?

The pages in the worktext are conveniently perforated so that your students can turn in their work. Or you may wish for your students to leave the pages in the book, but turn in the books to you on a daily or weekly basis for you to grade them.

The Lesson Reviews and Unit Reviews are designed so students can turn in the pages but still keep their annotated pages for reference when moving on to the next lesson or unit or for review before a lesson or unit test.

- Tour the classroom while students are writing in their worktexts. Address any issues you see immediately or make note of items that need to be addressed with students later.
- Have students do 'self checks' and 'partner checks.' Choose a question in the worktext, and have all students check their responses. Or, have students trade their worktext with a partner to check each other's responses.
- Once a week, have students copy five questions and their responses from the worktext onto a sheet of notebook paper. You can review student answers to ensure they're using the worktext correctly without having students turn in worktext pages or the books themselves.
- Use a document camera to show students correct worktext answers.
- Every two weeks, review and grade one class's worth of student worktext answers per day. Or, grade a class's worktexts while the students are taking a test.

Pacing Guide

You have options for covering the lesson materials: you may choose to follow the digital path, the print path, or a combination of the two. Customize your Pacing Guide to plan print, inquiry, digital, and assessment mini-blocks based on your teaching style and classroom needs.

Pressed for Time? Follow the faster-paced compressed schedule.

	Total Days			Customize Your Pacing Guide			
	Traditional 1 = 45 min	Block 1 = 90 min	Compressed (T/B)	Print Path	Inquiry Labs & Activities	Digital Path	Review & Assess
UNIT 1 Earth's Surface							
Unit Project	3	1.5	3 (1.5)				
Lesson 1 Earth's Spheres	6	3	5 (2.5)				
Lesson 2 Weathering	4	2	3 (1.5)				
Lesson 3 Erosion and Deposition by Water	6	3	5 (2.5)				
Lesson 4 Erosion and Deposition by Wind, Ice, and Gravity	5	2.5	4 (2)				
Lesson 5 Soil Formation	5	2.5	4 (2)				
Unit Review	2	1	1 (0.5)				
Total Days for Unit 1	**31**	**15.5**	**25 (12.5)**				
UNIT 2 Earth's History							
Unit Project	3	1.5	3 (1.5)				
Lesson 1 Geologic Change over Time	6	3	5 (2.5)				
Lesson 2 Relative Dating	5	2.5	4 (2)				
Lesson 3 Absolute Dating	5	2.5	4 (2)				
Lesson 4 The Geologic Time Scale	5	2.5	4 (2)				
Unit Review	2	1	1 (0.5)				
Total Days for Unit 2	**26**	**13**	**21 (10.5)**				

	Total Days			Customize Your Pacing Guide			
	Traditional 1 = 45 min	Block 1 = 90 min	Compressed (T/B)	Print Path	Inquiry Labs & Activities	Digital Path	Review & Assess
UNIT 3 Minerals and Rocks							
Unit Project	3	1.5	3 (1.5)				
Lesson 1 Minerals	6	3	5 (2.5)				
Lesson 2 The Rock Cycle	5	2.5	4 (2)				
Lesson 3 Three Classes of Rock	5	2.5	4 (2)				
Unit Review	2	1	1 (0.5)				
Total Days for Unit 3	**21**	**10.5**	**17 (8.5)**				
UNIT 4 The Restless Earth							
Unit Project	3	1.5	3 (1.5)				
Lesson 1 Earth's Layers	3	1	2 (1)				
Lesson 2 Plate Tectonics	6	3	5 (2.5)				
Lesson 3 Mountain Building	4	2	3 (1.5)				
Lesson 4 Volcanoes	5	2.5	4 (2)				
Lesson 5 Earthquakes	4	2	3 (1.5)				
Lesson 6 Measuring Earthquake Waves	6	3	5 (2.5)				
Unit Review	2	1	1 (0.5)				
Total Days for Unit 4	**33**	**16**	**26 (13)**				

Teacher Notes

UNIT 1 Earth's Surface

The Big Idea and Essential Questions

This Unit was designed to focus on this Big Idea and Essential Questions.

Big Idea **Continuous processes on Earth's surface result in the formation and destruction of landforms and the formation of soil.**

Lesson	ESSENTIAL QUESTION	Student Mastery	PD Professional Development	Lesson Overview
LESSON 1 Earth's Spheres	*How do matter and energy move through Earth's spheres?*	To describe Earth's spheres and their interactions, and explain the energy budget	Content Refresher, TE p. 6	TE p. 14
LESSON 2 Weathering	*How does weathering change Earth's surface?*	To analyze the effects of weathering on Earth's surface and give examples	Content Refresher, TE p. 7	TE p. 30
LESSON 3 Erosion and Deposition by Water	*How does water change Earth's surface?*	To relate the processes of erosion and deposition by water to the landforms that result from these processes	Content Refresher, TE p. 8	TE p. 44
LESSON 4 Erosion and Deposition by Wind, Ice, and Gravity	*How do wind, ice, and gravity change Earth's surface?*	To describe erosion and deposition by wind, ice, and gravity and identify landforms that result from these processes	Content Refresher, TE p. 9	TE p. 62
LESSON 5 Soil Formation	*How does soil form?*	To describe the physical and chemical characteristics of soil layers and identify the factors that affect soil formation, including the actions of living things	Content Refresher, TE p. 10	TE p. 76

Science Background

Use the keywords at right to access

- Professional Development from **The NSTA Learning Center**
- **SciLinks** for additional online content appropriate for students and teachers

Keywords
deposition
erosion
soil
weathering

NSTA National Science Teachers Association

Options for Instruction

Two parallel paths provide coverage of the Essential Questions, with a strong **Inquiry** strand woven into each. Follow the **Print Path**, the **Digital Path**, or your customized combination of print, digital, and inquiry.

	LESSON 1 Earth's Spheres	LESSON 2 Weathering	LESSON 3 Erosion and Deposition by Water
Essential Questions	***How do matter and energy move through Earth's spheres?***	***How does weathering change Earth's surface?***	***How does water change Earth's surface?***
Key Topics	• The Earth System and its Spheres • Interactions Between Spheres • Earth's Energy Budget	• Weathering • Physical Weathering • Chemical Weathering	• Erosion and Deposition • Erosion and Deposition by Streams • Formation of Landforms by Streams • Erosion and Deposition by Groundwater and Waves
Print Path	Teacher Edition pp. 14–28 Student Edition pp. 4–17	Teacher Edition pp. 30–42 Student Edition pp. 18–27	Teacher Edition pp. 44–58 Student Edition pp. 28–41
Inquiry Labs	Lab Manual **Quick Lab** Explaining Earth's Systems **Quick Lab** Model Earth's Spheres **S.T.E.M. Lab** Change and Balance Between Spheres	Lab Manual **Quick Lab** Mechanical Weathering **Quick Lab** Weathering Chalk **Quick Lab** How Can Materials on Earth's Surface Change?	Lab Manual **Quick Lab** Wave Action... **Quick Lab** Moving Sediment **Exploration Lab** Exploring Stream Erosion... Virtual Lab Erosion, Deposition by Rivers
Digital Path	Digital Path TS661402	Digital Path TS661000	Digital Path TS661021

LESSON 4
Erosion and Deposition by Wind, Ice, and Gravity

How do wind, ice, and gravity change Earth's surface?

- Erosion and Deposition by Wind
- Erosion and Deposition by Ice
- Erosion and Deposition by Gravity (Mass Movement)

Teacher Edition
pp. 62–75

Student Edition
pp. 44–55

Lab Manual

Quick Lab Modeling a Glacier

Quick Lab Modeling a Landslide

 Virtual Lab
Erosion and Deposition of Sand Dunes

Digital Path
TS661022

LESSON 5
Soil Formation

How does soil form?

- Soil Formation
- Soil Horizons
- Soil Characteristics

Teacher Edition
pp. 76–89

Student Edition
pp. 56–67

Lab Manual

Quick Lab Observing Life in Soil

Quick Lab Modeling, Soil Profile

Quick Lab Impact, Earthworms

Field Lab Comparing Soil...

Digital Path
TS692102

UNIT 1
Unit Projects

Citizen Science Project
Save a Beach

Teacher Edition p. 13

Student Edition
pp. 2–3

Unit Assessment

Formative Assessment

Strategies RTI
Throughout TE

Lesson Reviews SE

Unit PreTest

Summative Assessment

Alternative Assessment
(1 per lesson) RTI

Lesson Quizzes

Unit Tests A and B

Unit Review RTI
(with answer remediation)

Practice Tests
(end of module)

Project-Based Assessment

See the Assessment Guide for quizzes and tests.

Go Online to edit and create quizzes and tests.

Response to Intervention

See RTI teacher support materials on p. PD6.

Differentiated Instruction

English Language Proficiency

Strategies for **English Language Learners (ELL)** are provided for each lesson, under the Explain tabs.

LESSON 1 *Organisms,* TE p. 19

LESSON 2 *Different Ways to Weather,* TE p. 35

LESSON 3 *Coastline Landform Progression,* TE p. 49

LESSON 4 *Main Ideas,* TE p. 67

LESSON 5 *Mnemonic Device,* TE p. 81

Vocabulary strategies provided for all students can also be a particular help for ELL. Use different strategies for each lesson or choose one or two to use throughout the unit. Vocabulary strategies can be found under the Explain tab for each lesson (TE pp. 19, 35, 49, 67, and 81).

Leveled Inquiry

Inquiry labs, activities, probing questions, and daily demos provide a range of inquiry levels. Preview them under the Engage and Explore tabs starting on TE pp. 16, 32, 46, 64, and 78.

Levels of Inquiry

DIRECTED inquiry	**GUIDED** inquiry	**INDEPENDENT** inquiry
introduces inquiry skills within a structured framework.	develops inquiry skills within a supportive environment.	deepens inquiry skills with student-driven questions or procedures.

Each long lab has two inquiry options:

LESSON 1 **S.T.E.M. Lab** *Change and Balance Between Spheres*

LESSON 3 **Exploration Lab** *Exploring Stream Erosion and Deposition*

LESSON 5 **Field Lab** *Comparing Soil Characteristics*

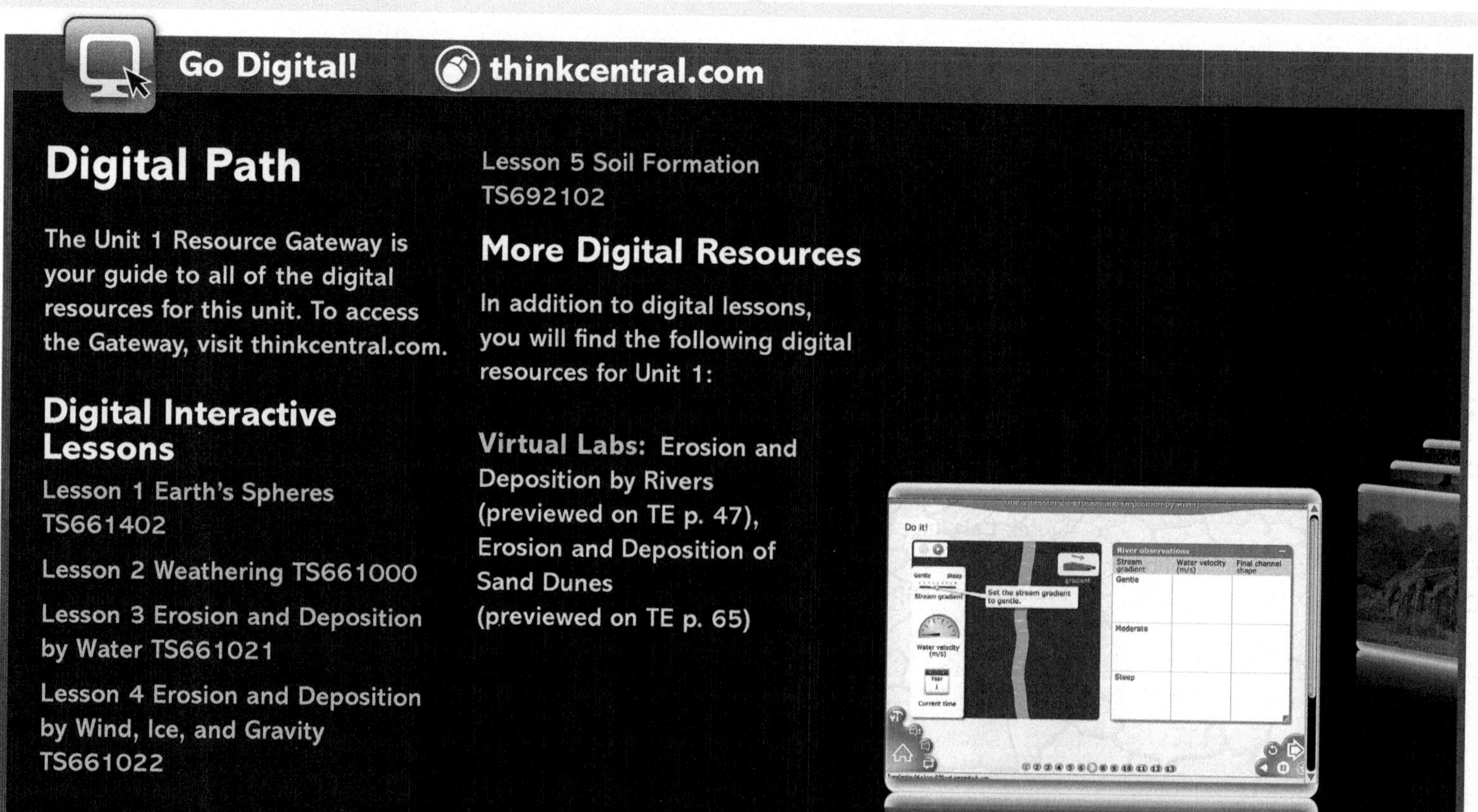

Go Digital! thinkcentral.com

Digital Path

The Unit 1 Resource Gateway is your guide to all of the digital resources for this unit. To access the Gateway, visit thinkcentral.com.

Digital Interactive Lessons

Lesson 1 Earth's Spheres TS661402

Lesson 2 Weathering TS661000

Lesson 3 Erosion and Deposition by Water TS661021

Lesson 4 Erosion and Deposition by Wind, Ice, and Gravity TS661022

Lesson 5 Soil Formation TS692102

More Digital Resources

In addition to digital lessons, you will find the following digital resources for Unit 1:

Virtual Labs: Erosion and Deposition by Rivers (previewed on TE p. 47), Erosion and Deposition of Sand Dunes (previewed on TE p. 65)

 Response to Intervention

Response to Intervention (RTI) is a process for identifying and supporting students who are not making expected progress toward essential learning goals. The following *ScienceFusion* components can be used to provide strategic and intensive intervention.

Component	Location	Strategies and Benefits
STUDENT EDITION Active Reading prompts, Visualize It!, Think Outside the Book	**Throughout each lesson**	Student responses can be used as screening tools to assess whether intervention is needed.
TEACHER EDITION Formative Assessment, Probing Questions, Learning Alerts	**Throughout each lesson**	Opportunities are provided to assess and remediate student understanding of lesson concepts.
TEACHER EDITION Extend Science Concepts	**Reinforce and Review, TE pp. 20, 36, 50, 68, 82** **Going Further, TE pp. 20, 36, 50, 68, 82**	Additional activities allow students to reinforce and extend their understanding of lesson concepts.
TEACHER EDITION Evaluate Student Mastery	**Formative Assessment, TE pp. 21, 37, 51, 69, 83** **Alternative Assessment, TE pp. 21, 37, 51, 69, 83**	These assessments allow for greater flexibility in assessing students with differing physical, mental, and language abilities, as well as varying learning and communication modes.
TEACHER EDITION Unit Review Remediation	**Unit Review, TE pp. 90–92**	Includes reference back to Lesson Planning pages for remediation activities and assignments.
INTERACTIVE DIGITAL LESSONS and VIRTUAL LABS	**thinkcentral.com** **Unit 1 Gateway** **Lesson 1 TS661402** **Lesson 2 TS661000** **Lesson 3 TS661021** **Lesson 4 TS661022** **Lesson 5 TS692102**	Lessons and labs make content accessible through simulations, animations, videos, audio, and integrated assessment. Useful for review and reteaching of lesson concepts.

Content Refresher

Lesson 1

Earth's Spheres

ESSENTIAL QUESTION

How do matter and energy move through Earth's spheres?

1. The Earth System and its Spheres

Students will learn that Earth is a system of interrelated spheres.

Earth's system is made up of spheres. Each sphere has a unique identity, but also interacts with the other spheres.

Geosphere

The geosphere includes the Earth's interior, landforms, rocks and minerals, and the processes that shape its surface. Earth's interior is made up of the mantle and the solid inner and liquid outer core. The outer core contains liquid iron, and is the main source of Earth's magnetic field.

The geosphere interacts with other spheres; for example, a volcanic eruption can emit particles into the atmosphere; this can encourage the formation of water droplets and thereby increase rainfall. This impact on the hydrosphere can affect the biosphere—for example, increased rainfall can stimulate increased plant growth, which could support increased animal populations.

Hydrosphere and cryosphere

Water covers about 70% of Earth's surface, and the majority of this is ocean water. The hydrologic cycle traces the path water takes through Earth's spheres.

The cryosphere plays an integral role in the global climate system; for example, it reflects solar radiation. The cryosphere affects the hydrosphere by seasonally storing water in snowpacks and then releasing it.

Atmosphere

Earth's atmosphere surrounds the planet and is divided into distinct layers. It becomes thinner with increased altitude, and there is no definitive boundary between the atmosphere and space. It protects us from harmful solar radiation.

Biosphere

The biosphere is made up of all living things on Earth. It extends to every part of Earth that can support life. The biosphere interacts with the other four spheres.

2. Interactions between spheres

Students will learn that interactions between spheres are essential for life on Earth.

Earth's spheres exchange matter and energy. Some of the most important interactions between spheres include the water cycle and the cycling of carbon dioxide by plants and animals. A change in one sphere can precipitate changes in other spheres. A forest fire that damages or destroys parts of the biosphere is an example of an interaction between the spheres. Smoke from the fire will temporarily pollute the atmosphere. The land may lose vital nutrients and become vulnerable to erosion. The area's water may become polluted. Interactions among Earth's spheres affect us every day.

3. Earth's energy budget

Students will learn that energy moves between Earth's spheres, but is never created or destroyed.

The vast majority of Earth's energy comes from the sun. Very small amounts come from other sources. After energy enters Earth's atmosphere, it moves between Earth's spheres. Energy lost by one sphere is gained by another. Energy is never destroyed.

The Earth's albedo is a measure of its reflectivity, or how much energy is reflected back into space. The average planetary albedo on Earth is 30% to 35%; that is, about 30% to 35% of the solar energy coming toward Earth is reflected back into space, and about 65% to 70% is absorbed. The exact albedos of specific areas on Earth vary widely; a glacier will reflect much more energy than a rainforest. As Earth's glaciers, ice caps, and snow-covered lands decrease in area, planetary albedo decreases and more energy is absorbed. This creates a positive feedback system, accelerating global temperature increases. For Earth to be in thermal equilibrium, the energy absorbed must equal the energy reflected.

Karen Cavalluzzi
Sunny Vale Middle School
Blue Springs, MO

Lesson 3 Erosion and Deposition by Water A great way to show students deposition by water is during a school parking lot field trip. Look along the gutters and a drain in your school's parking lot for evidence of water deposition. Sand and gravel will fall out of the water as it moves toward the drain. Look closely—you will see large particles dropping first, then smaller ones as you get close to the drain.

Lesson 2

Weathering

ESSENTIAL QUESTION

How does weathering change Earth's surface?

1. Weathering

Weathering is a process that breaks down rock materials.

Scientists classify weathering processes into two groups: physical weathering and chemical weathering. Weathering is caused by many different agents.

2. Physical Weathering

Physical weathering is the breakdown of rock through motion, force, and other physical processes.

Abrasion describes the wearing down or weathering of rock by other rock materials.

Exfoliation describes the process of large rock layers peeling away due to pressure changes. As outer layers of rock are removed, the ones underneath are exposed. The pressure they were under decreases as layers are removed, and therefore they expand.

There are several agents of physical weathering:

- Water that seeps into cracks in rock and then freezes and expands can cause the rock to split apart. This is called ice wedging. Ice, in the form of glaciers, can also cause weathering as particles in the glacier wear down Earth's surface.
- Wind can cause weathering by blowing particles against rock surfaces, wearing them down over time.
- The particles carried in moving water can wear away rock.
- Plants can cause weathering as their roots grow and develop, breaking up rocks.
- Animals can cause weathering by digging and burrowing in the ground, turning up rock materials and exposing new ones to other elements.

3. Chemical Weathering

Chemical weathering is the process by which rocks break down as a result of chemical reactions.

There are several forms of chemical weathering:

- Acids cause chemical weathering by reacting and breaking down molecules in rock. This process dissolves rock. Acids are found in precipitation, groundwater, soil, and living things.
- Oxygen causes weathering by reacting with some of the molecules in rock. This process is called oxidation. Oxidation can often result in color changes, such as in rust-colored rocks, which actually contain minerals that have been oxidized.

Ice Wedging

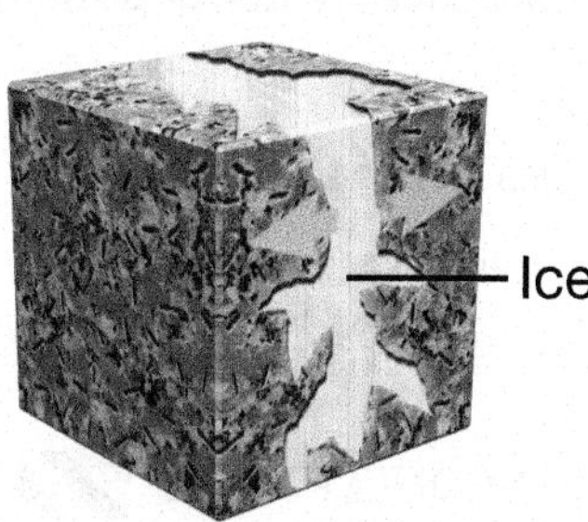

Content Refresher (continued)

Lesson 3

Erosion and Deposition by Water

ESSENTIAL QUESTION

How does water change Earth's surface?

1. Erosion and Deposition

Erosion and deposition change Earth's surface.

Erosion is the process through which sediment and other material are moved. Deposition is the process through which sediment and other material are deposited in a new place. These processes have occurred throughout Earth's history.

There are several agents that cause erosion and deposition.

Agents of erosion and deposition include water, gravity, wind and ice. As these agents interact with Earth's surface, they wear it away, move it, and deposit it elsewhere changing its shape.

2. Erosion and Deposition by Streams

These conditions produce faster erosion:

- faster flow
- steeper slopes (high gradient)
- greater discharge of water

These conditions produces faster deposition:

- slower flow
- more shallow slopes (low gradient)
- less discharge of water

3. Formation of Landforms by Streams

Some landforms result from stream erosion.

Streams erode soil and rock to form channels. Over many years, the erosion of sediment from the bottoms of channels may cause canyons and valleys to form. This is more likely to happen in locations where rock is softer and easily eroded.

Oxbow lakes form when a bend in a stream is eroded on its outer sides and deposits sediment on its inner side causing a sharper and sharper bend. Eventually the bend becomes cut off from the main stream as the stream forms a new channel.

Other landforms result from stream deposition.

- Floodplain: area of deposited sediment caused by flooding
- Alluvial fan: forms as a stream slows down, spreads out, and deposits sediment
- Delta: forms at the mouth of a river; as a stream enters an ocean and slows, sediment is deposited in a fan shape

4. Erosion and Deposition by Groundwater, Waves, and Currents

Groundwater erosion can change the land.

Groundwater can erode rock, forming underground caverns or spaces. The roof of a cavern may fall, producing a sinkhole.

Waves and currents can cause shoreline changes and land formations.

Wave action against coastal rock causes many formations—sea cliffs, headlands, sea caves, sea arches, sea stacks.

Beaches, sandbars, and barrier islands are formed and destroyed by erosion and deposition by waves and currents.

 COMMON MISCONCEPTIONS  

WATER AND ROCK Students may think of rock as more powerful than water because it is hard. This is true in the short term, but over long periods, water has a huge impact on rock.

This misconception is addressed on p. 52.

CONSERVATION Students may believe that when soil and rock are eroded, they disappear. The law of conservation states that matter cannot be created or destroyed. In this case, it simply moves.

This misconception is addressed on p. 52.

Lesson 4

Erosion and Deposition by Wind, Ice, and Gravity

ESSENTIAL QUESTION

How do wind, ice, and gravity change Earth's surface?

1. Erosion and Deposition by Wind

Wind causes erosion and deposition.

Wind can pick up particles and sediment. These moving particles can erode rock and also result in deposition. The particles and sediment carried by wind are blown against other surfaces, causing erosion through abrasion. Variables that increase these processes are the strength of the wind, the amount of loose particles, and the softness of the rock being eroded. The type of soil in an area also plays a part in determining how vulnerable the area is to wind erosion. Dry, loose soil erodes much more easily than moist, dense soil. Wind also acts as an agent of erosion by removing fine particles in a process called deflation. Wind erosion has the largest impacts in arid and semi-arid areas.

Wind also acts as an agent of deposition. Dunes and loess are features which result from wind deposition. Loess is a deposit of windblown silt and is important to agriculture because it tends to develop into fertile soil. Dunes result from strong winds carrying sand particles that slow down due to an obstacle in the wind's path. In general, wind does not carry and deposit larger-sized materials such as pebbles.

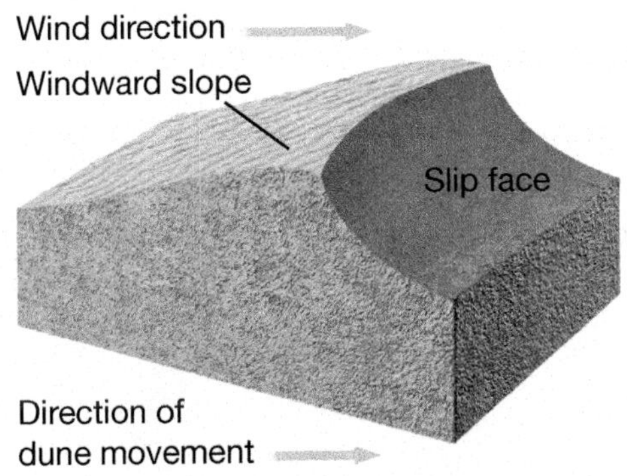

2. Erosion and Deposition by Ice

Ice expands and scrapes land, causing erosion.

Two types of glaciers are alpine glaciers and continental glaciers. Alpine glaciers form in mountainous areas. Continental glaciers form on flatter landscapes.

The famous Matterhorn in Switzerland is a classic example of a horn: a sharp, pyramid-shaped peak carved by alpine glaciation. Alpine glaction also forms cirques and arêtes. Cirques are bowl-shaped depressions and arêtes are jagged ridges between two or more cirques. If several cirques and arêtes meet at a peak, a horn is formed. U-shaped and hanging valleys result from alpine glaciation as well.

Continental glaciers expand to enormous sizes. Some continental glaciers are over 3 km thick. The sliding ice scrapes the surface of the land, eroding it away.

Ice carries and moves sediment, causing deposition.

All glaciers pick up and carry sediment and materials including large boulders. They can scrape rock, leaving striations, or parallel grooves and scratches. As glaciers melt and recede, sediments fall out and are deposited. This is called glacial drift. Large boulders that fall out of melting glaciers are called erratics. Kettle lakes form after a large chunk of ice breaks off and melts into a depression.

3. Erosion and Deposition by Gravity

Gravity causes erosion and deposition by pulling down on loose materials.

The constant downward pull of gravity is an agent of both erosion and deposition. When material is loose enough and land is sloped, gravity causes the land to move. Gravity can erode land on its own, but it is more likely to trigger a loosening of materials when it is coupled with other agents or events, such as heavy rains or earthquakes. Gravity working with other factors can cause a landscape to change very quickly, as it does during a rockfall, landslide, or mudflow. It can also contribute to very slow movement of material, as it does in a creep.

Content Refresher (continued)

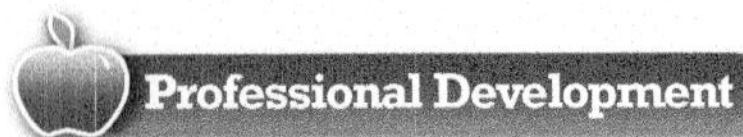

Lesson 5

Soil Formation

ESSENTIAL QUESTION

How does soil form?

1. Soil Formation

Students will learn how soil forms.

Soil is a loose mixture of rock fragments, organic matter, water, and air that can support the growth of vegetation. Soil begins to form as parent rock is weathered. The remains of living things provide organic matter that eventually forms humus, the organic component of soil. Microorganisms decompose these remains, releasing nutrients that plants need to grow. Animals such as earthworms and moles aerate, loosen, and mix soil as they burrow. They also bring partly weathered rock particles to the surface.

Soil formation and development take place over a long period of time. Often, the condition of the soil depends on how long the soil has been developing. The rate of soil development depends on these main factors:

- Rock type: Some rocks weather more slowly than others.
- Climate: The rate of weathering is higher in warm, wet areas.
- Topography: Soil on hillsides is easily eroded and does not develop as quickly as soil in flatter areas.
- Organisms: Plant roots stabilize soil. Soil full of life has a higher rate of decomposition and mixing.

2. Soil Horizons

Students will learn about soil horizons.

A soil horizon is a layer of soil with properties that differ from those of the soil layers above and below it. The A horizon is the upper layer of soil, or topsoil; it contains a large amount of organic matter. Decomposers are found in this horizon. The B horizon lies below the A horizon; it has little organic matter. Materials from the A horizon enter the B horizon through the process of leaching. The C horizon lies below the B horizon; it consists mainly of weathered parent rock. A soil profile refers to a vertical section that displays all soil horizons found in a particular location. Soil profiles vary from one area to another, and only the main soil horizons are covered here.

3. Soil Characteristics

Students will learn about the characteristics of soil.

Soil scientists study numerous soil characteristics, including texture, color, pore space, chemistry, and fertility. Soil texture is determined by a soil's relative amounts of particles. Soil scientists classify soil particles as sand, silt, and clay. Sand particles are the largest, silt particles are smaller, and clay particles are the smallest. The color of a soil reflects properties such as mineral composition and humus content. Color can also give environmental clues. Pore space refers to the spaces between soil particles. Water and air move easily through soils with many, well-connected pore spaces, which promotes plant growth. Chemistry refers to soil pH, which determines how well a soil will support the growth of certain plants. Soil fertility refers to the ability of a soil to support plant growth.

 COMMON MISCONCEPTIONS  RTI

SOIL TEXTURE Students may be confused about the meaning of the word *clay* in soil science. Here, *clay* refers to the smallest sized particle found in soils. Clay is too small to be seen with the naked eye. Soils with a lot of clay and little sand feel very smooth when rubbed between two fingers and are typically sticky when wet.

This misconception is addressed in the Activity on p. 78 and on p. 87.

Teacher Notes

Advance Planning

These activities may take extended time or special conditions.

Unit 1

Project Save a Beach, p. 13
plan and conduct an experiment

Graphic Organizers and Vocabulary pp. 19, 20, 35, 36, 49, 50, 67, 68, 81, 82
ongoing with reading

Lesson 1

S.T.E.M. Lab Change and Balance Between Spheres, p. 17
make ice blocks in advance

Lesson 2

Quick Lab Weathering Chalk, p. 33
observations over 2 weeks

Lesson 3

Quick Lab Modeling Stalactites and Stalagmites, p. 46
sodium carbonate; observations over several days

Exploration Lab Exploring Stream Erosion and Deposition, p. 47
multiple types of soil

Lesson 5

Field Lab Comparing Soil Characteristics, p. 79
requires outdoor sample collection

Quick Lab Observing Life in Soil, p. 79
observations over several days

Quick Lab Observing the Impact of Earthworms on Soil, p. 79
earthworms; observations over a week

Daily Demo Watch It Rot!, p. 79
yard waste or fruit/vegetable scraps; two 10- to 15-min periods

What Do You Think?

Have students consider the forces that could cause caves to form.

Ask: Do you think caves form quickly or slowly? Explain. Sample answer: I think they probably form slowly. Caves are carved out of solid rock. I think that process would take a long time.

Ask: What forces or events do you think could cause a cave to form? **Prompt:** What can cause rock to break apart or change? Sample answers: I know flowing water can wear away rock. Maybe water flowing underground can form caves by wearing away rock. Maybe caves can form when a volcano erupts. When lava hardens, there could be spaces under the surface that become caves.

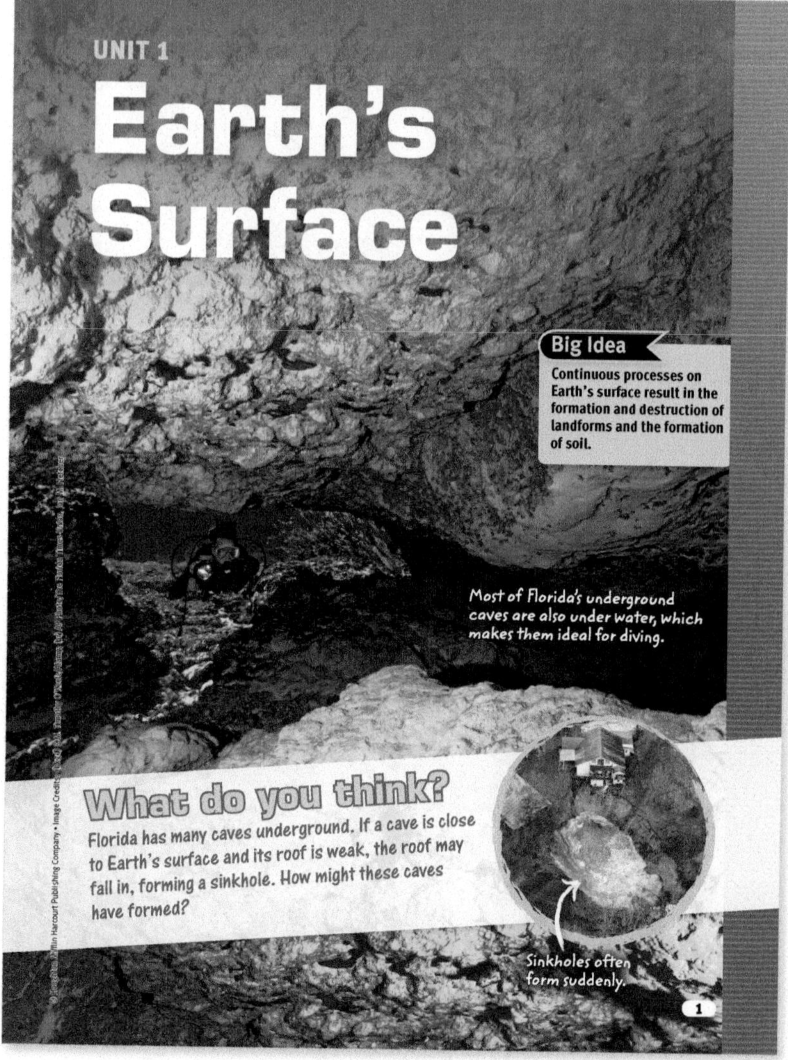

UNIT 1
Earth's Surface
Big Idea
Continuous processes on Earth's surface result in the formation and destruction of landforms and the formation of soil.
Most of Florida's underground caves are also under water, which makes them ideal for diving.
What do you think?
Florida has many caves underground. If a cave is close to Earth's surface and its roof is weak, the roof may fall in, forming a sinkhole. How might these caves have formed?
Sinkholes often form suddenly.
1

Ask: What forces near the shoreline might cause a cave to form? Explain. Sample answer: Ocean waves can wear away the land around the shore. Maybe over time, waves can carve holes in rock that fill with water and become underwater caves.

Interpreting Visuals

Have students look at the image of the sinkhole. **Ask:** What do you notice about this sinkhole? Sample answers: It is larger than a house. It looks deep. **Ask:** Look at the area around the sinkhole. What might have caused the sinkhole to form? Explain. Sample answer: There is a house near the sinkhole. Maybe human activity, such as construction, weakened the ground and caused the cave roof to fall in, forming the sinkhole.

For greater depth, tell students that sinkholes are common in some parts of the United States. They can be caused when water dissolves limestone or certain other types of rock, forming an underground cave. As the cave grows larger, the roof may fall in. Sinkholes can also be caused by human activity, such as groundwater pumping and construction.

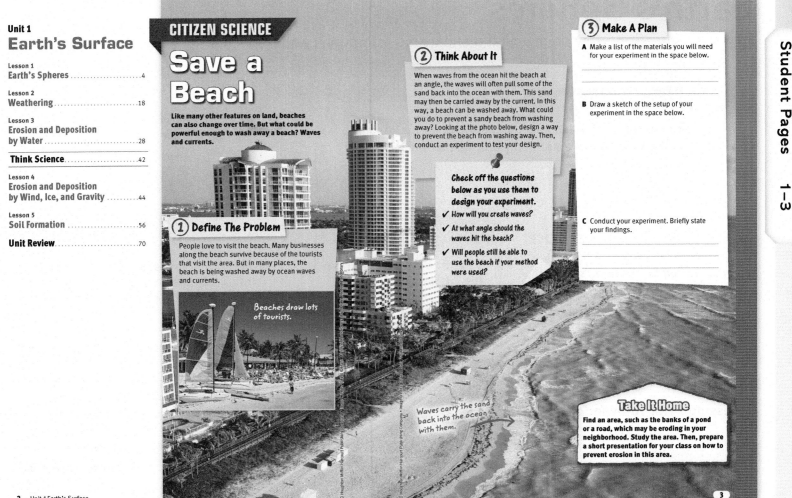

Unit 1
Earth's Surface

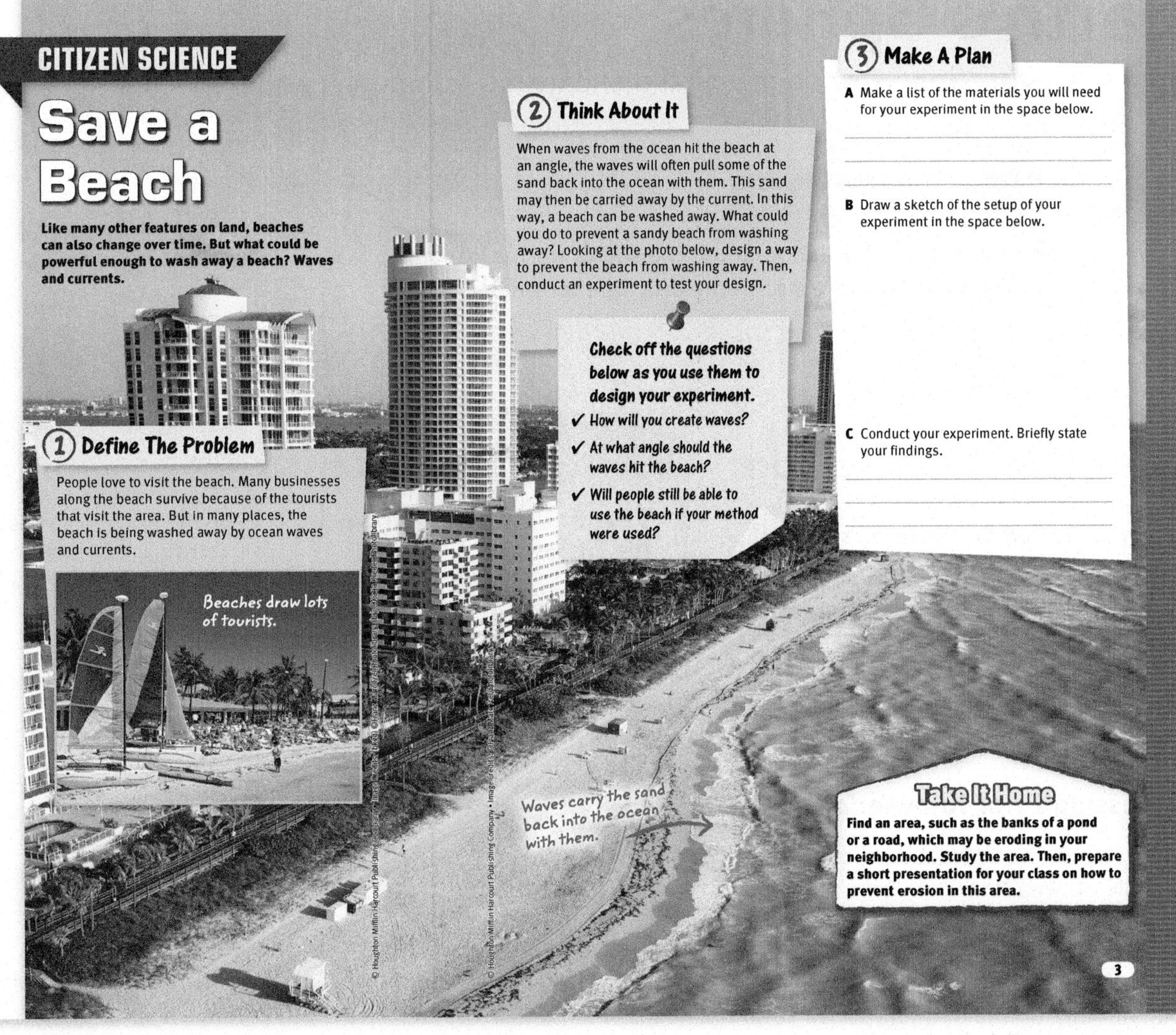

CITIZEN SCIENCE
Save a Beach
Like many other features on land, beaches can also change over time. But what could be powerful enough to wash away a beach? Waves and currents.
1 Define The Problem
People love to visit the beach. Many businesses along the beach survive because of the tourists that visit the area. But in many places, the beach is being washed away by ocean waves and currents.
Beaches draw lots of tourists.
2 Think About It
When waves from the ocean hit the beach at an angle, the waves will often pull some of the sand back into the ocean with them. This sand may then be carried away by the current. In this way, a beach can be washed away. What could you do to prevent a sandy beach from washing away? Looking at the photo below, design a way to prevent the beach from washing away. Then, conduct an experiment to test your design.
Check off the questions below as you use them to design your experiment.
✓ How will you create waves?
✓ At what angle should the waves hit the beach?
✓ Will people still be able to use the beach if your method were used?
Waves carry the sand back into the ocean with them.
3 Make A Plan
A Make a list of the materials you will need for your experiment in the space below.
B Draw a sketch of the setup of your experiment in the space below.
C Conduct your experiment. Briefly state your findings.
Take It Home
Find an area, such as the banks of a pond or a road, which may be eroding in your neighborhood. Study the area. Then, prepare a short presentation for your class on how to prevent erosion in this area.
3

CITIZEN SCIENCE

Unit Project Save a Beach

3. Make a Plan

A. Answers will vary. Students may choose materials such as a large plastic tub, sand, water, pieces of wood (to use as jetties), and objects to make a seawall. They also need a method of creating waves.

B. Students should create a setup that is similar to the beach and waves shown in the photo (i.e., the waves must hit the shoreline at an angle). Except for their erosion-prevention method, students should keep all of the other variables as consistent as possible.

C. Students should be able to clearly articulate their findings. Their conclusions must be based on the results of their tests.

Optional Online rubric: Design Your Own Investigations: Experiments

Take It Home

The presentation should include a description of the location, why erosion is occurring, the form in which it is occurring, and a solution to the erosion problem. For example, in an area behind a student's house, the banks of a drainage ditch may be collapsing and clogging up the drain. The student may suggest planting grass cover along the banks or lining the banks with a brick wall to prevent further erosion.

Optional Online rubric: Oral Presentations

Earth's Spheres

Essential Question How do matter and energy move through Earth's spheres?

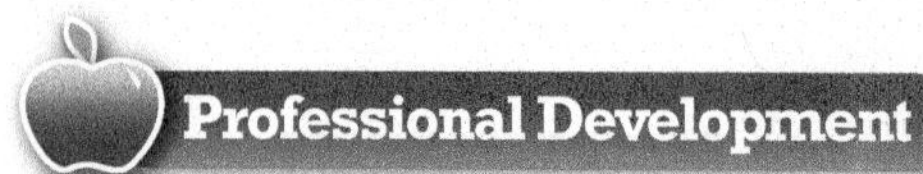

For more detailed information about the topics in this lesson, refer to the Content Refresher in the Unit Opener pages.

Opening Your Lesson

Begin the lesson by assessing students' prerequisite and prior knowledge.

Prerequisite Knowledge

- Many organisms live on Earth.
- The ground, air, and water are part of planet Earth.

Accessing Prior Knowledge

Ask: What do we know about water? Sample answer: Water can be a gas, a liquid, or a solid, and can go back and forth from one state to another.

Ask: What types of weather have you experienced where you live? What other types of weather do you know about but have not seen locally? Sample answers: rain, hail, snow, and sleet

Customize Your Opening

- ☐ **Accessing Prior Knowledge,** above
- ☐ **Print Path** Engage Your Brain, SE p. 5
- ☐ **Print Path** Active Reading, SE p. 5
- ☐ **Digital Path** Lesson Opener

Key Topics/Learning Goals	Supporting Concepts
The Earth System and its Spheres 1 Explain the Earth system. 2 Define *geosphere* and describe Earth's compositional layers. 3 Define *hydrosphere* and explain where it is found. 4 Define *cryosphere*, naming the forms solid water takes. 5 Explain *atmosphere* and its size and composition. 6 Define and explain *biosphere*.	• The Earth system is all of the living and nonliving things, processes, and spheres: the geosphere, hydrosphere, cryosphere, atmosphere, and biosphere. • Earth's compositional layers are the crust, mantle, and core, which have different chemical compositions. • The hydrosphere includes water in liquid form. Liquid water is found on and under Earth's surface and in the atmosphere as rain and clouds. • The cryosphere includes water in solid form, such as snow, glaciers, and permafrost. • Earth's atmosphere is the mixture of gases that surrounds Earth. • The biosphere is where life exists on Earth.
Interactions Between Spheres 1 Describe how Earth's spheres interact. 2 Give examples of interactions among Earth's spheres.	• Matter and energy are exchanged between Earth's spheres. • The biosphere and geosphere interact when byproducts of decaying organisms mix into soil and plants take in nutrients from the soil. • The atmosphere and hydrosphere interact when wind causes waves in the ocean.
Earth's Energy Budget 1 Identify the main source of energy in the Earth system. 2 Describe how Earth's energy budget explains the flow of energy in the Earth system. 3 Explain how an unbalanced energy budget can affect Earth's climate.	• The sun is the main source of energy on Earth. • Energy flows into Earth's system as sunlight and escapes from Earth's atmosphere as heat. • An unbalanced energy budget could increase or decrease global temperatures. • Increased greenhouse gases can trap energy in the atmosphere, increasing temperatures. • Melting polar ice caps absorb more energy, increasing global temperatures.

Options for Instruction

Two parallel paths provide coverage of the Essential Questions, with a strong **Inquiry** strand woven into each. Follow the **Print Path,** the **Digital Path,** or your customized combination of print, digital, and inquiry.

 **Print Path** *Teaching support for the Print Path appears with the Student Pages.*	 **Inquiry Labs and Activities**	 **Digital Path** *Digital Path shortcut: TS661402*
What on Earth?, SE pp. 6–7 **What is the Earth system?** **What is the geosphere?** **Got Water?,** SE pp. 8–9 **What is the hydrosphere?** **What is the cryosphere?** **What a Gas!,** SE pp. 10–11 **What is the atmosphere?** **What is the biosphere?**	**Quick Lab** **Model Earth's Spheres** **Quick Lab** **Explaining Earth's Systems** **Daily Demo** **A Peachy Model**	**Earth Spheres** **Interactive Graphics** **The Hydrosphere** **Interactive Images** **The Biosphere** **Interactive Images**
What's the Matter?, SE pp. 12–13 **How do Earth's spheres interact?** • By Exchanging Matter • By Exchanging Energy	**Activity** **Earth Factory** **Activity** **Why Change?**	**Energy Pyramid** **Interactive Image**
Balancing the Budget, SE pp. 14–15 **What is the source of Earth's energy?** **What can disturb Earth's energy budget?** • Greenhouse Gases • Melting Polar Ice	**S.T.E.M. Lab** **Change and Balance Between Spheres** **Activity** **Greenhouse Gas Reduction**	

Options for Assessment

See the Evaluate page for options, including Formative Assessment, Summative Assessment, and Unit Review.

Engage and Explore

Activities and Discussion

Activity *Earth Factory*

Engage

Interactions Between Spheres

 individuals
 20 min
 **GUIDED** inquiry

We can think of the Earth system as a kind of factory. **Prompt:** We will create our own factories that show how the different parts and processes that make up the Earth system work together. Have students draw a diagram to show the spheres of Earth as if they were components of a factory. Diagrams should label each representation and include a description of the role of each component. **Ask:** What can we learn about the Earth system from the machine we created? Sample answer: The different spheres that make up the Earth system are interdependent. What happens in one sphere affects what happens throughout the system.

Activity *Greenhouse Gas Reduction*

Earth's Energy Budget

 individuals or pairs
20 min
GUIDED inquiry

Remind students that greenhouse gases can affect Earth's energy budget. Tell students that greenhouse gases occur naturally; however, they are also a byproduct of human activity. Burning fossil fuels, such as coal, oil, and natural gas, produces the greenhouse gas carbon dioxide. Another type of greenhouse gas—methane—is produced by cattle and other animals. These gases can affect Earth's energy budget balance. Have students, either individually or in pairs, brainstorm ways that humans could reduce their production of greenhouse gases. Encourage students to share their ideas with the class.

Probing Questions *Our School System*

Interactions Between Spheres

 small groups
 20 min
 **GUIDED** inquiry

Recognizing Remind students that Earth is a system of interacting parts and processes. Invite them to think about their school as a system. **Ask:** What are the parts and processes that work together in our school? Have students create a diagram of their school's network and label the various parts and processes.

Variation Have each group show their diagram and compare what components they included. Did some groups include other schools in the district or in the state? Discuss how a system can be defined in narrow or broad terms.

Discussion *Pollution*

Interactions Between Spheres

 whole class
40 min

What happens in one sphere affects others. Pollution that gets into the air can fall to the ground in the form of acid rain; in this way, pollution in the air can also affect water supplies. Have students discuss pollution as it relates to Earth's spheres.

©Alamy Images

Customize Your Labs

 *See the Lab Manual for lab datasheets.*

 *Go Online for editable lab datasheets.*

Levels of Inquiry

DIRECTED inquiry introduces inquiry skills within a structured framework.

GUIDED inquiry develops inquiry skills within a supportive environment.

INDEPENDENT inquiry deepens inquiry skills with student-driven questions or procedures.

Labs and Demos

Daily Demo *A Peachy Model*

Engage

The Earth System and its Spheres

 whole class
 15 min
 **GUIDED** inquiry

PURPOSE **To model the geosphere**

MATERIALS

- **1 peach**
- **knife**

1 Hold up the peach for students. Tell them that the peach makes a good model for Earth's compositional layers.

2 **Observing** Cut the peach in half so that the pit can be seen, and display it to students. Tell them that the geosphere's crust is represented by the peach skin, the mantle is represented by the fruit of the peach, and Earth's core by the peach's pit, although unlike the pit, Earth's core has two parts—liquid and solid.

3 **Evaluating** Ask students to explain why a peach serves as a good model of Earth's geosphere. Sample answers: Like Earth's crust, the skin is very thin compared to the other parts of the peach; like Earth's mantle, the peach fruit makes up the largest part of the peach; like Earth's inner core, the pit is solid and dense and at the center of the peach; the peach is solid; the peach is round.

Quick Lab *Model Earth's Spheres*

PURPOSE **To examine Earth's spheres**

See the Lab Manual or go Online for planning information.

Quick Lab *Explaining Earth's Systems*

The Earth System and its Spheres

 individuals
 15 min/day for 2 days
 **GUIDED** inquiry

Students will use media to teach about Earth's geosphere, hydrosphere, cryosphere, atmosphere, and biosphere.

PURPOSE **To describe the characteristics of Earth's systems**

MATERIALS

- **glue sticks**
- **markers**
- **paper, 11 x 14 in.**
- **pencils**
- **scissors**
- **selection of nature magazines to cut**

S.T.E.M. Lab *Change and Balance Between Spheres*

Earth's Energy Budget

 small groups
 45 min
DIRECTED or GUIDED inquiry

Students will model different spheres of the Earth in an aquarium, make predictions, simulate imbalances, then revise predictions.

PURPOSE **To examine interactions and imbalances among Earth's systems**

MATERIALS

- **aquarium, with lid**
- **clay, modeling (two colors)**
- **graduated cylinder, 100 mL**
- **block of ice**
- **hair dryer**
- **stopwatch**
- **water**

Activities and Discussion

- ☐ **Activity** Earth Factory
- ☐ **Probing Question** Our School System
- ☐ **Activity** Greenhouse Gas Reduction
- ☐ **Discussion** Pollution

Labs and Demos

- ☐ **Daily Demo** A Peachy Model
- ☐ **Quick Lab** Model Earth's Spheres
- ☐ **Quick Lab** Explaining Earth's Systems
- ☐ **S.T.E.M. Lab** Change and Balance Between Spheres

Your Resources

Explain Science Concepts

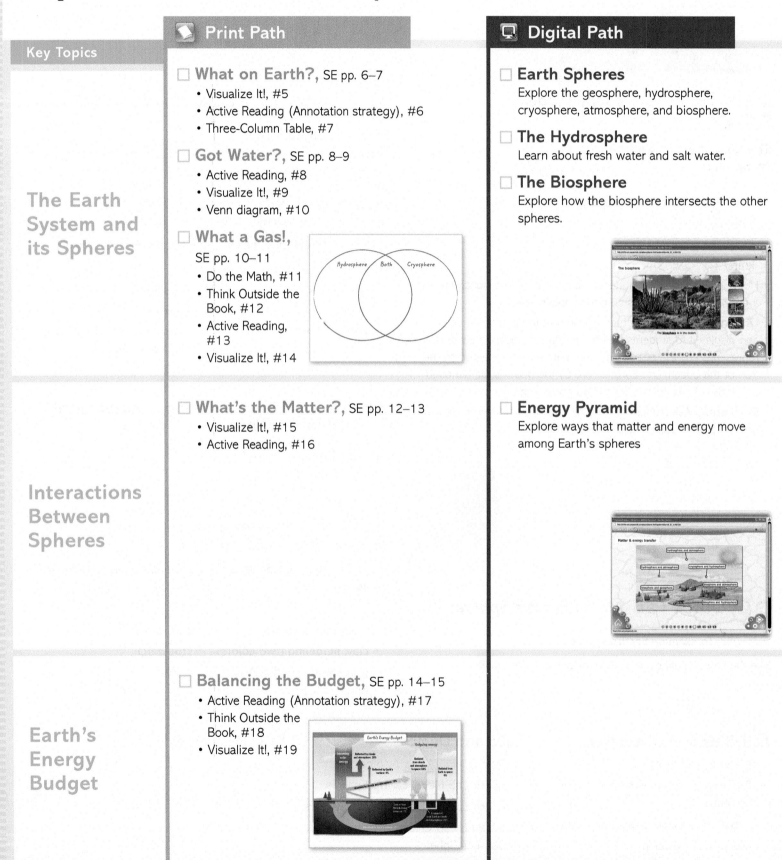

Key Topics	Print Path	Digital Path
The Earth System and its Spheres	☐ **What on Earth?,** SE pp. 6–7 • Visualize It!, #5 • Active Reading (Annotation strategy), #6 • Three-Column Table, #7 ☐ **Got Water?,** SE pp. 8–9 • Active Reading, #8 • Visualize It!, #9 • Venn diagram, #10 ☐ **What a Gas!,** SE pp. 10–11 • Do the Math, #11 • Think Outside the Book, #12 • Active Reading, #13 • Visualize It!, #14 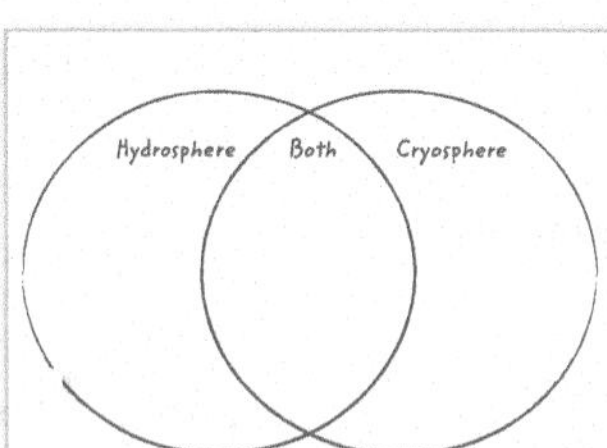 	☐ **Earth Spheres** Explore the geosphere, hydrosphere, cryosphere, atmosphere, and biosphere. ☐ **The Hydrosphere** Learn about fresh water and salt water. ☐ **The Biosphere** Explore how the biosphere intersects the other spheres. 
Interactions Between Spheres	☐ **What's the Matter?,** SE pp. 12–13 • Visualize It!, #15 • Active Reading, #16	☐ **Energy Pyramid** Explore ways that matter and energy move among Earth's spheres 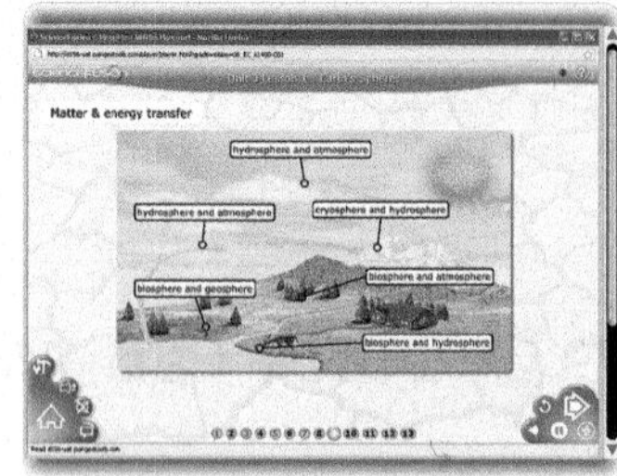
Earth's Energy Budget	☐ **Balancing the Budget,** SE pp. 14–15 • Active Reading (Annotation strategy), #17 • Think Outside the Book, #18 • Visualize It!, #19 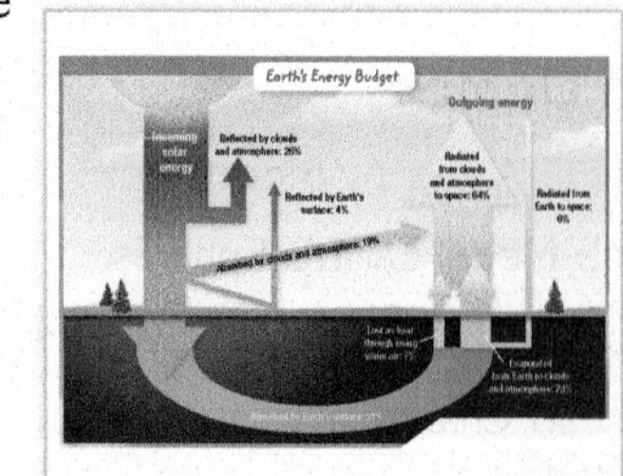 	

Differentiated Instruction

Basic *Where Is the Water?*

Introducing Key Topics

 individuals
15 min

Have students use a Venn diagram to compare and contrast two of Earth's spheres. Provide examples or images to help students think of details to include in the graphic organizer.

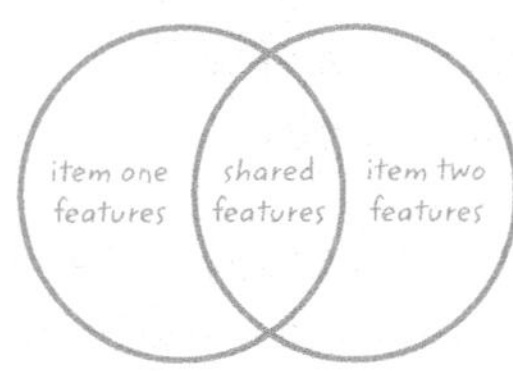

Advanced *Tundra in Trouble*

Earth's Energy Budget

 individuals
 40 min

Case Study Present to students information about what is happening to the permafrost underlying the Siberian tundra. Describe what changes are taking place in the tundra and what factors scientists think are causing these changes. Have students write an analysis of the impact these changes in the cryosphere might have on the biosphere, atmosphere, and hydrosphere.

ELL *Organisms*

The Earth System and its Spheres

 individuals
 20 min

Description Wheel Struggling students or English language learners may be unfamiliar with the word *organism*, which is central to understanding the biosphere. Provide students with this definition of an organism: "a living thing." Then have students make a Description Wheel in which *organism* is the central word, with examples, details, or drawings on the spokes.

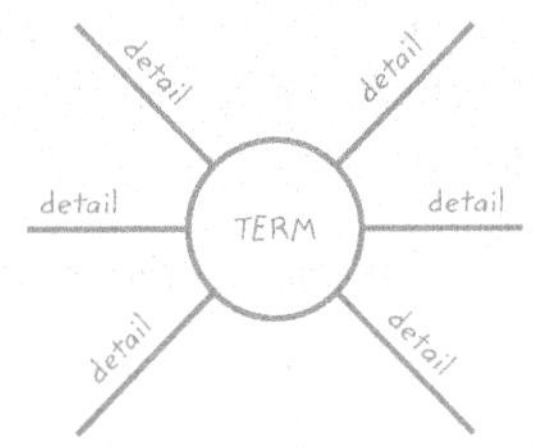

Lesson Vocabulary

Earth system **geosphere** **hydrosphere** **cryosphere**
atmosphere **biosphere** **energy budget**

Previewing Vocabulary

whole class
5 min

Word Roots Share the following to help students understand these terms:

- **Biosphere** comes from the Greek word *bios*, which means "live together."
- **Cryosphere** comes from the Greek word *kryos,* meaning "icy cold."
- **Geosphere** comes from the Greek word *geo*, meaning "earth."
- **Hydrosphere** is from the Greek word *hydros*, meaning "water."

Reinforcing Vocabulary

 individuals
ongoing

Frame Game To help students understand the terms introduced in this lesson, have them create a frame for each one. Students can then use the frames to compare and contrast the terms. **Prompt:** Write the term in the center of a frame. Fill in the surrounding cells with information about that term.

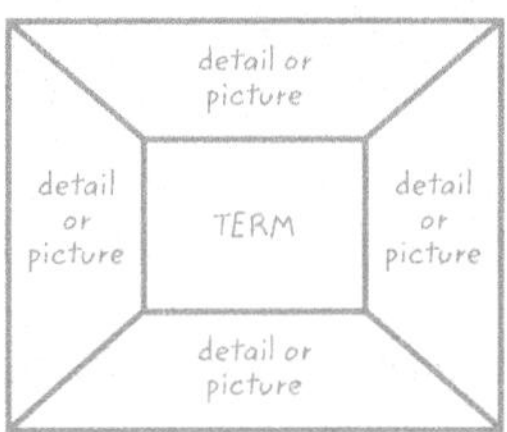

Customize Your Core Lesson

Core Instruction

- ☐ Print Path choices
- ☐ Digital Path choices

Vocabulary

- ☐ Previewing Vocabulary Word Roots
- ☐ Reinforcing Vocabulary Frame Game

Your Resources

Differentiated Instruction

- ☐ Basic Where is the Water?
- ☐ Advanced Tundra in Trouble
- ☐ ELL Organisms

Extend Science Concepts

Reinforce and Review

Activity *Why Change?*

Interactions Between Spheres | pairs, small groups | 30 min

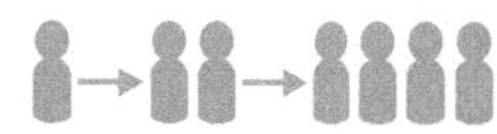

Think, Pair, Share Encourage pairs of students to discuss this question: Is one of Earth's spheres more important for life than the others, could life exist without one sphere, or is it essential that all spheres work together? Defend your answer with details and facts. **Prompt:** Share your thoughts about this question to see if you agree or disagree with your partner. Can you persuade your partner to agree with your point of view? Have student pairs form small groups of four. **Prompt:** Share your ideas with the other people in your group. Do you have similar or new ideas? Are you able to agree on what is a fact and what is an opinion? What additional information do you need? What ideas are causing you to change your mind?

Optional Online resource: Think, Pair, Share support

Graphic Organizer

Earth's Energy Budget | individuals | ongoing

Cluster Diagram After students have learned about Earth's energy budget, have them create a cluster diagram. Diagrams should include information on where Earth's energy comes from, how it moves, how it remains in balance, and how it can become unbalanced.

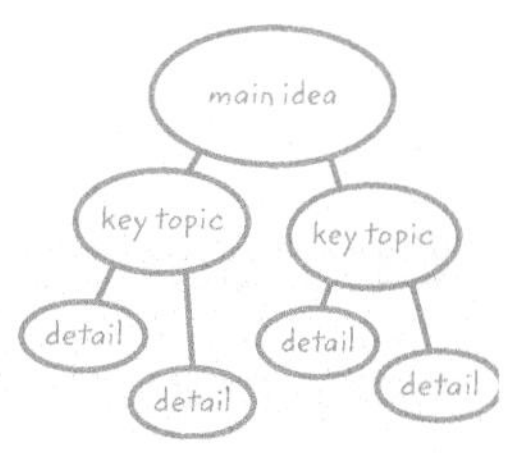

Optional Online resource: Cluster Diagram support

Going Further

Language Arts Connection

Synthesizing Key Topics | whole class | 30 min

Journal Study Invite students to imagine a time in the future when there is a widespread, prolonged drought. **Prompt:** Imagine that you have been keeping a journal during the drought. Use your imagination, your knowledge of how spheres interact, and your knowledge of the energy budget to write a one-page entry in your journal. Describe the changes you have seen, and why you think they have occurred. Show how the disruption in the hydrosphere has affected the other spheres. For example, no rain would mean crops drying up, causing food shortages.

Optional Online rubric: Written Pieces

Real World Connection

Synthesizing Key Topics | pairs | 45 min

Cause-and-Effect Chain Have pairs of students research the effects of an infestation by an organism. Encourage them to discuss how different parts of the biosphere have been affected. One example is an infestation by the mountain pine beetle, a tiny beetle the size of a rice grain, which has had a big impact in North America. Direct students to create a cause-and-effect chain for the infestation they have chosen.

Optional Online resource: Cause-and-Effect Chain support

Customize Your Closing

See the Assessment Guide for quizzes and tests.

Go Online to edit and create quizzes and tests.

Reinforce and Review

- [ ] **Activity** Why Change?
- [ ] **Graphic Organizer** Cluster Diagram
- [ ] **Print Path** Visual Summary, SE p. 16
- [ ] **Print Path** Lesson Review, SE p. 17
- [ ] **Digital Path** Lesson Closer

Evaluate Student Mastery

Formative Assessment

See the teacher support below the Student pages for additional Formative Assessment questions.

Have students review the information about emperor penguins from the beginning of the print lesson or provide another example that describes how organisms interact with their environment. **Ask:** How do these organisms interact with each of Earth's spheres? Sample answer: Penguins are living things and belong to the biosphere; they live on the geosphere and the cryosphere; they swim and go hunting in the hydrosphere; they breathe the air in the atmosphere. **Ask:** What is the energy budget? Sample answer: the Earth is a system that maintains a balance. If energy is taken away from one area, it is added to another. If energy enters the system, an equivalent amount of energy should leave the system.

Reteach

Formative assessment may show that students need reinforcement for certain topics. The resources below are recommended for reteaching. If students were introduced to a topic through the Print Path, you can also use the Digital Path to reteach, or vice versa.
Can be assigned to individual students

The Earth System and its Spheres

Quick Lab Explaining Earth's Systems

Interactions Between Spheres

Activity Earth Factory

Earth's Spheres Interact

Activity Greenhouse Gas Reduction

S.T.E.M. Lab Change and Balance Between Spheres

Summative Assessment

Alternative Assessment

Earth's System and Earth's Spheres

Online resources: student worksheet, optional rubrics

Earth's Spheres

Choose Your Meal: *Earth's System and Earth's Spheres*
Complete the activities to show what you've learned about the Earth system, Earth's spheres, and Earth's energy budget.

1. Work on your own, with a partner, or with a small group.
2. Choose one item from each section of the menu, with an optional dessert. Check your choices.
3. Have your teacher approve your plan.
4. Submit or present your results.

Appetizers

____ **What's in a Sphere?** Write a poem about Earth's spheres. Include all spheres in your poem.

____ **Promoting Earth** Compose a brochure that encourages an alien species to move to the planet Earth. Include information about the Earth system and the ways living things, nonliving things, and Earth's spheres work together to make it a good planet to live on. Include an illustration of Earth.

____ **Peeling Back the Layers** Create a PowerPoint presentation in which you describe the layers of Earth's geosphere. You may want to feature one layer on each slide. Include pictures or diagrams.

Main Dish

____ **Earth's Description** Write a description from Earth's point of view. Have Earth give an overview of its systems and give examples of the ways the systems work together.

Side Dishes

____ **Fan Club** Suppose you run the atmosphere's fan club. Design a Web page for your club. Include information on the atmosphere's composition and size, and on how it helps us.

____ **Job Description** Imagine you are hiring an accountant to balance Earth's energy budget. Write a job description, explaining what needs to be balanced and why it is so important.

Desserts (optional)

____ **Where's the Water?** Create a poster of Earth's hydrosphere. Include all the parts of the hydrosphere including water underground and in clouds. Label the parts.

____ **Composing Questions** Write a quiz about the cryosphere. Include at least five questions or activities on your quiz and include an answer key.

Going Further

- ☐ Language Arts Connection
- ☐ Real World Connection

Formative Assessment

- ☐ Strategies Throughout TE
- ☐ Lesson Review SE

Summative Assessment

- ☐ Alternative Assessment Earth's System and Earth's Spheres
- ☐ Lesson Quiz
- ☐ Unit Tests A and B
- ☐ Unit Test SE End-of-Unit

Your Resources

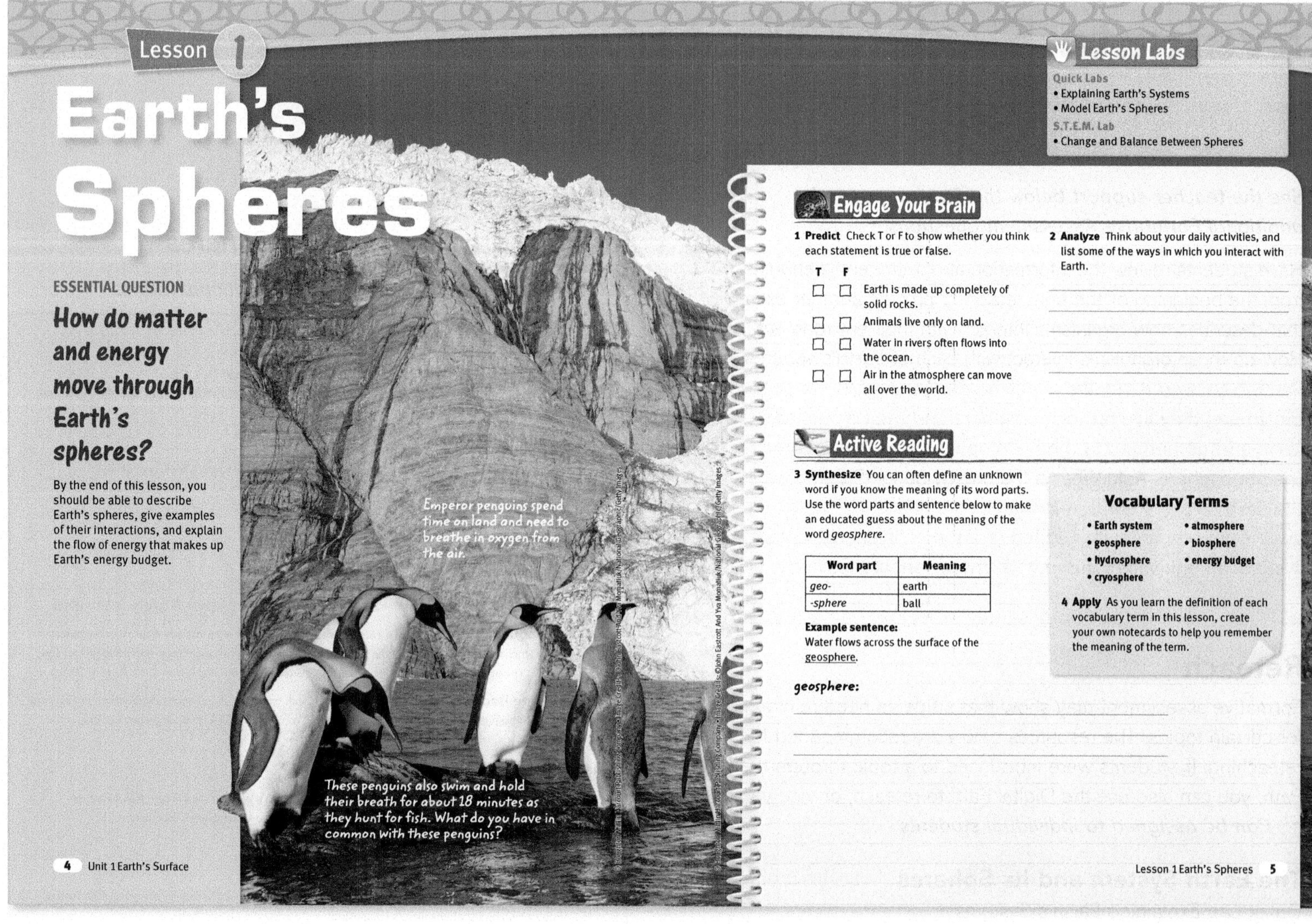

Answers

Answers for 1–3 should represent students' current thoughts, even if incorrect.

1. F; F; T; T
2. Sample answer: I throw out trash that will end up in a landfill. I use water that flows through the drains and into the water system.
3. Sample answer: planet Earth
4. Students' annotations will vary.

Opening Your Lesson

Discuss some of the ways in which students interact with different parts of Earth on a daily basis.

Preconceptions Students may think of Earth only as the solid planet, disregarding water and air. They may also only know the meaning of *sphere* as something round.

Accessing Prior Knowledge Invite students to give examples of evidence that show that Earth is not just made of solid rock. **Ask:** What are some types of animals that live in more than one type of environment?

Learning Alert

Everyday Definitions We tend to think of Earth as one unit but in this lesson we will learn that our planet is made up of five spheres that work together. Earth is not only the ground we stand on; it is a complex system that includes air, liquid and frozen forms of water, and all forms of life. We also tend to think of a sphere as a round shape, but in this lesson we will learn that the word *sphere* also means an environment in which something can be found.

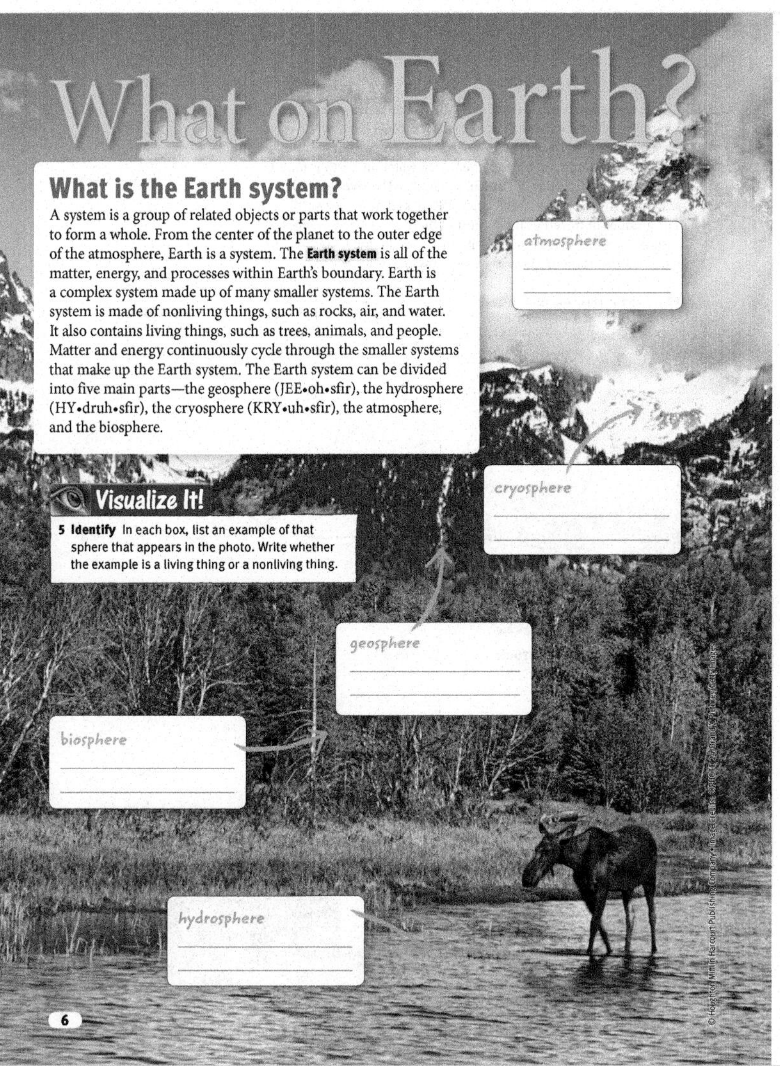

What on Earth?

What is the Earth system?

A system is a group of related objects or parts that work together to form a whole. From the center of the planet to the outer edge of the atmosphere, Earth is a system. The **Earth system** is all of the matter, energy, and processes within Earth's boundary. Earth is a complex system made up of many smaller systems. The Earth system is made of nonliving things, such as rocks, air, and water. It also contains living things, such as trees, animals, and people. Matter and energy continuously cycle through the smaller systems that make up the Earth system. The Earth system can be divided into five main parts—the geosphere (JEE•oh•sfir), the hydrosphere (HY•druh•sfir), the cryosphere (KRY•uh•sfir), the atmosphere, and the biosphere.

Visualize It!

5 Identify In each box, list an example of that sphere that appears in the photo. Write whether the example is a living thing or a nonliving thing.

atmosphere
cryosphere
geosphere
biosphere
hydrosphere

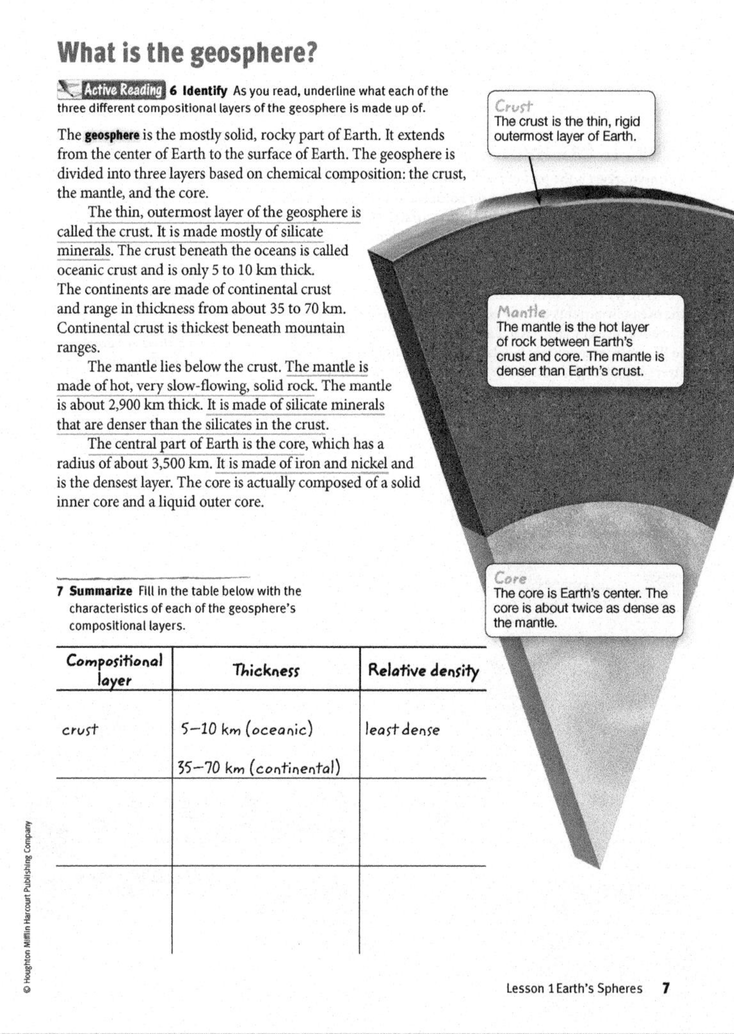

What is the geosphere?

Active Reading **6 Identify** As you read, underline what each of the three different compositional layers of the geosphere is made up of.

The **geosphere** is the mostly solid, rocky part of Earth. It extends from the center of Earth to the surface of Earth. The geosphere is divided into three layers based on chemical composition: the crust, the mantle, and the core.

The thin, outermost layer of the geosphere is called the crust. It is made mostly of silicate minerals. The crust beneath the oceans is called oceanic crust and is only 5 to 10 km thick. The continents are made of continental crust and range in thickness from about 35 to 70 km. Continental crust is thickest beneath mountain ranges.

The mantle lies below the crust. The mantle is made of hot, very slow-flowing, solid rock. The mantle is about 2,900 km thick. It is made of silicate minerals that are denser than the silicates in the crust.

The central part of Earth is the core, which has a radius of about 3,500 km. It is made of iron and nickel and is the densest layer. The core is actually composed of a solid inner core and a liquid outer core.

Crust
The crust is the thin, rigid outermost layer of Earth.
Mantle
The mantle is the hot layer of rock between Earth's crust and core. The mantle is denser than Earth's crust.
Core
The core is Earth's center. The core is about twice as dense as the mantle.

7 Summarize Fill in the table below with the characteristics of each of the geosphere's compositional layers.

Compositional layer	Thickness	Relative density
crust	5–10 km (oceanic) 35–70 km (continental)	least dense

Answers

5. Sample answer: geosphere: soil, nonliving thing; biosphere: trees, living thing; cryosphere: snow, nonliving thing; hydrosphere: river, nonliving thing; atmosphere: air, nonliving thing.
6. *See students' pages for annotations.*
7. Students should fill in the table with the following: mantle (middle left), 2,900 km (middle center), more dense than crust (middle right), core (bottom left), 3,500 km (bottom center), most dense (bottom right).

Interpreting Visuals

Have students identify specific forms of life in the photograph. Ask them what other parts of the biosphere might not be visible in the photo. Sample answers: The moose, trees, and grass are pictured; other living things not visible in the photo might include birds, insects, small animals, fish, underwater vegetation, and microscopic organisms. Ask students to then identify some of the nonliving things in the photograph. Sample answers: The water, soil, mountains, and clouds are nonliving.

Learning Alert

Lithosphere Although this lesson does not discuss the lithosphere, it is an important concept for scientists studying the geosphere. The lithosphere is the rigid outer layer of Earth. It includes the crust and the upper mantle, and is about 100 km thick. The lithosphere is divided into tectonic plates. When these plates interact with one another, many different geologic events are possible, such as volcanic eruptions, earthquakes, and the formation of mountains. Encourage students to relate what they know about plate tectonics to the composition of Earth's geosphere.

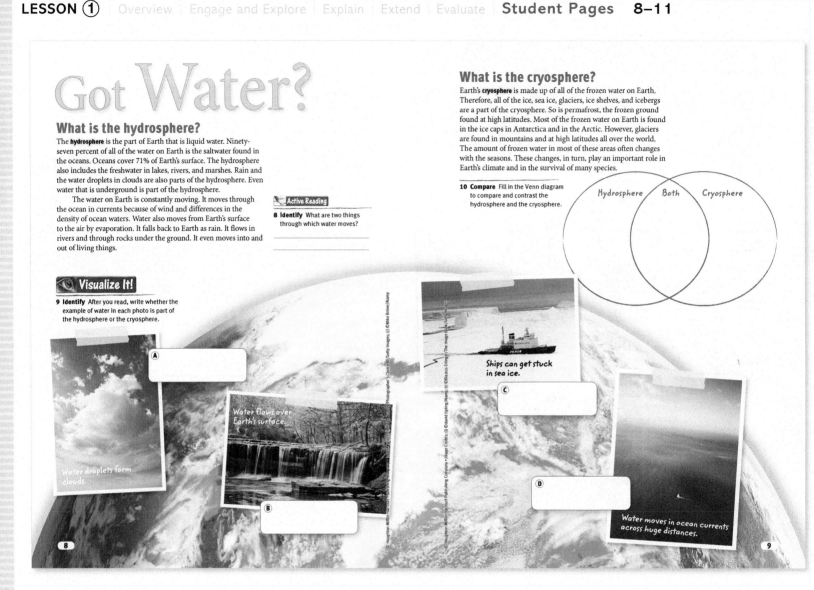

Got Water?

What is the hydrosphere?

The **hydrosphere** is the part of Earth that is liquid water. Ninety-seven percent of all of the water on Earth is the saltwater found in the oceans. Oceans cover 71% of Earth's surface. The hydrosphere also includes the freshwater in lakes, rivers, and marshes. Rain and the water droplets in clouds are also parts of the hydrosphere. Even water that is underground is part of the hydrosphere.

The water on Earth is constantly moving. It moves through the ocean in currents because of wind and differences in the density of ocean waters. Water also moves from Earth's surface to the air by evaporation. It falls back to Earth as rain. It flows in rivers and through rocks under the ground. It even moves into and out of living things.

Active Reading

8 Identify What are two things through which water moves?

What is the cryosphere?

Earth's **cryosphere** is made up of all of the frozen water on Earth. Therefore, all of the ice, sea ice, glaciers, ice shelves, and icebergs are a part of the cryosphere. So is permafrost, the frozen ground found at high latitudes. Most of the frozen water on Earth is found in the ice caps in Antarctica and in the Arctic. However, glaciers are found in mountains and at high latitudes all over the world. The amount of frozen water in most of these areas often changes with the seasons. These changes, in turn, play an important role in Earth's climate and in the survival of many species.

10 Compare Fill in the Venn diagram to compare and contrast the hydrosphere and the cryosphere.

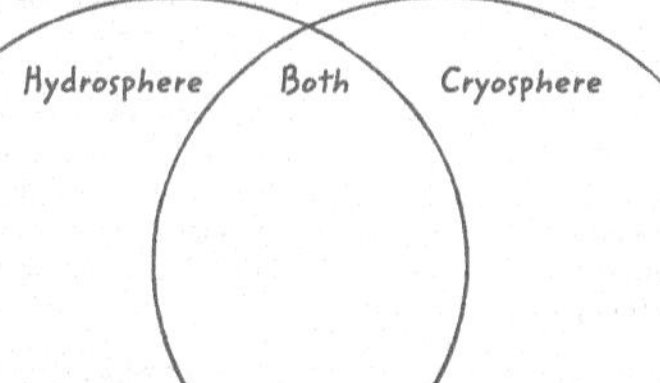

Visualize It!

9 Identify After you read, write whether the example of water in each photo is part of the hydrosphere or the cryosphere.

Water droplets form clouds.

Water flows over Earth's surface.

Ships can get stuck in sea ice.

Water moves in ocean currents across huge distances.

8 9

Answers

8. Any two of the following examples: oceans, lakes, rivers, marshes, atmosphere, underground/rocks, and living things.
9. A: hydrosphere; B: hydrosphere; C: cryosphere; D: hydrosphere
10. Students should fill out the Venn diagram with variations of the following: liquid water accounts for most of the water on Earth (under heading, Hydrosphere); composed of water molecules, and one of Earth's spheres (under heading, Both); frozen water on Earth in various forms of ice and snow (under heading, Cryosphere).

Formative Assessment

Ask: What are some examples of the hydrosphere that are not shown in the image? Sample answers: marshes, streams, swamps, groundwater

Learning Alert

Melting Ice The Greenland ice sheet is the world's second largest body of ice. It covers about 80% of Greenland's surface. Only the Antarctic ice sheet is larger. Scientists have discovered that the Greenland ice sheet is melting at a fast rate. This melting is a strong indicator of climate change and a major reason for rising sea levels around the world. As melting occurs, the hydrosphere grows while the cryosphere shrinks.

Probing Questions GUIDED Inquiry

Examining Why do you think most of the frozen water on Earth is found in the polar ice caps? Sample answer: The polar regions receive less sunlight than other parts of Earth so they are colder than other regions and ice stays frozen for longer.

Interpreting Can you think of ways in which the hydrosphere and cryosphere are changing? Sample answers: Some glaciers are melting. Sea levels are rising.

What a Gas!

What is the atmosphere?

The **atmosphere** is mostly made of invisible gases that surround Earth. The atmosphere extends outward about 500 to 600 km from the surface of Earth. But most of the gases lie within 8 to 50 km of Earth's surface. The main gases that make up the atmosphere are nitrogen and oxygen. About 78% of the atmosphere is nitrogen. Oxygen makes up 21% of the atmosphere. The remaining 1% is made of many other gases, including argon, carbon dioxide, and water vapor.

The atmosphere contains the air we breathe. The atmosphere also absorbs some of the energy from the sun's rays. This energy helps keep Earth warm enough for living things to survive and multiply. Uneven warming by the sun gives rise to winds and air currents that move air and energy around the world.

Some gases in the atmosphere absorb and reflect harmful ultraviolet (UV) rays from the sun, protecting Earth and its living things. The atmosphere also causes space debris to burn up before reaching Earth's surface and causing harm. Have you ever seen the tail of a meteor across the sky? Then you have seen a meteoroid burning up as it moves through the atmosphere!

Do the Math You Try It

11 Identify Fill in the blank in the key with the percentage of oxygen in the atmosphere.

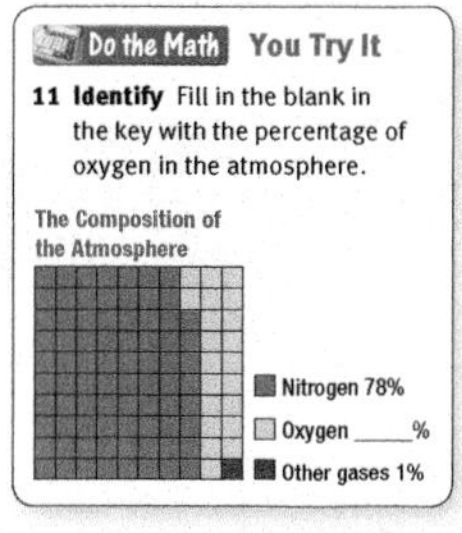

The atmosphere is a very thin layer around Earth. It is made up of a mixture of gases.

Think Outside the Book

12 Apply Design a magazine ad for the atmosphere to show what it does for Earth.

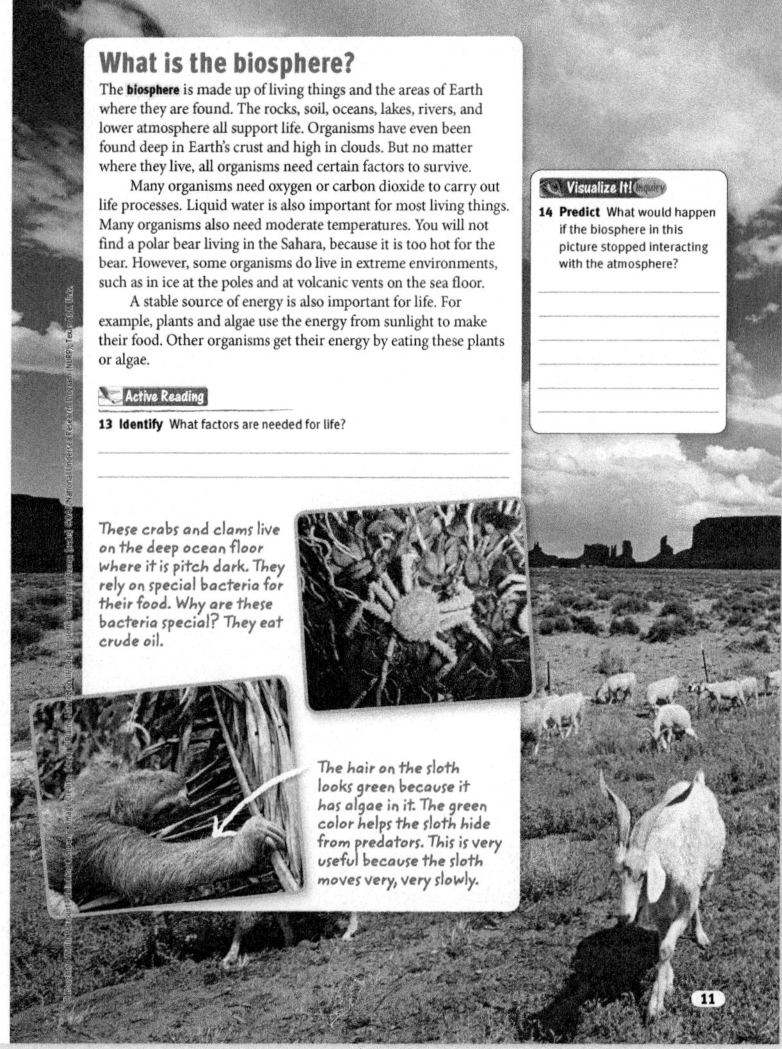

What is the biosphere?

The **biosphere** is made up of living things and the areas of Earth where they are found. The rocks, soil, oceans, lakes, rivers, and lower atmosphere all support life. Organisms have even been found deep in Earth's crust and high in clouds. But no matter where they live, all organisms need certain factors to survive.

Many organisms need oxygen or carbon dioxide to carry out life processes. Liquid water is also important for most living things. Many organisms also need moderate temperatures. You will not find a polar bear living in the Sahara, because it is too hot for the bear. However, some organisms do live in extreme environments, such as in ice at the poles and at volcanic vents on the sea floor.

A stable source of energy is also important for life. For example, plants and algae use the energy from sunlight to make their food. Other organisms get their energy by eating these plants or algae.

Active Reading

13 Identify What factors are needed for life?

These crabs and clams live on the deep ocean floor where it is pitch dark. They rely on special bacteria for their food. Why are these bacteria special? They eat crude oil.

The hair on the sloth looks green because it has algae in it. The green color helps the sloth hide from predators. This is very useful because the sloth moves very, very slowly.

Visualize It! Inquiry

14 Predict What would happen if the biosphere in this picture stopped interacting with the atmosphere?

Answers

11. 21
12. Students' ads might show an image of Earth's atmosphere with callouts of how it protects living things and how living things interact with it.
13. Oxygen or carbon dioxide, liquid water, moderate temperatures, and a stable source of energy.
14. Sample answer: The amount of available oxygen would decrease, while the amount of carbon dioxide would increase. Reduced amounts of oxygen would mean that most organisms would start to die.

Building Reading Skills

Cause and Effect Have students identify the effects of the relationship between Earth's atmosphere and the sun's energy. Sample answers: Earth is warmed as solar energy is trapped by the atmosphere. Harmful radiation is reflected away from Earth. Wind and air currents are created. **Ask:** How does this cause-and-effect relationship affect life on Earth? The atmosphere keeps Earth at a temperature that organisms can live in.

Building Graphing Skills

Drawing Conclusions Tell students that graphs like the one that shows the composition of Earth's atmosphere can be used to draw conclusions without looking at exact data. Ask students to point out some conclusions they can draw just by quickly glancing at the graph. The atmosphere is made up mostly of nitrogen. Other gases make up only a very small percentage of the atmosphere. Two gases make up most of the atmosphere.

Learning Alert

Giant Tube Worms Scientists have discovered a species of worm living near volcanic vents on the ocean floor. Unlike most organisms, which require energy from sunlight, the tube worm and other species living in deep oceans depend on energy from the geosphere.

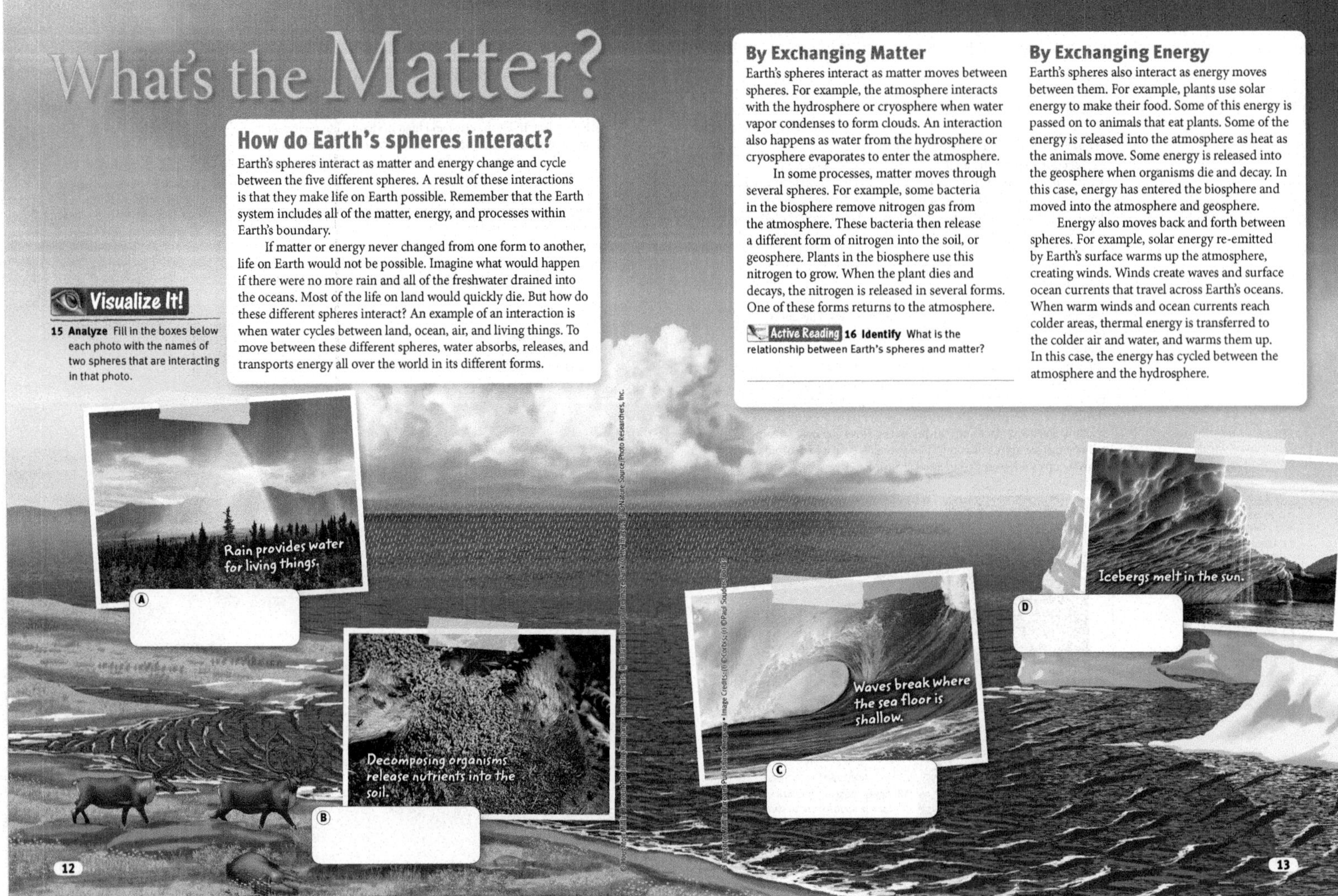

What's the Matter?
How do Earth's spheres interact?
Earth's spheres interact as matter and energy change and cycle between the five different spheres. A result of these interactions is that they make life on Earth possible. Remember that the Earth system includes all of the matter, energy, and processes within Earth's boundary.
If matter or energy never changed from one form to another, life on Earth would not be possible. Imagine what would happen if there were no more rain and all of the freshwater drained into the oceans. Most of the life on land would quickly die. But how do these different spheres interact? An example of an interaction is when water cycles between land, ocean, air, and living things. To move between these different spheres, water absorbs, releases, and transports energy all over the world in its different forms.
Visualize It!
15 Analyze Fill in the boxes below each photo with the names of two spheres that are interacting in that photo.
By Exchanging Matter
Earth's spheres interact as matter moves between spheres. For example, the atmosphere interacts with the hydrosphere or cryosphere when water vapor condenses to form clouds. An interaction also happens as water from the hydrosphere or cryosphere evaporates to enter the atmosphere.
In some processes, matter moves through several spheres. For example, some bacteria in the biosphere remove nitrogen gas from the atmosphere. These bacteria then release a different form of nitrogen into the soil, or geosphere. Plants in the biosphere use this nitrogen to grow. When the plant dies and decays, the nitrogen is released in several forms. One of these forms returns to the atmosphere.
Active Reading 16 Identify What is the relationship between Earth's spheres and matter?
By Exchanging Energy
Earth's spheres also interact as energy moves between them. For example, plants use solar energy to make their food. Some of this energy is passed on to animals that eat plants. Some of the energy is released into the atmosphere as heat as the animals move. Some energy is released into the geosphere when organisms die and decay. In this case, energy has entered the biosphere and moved into the atmosphere and geosphere.
Energy also moves back and forth between spheres. For example, solar energy re-emitted by Earth's surface warms up the atmosphere, creating winds. Winds create waves and surface ocean currents that travel across Earth's oceans. When warm winds and ocean currents reach colder areas, thermal energy is transferred to the colder air and water, and warms them up. In this case, the energy has cycled between the atmosphere and the hydrosphere.
Rain provides water for living things.
A
Decomposing organisms release nutrients into the soil.
B
Waves break where the sea floor is shallow.
C
Icebergs melt in the sun.
D
12
13

Answers

15. Sample answers: A: biosphere and hydrosphere; B: biosphere and geosphere; C: hydrosphere and geosphere; D: cryosphere and hydrosphere
16. Matter moves between Earth's spheres.

Building Reading Skills

Diagrams Diagrams can help students organize their thoughts and develop a more complete understanding of complex ideas. Encourage students to choose one of the descriptions of interactions among spheres from the text and use it to create a diagram that illustrates the ideas presented in the text.

Formative Assessment

Ask: How does energy from the sun become part of our bodies? Sample answer: Plants absorb solar energy to make their own food. When we eat vegetables and fruit, some of this energy passes into us. **Prompt:** Think about how you get energy for all the things you do. **Ask:** How do the biosphere and geosphere interact when organisms die? Sample answer: When organisms die, their bodies decompose. This process adds nutrients to the soil. This nutrient-rich soil is the perfect place for plants to begin growing. The plants provide food for animals. In this way, the cycle goes on and on.

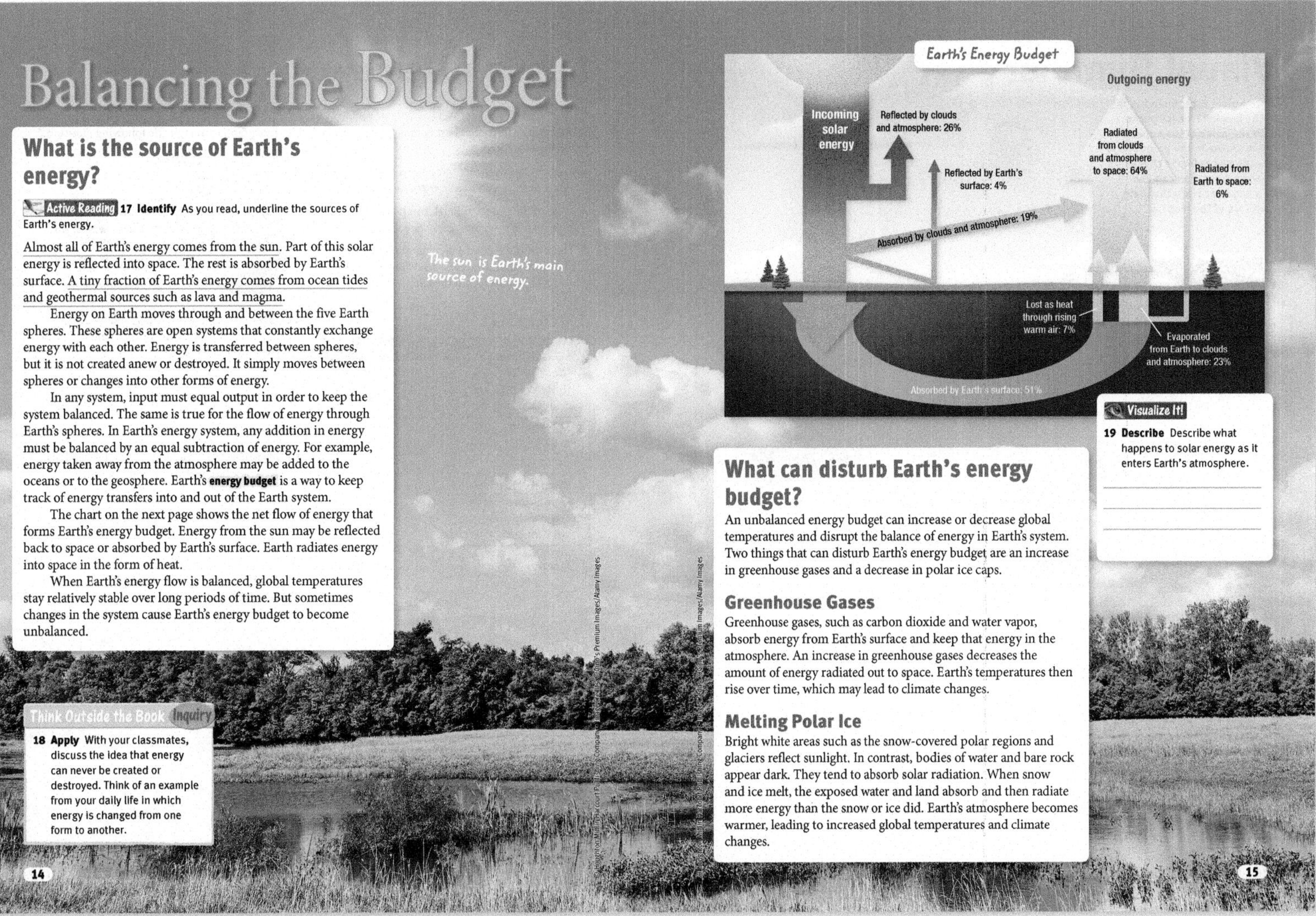

Balancing the Budget

What is the source of Earth's energy?

Active Reading **17 Identify** As you read, underline the sources of Earth's energy.

Almost all of Earth's energy comes from the sun. Part of this solar energy is reflected into space. The rest is absorbed by Earth's surface. A tiny fraction of Earth's energy comes from ocean tides and geothermal sources such as lava and magma.

Energy on Earth moves through and between the five Earth spheres. These spheres are open systems that constantly exchange energy with each other. Energy is transferred between spheres, but it is not created anew or destroyed. It simply moves between spheres or changes into other forms of energy.

In any system, input must equal output in order to keep the system balanced. The same is true for the flow of energy through Earth's spheres. In Earth's energy system, any addition in energy must be balanced by an equal subtraction of energy. For example, energy taken away from the atmosphere may be added to the oceans or to the geosphere. Earth's **energy budget** is a way to keep track of energy transfers into and out of the Earth system.

The chart on the next page shows the net flow of energy that forms Earth's energy budget. Energy from the sun may be reflected back to space or absorbed by Earth's surface. Earth radiates energy into space in the form of heat.

When Earth's energy flow is balanced, global temperatures stay relatively stable over long periods of time. But sometimes changes in the system cause Earth's energy budget to become unbalanced.

The sun is Earth's main source of energy.

Think Outside the Book Inquiry

18 Apply With your classmates, discuss the idea that energy can never be created or destroyed. Think of an example from your daily life in which energy is changed from one form to another.

14

Visualize It!

19 Describe Describe what happens to solar energy as it enters Earth's atmosphere.

What can disturb Earth's energy budget?

An unbalanced energy budget can increase or decrease global temperatures and disrupt the balance of energy in Earth's system. Two things that can disturb Earth's energy budget are an increase in greenhouse gases and a decrease in polar ice caps.

Greenhouse Gases

Greenhouse gases, such as carbon dioxide and water vapor, absorb energy from Earth's surface and keep that energy in the atmosphere. An increase in greenhouse gases decreases the amount of energy radiated out to space. Earth's temperatures then rise over time, which may lead to climate changes.

Melting Polar Ice

Bright white areas such as the snow-covered polar regions and glaciers reflect sunlight. In contrast, bodies of water and bare rock appear dark. They tend to absorb solar radiation. When snow and ice melt, the exposed water and land absorb and then radiate more energy than the snow or ice did. Earth's atmosphere becomes warmer, leading to increased global temperatures and climate changes.

15

Answers

17. *See students' pages for annotations.*
18. Sample answer: electrical energy to radiant energy – a light bulb; electrical energy to sound energy – a radio broadcast
19. Sample answer: Part of the sun's energy is reflected back into space, part of it is absorbed by the land and oceans, and part of it is absorbed by the clouds and atmosphere.

Learning Alert

Greenhouse Gases Students have likely heard the term *greenhouse gases* before, but may not know exactly what they are. Ask if any students have ever seen a real greenhouse, and have them describe what a greenhouse looks like. Explain that Earth's atmosphere acts much like the glass in a real greenhouse: it lets energy in, then traps some of that energy. Without greenhouse gases, Earth would not be warm enough for humans to live. However, an increase in greenhouse gases can change Earth's energy budget.

Interpreting Visuals

Have students look at the chart showing the flow of energy to and away from Earth. **Ask:** Does all of the incoming energy enter Earth's spheres? How can you tell? Sample answer: No. I can tell because of the small arrow that splits off from the large incoming orange arrow. That arrow shows the energy turning around and heading back into space. Also, that arrow's label says that 26% of the incoming energy is reflected by the clouds and atmosphere. How can you confirms that 100% of the energy that entered Earth's atmosphere Leaves Earth and its atmosphere? Sample answer: I can add up all the percentages leaving Earth: 7%, 23%, 6% and 64%—these add up to 100%.

Visual Summary
To complete this summary, fill in the box below each photo with the name of the sphere being shown in the photo. Then use the key below to check your answers. You can use this page to review the main concepts of the lesson.
Earth's Spheres
20
21
22
23
24
Answers: 20 geosphere; 21 biosphere; 22 cryosphere; 23 hydrosphere; 24 atmosphere
25 Synthesize Diagram an interaction between any two of Earth's spheres.

Lesson Review

Lesson 1

Vocabulary

Underline the term that best completes each of the following sentences.

1 The ice caps in the Antarctic and the Arctic are a part of the *geosphere/cryosphere/biosphere.*

2 Most of the water on Earth can be found in the *biosphere/hydrosphere/geosphere.*

3 The *hydrosphere/geosphere/atmosphere* protects organisms that live on Earth by blocking out harmful UV rays from the sun.

Key Concepts

Location	Sphere
4 Identify Forms a thin layer of gases around Earth	
5 Identify Extends from Earth's core to Earth's surface	
6 Identify Extends from inside Earth's crust to the lower atmosphere	

7 Describe What does the Earth system include?

8 Analyze Which spheres are interacting when a volcano erupts and releases gases into the air?

9 Identify What are the two most abundant gases in the atmosphere?

10 Describe How do Earth's spheres interact?

Critical Thinking

Use this graph to answer the following question.

Earth's Solar Energy Balance

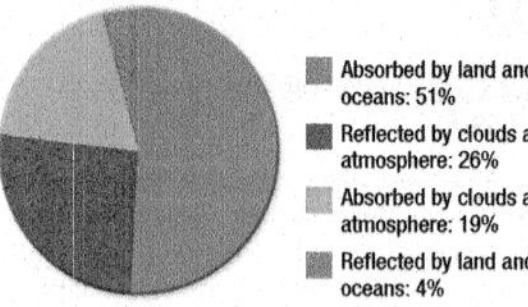

11 Infer Which parts of the graph would increase if all of Earth's polar ice melts? Which parts would decrease?

12 Identify Name two ways in which the Earth system relies on energy from the sun.

13 Analyze How does the biosphere rely on the other spheres for survival?

14 Infer Where is most of Earth's liquid water? What must be done so humans can drink it?

Visual Summary Answers

20. geosphere
21. biosphere
22. cryosphere
23. hydrosphere
24. atmosphere
25. Students' diagrams should clearly show an interaction between any two spheres. For example: an animal digging a burrow or drinking water.

Lesson Review Answers

1. cryosphere
2. hydrosphere
3. atmosphere
4. atmosphere
5. geosphere
6. biosphere
7. all of the matter, energy and processes within Earth's boundary
8. geosphere and atmosphere
9. nitrogen and oxygen
10. matter and energy move between Earth's spheres
11. increase: absorbed by land and oceans; decrease: reflected from land and oceans
12. Sample answer: The Earth system relies on energy from the sun for plants to make food and for winds and ocean currents.
13. Sample answer: The biosphere relies on the matter and energy that cycles between all of the spheres.
14. Sample answer: Most of the liquid water on Earth is in the oceans. The salts would have to be removed from this water before humans could drink it.

Teacher Notes

Weathering

Essential Question How does weathering change Earth's surface?

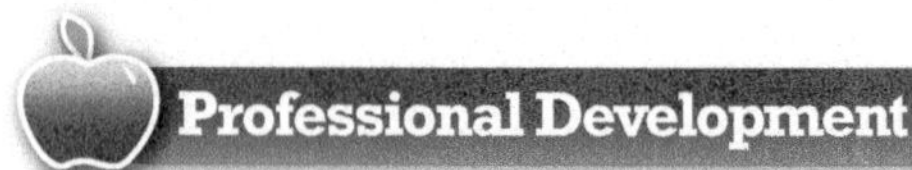

For more detailed information about the topics in this lesson, refer to the Content Refresher in the Unit Opener pages.

Opening Your Lesson

Begin the lesson by assessing students' prerequisite and prior knowledge.

Prerequisite Knowledge

- Physical properties
- Physical and chemical changes

Accessing Prior Knowledge

Ask: What is a physical property? a trait that can be observed without changing a substance into a new substance, such as size, texture, shape, color, mass

Ask: What is the difference between a physical change and a chemical change? A physical change changes a physical property. It does not change a substance into a new substance. A chemical change changes one substance into a different one with new properties.

Customize Your Opening

- ☐ **Accessing Prior Knowledge,** above
- ☐ **Print Path** Engage Your Brain, SE p. 19 #1–2
- ☐ **Print Path** Active Reading, SE p. 19 #3–4
- ☐ **Digital Path** Lesson Opener

Key Topics/Learning Goals	Supporting Concepts
Weathering 1 Define *weathering*. 2 Recognize that there are two kinds of weathering.	• Weathering is the process by which rock materials are broken down by the action of physical and chemical processes. • The two kinds of weathering are physical weathering and chemical weathering.
Physical Weathering 1 Define *physical weathering*. 2 Identify agents of physical weathering. 3 List examples of physical weathering.	• Physical weathering is the breaking down of rocks into smaller pieces by physical means. • Agents of physical weathering include temperature change, pressure change, wind, water, gravity, and plant and animal actions. • Weathering can be caused by ice wedging, abrasion, exfoliation, plant growth, and animal burrowing.
Chemical Weathering 1 Define *chemical weathering*. 2 Identify agents of chemical weathering. 3 List examples of the results of chemical weathering.	• Chemical weathering is the process by which rocks break down as a result of chemical reactions. • Agents of chemical weathering include water, acids, and oxygen. • Acids cause chemical weathering through acid precipitation, acids in groundwater, and acids in living things. • Oxidation occurs when oxygen reacts with compounds that make up rock. Rock surfaces can change color because of oxidation, such as when iron in rocks turns reddish orange.

Options for Instruction

Two parallel paths provide coverage of the Essential Questions, with a strong **Inquiry** strand woven into each. Follow the **Print Path**, the **Digital Path**, or your customized combination of print, digital, and inquiry.

Print Path

Teaching support for the Print Path appears with the Student Pages.

Inquiry Labs and Activities

Digital Path

Digital Path shortcut: TS661000

Print Path	Inquiry Labs and Activities	Digital Path
Break It Down, SE p. 20 **What is weathering?**	**Activity** **Physical vs. Chemical** **Activity** **Weathering in Action** **Quick Lab** **How Can Materials on Earth's Surface Change?**	**Physical vs. Chemical** **Interactive Image**
Break It Down, SE pp. 20–23 **What causes physical weathering?** • Temperature Change • Exfoliation • Animal Action • Abrasion • Plant Growth	**Quick Lab** **Mechanical Weathering** **Daily Demo** **Weathering Model**	**Physical Weathering** **Interactive Image**
Reaction, SE pp. 24–25 **What causes chemical weathering?** • Reactions with Oxygen in Air • Reactions with Acid Precipitation • Reactions with Acids in Ground Water • Reactions with Acids in Living Things	**Quick Lab** **Weathering Chalk**	**Chemical Weathering** **Interactive Image** **Making Caves** **Animation** **Sinkholes** **Interactive Images**

Options for Assessment

See the Evaluate page for options, including Formative Assessment, Summative Assessment, and Unit Review.

Engage and Explore

Activities and Discussion

Activity *Physical vs. Chemical*

Engage

Introducing Key Topics

 small groups
 15 min
 DIRECTED or INDEPENDENT inquiry

Review the concepts of physical and chemical changes of matter. Do a simple demonstration of a chemical change such as lighting a match or combining vinegar with baking soda. Then give each small group a different combination of simple materials, such as steel wool, masking tape, aluminum foil, a pencil, or an eraser, and have them come up with a physical change on their own to show and explain to the class. Conclude by having students discuss the differences between the two types of changes. Point out that weathering changes are caused by both physical and chemical agents. In addition, point out to students that the terms *physical weathering* and *mechanical weathering* are often used to refer to the same processes.

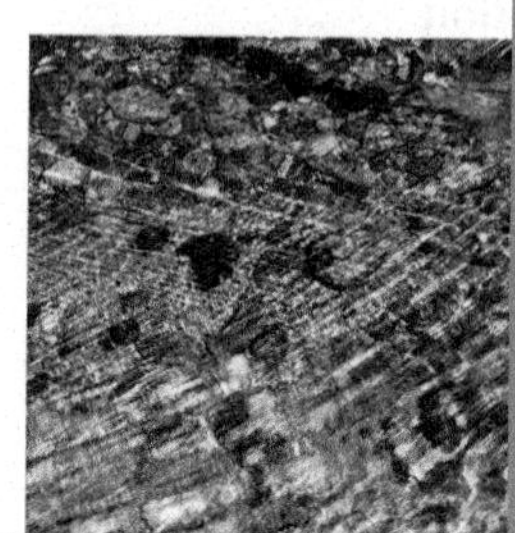

Discussion *When Water Expands*

Physical Weathering

 whole class
 15 min

Use this discussion *prior* to teaching wedging to see if students can figure out wedging using their own logic.

Nearly every type of matter follows a simple pattern: When it gets cold, it contracts and gets smaller; when it gets hot, it spreads out and gets bigger. Water, however, does the opposite—when it freezes, it gets bigger. What happens if you fill a plastic bottle with water and then put it in the freezer? Sample answer: It expands and pushes against the sides of the bottle. A similar process happens when water seeps into cracks found in rocks. When it freezes, the water expands, spreading apart the cracks. Eventually, the rocks can break apart. This is called ice wedging or frost wedging.

Labs and Demos

Probing Question *Weathering by Car*

Chemical Weathering

 small groups or whole class
 20 min
Inquiry GUIDED inquiry

Burning fossil fuels, such as those used to power cars, has been identified as a cause of air pollution and acid rain. Have students describe the sequence of events that connects cars to chemical weathering. Sample answer: Cars burn fossil fuels. Chemicals in car exhaust combine with water in the atmosphere to forms acids. When water in the air falls back to Earth, it contains acids. Have students list ways to reduce weathering by acid precipitation.

Quick Lab *How Can Materials on Earth's Surface Change?*

Engage

Introducing Key Topics

 small groups
 15 min
 INDEPENDENT inquiry

Students will use chalk and sand as models to investigate ways that materials at Earth's surface can be changed through physical or chemical weathering.

PURPOSE To explore how weathering can change Earth's surface

MATERIALS

- bowls, small (2)
- chalk
- food coloring
- eyedropper
- sand
- sandpaper
- vinegar
- water

DIRECTED inquiry introduces inquiry skills within a structured framework.

GUIDED inquiry develops inquiry skills within a supportive environment.

INDEPENDENT inquiry deepens inquiry skills with student-driven questions or procedures.

Daily Demo *Weathering Model*

Physical Weathering

 whole class
 10 min
 **GUIDED** inquiry

PURPOSE **To demonstrate weathering**

MATERIALS

- **crackers**
- **water**

1 Hold up a cracker and tell students that it represents rock.
2 Break the rock into pieces and tell students that the same thing occurs when rock is weathered—it breaks into smaller pieces. Point out that the pieces are still crackers, they're just broken into smaller pieces.
3 Add a few tablespoons of water to another cracker and show students how the water weakens the cracker and makes it easier to break up. Point out that the same is true of rock.
4 **Applying** Have students brainstorm other weathering processes that could be modeled with the crackers. Sample answers: using a fan to show how wind blows pieces away, wetting and then freezing a cracker to model ice or frost wedging, rubbing two crackers together

Quick Lab *Weathering Chalk*

Chemical Weathering

 small groups
 5 min/day up to 2 weeks
 **DIRECTED** inquiry

Students will examine the effects of chemical weathering on chalk. Chalk has the same chemical composition as limestone and provides a good example for chemical weathering of rocks.

PURPOSE **To describe how chemicals can weather chalk**

MATERIALS

- **chalk**
- **paper**
- **plastic container with lid**
- **vinegar (full strength and diluted)**
- **water**

Quick Lab *Mechanical Weathering*

Physical Weathering

 individuals
 10 min
 **GUIDED** inquiry

Students investigate abrasion, a form of physical weathering, using colored chalk and salt. Students also make observations about the mixing of sediment.

PURPOSE **To model abrasion and understand that abrasion is one form of mechanical weathering**

MATERIALS

- **chalk (colored)**
- **ruler**
- **safety goggles**
- **salt, table**
- **plate, paper**
- **spoon**

Customize Your Labs

See the Lab Manual for lab datasheets.

Go Online for editable lab datasheets.

Activities and Discussion

- ☐ **Activity** Physical vs. Chemical
- ☐ **Discussion** When Water Expands
- ☐ **Probing Question** Weathering by Car

Labs and Demos

- ☐ **Daily Demo** Weathering Model
- ☐ **Quick Lab** Weathering Chalk
- ☐ **Quick Lab** Mechanical Weathering
- ☐ **Quick Lab** How Can Materials on Earth's Surface Change?

Explain Science Concepts

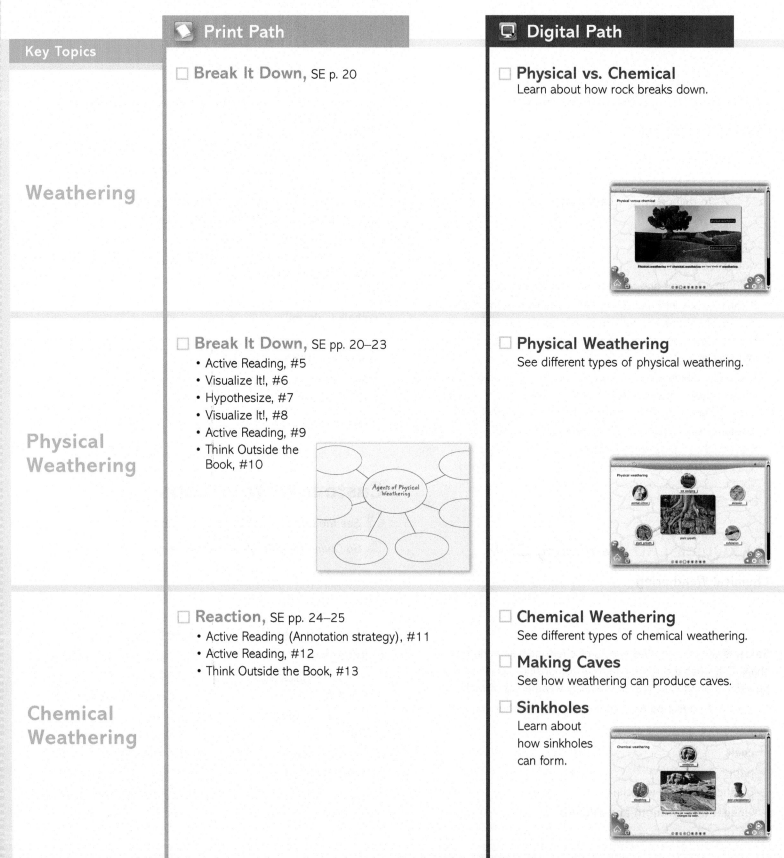

Key Topics	Print Path	Digital Path
Weathering	☐ **Break It Down,** SE p. 20	☐ **Physical vs. Chemical** Learn about how rock breaks down.
Physical Weathering	☐ **Break It Down,** SE pp. 20–23 • Active Reading, #5 • Visualize It!, #6 • Hypothesize, #7 • Visualize It!, #8 • Active Reading, #9 • Think Outside the Book, #10	☐ **Physical Weathering** See different types of physical weathering.
Chemical Weathering	☐ **Reaction,** SE pp. 24–25 • Active Reading (Annotation strategy), #11 • Active Reading, #12 • Think Outside the Book, #13	☐ **Chemical Weathering** See different types of chemical weathering. ☐ **Making Caves** See how weathering can produce caves. ☐ **Sinkholes** Learn about how sinkholes can form.

Differentiated Instruction

Basic *Now and Then*

Chemical Weathering

 individuals, then pairs
20 min

Think, Pair, Share Discuss briefly with students how human use of fossil fuels contributes to acid precipitation and chemical weathering. Tell students that natural events, such as volcanic eruptions and the decomposition of dead organisms also add chemicals to the environment that can form acid precipitation. **Ask:** Do you think human contribution to acid weathering is okay because it is something that happens naturally? After they have had time to think, pair students. Have them discuss their ideas. Call on various pairs to share their ideas and offer explanations.

Advanced *Spectacular Weathering*

Physical Weathering

 individuals
 ongoing

Display Invite students to research some of the world's most spectacular examples of physical weathering. Tell students that different types of rock formations are created by different types of physical weathering. For example, natural bridges are often formed by flowing water. Invite students to make a poster or display showing a particular natural formation with an explanation of how it was formed. Some areas that students could research include formations in Bryce Canyon, Utah; the Garden of the Gods in Colorado; the Devils Marbles Conservation Reserve in Australia; or the Wave in North Coyote Buttes in Utah. Display finished presentations around the classroom.

ELL *Different Ways to Weather*

Weathering

 individuals
 15 min

Venn Diagram To help students understand the terms and concepts in the lesson, have them create a Venn diagram. In the center, have them write terms that apply to both physical and chemical weathering (*water, rock, breakdown*). On one side, have them write physical weathering terms (*abrasion, exfoliation, plant growth, animal actions*); on the other, chemical ones (*oxidation, acid precipitation*).

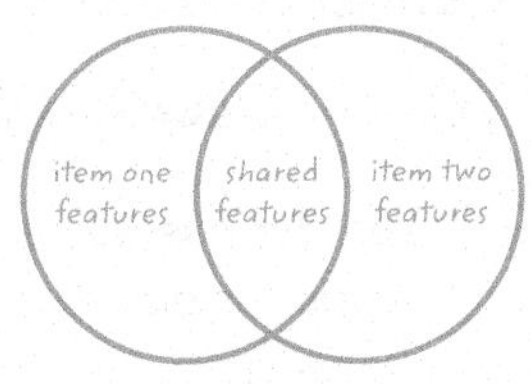

Lesson Vocabulary

weathering	physical weathering	chemical weathering
abrasion	oxidation	acid precipitation

Previewing Vocabulary

 individuals or whole class
20 min

Everyday vs. Scientific Many words used in science are similar to words that we use every day. This can sometimes lead to confusion because the scientific meaning of a word is often very different from its everyday meaning. Have students discuss the differences between the scientific and everyday meanings of the word *weather.* Ask students to look for other words in the lesson that are similarly confusing. Discuss these words too.

Reinforcing Vocabulary

 individuals
ongoing

Description Wheel To help students learn the terms introduced in this lesson, have them make a Description Wheel for each key term. Encourage them to add details using their own words. Details can be definitions, characteristics, examples, nonexamples, and any other details the students want to include.

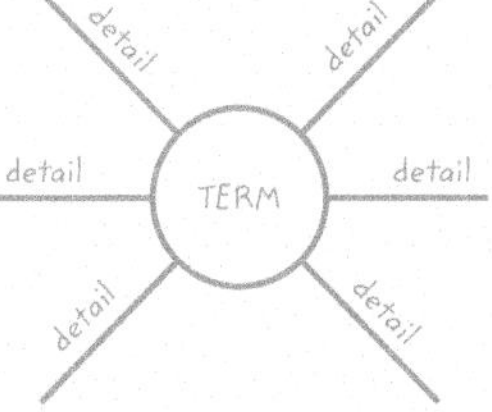

Customize Your Core Lesson

Core Instruction

- ☐ **Print Path** choices
- ☐ **Digital Path** choices

Vocabulary

- ☐ **Previewing Vocabulary** Everyday vs. Scientific
- ☐ **Reinforcing Vocabulary** Description Wheel

Your Resources

Differentiated Instruction

- ☐ **Basic** Now and Then
- ☐ **Advanced** Spectacular Weathering
- ☐ **ELL** Different Ways to Weather

Extend Science Concepts

Reinforce and Review

Activity *Name That Term*

Synthesizing Key Topics

pairs
30 min

Role-Playing Assign a key term or weathering agent to each pair. Give them 10 min to come up with a plan to act out their word. Encourage students to look back in the lesson to clarify any confusion about their word. They can either use a silent charade presentation or give clues that describe their term without giving away too much information. For example, "I fall to Earth but am not very clean. I can wear away stones and buildings, and even pollute streams. What am I?" acid precipitation
Include the following terms:

- weathering
- physical weathering
- ice wedging
- exfoliation
- animal action
- abrasion
- plant growth
- chemical weathering
- oxidation
- acid precipitation
- acid in groundwater
- acids from living things

Graphic Organizer

Synthesizing Key Topics

individuals
20 min

Cause and Effect Diagram Point out to students that multiple causes can have the same effect. Have students use concepts from the lesson in a Cause and Effect Diagram to show how multiple factors cause the same result—weathering. For extra support, give students sets of two or three words and have them use the words to make a Cause and Effect Diagram.

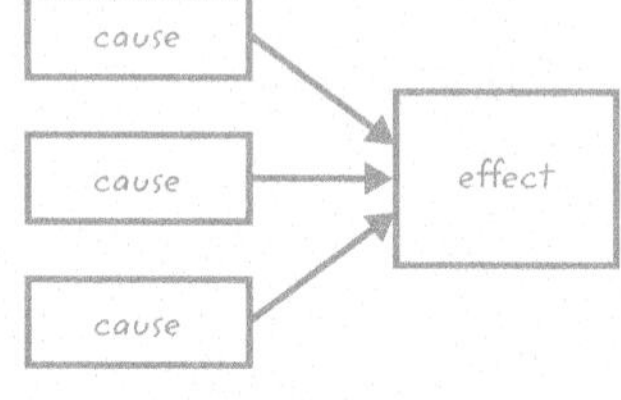

Optional Online resource: Cause and Effect Diagram support

Going Further

Real World Connection

Chemical Weathering

whole class
20 min

Discussion Humans use fossil fuels for many daily activities. A large amount of the electricity that people use is generated from burning coal. Cars, buses, and planes run on fuel from fossil fuels. Products that people buy and use are made in factories that use large amounts of fossil fuels. Hold a class discussion to come up with a list of things in students' daily lives that can be linked to the use of fossil fuels, and therefore to acid precipitation. Prompt the students to discuss why it is important to reduce the amount of pollutants put into the environment.

Fine Arts Connection

Weathering

whole class

15 min

Art Study The ancient art of sculpture relies on some of the same processes that causes weathering. Share with students images of several examples of rock-carved sculptures, such as Mount Rushmore, the Crazy Horse Memorial, the works of Renaissance sculptors, and others. Have students discuss how they think the artists created these works of art. Which tools might they have used? Then ask students to discuss how the methods that sculptors use mimic some of the weathering processes that have been discussed in the lesson.

Customize Your Closing

See the Assessment Guide for quizzes and tests.

Go Online to edit and create quizzes and tests.

Reinforce and Review

- ☐ Activity Name That Term
- ☐ Graphic Organizer Cause and Effect Diagram
- ☐ **Print Path** Visual Summary, SE p. 26
- ☐ **Digital Path** Lesson Closer

Evaluate Student Mastery

Formative Assessment

See the teacher support below the Student Pages for additional Formative Assessment questions.

Collect a series of images from the Internet that shows various examples of weathering. For each image, determine what types of weathering have occurred and the likely agents. Try to use both urban and natural settings.

Reteach

Formative assessment may show that students need reinforcement for certain topics. The resources below are recommended for reteaching. If students were introduced to a topic through the Print Path, you can also use the Digital Path to reteach, and vice versa.
Can be assigned to individual students

Weathering
Activity Physical vs. Chemical

Physical Weathering
Quick Lab Mechanical Weathering
Discussion When Water Expands
Daily Demo Weathering Model

Chemical Weathering
Probing Question Weathering by Car
Quick Lab Weathering Chalk

Summative Assessment

Alternative Assessment

Weathering

Online resources: student worksheet, optional rubrics

Weathering

Take Your Pick: *Weathering*
Weathering can be either physical or chemical. These activities will help you learn more about both.

1. Work on your own, with a partner, or with a small group.
2. Choose one or more items for a total of at least 10 points. Check your choices.
3. Have your teacher approve your plan.
4. Submit or present your results.

2 Points

____ **Crossword Puzzle** Make a crossword puzzle that includes the different agents of weathering. Use definitions and descriptions of the specific types of weathering caused by the agent.

____ **Illustration of Agents** Weathering occurs through many different agents. Make an illustration of a landscape that includes several agents of weathering.

5 Points

____ **Wanted Poster** Chemical weathering occurs through many different agents. Make a Wanted poster identifying these agents. You poster could be for a criminal (Agent Wanted), a star agent (Star Agent Wanted), or jobs needed to make the weathering occur (Jobs Wanted). Include pictures and descriptions about how each causes weathering.

____ **Model** Using recycled materials, make a model of an area that has experienced at least two kinds of chemical weathering. Be sure to include labeled descriptions of how the weathering occurred.

____ **Quiz** Write your own quiz on physical weathering. Make sure you ask questions about agents of physical weathering, how the physical weathering occurs, and what the results of physical weathering are. Include an answer key.

____ **Newspaper Article** Invent a newsworthy example of chemical weathering. Then write a newspaper article about it. As background for your article, explore other types of weathering, too.

8 Points

____ **Interview with a Landform** Write a interview between you and an outcrop of bedrock that has experienced chemical and physical weathering. Ask the outcrop about its weathering from the past, and what it expects in the future. Include a picture of the outcrop showing the weathering it has experienced.

____ **Timeline** Create an imagined timeline of physical and chemical weathering that has occurred to a material. Show what the material looks like at different points along the timeline.

Going Further
- [ ] Real World Connection
- [ ] Fine Arts Connection

Formative Assessment
- [ ] Strategies Throughout TE
- [ ] Lesson Review SE

Summative Assessment
- [ ] Alternative Assessment Weathering
- [ ] Lesson Quiz
- [ ] Unit Tests A and B
- [ ] Unit Review SE End-of-Unit

Your Resources

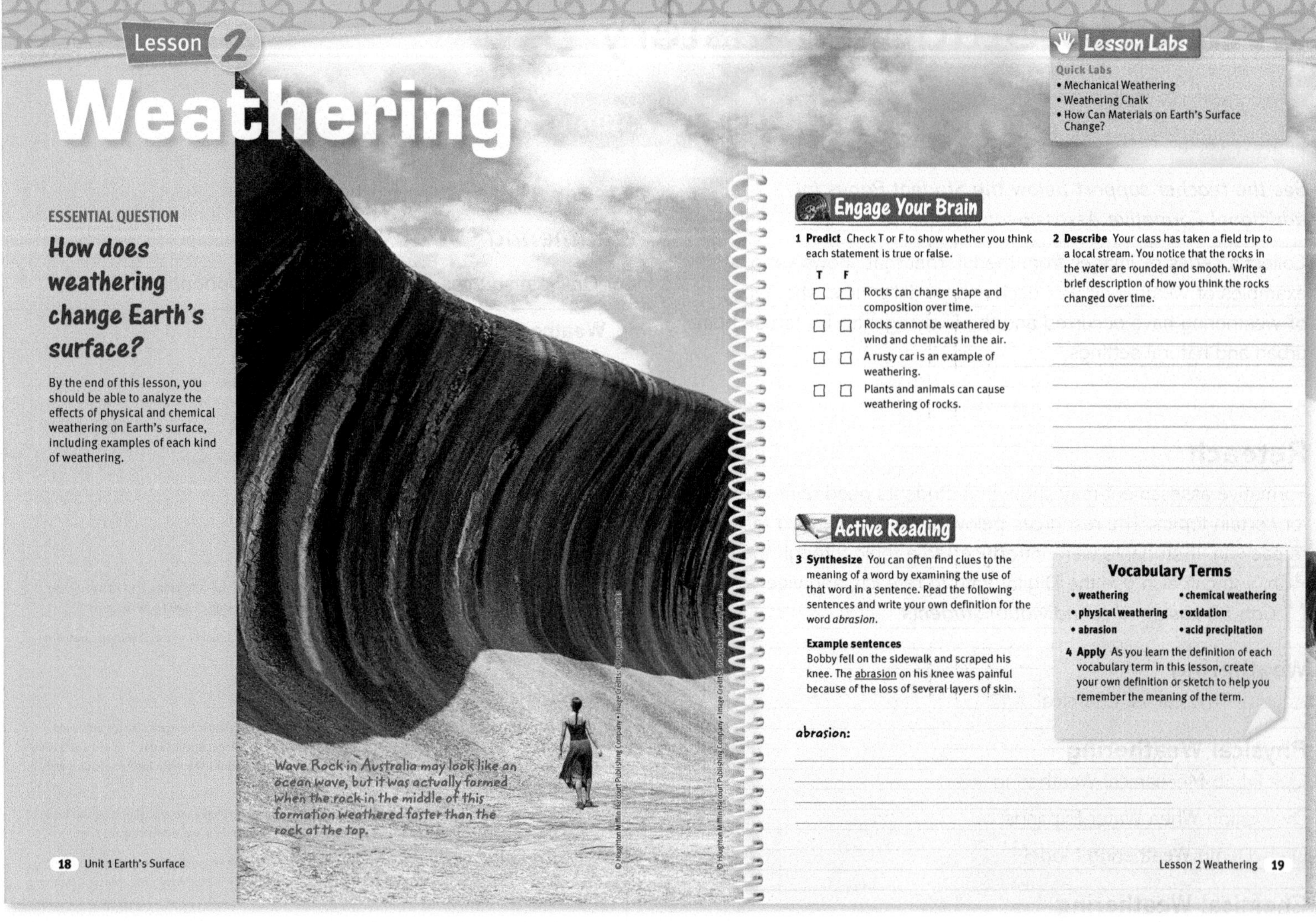

Lesson 2
Weathering
ESSENTIAL QUESTION
How does weathering change Earth's surface?
By the end of this lesson, you should be able to analyze the effects of physical and chemical weathering on Earth's surface, including examples of each kind of weathering.
Wave Rock in Australia may look like an ocean wave, but it was actually formed when the rock in the middle of this formation weathered faster than the rock at the top.
18 Unit 1 Earth's Surface
Lesson Labs
Quick Labs
• Mechanical Weathering
• Weathering Chalk
• How Can Materials on Earth's Surface Change?
Engage Your Brain
1 Predict Check T or F to show whether you think each statement is true or false.
T F
Rocks can change shape and composition over time.
Rocks cannot be weathered by wind and chemicals in the air.
A rusty car is an example of weathering.
Plants and animals can cause weathering of rocks.
2 Describe Your class has taken a field trip to a local stream. You notice that the rocks in the water are rounded and smooth. Write a brief description of how you think the rocks changed over time.
Active Reading
3 Synthesize You can often find clues to the meaning of a word by examining the use of that word in a sentence. Read the following sentences and write your own definition for the word abrasion.
Example sentences
Bobby fell on the sidewalk and scraped his knee. The abrasion on his knee was painful because of the loss of several layers of skin.
abrasion:
Vocabulary Terms
• weathering
• physical weathering
• abrasion
• chemical weathering
• oxidation
• acid precipitation
4 Apply As you learn the definition of each vocabulary term in this lesson, create your own definition or sketch to help you remember the meaning of the term.
Lesson 2 Weathering 19

Answers

Answers for 1–3 should represent students' current thoughts, even if incorrect.

1. T; F; T; T
2. Sample answer: The rocks may have become rounded as the water ran over the rocks. Tiny particles are worn away over time making the rocks smooth.
3. Abrasion is the loss of layers of rock from an exposed surface.
4. Students should define or sketch each vocabulary term in the lesson.

Opening Your Lesson

Preconceptions: Students may believe that rocks are worn down only by physical means, and may not consider chemical interactions, because these may be difficult to observe.

Prerequisites: Students should understand physical and chemical changes of matter, and how to distinguish between them.

Learning Alert

Chemical Weathering Students may not have a clear understanding of what acids are. However, they likely think of an acid as a substance that causes change. Ask students to share their ideas about what an acid is and what it can do. Encourage students to think of acidic substances, such as vinegar, lemon juice, orange juice, and other such substances. Have students brainstorm the qualities that acidic substances have in common. **Ask:** What is it about acids that make them good at weathering rock? Sample answer: Acids can weather some types of rock because acids can react with some rocks more easily than water does.

Break It Down

What is weathering?

Did you know that sand on a beach may have once been a part of a large boulder? Over millions of years, a boulder can break down into many smaller pieces. The breakdown of rock material by physical and chemical processes is called **weathering**. Two kinds of weathering are *physical weathering* and *chemical weathering*.

What causes physical weathering?

Rocks can get smaller and smaller without a change in the composition of the rock. This is an example of a physical change. The process by which rock is broken down into smaller pieces by physical changes is **physical weathering**. Temperature changes, pressure changes, plant and animal actions, water, wind, and gravity are all agents of physical weathering.

As materials break apart, they can become even more exposed to physical changes. For instance, a large boulder can be broken apart by ice and water over time. Eventually, the boulder can split in two. Now there are two rocks exposed to the agents of physical weathering. In other words, the amount of surface area exposed to the agents of physical weathering increases. The large boulder can become thousands of tiny rocks over time as each new rock increases the amount of surface area able to be weathered.

Active Reading

5 Identify As you read, place the names of some common agents of physical weathering in the graphic organizer below.

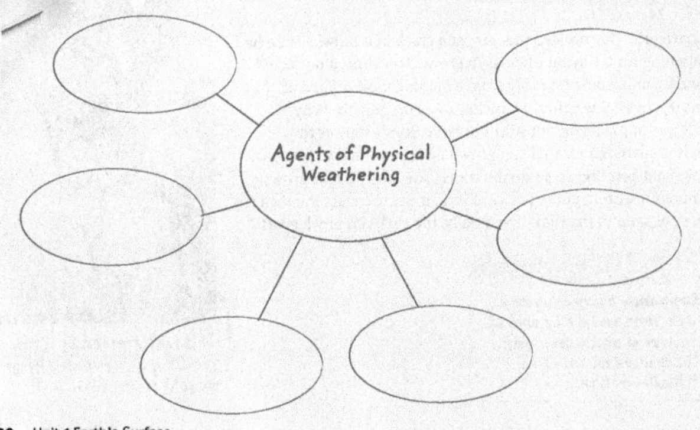

Visualize It!

6 Describe Write a caption for each of the images to describe the process of ice wedging

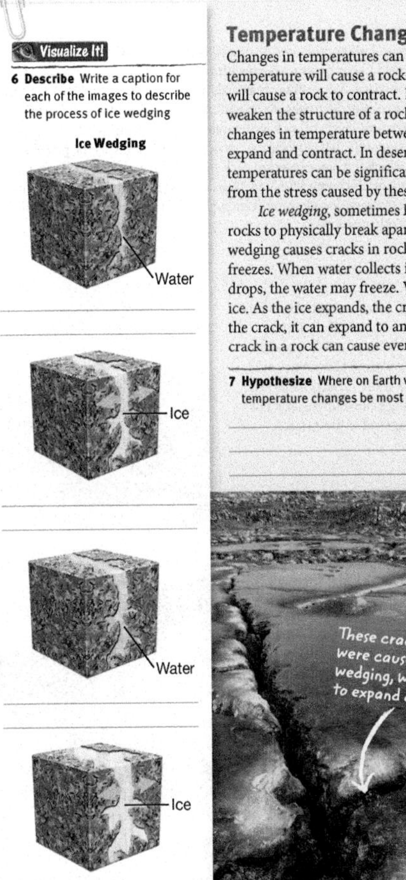

Temperature Change

Changes in temperatures can cause a rock to break apart. A rise in temperature will cause a rock to expand. A decrease in temperature will cause a rock to contract. Repeated temperature changes can weaken the structure of a rock, causing the rock to crumble. Even changes in temperature between day and night can cause rocks to expand and contract. In desert regions differences in day and night temperatures can be significant. Rocks can weaken and crumble from the stress caused by these temperature changes.

Ice wedging, sometimes known as *frost wedging*, can also cause rocks to physically break apart, as shown in the image below. Ice wedging causes cracks in rocks to expand as water seeps in and freezes. When water collects in cracks in rock and the temperature drops, the water may freeze. Water expands as it freezes to become ice. As the ice expands, the crack will widen. As more water enters the crack, it can expand to an even larger size. Eventually, a small crack in a rock can cause even the largest of rocks to split apart.

7 Hypothesize Where on Earth would physical weathering from temperature changes be most common? Least common? Explain.

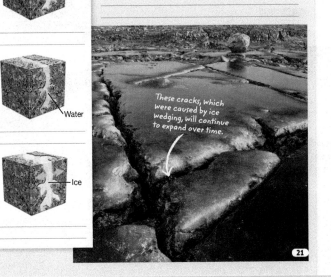

These cracks, which were caused by ice wedging, will continue to expand over time.

Answers

5. temperature changes; pressure changes; plant and animal actions; water; wind; gravity
6. Water seeps into a crack in a rock; The water freezes inside the rock and expands the size of the crack; More water seeps into the expanded crack; The water freezes again causing the crack to expand to an even larger size.
7. In desert regions, vast temperature changes from day to night can cause rock to crumble. Tropical and polar climates would have less changes because of less temperature variation.

Learning Alert

Surface Area Students may have a hard time understanding that after a rock breaks apart, it has even more surface area that is exposed and will therefore weather even faster. **Ask:** Which would dissolve faster in water, a sugar cube or sugar that has already been broken into pieces? The smaller pieces would probably dissolve faster.

Probing Questions GUIDED Inquiry

Comparing Weathering can be caused by temperature changes in rocks and water. Describe a major difference between how weathering is caused by temperature changes in rocks and how it is caused by temperature changes in water. Describe a similarity. Sample answer: When rock warms, it expands; when it cools, it contracts. Water expands when it freezes. Both cause weathering by expanding and contracting, which results in the rocks breaking apart.

Interpreting Visuals

Do you think ice wedging can break apart a large rock in a single season? Explain. Sample answer: For ice wedging to break a large rock, there must be many cycles of freezing followed by a defrost and more water added to the crack. This is not likely to happen in a single season.

Enchanted Rock was once buried deep inside Earth.

Pressure Change

Physical weathering can be caused by pressure changes. Rocks formed under pressure deep within Earth can become exposed at the surface. As overlying materials are removed above the rock, the pressure decreases. As a result, the rock expands, causing the outermost layers of rock to separate from the underlying layers, as shown to the left. *Exfoliation* (ex•foh•lee•AY•shun) is the process by which the outer layers of rock slowly peel away due to pressure changes. Enchanted Rock in Texas is a 130 m-high dome of granite that is slowly losing the outermost layers of rock due to exfoliation and other processes.

Animal Action

Animals can cause physical weathering. Many animals dig burrows into the ground, allowing more rock to be exposed. Common burrowing animals include ground squirrels, prairie dogs, ants, and earthworms. These animals move soils and allow new rocks, soils, and other materials to be exposed at the surface, as shown below. Materials can undergo weathering below the surface, but are more likely to be weathered once exposed at the surface.

Visualize It!

8 Describe Write a caption for each animal describing how it might cause physical weathering.

Prairie dog

A

B

C

Wind, Water, and Gravity

Rock can be broken down by the action of other rocks over time. **Abrasion** (uh•BRAY•zhuhn) is the breaking down and wearing away of rock material by the mechanical action of other rock. Three agents of physical weathering that can cause abrasion are moving water, wind, and gravity. Also, rocks suspended in the ice of a glacier can cause abrasion of other rocks on Earth's surface.

In moving water, rock can become rounded and smooth. Abrasion occurs as rocks are tumbled in water, hitting other rocks. Wind abrasion occurs when wind lifts and carries small particles in the air. The small particles can blast away at surfaces and slowly wear them away. During a landslide, large rocks can fall from higher up a slope and break more rocks below, causing abrasion.

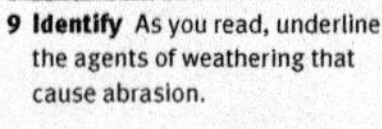

9 Identify As you read, underline the agents of weathering that cause abrasion.

Rocks are tumbled in water, causing abrasion.

Wind-blown sand can blast small particles away.

Rocks can be broken down in a landslide.

Plant Growth

You have probably noticed that just one crack in a sidewalk can be the opening for a tiny bit of grass to grow. Over time, a neglected sidewalk can become crumbly from a combination of several agents of physical weathering, including plant growth. Why?

Roots of plants do not start out large. Roots start as tiny strands of plant matter that can grow inside small cracks in rocks. As the plant gets bigger, so do the roots. The larger a root grows, the more pressure it puts on rock. More pressure causes the rock to expand, as seen to the right. Eventually, the rock can break apart.

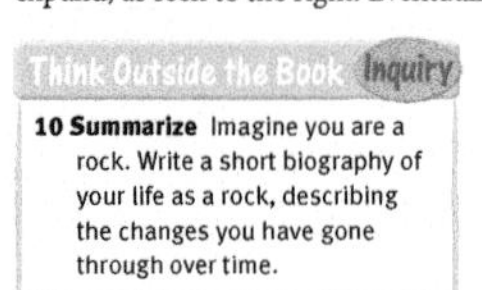

10 Summarize Imagine you are a rock. Write a short biography of your life as a rock, describing the changes you have gone through over time.

This tree started as a tiny seedling and eventually grew to split the rock in half.

Answers

8. A: A prairie dog digs holes and brings new sediments, rock, and other materials to the surface; B: The earthworm moves soils and creates spaces for water and air to weather rocks; C: Pocket gophers can dig burrows, exposing rock under the surface.
9. *See students' pages for annotations.*
10. Sample answer: I was born sharp and large. I was a strong boulder, but then I met a gopher that slowly exposed me to the surface. I was later broken down as abrasion in water caused me to smash into many other rocks.

Learning Alert

Exfoliation Students may have difficulty understanding how rock can expand after layers peel away. When the overlying rock is removed, the pressure on the rock decreases and it can expand upward and outward. To help students understand this change in pressure, use a soft object that can be squashed down but then expands when released, such as a foam ball. Explain that a similar, but much slower, process occurs during exfoliation.

Formative Assessment

Ask: How can a tiny animal, such as a worm, cause weathering of rocks? Worms wiggle through soil, churning it up. This can expose rocks to the surface. Once this happens, air, wind, and other agents can affect the rock. **Ask:** Is abrasion an agent of weathering? No, abrasion is a type of weathering that involves rock wearing down by friction from other rocks. Wind, moving water, ice, and gravity are agents of weathering that cause abrasion.

Building Reading Skills

Identifying Cause and Effect Help students identify cause-and-effect relationships between agents and types of weathering. As they read the text, have students write down agents, such as water or plants, on the left side of a piece of paper. On the right side, have them write what type of weathering that agent causes, such as abrasion.

Reaction

What causes chemical weathering?

Chemical weathering changes both the composition and appearance of rocks. **Chemical weathering** is the breakdown of rocks by chemical reactions. Agents of chemical weathering include oxygen in the air and acids.

Active Reading

11 Identify As you read, underline examples of chemical weathering.

Reactions with Oxygen

Oxygen in the air or in water can cause chemical weathering. Oxygen reacts with the compounds that make up rock, causing chemical reactions. The process by which other chemicals combine with oxygen is called **oxidation** (ahk•si•DAY•shun).

Rock surfaces sometimes change color. A color change can mean that a chemical reaction has taken place. Rocks containing iron can easily undergo chemical weathering. Iron in rocks and soils combines quickly with oxygen that is dissolved in water. The result is a rock that turns reddish orange. This is rust! The red color of much of the soil in the southeastern United States and of rock formations in the southwestern United States is due to the presence of rust, as seen in the image below.

Reactions with Acid Precipitation

Acids break down most minerals faster than water alone. Increased amounts of acid from various sources can cause chemical weathering of rock. Acids in the atmosphere are created when chemicals combine with water in the air. Rain is normally slightly acidic. When fossil fuels are burned, other chemicals combine with water in the atmosphere to produce even stronger acids. When these stronger acids fall to Earth, they are called **acid precipitation** (AS•id prih•sip•ih•TAY•shun). Acid precipitation is recognized as a problem all around the world and causes rocks to break down and change composition.

Active Reading **12 Describe** How does acid precipitation cause rocks to weather faster?

These rocks in Arizona are red because of oxidation.

Reactions with Acids in Groundwater

Water in the ground, or groundwater, can cause chemical weathering. As groundwater moves through spaces or cracks in rock, acids in the water can cause rocks to dissolve. A small crack in a rock can result in the formation of extensive cave systems that are carved out over time under Earth's surface, as shown to the right. The dissolved rock material is carried in water until it is later deposited. Stalactites (stuh•LAHK•tyt) and stalagmites (stuh•LAHG•myt) are common features in cave systems as dissolved chemicals are deposited by dripping water underground.

Reactions with Acids in Living Things

Acids are produced naturally by certain living organisms. For instance, lichens (LY•kuhns) and mosses often grow on rocks and trees. As they grow on rocks, they produce weak acids that can weather the rock's surface. As the acids move through tiny spaces in the rocks, chemical reactions can occur. The acids will eventually break down the rocks. As the acids seep deeper into the rocks, cracks can form. The rock can eventually break apart when the cracks get too large.

Stalactites

Stalagmites

The dissolved rock from acidic groundwater can later be deposited in different locations.

This gear is rusted, which indicates that a chemical reaction has taken place.

Think Outside the Book

13 Apply Think of an item made by humans that could be broken down by the agents of physical and chemical weathering. Describe to your classmates all of the ways the item could change over time.

Answers

11. *See students' pages for annotations.*
12. Acids can cause materials to break down faster because some rocks are more easily dissolved in acids than others.
13. Sample answer: A building made of bricks or stones can break down over time as acid precipitation and the action of wind and water cause the building to be slowly worn away.

Learning Alert

Chemical Weathering The word *reactions* is used frequently in this section. Students may not understand what a chemical reaction is. Explain that when a person encounters a new or surprising situation, he or she reacts. Explain that substances can also react when combined with other substances or when their physical environment changes. In a chemical reaction, one or more substances change to make one or more new substances. After that reaction takes place, the changed rock material has been weathered.

Probing Questions GUIDED Inquiry

Predicting Imagine large rocks with plants growing on them. Do you think the physical weathering from the plants is greater in the summer or the winter? Explain. Sample answer: In the summer, the plants are growing, including their roots. In the winter, the plants grow less or not at all, so they will affect the rock less.

Visual Summary

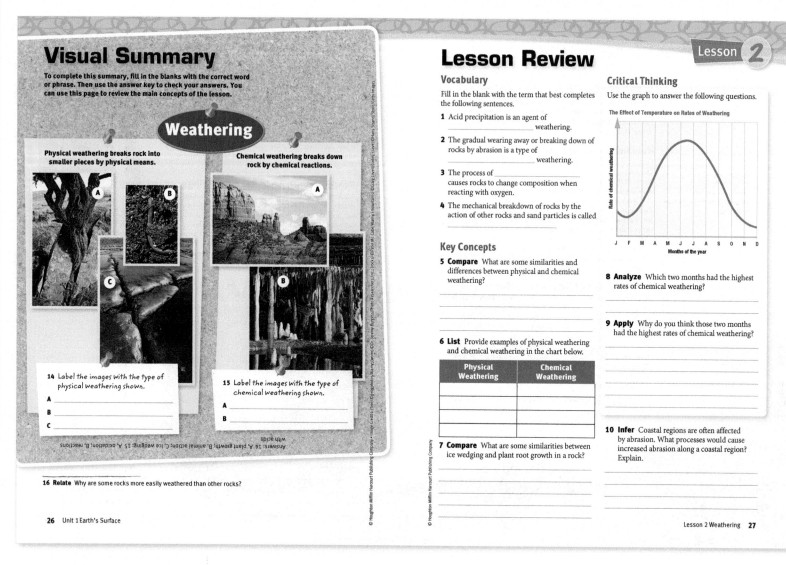

To complete this summary, fill in the blanks with the correct word or phrase. Then use the answer key to check your answers. You can use this page to review the main concepts of the lesson.

Weathering

Physical weathering breaks rock into smaller pieces by physical means.

Chemical weathering breaks down rock by chemical reactions.

14 Label the images with the type of physical weathering shown.

A ______

B ______

C ______

15 Label the images with the type of chemical weathering shown.

A ______

B ______

Answers: 14 A, plant growth; B, animal action; C, ice wedging; 15 A, oxidation; B, reactions with acids

16 Relate Why are some rocks more easily weathered than other rocks?

26 Unit 1 Earth's Surface

Lesson 2

Lesson Review

Vocabulary

Fill in the blank with the term that best completes the following sentences.

1 Acid precipitation is an agent of ______ weathering.

2 The gradual wearing away or breaking down of rocks by abrasion is a type of ______ weathering.

3 The process of ______ causes rocks to change composition when reacting with oxygen.

4 The mechanical breakdown of rocks by the action of other rocks and sand particles is called ______

Key Concepts

5 Compare What are some similarities and differences between physical and chemical weathering?

6 List Provide examples of physical weathering and chemical weathering in the chart below.

Physical Weathering	Chemical Weathering

7 Compare What are some similarities between ice wedging and plant root growth in a rock?

Critical Thinking

Use the graph to answer the following questions.

The Effect of Temperature on Rates of Weathering

Rate of chemical weathering

J F M A M J J A S O N D

Months of the year

8 Analyze Which two months had the highest rates of chemical weathering?

9 Apply Why do you think those two months had the highest rates of chemical weathering?

10 Infer Coastal regions are often affected by abrasion. What processes would cause increased abrasion along a coastal region? Explain.

Lesson 2 Weathering 27

Visual Summary Answers

14. A: plant growth; B: animal action; C: ice wedging
15. A: oxidation; B: reactions with acids
16. The composition, size, and shape of a rock can determine whether it is more easily weathered than other rocks.

Lesson Review Answers

1. chemical
2. physical
3. oxidation
4. abrasion
5. Physical weathering is the break down of rock materials by physical means without changing rock composition. Chemical weathering causes changes to rock composition.
6. Physical: plant root growth; abrasion by gravity; wind movements; temperature changes; moving water.

   Chemical: oxidation of materials containing iron, acids in groundwater, acids in living things.
7. In both instances, the crack in a rock can slowly grow larger over time. Both can cause a rock to break as a crack becomes progressively larger.
8. June and July
9. Higher temperatures in June and July would mean that the rate of chemical reactions is increased. Therefore, the rate of chemical weathering is increased.
10. Coastal regions are close to large bodies of water, such as oceans. Rocks near a coastline can be tumbled by abrasion in the water.

Teacher Notes

Erosion and Deposition by Water

Essential Question How does water change Earth's surface?

For more detailed information about the topics in this lesson, refer to the Content Refresher in the Unit Opener pages.

Opening Your Lesson

Begin the lesson by assessing students' prerequisite and prior knowledge.

Prerequisite Knowledge

- Weathering
- Waves

Accessing Prior Knowledge

Ask: Water is a force that constantly changes Earth's surface. Why is water a weathering agent? As water washes over rock material, it loosens and breaks off pieces of rock over time. As water freezes, it expands in rock cracks, breaking them open over time.

Ask: What characteristics of waves likely cause the most weathering? the back-and-forth motion, the speed, the amount of water

Customize Your Opening

- ☐ **Accessing Prior Knowledge,** above
- ☐ **Print Path** Engage Your Brain, SE p. 29 #1–2
- ☐ **Print Path** Active Reading, SE p. 29 #3–4
- ☐ **Digital Path** Lesson Opener

Key Topics/Learning Goals	Supporting Concepts
Erosion and Deposition 1 Define and describe the processes of *erosion* and *deposition.*	• Erosion occurs as sediment and other materials are moved from one location to another. • The laying down of those materials is deposition.
Erosion and Deposition by Streams 1 Relate gravity, gradient, discharge, and load to stream erosion and deposition. 2 Describe what happens to sediment as a stream slows.	• Gravity causes water to move downward. • High gradients cause streams to move faster and cause more erosion. Streams that carry large loads have higher rates of erosion. • A high-discharge stream moves faster than a low-discharge stream does. High discharge may result from greater speed or volume. • As streams slow, they deposit sediment.
Formation of Landforms by Streams 1 Describe the role of stream erosion and deposition in building landforms.	• Stream erosion plays a part in the formation of channels, oxbow lakes, valleys, and canyons. • Floodplains, alluvial fans, and deltas are formed by deposition of stream sediment.
Erosion and Deposition by Groundwater, Waves, and Currents 1 Describe the effects of erosion by groundwater. 2 Describe how erosion and deposition by waves and currents shape shorelines.	• Groundwater erosion may cause underground caverns and sinkholes to form. • Erosion and deposition by waves and currents cause many shoreline formations. • Shoreline erosion and deposition depends on the hardness of the rock and wave energy.

Options for Instruction

Two parallel paths provide coverage of the Essential Questions, with a strong **Inquiry** strand woven into each. Follow the **Print Path,** the **Digital Path,** or your customized combination of print, digital, and inquiry.

 Print Path *Teaching support for the Print Path appears with the Student Pages.*	 Inquiry Labs and Activities	 Digital Path *Digital Path shortcut: TS661021*
Go with the Flow, SE p. 30 **How does flowing water change Earth's surface?**	**Activity** Take It or Leave It **Quick Lab** Modeling Stalactites and Stalagmites	**Erosion and Deposition** Interactive Images
Go with the Flow, SE p. 31 **What factors relate to a stream's ability to erode material?**	**Exploration Lab** Exploring Stream Erosion and Deposition **Virtual Lab** Erosion and Deposition by Rivers	**Erosion and Deposition** Interactive Images
Run of a River, SE pp. 32–33 **What landforms can streams create?**	**Activity** Washed Up **Quick Lab** Moving Sediment	**A Lot of Sediment** Diagram
More Waterworks, SE pp. 34–35 Ground water erosion What forces shape a shoreline? **Surf Versus Turf,** SE pp. 36–37 Coastal landforms made by erosion **Shifting Sands,** SE p. 38 Coastal landforms made by deposition	**Activity** Now You Sea It, Now You Don't **Daily Demo** Groundwater **Quick Lab** Wave Action on the Shoreline	**Groundwater and Waves** Interactive Images **Effects on Environment** Diagram **Breaking Waves** Interactive Images

Options for Assessment

See the Evaluate page for options, including Formative Assessment, Summative Assessment, and Unit Review.

Engage and Explore

Activities and Discussion

Activity *Take It or Leave It*

Erosion and Deposition

 whole class
 15 min
 **GUIDED** inquiry

After defining *erosion* and *deposition,* write both words on the board. List agents of erosion and deposition (water, wind, ice, gravity) between them. Have students provide examples of erosion and deposition by drawing sketches or finding photographs. Then, as a class, classify each as an example of erosion or deposition, and identify the agent(s) involved. To help clarify the misconception that rock that has worn away disappears, point out that matter is neither created nor destroyed in these processes; it just changes and moves.

Activity *Washed Up*

Formation of Landforms by Streams

 small groups
 30 min
 **GUIDED** inquiry

Map Study Break students into small groups. Have each group draw a map showing the course of a stream. Tell students to draw and label features that the stream could have. Labels should include a description of how and why the features form.

Activity *Now You Sea It, Now You Don't*

Erosion and Deposition by Groundwater, Waves, and Currents

 small groups or pairs
30–40 min
 **GUIDED** inquiry

Process Posters Help students correct the common misconception that rock is strong and water is weak. Give each group or pair a poster to sketch a group of related formations. Students can choose the rock group, which includes sea cliffs, sea stacks, sea arches, sea caves, and headlands, or the sand group, which includes sandbars and barrier islands. Have students describe the characteristics of the group of landforms and explain the process by which they form.

Labs and Demos

Daily Demo *Groundwater*

Engage

Erosion and Deposition by Groundwater, Waves, and Currents

 whole class
 10 min
 **DIRECTED** inquiry

PURPOSE **To model how groundwater can cause erosion**

MATERIALS
- cup, clear plastic
- sugar cubes
- gravel
- water

To help students understand groundwater and how it can cause erosion, use the following model: Punch holes in the bottom of a clear plastic cup. Fill the cup with gravel. Explain that the cup represents the top layer of the ground. Place the cup on the sugar cubes, which represents rock located under the top layer. Add water to the cup, pointing out that water is flowing through the gravel down to the lower layer. The sugar should start to dissolve and the cup may shift. Explain that the same process can occur in the ground if acidic water weakens soft rock.

Quick Lab *Modeling Stalactites and Stalagmites*

Erosion and Deposition

 individuals
 ongoing
 **DIRECTED** inquiry

Students use household materials to model stalactites and stalagmites.

PURPOSE **To model the formation of stalactites and stalagmites**

MATERIALS
- beakers (2)
- glass stirring rod
- gloves
- hot water, 3 cups
- paper clips (2)
- plate
- safety goggles
- sand
- scale
- sodium carbonate, 120 g
- yarn, 45 cm

DIRECTED inquiry introduces inquiry skills within a structured framework.

GUIDED inquiry develops inquiry skills within a supportive environment.

INDEPENDENT inquiry deepens inquiry skills with student-driven questions or procedures.

Quick Lab *Moving Sediment*

Erosion and Deposition by Groundwater, Waves, and Currents

 small groups
 15 min
 **DIRECTED** inquiry

Students build, measure, and erode a model hillside to investigate angle of repose and mass movement.

PURPOSE To model how water can cause a landslide

MATERIALS
- beaker
- protractor
- sand (1 L)
- plastic washtub
- water (2 L)

Exploration Lab *Exploring Stream Erosion and Deposition*

Erosion and Deposition by Streams

 small groups
 45 min
 **DIRECTED or GUIDED** inquiry

Students design, create, and test model waterways to investigate factors that contribute to stream erosion and deposition.

PURPOSE To model erosion and deposition by streams

MATERIALS
- cup, plastic
- paper towels
- ruler
- water
- books or blocks of wood
- beaker or measuring cup, plastic
- duct tape
- aluminum pan
- soil
- spray bottle

Quick Lab *Wave Action on the Shoreline*

PURPOSE To observe the power of waves against a shoreline

See the Lab Manual or go Online for planning information.

Virtual Lab *Erosion and Deposition by Rivers*

Erosion and Deposition by Streams

flexible
45 min
GUIDED inquiry

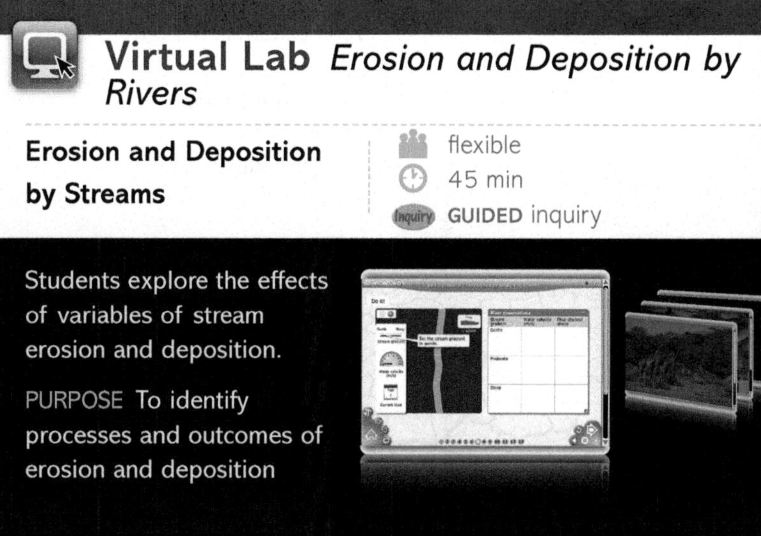

Students explore the effects of variables of stream erosion and deposition.

PURPOSE To identify processes and outcomes of erosion and deposition

Customize Your Labs

See the Lab Manual for lab datasheets.

Go Online for editable lab datasheets.

Activities and Discussion

- ☐ **Activity** Take It or Leave It
- ☐ **Activity** Washed Up
- ☐ **Activity** Now You Sea It, Now You Don't

Labs and Demos

- ☐ **Daily Demo** Groundwater
- ☐ **Quick Lab** Modeling Stalactites and Stalagmites
- ☐ **Exploration Lab** Exploring Stream Erosion and Deposition
- ☐ **Quick Lab** Wave Action on the Shoreline
- ☐ **Virtual Lab** Erosion and Deposition by Rivers
- ☐ **Quick Lab** Moving Sediment

Your Resources

Explain Science Concepts

Key Topics	Print Path	Digital Path
Erosion and Deposition	☐ **Go with the Flow,** SE p. 30 • Venn Diagram, #5 *Optional Online resource: Venn Diagram support* 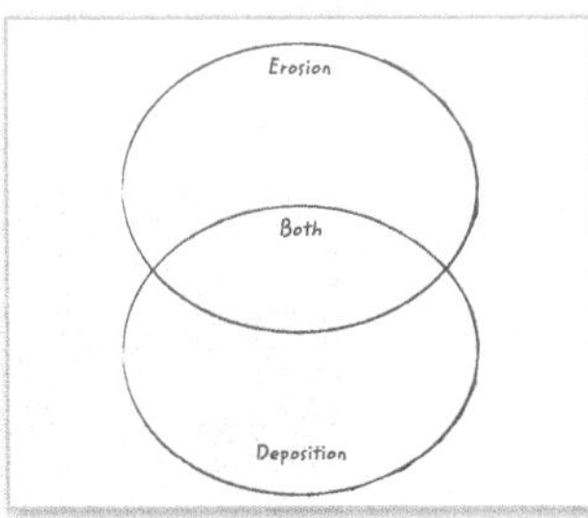 	☐ **Erosion and Deposition** Explore the different agents that move material. 
Erosion and Deposition by Streams	☐ **Go with the Flow,** SE p. 31 • Active Reading, #6 • Do the Math, #7, 8, 9	☐ **Erosion and Deposition** Watch how water can change the shape of land. 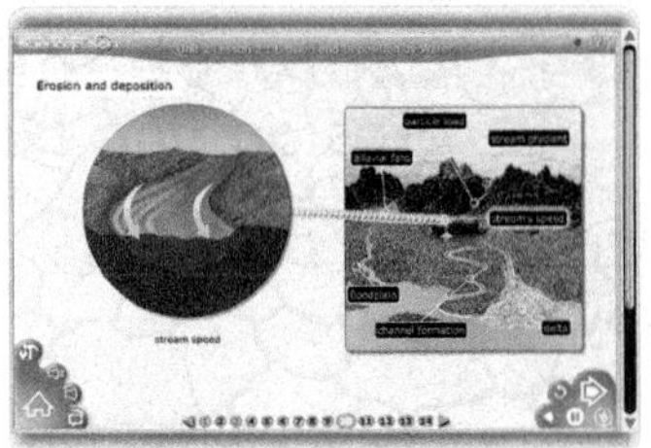
Formation of Landforms by Streams	☐ **Run of a River,** SE pp. 32–33 • Think Outside the Book, #10 • Visualize It!, #11 • Active Reading (Annotation strategy), #12 • Compare and Contrast, #13	☐ **A Lot of Sediment** See how running water can affect landforms.
Erosion and Deposition by Groundwater, Waves, and Currents	☐ **More Waterworks,** SE pp. 34–35 • Active Reading, #14 • Visualize It!, #15 • Visualize It!, #16 ☐ **Surf Versus Turf,** SE pp. 36–37 • Active Reading (Annotation strategy), #17 • Two-column Chart, #18 • Analyze, #19 ☐ **Shifting Sands,** SE p. 38 • Visualize It!, #20	☐ **Groundwater and Waves** Learn about caves, sinkholes, and shoreline features. ☐ **Effects on Environment** Learn what happens as soil is carried into bodies of water. ☐ **Breaking Waves** Learn more about how waves and currents can shape shorelines.

Differentiated Instruction

Basic *Break Down and Build Up*

Synthesizing Key Topics

small groups or individuals
20 min

Sequence Diagram Show students images of landforms built by erosion and deposition. Have students make a sequence diagram, for a landform formed by erosion and deposition processes. Have them describe the likely events that caused the formation of the landform, and the events that will likely occur in the future.

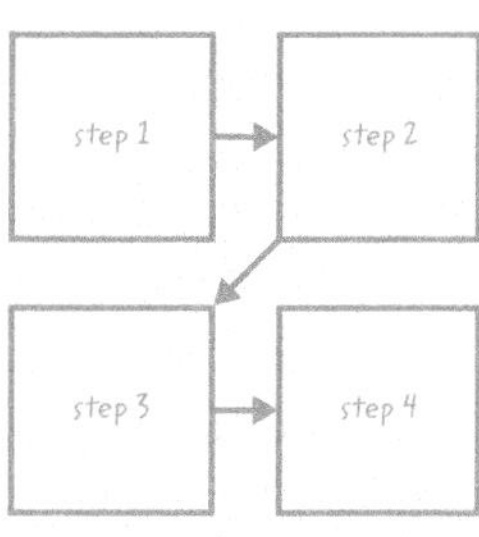

Advanced *Coastline Erosion*

Erosion and Deposition by Groundwater, Waves, and Currents

pairs or individuals
30 min

Quick Research Beach and coastline erosion is a major concern. Have students choose a stretch of coastline and prepare a poster on it. Posters should show the coastlines current condition, how it came to be that way, and possible solutions to any problems that might exist. Posters should include terms and concepts from the lesson.

ELL *Coastline Landform Progression*

Erosion and Deposition by Groundwater, Waves, and Currents

individuals
15–20 min

Process Chart Write the following terms on the board: *sea cliff, sea stack, sea arch, sea cave.* Have students use a process chart to make a series of drawings that show the sequence in which the landforms form; for example, a sea arch forms from a sea cave. Have students use the charts to describe how the landforms are built.

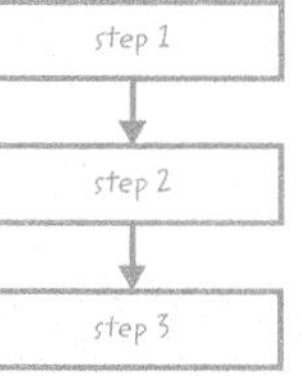

Lesson Vocabulary

erosion	**deposition**	**floodplain**	**delta**
alluvial fan	**groundwater**	**shoreline**	**beach**
sandbar	**barrier island**		

Previewing Vocabulary

whole class 15 min

Word Origins Many of the words in this lesson are either commonly known or are compound words formed from common word parts. The term *alluvial fan,* however, may be unfamiliar to many students. Share the following to help students understand and remember the term *alluvial fan: Alluvial* comes from the Latin word *alluvius,* which means "to wash against." The sediment that forms an alluvial fan has been "washed against" the plain on which it is deposited.

Reinforcing Vocabulary

individuals 20–30 min

Magnet Word Encourage students to make two magnet word organizers, one with *erosion* in the center and the other with *deposition* in the center. Ask students to write the rest of the vocabulary terms around the magnet words. Remind students that some words may go with both *erosion* and *deposition.*

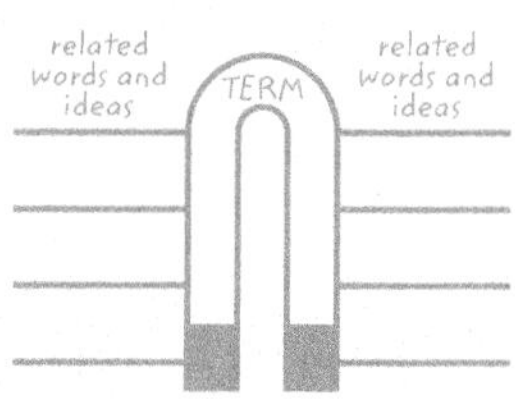

Customize Your Core Lesson

Core Instruction

- ☐ Print Path choices
- ☐ Digital Path choices

Vocabulary

- ☐ Previewing Vocabulary Word Origins
- ☐ Reinforcing Vocabulary Magnet Word

Differentiated Instruction

- ☐ Basic Break Down and Build Up
- ☐ Advanced Coastline Erosion
- ☐ ELL Coastline Landform Progression

Your Resources

Extend Science Concepts

Reinforce and Review

Activity *Formation Facts*

Synthesizing Key Topics | whole class | 20 min

Write Fast Use the list below or prepare your own list of landforms formed from both erosion and deposition. For each one, have students list the source of water that likely caused it (stream, ground, ocean) and quickly write two or three key words related to the process that produced it. Provide only a short time (approximately 30 seconds per word).

1. channel
2. cavern
3. barrier island
4. floodplain
5. oxbow lake
6. sea stack
7. beach
8. valley

Graphic Organizer

Synthesizing Key Topics | individuals | ongoing

Concept Map After students have studied the lesson, have them create a concept map with water in the center oval. Encourage students to use the types of water (stream, ground, ocean) and landforms in their concept maps. Encourage students to color-code their concept map and create a key to explain what each color represents.

Going Further

Engineering Connection

Synthesizing Key Topics | small groups | 30–40 min

Problem Solver Erosion is a major concern on land, on farms, and along coastlines. Present a scenario to students that highlights a community that is negatively affected by erosion. Explain the processes that have caused the problem. Then have students design a potential solution for the situation.

Real World Connection

Erosion and Deposition by Streams |  individuals | varied

Exploration The Grand Canyon is probably the most famous landform in the world formed by erosion. It took millions of years to form the steep sides of the massive canyon. Have students study photos, maps, reports, and online videos about the Grand Canyon. Then have each student prepare a diagram explaining how erosion by the Colorado River formed the Grand Canyon.

Customize Your Closing

See the Assessment Guide for quizzes and tests.

Go Online to edit and create quizzes and tests.

Reinforce and Review

- ☐ **Activity** Formation Facts
- ☐ **Graphic Organizer** Concept Map
- ☐ **Print Path** Visual Summary, SE p. 40
- ☐ **Digital Path** Lesson Closer

Evaluate Student Mastery

Formative Assessment

See the teacher support below the Student Pages for additional Formative Assessment questions.

Obtain a map showing geological features. **Ask:** Where on this map might erosion occur? Erosion occurs along shorelines and near rivers. Why? Waves erode land along shorelines; rivers erode the sides of their banks. Where might deposition occur? Deposition occurs where streams enter larger bodies of water and along shorelines. Why? Slowing streams deposit sediment; coastal waves pick up sand and deposit it in different places.

Reteach

Formative assessment may show that students need reinforcement for certain topics. The resources below are recommended for reteaching. If students were introduced to a topic through the Print Path, you can also use the Digital Path to reteach, and vice versa.
Can be assigned to individual students

Erosion and Deposition

Activity Take It or Leave It

Erosion and Deposition by Streams

Exploration Lab Exploring Stream Erosion and Deposition

Formation of Landforms by Streams

Activity Washed Up

Erosion and Deposition by Groundwater, Waves and Currents

Daily Demo Groundwater

Activity Now You Sea It, Now You Don't

Summative Assessment

Alternative Assessment
Pathways of Erosion and Deposition

Online resources: student worksheet, optional rubrics

Erosion and Deposition by Water

Mix and Match: ***Pathways of Erosion and Deposition***
Mix and match ideas to show what you've learned about erosion and deposition.

1. Work on your own, with a partner, or with a small group.
2. Choose one information source from Column A, two topics from Column B, and one option from Column C. Check your choices.
3. Have your teacher approve your plan.
4. Submit or present your results.

A. Choose One Information Source	B. Choose Two Things to Analyze	C. Choose One Way to Communicate Analysis
___ photograph of a landform	___ pathway, size, and speed of water	___ diagram or illustration
___ observations of a stream or coast	___ origin and destination of material	___ colors, arrows, or symbols marked on a visual, with a key
___ an aerial photograph of an alluvial fan	___ past history	___ model, such as drawings or simulations with sand or clay
___ observations of a local farm	___ future prediction	___ booklet, such as a field guide, travel brochure, playbook, or set of instructions
___ website describing national parks	___ speed of landform change and why	___ game
___ descriptions or photographs of a flood		___ story, song, or poem, with supporting details
___ topographical map		___ skit, chant, or dance, with supporting details
___ descriptions or photographs of a coastline before and after a big storm		___ Multimedia presentation
___ geological map		___ mathematical depiction
___		___

Going Further

☐ Engineering Connection
☐ Real World Connection
☐ Print Path Why it Matters, SE p. 39

Formative Assessment

☐ Strategies Throughout TE
☐ Lesson Review SE

Summative Assessment

☐ Alternative Assessment Pathways of Erosion and Deposition
☐ Lesson Quiz
☐ Unit Tests A and B
☐ Unit Review SE End-of-Unit

Your Resources

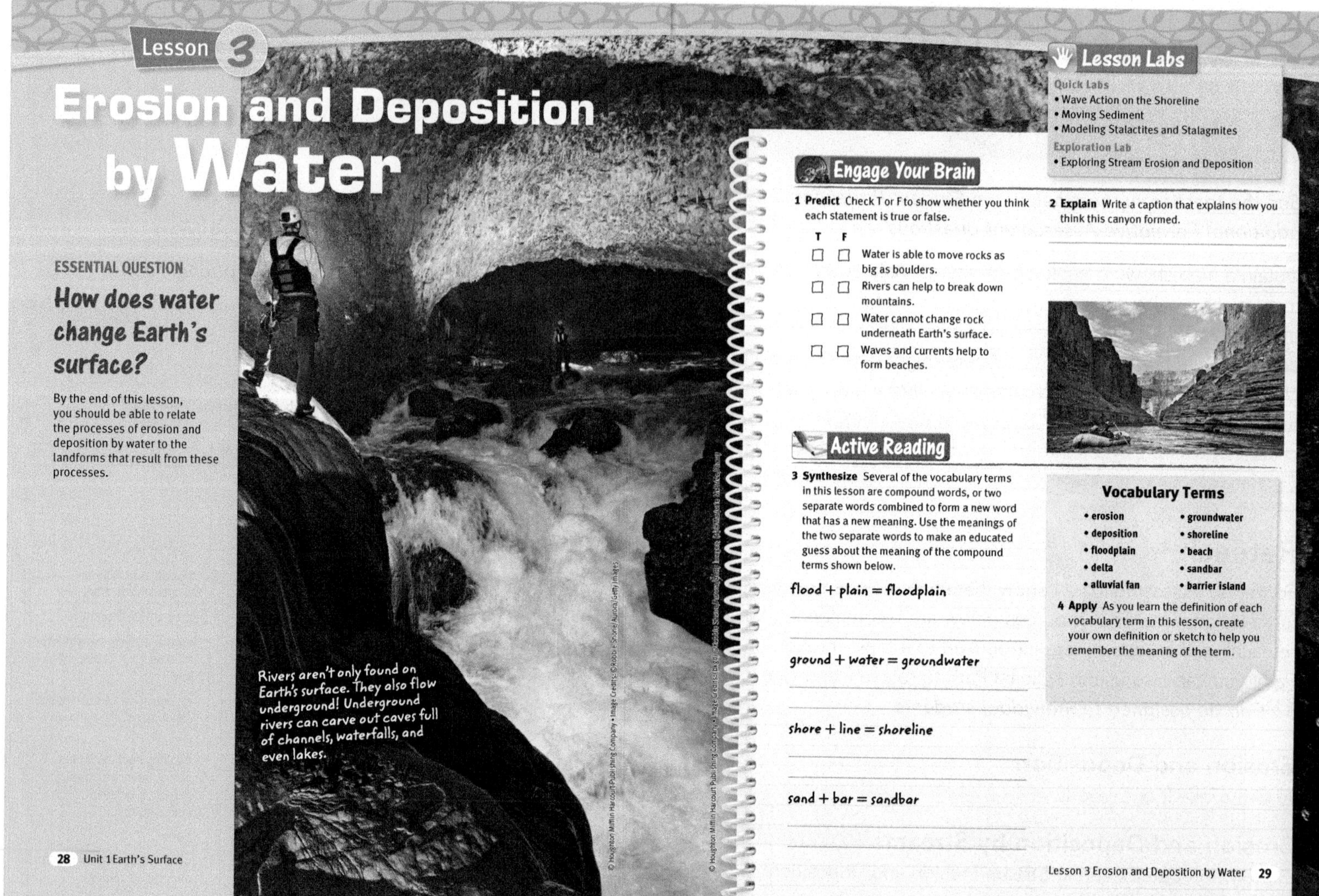

Answers

Answers for 1–3 should represent students' current thoughts, even if incorrect.

1. T; T; F; T
2. Over time, the river washed away soil and rocks from its banks, cutting out the canyon.
3. (floodplain) a plain made by floods; (ground water) water found underground; (shoreline) the edge of a body of water; (sandbar) a mounded strip of sand
4. Students should define or sketch each vocabulary term in the lesson.

Opening Your Lesson

Discuss the Engage Your Brain questions to assess students' preconceived notions about water. Have students study the photo of the canyon. Ask students what they already know about how water affects rock.

Preconceptions: Students may perceive water as weak, and rock as strong.

Prerequisites: Students should understand that water is a weathering agent.

Learning Alert MISCONCEPTION

Water and Rock Students may think of water as weaker than rock. Use the Engage Your Brain questions to be sure they realize water can be a powerful force. Even slow-moving water over time causes erosion and deposition.

Conservation Students may tend to think that when rock or soil is worn away, it disappears. Remind students about the law of conservation, which states that matter can neither be created nor destroyed. Tell students to keep this in mind as they read the lesson.

Go with the Flow

How does flowing water change Earth's surface?

If your job was to carry millions of tons of rock and soil across the United States, how would you do it? You might use a bulldozer or a dump truck, but your job would still take a long time. Did you know that rivers and other bodies of flowing water do this job every day? Flowing water, as well as wind and ice, can move large amounts of material, such as soil and rock. Gravity also has a role to play. Gravity causes water to flow and rocks to fall downhill.

By Erosion

Acting as liquid conveyor belts, rivers and streams erode soil, rock, and sediment. *Sediment* is tiny grains of broken-down rock. **Erosion** is the process by which sediment and other materials are moved from one place to another. Eroded materials in streams may come from the stream's own bed and banks or from materials carried to the stream by rainwater runoff. Over time, erosion causes streams to widen and deepen.

By Deposition

After streams erode rock and soil, they eventually drop, or deposit, their load downstream. **Deposition** is the process by which eroded material is dropped. Deposition occurs when gravity's downward pull on sediment is greater than the push of flowing water or wind. This usually happens when the water or wind slows down. A stream deposits materials along its bed, banks, and mouth, which can form different landforms.

5 Compare Fill in the Venn diagram to compare and contrast erosion and deposition.

Erosion

Both

Deposition

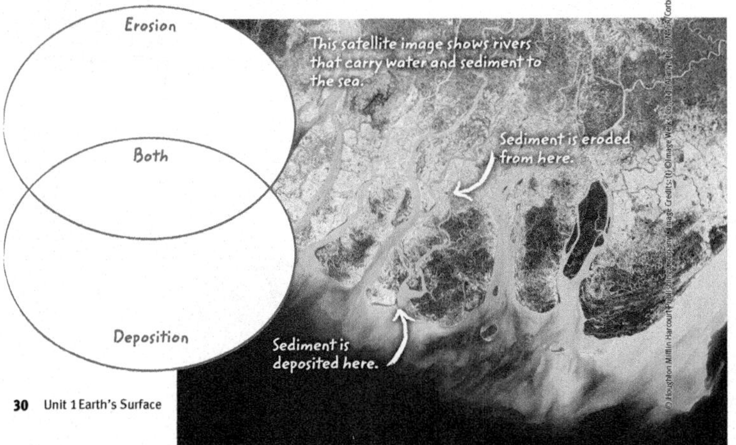

Sediment is eroded from here.
Sediment is deposited here.

This satellite image shows rivers that carry water and sediment to the sea.

What factors relate to a stream's ability to erode material?

Some streams are able to erode large rocks, while others can erode only very fine sediment. Some streams move many tons of material each day, while others move very little sediment. So what determines how much material a stream can erode? A stream's gradient, discharge, and load are the three main factors that control what sediment a stream can carry.

Gradient

Gradient is the measure of the change in elevation over a certain distance. You can think of gradient as the steepness of a slope. The water in a stream that has a high gradient—or steep slope—moves very rapidly because of the downward pull of gravity. This rapid water flow gives the stream a lot of energy to erode rock and soil. A river or stream that has a low gradient has less energy for erosion, or erosive energy.

Load

Materials carried by a stream are called the stream's *load*. The size of the particles in a stream's load is affected by the stream's speed. Fast-moving streams can carry large particles. The large particles bounce and scrape along the bottom and sides of the streambed. Thus, a stream that has a load of large particles has a high erosion rate. Slow-moving streams carry smaller particles and have less erosive energy.

Discharge

The amount of water that a stream carries in a given amount of time is called *discharge*. The discharge of a stream increases when a major storm occurs or when warm weather rapidly melts snow. As the stream's discharge increases, its erosive energy, speed, and load increase.

Active Reading

6 Explain Why do some streams and rivers cause more erosion and deposition than others?

Do the Math

River Gradient Plot

Altitude (m): 2,000; 1,800; 1,600; 1,400; 1,200

Stream distance (m): 0; 500; 1,000; 1,500; 2,000

A river gradient plot shows how quickly the elevation of a river falls along its course. The slope of the line is the river's gradient. The line has a steep slope at points along the river where the gradient is steep. The line has a nearly level slope where the river gradient is shallow.

Identify

7 Along this river, at which two approximate altitude ranges are the gradients the steepest?

8 At which altitude ranges would you expect the highest streambed erosion rate?

9 At which altitude ranges would you expect the slowest streambed erosion rate?

Answers

5. (under erosion) carries away materials, (under both) change Earth's surface (under deposition) drops materials
6. Some streams have a steeper gradient, a larger load, and/or a greater discharge.
7. at ranges of approximately 1,750 m to 1,550 m and 1,500 m to 1,400 m.
8. at ranges of approximately 1,750 m to 1,500 m and 1,500 m to 1,400 m.
9. at ranges of approximately 1,900 m to 1,800 m and 1,300 m to 1,200 m

Probing Questions INDEPENDENT Inquiry

Drawing Conclusions Imagine two streams. One is much more erosive than the other. What factors or combination of factors might affect the rate of erosion? Sample answer: The water in the more erosive stream may have a steeper gradient, so it is faster and causes more erosion; the stream's fast speed may also increase its load, which causes even more erosion. Finally, the stream may also have a high discharge—another factor that affects erosion.

Learning Alert

Rate of Erosion and Deposition Students may believe that erosion and deposition only occur over long periods of time. However, in some locations, such as certain beaches, erosion and deposition can cause noticeable changes in a single day.

Interpreting Visuals

Have students look at the graph. **Ask:** What would a graphic representation of a stream with a lower gradient look like? The line on the graph would be flatter. What would a stream with a higher gradient look like? The line would be steeper.

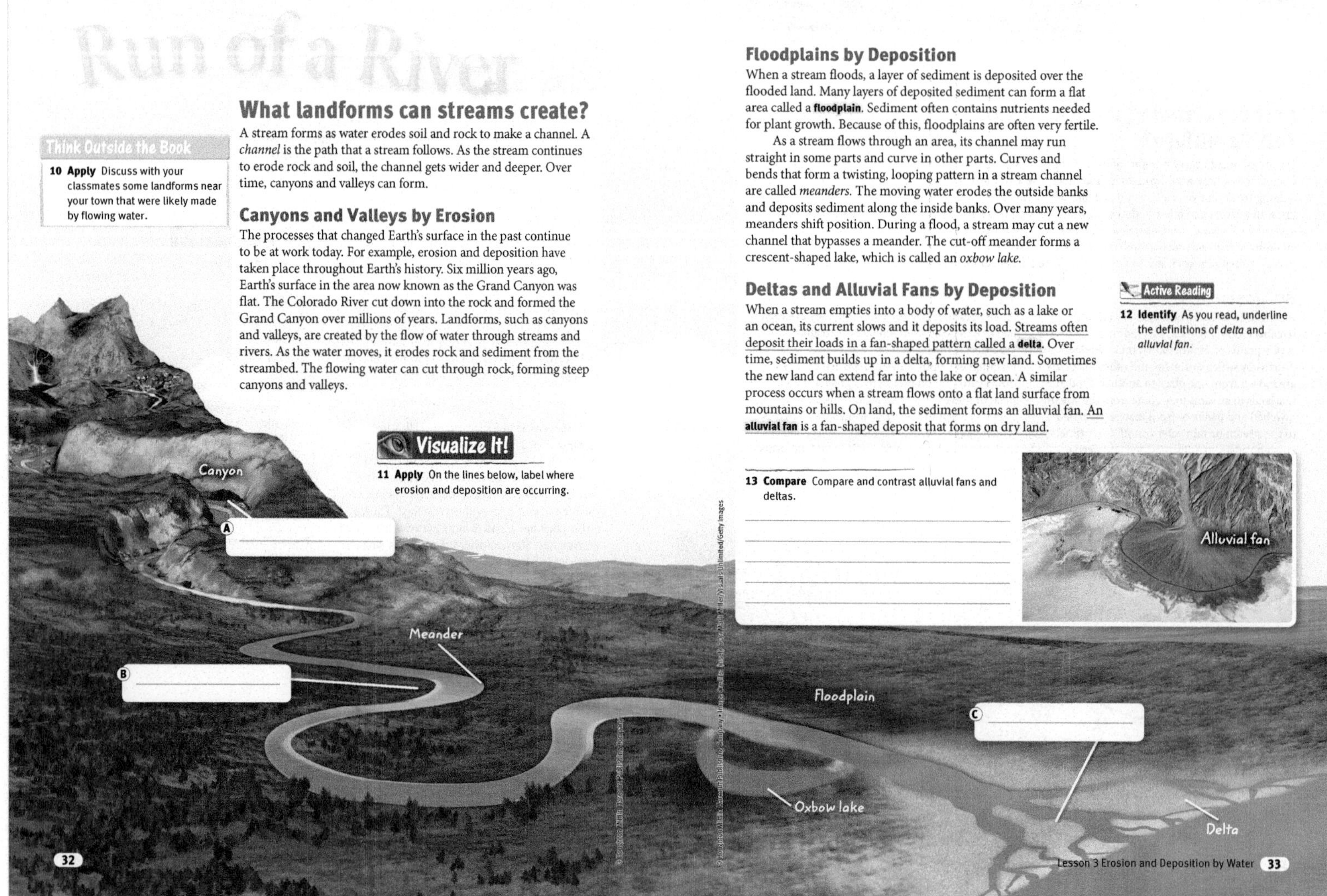

Run of a River

What landforms can streams create?

A stream forms as water erodes soil and rock to make a channel. A *channel* is the path that a stream follows. As the stream continues to erode rock and soil, the channel gets wider and deeper. Over time, canyons and valleys can form.

Think Outside the Book

10 Apply Discuss with your classmates some landforms near your town that were likely made by flowing water.

Canyons and Valleys by Erosion

The processes that changed Earth's surface in the past continue to be at work today. For example, erosion and deposition have taken place throughout Earth's history. Six million years ago, Earth's surface in the area now known as the Grand Canyon was flat. The Colorado River cut down into the rock and formed the Grand Canyon over millions of years. Landforms, such as canyons and valleys, are created by the flow of water through streams and rivers. As the water moves, it erodes rock and sediment from the streambed. The flowing water can cut through rock, forming steep canyons and valleys.

Visualize It!

11 Apply On the lines below, label where erosion and deposition are occurring.

Floodplains by Deposition

When a stream floods, a layer of sediment is deposited over the flooded land. Many layers of deposited sediment can form a flat area called a **floodplain**. Sediment often contains nutrients needed for plant growth. Because of this, floodplains are often very fertile.

As a stream flows through an area, its channel may run straight in some parts and curve in other parts. Curves and bends that form a twisting, looping pattern in a stream channel are called *meanders*. The moving water erodes the outside banks and deposits sediment along the inside banks. Over many years, meanders shift position. During a flood, a stream may cut a new channel that bypasses a meander. The cut-off meander forms a crescent-shaped lake, which is called an *oxbow lake*.

Deltas and Alluvial Fans by Deposition

When a stream empties into a body of water, such as a lake or an ocean, its current slows and it deposits its load. Streams often deposit their loads in a fan-shaped pattern called a **delta**. Over time, sediment builds up in a delta, forming new land. Sometimes the new land can extend far into the lake or ocean. A similar process occurs when a stream flows onto a flat land surface from mountains or hills. On land, the sediment forms an alluvial fan. An **alluvial fan** is a fan-shaped deposit that forms on dry land.

Active Reading

12 Identify As you read, underline the definitions of *delta* and *alluvial fan*.

13 Compare Compare and contrast alluvial fans and deltas.

32

Lesson 3 Erosion and Deposition by Water 33

Answers

10. Answers will vary. Students will likely discuss local canyons, valleys, floodplains, or deltas.
11. A. Erosion, B. Deposition, C. Deposition
12. *See students' pages for annotations.*
13. Both deltas and alluvial fans are fan-shaped landforms made by stream deposition. Deltas form at the mouth of a river. Alluvial fans form on dry land.

Formative Assessment

Ask: What is similar about how floodplains and alluvial fans form? What is different? Sample answer: Both form when a stream deposits sediment. They are different because a floodplain forms along the sides of a stream, and an alluvial fan forms where streambeds flatten out. **Ask:** Why are floodplains often very good areas for farming? When a stream floods, it spreads out over the land nearby and deposits sediment. This sediment can make the land very fertile.

Probing Questions GUIDED Inquiry

Synthesizing Can you think of a reason some streams and rivers form deep canyons, and others do not? Sample answer: Some rivers might flow over softer rock that erodes more easily and form canyons. Other rivers might flow over harder rock that does not erode easily. If floodplains form, streams and rivers get shallower and do not cause as much erosion.

Interpreting Visuals

Have students identify the oxbow lake in the illustration. Then have them identify the likely path of the stream before the oxbow was cut off by drawing dashed lines to show its path.

More Waterworks

What landforms are made by groundwater erosion?

As you have learned, rivers cause erosion when water picks up and moves rock and soil. The movement of water underground can also cause erosion. **Groundwater** is the water located within the rocks below Earth's surface. Slightly acidic groundwater can cause erosion by dissolving rock. When underground erosion happens, caves can form. Most of the world's caves formed over thousands of years as groundwater dissolved limestone underground. Although caves are formed by erosion, they also show signs of deposition. Water that drips from cracks in a cave's ceiling leaves behind icicle-shaped deposits known as *stalactites* and *stalagmites*. When the groundwater level is lower than the level of a cave, the cave roof may no longer be supported by the water underneath. If the roof of a cave collapses, it may leave a circular depression called a *sinkhole*.

Active Reading **14 Explain** How does groundwater cause caves to form?

Stalactites are caused by deposition.

Groundwater can erode rock, causing caves to form.

Visualize It!

15 Apply Describe what may have happened underground to cause this sinkhole to form.

34

What forces shape a shoreline?

A **shoreline** is the place where land and a body of water meet. Ocean water along a shoreline moves differently than river water moves. Ocean waves crashing against the shoreline have a great deal of energy. Strong waves may erode material. Gentle waves may deposit materials. In addition to waves, ocean water has *currents*, or streamlike movements of water. Like waves, currents can also erode and deposit materials.

Waves

Waves play a major part in building up and breaking down a shoreline. Waves slow down as they approach a shoreline. The first parts of the shoreline that waves meet are the *headlands*, or pieces of land that project into the water. The slowing waves bend toward the headlands, which concentrates the waves' energy. A huge amount of energy is released when waves crash into headlands, causing the land to erode. The waves striking the areas between headlands have less energy. Therefore, these waves are more likely to deposit materials rather than erode materials.

Currents

When water travels almost parallel to the shoreline very near shore, the current is called a *longshore current*. Longshore currents are caused by waves hitting the shore at an angle. Waves that break at angles move sediment along the coast. The waves push the sand in the same angled direction in which they break. But the return water flow moves sand directly away from the beach. The end result is a zigzag movement of the sand. As sand moves down a beach, the upcurrent end of the beach is eroded away while the downcurrent end of the beach is built up.

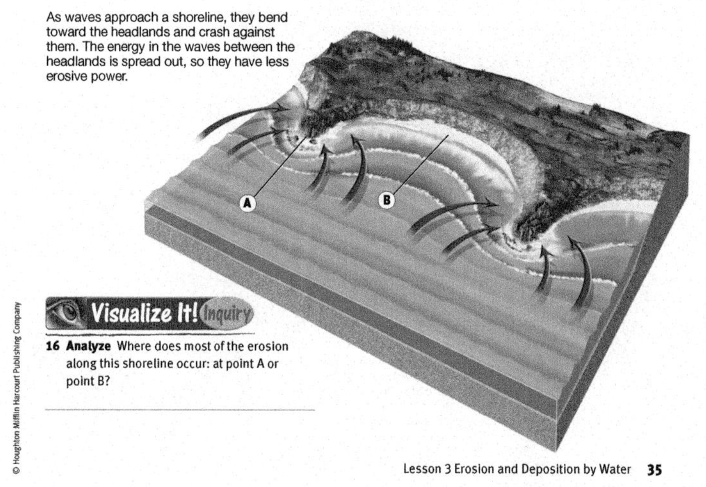

As waves approach a shoreline, they bend toward the headlands and crash against them. The energy in the waves between the headlands is spread out, so they have less erosive power.

Visualize It! Inquiry

16 Analyze Where does most of the erosion along this shoreline occur: at point A or point B?

Lesson 3 Erosion and Deposition by Water 35

Answers

14. Groundwater can dissolve and carry away rock.
15. The groundwater level in a cave lowered and the cave's roof collapsed.
16. point A

Interpreting Visuals

Look at the illustration of a shoreline. Point out the beach where sediment has been deposited and point out the arrows, which show the strongest wave action. Where is the greatest amount of erosion taking place? The greatest amount of erosion occurs where the land juts out into the water. Why do you think this is so? Sample answers: More land is exposed to the action of the waves; the waves hit this land first.

Probing Questions INDEPENDENT Inquiry

Predicting If the level of the oceans rose, what would likely happen to the shorelines? Describe two changes. Sample answers: Part of the beaches would be underwater. A new shoreline would be established. The waves would hit farther up on the land, causing new erosion and eventually making new beaches.

Synthesizing Groundwater is present almost everywhere. Can you think of a way that people use groundwater for survival? People dig wells so they can get water from the ground for drinking and bathing.

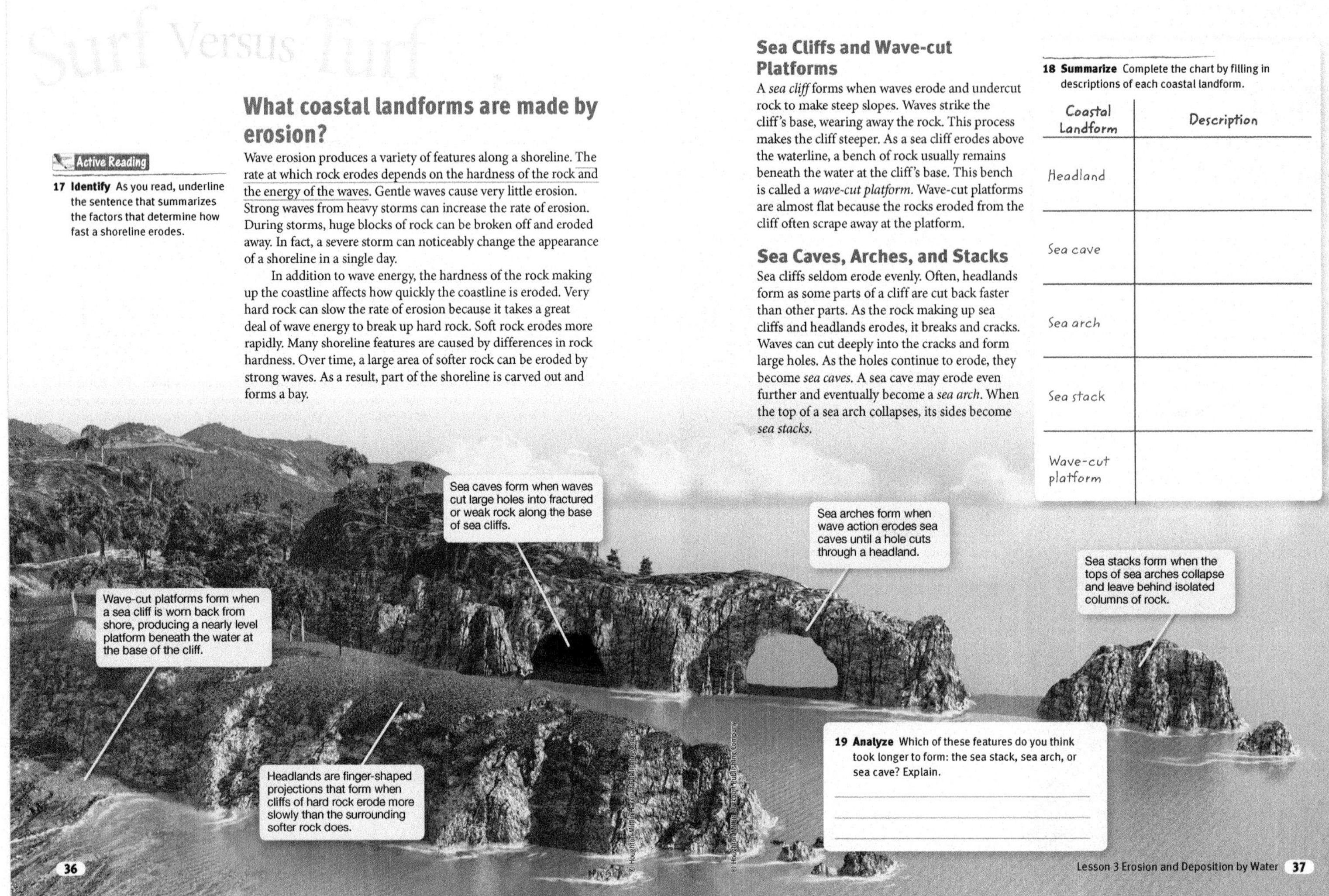

Surf Versus Turf

What coastal landforms are made by erosion?

Active Reading

17 Identify As you read, underline the sentence that summarizes the factors that determine how fast a shoreline erodes.

Wave erosion produces a variety of features along a shoreline. The rate at which rock erodes depends on the hardness of the rock and the energy of the waves. Gentle waves cause very little erosion. Strong waves from heavy storms can increase the rate of erosion. During storms, huge blocks of rock can be broken off and eroded away. In fact, a severe storm can noticeably change the appearance of a shoreline in a single day.

In addition to wave energy, the hardness of the rock making up the coastline affects how quickly the coastline is eroded. Very hard rock can slow the rate of erosion because it takes a great deal of wave energy to break up hard rock. Soft rock erodes more rapidly. Many shoreline features are caused by differences in rock hardness. Over time, a large area of softer rock can be eroded by strong waves. As a result, part of the shoreline is carved out and forms a bay.

Sea Cliffs and Wave-cut Platforms

A *sea cliff* forms when waves erode and undercut rock to make steep slopes. Waves strike the cliff's base, wearing away the rock. This process makes the cliff steeper. As a sea cliff erodes above the waterline, a bench of rock usually remains beneath the water at the cliff's base. This bench is called a *wave-cut platform.* Wave-cut platforms are almost flat because the rocks eroded from the cliff often scrape away at the platform.

Sea Caves, Arches, and Stacks

Sea cliffs seldom erode evenly. Often, headlands form as some parts of a cliff are cut back faster than other parts. As the rock making up sea cliffs and headlands erodes, it breaks and cracks. Waves can cut deeply into the cracks and form large holes. As the holes continue to erode, they become *sea caves.* A sea cave may erode even further and eventually become a *sea arch.* When the top of a sea arch collapses, its sides become *sea stacks.*

18 Summarize Complete the chart by filling in descriptions of each coastal landform.

Coastal Landform	Description
Headland	
Sea cave	
Sea arch	
Sea stack	
Wave-cut platform	

Sea caves form when waves cut large holes into fractured or weak rock along the base of sea cliffs.
Sea arches form when wave action erodes sea caves until a hole cuts through a headland.
Sea stacks form when the tops of sea arches collapse and leave behind isolated columns of rock.
Wave-cut platforms form when a sea cliff is worn back from shore, producing a nearly level platform beneath the water at the base of the cliff.
Headlands are finger-shaped projections that form when cliffs of hard rock erode more slowly than the surrounding softer rock does.

19 Analyze Which of these features do you think took longer to form: the sea stack, sea arch, or sea cave? Explain.

36

Lesson 3 Erosion and Deposition by Water 37

Answers

17. *See students' pages for annotations.*
18. Headland: projection formed when hard rock erodes more slowly than surrounding soft rock; Sea cave: hole formed when waves erode rock around a crack in a sea cliff; Sea arch: arch formed when wave action cuts all the way through a cave; Sea stack: column of rock formed when the top of a sea arch collapses; Wave-cut platform: flat platform of rock formed at base of sea cliff
19. A sea stack takes the longest because it forms from a collapsed sea arch, which formed from a sea cave.

Interpreting Visuals

Ask students to look at the visual. Have students describe how water can turn one landform into another. The power of the waves wears away at the rock. Caves can form in headlands; arches can form from caves; sea stacks are left when an arch is eroded.

Probing Questions GUIDED Inquiry

Justifying Why is it more likely that a sea cave becomes a sea arch before becoming a sea stack? Sample answer: Water flows into the cave and hits the back of the cave directly. The ceiling of the cave probably only has contact with the water during high tide or storms.

Synthesizing The cracks, crevices, caves, and spaces made by erosion make perfect homes for many plants and animals. How do you think living things might play a role in erosion? Sample answer: The roots of plants can break up soil and make it more likely to erode. Animals also break up soil as they build homes and forage for food.

Student Pages 36–39

Shifting Sands

What coastal landforms are made by deposition?

Waves and currents carry a variety of materials, including sand, rock, dead coral, and shells. Often, these materials are deposited on a shoreline, where they form a beach. A **beach** is an area of shoreline that is made up of material deposited by waves and currents. A great deal of beach material is also deposited by rivers and then is moved down the shoreline by currents.

Beaches

You may think of beaches as sandy places. However, not all beaches are made of sand. The size and shape of beach material depend on how far the material has traveled from its source. Size and shape also depend on the type of material and how it is eroded. For example, in areas with stormy seas, beaches may be made of pebbles and boulders deposited by powerful waves. These waves erode smaller particles such as sand.

Visualize It!

20 Infer Would it take more wave energy to deposit sand or the rocks shown on this beach? Explain.

Barrier islands lie nearly parallel to the shore.
Barrier islands are ridges of sand.

Sandbars and Barrier Islands

When waves erode material from the shoreline, longshore currents can transport and deposit this material offshore. This process creates landforms in open water.

A **sandbar** is an underwater or exposed ridge of sand, gravel, or shell material. A **barrier island** is a long, narrow island, usually made of sand, that forms parallel to the shoreline a short distance offshore.

38

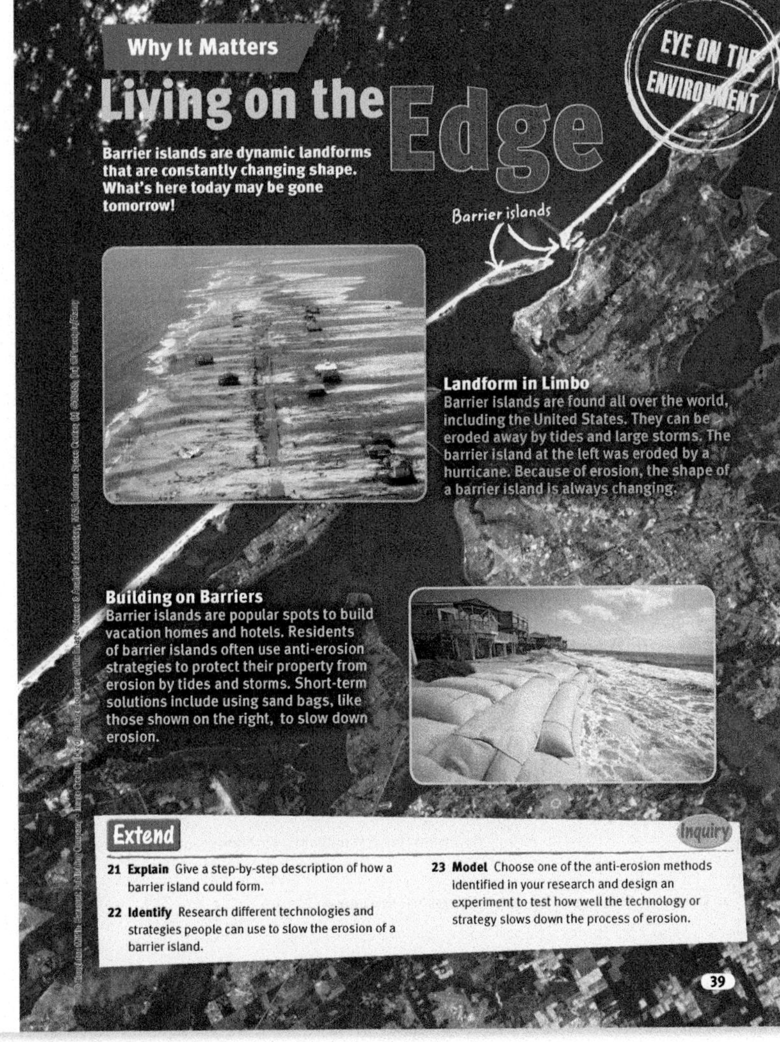

Why It Matters

Living on the Edge

Barrier islands are dynamic landforms that are constantly changing shape. What's here today may be gone tomorrow!

Landform in Limbo

Barrier islands are found all over the world, including the United States. They can be eroded away by tides and large storms. The barrier island at the left was eroded by a hurricane. Because of erosion, the shape of a barrier island is always changing.

Building on Barriers

Barrier islands are popular spots to build vacation homes and hotels. Residents of barrier islands often use anti-erosion strategies to protect their property from erosion by tides and storms. Short-term solutions include using sand bags, like those shown on the right, to slow down erosion.

Extend Inquiry

21 Explain Give a step-by-step description of how a barrier island could form.

22 Identify Research different technologies and strategies people can use to slow the erosion of a barrier island.

23 Model Choose one of the anti-erosion methods identified in your research and design an experiment to test how well the technology or strategy slows down the process of erosion.

39

Answers

20. It would take more energy to deposit the rocks because they are heavier, and thus would take more force to move.
21. Sample answer: Sediment could be eroded into the ocean by rivers. Longshore currents transport the sediment offshore. Over time, sediment builds up, forming barrier islands.

Formative Assessment

Ask: How does the sand and other material on a beach get there? Sample answer: Sand and other materials are deposited by waves; most material is deposited by rivers, and then moved onto a shoreline by waves. **Ask:** How does the sediment and other material in oceans get there? Sample answer: Rivers and streams carry sediment and materials into oceans; waves erode material from shorelines.

Why It Matters

Most people know that living on barrier islands has a downside, but they do it anyway. Ask students to discuss the benefits and risks of living on a barrier island. Sample answer: Living on a barrier island would be nice because you would have ocean all around you. It would be risky though; a hurricane could quickly wipe out your house or the action of wave erosion could slowly erode your property away.

Visual Summary

To complete this summary, fill in the blanks. Then use the key below to check your answers. You can use this page to review the main concepts of the lesson.

Erosion and Deposition by Water

Streams alter the shape of Earth's surface.

24 Caused by erosion: canyons, valleys
Caused by deposition: floodplains, deltas, ______

Groundwater erodes and deposits materials.

25 Caused by erosion: caves, ______
Caused by deposition: stalactites, stalagmites

Waves and currents change the shape of the shoreline.

26 Caused by erosion: bays, inlets, headlands, wave-cut platforms, sea cliffs, sea caves, sea stacks, ______
Caused by deposition: beaches, sandbars, barrier islands

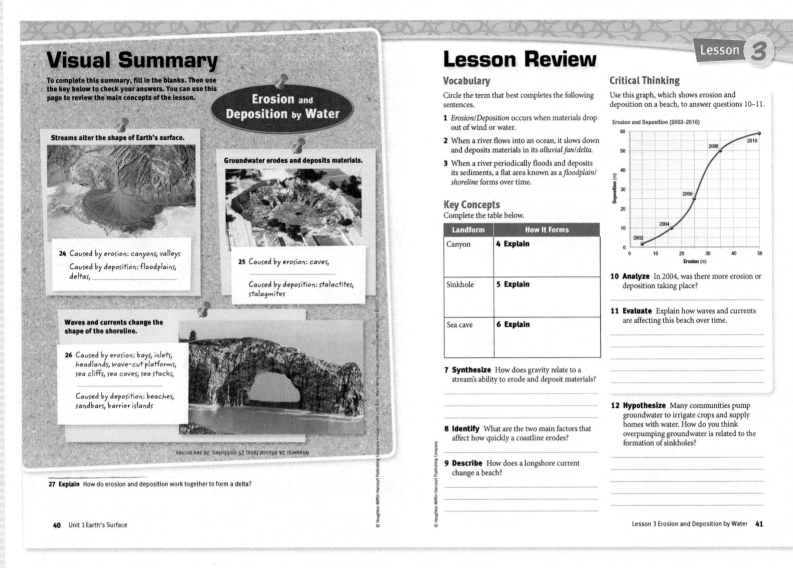

Answers: 24 alluvial fans; 25 sinkholes; 26 sea arches

27 Explain How do erosion and deposition work together to form a delta?

40 Unit 1 Earth's Surface

Lesson Review

Lesson 3

Vocabulary

Circle the term that best completes the following sentences.

1 *Erosion/Deposition* occurs when materials drop out of wind or water.

2 When a river flows into an ocean, it slows down and deposits materials in its *alluvial fan/delta.*

3 When a river periodically floods and deposits its sediments, a flat area known as a *floodplain/shoreline* forms over time.

Key Concepts

Complete the table below.

Landform	How It Forms
Canyon	**4 Explain**
Sinkhole	**5 Explain**
Sea cave	**6 Explain**

7 Synthesize How does gravity relate to a stream's ability to erode and deposit materials?

8 Identify What are the two main factors that affect how quickly a coastline erodes?

9 Describe How does a longshore current change a beach?

Critical Thinking

Use this graph, which shows erosion and deposition on a beach, to answer questions 10–11.

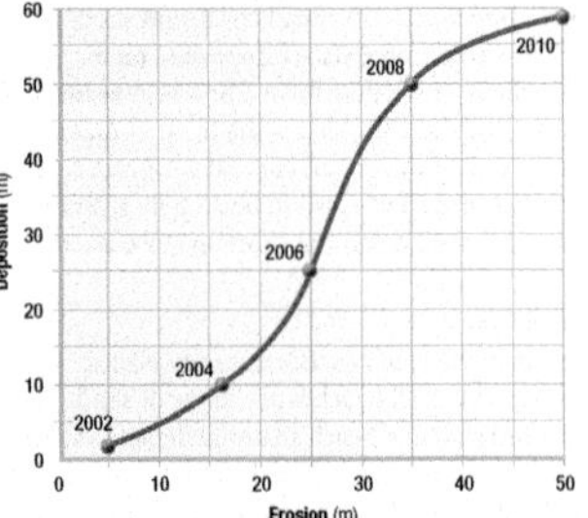

10 Analyze In 2004, was there more erosion or deposition taking place?

11 Evaluate Explain how waves and currents are affecting this beach over time.

12 Hypothesize Many communities pump groundwater to irrigate crops and supply homes with water. How do you think overpumping groundwater is related to the formation of sinkholes?

Lesson 3 Erosion and Deposition by Water 41

Visual Summary Answers

24. alluvial fans
25. sinkholes
26. sea arches
27. Upstream, rivers erode materials. The eroded materials are carried to the river's mouth, where the river water slows, causing the eroded materials to be deposited.

Lesson Review Answers

1. Deposition
2. delta
3. floodplain
4. A river erodes materials from its banks.
5. Ground water erodes a cave. Water levels drop, and the cave's roof collapses.
6. Waves erode and widen a crack in a sea cliff or headland.
7. Some streams have a steeper gradient than others. Gravity causes water to flow faster down steep slopes.
8. wave energy and rock hardness
9. It causes sand to move down the beach in a zig-zag pattern.
10. erosion
11. Before 2006, there was more erosion than deposition. In 2006, an equal amount of erosion and deposition occurred. After 2006, there was more deposition than erosion.
12. Over-pumping groundwater would lower the level of groundwater. If there was a cave in the ground, the cave's roof may no longer be supported and could possibly collapse.

Teacher Notes

Searching the Internet

Purpose To learn about how to use the Internet to find scientific information and reference material

Learning Goals

- Identify and use appropriate Internet reference materials.

Informal Vocabulary

keyword, search engine, organization, biased

Prerequisite Knowledge

- Understanding of the processes that cause weathering, erosion, and deposition
- Understanding of the landforms created by weathering, erosion, and deposition

Discussion *Using the Internet*

 whole class

 15 min

Inquiry **GUIDED** inquiry

Have students think about what they already know about using the Internet to find information. **Ask:** What do you do when you want to look something up on the Internet? Sample answers: I use a search engine to find a webpage with the information I need. I go to a webpage that I think will have the answer. **Ask:** Do you trust some webpages more than others? What are some signs that a webpage is trustworthy? Not trustworthy? Sample answers: Trustworthy: is well-written and well-designed, cites sources, is made by a well-known organization; Not trustworthy: poorly written or poorly designed, does not cite sources, has information that seems wrong or cannot be verified by another source

Optional Online resource: Class discussion support

Differentiated Instruction

Basic *Search It!*

 individuals

 20 min

Assign each student a science topic related to weathering, erosion, or deposition. Have them use a search engine to find webpages about their assigned topic. Remind them to use steps 2 and 3 in the tutorial as a guide. Ask them to list the five best webpages that appeared in their search and explain why they thought these sources would be the most useful and reliable.

Advanced *Website Critic*

small groups

 45 min

Multimedia Presentations Assign each group a science webpage to evaluate. Try to assign a mix of reliable and unreliable sites. Using the tutorial as a guide, have them evaluate their assigned webpage. Group presentations should include images of the page that highlight features or information they judged to be reliable or unreliable. When students give their presentations, have them imagine they work for a student-run webpage that rates science webpages by their usefulness and accuracy.

ELL *Brainstorming Keywords*

pairs

10–20 min

Concept Map Have pairs use a Concept Map to brainstorm keywords that they could use to search for information about physical weathering. Have them put *physical weathering* in the center oval of the Concept Map. Then they should add details related to the concept in the smaller ovals. Remind them to write linking words on arrows that connect the ovals. Point out that their keywords could come from the ovals or from the arrow labels.

Customize Your Feature

- ☐ **Discussion** Using the Internet
- ☐ **Basic** Search It!
- ☐ **Advanced** Webpage Critic
- ☐ **ELL** Brainstorming Keywords
- ☐ **Written Pieces**

Student Pages 42–43

Think Science

Searching the Internet

The Internet can be a great tool for finding scientific information and reference material. But, because the Internet contains so much information, finding useful information on it may be difficult. Or, you may find information that is unreliable or not suitable.

Tutorial

The procedure below can help you retrieve useful, reliable information from the Internet.

Choose a search engine There are many search engines available for finding information. Evaluate different search engines using the following criteria:

- number of relevant sites listed in search results;
- how easy the search engine is to use;
- how fast the search is; and
- how easy the documents on the site are to access, and what type of documents they are.

Choose and enter keywords Identify specific keywords for the topic of interest. You can make lists or draw concept maps to help you think of keywords or key phrases. Enter your keyword(s) into the search engine. You can enter one keyword at a time, or you can enter multiple keywords. You can put the word *and* or + between two keywords to find both words on the site. Use the word *or* between two keywords to find at least one of the keywords on the site. Use quotations ("like this") around keywords to find exact matches.

Search Engine | erosion + water | GO!

Water Erosion
Water erosion is what destroys houses and landscapes due to rain, which erodes the soil and causes things like rill, gully and stream erosion...
www.floodaware.net

Rangeland Soil Quality—Water Erosion
Water erosion is the detachment and removal of soil material by water. ... Water erosion wears away the earth's surface. Sheet erosion...
www.soilsolutions.com

Water Erosion
Erosion is the detachment of earth material from the surface. Once detached, agents like water or wind transport the material to a new...
www.geology101/erosion/university.edu

Look at the URL Examine the address in the search results list. Ask yourself if a reliable organization is behind the webpage such as government agencies (.gov or .mil), educational institutions (.edu), and non-profit organizations (.org). Avoid personal sites and biased sources, which may tell only one side of a story. These types of sources may lead to inaccurate information or a false impression.

Look at the content of the webpage Decide whether the webpage contains useful information. Read the page's title and headings. Read the first sentences of several paragraphs. Look at tables and diagrams. Ask yourself: How current is the webpage?; Are the sources documented?; and Are there links to more information? Decide whether the webpage contains the kind of information that you need.

You Try It!

Weathering is the physical and chemical alteration of rock. Weathering processes have led to the formations you see here in Bryce Canyon. Study the photo and then do some research on the Internet to find out more about weathering processes.

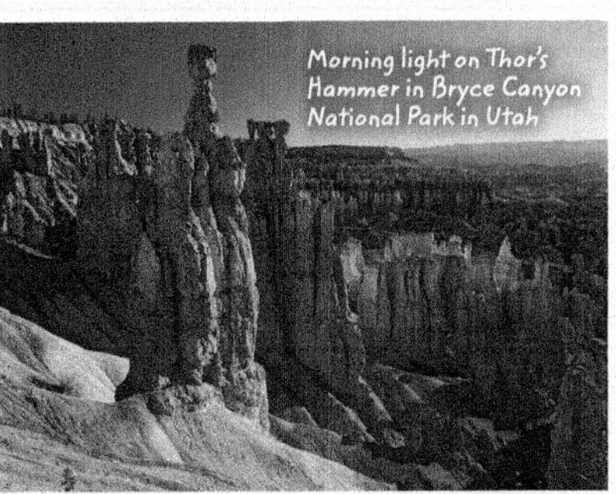
Morning light on Thor's Hammer in Bryce Canyon National Park in Utah

1 Choosing Keywords Think about what you want to learn about mechanical weathering. You may want to focus on one topic, such as frost wedging, exfoliation, or thermal expansion. Choose relevant keyword(s) or phrases for the topic that you are researching.

2 Searching the Internet Enter the keywords in a search engine. Which keywords or phrases prompted the most relevant and reliable sites?

3 Evaluating Websites Use the table below to evaluate websites on how useful they are and on the quality of the information. As you visit different websites for your research, make notes about each site's relevance and suitability.

Webpage	Comments

Answers

1. Students should write down keywords or phrases that relate to one specific topic of mechanical weathering. Some examples are "weathering," "geological processes," and "weathering + canyon."
2. Students should list the keywords or phrases that yielded the best results. They should be topic-specific, and have been listed for question one.
3. Students should list the webpages they visited on the left side of the chart, and comments about how reliable and relevant the web sites were on the right side. Students should also comment on content quality.

Written Pieces

Have students use information from the most reliable webpages they found to write a brief report about their topic. Help them create a bibliography that properly documents the sources they used in the report. Encourage volunteers to share their reports with the class and explain how they decided which sources to use. After all students have presented their reports, discuss with the class why bibliographies or works cited pages are an important part of presenting research.

Optional Online resource: Written Pieces

Erosion and Deposition by Wind, Ice, and Gravity

Essential Question How do wind, ice, and gravity change Earth's surface?

For more detailed information about the topics in this lesson, refer to the Content Refresher in the Unit Opener pages.

Opening Your Lesson

Begin the lesson by assessing students' prerequisite and prior knowledge.

Prerequisite Knowledge

- Erosion and deposition by water

Accessing Prior Knowledge

Ask: What can result from water erosion? channels, valleys, canyons, caverns, sink-holes, shorelines, cliffs, sea stacks, sea caves, and sea arches

Ask: What can result from water deposition? floodplains, alluvial fans, deltas, barrier islands, and sand bars

Customize Your Opening

- ☐ **Accessing Prior Knowledge,** above
- ☐ **Print Path** Engage Your Brain, SE p. 45 #1–2
- ☐ **Print Path** Active Reading, SE p. 45 #3–4
- ☐ **Digital Path** Lesson Opener

Key Topics/Learning Goals	Supporting Concepts
Erosion and Deposition by Wind 1 Describe how wind speed affects sediment movement. 2 Define and describe *dunes*. 3 Define and describe *loess*. 4 Explain what desert pavement is and how it is formed.	• Stronger winds cause more change. • Dunes are mounds of wind-deposited sand that form in places with strong winds and a large supply of sand. They are gently sloped on the side where the wind blows and steeply sloped on the other side. • Loess is a thick deposit of windblown, fine-grained sediment. • Desert pavement describes the rocky surface left after wind erodes layers of sand.
Erosion and Deposition by Ice 1 Describe glacier formation. 2 Describe how glaciers shape the land.	• Glaciers are masses of moving ice. They form as snow buildup changes into ice. • Expanding glaciers shape land as they push masses of sediment to their sides and front. • On mountains, glaciers move downward, forming valleys; on flat land, they spread out in sheets. • As a glacier retreats, a glacial drift remains. Many landforms result from glacial drifts.
Erosion and Deposition by Gravity (Mass Movement) 1 Describe the processes of erosion and deposition by gravity (mass movement). 2 Explain how mass movement can occur. 3 Define and describe: *rockfall*, *landslide*, *mudflow*, and *creep*.	• Gravity causes materials to move downhill, either slowly or rapidly. Events such as rain or earthquakes can quicken this process. • In a landslide or rockfall, a large mass of earth material slides as a unit down a slope. • Mudflows occur as water mixes with material and causes a mass of mud to flow downhill. • Creep is a slow form of mass movement. It occurs when soil close to the surface moves faster than the soil farther down.

Options for Instruction

Two parallel paths provide coverage of the Essential Questions, with a strong **Inquiry** strand woven into each. Follow the **Print Path,** the **Digital Path,** or your customized combination of print, digital, and inquiry.

 Print Path *Teaching support for the Print Path appears with the Student Pages.*	 Inquiry Labs and Activities	 Digital Path *Digital Path shortcut: TS661022*
Gone with the Wind, SE pp. 46–47 **How can wind shape Earth?** • Abraded Rock • Desert Pavement • Dunes • Loess	**Activity** **Think About It** **Activity** **Alike and Different** **Virtual Lab** **Erosion and Deposition of Sand Dunes**	**Wind Shapes the Land** **Animation**
Groovy Glaciers, SE pp. 48–50 **What kinds of ice shape Earth?** • Flowing Ice • Alpine Glaciers • Continental Glaciers	**Daily Demo** **Erosion in Fast Forward** **Quick Lab** **Modeling a Glacier**	**Ice Shapes the Land** **Interactive Images** **Ice Wedging** **Interactive Images**
Slippery Slopes, SE pp. 52–53 **How can gravity shape Earth?** • Slow Mass Movement • Rapid Mass Movement	**Activity** **Flipping Through Time** **Quick Lab** **Modeling a Landslide**	**Gravity Shapes Land** **Interactive Images**

Options for Assessment

See the Evaluate page for options, including Formative Assessment, Summative Assessment, and Unit Review.

Engage and Explore

Activities and Discussion

Discussion *Logical Motion*

Introducing Key Topics

 whole class
 15 min
GUIDED inquiry

This lesson and the previous one include many new terms relating to erosion and deposition, especially many new landforms. Help students see that all of these formations follow logical patterns of motion. Describe a couple of simple scenarios with a ball: how it would move if dropped from above your head, and how it would move if placed on the ground and kicked. Then, compare movement of sediment to many tiny balls moving over Earth's surface. Introduce the agents of wind, ice, and gravity and ask how students think these things could cause sediment to move.

Activity *Think About It*

Introducing Key Topics

 whole class
 15 min
GUIDED inquiry

Compare water to wind, ice, and gravity as agents of erosion and deposition. Ask students to compare the agents featured in this lesson to how water acts as an agent of erosion and deposition. As students come up with ideas, list the similarities and differences on the board.

Agent	Similarity	Difference
Wind	Moves sediment around	Not as likely to carry big pieces
Ice	Can get into rock cracks	Flows much slower than liquid water
Gravity	Pulls sediment	Gravity only pulls downward, water can pull down and horizontally

Probing Question *Conservation and Change*

Introducing Key Topics

 whole class or small groups
 10 min
 GUIDED inquiry

Recognizing Relationships The word *conservation* can be used to describe how the amount of matter stays the same during a change. The processes of erosion and deposition change the land, but they also play a role in the conservation of matter on Earth. How can erosion and deposition be both processes of change and conservation at the same time?

Activity *Flipping Through Time*

Erosion and Deposition by Gravity

 individuals
 30–40 min
DIRECTED inquiry

Flip Book Provide students with blank flip books. Have them choose a landform caused by processes of erosion and deposition from gravity. Then have them draw out an animated sequence. The sequence should show the processes of erosion followed by deposition and should end with the formation of a landform. Sequences should include labels for erosion, deposition, and the resulting landform. Encourage them to use color and to show two different landforms if they have extra time.

Customize Your Labs

 *See the Lab Manual for lab datasheets.*

 *Go Online for editable lab datasheets.*

Levels of Inquiry

DIRECTED inquiry introduces inquiry skills within a structured framework.

GUIDED inquiry develops inquiry skills within a supportive environment.

INDEPENDENT inquiry deepens inquiry skills with student-driven questions or procedures.

Labs and Demos

Quick Lab *Modeling a Glacier*

Engage

Erosion and Deposition by Ice

 small groups

 20 min

 **DIRECTED** inquiry

Students will model a glacier to study how it affects land over which it moves. They will use a block of ice with sand and gravel embedded in it to represent the glacier, and clay to represent land.

PURPOSE **To describe how ice causes erosion and deposition**

MATERIALS

- clay, stick
- gravel
- paper towel
- paper cup
- rolling pin
- sand
- water

Daily Demo *Erosion in Fast Forward*

Erosion and Deposition by Ice

 pairs or small groups

 20 min

 **DIRECTED** inquiry

PURPOSE **To show features and landforms formed by glaciers**

MATERIALS

- clay, modeling or any soft clay

1 Tell students you are going to use clay to show them landforms created by alpine glaciers.

2 **Observing** Use the clay to create landforms in the order they would form naturally. As you form each one, have students name the landform you are sculpting. Begin with a cirque and continue by showing how cirques form an arête and eventually a horn. Continue with U-shaped and hanging valleys.

Quick Lab *Modeling a Landslide*

Erosion and Deposition by Gravity

 small groups

 20 min

 **GUIDED** inquiry

Students will use a wooden board with a sample of rocks on it to model a hillside. They will change the slope of the board and observe what happens to the rocks.

PURPOSE **To describe how the angle of a slope affects the movement of sediment**

MATERIALS

- board, wooden, 1 m long
- protractor
- rocks, various sizes
- safety goggles

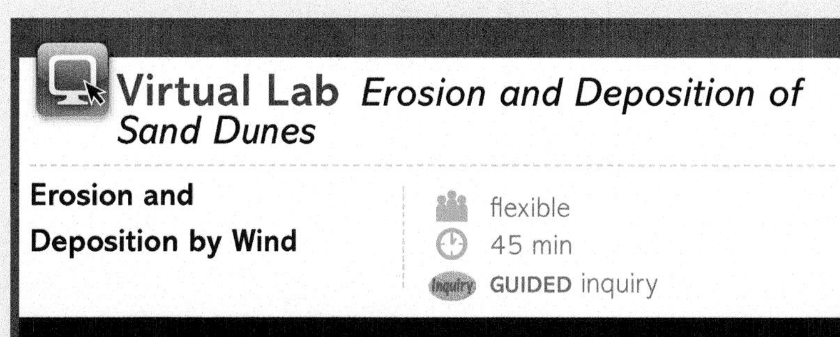

Virtual Lab *Erosion and Deposition of Sand Dunes*

Erosion and Deposition by Wind

flexible

45 min

GUIDED inquiry

Students change different wind parameters and see the results.

PURPOSE To observe and analyze the effects of wind on sand dunes

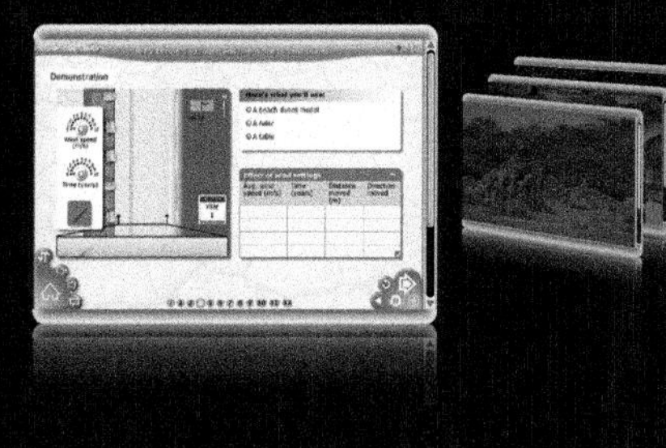

Activities and Discussion

- ☐ **Discussion** Logical Motion
- ☐ **Activity** Think About It
- ☐ **Probing Question** Conservation and Change
- ☐ **Activity** Flipping Through Time

Labs and Demos

- ☐ **Quick Lab** Modeling a Glacier
- ☐ **Daily Demo** Erosion in Fast Forward
- ☐ **Quick Lab** Modeling a Landslide
- ☐ **Virtual Lab** Erosion and Deposition of Sand Dunes

Your Resources

Explain Science Concepts

Key Topics	Print Path	Digital Path
Erosion and Deposition by Wind	☐ **Gone with the Wind,** SE pp. 46–47 • Visualize It!, #5 • Active Reading, #6 • Visualize It!, #7–8	☐ **Wind Shapes the Land** Learn how wind causes erosion and deposition.
Erosion and Deposition by Ice	☐ **Groovy Glaciers,** SE pp. 48–50 • Think Outside the Book, #9 • Active Reading, #10 • Visualize It!, #11 • Visualize It!, #12	☐ **Ice Shapes the Land** Learn about the different landforms shaped by glaciers. ☐ **Ice Wedging** Learn how freezing and thawing of water can erode surfaces.
Erosion and Deposition by Gravity	☐ **Slippery Slopes,** SE pp. 52–53 • Visualize It!, #16 • Identify, #17 • Visualize It!, #18	☐ **Gravity Shapes Land** Explore ways that gravity changes the shape of landforms.

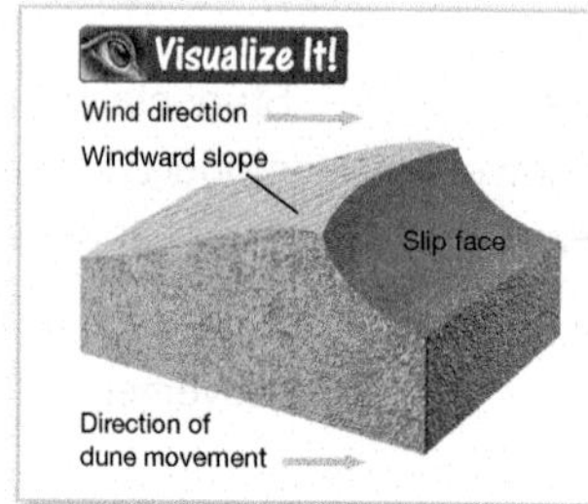

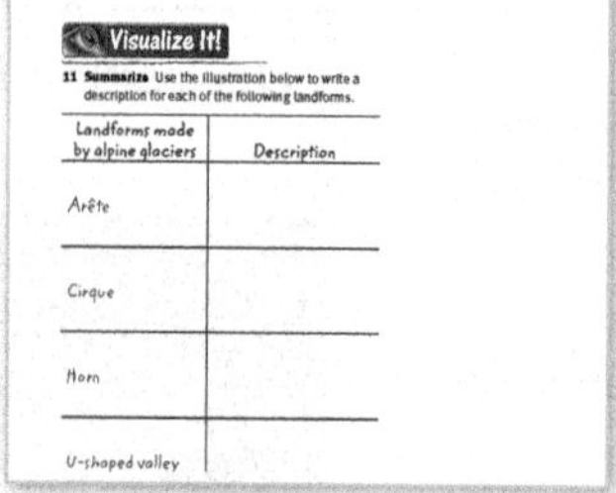
Visualize It!

11 Summarize Use the illustration below to write a description for each of the following landforms.

Landforms made by alpine glaciers	Description
Arête	
Cirque	
Horn	
U-shaped valley	

Differentiated Instruction

Basic *Alpine vs. Continental*

Erosion and Deposition by Ice

individuals
30 min

Once students have learned about the two types of glaciers and the types of landforms each creates, encourage them to create a Venn diagram comparing and contrasting the two types. Students should include in their diagrams characteristics of the glaciers as well as the landforms and landscapes they create.

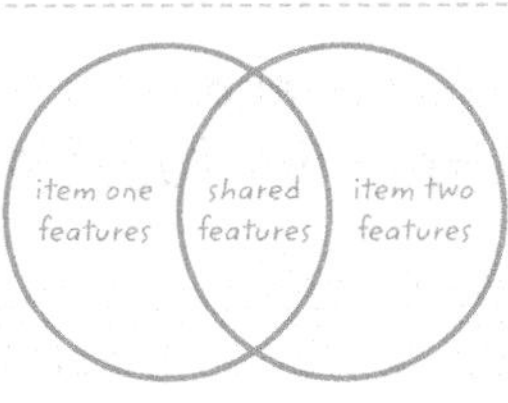

Advanced *Before and After*

Synthesizing Key Topics

individuals
30 min

Quick Project Ask students to find three or four pictures of landscapes. Encourage them to think about whether wind, ice, gravity, or some combination of these agents caused erosion and deposition in each landscape. Have students draw pictures to show what they think the landscapes might have looked like before these processes occurred. Students can display their before-and-after pictures on posters or in booklets. Remind students to include explanations of what agent or agents acted on their landscapes, and what occurred.

ELL *Main Ideas*

Synthesizing Key Topics

individuals

30 min

Supporting Main Ideas Encourage students to create Main Idea Webs for some of the topics introduced in the lesson. Have students write details about each topic in the branches of the web. Details can include definitions, examples, drawing, and anything else that helps students organize their thoughts. Students can focus on Lesson Vocabulary or names of landforms.

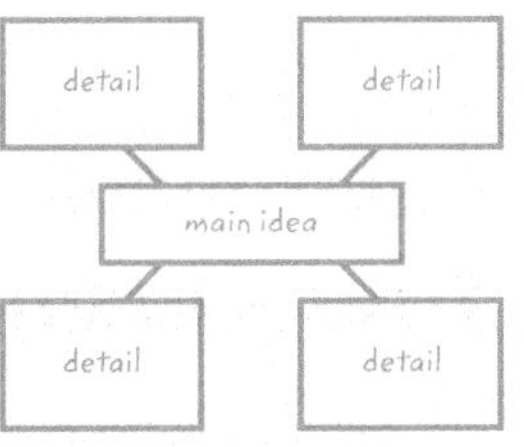

Lesson Vocabulary

dune	loess	glacier	glacial drift
creep	rockfall	landslide	mudflow

Previewing Vocabulary

whole class
10 min

Categories Write three columns on the board, one for wind, one for ice, and one for gravity. As a class, sort the vocabulary terms into the columns. Leave the word sort on display. Encourage students to refer to it as they go through the lesson to help keep details in order. wind: dune, loess; ice: glacier, glacial drift; gravity: landslide, rock fall, mudflow, creep

Reinforcing Vocabulary

individuals
ongoing

Word Squares To help students remember the terms introduced in this lesson, have them create a booklet with a Word Square for each term on each page. Students write the term in one of the cells and then fill in the remaining cells with additional information.

TERM translation	symbol or picture
my meaning dictionary definition	sentence

Customize Your Core Lesson

Core Instruction

- ☐ **Print Path** choices
- ☐ **Digital Path** choices

Vocabulary

- ☐ **Previewing Vocabulary** Categories
- ☐ **Reinforcing Vocabulary** Word Squares

Your Resources

Differentiated Instruction

- ☐ **Basic** Alpine vs. Continental
- ☐ **Advanced** Before and After
- ☐ **ELL** Main Ideas

Extend Science Concepts

Reinforce and Review

Activity *Alike and Different*

Synthesizing Key Topics

 pairs or individuals
30–40 min

Compare and Contrast Divide students into two teams. Tell them that you are going to say two terms. Teams then find something that the two terms have in common, and something that is different. The team that comes up with one similarity and one difference first wins a point. Use the following pairs of terms, or come up with your own.

desert pavement/loess both caused by wind; desert pavement consists of large rocks; loess is made of fine particles

glacial drift and glacier both related to ice; glacier is a large mass of ice; a glacial drift is left after the glacier melts

hanging valley/U-shaped valley both are created by alpine glaciers and are U-shaped; a hanging valley is formed by a tributary of a main glacier; a U-shaped valley is formed by a main glacier

arêtes/horn both are formed by alpine glaciers; an arête is a sharp ridge; a horn is the point where arêtes join

kettle lakes/cirques both are bowl-shaped depressions formed by ice; kettle lakes are water-filled depressions on flat land; a cirque cuts into a mountain wall

alpine glacier/continental glacier both are ice; alpine glaciers form in mountain areas; continental glaciers form on large, flat areas

rockfall/creep both are caused by gravity, both involve materials falling down a slope; creep is slow; rockfalls happen quickly

mudflow/lahar both involve mud moving downhill; a mudflow includes water, soil, and rocks; a lahar also includes volcanic ash

Graphic Organizer

Synthesizing Key Topics

 individuals
ongoing

Cause and Effect Chains As students study the lesson, ask them to draw cause and effect chains for the creation of landforms.

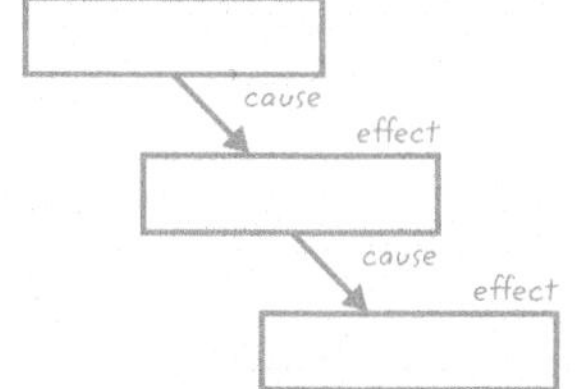

Going Further

Real World Connection

Erosion and Deposition by Wind

 individuals
40 min

Quick Research The lesson mentions that formation of loess can be a positive thing because it brings fertile soil into an area. However, soil that forms loess was eroded from another area. Have students research a specific loess formation. Then have them prepare a short report on the impacts to the area where the loess formed and to the area from which sediment was eroded.

Social Studies Connection

Erosion and Deposition by Gravity

 whole class
varied

Discussion Present information about a specific major mudflow, landslide, or lahar—for example, the lahar that occurred at Nevado del Huila Volcano, Colombia—that changed the history of an area. Describe the causes of the event, details about the event, and what the situation is like today. Include pictures if possible. Then discuss with students how events like the one presented have huge impacts on an area's environment and the people who live there. Have students give examples of ways they imagine such an event would affect an area.

Customize Your Closing

 *See the Assessment Guide for quizzes and tests.*

 *Go Online to edit and create quizzes and tests.*

Reinforce and Review

- ☐ **Activity** Alike and Different
- ☐ **Graphic Organizer** Cause and Effect Chains
- ☐ **Print Path** Visual Summary, SE p. 54
- ☐ **Digital Path** Lesson Closer

Evaluate Student Mastery

Formative Assessment

See the teacher support below the Student Pages for additional Formative Assessment questions.

Write Fast Read the following descriptions twice. Give students a few seconds to write the landform or process it is describing.

- All the material dropped by a glacier glacial drift
- Sand dropped by wind when it hits an obstacle dune
- Hills formed from piles of glacial drift drumlins
- A glacier in a mountainous area alpine glacier
- Rapid downhill movement of mud mudflow
- Bowl-shaped depression cut by a glacier into a mountain cirque
- Jagged ridges between two or more cirques arêtes

Reteach

Formative assessment may show that students need reinforcement for certain topics. The resources below are recommended for reteaching. If students were introduced to a topic through the Print Path, you can also use the Digital Path to reteach, and vice versa.

Can be assigned to individual students

Erosion and Deposition by Wind

Activity Think About It

Erosion and Deposition by Ice

Quick Lab Modeling a Glacier

Daily Demo Erosion in Fast Forward

Erosion and Deposition by Gravity

Quick Lab Modeling a Landslide

Activity Flipping Through Time

Summative Assessment

Alternative Assessment

Make a Board Game

Online resources: student worksheet, optional rubrics

Erosion and Deposition by Wind, Ice, and Gravity

Tic-Tac-Toe: *Make a Board Game*

You are designing a board game in which players must explain forms of erosion and deposition situations. You must test your game's questions before your game is manufactured.

1. Work on your own, with a partner, or with a small group.
2. Choose three quick activities from the game. Check the boxes you plan to complete. They must form a straight line in any direction.
3. Have your teacher approve your plan.
4. Do each activity, and turn in your results.

__ **Desert Pavement**	__ **Dunes**	__ **Loess**
Your game includes an area of harsh desert pavement. Game questions: What does desert pavement look like? Why does it look this way?	Your players must cross areas of dunes. Game questions: Do dunes stay the same over time? Why or why not?	In your game, there is an area of loess your players must go around. Game question: How did this loess get so fertile?
__ **Alpine Glacier** Players must cross an area with an alpine glacier and all of the features it can create. Game questions: What features can an alpine glacier create? How does this happen?	__ **Continental Glacier** A continental glacier covers part of your board. Game questions: How big can a continental glacier be? Where can you find a continental glacier? How is a continental glacier different than an alpine glacier?	__ **Glacial Drift** Glacial drift makes some areas of your game board difficult to move across. Game question: How did all this material get here?
__ **Creep** Players can only cross slopes experiencing creep if they explain what it is. Game question: What is creep?	__ **Rock Fall and Landslides** Rock falls and landslides form some difficult terrain for players. Game question: What conditions are perfect for creating rock falls and landslides?	__ **Mudflows and Lahars** Hazardous areas of your game include mudflows and lahars. Game questions: Why is a mudflow dangerous? Where can a mudflow occur? What is the difference between a mudflow and a lahar?

Going Further

- ☐ Real World Connection
- ☐ Social Studies Connection
- ☐ Print Path Why it Matters, SE p. 51

Formative Assessment

- ☐ Strategies Throughout TE
- ☐ Lesson Review SE

Summative Assessment

- ☐ Alternative Assessment Make a Board Game
- ☐ Lesson Quiz
- ☐ Unit Tests A and B
- ☐ Unit Review SE End-of-Unit

Your Resources

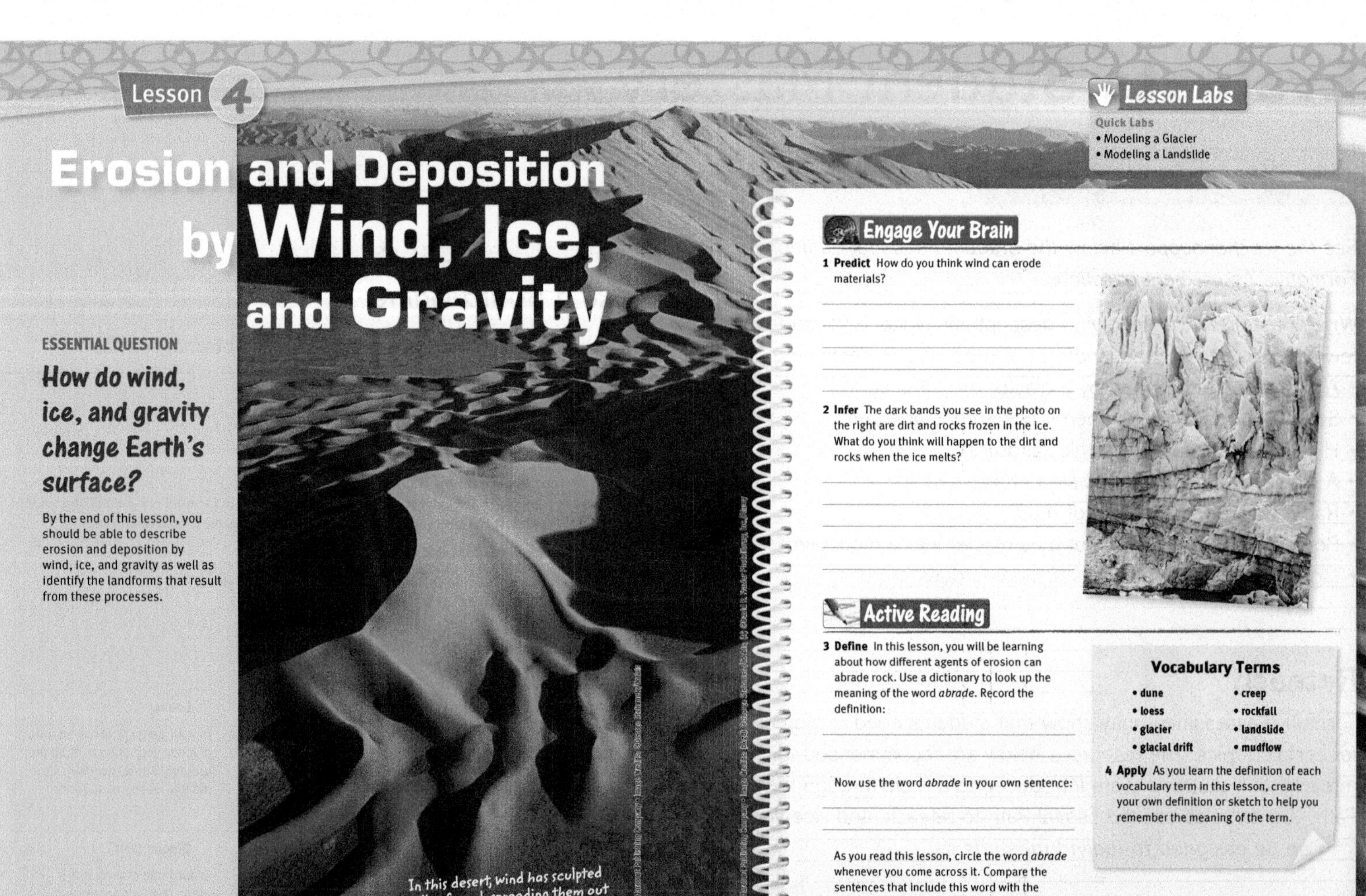

Answers

Answers for 1–3 should represent students' current thoughts, even if incorrect.

1. Wind can pick up very fine materials and blow them away.
2. When the ice melts, the dirt and rock will be deposited on the ground.
3. Definition of abrade: the process of wearing down or rubbing away by friction, Sample sentence: Sand paper is used to abrade wood.

Opening Your Lesson

Discuss items 1 and 2 to activate students' everyday understanding of wind, ice, and gravity. Show them how this basic knowledge will help them throughout the lesson—wind blows things around, things can become frozen in ice, and gravity is at play any time things fall down.

Preconceptions: Students may think that wind cannot affect rocks or that ice always holds materials still by freezing them in place.

Prerequisites: Students should already be familiar with the processes of erosion and deposition and that different agents can cause these processes to occur.

Learning Alert

Terminology This lesson contains many new terms related to erosion and deposition. Encourage students to use strategies to associate the terms with the correct agent of erosion and deposition. One effective strategy is simple repetition. Students can make lists of related terms, such as *wind, abrasion, deflation, dunes, loess, desert pavement*, and read them repeatedly. Reading a list of related terms five to ten times per day can greatly improve recall.

Gone with the Wind

How can wind shape Earth?

Have you ever been outside and had a gust of wind blow a stack of papers all over the place? If so, you have seen how wind erosion works. In the same way that wind moved your papers, wind moves soil, sand, and rock particles. When wind moves soil, sand, and rock particles, it acts as an agent of erosion.

Abraded Rock

When wind blows sand and other particles against a surface, it can wear down the surface over time. The grinding and wearing down of rock surfaces by other rock or by sand particles is called *abrasion*. Abrasion happens in areas where there are strong winds, loose sand, and soft rocks. The blowing of millions of grains of sand causes a sandblasting effect. The sandblasting effect slowly erodes the rock by stripping away its surface. Over time, the rock can become smooth and polished.

Desert Pavement

The removal of fine sediment by wind is called *deflation*. This process is shown in the diagram below. During deflation, wind removes the top layer of fine sediment or soil. Deflation leaves behind rock fragments that are too heavy to be lifted by the wind. After a while, these rocks may be the only materials left on the surface. The resulting landscape is known as desert pavement. As you can see in the photo below, desert pavement is a surface made up mostly of pebbles and small, broken rocks.

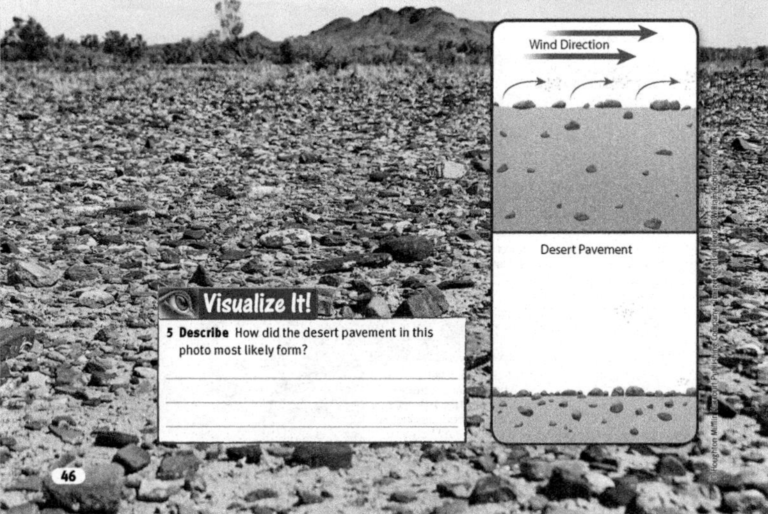

Visualize It!

5 Describe How did the desert pavement in this photo most likely form?

Dunes

Wind carries sediment in much the same way that rivers do. Just as rivers deposit their loads, winds eventually drop the materials that they are carrying. For example, when wind hits an obstacle, it slows and drops materials on top of the obstacle. As the material builds up, the obstacle gets larger. This obstacle causes the wind to slow more and deposit more material, which forms a mound. Eventually, the original obstacle is buried. Mounds of wind-deposited sand are called **dunes**. Dunes are common in deserts and along the shores of lakes and oceans.

Generally, dunes move in the same direction the wind is blowing. Usually, a dune's gently sloped side faces the wind. Wind constantly moves material up this side of the dune. As sand moves over the crest of the dune, the sand slides down the slip face and makes a steep slope.

Loess

Wind can carry extremely fine material long distances. Thick deposits of this windblown, fine-grained sediment are known as **loess** (LOH•uhs). Loess can feel like the talcum powder a person may use after a shower. Because wind carries fine-grained material much higher and farther than it carries sand, loess deposits are sometimes found far away from their source. Loess deposits can build up over thousands and even millions of years. Loess is a valuable resource because it forms good soil for growing crops.

Inquiry

6 Infer Why do you think loess can be carried further than sand?

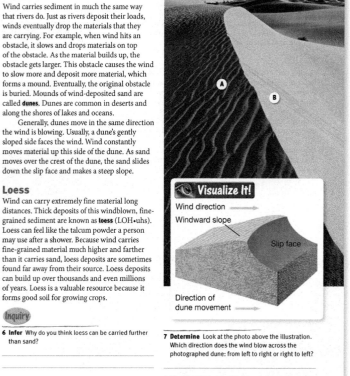

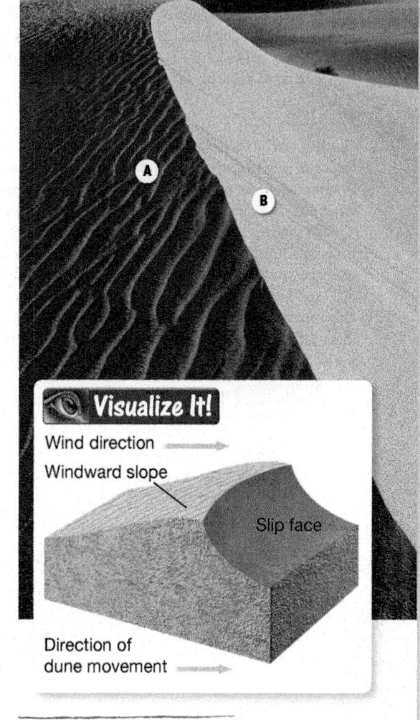

7 Determine Look at the photo above the illustration. Which direction does the wind blow across the photographed dune: from left to right or right to left?

8 Identify Which side of the dune in the photograph is the slip face: A or B?

Answers

5. Deflation caused fine sediments to blow away, leaving behind a layer of rocks.
6. Loess is smaller and finer than sand, so it can be carried by slower winds.
7. The wind is blowing left to right.
8. B

Probing Questions

Synthesizing Why does a dune form over another object or obstacle, and not on flat ground? On flat ground, the wind just blows the sand away; when there is an obstacle, the sand gets caught. The wind keeps blowing more and more sand, some of which gets caught, and over time a dune is formed.

Interpreting Visuals

Have students look at the image of the desert pavement. **Ask:** Could dunes form here? Sample answer: Yes, if enough sand blew into the area, because it could build up on the larger rock pieces over time.

Learning Alert

Deflation The word *deflation* has a different meaning in this context than the more common definition—"the act of deflating." *Deflation* also has a third meaning—"a decline in consumer prices." Point out the different meanings and discuss how they differ from the meaning of *deflation* in this lesson.

Desert Pavement This term can be confusing, as students generally think of pavement as something smooth, such as a sidewalk or a street. Point this out and discuss how the two uses of *pavement* differ.

Groovy Glaciers

What kinds of ice shape Earth?

Have you ever made a snowball from a scoop of fluffy snow? If so, you know that when the snow is pressed against itself, it becomes harder and more compact. The same idea explains how a glacier forms. A **glacier** is a large mass of moving ice that forms by the compacting of snow by natural forces.

Think Outside the Book

9 Apply Find out whether glaciers have ever covered your state. If so, what landforms did they leave behind?

Flowing Ice

Glaciers can be found anywhere on land where it is cold enough for ice to stay frozen year round. Gravity causes glaciers to move. When enough ice builds up on a slope, the ice begins to move downhill. The steeper the slope is, the faster the glacier moves.

As glaciers move, they pick up materials. These materials become embedded in the ice. As the glacier moves forward, the materials scratch and abrade the rock and soil underneath the glacier. This abrasion causes more erosion. Glaciers are also agents of deposition. As a glacier melts, it drops the materials that it carried. **Glacial drift** is the general term for all of the materials carried and deposited by a glacier.

Active Reading 10 Infer Where in North America would you expect to find glaciers?

As a glacier flowed over this rock, it scratched out these grooves.

This glacier is moving down the valley like a river of ice.

Alpine Glaciers

An alpine glacier is a glacier that forms in a mountainous area. Alpine glaciers flow down the sides of mountains and create rugged landscapes. Glaciers may form in valleys originally created by stream erosion. The flow of water in a stream forms a V-shaped valley. As a glacier slowly flows through a V-shaped valley, it scrapes away the valley floor and walls. The glacier widens and straightens the valley into a broad U-shape. An alpine glacier can also carve out bowl-shaped depressions, called *cirques* (surks), at the head of a valley. A sharp ridge called an *arête* (uh•RAYT) forms between two cirques that are next to each other. When three or more arêtes join, they form a sharp peak called a *horn*.

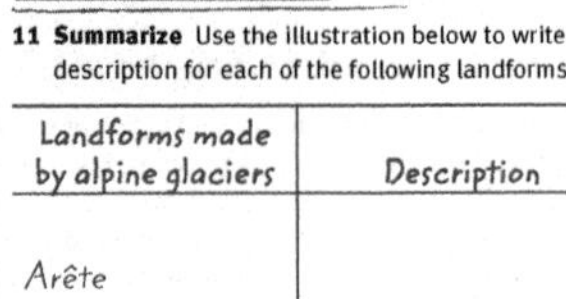

Visualize It!

11 Summarize Use the illustration below to write a description for each of the following landforms.

Landforms made by alpine glaciers	Description
Arête	
Cirque	
Horn	
U-shaped valley	

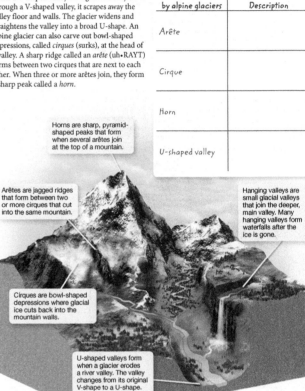

Horns are sharp, pyramid-shaped peaks that form when several arêtes join at the top of a mountain.

Arêtes are jagged ridges that form between two or more cirques that cut into the same mountain.

Hanging valleys are small glacial valleys that join the deeper, main valley. Many hanging valleys form waterfalls after the ice is gone.

Cirques are bowl-shaped depressions where glacial ice cuts back into the mountain walls.

U-shaped valleys form when a glacier erodes a river valley. The valley changes from its original V-shape to a U-shape.

Answers

9. Answers will vary depending on which state you live in. During the last ice age, glaciers covered the United States as far south as Kansas and Nebraska.
10. Sample answer: Glaciers could likely be found far north in Alaska and Canada, as well as high up on some mountains.
11. Arête: a jagged ridge that forms between two or more cirques; Cirque: a bowl-shaped depression where a glacier cut into a mountain wall; Horn: a pyramid-shaped peak formed where several arêtes join; U-shaped valley: a valley carved out by a glacier

Interpreting Visuals

Which structures can form only *after* cirques have formed? Sample answer: Horns and arêtes can form only after several cirques have formed on the same mountain.

Learning Alert

Glaciers Students may have the preconceived notion that glaciers are shaped like a block of ice. Discuss how glaciers can assume a wide variety of shapes.

Probing Questions GUIDED Inquiry

Predicting Do you think the landforms shown in the photograph could ever be erased? Why or why not? Sample answer: Erosion will most likely affect the landforms, and if a great deal of erosion took place over hundreds of thousands of years, the landscape could become flatter and many of the features sculpted by glaciers could be smoothed or erased.

Continental Glaciers

Continental glaciers are thick sheets of ice that may spread over large areas, including across entire continents. These glaciers are huge, continuous masses of ice. Continental glaciers create very different landforms than alpine glaciers do. Alpine glaciers form sharp and rugged features, whereas continental glaciers flatten and smooth the landscape. Continental glaciers erode and remove features that existed before the ice appeared. These glaciers smooth and round exposed rock surfaces in a way similar to the way that bulldozers can flatten landscapes.

Erosion and deposition by continental glaciers result in specific, recognizable landforms. Some of the landforms are shown below. Similar landforms can be found in the northern United States, which was once covered by continental glaciers.

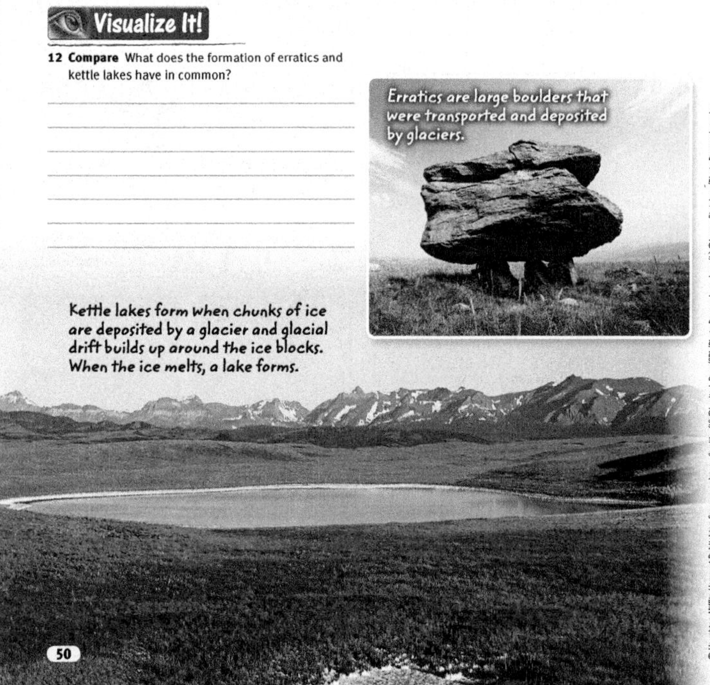

Visualize It!

12 Compare What does the formation of erratics and kettle lakes have in common?

Erratics are large boulders that were transported and deposited by glaciers.

Kettle lakes form when chunks of ice are deposited by a glacier and glacial drift builds up around the ice blocks. When the ice melts, a lake forms.

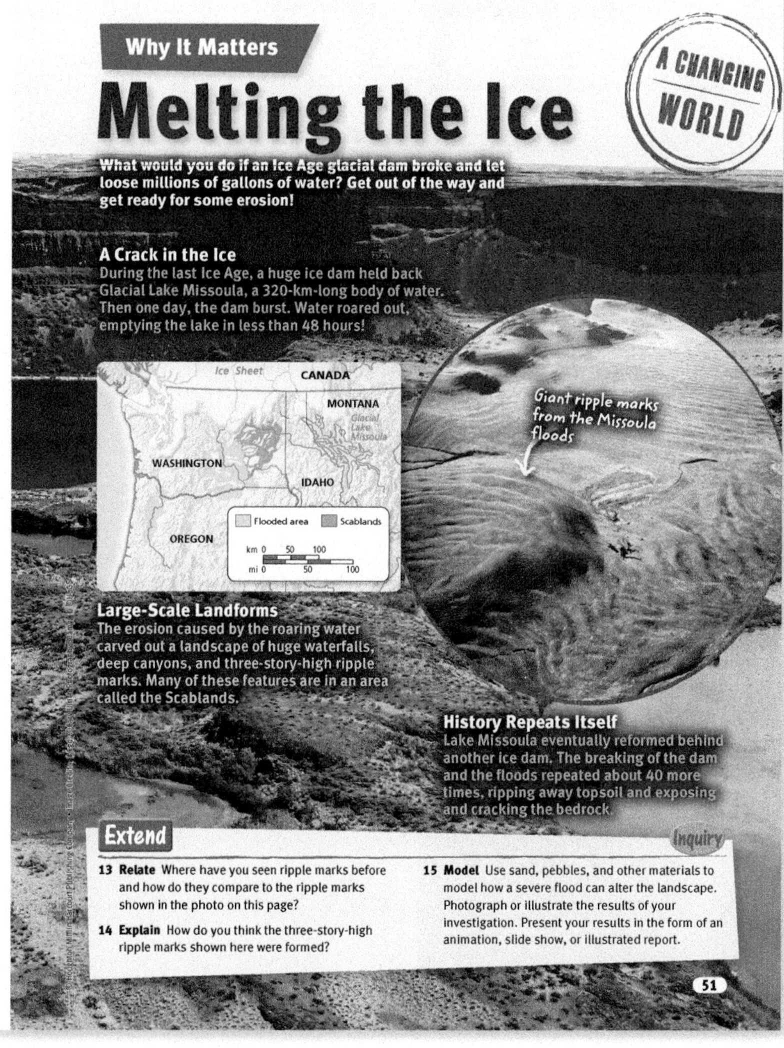

Why It Matters

Melting the Ice

What would you do if an Ice Age glacial dam broke and let loose millions of gallons of water? Get out of the way and get ready for some erosion!

A Crack in the Ice

During the last Ice Age, a huge ice dam held back Glacial Lake Missoula, a 320-km-long body of water. Then one day, the dam burst. Water roared out, emptying the lake in less than 48 hours!

Large-Scale Landforms

The erosion caused by the roaring water carved out a landscape of huge waterfalls, deep canyons, and three-story-high ripple marks. Many of these features are in an area called the Scablands.

History Repeats Itself

Lake Missoula eventually reformed behind another ice dam. The breaking of the dam and the floods repeated about 40 more times, ripping away topsoil and exposing and cracking the bedrock.

Extend Inquiry

13 Relate Where have you seen ripple marks before and how do they compare to the ripple marks shown in the photo on this page?

14 Explain How do you think the three-story-high ripple marks shown here were formed?

15 Model Use sand, pebbles, and other materials to model how a severe flood can alter the landscape. Photograph or illustrate the results of your investigation. Present your results in the form of an animation, slide show, or illustrated report.

Answers

12. Both kettle lakes and erratics are the result of materials (large boulders and chunks of ice, respectively) that were deposited by a glacier as it retreated.
13. Students may have seen ripple marks on land that has previously flooded or at the beach. Students should relate their observations and experiences to the story of the Missoula flood described on this page.
14. The extreme ripple marks were formed by a huge flood event during the last ice age.
15. Student output should demonstrate an understanding of how a severe flood can alter a landscape, and relate the processes of erosion and deposition.

Probing Questions GUIDED Inquiry

Predicting Even though continental glaciers tend to smooth landscapes, why is it unlikely a glacier would leave an area completely smooth? Sample answer: A lot of deposition occurs when a glacier moves and then melts. Kettle lakes and erratics are examples of features left on a landscape after a continental glacier retreats.

Why It Matters

The events and features described in the text would have caused dramatic processes of erosion and deposition. Some processes would have happened slowly, some would have happened very quickly. Describe some of the forces that would have shaped the land during the events described. Sample answer: The glacier that dammed the lake would have moved slowly, eroding the land in some places and depositing glacial drift in other places. These processes would have happened slowly. The huge gush of water that erupted over the land when the dam broke would have caused erosion and deposition throughout the area. These processes would have happened very quickly.

Slippery Slopes

The shape of this tree trunk indicates that creep has occurred along the slope.

How can gravity shape Earth?

Although you can't see it, the force of gravity, like water, wind, and ice, is an agent of erosion and deposition. Gravity not only influences the movement of water and ice, but it also causes rocks and soil to move downslope. This shifting of materials is called *mass movement.* Mass movement plays a major role in shaping Earth's surface.

Slow Mass Movement

Even though most slopes appear to be stable, they are actually undergoing slow mass movement. In fact, all the rocks and soil on a slope travel slowly downhill. The ground beneath the tree shown on the left is moving so slowly that the tree trunk curved as the tree grew. The extremely slow movement of material downslope is called **creep**. Many factors contribute to creep. Water loosens soil and allows the soil to move freely. In addition, plant roots act as wedges that force rocks and soil particles apart. Burrowing animals, such as gophers and groundhogs, also loosen rock and soil particles, making it easier for the particles to be pulled downward.

Visualize It!

16 Analyze As the soil on this hill shifts, how is the tree changing so that it continues to grow upright?

Rapid Mass Movement

The most destructive mass movements happen suddenly and rapidly. Rapid mass movement can be very dangerous and can destroy everything in its path. Rapid mass movement tends to happen on steep slopes because materials are more likely to fall down a steep slope than a shallow slope.

While traveling along a mountain road, you may have noticed signs along the road that warn of falling rocks. A **rockfall** happens when loose rocks fall down a steep slope. Steep slopes are common in mountainous areas. Gravity causes loosened and exposed rocks to fall down steep slopes. The rocks in a rockfall can range in size from small fragments to large boulders.

Another kind of rapid mass movement is a landslide. A **landslide** is the sudden and rapid movement of a large amount of material downslope. As you can see in the photo on the right, landslides can carry away plants. They can also carry away animals, vehicles, and buildings. Heavy rains, deforestation, construction on unstable slopes, and earthquakes increase the chances of a landslide.

A rapid movement of a large mass of mud is a **mudflow**. Mudflows happen when a large amount of water mixes with soil and rock. The water causes the slippery mud to flow rapidly downslope. Mudflows happen in mountainous regions after deforestation has occurred or when a long dry season is followed by heavy rains. Volcanic eruptions or heavy rains on volcanic ash can produce some of the most dangerous mudflows. Mudflows of volcanic origin are called lahars. Lahars can travel at speeds greater than 80 km/h and can be as thick as wet cement.

17 Identify List five events that can trigger a mass movement.

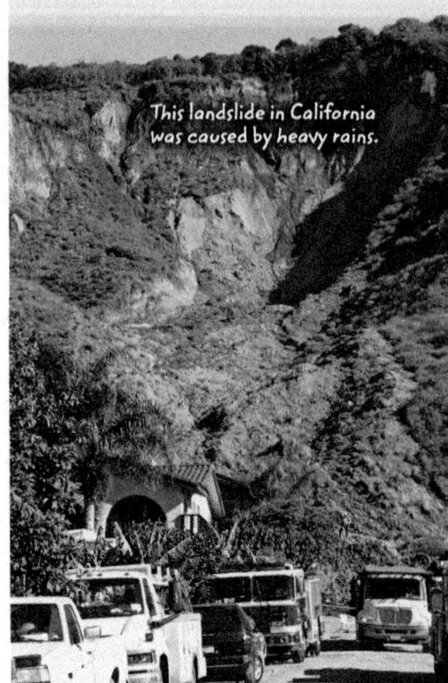
This landslide in California was caused by heavy rains.

A

B

Visualize It!

18 Infer On which slope, A or B, would a landslide be more likely to occur? Explain.

Answers

16. The tree trunk bends so that the tree will continue to grow upward toward the strongest light source.
17. heavy rains, deforestation, construction on unstable slopes, earthquakes, and volcanic eruptions
18. A landslide would more likely occur on slope B, because it is steeper.

Formative Assessment

Ask: What factors work with gravity to contribute to creep? Water, plant roots, and animals contribute to creep. **Ask:** Why do tree roots not act as anchors, holding soil in place on slopes? On a slope, gravity is pulling everything downward. The roots break up rock and soil, making it easier for gravity to pull them down. **Ask:** What is the difference between a rockfall and a landslide? A rockfall involves loose rocks that fall off a steep slope, often in a mountainous area. A landslide can occur on a slope that is not as steep. It moves along the ground, picking up more and more material as it goes. A landslide is not just rocks; it may involve large amounts of soil, water, and other material. Landslides may carry away plants and even buildings.

Probing Questions DIRECTED Inquiry

Identifying All three forms of rapid mass movement are two-part words. Identify a pattern in these word parts. The first part of each word *(rock, land, mud)* refers to the materials or sediment that is moving. The second part of each word *(fall, slide, flow)* refers to different actions caused by gravity, all of which can be forms of downward movement.

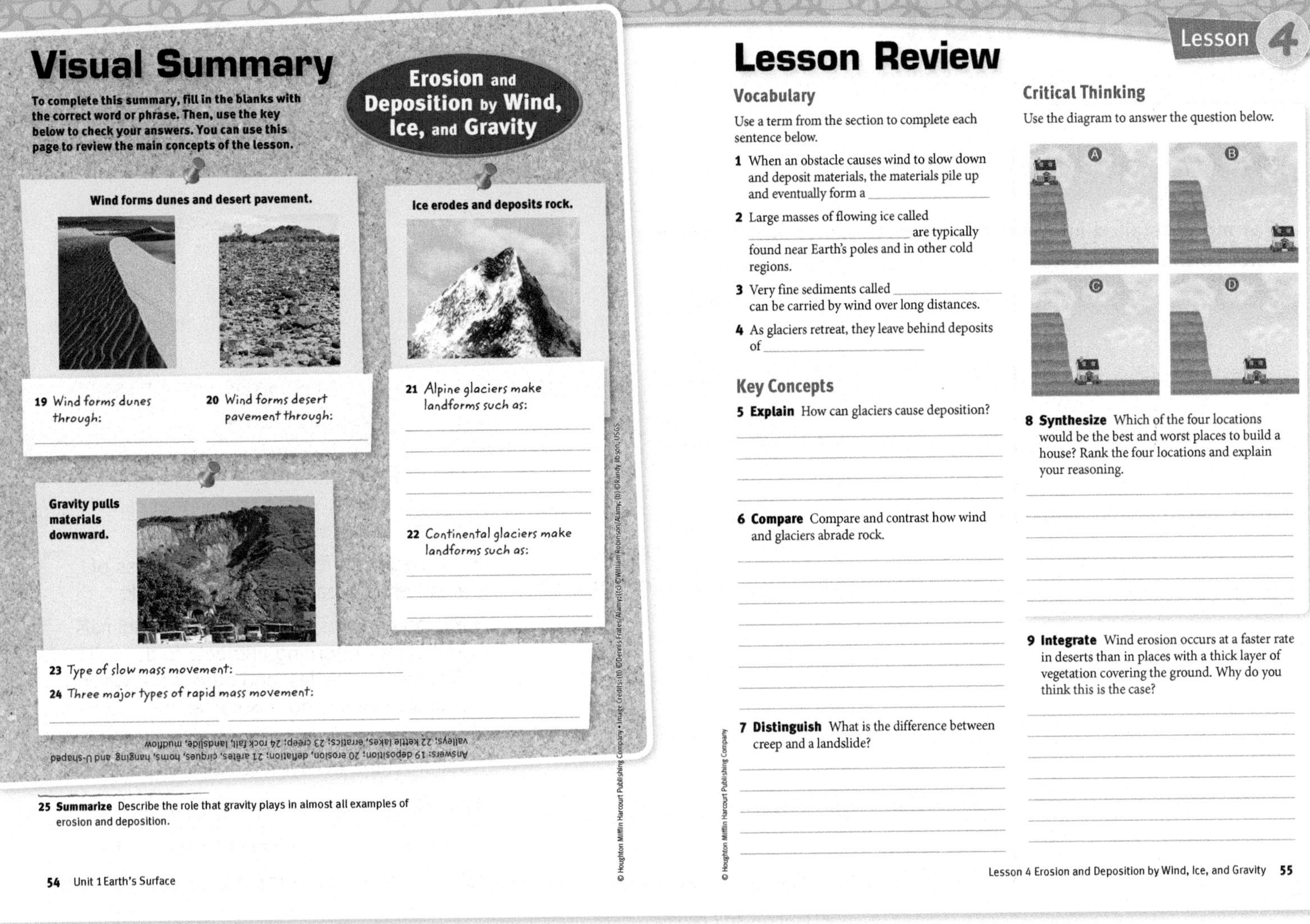

Student Pages 52–55

Visual Summary Answers

19. deposition
20. erosion (and deflation)
21. arêtes, cirques, horns, hanging valleys, U-shaped valleys
22. kettle lakes, erratics
23. creep
24. rock fall, landslide, mudflow (could also list lahar)
25. Gravity causes materials being carried in wind, ice, and water to drop out and be deposited. Gravity also causes ice and water to flow downhill.

Lesson Review Answers

1. dune
2. glaciers
3. loess
4. glacial drift
5. As glaciers melt, material frozen in them can drop out.
6. Both wind and glaciers can drag sand, dirt, and other materials against the surface of exposed rocks. The rate of erosion by wind abrasion would typically be slower than by glacial abrasion, because wind cannot carry heavy materials and wind does not press the materials into the rock like glaciers do.
7. Creep occurs very slowly as land slumps down a slope. A landslide occurs rapidly as soil and rock materials fall down a slope.
8. The best location is B because it is far enough from the cliff face to avoid severe damage if a rockfall occurs. Location D would be next best. Location A is third best because the house would not be endangered from a rockfall, but it could be damaged by a landslide. The worst location is C because it would be directly in the path of landslides and rockfalls.
9. Vegetation can act as a wind breaker and covers the soil so that wind cannot pick it up and carry it away.

Soil Formation

Essential Question How does soil form?

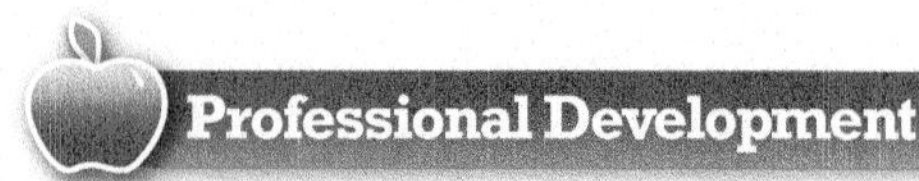

For more detailed information about the topics in this lesson, refer to the Content Refresher in the Unit Opener pages.

Opening Your Lesson

Begin the lesson by assessing students' prerequisite and prior knowledge.

Prerequisite Knowledge

- The physical weathering of rock
- The chemical weathering of rock by living organisms
- Knowledge that plants grow in soil and get nutrients from soil

Accessing Prior Knowledge

Ask: What are some other words for soil? Sample answers: dirt, mud, earth

Ask: Why is soil important? Sample answers: Plants need soil to grow; water is filtered by soil.

Ask: What might you expect to find in soil? Sample answers: rocks, tree roots, insects, worms, bones, water, trash

Customize Your Opening

- ☐ **Accessing Prior Knowledge** above
- ☐ **Print Path** Engage Your Brain, SE p. 57 #1–2
- ☐ **Print Path** Active Reading, SE p. 57 #3–4
- ☐ **Digital Path** Lesson Opener

Key Topics/Learning Goals	Supporting Concepts
Soil Formation 1 Define *soil.* 2 Explain how soil forms. 3 Identify the factors that affect soil development, including living things. 4 Define *humus.*	• Soil is a loose mixture of rock fragments, organic matter, water, and air that can support the growth of vegetation. • Soil begins to form when the process of weathering breaks down parent rock. • Microorganisms decompose dead animals and plants, returning nutrients to the soil. Earthworms, moles, and other soil-dwelling animals loosen and mix soil as they burrow. • Humus is dark, organic material formed in soil from the decayed remains of plants and animals.
Soil Horizons 1 Define *soil horizon.* 2 Define *soil profile.* 3 Describe a typical soil profile.	• A soil horizon is a distinct layer of soil. • A soil profile is a vertical section of soil that shows the horizons. • A typical soil profile, from top to bottom, has an A horizon containing humus, a B horizon containing leached materials and little to no humus, and a C horizon of partially weathered parent rock.
Soil Characteristics 1 Explain how soil characteristics are influenced by the process of soil formation and living things.	• Soils differ in texture, color, chemistry, pore space, and fertility. • Relative amounts of sand, silt, and clay determine soil texture. • Soil pH tells how acidic or basic soil is. • Pore space describes spaces between soil particles. • Minerals and humus determine soil color. • Soil fertility depends on climate, topography, amount of humus, minerals, and nutrients.

Options for Instruction

Two parallel paths provide coverage of the Essential Questions, with a strong **Inquiry** strand woven into each. Follow the **Print Path,** the **Digital Path,** or your customized combination of print, digital, and inquiry.

 Print Path *Teaching support for the Print Path appears with the Student Pages.*	 Inquiry Labs and Activities	 Digital Path *Digital Path shortcut: TS692102*
The Dirt on Soil, SE pp. 58–59 **What causes soil to form?** • Weathering of Parent Rock • Decomposition . . . by Living Things **Thick Tops, Rocky Bottoms,** SE p. 60 **What factors determine how long it takes for soils to form?**	**Daily Demo** Watch It Rot! **Quick Lab** Observing Life in Soil **Quick Lab** Observing the Impact of Earthworms on Soil	**What is Soil?** Video **Physical Characteristics of Soil** Interactive Graphics **Development and Erosion of Soil** Interactive Images
Thick Tops, Rocky Bottoms, SE p. 61 **What are the main soil horizons?** • A Horizon • B Horizon • C Horizon	**Quick Lab** Modeling a Soil Profile **Activity** On the Horizon	**Soil Profile and Soil Horizon** Interactive Graphic
All About Soil, SE pp. 62–65 **What are some properties of soil?** • Soil Texture • Soil Color • Soil Chemistry • Pore Space • Soil Fertility	**Field Lab** Comparing Soil Characteristics **Activity** Sand, Silt, Clay **Activity** Separating Soil Components **Activity** Soil Game	**Physical Characteristics of Soil** Interactive Images **Chemical Characteristics of Soil** Slideshow

Options for Assessment

See the Evaluate page for options, including Formative Assessment, Summative Assessment, and Unit Review.

Engage and Explore

Activities and Discussion

Activity *On the Horizon*

Engage

Soil Horizons

 individuals or pairs

 10 min

 **GUIDED** inquiry

Bring potting soil, sand, gravel, rocks, and clear, plastic cups to class. Make sure there is a rock for each cup and that it can fit in the bottom of the cup. Ask students to arrange the materials into a soil profile and parent rock, with A, B, and C horizons. Have students explain their models. From top to bottom: potting soil is rich in organic matter and represents the A horizon. Sand represents the B horizon. Gravel represents the C horizon, and the rock represents the parent rock.

Activity *Separating Soil Components*

Soil Characteristics

pairs or small groups

10 min

INDEPENDENT inquiry

Challenge students to devise a method that will allow them to separate the components of a soil that includes rock fragments of various sizes and organic matter. You may wish to mix your own "soil" by adding fine, medium, and coarse sand and fine gravel to a sample of soil dug from your area or to a bag of potting soil. Encourage students to think creatively about tools they can use to separate the soil components. After students present their ideas, you may wish to show them or describe to them the graduated sieves and a sieve shaker that geologists use for the task.

Activity *Sand, Silt, Clay*

Soil Characteristics

 pairs or small groups

 10 min

 **DIRECTED** inquiry

Give each group samples of salt, powdered sugar, and flour. Allow students to feel the materials' different textures. **Ask:** Which soil particle does each material model, and why? salt: sand, coarse texture; powdered sugar: silt, smooth texture, flour: clay, sticky when wet

Probing Question *Organic Matters*

Soil Formation

whole class

5 min

GUIDED inquiry

Inferring To help students recognize how the activities of organisms affect a soil's characteristics, **Ask:** What might happen to the process of soil formation if all microorganisms disappeared? Sample answer: These organisms decompose organic matter. Without them, the rate of soil formation would slow drastically, and soils would consist mainly of weathered rock.

Take It Home *Soil Study*

Soil Characteristics

 adult-student pairs

 30 min

GUIDED inquiry

Working with an adult, students will collect a small sample of soil from their yards, a park, or from school. They will then closely examine the sample and record their observations about the characteristics of the soil.

Optional Online resource: student worksheet

Customize Your Labs

 *See the Lab Manual for lab datasheets.*

 *Go Online for editable lab datasheets.*

Levels of Inquiry

DIRECTED inquiry introduces inquiry skills within a structured framework.

GUIDED inquiry develops inquiry skills within a supportive environment.

INDEPENDENT inquiry deepens inquiry skills with student-driven questions or procedures.

Labs and Demos

Field Lab *Comparing Soil Characteristics*

Soil Characteristics

 pairs
 45 min
 **DIRECTED/GUIDED** inquiry

Students will compare soil from two different sites.

PURPOSE **To observe different soil characteristics**

MATERIALS

- **bucket**
- **magnifying lens**
- **pH testing kit or pH paper**
- **shovel**
- **sieve**
- **spray bottle**
- **distilled water**

Quick Lab *Observing Life in Soil*

PURPOSE **To determine the type of soil most likely to support mold growth and to observe fungi action in soil**

See the Lab Manual or go Online for planning information.

Quick Lab *Observing the Impact of Earthworms on Soil*

PURPOSE **To observe the effects of earthworms on soil quality**

See the Lab Manual or go Online for planning information.

Daily Demo *Watch It Rot!*

Engage

Soil Formation

 whole class
 two 10–15 min periods
 **DIRECTED** inquiry

Use this short demo after you have discussed the role of organic matter in soil.

PURPOSE **To observe how living things decompose materials**

MATERIALS

- **beakers or plastic containers**
- **samples of items to decompose, such as yard waste or fruit or vegetable scraps**

1 Place the organic items in separate containers. Point out that each item comes from a living thing.

2 **Predicting Ask:** What do you think will happen to these items after a few days? Sample answer: They will start to rot and change color. **Ask:** If these items were on the ground of a forest, how would such a process affect the soil? As the items decomposed, they would add nutrients to the soil.

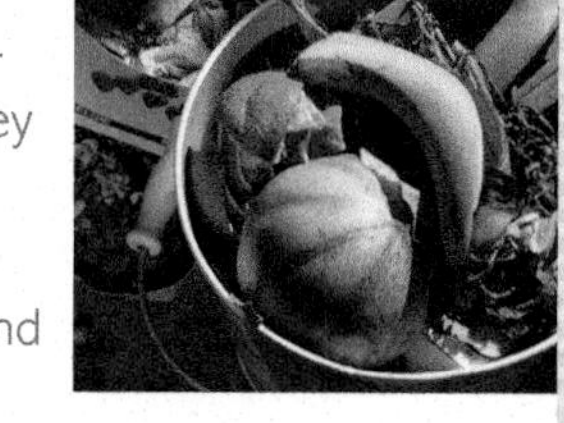

3 After 2 or 3 days, display the items again.

4 **Observing Ask:** What do you notice? Sample answer: The items have turned color, they smell, and they look rotten. These items are decomposing. **Ask:** Would this be good for soil? Yes. It would make the soil healthier, and the nutrients would be available for plants.

Quick Lab *Modeling a Soil Profile*

PURPOSE **To make a model of a soil profile**

See the Lab Manual or go Online for planning information.

Activities and Discussion

- ☐ **Activity** On the Horizon
- ☐ **Activity** Sand, Silt, Clay
- ☐ **Take It Home** Soil Study
- ☐ **Activity** Separating Soil Components
- ☐ **Probing Question** Organic Matters

Labs and Demos

- ☐ **Field Lab** Comparing Soil
- ☐ **Quick Lab** Observing Life in Soil
- ☐ **Quick Lab** Observing the Impact of...
- ☐ **Daily Demo** Watch It Rot!
- ☐ **Quick Lab** Modeling a Soil Profile

Your Resources

Explain Science Concepts

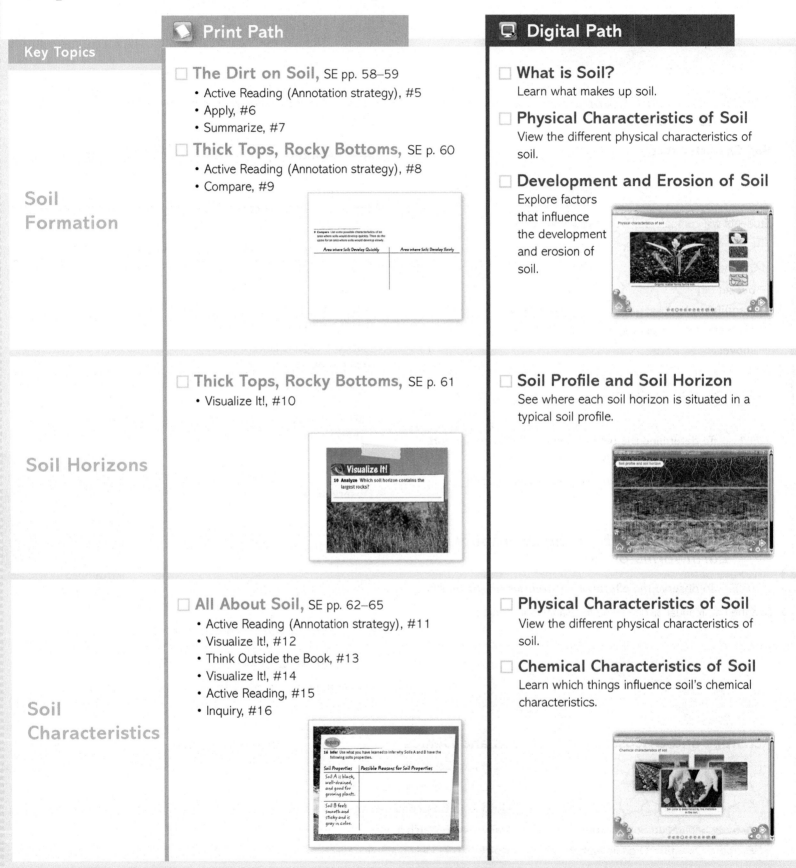

Key Topics	Print Path	Digital Path
Soil Formation	☐ **The Dirt on Soil,** SE pp. 58–59 • Active Reading (Annotation strategy), #5 • Apply, #6 • Summarize, #7 ☐ **Thick Tops, Rocky Bottoms,** SE p. 60 • Active Reading (Annotation strategy), #8 • Compare, #9	☐ **What is Soil?** Learn what makes up soil. ☐ **Physical Characteristics of Soil** View the different physical characteristics of soil. ☐ **Development and Erosion of Soil** Explore factors that influence the development and erosion of soil. 
Soil Horizons	☐ **Thick Tops, Rocky Bottoms,** SE p. 61 • Visualize It!, #10 	☐ **Soil Profile and Soil Horizon** See where each soil horizon is situated in a typical soil profile. 
Soil Characteristics	☐ **All About Soil,** SE pp. 62–65 • Active Reading (Annotation strategy), #11 • Visualize It!, #12 • Think Outside the Book, #13 • Visualize It!, #14 • Active Reading, #15 • Inquiry, #16 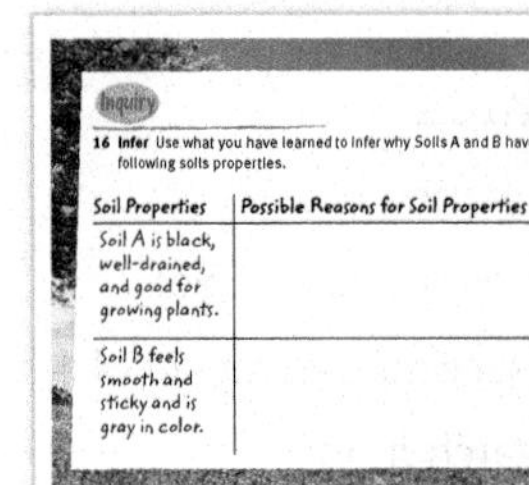	☐ **Physical Characteristics of Soil** View the different physical characteristics of soil. ☐ **Chemical Characteristics of Soil** Learn which things influence soil's chemical characteristics. 

Differentiated Instruction

Basic *Soil Concepts*

Soil Formation

individuals
 15 min

Concept Map Have students make concept maps showing how nutrients are cycled through soil. Concept maps should show several ovals containing statements linked by arrows. The statements within the ovals might read: *Plant and animal remains are broken down into humus by decomposers. Humus adds nutrients to soil. Plants take up nutrients and use them to grow.*

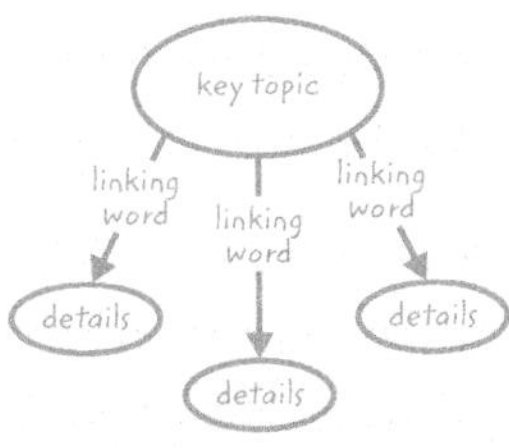

 *Optional Online resource: Concept Map support*

Advanced *Using Data*

Synthesizing Key Topics

 individuals or pairs
 varied

Soil-quality indicators are used by the USDA Natural Resources Conservation Service to monitor changes in soil. The indicators include physical, chemical, and biological characteristics of soil. Have interested students obtain information about soil-quality indicators and explain how they are used. The indicators provide information that helps guide land-use decisions. They allow scientists to evaluate conservation techniques, monitor trends, assess soil health, and improve soil quality.

ELL *Mnemonic Device*

Soil Formation

 individuals or pairs
 15 min

The factors that affect the rate of soil development and formation include rock type, climate, topography, and living things. Use the first letter of each factor to make a mnemonic statement, such as this: *Really clever teens listen.* Encourage students to develop other memory devices to help them remember key concepts throughout the chapter.

Lesson Vocabulary

soil	**humus**
soil profile	**soil horizon**

Previewing Vocabulary

whole class
5 min

Multiple Meanings Many of the terms in this lesson have more than one meaning. Share the following with students:

- **Soil** can refer to the matter that covers Earth, but can also refer to making something dirty when used as a verb.
- **Horizon** refers to distinct layers of soil, but can also refer to the apparent boundary between the land and sky.
- **Profile** can refer to a section of soil horizons from top to bottom, but can also refer to the outline of a person's face when viewed from the side.

Reinforcing Vocabulary

 individuals
15 min

Word Triangle Have students complete word triangles for each new term. Students can write the term and its definition in the bottom layer, a sentence using the term in the center, and an illustration in the top.

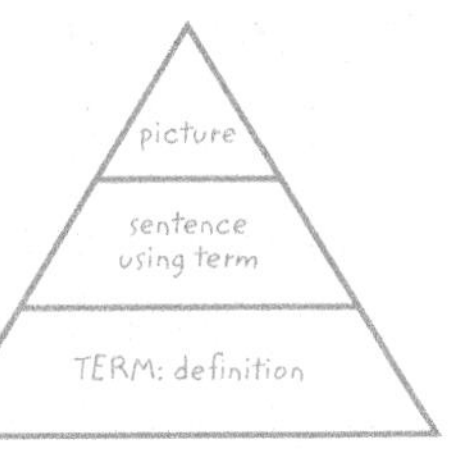

Optional Online resource: Word Triangle support

Customize Your Core Lesson

Core Instruction

☐ Print Path choices

☐ Digital Path choices

Vocabulary

☐ Previewing Vocabulary Multiple Meanings

☐ Reinforcing Vocabulary Word Triangle

Differentiated Instruction

☐ Basic Soil Concepts

☐ Advanced Using Data

☐ ELL Mnemonic Device

Your Resources

Extend Science Concepts

Reinforce and Review

Activity *Soil Game*

Synthesizing Key Topics

 small groups
 15 min

Competitive Game

1 Divide students into groups of four or five and give each group a piece of paper.
2 Have groups sit together and elect one student who will be the writer for the group.
3 One at a time, ask 5-10 questions pertaining to this lesson. They can be your own or borrowed from exercises in the book.
4 After asking each question, give groups a few minutes to quietly discuss their responses and have the writer write the answer down.
5 After all of the questions are asked, have groups trade papers and take score while you give the correct answers.
6 The group with the most points at the end of the game wins.

Sample Questions:

- Which four materials make up soil? rock fragments, organic matter, water, and air
- What are three types of soil particles? sand, silt, and clay
- Why are the top layers of soil darker in color than the lower layers? They contain more organic matter.
- What is another word for the organic matter found in soil? humus
- True or false: Plants and animals are bad for soil. false
- Which of the soil particles is largest? sand
- Where do the rock particles in soil come from? from parent rock that has been weathered

FoldNote

Synthesizing Key Topics

 individuals
ongoing

Layered Book Have students create a Layered Book FoldNote to cover the three key topic areas—*Soil Formation, Soil Horizons,* and *Soil Characteristics.* As students read each topic, have them use the Layered Book to take notes.

Online resource: Layered Book support

Going Further

Real World Connection

Synthesizing Key Topics

 whole class
10 min

Discussion Gardeners often use compost to add organic matter to soils with thin top layers. Compost consists of leaves, grass clippings, food scraps, and other organic materials that decompose into a rich fertilizer for plants. Have students brainstorm a list of common items from home and school that could be used for compost.

Social Studies Connection

Synthesizing Key Topics

 individuals
varied

Irrigation Diagram For thousands of years, people have looked for ways to improve the soils in their area. Desert soils, for example, are not naturally suited for growing most crops. As early as 2000 B.C., Egyptian farmers overcame this problem by building canals to transport water from the Nile River to their crops. Irrigation is still used today to change dry landscapes into fertile fields. Have interested students research a historical or current method of irrigation and draw a picture showing how water is transported to soil with that method. Have them list advantages and disadvantages of that method.

Customize Your Closing

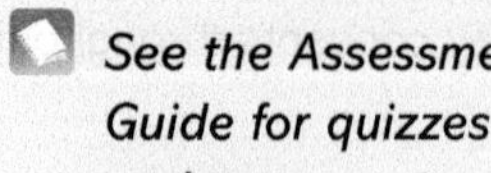

See the Assessment Guide for quizzes and tests.

Go Online to edit and create quizzes and tests.

Reinforce and Review

- ☐ **Activity** Soil Game
- ☐ **FoldNote** Layered Book
- ☐ **Print Path** Visual Summary, SE p. 66
- ☐ **Digital Path** Lesson Closer

Evaluate Student Mastery

Formative Assessment

See the teacher support below the Student Pages for additional Formative Assessment questions.

Have students draw a diagram of a soil profile. Diagrams should include the following, with labels: A horizon, B horizon, C horizon, humus, decomposers. Students should include arrows showing nutrients cycling between organisms and soil. Diagrams should correctly label all parts and should show nutrients flowing down from decaying plants into the soil and back up into plant roots.

Reteach

Formative assessment may show that students need reinforcement for certain topics. The resources below are recommended for reteaching. If students were introduced to a topic through the Print Path, you can also use the Digital Path to reteach and vice versa.
Can be assigned to individual students

Soil Formation
Daily Demo Watch It Rot!
Basic Soil Concepts

Soil Horizons
Activity On the Horizon
Quick Lab Modeling a Soil Profile

Soil Characteristics
Activity Sand, Silt, Clay
FoldNote Layered Book

Summative Assessment

Alternative Assessment

All About Soil

Online resources: student worksheet, optional rubrics

Soil Formation

Mix and Match: *All About Soil*
Mix and match ideas to show what you've learned about soil and how it forms.

1. Work on your own, with a partner, or with a small group.
2. Choose one information source from Column A, two topics from Column B, and one option from Column C. Check your choices.
3. Have your teacher approve your plan.
4. Submit or present your results.

A. Choose One or More Information Sources	B. Choose Two or More Things to Analyze	C. Choose One Way to Communicate Analysis
___ direct observations of soil in a natural environment	___ soil horizons	___ realistic illustration
___ direct observation of modified soil, such as from a garden or a potted plant	___ soil characteristics (texture, color, moisture, organic matter, fertility)	___ schematic diagram with a key
___ observations of soil from a photograph, video, or similar source	___ soil chemistry	___ model
___ records of observations of soil, such as from a naturalist's journal or a geological survey	___ formation, including possible parent rock or transport	___ informational booklet, such as a field guide
___________	___ actions of living things	___ multimedia presentation
		___________

Going Further
- [ ] Real World Connection
- [ ] Social Studies Connection

Formative Assessment
- [ ] Strategies Throughout TE
- [ ] Lesson Review SE

Summative Assessment
- [ ] Alternative Assessment All About Soil
- [ ] Lesson Quiz
- [ ] Unit Tests A and B
- [ ] Unit Review SE End-of-Unit

Your Resources ___________

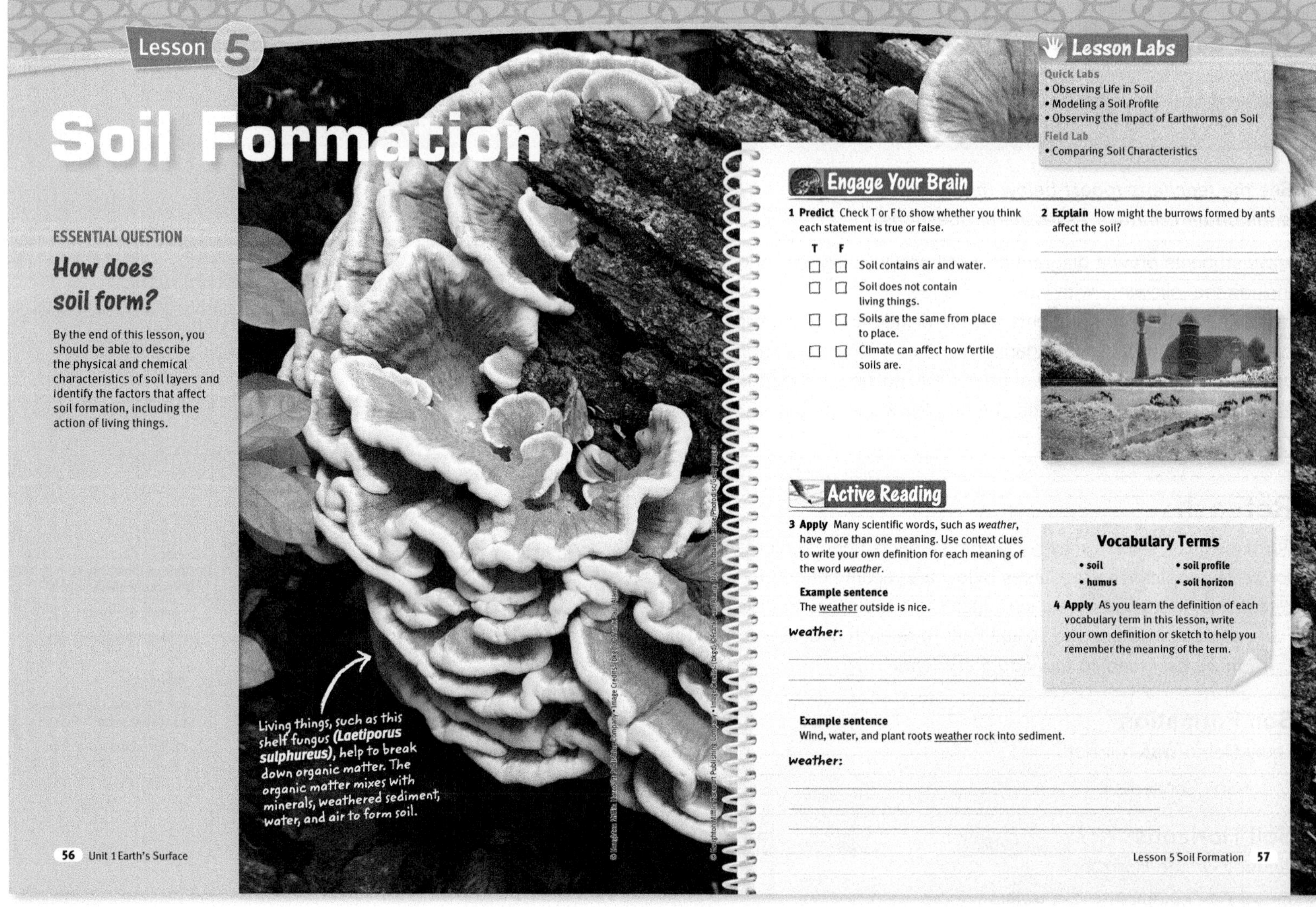

Lesson 5
Soil Formation
ESSENTIAL QUESTION
How does soil form?
By the end of this lesson, you should be able to describe the physical and chemical characteristics of soil layers and identify the factors that affect soil formation, including the action of living things.
Living things, such as this shelf fungus (Laetiporus sulphureus), help to break down organic matter. The organic matter mixes with minerals, weathered sediment, water, and air to form soil.
56 Unit 1 Earth's Surface
Lesson Labs
Quick Labs
• Observing Life in Soil
• Modeling a Soil Profile
• Observing the Impact of Earthworms on Soil
Field Lab
• Comparing Soil Characteristics
Engage Your Brain
1 Predict Check T or F to show whether you think each statement is true or false.
T F
Soil contains air and water.
Soil does not contain living things.
Soils are the same from place to place.
Climate can affect how fertile soils are.
2 Explain How might the burrows formed by ants affect the soil?
Active Reading
3 Apply Many scientific words, such as weather, have more than one meaning. Use context clues to write your own definition for each meaning of the word weather.
Example sentence
The weather outside is nice.
weather:
Example sentence
Wind, water, and plant roots weather rock into sediment.
weather:
Vocabulary Terms
• soil
• soil profile
• humus
• soil horizon
4 Apply As you learn the definition of each vocabulary term in this lesson, write your own definition or sketch to help you remember the meaning of the term.
Lesson 5 Soil Formation 57

Answers

Answers for 1–3 should represent students' current thoughts, even if incorrect.

1. T; F; F; T
2. Sample answer: The burrowing loosens and mixes the soil.
3. Sample answer: the state of the atmosphere at a given time and place; Sample answer: to break down into smaller pieces
4. Students should define or sketch each vocabulary term in the lesson.

Opening Your Lesson

Discuss student responses to items 1 and 2 to assess students' prerequisite knowledge and to estimate what they already know about soil formation.

Prerequisites: Students should be familiar with the physical weathering and chemical weathering of rock. Students should also be familiar with the role that soil plays in the growth of plants.

Accessing Prior Knowledge

Anticipation Guide Anticipation guides help students review what they already know about a topic before reading the lesson. Invite students to make an anticipation guide about soil formation. Provide students with some statements that are true and other statements that sound plausible but are untrue. These statements can also be generated by a class discussion. Then have students write whether they agree or disagree before and after reading the lesson.

Optional Online resource: Anticipation Guide support

The Dirt on Soil

What causes soil to form?

Soil is important to your life. You walk on grass that is rooted in soil. You eat foods that need soil in order to grow. But what exactly is soil? Where does it come from? How does it form?

A scientist might define **soil** as a loose mixture of small rock fragments, organic matter, water, and air that can support the growth of vegetation. The very first step in soil formation is the weathering of *parent rock*. Parent rock is the source of inorganic soil particles. Soil forms directly above the parent rock. Soil either develops here, or it is eroded and transported to another location.

Active Reading

5 Identify As you read, underline the different substances that make up soil.

Weathering of Parent Rock

Weathering breaks down parent rock into smaller and smaller pieces. These pieces of rock eventually become very small particles that are mixed in with organic matter to form soil. The process of soil formation can take a very long time. The amount of time it takes depends on many factors that you will learn about later in this lesson.

Decomposition and Mixing by Living Things

Some microorganisms, such as bacteria and fungi, are decomposers that live in soil. These tiny decomposers perform the important task of breaking down the remains of plants and animals. These remains are decayed organic matter called **humus**. Humus is found in the top layer of soils. It is important because it contains nutrients that plants need to grow. Plants take up these nutrients through their roots. When plants or animals die, they are broken down by decomposers, and the nutrients are returned to the soil.

Larger animals, such as earthworms and moles, also live in soil. They loosen and mix the soil as they burrow through it. The mixing increases the amount of air in soil and improves the ability of soil to drain water.

6 Apply How might a fallen leaf eventually become part of soil?

7 Summarize How do decomposers and plants cycle nutrients in soil?

Soil formation begins when parent rock weathers into small fragments.
Plant roots grow and can break down sediment even further.
Burrowing animals increase the rate of weathering. They mix the soil, allowing more air to enter. They bring sediment to the surface where it is weathered more quickly by water, wind, and organisms.
At least a million microorganisms can fit into one spoonful of soil! These tiny organisms have the big job of decomposing plant and animal remains.

58 59

Student Pages 56–59

Answers

5. *See students' pages for annotations.*
6. Decomposers break down the leaf. Over time the leaf becomes humus, then that resulting organic matter mixes with weathered rock fragments to form soil.
7. Decomposers add nutrients to soil when they break down organic matter. Plants take up the nutrients through their roots. When plants die, they are broken down by decomposers and the nutrients are returned to the soil.

Building Reading Skills

Student Vocabulary Ask: Which context clues helped you determine the meaning of some of the unfamiliar words on these pages? Sample answers: soil: mixture of rock fragments, organic matter, water, air; weathering: breaks rocks into smaller pieces; microorganisms: living things, bacteria, fungi, tiny, decomposers; humus: decayed organic matter, contains nutrients that plants need

Learning Alert

Underground Life Organisms that live in soil have to survive changes such as variations in temperature and water level. Earthworms, for example, are well adapted to life underground. They respond to changes in their environment by estivation, a state similar to hibernation. Some earthworms secrete a mucus that protects their tightly curled bodies during estivation.

Formative Assessment

Ask: What are the main ingredients of soil? rock fragments, organic matter, water, and air **Ask:** How do activities of organisms affect soil? They decompose organic matter, help to cycle nutrients, mix and loosen soil, and form humus as they decompose.

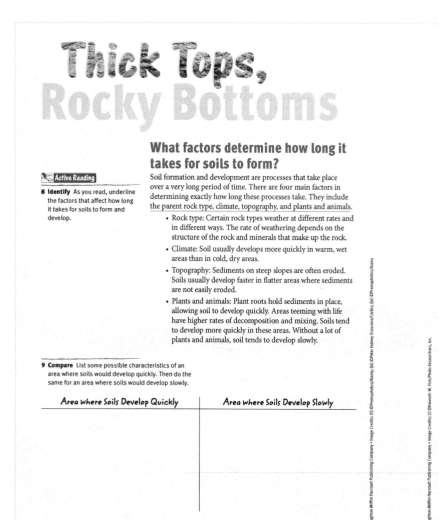

Thick Tops, Rocky Bottoms

What factors determine how long it takes for soils to form?

Active Reading

8 Identify As you read, underline the factors that affect how long it takes for soils to form and develop.

Soil formation and development are processes that take place over a very long period of time. There are four main factors in determining exactly how long these processes take. They include the parent rock type, climate, topography, and plants and animals.

- Rock type: Certain rock types weather at different rates and in different ways. The rate of weathering depends on the structure of the rock and minerals that make up the rock.
- Climate: Soil usually develops more quickly in warm, wet areas than in cold, dry areas.
- Topography: Sediments on steep slopes are often eroded. Soils usually develop faster in flatter areas where sediments are not easily eroded.
- Plants and animals: Plant roots hold sediments in place, allowing soil to develop quickly. Areas teeming with life have higher rates of decomposition and mixing. Soils tend to develop more quickly in these areas. Without a lot of plants and animals, soil tends to develop slowly.

9 Compare List some possible characteristics of an area where soils would develop quickly. Then do the same for an area where soils would develop slowly.

Area where Soils Develop Quickly	Area where Soils Develop Slowly

60

What are the main soil horizons?

Picture the rich, dark soil in a garden. Now imagine what the soil looks like as you dig deeper beneath the surface. Does the soil look and feel the same as you dig deeper? A vertical section of soil that shows all of the different layers is a **soil profile**. Each layer in the soil profile that has different physical properties is called a **soil horizon**. The main horizons include the A horizon, B horizon, and C horizon. There are many other horizons as well.

A Horizon

The A horizon is at the top of the soil profile. It is often referred to as *topsoil*. Decomposers live in this horizon, so it has the most decayed organic matter. This humus gives it a dark color. Plant roots break up fragments and animals burrow and mix the the soil. These processes increase the rate of weathering, so the A horizon is usually the most developed. As you'll learn later in this lesson, rich soils generally have high amounts of humus. Dead leaves, branches, and other organic matter may cover the surface of the A horizon.

B Horizon

The B horizon lies below the A horizon. It is not as developed as the A horizon and has less humus. Following precipitation events, water seeps down through the A horizon. Water carries material, such as iron minerals and clay, from the A horizon down to the B horizon. This is known as *leaching*. The leached materials commonly give the B horizon a reddish or brownish color.

C Horizon

The C horizon lies below the B horizon. It is the least-developed soil horizon. It contains the largest rock fragments and usually has no organic matter. The C horizon lies directly above the parent rock. Recall that this is the weathered rock from which the soil was formed.

Visualize It!

10 Analyze Which soil horizon contains the largest rocks?

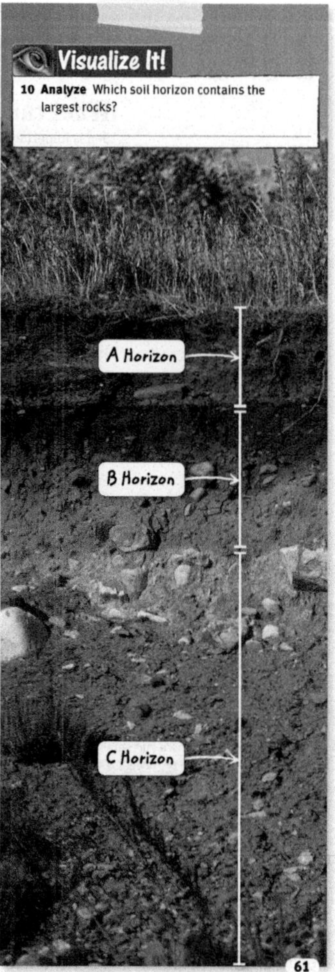

61

Answers

8. *See students' pages for annotations.*
9. Area where Soils Develop Quickly: An example of an area where soils would develop quickly is a flat area or valley bottom in a place with moderate precipitation and a warm climate. There would be a lot of plants and animals. The rock type here could be one that weathers quickly.

   Area where Soils Develop Slowly: An example of an area where soils would develop slowly is a steep slope in a cold, dry place where there are few plants and animals. The rock making up the steep slope may be one that weathers very slowly.
10. C horizon

Probing Question GUIDED Inquiry

Inferring Instruct students to use what they have learned thus far about soil composition to make inferences about soils for growing crops. **Ask:** Which soil is better for crops, soil with or without a lot of worms? The soil with a lot of worms would be best for crops because these organisms mix the soil, allowing in more air and water.

Interpreting Visuals

To help students interpret the visual of a soil profile, **Ask**: Why are there vertical lines in the visual? to show the depth of each horizon **Ask**: Where would you find the most organic matter? The least? most: A horizon; least: C horizon **Ask**: In which horizon are the most rock fragments found? C horizon

Building Graphing Skills

Have students visualize a line graph that shows the amount of organic matter in samples of soil taken from soil layers at different depths in a soil sequence. The graph would show how much organic matter was present at different depths. **Ask:** What would the graph look like, and what would it show? The line on the graph would be highest at the points that represent the layers closest to the surface; the line would go down as the samples got deeper.

All About Soil

What are some properties of soil?

Plants grow well in some soils and poorly in others. Soils look and feel different. They also contain different minerals and particles. Soil properties are used to classify different soils. These properties include soil texture, color, chemistry, pore space, and fertility.

Active Reading

11 Identify As you read, underline the three kinds of soil particles.

Soil Texture

The term *soil texture* is a property that describes the relative amounts of differently sized soil particles. Soil particles are classified as sand, silt, or clay. Most soils are a mixture of all three. Sand is the largest particle, ranging from 0.05 mm to 2 mm. Soils containing a lot of sand feel coarse. Silt particles are smaller than sand particles. They range from 0.002 mm to 0.05 mm. Silty soils have a smooth, silky feel. At less than 0.002 mm, clay particles are the smallest soil particles. Clayey soils feel very smooth and are usually sticky when they are wet.

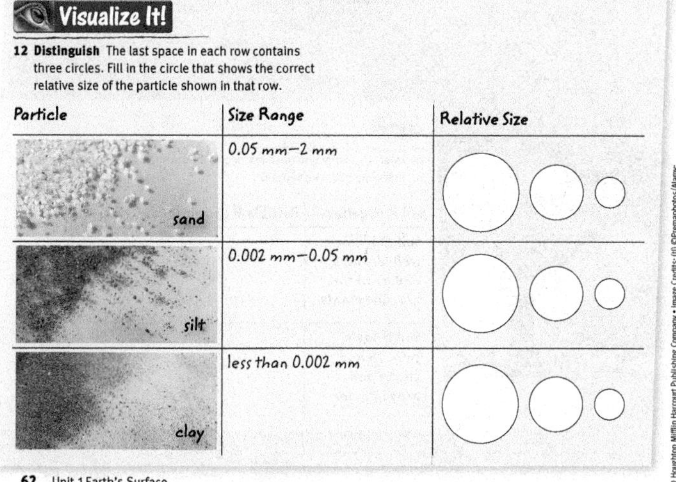

Visualize It!

12 Distinguish The last space in each row contains three circles. Fill in the circle that shows the correct relative size of the particle shown in that row.

Particle	Size Range	Relative Size
sand	0.05 mm–2 mm	◯ ◯ ◯
silt	0.002 mm–0.05 mm	◯ ◯ ◯
clay	less than 0.002 mm	◯ ◯ ◯

Soil Color

Soils can be black, brown, red, orange, yellow, gray, and even white. Soil color is a clue to the types and amounts of minerals and organic matter in the soil. Iron minerals make soil orange or reddish. Soils that contain a lot of humus are black or brown. Color can also be a clue about the environmental conditions. Gray soil can indicate that an area is often wet and has poor drainage.

Soils are usually a mixture of colors, such as reddish brown. Scientists use the Munsell System of Color Notation to describe soil colors. The system uses a book of color chips, much like the paint chips found in a paint store. Scientists compare a soil to the color chips in the book to classify soils.

Think Outside the Book

13 Apply Find out about the qualities of your local soil. Describe its texture, color, chemistry, pore space, and fertility. Choose one of these activities to present your description: draw a poster or diagram, create a brochure, or write a poem.

Soil and Climate

Climate can affect how soil forms in different regions on Earth. Warm, rainy regions produce tropical soils and temperate soils. Dry regions produce desert soils and arctic soils.

Tropical Soils form in warm, wet regions. Heavy rains wash away and leach soils, leaving only a thin layer of humus. Soil development is fast in these regions. They are not suitable for growing most crops.

Desert Soils form in dry regions. These soils are shallow and contain little organic matter. Because of the low rainfall, chemical weathering and soil development is slow in desert regions.

Temperate Soils form in regions with moderate rainfall and temperatures. Some temperate soils are dark-colored, rich in organic matter and minerals, and good for growing crops.

Arctic Soils form in cold, dry regions where chemical weathering is slow. They typically do not have well-developed horizons. Arctic soils may contain many rock fragments.

Answers

11. *See students' pages for annotations.*
12. Students should fill in the largest circle to represent the relative size of a sand particle in row 1, the middle circle to represent the relative size of a silt particle in row 2, and the smallest circle to represent the relative size of a clay particle in row 3.
13. Answers will depend on students' location.

Learning Alert MISCONCEPTION

Clay To help clarify the misconception that the only type of clay is modeling clay, **Ask**: What is clay? If student responses refer to modeling clay, they may not realize that clay occurs naturally. Discuss all experiences that students have had with clay, such as digging it up in a garden or backyard, seeing it in a soil profile at a construction site, or working with modeling clay. Explain that natural clay is composed of one or more minerals formed as a result of the weathering of rock and other minerals. For example, the mineral feldspar weathers into a variety of clays. Clay particles are microscopic and almost always stuck together to form clumps of different sizes. Some modeling clays that artists use are natural. Others, such as children's modeling clay, are made from waxes and other materials.

Interpreting Visuals

Comparisons Point out that the circles that represent the sizes of the soil particles are relative, meaning they are used to show how the sizes of the soil particles relate to each other but may not show an exact comparison. **Ask:** Are the circle sizes shown accurate? No, the sizes show a relative, or rough comparison, but the differences in the sizes are much greater. For example, a clay particle would be much smaller than is shown.

Soil Chemistry

Soil pH is determined by the combination of minerals, sediment, and organic matter found in soil. The pH of soil is a measure of how acidic or basic a soil is. The pH is based on a scale of 0 to 14. If pH is less than 7, the soil is acidic. If pH is above 7, the soil is basic. In the middle of the pH scale is 7, which means the soil is neither acidic nor basic; it is neutral. Scientists measure soil pH to determine whether the soil can support different plants. For example, soybeans grow best in a soil with a pH between 6.0 and 7.0. Peanuts thrive when the pH of soil is between 5.3 and 6.6.

Farmers can adjust the pH of soil to meet the needs of their plants. They can add lime to make acidic soils more basic. They can add acids to make basic soils more acidic.

The pH of a soil can be tested to make sure it will support the plants being grown.

Pore Space

Pore space describes the spaces between soil particles. Water and air are found in the pore spaces of soils. Water and air move easily through soils with many well-connected pore spaces. Soils with this property are well-drained and typically good for plant growth.

Plants need both water and air to grow. About 25 to 60 percent of the volume of most soils is pore space. The best soil for growing most plants has about 50 percent of its volume as pore space, with that volume equally divided between water and air.

Visualize It!

14 Describe Write a caption that describes the pore space for each diagram below.

A ______

B ______

Soil Fertility

Soil fertility describes how well a soil can support plant growth. This quality is affected by factors that include the climate of the area; the amount of humus, minerals, and nutrients in the soil; and the topography of the area.

Fertile soils are often found in areas with moderate rainfall and temperatures. Soils with a lot of humus and the proper proportions of minerals and nutrients have high soil fertility. Soils found in dry areas or on steep hillsides often have low fertility. Farmers can add chemical fertilizers or organic material to soils to improve soil fertility. They also can grow crops, such as legumes, to restore certain nutrients to soil or leave cropland unplanted for a season to replenish its fertility.

Active Reading 15 Apply What could you do to improve the fertility of the soil in your garden?

______

This meadow's bluebonnets thrive in well-drained soil. Bluebonnets also grow best in slightly basic soils.

Inquiry

16 Infer Use what you have learned to infer why Soils A and B have the following soils properties.

Soil Properties	Possible Reasons for Soil Properties
Soil A is black, well-drained, and good for growing plants.	
Soil B feels smooth and sticky and is gray in color.	

Answers

14. Sample caption on the left: "This diagram shows a soil with plenty of pore space." Sample caption on the right: "This diagram shows a soil with little pore space."
15. Sample answer: You could add organic materials or plant legumes in the soil to improve its fertility.
16. Sample answer: Soil A probably has a lot of humus because it is black. It is probably an A horizon. To be well drained, it has a large volume of well-connected pore spaces. It has a high fertility since it is good for growing plants. Soil B has a lot of clay with very little sand since its texture is smooth and sticky. It may be poorly drained and in a wet environment because it is gray.

Formative Assessment

Ask: Which would you expect to be more fertile, the soil on a steep slope or the soil on a plain? Why? on a plain, because the soil on a steep slope would be eroded away by wind and water, so it would be thin and lack nutrients. **Ask:** Describe five properties of soil. texture: relative amounts of soil particles; color: indication of content and water mobility; pore space: spaces between particles that hold water; chemistry: pH of soil; fertility: ability to support plant growth

Building Reading Skills

Problem-Solution Notes Point out that there are several examples of soil problems and potential solutions. Invite students to make Problem-Solution Notes using the examples to improve poor or unhealthy soil. Sample answers: problem: soil contains too much sand, silt, or clay, solution: mix in particles of other sizes; problem: soil pH is too high or low, solution: add a basic or acidic substance to the soil to change the pH; problem: there is too little pore space in soil, solution: introduce worms or other animals that can burrow and loosen the soil; problem: soil is not fertile, solution: add humus or compost to the soil or grow certain crops that will restore nutrients to the soil

Optional Online resource: Problem-Solution Notes support

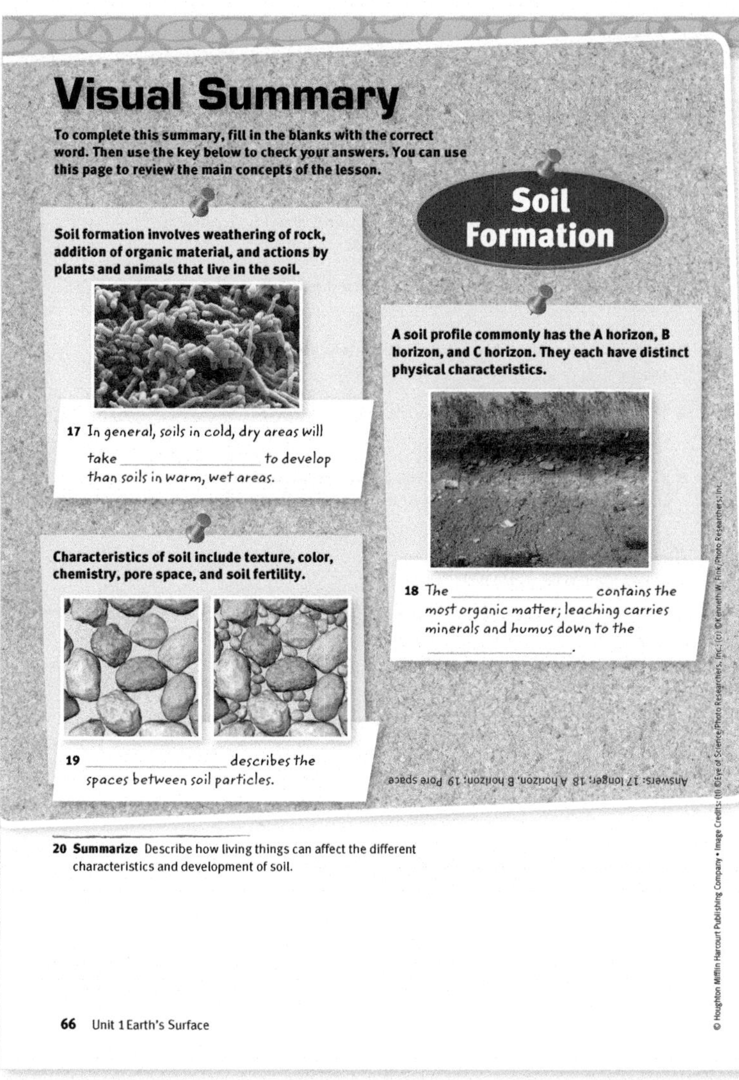

Visual Summary

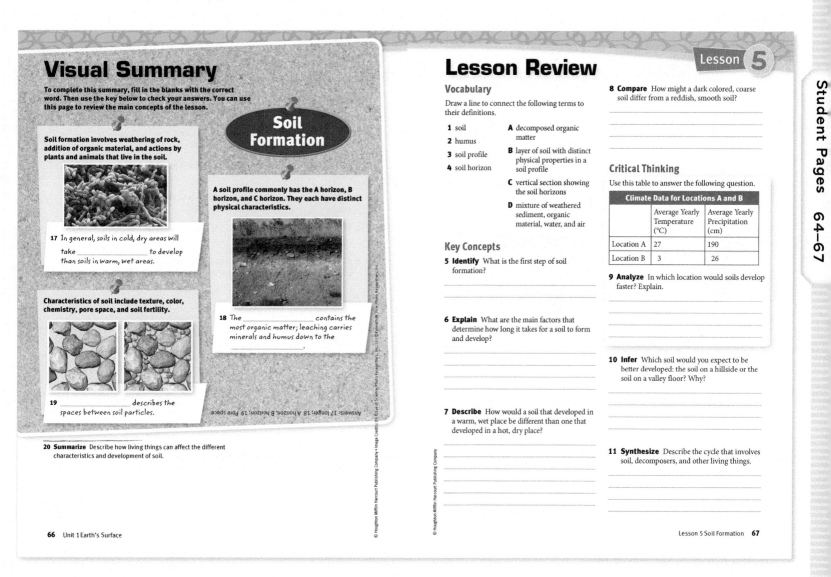

To complete this summary, fill in the blanks with the correct word. Then use the key below to check your answers. You can use this page to review the main concepts of the lesson.

Soil Formation

Soil formation involves weathering of rock, addition of organic material, and actions by plants and animals that live in the soil.

17 In general, soils in cold, dry areas will take ________ to develop than soils in warm, wet areas.

Characteristics of soil include texture, color, chemistry, pore space, and soil fertility.

19 ________ describes the spaces between soil particles.

A soil profile commonly has the A horizon, B horizon, and C horizon. They each have distinct physical characteristics.

18 The ________ contains the most organic matter; leaching carries minerals and humus down to the ________.

Answers: 17 longer; 18 A horizon, B horizon; 19 Pore space

20 **Summarize** Describe how living things can affect the different characteristics and development of soil.

Lesson Review

Vocabulary

Draw a line to connect the following terms to their definitions.

1 soil	A decomposed organic matter
2 humus	B layer of soil with distinct physical properties in a soil profile
3 soil profile	C vertical section showing the soil horizons
4 soil horizon	D mixture of weathered sediment, organic material, water, and air

Key Concepts

5 **Identify** What is the first step of soil formation?

6 **Explain** What are the main factors that determine how long it takes for a soil to form and develop?

7 **Describe** How would a soil that developed in a warm, wet place be different than one that developed in a hot, dry place?

8 **Compare** How might a dark colored, coarse soil differ from a reddish, smooth soil?

Critical Thinking

Use this table to answer the following question.

Climate Data for Locations A and B		
	Average Yearly Temperature (°C)	Average Yearly Precipitation (cm)
Location A	27	190
Location B	3	26

9 **Analyze** In which location would soils develop faster? Explain.

10 **Infer** Which soil would you expect to be better developed: the soil on a hillside or the soil on a valley floor? Why?

11 **Synthesize** Describe the cycle that involves soil, decomposers, and other living things.

Visual Summary Answers

17. longer
18. A horizon, B horizon
19. Pore space
20. Sample answer: As plant roots grow, they break down rocks into sediment. Plant roots can also hold soil and sediments in place. Burrowing animals mix the soil and increase rates of weathering. This speeds up soil development.

Lesson Review Answers

1. D
2. A
3. C
4. B
5. weathering of parent rock into smaller fragments
6. rock type; climate; topography; plants and animals
7. Tropical soils form in warm, wet climates and develop quickly but are often devoid of nutrients. Desert soils form in hot, dry climates and develop slowly.
8. A dark, coarse soil could be rich in organic material/humus, and mostly contain sand-sized particles. It may be the A horizon of a soil profile. A reddish, smooth soil may contain iron minerals and mostly silt or clay. This would probably be a B horizon.
9. Soils would develop faster in Location A because warm, wet areas have higher rates of weathering.
10. the soil on the valley floor because there are more organisms and water; The hillside experiences more erosion and has less organisms, so soil doesn't develop as quickly.
11. Decomposers break down organic matter, releasing nutrients into the soil. Plants obtain these nutrients through their roots. When the plant dies, decomposers break down the organic matter and return the nutrients to the soil.

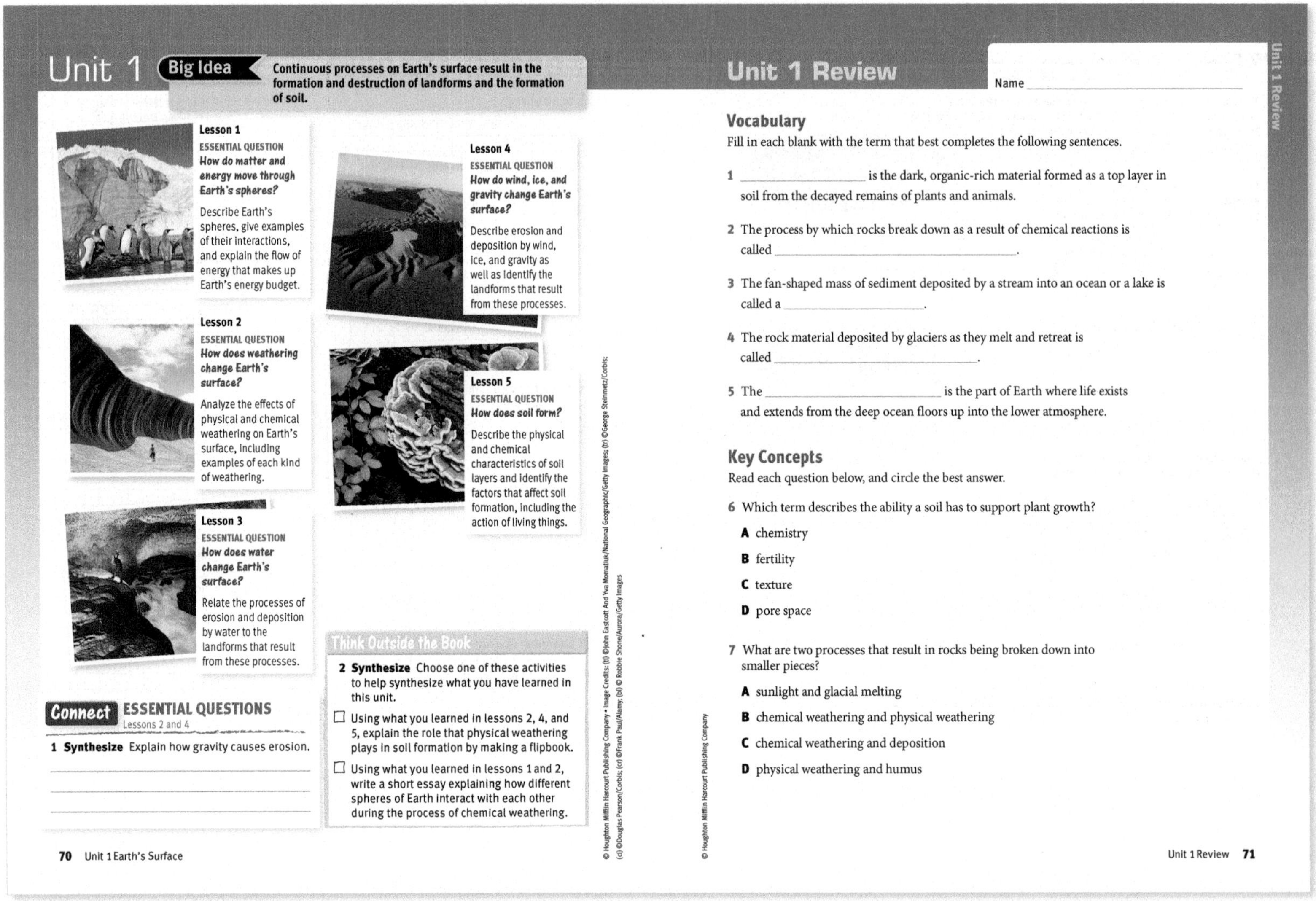

Unit 1 Big Idea

Continuous processes on Earth's surface result in the formation and destruction of landforms and the formation of soil.

Lesson 1
ESSENTIAL QUESTION
How do matter and energy move through Earth's spheres?
Describe Earth's spheres, give examples of their interactions, and explain the flow of energy that makes up Earth's energy budget.

Lesson 2
ESSENTIAL QUESTION
How does weathering change Earth's surface?
Analyze the effects of physical and chemical weathering on Earth's surface, including examples of each kind of weathering.

Lesson 3
ESSENTIAL QUESTION
How does water change Earth's surface?
Relate the processes of erosion and deposition by water to the landforms that result from these processes.

Lesson 4
ESSENTIAL QUESTION
How do wind, ice, and gravity change Earth's surface?
Describe erosion and deposition by wind, ice, and gravity as well as identify the landforms that result from these processes.

Lesson 5
ESSENTIAL QUESTION
How does soil form?
Describe the physical and chemical characteristics of soil layers and identify the factors that affect soil formation, including the action of living things.

Connect ESSENTIAL QUESTIONS
Lessons 2 and 4

1 **Synthesize** Explain how gravity causes erosion.

Think Outside the Book

2 **Synthesize** Choose one of these activities to help synthesize what you have learned in this unit.

☐ Using what you learned in lessons 2, 4, and 5, explain the role that physical weathering plays in soil formation by making a flipbook.

☐ Using what you learned in lessons 1 and 2, write a short essay explaining how different spheres of Earth interact with each other during the process of chemical weathering.

70 Unit 1 Earth's Surface

Unit 1 Review

Name ____________

Unit 1 Review

Vocabulary

Fill in each blank with the term that best completes the following sentences.

1 ____________ is the dark, organic-rich material formed as a top layer in soil from the decayed remains of plants and animals.

2 The process by which rocks break down as a result of chemical reactions is called ____________.

3 The fan-shaped mass of sediment deposited by a stream into an ocean or a lake is called a ____________.

4 The rock material deposited by glaciers as they melt and retreat is called ____________.

5 The ____________ is the part of Earth where life exists and extends from the deep ocean floors up into the lower atmosphere.

Key Concepts

Read each question below, and circle the best answer.

6 Which term describes the ability a soil has to support plant growth?
A chemistry
B fertility
C texture
D pore space

7 What are two processes that result in rocks being broken down into smaller pieces?
A sunlight and glacial melting
B chemical weathering and physical weathering
C chemical weathering and deposition
D physical weathering and humus

Unit 1 Review 71

Unit Summary Answers

1. Gravity causes water, ice, soil, and rocks to move downslope, eroding materials in their paths.
2. Option 1: Flipbooks can show how different agents of physical weathering, such as water (and ice, as in freeze-thaw), wind, gravity, and plant and animal actions, contribute to soil formation.

   Option 2: Oxygen in the atmosphere interacts with rocks in the geosphere during the process of oxidation.

   Acid precipitation begins in the biosphere, with chemicals generated by humans. These chemicals enter the atmosphere and combine with water in the hydrosphere to form acid precipitation. Acid precipitation falls to Earth and causes rocks in the geosphere to break down.

   Acids in water, which is part of the hydrosphere, interact with rock, which is part of the geosphere.

   Acids in living things, which are part of the biosphere, interact with rock, which is part of the geosphere.

Unit Review **Response to Intervention**

A Quick Grading Chart follows the Answers. See the Assessment Guide for more detail about correct and incorrect answer choices. Refer back to the Lesson Planning pages for activities and assignments that can be used as remediation for students who answer questions incorrectly.

Answers

1. humus Humus is the final product of the breakdown of organic matter and results as the top layer in certain soil horizons. (Lesson 5)
2. chemical weathering Chemical weathering is most commonly due to chemical reactions caused by the interactions between rock, water, and the atmosphere. (Lesson 2)
3. delta As streams enter a standing body of water, they slow down and lose energy, hence depositing their sediment load. Over time this forms a fan-shaped deposit called a delta. (Lesson 3)

Name ______________________

8 This diagram shows a landform called an alluvial fan.

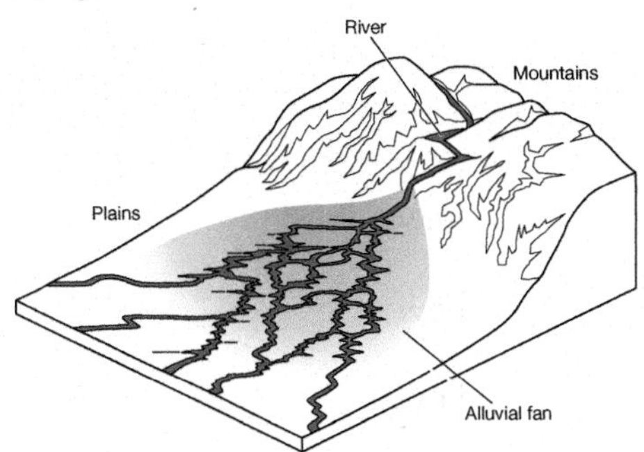

How does an alluvial fan form?

A It forms where a stream enters an ocean or lake, slows down, and deposits sediments there over time.

B It forms from a stream overflowing and depositing sediments.

C It forms where part of a meandering stream is cut off.

D It forms where a stream reaches a flat area of land, slows down, and deposits sediments there over time.

9 While walking along a seashore, Antonio determined that the shore has been affected by stormy seas and rough waves. What did Antonio observe?

A The beach was sandy.
B There were sandbars.
C The beach was rocky.
D There was a sea stack.

10 Landslides, rockfalls, and creep are examples of erosion and deposition by which erosion agent?

A gravity
B solar energy
C oxidation
D wind

11 The diagram below shows a landform called a sinkhole.

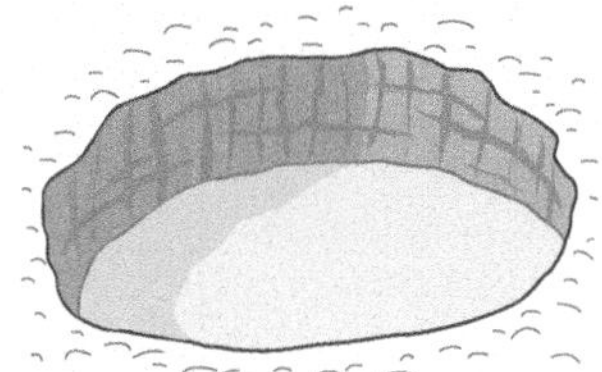

How does a sinkhole form?

A Stalactites erode the ceiling of a cavern.

B A flowing stream in the mountains erodes sediment and the ground caves in.

C Underground water erodes rock forming a cavern, and over time the cavern's roof collapses.

D A flowing stream erodes soil and rock making the stream deeper and wider.

12 A glacier is a large mass of moving ice. What conditions are necessary for a glacier to form?

A The weather must be below freezing and very dry.

B The weather must be below freezing, and more snow must fall than melt.

C The weather must be mild, and there must be a lot of precipitation.

D The weather must be below freezing, and more snow must melt than fall.

Critical Thinking

Answer the following questions in the space provided.

13 Explain whether water is a cause of either chemical weathering, physical weathering, or both.

____

____

____

____

Answers *(continued)*

4. glacial drift Sediment is picked up as glaciers advance. When they retreat, they deposit glacial drift, or sediment. (Lesson 4)
5. biosphere The biosphere extends to wherever life can be found on Earth. (Lesson 1)
6. Answer B is correct because soil fertility is the ability of the soil to support plant growth. (Lesson 5)
7. Answer B is correct because rocks are broken down by chemical and physical weathering, such as dissolution and freeze-thaw. (Lesson 2)
8. Answer D is correct because an alluvial fan is a fan-shaped deposit of sediment that is formed over time as a stream deposits its load. Typically, this is due to the stream slowing down when entering a flat area of land. (Lesson 3)
9. Answer C is correct because stormy seas and rough waves would erode all of the smaller sediment leaving larger sediments such as pebbles and rocks. (Lesson 5)
10. Answer A is correct because gravity is a cause of landslides, rockfalls, and creep. (Lesson 4)
11. Answer C is correct because a sinkhole forms when the roof of a cavern collapses and results in a formation like what is shown in the diagram. (Lesson 3)
12. Answer B is correct because for a glacier to form, the temperature must be below freezing and snow must fall and be compacted into a glacier. (Lesson 4)
13. Key Elements:
    - Water is a cause of both physical and chemical weathering.
    - Water can cause physical weathering by causing abrasion, in which rocks bump into each other and break down into smaller pieces. Water causes physical weathering in other ways as well.
    - Water can cause chemical weathering by dissolving certain minerals in the rocks. (Lessons 2, 3)

Unit 1 Review continued

14 Below is a diagram of the soil profile of three layers of soil.

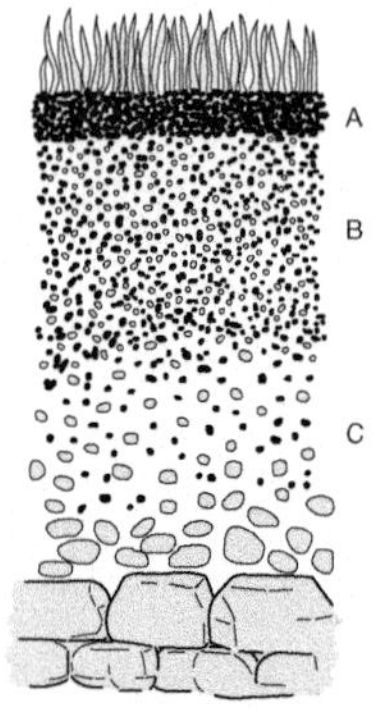

A

B

C

Describe the characteristics and properties of the three layers of soil.

Connect ESSENTIAL QUESTIONS
Lessons 3 and 4

Answer the following question in the space provided.

15 How can water and gravity work together to erode soil, sediment, and rock? Give two examples.

Explain how water deposits soil, sediment, and rock. Give two examples.

74 Unit 1 Earth's Surface

Answers *(continued)*

14. Key Elements:

- The A horizon is the top layer with the most humus, which gives it a dark color. Plants and animals affect this horizon the most.
- The B horizon is below A. Materials from the A horizon leach down to B. B contains less organic matter than A.
- C is below B. It is partially weathered parent rock, with little to no organic matter and usually larger particles. (Lesson 5)

15. Key Elements:

A. Gravity causes water to flow downward, which can cause erosion. Over time, streams can carve valleys. Gravity causes glaciers to move downslope and erode rock underneath them.

B. Water erodes, transports, and deposits the materials. A stream can carry a sediment load; when it slows, some sediment is deposited (for example, a delta or an alluvial fan). When a glacier melts, sediment it has eroded and picked up is deposited (for example, glacial drift). (Lessons 3, 4)

Quick Grading Chart

Use the chart below for quick test grading. The lesson correlations can help you target reteaching for missed items.

Item	Answer	Cognitive Complexity	Lesson
1.	—	Low	5
2.	—	Low	2
3.	—	Low	3
4.	—	Low	4
5.	—	Low	1
6.	B	Moderate	5
7.	B	Moderate	2
8.	D	Moderate	3
9.	C	Moderate	5
10.	A	Moderate	4
11.	C	Moderate	3
12.	B	Moderate	4
13.	—	Moderate	2, 3
14.	—	Moderate	5
15.	—	Moderate	3, 4

Cognitive Complexity refers to the demand on thinking associated with an item, and may vary with the answer choices, the number of steps required to arrive at an answer, and other factors, but not the ability level of the student.

UNIT 2 Earth's History

The Big Idea and Essential Questions

This Unit was designed to focus on this Big Idea and Essential Questions.

Big Idea **Rock, fossils, and other types of natural evidence are used to study Earth's history and measure geologic time.**

Lesson	ESSENTIAL QUESTION	Student Mastery	PD Professional Development	Lesson Overview
LESSON 1 Geologic Change Over Time	*How do we learn about Earth's history?*	To explain how Earth materials, such as rock, fossils, and ice, show that Earth has changed over time	Content Refresher, TE p. 98	TE p. 104
LESSON 2 Relative Dating	*How are the relative ages of rock measured?*	To summarize how scientists measure the relative ages of rock layers and identify gaps in the rock record	Content Refresher, TE p. 99	TE p. 120
LESSON 3 Absolute Dating	*How is the absolute age of rock measured?*	To summarize how scientists measure the absolute age of rock layers, including by radiometric dating	Content Refresher, TE p. 100	TE p. 136
LESSON 4 The Geologic Time Scale	*What is the geologic time scale?*	To understand how geologists use the geologic time scale to divide Earth's history	Content Refresher, TE p. 101	TE p. 150

Science Background

Use the key words at right to access

- Professional Development from **The NSTA Learning Center**
- **SciLinks** for additional online content appropriate for students and teachers

Key words

absolute dating
fossils
geologic time scale
relative dating

SCILINKS. THE WORLD'S A CLICK AWAY

Options for Instruction

Two parallel paths provide coverage of the Essential Questions, with a strong **Inquiry** strand woven into each. Follow the **Print Path,** the **Digital Path,** or your customized combination of print, digital, and inquiry.

	LESSON 1 Geologic Change Over Time	LESSON 2 Relative Dating	LESSON 3 Absolute Dating
Essential Questions	***How do we learn about Earth's history?***	***How are the relative ages of rocks measured?***	***How is the absolute age of rock measured?***
Key Topics	• Uniformitarianism and Fossils • The Rock Record • Earth's Changing Climate	• Dating Undisturbed Rock Layers • Dating Disturbed Rock Layers • Fossils and Relative Dating • Geologic Columns	• Absolute Dating • Radiometric Dating • The Age of Earth • Index Fossils
Print Path	Teacher Edition pp. 104–118 Student Edition pp. 78–91	Teacher Edition pp. 120–133 Student Edition pp. 92–103	Teacher Edition pp. 136–149 Student Edition pp. 106–117
Inquiry Labs	Lab Manual **Quick Lab** Modeling the Fossil... **Quick Lab** Fossil Flipbook **S.T.E.M. Lab** Exploring Landforms Virtual Lab Earth's History	Lab Manual **Quick Lab** Layers of Sedimentary Rock **Exploration Lab** Earth's History Virtual Lab Ordering Rock Layers	Lab Manual **Quick Lab** Index Fossils **Quick Lab** Radioactive Decay
Digital Path	Digital Path TS671280	Digital Path TS671210	Digital Path TS671220

LESSON 4
The Geologic Time Scale

What is the geologic time scale?

- A Historical Perspective of Geologic Change
- The Geologic Time Scale
- Milestones in Earth History

Teacher Edition
pp. 150–163

Student Edition
pp. 118–129

Lab Manual
Quick Lab Timeline of Earth's History

Quick Lab Investigating Events...

Virtual Lab
How, Divide Earth's History?

Digital Path
TS671155

UNIT 2
Unit Projects

Citizen Science Project
Preserving the Past

Teacher Edition p. 103

Student Edition
pp. 76–77

Transforming Earth

Unit Assessment

Formative Assessment

Strategies RTI
Throughout TE

Lesson Reviews SE

Unit PreTest

Summative Assessment

Alternative Assessment
(1 per lesson) RTI

Lesson Quizzes

Unit Tests A and B

Unit Review RTI
(with answer remediation)

Practice Tests
(end of module)

Project-Based Assessment

See the Assessment Guide for quizzes and tests.

Go Online to edit and create quizzes and tests.

Response to Intervention
See RTI teacher support materials on p. PD6.

Teacher Notes

Differentiated Instruction

English Language Proficiency

Strategies for **English Language Learners (ELL)** are provided for each lesson, under the Explain tabs.

LESSON 1 *Diagramming Fossil Formation,* TE p.109

LESSON 2 *Concept Mapping,* TE p.125

LESSON 3 *Note Taking,* TE p.141

LESSON 4 *Important Milestones,* TE p.155

Vocabulary strategies provided for all students can also be a particular help for ELL. Use different strategies for each lesson or choose one or two to use throughout the unit. Vocabulary strategies can be found under the Explain tab for each lesson (TE pp. 109, 125, 141, and 155).

Leveled Inquiry

Inquiry labs, activities, probing questions, and daily demos provide a range of inquiry levels. Preview them under the Engage and Explore tabs starting on TE pp. 106, 122, 138, and 152.

Levels of Inquiry

DIRECTED inquiry	**GUIDED** inquiry	**INDEPENDENT** inquiry
introduces inquiry skills within a structured framework.	develops inquiry skills within a supportive environment.	deepens inquiry skills with student-driven questions or procedures.

Each long lab has two inquiry options:

LESSON 1 S.T.E.M. Lab *Exploring Landforms*

LESSON 2 Exploration Lab *Earth's History*

Go Digital! thinkcentral.com

Digital Path

The Unit 2 Resource Gateway is your guide to all of the digital resources for this unit. To access the Gateway, visit thinkcentral.com.

Digital Interactive Lessons

Lesson 1 Geologic Change Over Time TS671280

Lesson 2 Relative Dating TS671210

Lesson 3 Absolute Dating TS671220

Lesson 4 The Geologic Time Scale TS671155

More Digital Resources

In addition to digital lessons, you will find the following digital resources for Unit 2:

Video-Based Project: Transforming Earth (previewed on TE p. 102)

Virtual Labs: Earth's History (previewed on TE p. 107)
Ordering Rock Layers (previewed on TE p. 123)
How Do We Divide Earth's History? (previewed on TE p. 153)

Response to Intervention

Response to Intervention (RTI) is a process for identifying and supporting students who are not making expected progress toward essential learning goals. The following *ScienceFusion* components can be used to provide strategic and intensive intervention.

Component	Location	Strategies and Benefits
STUDENT EDITION Active Reading prompts, Visualize It!, Think Outside the Book	**Throughout each lesson**	Student responses can be used as screening tools to assess whether intervention is needed.
TEACHER EDITION Formative Assessment, Probing Questions, Learning Alerts	**Throughout each lesson**	Opportunities are provided to assess and remediate student understanding of lesson concepts.
TEACHER EDITION Extend Science Concepts	**Reinforce and Review, TE pp. 110, 126, 142, 156** **Going Further, TE pp. 110, 126, 142, 156**	Additional activities allow students to reinforce and extend their understanding of lesson concepts.
TEACHER EDITION Evaluate Student Mastery	**Formative Assessment, TE pp. 111, 127, 143, 157** **Alternative Assessment, TE pp. 111, 127, 143, 157**	These assessments allow for greater flexibility in assessing students with differing physical, mental, and language abilities as well as varying learning and communication modes.
TEACHER EDITION Unit Review Remediation	**Unit Review, TE pp. 164–166**	Includes reference back to Lesson Planning pages for remediation activities and assignments.
INTERACTIVE DIGITAL LESSONS and VIRTUAL LABS	**thinkcentral.com** **Unit 2 Gateway** **Lesson 1 TS671280** **Lesson 2 TS671210** **Lesson 3 TS671220** **Lesson 4 TS671155**	Lessons and labs make content accessible through simulations, animations, videos, audio, and integrated assessment. Useful for review and reteaching of lesson concepts.

Content Refresher

Lesson 1

Geologic Change over Time

ESSENTIAL QUESTION

How do we learn about Earth's history?

1. Uniformitarianism and Fossils

Fossils are one source of information about Earth's history.

Uniformitarianism is the theory that the same geologic processes shaping Earth today have been at work throughout Earth's history. This theory was proposed in 1788 by James Hutton. At the time, the theory was not well accepted because most scientists subscribed to the theory of catastrophism, which held that all geologic change occurs suddenly as a result of catastrophic events. In 1833, Charles Lyell published *Principles of Geology*. Lyell supported Hutton's proposal that present geologic change happens in the same ways it did in the past. Lyell also supported the idea that geologic change happened gradually. Today's scientists know that geologic change happens both gradually and quickly.

Fossils are the traces or remains of organisms that lived in the past, most commonly preserved in sedimentary rock. Fossils also include remains of organisms preserved in asphalt, amber, or ice. Some fossils form by petrification, a process in which an organism's tissues are completely replaced by minerals.

This ant was preserved in amber.

COMMON MISCONCEPTIONS  

FOSSILS AND ORGANISM REMAINS Students often think that all fossils are the remains of organisms. Most fossils are actually rock or mineral impressions that formed from the hard parts of organisms before the organisms decomposed.

2. The Sedimentary Rock Record

Fossils tell scientists much about the past.

For example, fossils of tropical flora in a temperate area provide evidence that the area once had a tropical climate; fossils of shells suggest an area was once covered in sea water. Fossils also provide clues about evolution. ***Evolution*** is the gradual development of new organisms from preexisting organisms. Scientists compare fossils of organisms from the past to those of today to build a record of how species have changed over time and how species of the past are related to those of today.

Sedimentary rock also provides clues about Earth's history. For example, the composition of sedimentary rock indicates the source from which the rock eroded. Its texture can provide clues about the environment in which the sediment was transported and deposited.

3. Earth's Changing Landforms and Climate

Landforms and the shapes of the continents are clues about Earth's past.

The continents have been moving throughout Earth's history. At one time, the continents were a single landmass, which eventually drifted apart to form today's continents. The shape of the continental edges and rock and mineral samples taken from opposite coasts have substantiated the claims that there was once only one landmass.

As tectonic plates move across Earth, they collide to form mountains, volcanoes, and deep trenches, and to change the course of rivers. All these events give scientists clues about what Earth may have once looked like.

Climatologists know that Earth's climate has changed several times throughout its 4.6 billion-year history. Scientists use clues from trees, ice, and sea-floor sediments to help them uncover the climate patterns of the past. Tree rings indicate fluctuations in climate such as drought or periods of ample rainfall and moderate temperatures. Ice cores provide clues about atmospheric conditions in the past. Climate and atmospheric data are also revealed through analysis of sea-floor sediment composition.

Pamela Sweeney
Smith-Hale Middle School
Kansas City, MO

Lesson 3 Absolute Dating For a clearer understanding of how items can be dated based on radioactive decay, begin by giving each student 20 small objects, such as pennies or beans. Ask students to arrange the objects into rows of 5 and columns of 4. Have students remove half of the objects to represent the daughter isotope after one half-life. Then, have the students remove another half for a second half-life. Have students determine the percentage of isotope left.

Lesson 2

Relative Dating

ESSENTIAL QUESTION

How are the relative ages of rocks measured?

1. Dating Undisturbed Rock Layers

Relative age is used to date rock layers.

Dating rock layers by comparing their relative age helps scientists build a sequence of events that facilitates an understanding of the geologic history of Earth. Scientists apply various principles when dating undisturbed layers of sedimentary rock. The first is horizontality. This principle states that sediments are usually deposited in horizontal layers and cement together to form sedimentary rocks.

The second is the law of superposition. This law states that in a section of sedimentary rock, older layers are at the bottom, and younger rocks lie on top of them. This can give scientists a general understanding of when an event occurred on Earth relative to other events.

2. Dating Disturbed Rock Layers

Disturbed rock layers can be dated using relative dating methods.

Dating disturbed rock layers is a bit more difficult. Rocks can be displaced along fault lines. When this happens, older layers may be placed on top of or beside younger rock layers. However, the law of crosscutting relationships states that a fault or crack that cuts into a rock layer is younger than the rock it cuts into.

Scientists also use principles of inclusion and correlation to help them date rocks. An inclusion is a part of an older rock unit that is mixed and deposited into a younger unit. Inclusions occur when rocks have been eroded and create conditions in which particles from an older rock or layer can mix with younger sediments. For example, a geologist might find a cobble from an older metamorphic unit incorporated into a sedimentary rock. In this case, the geologist knows that the inclusion, metamorphic cobble, represents a unit that is older than the sedimentary rock in which it is contained. Correlation helps when scientists find layers far away from one another. They can compare fossils and minerals in rock layers and correlate them to rock layers that were formed around the same time.

3. Fossils and Relative Dating

Fossils can be used to date rock layers.

Fossils can play an important role in helping scientists to determine relative ages of rock layers. Fossils can also help scientists understand the conditions that existed during the time when the rock layer in which the fossil is present formed.

4. Geologic Column

Geologic columns provide clues to Earth's past.

Information about rock strata can be arranged in a geologic column, an organizational system that depicts the various periods in Earth's past. This organizational system is based on relative ages of the rocks. This scale allows scientists to compare and correlate rock layers from different regions.

Rock layers from different places can be compared to a geologic column.

Content Refresher (continued)

Lesson 3

Absolute Dating

ESSENTIAL QUESTION

How is the absolute age of rock measured?

1. Absolute Dating

Absolute dating provides actual ages of Earth materials.

Absolute dating is any method of measuring the age of an event or object, such as a rock or fossil, in years. Unlike relative dating, which provides only an estimate of when rocks or fossils formed or geologic events occurred relative to other objects or events, absolute dating provides quantitative data for describing the actual age of a rock or fossil.

2. Radiometric Dating

Time can be measured using radioactive decay.

Radiometric dating is a method of determining the age of an object by estimating the relative percentages of a radioactive (parent) isotope and a stable (daughter) isotope. Thus, the process uses the radioactivity of isotopes as a means for dating objects. Radioactive isotopes are composed of unstable atoms that emit particles and energy. When these particles are emitted, the unstable isotope is changed into a more stable isotope (often of a different element). The process in which an unstable isotope breaks down and releases particles to form a more stable isotope is called radioactive decay.

Radioactive decay occurs at a predictable rate. The rate of decay is described by the half-life of the isotope, which is the average time required for one-half of a quantity of a radioactive material to decay. Using the known half-life of a radioisotope, scientists are able to determine the age of a material by comparing the amount of radioactive isotope contained in a sample to the amount of its decay product.

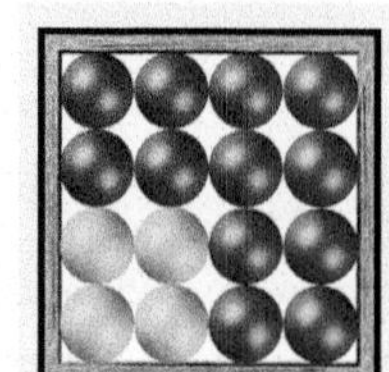

After 2 half-lives
Parent isotope = 4
Daughter isotope = ___
25%, or $\frac{1}{4}$, of the sample is parent isotope.

3. The Age of Rock

Different isotopes are used for measuring different matter.

Radiometric dating works best with igneous rock—rock formed when magma cools. When igneous rock forms, the elements contained in the magma separated into different minerals in the rock. As a result, newly formed igneous rock often contains only the parent isotope and none of the daughter isotope. By determining the ratio of the parent isotope to the daughter isotope in an igneous rock sample, it is possible to calculate the sample's age.

Scientists use different radiometric dating methods to study different types of samples. Each method is most useful on a particular type of material (rock or fossil) and has a unique time range for when it is useful. For example potassium-argon dating is useful for dating igneous rock that ranges from about 10,000 to billions of years old. Uranium-lead dating is used for dating igneous rock between 65 million and 3.8 billion years old. Other methods used to date rock include argon-argon dating and thorium-lead dating. By contrast, radiocarbon dating is useful for determining the ages of fossilized organisms that existed only within the past 70,000 years.

4. Index Fossils

Scientists use index fossils to help study Earth's history.

An *index fossil* is a fossil that can be used to establish the absolute age of a rock layer because the fossil is distinct, abundant, and widespread, and existed for only a very short span of geologic time. For example, nearly half of the discovered fossils representing the Paleozoic era are trilobites. Trilobites are found only in rock layers that are older than the Permian period.

Index fossils cannot be dated directly, however igneous rock layers on either side of the fossil layer can be dated radiometrically. Thus, scientists can use the ages of these layers to establish a numeric age range for an index fossil. This age can then be applied to the rock layer in which the index fossil was discovered.

Lesson 4

The Geologic Time Scale

ESSENTIAL QUESTION

What is the geologic time scale?

1. An Historical Perspective of Geologic Change

Students will learn that scientists' understanding of geologic change has evolved over time.

In the late 18th century and early 19th century, scientists developed two conflicting theories to explain how Earth changed over time: catastrophism and uniformitarianism. Baron Georges Cuvier proposed catastrophism. He believed that sudden, catastrophic events accounted for changes to Earth's surface. Charles Lyell and James Hutton countered with the theory of uniformitarianism, which states that changes to Earth's surface occur at the same gradual rate in the present as they have in the past. This theory also proposes that the events that cause changes have always occurred throughout Earth's long history.

In the end, both theories were partly correct. Modern geologists know that some changes to Earth's surface happen because of catastrophic events, such as volcanic eruptions. At the same time, weathering, erosion, mountain building, and other processes work slowly and steadily to change Earth's surface over time.

2. The Geologic Time Scale

Students will learn that the geologic time scale divides Earth's history into intervals of time.

The geologic time scale divides Earth's long history into manageable units of time. The largest unit is the eon, which can span billions of years. The next smallest unit is the era, which usually spans hundreds of millions of years. Eras are divided into periods, and periods are divided into epochs. The epochs of the Cenozoic era are named. Epochs for other eras are sometimes given general names, such as *Early, Middle,* and *Late.*

The geologic time scale undergoes periodic "fine-tuning" as additional information is gathered about the rock and fossil record. In the United States, the USGS Geologic Names Committee and the Association of American State Geologists work together to develop a consistent geologic time scale.

3. Milestones in Earth History

Students will learn that Earth's climate, geology, and life forms changed throughout its history.

The main divisions of the geologic time scale are distinguished by major events or changes on Earth. Precambrian time, for example, ended 542 million years ago when most major kinds of organisms appeared in the fossil record. The Paleozoic era ended 251 million years ago with the Permian mass extinction. The Mesozoic era ended 65.5 million years ago with the Cretaceous mass extinction.

In addition to changes in life forms, certain geologic events are associated with different time divisions. Precambrian time saw the formation of landmasses. The great supercontinent Pangaea began forming during the late Paleozoic and broke up during the Mesozoic. The continents assumed their current positions during the Cenozoic, which also saw the formation of the Himalayas (as the Indian subcontinent collided with Asia) and the formation of the Alps (as Africa collided with Europe).

Advance Planning

These activities may take extended time or special conditions.

Unit 2

Video-Based Project Transforming Earth, p. 102
multiple activities spanning several lessons

Project Preserving the Past, p. 103
research and writing time

Graphic Organizers and Vocabulary pp. 109, 110, 125, 126, 141, 142, 155, 156
ongoing with reading

Lesson 1

Activity Reconstructing Pangaea, p. 106
requires 45 min first day, then 20 min second day

Lesson 2

Exploration Lab Earth's History, p. 123
requires 90 min

Lesson 3

Quick Lab Index Fossils, p. 139
chart of geologic timescale, chart of index fossils

Lesson 4

Quick Lab Investigating Events in Earth's History, p. 153
prepare index cards describing events in Earth's history

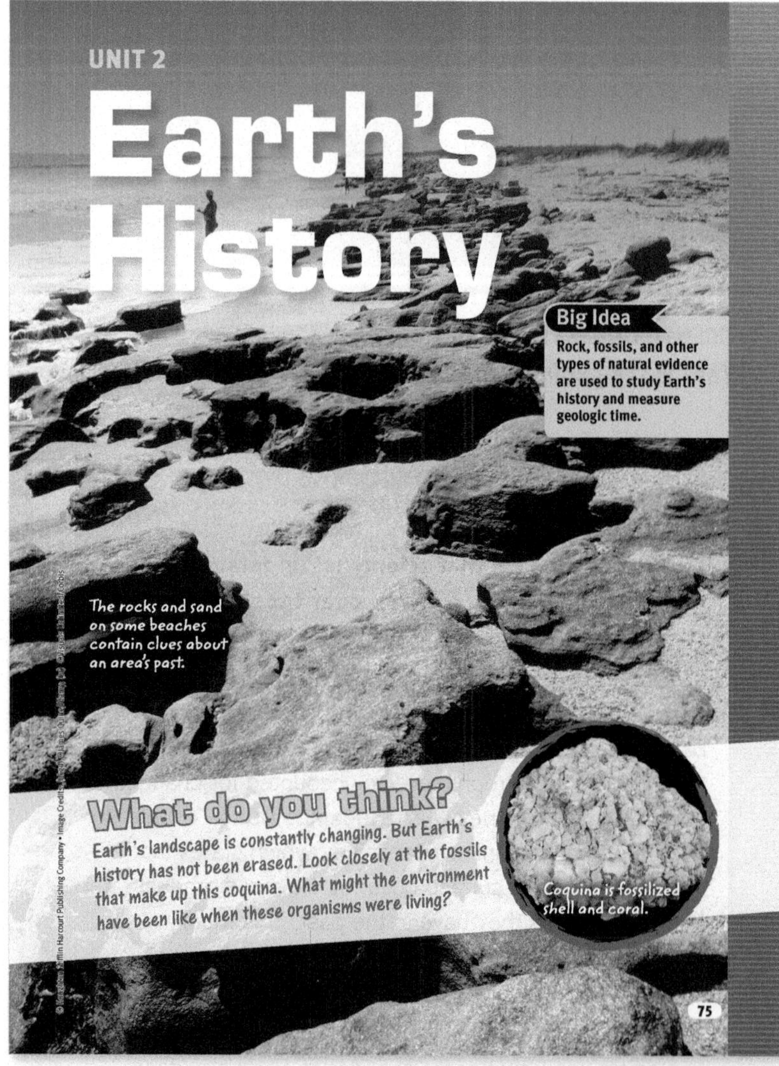
UNIT 2

Earth's History

Big Idea

Rock, fossils, and other types of natural evidence are used to study Earth's history and measure geologic time.

The rocks and sand on some beaches contain clues about an area's past.

What do you think?

Earth's landscape is constantly changing. But Earth's history has not been erased. Look closely at the fossils that make up this coquina. What might the environment have been like when these organisms were living?

Coquina is fossilized shell and coral.

75

What Do You Think?

Invite students to think about what we can learn from fossils.

Ask: What can the fossil of an organism tell us about what the world was like when the organism was alive? Sample answer: A fossil can indicate how Earth's environments have changed. For example, finding the fossil of a marine animal in a place that is now dry land is an indication that salt water once covered that area.

Ask: How can we figure out how old a fossil is? Sample answers: by the rock layer in which it is found; by using dating methods; by linking it to a period in which other organisms lived

Ask: Are you more likely to find fossils in sedimentary rocks or igneous rocks? Why? Sample answer: Fossils are more likely to be found in sedimentary rocks. An organism buried in sediments is sometimes preserved as the sediments harden into sedimentary rock. Igneous rock forms as magma or lava cools and solidifies, which may destroy the remains of an organism.

Video-Based Project

Transforming Earth

Go Online to preview the videos, access teacher support pages, and print student activity worksheets.

Dr. Mike Heithaus introduces students to some very unusual features that result from important processes that shape Earth's surface.

Activities

1 Early Life and Changes in the Atmosphere
2 What Affects Soils?
3 The Pinnacles

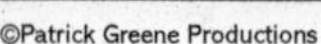
©Patrick Greene Productions

Student Pages 75–77

Earth's History

CITIZEN SCIENCE

Preserving the Past

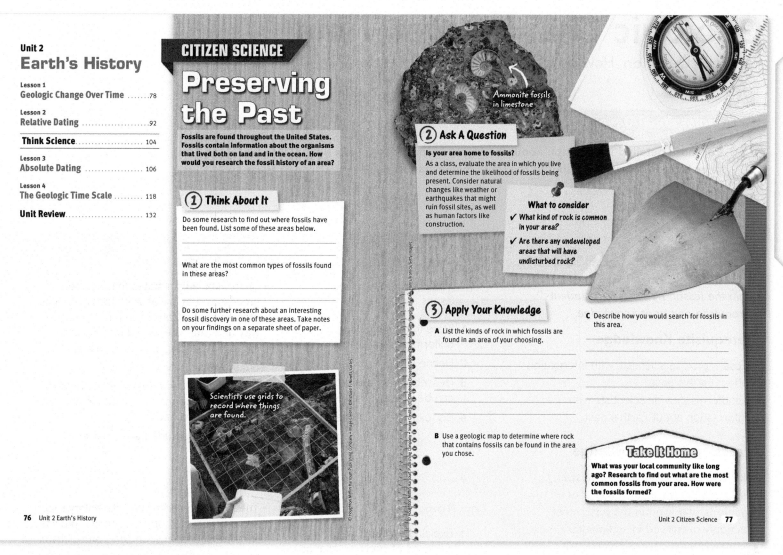

Fossils are found throughout the United States. Fossils contain information about the organisms that lived both on land and in the ocean. How would you research the fossil history of an area?

1 Think About It

Do some research to find out where fossils have been found. List some of these areas below.

What are the most common types of fossils found in these areas?

Do some further research about an interesting fossil discovery in one of these areas. Take notes on your findings on a separate sheet of paper.

Scientists use grids to record where things are found.

Ammonite fossils in limestone

2 Ask A Question

Is your area home to fossils?

As a class, evaluate the area in which you live and determine the likelihood of fossils being present. Consider natural changes like weather or earthquakes that might ruin fossil sites, as well as human factors like construction.

What to consider

- ✓ What kind of rock is common in your area?
- ✓ Are there any undeveloped areas that will have undisturbed rock?

3 Apply Your Knowledge

A List the kinds of rock in which fossils are found in an area of your choosing.

B Use a geologic map to determine where rock that contains fossils can be found in the area you chose.

C Describe how you would search for fossils in this area.

Take It Home

What was your local community like long ago? Research to find out what are the most common fossils from your area. How were the fossils formed?

CITIZEN SCIENCE

Unit Project Preserving the Past

1. Think About It

- Students' answers will vary. They should list a few different areas where fossils have been found.
- Students' answers will vary. They should list any common fossils found in the areas they listed.
- Students' answers will vary. They should choose an area from their list to research further and identify the fossil(s) discovered there.

2. Ask a Question

Students need to consider the types of rock found near where they live and the likelihood that fossils would be preserved in this type of environment. Encourage a class discussion to evaluate this question.

Optional Online rubric: Class Discussion

3. Apply Your Knowledge

A. Students' answers will vary but should include the main types of rock.

B. Students should identify an area on a geologic map and explain why fossils can be found there.

C. Students' plans should identify transportation, equipment, and strategies for finding fossils. Encourage students to consider what types of permission they might need in order to work in their target area.

Take It Home

Students may be able to find information about local fossil discoveries at a museum or park. Direct students to resources that can help them investigate local fossils. Discuss student findings in class.

Optional Online rubric: Class Discussion

Geologic Change over Time

Essential Question How do we learn about Earth's History?

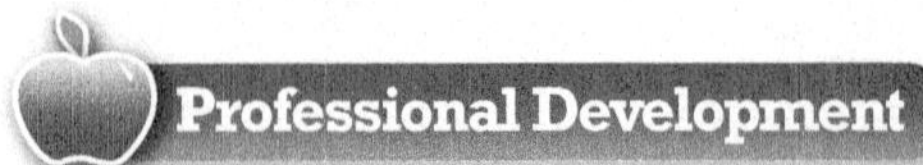

For more detailed information about the topics in this lesson, refer to the Content Refresher in the Unit Opener pages.

Opening Your Lesson

Begin the lesson by assessing students' prerequisite and prior knowledge.

Prerequisite Knowledge

- Fossils provide scientists with information about Earth's past.
- Landforms provide scientists with information about Earth's past.

Accessing Prior Knowledge

Ask: What are fossils? Sample answer: Fossils are the traces or remains of organisms that lived in the past, most commonly preserved in sedimentary rock.

Ask: What can scientists learn from fossils? Sample answer: They can use fossils to learn about organisms that once lived on Earth.

Customize Your Opening

- ☐ **Accessing Prior Knowledge,** above
- ☐ **Print Path** Engage Your Brain, SE p. 79 #1–2
- ☐ **Print Path** Active Reading, SE p. 79 #3–4
- ☐ **Digital Path** Lesson Opener

Key Topics/Learning Goals	Supporting Concepts
Uniformitarianism and Fossils 1 State the principle of uniformitarianism. 2 Define *fossils*. 3 Describe the ways organisms can be preserved as fossils. 4 List examples of trace fossils.	• Uniformitarianism states that geologic processes that are at work today, such as erosion and volcanism, occur in a similar way and rate as they did in the past. • Fossils are the traces or remains of organisms that lived long ago. • Organisms become fossilized by being buried in rock, frozen, trapped in amber or asphalt, or petrified. • Trace fossils include tracks, burrows, and coprolites.
The Rock Record 1 Explain how fossils supply evidence of geologic change. 2 Relate the composition and texture of sedimentary rocks to the environment in which the rocks formed. 3 Describe and give evidence for the movement of continents over time.	• The fossils preserved in sedimentary rock serve as a record of evolution and provide data about past environments and climate. • The composition of sedimentary rock indicates the erosive sources of the sediment. Its texture indicates the environment in which the sediment was transported and deposited. • The continents have been moving throughout Earth's history. At one time, they formed a single landmass, which is evident by the shapes of continents and the distribution of rock types, mountains, and fossils.
Earth's Changing Climate 1 List types of evidence that support that Earth's climate has changed over time.	• Ice cores, sea-floor sediments, and tree rings provide evidence that Earth's climate has changed over time.

Options for Instruction

Two parallel paths provide coverage of the Essential Questions, with a strong **Inquiry** strand woven into each. Follow the **Print Path,** the **Digital Path,** or your customized combination of print, digital, and inquiry.

Print Path

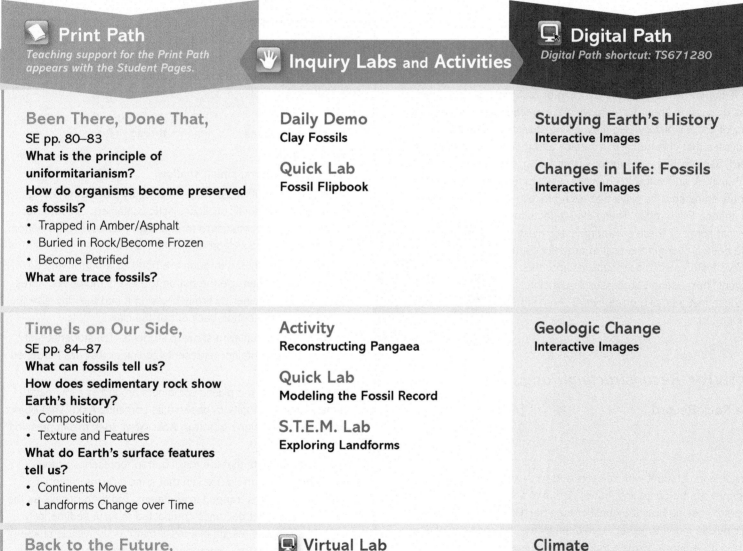

Teaching support for the Print Path appears with the Student Pages.

Been There, Done That,

SE pp. 80–83

What is the principle of uniformitarianism?

How do organisms become preserved as fossils?

- Trapped in Amber/Asphalt
- Buried in Rock/Become Frozen
- Become Petrified

What are trace fossils?

Time Is on Our Side,

SE pp. 84–87

What can fossils tell us?

How does sedimentary rock show Earth's history?

- Composition
- Texture and Features

What do Earth's surface features tell us?

- Continents Move
- Landforms Change over Time

Back to the Future,

SE pp. 88–89

What other materials tell us about Earth's climate history?

- Trees
- Ice
- Sea-Floor Sediments

Inquiry Labs and Activities

Daily Demo

Clay Fossils

Quick Lab

Fossil Flipbook

Activity

Reconstructing Pangaea

Quick Lab

Modeling the Fossil Record

S.T.E.M. Lab

Exploring Landforms

Virtual Lab

Earth's History

Digital Path

Digital Path shortcut: TS671280

Studying Earth's History

Interactive Images

Changes in Life: Fossils

Interactive Images

Geologic Change

Interactive Images

Climate

Interactive Graphics

Options for Assessment

See the Evaluate page for options, including Formative Assessment, Summative Assessment, and Unit Review.

Engage and Explore

Activities and Discussion

Discussion *The Key to the Past*

Engage

Uniformitarianism and Fossils

 whole class
 20 min

Write, *The present is the key to the past* on the board. Explain that this is the cornerstone of the principle of uniformitarianism. Lead a class discussion about how studying the present can help reveal the story of Earth's history. Begin by asking students to brainstorm the processes that change Earth's surface and to list their ideas on the board. Sample ideas may include weathering, erosion, deposition, earthquakes, and volcanic eruptions. Ask students to use the list to identify some specific ways that each process can change Earth today. Then help students to see that some of these same processes must have been at work in the past in order for Earth to have features such as mountains and deep canyons, because the processes responsible for these features take place over a very long time period.

Activity *Reconstructing Pangaea*

The Rock Record

individuals
 45 min first day, then 20 min second day

Provide each student with scissors and two world maps. Have students cut the continents out of one map and treat them as puzzle pieces by seeing how they best fit together. Once students have fit their puzzle maps together, have them locate the positions of Africa and South America. Explain that scientists have discovered fossils of a small, aquatic reptile called *Mesosaurus* and an ancient plant known as *Glossopteris* on both continents. **Ask:** What do the similar fossil findings and the complementary shapes of these two continents suggest? Sample answer: The continents were once joined together.

Labs and Demos

Daily Demo *Clay Fossils*

Engage

Uniformitarianism and Fossils

 whole class
 15 min
 **GUIDED** inquiry

PURPOSE **To demonstrate how a fossil makes an impression in soft sediment**

MATERIALS

- **button with holes**
- **modeling clay**
- **plastic containers, small, shallow**
- **thread**

1 Prepare the "fossil" molds prior to class by placing modeling clay into several small, shallow plastic containers. Smooth out the clay in each container to form a layer that covers the bottom of the container to a depth of about 1.5 cm.

2 Feed a piece of thread through the holes of a button and tie off the thread. Then use the button to make a mold-like impression in each container by firmly pressing it into the clay. Use the thread to pull the button back out of the clay.

3 Hold up one container to show to students. Tell students that the clay in the container represents sediment that has hardened to form rock.

4 **Observing** Pass the plastic containers around to allow each student an opportunity to observe its contents. **Ask:** What object made the impression? a button **Ask:** What does this impression represent? a fossil

5 Explain to students that the fossil button represents a type of fossil known as a mold. Explain that a mold forms when an organism becomes trapped in sediment, and then decays as the sediment around it becomes compacted to form sedimentary rock. This process results in a fossil that has the visible shape of the organism that was entrapped in the sediment.

6 Save one clay mold for use in the next demonstration.

Quick Lab *Fossil Flipbook*

PURPOSE **To model how a fossilized fish could form in what is now desert**

See the Lab Manual or go Online for planning information

DIRECTED inquiry introduces inquiry skills within a structured framework.

GUIDED inquiry develops inquiry skills within a supportive environment.

INDEPENDENT inquiry deepens inquiry skills with student-driven questions or procedures.

Daily Demo *Cast in Wax*

Engage

Uniformitarianism and Fossils

 whole class
 15 min
 **GUIDED** inquiry

PURPOSE **To demonstrate that most fossils are not the actual remains of organisms**

MATERIALS

- candle
- clay mold from previous demonstration
- matches
- safety goggles
- small knife

1 Show students a clay mold from the previous demonstration.
2 Put on safety goggles and light the candle. While students observe, hold the candle over the tray to allow the candle wax to drip into the mold. Tell students that the wax represents minerals that seep into and fill the void left by the mold.
3 Once the wax hardens, use the knife to carefully cut away the clay and remove the wax from the mold.
4 Explain that the wax object represents a kind of fossil called a cast, which forms when minerals fill a mold and harden.

S.T.E.M. Lab *Exploring Landforms*

The Rock Record

 small groups
 45 min
 **GUIDED/INDEPENDENT** inquiry

Students will study the landforms that make up Earth's terrestrial surface.

PURPOSE To make models of landforms

MATERIALS

- card stock
- clay or salt dough
- ice, large block
- measuring cups
- plastic container
- plastic tray
- sand
- potting soil
- state map

Quick Lab *Modeling the Fossil Record*

The Rock Record

 individuals
 30 min
 **DIRECTED** inquiry

Students will look at and examine drawings representing what one area might have looked like 300 million years ago and 150 million years ago. They will then use these pictures to draw a model fossil record.

PURPOSE **To draw a picture to represent the fossil record over 300 million years**

MATERIALS

- colored pencils

Customize Your Labs

See the Lab Manual for lab datasheets.

Go Online for editable lab datasheets.

Activities and Discussion

- ☐ **Discussion** The Key to the Past
- ☐ **Activity** Reconstructing Pangaea

Labs and Demos

- ☐ **Daily Demo** Clay Fossils
- ☐ **Quick Lab** Fossil Flipbook
- ☐ **Daily Demo** Cast in Wax
- ☐ **S.T.E.M. Lab** Exploring Landforms
- ☐ **Quick Lab** Modeling the Fossil Record

Your Resources

Explain Science Concepts

Key Topics	Print Path	Digital Path
Uniformitarianism and Fossils	☐ **Been There, Done That,** SE pp. 80–83 • Active Reading, # 5 • Visualize It!, #6 • Visualize It!, #7–8 • Visualize It!, #9 • Visualize It!, #10 • Active Reading (Annotation strategy), #11 • Visualize It!, #12 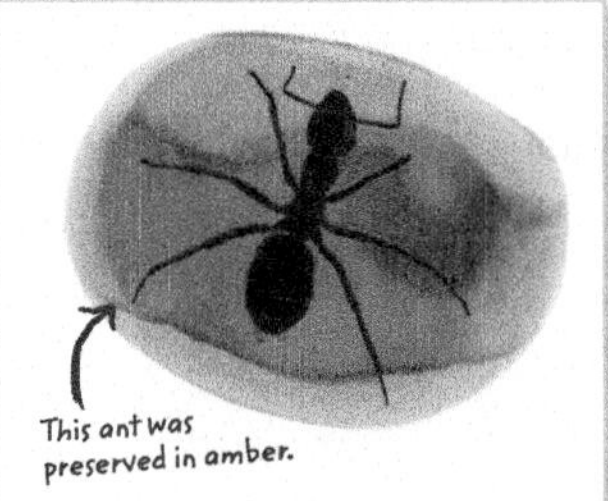	☐ **Studying Earth's History** Learn about the ways Earth changes. ☐ **Changes in Life: Fossils** Learn about different types of fossils. 
The Rock Record	☐ **Time Is on Our Side,** SE pp. 84–87 • Visualize It!, # 13 • Active Reading (Annotation strategy), #14 • Active Reading, #15 • Visualize It!, #16 • Visualize It!, #17 • Visualize It!, #18 • Think Outside the Book!, #19 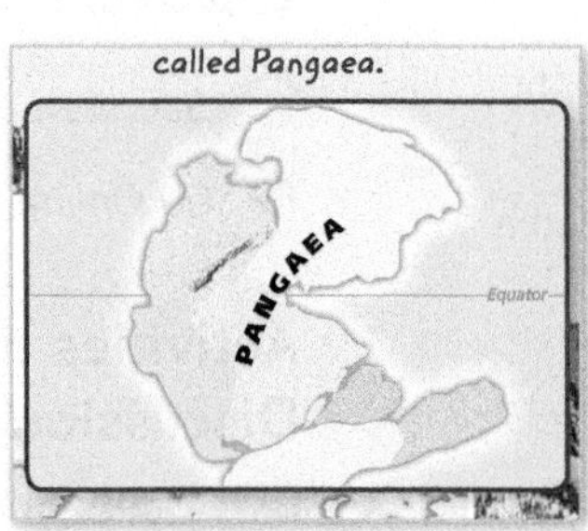	☐ **Geologic Change** Explore the evidence that continents have changed positions over time. 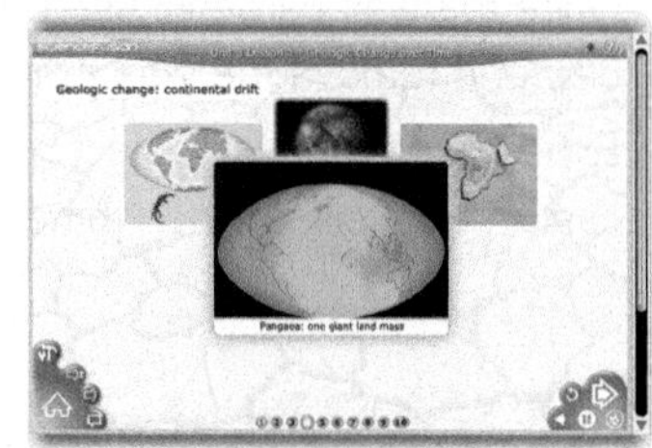
Earth's Changing Climate	☐ **Back to the Future,** SE pp. 88–89 • Active Reading (Annotation strategy), #20 • Visualize It!, #21 • Evaluate, #22 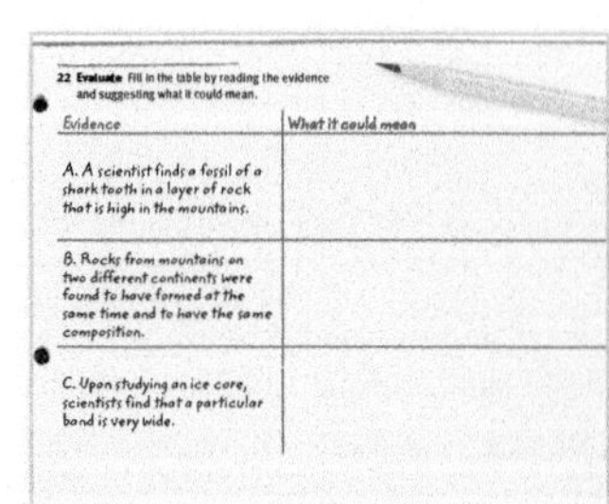 22 **Evaluate** Fill in the table by reading the evidence and suggesting what it could mean. Evidence / What it could mean A. A scientist finds a fossil of a shark tooth in a layer of rock that is high in the mountains. B. Rocks from mountains on two different continents were found to have formed at the same time and to have the same composition. C. Upon studying an ice core, scientists find that a particular band is very wide.	☐ **Climate** Explore types of evidence that support that Earth's climate has changed over time. 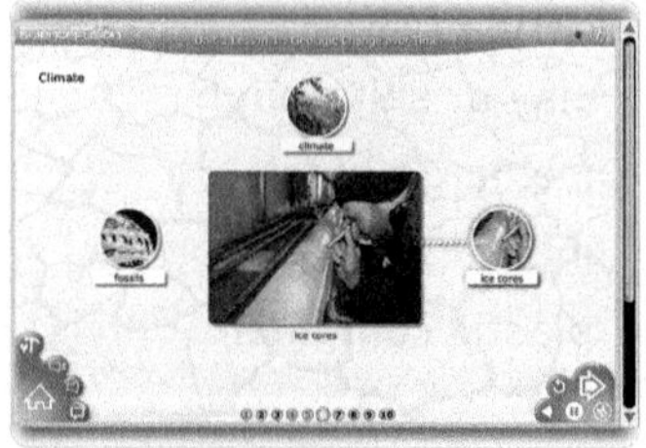

Differentiated Instruction

Basic *Recipe for Fossilization*

Uniformitarianism and Fossils

 individuals
 35 min

Have students develop a table to compare the five ways that organisms become preserved as fossils. Encourage students to include details and sketches that help to describe each method of fossilization.

Advanced *Rarity of Fossils*

The Rock Record

whole class
20 min

Have students evaluate and discuss why fossils are uncommon. Point out that many animals and plants thrived in prehistoric times. **Ask:** Why don't we find more evidence of ancient organisms everywhere we travel? Sample answer: Conditions have to be just right for fossils to form. Because of this, most organisms die and decompose without forming fossils.

ELL *Diagramming Fossil Formation*

Uniformitarianism and Fossils

 individuals
30 min

Have students use the text descriptions of the different ways organisms become preserved as fossils to make easy-to-understand diagrams. For example, students can outline the steps of petrification and draw arrows between each step in the process. Assign each student a different type of fossilization to diagram. Allow them to display their diagrams for all to see.

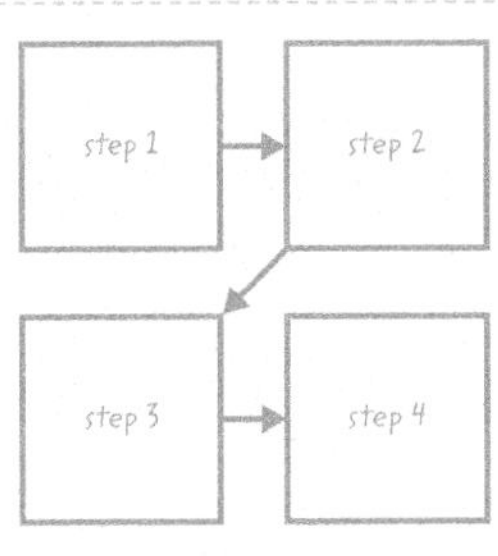

Optional Online resource: Text Details: Sequence support

Lesson Vocabulary

uniformitarianism **fossil** **trace fossil**
climate **ice core**

Previewing Vocabulary

 small groups  35 min

Word Triangles Have students make Word Triangles for each vocabulary term. In their triangles, they should write the term and its definition, a sentence using the term, and an illustration. Have them share their Word Triangles with a partner.

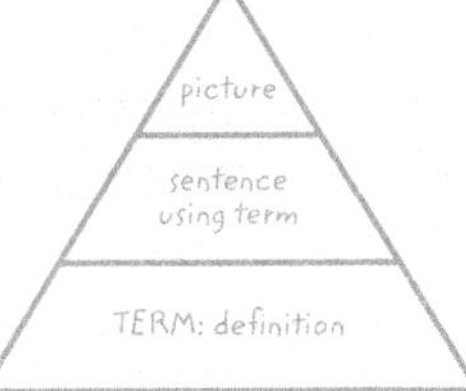

Online Resource: Word Triangle support

Reinforcing Vocabulary

 individuals 30 min

Paragraphs To help students remember the vocabulary words introduced in this lesson, have them write a paragraph or two, describing the ways scientists learn about Earth's geologic and climatic past. Encourage them to use at least five of the vocabulary words in their paragraphs. Explain that they are to come up with descriptive paragraphs, not merely to list each term and its definition.

Customize Your Core Lesson

Core Instruction

- [ ] Print Path choices
- [ ] Digital Path choices

Vocabulary

- [ ] Previewing Vocabulary Word Triangles
- [ ] Reinforcing Vocabulary Paragraphs

Differentiated Instruction

- [ ] Basic Recipe for Fossilization
- [ ] Advanced Rarity of Fossils
- [ ] ELL Diagramming Fossil Formation

Your Resources

Extend Science Concepts

Reinforce and Review

Activity *Geologic Time Review Game*

Synthesizing Key Topics

small groups
25 min

Carousel Review Set up four sheets of chart paper. At the top of the first, write, *What is the principle of uniformitarianism?* On the second, write, *How do fossils form?* On the third, write, *What are some ways that scientists can learn about Earth's geologic past?* And on the last, write, *What are some ways that scientists can learn about Earth's climatic history?*

Divide students into small groups, and assign each group a chart. Give each group a different colored marker. Have groups review their question, discuss their answer, and write a response. After 5 or 10 min, have each group rotate to the next station. Groups should place a check next to each answer they agree with, comment on those they don't agree with, and add their own answers. Continue until all groups have reviewed all charts. Invite each group to share information with the class.

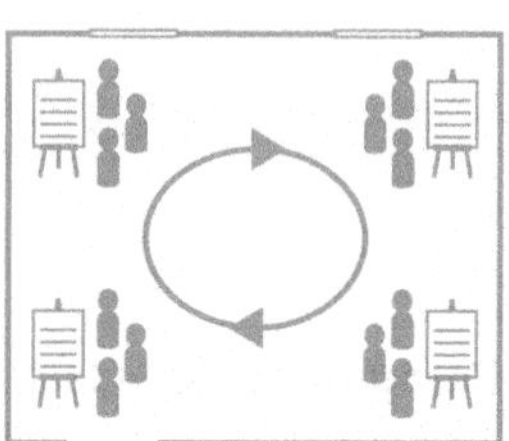

Graphic Organizer

Synthesizing Key Topics

individuals
35 min

Concept Map After students have studied the lesson, ask them to develop a Concept Map that identifies ways scientists study Earth's geologic history. Encourage students to use these terms in their concept maps: ***fossils, ice cores, climate,*** and ***landforms.***

Optional Online resources: Graphic Organizer support

Going Further

Social Studies Connection

Amateur Paleontologists

individuals
varied

Bucky Derflinger, Johnny Maurice, Brad Riney, and Wendy Sloboda are all young people who have made contributions to the field of paleontology. Have students choose one of these young scientists and research their lives, findings, and contributions to paleontology. Then have them write a short report detailing what they found.

Optional Online rubric: Written Pieces

Language Arts Connection

Dinosaur Names

individuals
varied

Paleontologists often give dinosaurs names that describe something unusual about the animal's head, body, feet, or size. These names have Greek or Latin roots. Have students use books or the Internet to choose two dinosaurs. Have them research the names of those dinosaurs to find out what the names mean and how they got their names.

Customize Your Closing

See the Assessment Guide for quizzes and tests.

Go Online to edit and create quizzes and tests.

Reinforce and Review

- ☐ **Activity** Geologic Time Review Game
- ☐ **Graphic Organizer** Concept Map
- ☐ **Print Path** Visual Summary, SE p. 90
- ☐ **Digital Path** Lesson Closer

Evaluate Student Mastery

Formative Assessment

See the teacher support below the Student Pages for additional Formative Assessment questions.

Describe or have students review the ways scientists learn about Earth's past history. **Ask:** What are some ways that organisms are preserved as fossils? Sample answer: by being trapped in amber or asphalt, by being buried in rock, and by becoming frozen or petrified. **Ask:** Besides fossils, what are some ways scientists learn about how Earth has changed over time? Sample answer: by studying its landforms and by examining ice cores, trees, and sea-floor sediments for evidence of climate change

Reteach

Formative assessment may show you that students need reinforcement for certain topics. The resources below are recommended for reteaching. If students were introduced to topics through the Print Path, you can also use the Digital Path for reteaching, and vice versa.

Can be assigned to individual students

Uniformitarianism and Fossils

Discussion The Key to the Past

Daily Demo Clay Fossils

The Rock Record

Activity Reconstructing Pangaea

Quick Lab Modeling the Fossil Record

Earth's Changing Climate

Activity Geologic Time Review Game

Summative Assessment

Alternative Assessment

Fossil Hunters

Online resources: student worksheet; optional rubrics

Geologic Change Over Time

Climb the Ladder: *Fossil Hunters*

You are a member of a local fossil-hunting club that enjoys searching for different types of fossils and learning about Earth's geologic history.

1. Work on your own, with a partner, or with a small group.
2. Choose one item from each rung of the ladder. Check your choices.
3. Have your teacher approve your plan.
4. Submit or present your results.

__ **Fossil Club** Design a Web page for the fossil-hunting club. The page should summarize the ways fossils form. Include pictures of at least two types of fossils on your page.	__ **Club Headquarters** Design a poster for your club's headquarters. On the poster, describe how sedimentary rock can give scientists information about Earth's past. Include at least two images of sedimentary rocks on your poster.
__ **Climate Quiz** Compose a quiz to test your club members' knowledge about the materials that tell us about Earth's climate history. Include at least five questions on your quiz. The answers can be multiple-choice, short answer, or true/false.	__ **Climate Clues** Imagine that members of your club found some fossils. Many of the fossils are of tropical palm fronds and ferns. Present a news report about your club's findings. In your report, explain what these fossils might indicate about the climate in the past.
__ **The Aging Earth** Imagine that your club has been asked to speak at a conference about Earth's age. Present a speech about uniformitarianism. In your speech, define uniformitarianism and explain how it relates to determining Earth's age.	__ **Move Along** Imagine your club is going to perform a short play about the break-up of Pangaea. Write the script. Start your script about 200 million years ago, and include evidence that the continents have been drifting apart since that time.

Going Further

- ☐ Social Studies Connection
- ☐ Language Arts Connection

Formative Assessment

- ☐ Strategies Throughout TE
- ☐ Lesson Review SE

Summative Assessment

- ☐ Alternative Assessment Fossil Hunters
- ☐ Lesson Quiz
- ☐ Unit Tests A and B
- ☐ Unit Review SE End-of-Unit

Your Resources

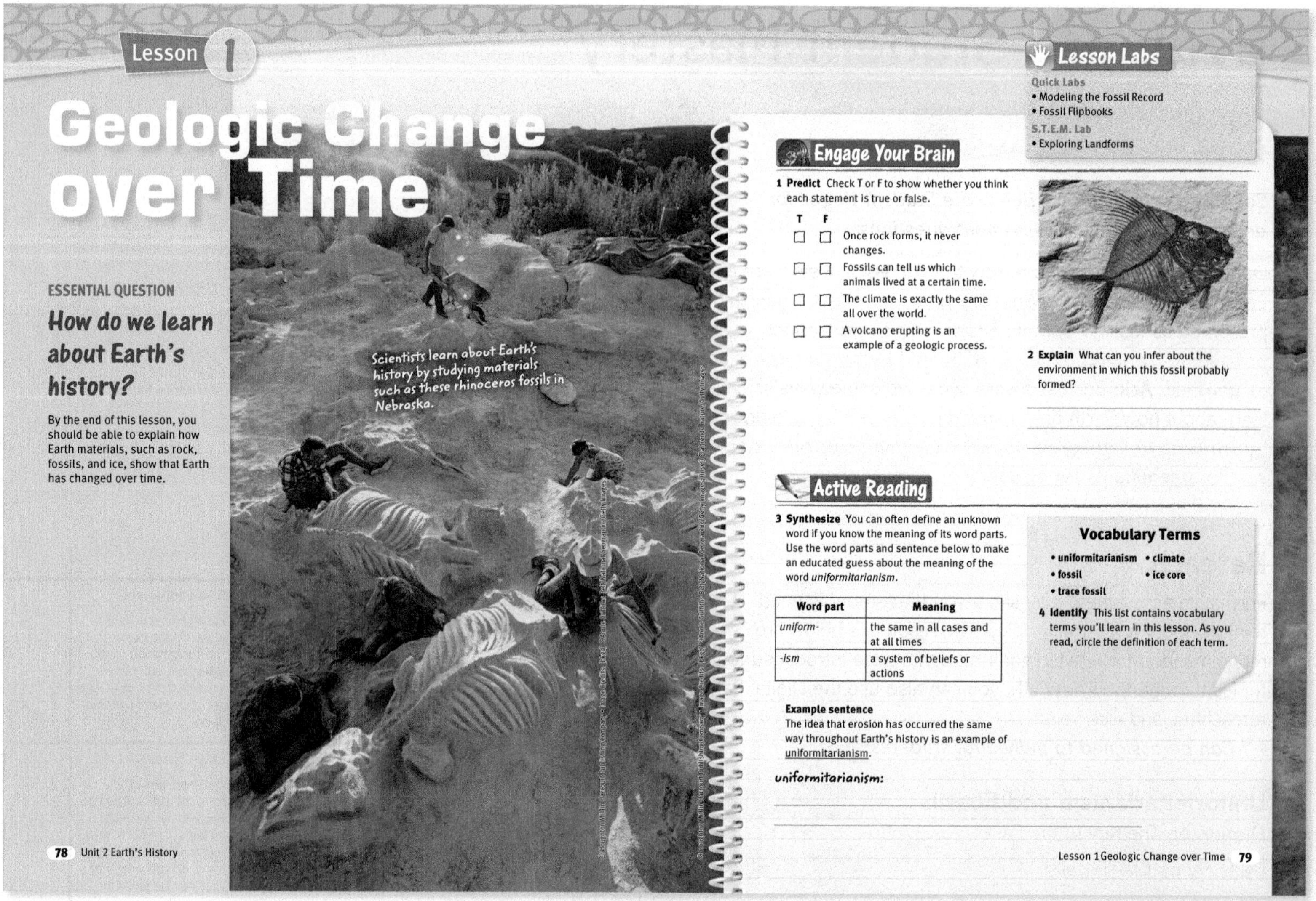

Lesson 1

Geologic Change over Time

ESSENTIAL QUESTION

How do we learn about Earth's history?

By the end of this lesson, you should be able to explain how Earth materials, such as rock, fossils, and ice, show that Earth has changed over time.

Scientists learn about Earth's history by studying materials such as these rhinoceros fossils in Nebraska.

78 Unit 2 Earth's History

Lesson Labs

Quick Labs
- Modeling the Fossil Record
- Fossil Flipbooks

S.T.E.M. Lab
- Exploring Landforms

Engage Your Brain

1 Predict Check T or F to show whether you think each statement is true or false.

T	F	
☐	☐	Once rock forms, it never changes.
☐	☐	Fossils can tell us which animals lived at a certain time.
☐	☐	The climate is exactly the same all over the world.
☐	☐	A volcano erupting is an example of a geologic process.

2 Explain What can you infer about the environment in which this fossil probably formed?

Active Reading

3 Synthesize You can often define an unknown word if you know the meaning of its word parts. Use the word parts and sentence below to make an educated guess about the meaning of the word *uniformitarianism*.

Word part	Meaning
uniform-	the same in all cases and at all times
-ism	a system of beliefs or actions

Example sentence
The idea that erosion has occurred the same way throughout Earth's history is an example of uniformitarianism.

uniformitarianism:

Vocabulary Terms
- uniformitarianism
- climate
- fossil
- ice core
- trace fossil

4 Identify This list contains vocabulary terms you'll learn in this lesson. As you read, circle the definition of each term.

Lesson 1 Geologic Change over Time 79

Answers

Answers for 1–3 should represent students' current thoughts, even if incorrect.

1. F; T; F; T
2. It tells me that the area was under water, because this is a fossil of a fish.
3. Sample answer: believing that things that are happening now have always happened in the same way
4. Students' annotations will vary.

Opening Your Lesson

Have students share their ideas about the fossil (item 2) to assess their prior knowledge of the Key Topics.

Prerequisites: Students should already know how sedimentary rock forms and that rocks on Earth's surface are continually broken down through weathering and transported to new locations through erosion.

Accessing Prior Knowledge: Develop an Anticipation Guide for this lesson. These guides are useful for topics about which students already have some knowledge. The key to the guide is to choose some statements that seem plausible, such as "Most organisms form fossils when they die," but that students will discover to be untrue after they read the material. Have students revisit the statements at the end of the lesson to allow students to evaluate the accuracy of their initial responses.

Optional Online resource: Anticipation Guide support

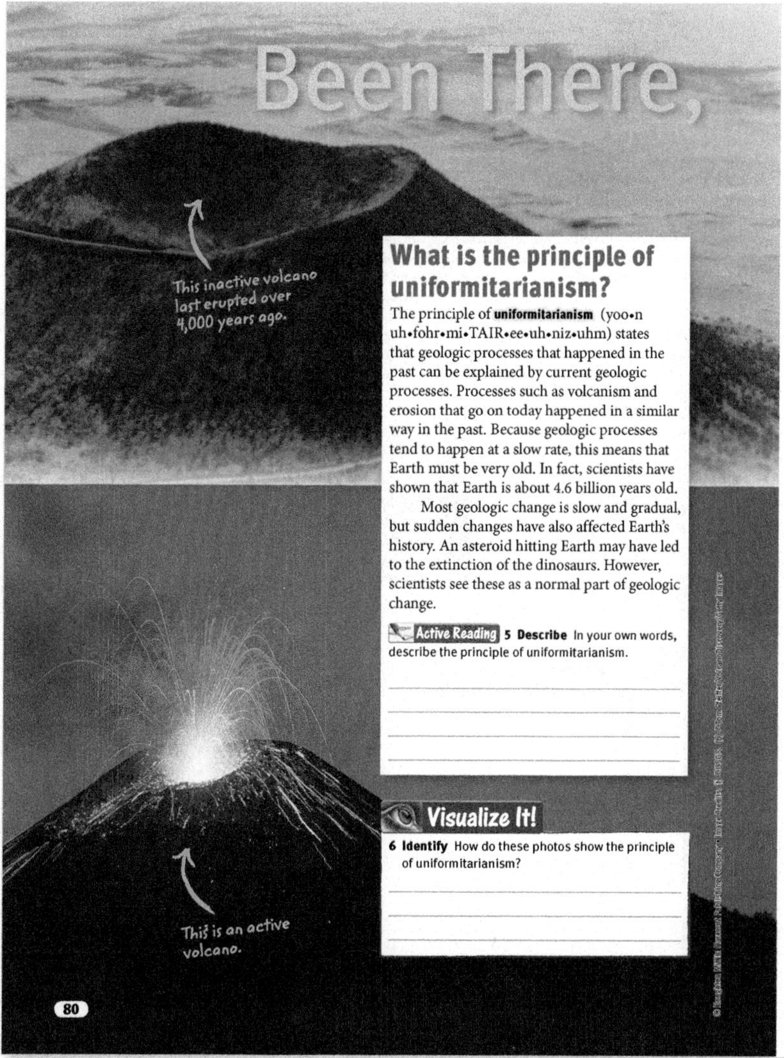

Been There,
This inactive volcano last erupted over 4,000 years ago.
This is an active volcano.

Done That

What is the principle of uniformitarianism?

The principle of **uniformitarianism** (yoo•n uh•fohr•mi•TAIR•ee•uh•niz•uhm) states that geologic processes that happened in the past can be explained by current geologic processes. Processes such as volcanism and erosion that go on today happened in a similar way in the past. Because geologic processes tend to happen at a slow rate, this means that Earth must be very old. In fact, scientists have shown that Earth is about 4.6 billion years old.

Most geologic change is slow and gradual, but sudden changes have also affected Earth's history. An asteroid hitting Earth may have led to the extinction of the dinosaurs. However, scientists see these as a normal part of geologic change.

Active Reading **5 Describe** In your own words, describe the principle of uniformitarianism.

Visualize It!

6 Identify How do these photos show the principle of uniformitarianism?

How do organisms become preserved as fossils?

Organisms can leave evidence of themselves in different ways. **Fossils** are the trace or remains of an organism that lived long ago, most commonly preserved in sedimentary rock. Fossils may be skeletons or body parts, shells, burrows, or ancient coral reefs. Fossils form in many different ways.

Visualize It!

Trapped in Amber

Imagine that an insect is caught in soft, sticky tree sap. Suppose that the insect is covered by more sap, which hardens with the body of the insect inside. Amber is formed when hardened tree sap is buried and preserved in sediment. Some of the best insect fossils, such as the one shown below, are found in amber. Fossil spiders, frogs, and lizards have also been found in amber.

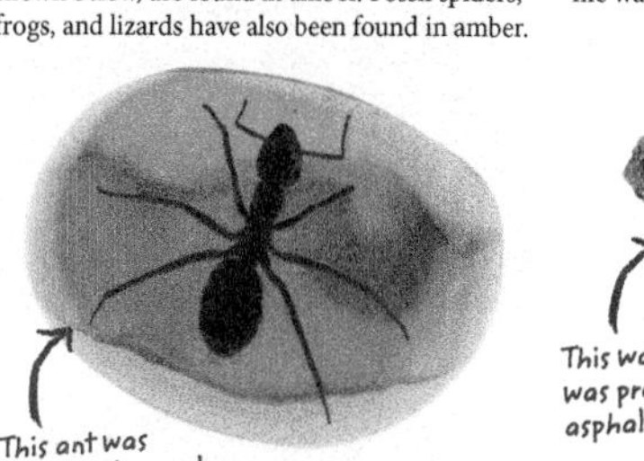

7 Analyze What features of the ant can you still see in this fossil?

Trapped in Asphalt

There are places where asphalt wells up at Earth's surface in thick, sticky pools. One such place is La Brea Tar Pits in California. These asphalt pools have trapped and preserved many fossils over the past 40,000 years, such as the one shown below. Fossils such as these show a lot about what life was like in Southern California in the past.

8 Describe How did this organism become a fossil?

Answers

5. Sample answer: The way that processes like erosion affect Earth today is the same way they did in the past.
6. Volcanism that goes on today (picture on the bottom) happened in a similar way in the past to produce structures like the inactive volcano (picture on the top).
7. Almost all of this ant's features have been preserved: for example, legs, body, head, and antennae.
8. It got trapped in asphalt and was preserved in it.

Probing Questions GUIDED Inquiry

Apply Scientists think Earth's surface changes today in the same ways it has always changed, and that by applying what they have come to know about these changes, they can accurately determine what Earth was like in the past. **Ask:** What example can you provide of a surface change that occurs on Earth today that has probably happened in the same way in the past? Sample answer: erosion and deposition, volcanic eruptions

Building Reading Skills

Concept Map Have students develop a Concept Map that describes ways organisms become preserved as fossils. The core of the Concept Map should read, *How Organisms Are Preserved as Fossils.* Students can then add connecting lines and circles to identify the different ways fossils form as they continue the lesson.

Optional Online resource: Concept Map support

Learning Alert

Rancho La Brea Tar Pits Although called tar pits, this famous landmark actually contains asphalt, not tar. Asphalt is a type of bitumen found in a natural state or obtained by distilling oil. Tar is obtained by the distillation of coal, wood, or slate.

Buried in Rock

When an organism dies, it often starts to decay or is eaten by other organisms. Sometimes, however, organisms are quickly buried by sediment when they die. The sediment slows down decay and can protect parts of the body from damage. Hard parts of organisms, such as shells and bones, do not break down as easily as soft parts do. So, when sediments become rock, the hard parts of animals are preserved and become part of the rock as the sediments harden.

Visualize It! 9 **Analyze** What part of the organism was preserved as a fossil in this rock?

Ammonites once lived in shells in ancient seas.

Become Frozen

In very cold places on Earth, the soil can be frozen all the time. An animal that dies there may also be frozen. It is frozen with skin and flesh, as well as bones. Because cold temperatures slow down decay, many types of frozen fossils are preserved from the last ice age.

Visualize It! 10 **Compare** What information can this fossil give that fossils preserved in rock cannot?

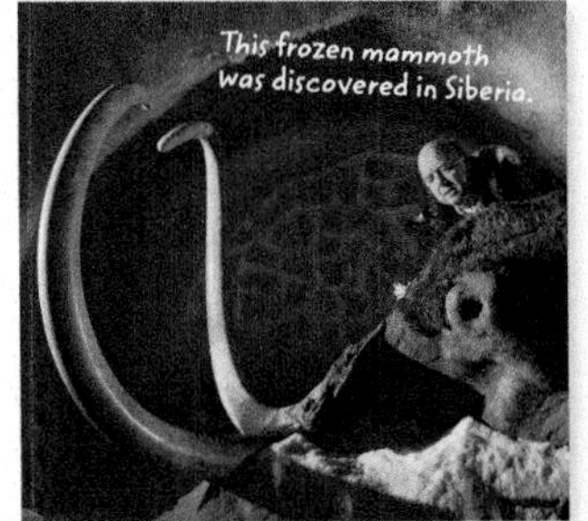
This frozen mammoth was discovered in Siberia.

Become Petrified

Petrification (pet•ruh•fi•KAY•shuhn) happens when an organism's tissues are replaced by minerals. In some petrified wood, minerals have replaced all of the wood. A sample of petrified wood is shown at the right. This wood is in the Petrified Forest National Park in Arizona.

A similar thing happens when the pore space in an organism's hard tissue, such as bone, is filled up with minerals.

This petrified wood is in Arizona.

82 Unit 2 Earth's History

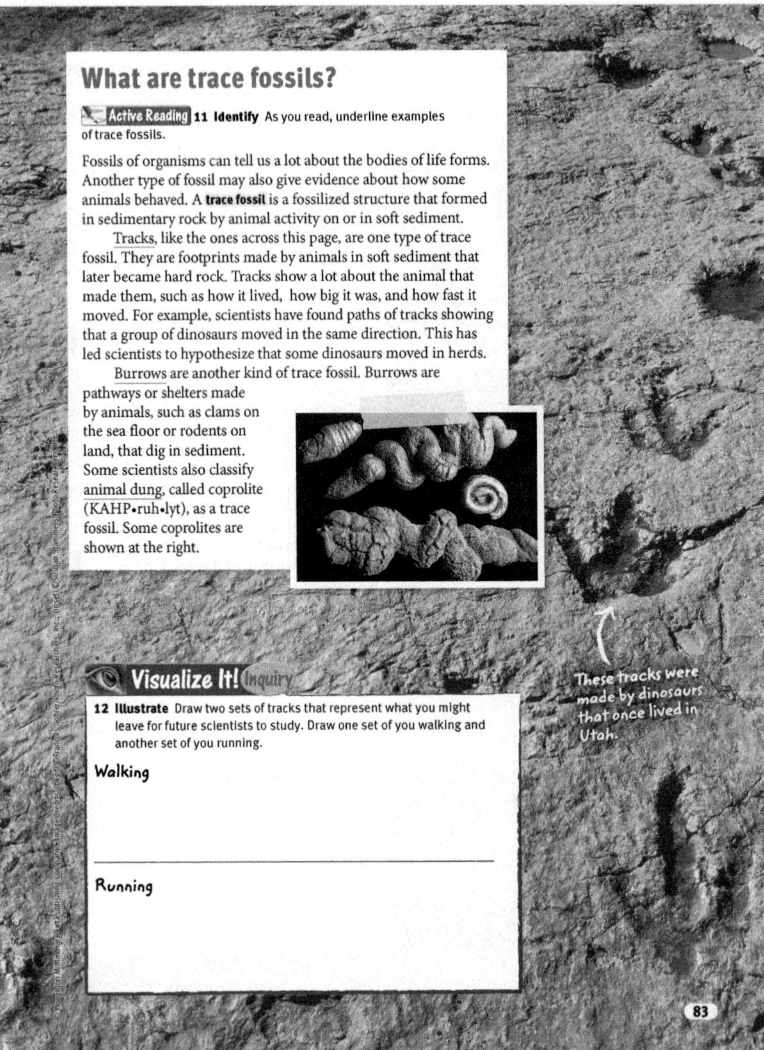

What are trace fossils?

Active Reading 11 **Identify** As you read, underline examples of trace fossils.

Fossils of organisms can tell us a lot about the bodies of life forms. Another type of fossil may also give evidence about how some animals behaved. A **trace fossil** is a fossilized structure that formed in sedimentary rock by animal activity on or in soft sediment.

Tracks, like the ones across this page, are one type of trace fossil. They are footprints made by animals in soft sediment that later became hard rock. Tracks show a lot about the animal that made them, such as how it lived, how big it was, and how fast it moved. For example, scientists have found paths of tracks showing that a group of dinosaurs moved in the same direction. This has led scientists to hypothesize that some dinosaurs moved in herds.

Burrows are another kind of trace fossil. Burrows are pathways or shelters made by animals, such as clams on the sea floor or rodents on land, that dig in sediment. Some scientists also classify animal dung, called coprolite (KAHP•ruh•lyt), as a trace fossil. Some coprolites are shown at the right.

These tracks were made by dinosaurs that once lived in Utah.

Visualize It! Inquiry

12 **Illustrate** Draw two sets of tracks that represent what you might leave for future scientists to study. Draw one set of you walking and another set of you running.

Walking

Running

83

Answers

9. Its shell was preserved.
10. Things like skin and fur are still visible. These are not in fossils that are preserved in rock.
11. *See students' pages for annotations.*
12. Students should draw human footprints that are spaced further apart in the running set of tracks than in the walking set of tracks.

Interpreting Visuals

Ask students to compare and contrast the images of the fossils formed in different ways. **Ask:** Which methods seem to preserve fossils in a way that provide the most information about the organism? Sample answer: Fossils preserved in amber or that had been frozen, because they provide the most complete specimens.

Building Reading Skills

Idea Wheel Have students draw a large circle with a smaller circle inside. Have them divide the outer ring into five sections. Have them write the word *fossils* in the center ring. Have them label the sections of the outer ring with these preservation methods: *amber, asphalt, rocks, ice, petrification*. Then have them describe how a fossil is preserved by each method.

Using Annotations

Text Structure: Details Many types of fossils are discussed in this section. The annotation asks students to underline examples of trace fossils. **For greater depth**, have students underline the details about each of the different types of fossils on the previous two pages and make a chart that summarizes each fossil type.

Time Is on Our Side

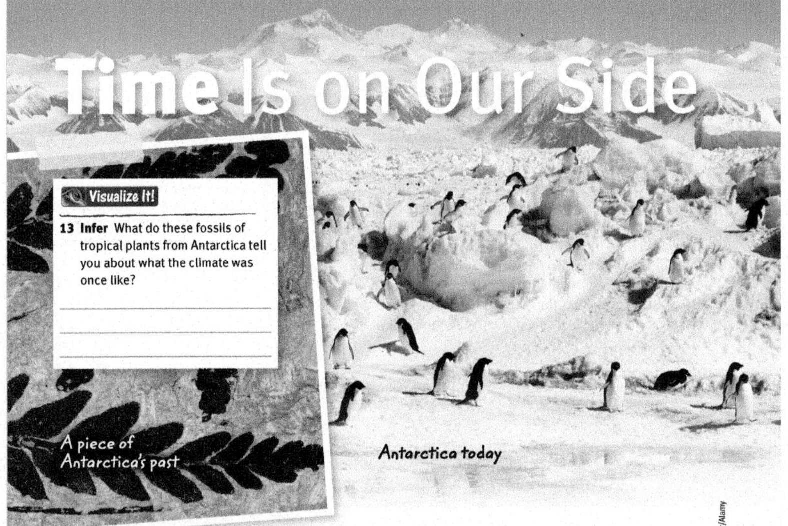

Visualize It!

13 Infer What do these fossils of tropical plants from Antarctica tell you about what the climate was once like?

A piece of Antarctica's past

Antarctica today

What can fossils tell us?

Active Reading

14 Identify As you read, underline two types of changes on Earth that fossils can give information about.

All of the fossils that have been discovered on Earth are called the *fossil record*. The fossil record shows part of the history of life on Earth. It is only part of the history because some things are still unknown. Not all the organisms that ever lived have left behind fossils. Also, there are many fossils that have not been discovered yet. Even so, fossils that are available do provide important information about Earth's history.

Fossils can tell scientists about environmental changes over time. The types of fossils preserved in sedimentary rock show what the environment was like when the organisms were alive. For example, fish fossils indicate that an aquatic environment was present. Palm fronds mean a tropical environment was present. Scientists have found fossils of trees and dinosaurs in Antarctica, so the climate there must have been warm in the past.

Fossils can also tell scientists how life forms have changed over time. Major changes in Earth's environmental conditions and surface can influence an organism's survival and the types of adaptations that a species must have to survive. To learn about how life on Earth has changed, scientists study relationships between different fossils and between fossils and living organisms.

How does sedimentary rock show Earth's history?

Rock and mineral fragments move from one place to another during erosion. Eventually, this sediment is deposited in layers. As new layers of sediment are deposited, they cover older layers. Older layers become compacted. Dissolved minerals, such as calcite and quartz, separate from water that passes through the sediment. This forms a natural cement that holds the rock and mineral fragments together in sedimentary rock.

Scientists use different characteristics to classify sedimentary rock. These provide evidence of the environment that the sedimentary rock formed in.

Composition

The composition of sedimentary rock shows the source of the sediment that makes up the rock. Some sedimentary rock forms when rock or mineral fragments are cemented together. Sandstone, shown below, forms when sand grains are deposited and buried, then cemented together. Other sedimentary rock forms from the remains of once-living plants and animals. Most limestone forms from the remains of animals that lived in the ocean. Another sedimentary rock, called coal, forms underground from partially decomposed plant material that is buried beneath sediment.

Active Reading **15 Describe** What processes can cause rock to break apart into sediment?

Texture and Features

The texture of sedimentary rock shows the environment in which the sediment was carried and deposited. Sedimentary rock is arranged in layers. Layers can differ from one another, depending on the kind, size, and color of their sediment. Features on sedimentary rock called *ripple marks* record the motion of wind or water waves over sediment. An example of sedimentary rock with ripple marks is shown below. Other features, called *mud cracks*, form when fine-grained sediments at the bottom of a shallow body of water are exposed to the air and dry out. Mud cracks show that an ancient lake, stream, or ocean shoreline was once a part of an area.

Visualize It!

16 Identify Which arrow shows the direction that water was moving to make these ripple marks?

Sandstone

These are ripple marks in sandstone.

Answers

13. Sample answer: Antarctica was once a very warm environment.
14. *See students' pages for annotations.*
15. Processes like weathering and erosion can cause rock to break apart into sediment.
16. C

Discussion

Amateur Fossil Collecting Have students debate the pros and cons of amateur fossil collecting. Tell them that many amateur fossil collectors have made amazing discoveries that have helped to advance the field of paleontology. In other cases, amateur fossil collectors have lost important information by improperly removing fossils, by not recording data about locations or associated fossils, or by failing to share specimens with research institutions for further study. Point out that it is illegal to collect fossils from national or state parks without a permit that allows you to do so. It is also illegal to remove vertebrate fossils from public lands without a permit.

Learning Alert MISCONCEPTION

Fossils and Organism Remains Many people think fossils are the actual remains of organisms, but this is rarely true. Many fossils are molds, an impression or cavity in the shape of the organism that forms before the actual remains of the organism decompose. Fossil casts form as sediments or minerals fill a cavity left by a decomposed organism, creating a fairly accurate replica of the body part or organism that left the initial impression. Replacement of an organism's tissues by minerals is one of the ways in which fossils look like an organism but are not the actual tissue of the organism.

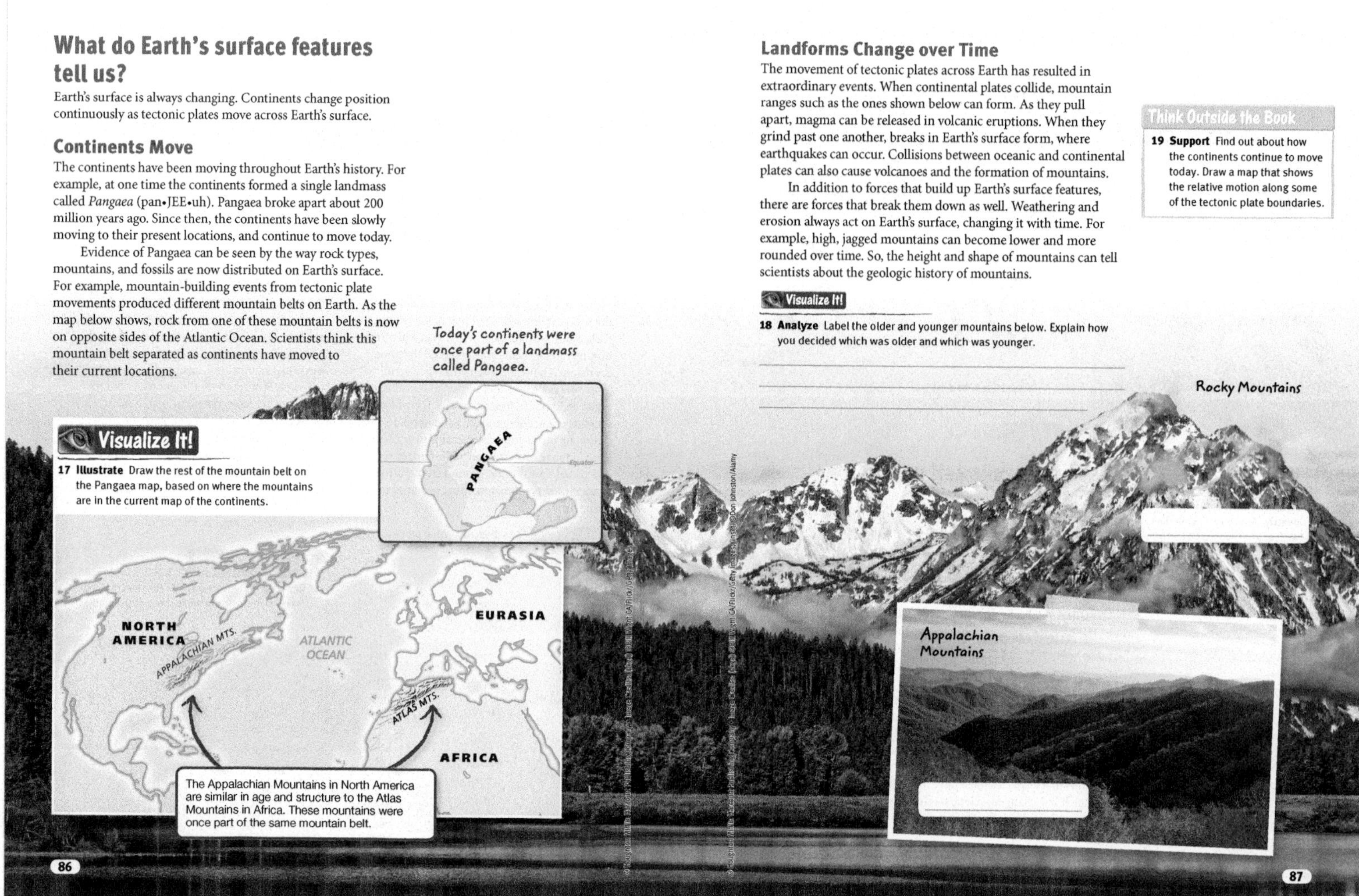

What do Earth's surface features tell us?

Earth's surface is always changing. Continents change position continuously as tectonic plates move across Earth's surface.

Continents Move

The continents have been moving throughout Earth's history. For example, at one time the continents formed a single landmass called *Pangaea* (pan•JEE•uh). Pangaea broke apart about 200 million years ago. Since then, the continents have been slowly moving to their present locations, and continue to move today.

Evidence of Pangaea can be seen by the way rock types, mountains, and fossils are now distributed on Earth's surface. For example, mountain-building events from tectonic plate movements produced different mountain belts on Earth. As the map below shows, rock from one of these mountain belts is now on opposite sides of the Atlantic Ocean. Scientists think this mountain belt separated as continents have moved to their current locations.

Today's continents were once part of a landmass called Pangaea.

Visualize It!

17 Illustrate Draw the rest of the mountain belt on the Pangaea map, based on where the mountains are in the current map of the continents.

The Appalachian Mountains in North America are similar in age and structure to the Atlas Mountains in Africa. These mountains were once part of the same mountain belt.

86

Landforms Change over Time

The movement of tectonic plates across Earth has resulted in extraordinary events. When continental plates collide, mountain ranges such as the ones shown below can form. As they pull apart, magma can be released in volcanic eruptions. When they grind past one another, breaks in Earth's surface form, where earthquakes can occur. Collisions between oceanic and continental plates can also cause volcanoes and the formation of mountains.

In addition to forces that build up Earth's surface features, there are forces that break them down as well. Weathering and erosion always act on Earth's surface, changing it with time. For example, high, jagged mountains can become lower and more rounded over time. So, the height and shape of mountains can tell scientists about the geologic history of mountains.

Think Outside the Book

19 Support Find out about how the continents continue to move today. Draw a map that shows the relative motion along some of the tectonic plate boundaries.

Visualize It!

18 Analyze Label the older and younger mountains below. Explain how you decided which was older and which was younger.

87

Answers

17. Students should draw the mountains as a continuous belt that includes parts of Pangaea that are near the center of the landmass; look for corresponding colors on the maps of today's continents to identify corresponding areas.
18. Students should indicate the Appalachians as older and the Rocky Mountains as younger. Sample answer: I decided that the Appalachian Mountains are older because they are more rounded looking than the Rocky Mountains are.
19. Students should demonstrate that Earth's landmasses are still continually moving and not just part of Earth's history.

Formative Assessment

Ask: What are two pieces of evidence that help to support the fact that at one time, Earth's continents formed a single landmass? Sample answer: The shapes of the coastlines of some continents appear as if they fit together; rocks types, mountains, and fossils from different parts of the world that appear to have once been joined are similar. **Prompt:** Use the information presented in the maps of the continents and Pangaea to support your response.

Interpreting Visuals

Have students look at the images of the Rocky Mountains and the Appalachian Mountains. Ask them to compare them. **Ask:** What differences do you observe in the shapes of the mountains in each range? Sample answer: The Appalachian Mountains have a gentler slope than the Rocky Mountains. **Ask:** What processes account for the difference in shape? Sample answer: Weathering has more greatly affected (worn down) the Appalachian Mountains and erosion has carried the weathered particles away. **Ask:** What does this suggest about the ages of the two mountain ranges? Sample answer: The Appalachian Mountains are older because their gentle peaks suggest that they have been more greatly affected by weathering and erosion than the steep peaks of the Rocky Mountains.

Back to the Future

What other materials tell us about Earth's climate history?

The **climate** of an area describes the weather conditions in the area over a long period of time. Climate is mostly determined by temperature and precipitation. In addition to using fossils, scientists also analyze other materials to study how Earth's climate and environmental conditions have changed over time.

Active Reading

20 Identify As you read the next two pages, underline the evidence that scientists use to learn about Earth's climate history.

Trees

When most trees grow, a new layer of wood is added to the trunk every year. This forms rings around the circumference (suhr•KUHM•fuhr•uhns) of the tree, as shown at the right. These rings tell the age of the tree. Some trees are over 2,000 years old. Scientists can use tree rings to find out about the climate during the life of the tree. If a tree ring is thick, it means the tree grew well—there was plenty of rain and favorable temperatures existed at that time. Thin tree rings mean the growing conditions were poor.

Tree rings tell the age of a tree and what the climate was like.

Visualize It! **21 Analyze** What is the time frame for which this tree can give information about Earth's climate?

Sea-Floor Sediments

Evidence about past climates can also be found deep beneath the ocean floor. Scientists remove and study long cylinders of sediment from the ocean floor, such as the one shown at the right. Preserved in these sediments are fossil remains of microscopic organisms that have died and settled on the ocean floor. These remains build up in layers, over time. If certain organisms are present, it can mean that the climate was particularly cold or warm at a certain time. The chemical composition of sediments, especially of the shells of certain microorganisms, can also be important. It shows what the composition was of the ocean water and atmosphere when the organisms were alive.

These scientists are studying sediment from the Ross Sea in Antarctica.

Ice

Icecaps are found in places such as Iceland and islands in the Arctic. The icecaps formed as older snow was squeezed into ice by new snow falling on top of it. Scientists can drill down into icecaps to collect a long cylinder of ice, called an **ice core**.

Ice cores, such as the ones shown in these photographs, give a history of Earth's climate over time. Some ice cores have regular layers, called bands, which form each year. Band size shows how much precipitation fell during a given time. The composition of water and concentration of gases in the ice core show the conditions of the atmosphere at the time that the ice formed.

Scientists study ice cores to find out about amounts of precipitation in the past.

22 Evaluate Fill in the table by reading the evidence and suggesting what it could mean.

Evidence	What it could mean
A. A scientist finds a fossil of a shark tooth in a layer of rock that is high in the mountains.	
B. Rocks from mountains on two different continents were found to have formed at the same time and to have the same composition.	
C. Upon studying an ice core, scientists find that a particular band is very wide.	

Answers

20. *See students' pages for annotations.*
21. This tree can give information about Earth's climate between 1796 and 1996.
22. A. This might mean that the area that is now high on a mountain was once under water.

    B. This might mean that the mountains were once on the same continent.

    C. This might mean that during the time frame that the band formed, there was a great deal of precipitation.

Interpreting Visuals

Have students look at the images of the tree rings and the ice core sample. **Ask:** How can ice cores and tree rings reveal conditions and changes in the environment? Sample answer: Tree rings vary in width, with the thickest rings indicating wet years; therefore, tree rings record changes in climate over time. Ice cores have regular layers called bands that form each year. Band size shows how much precipitation fell within a year. The composition of water and concentrations of gases in the ice core identify the conditions of the atmosphere at the time the ice formed.

Formative Assessment

Ask: What are three ways that scientists learn about past climate conditions on Earth? Sample answer: by studying tree rings, by studying sea-floor sediments, and by studying ice cores **Ask:** What is a limitation of using tree rings to determine past climate conditions? Sample answer: The rings provide information about climate conditions only during the period when the tree was living and growing.

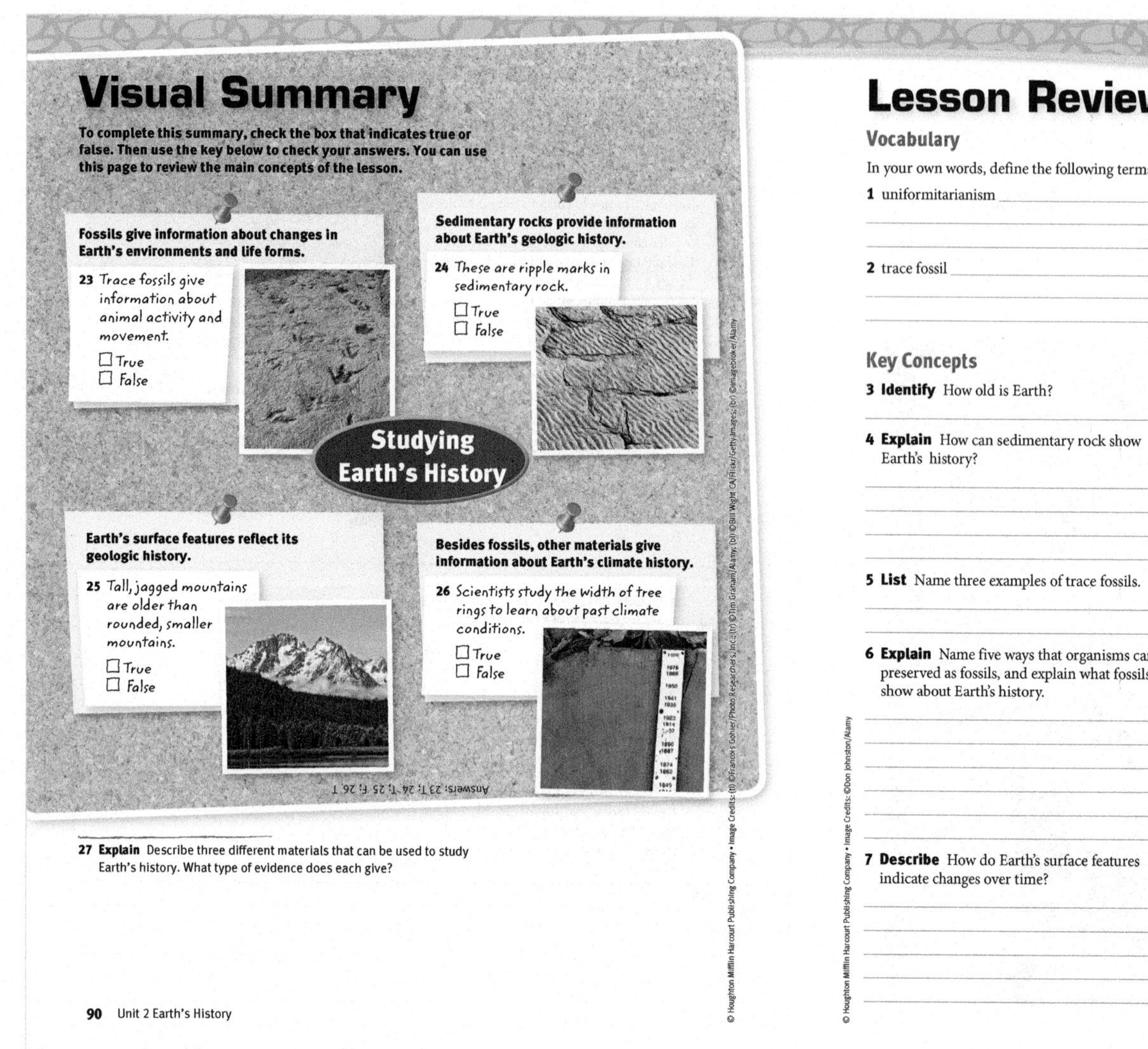

Visual Summary

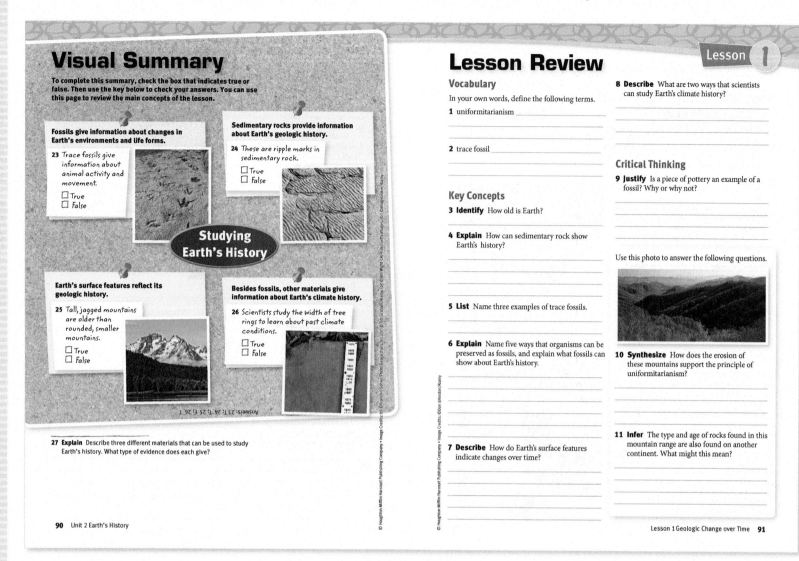

To complete this summary, check the box that indicates true or false. Then use the key below to check your answers. You can use this page to review the main concepts of the lesson.

Studying Earth's History

Fossils give information about changes in Earth's environments and life forms.

23 Trace fossils give information about animal activity and movement.
☐ True
☐ False

Sedimentary rocks provide information about Earth's geologic history.

24 These are ripple marks in sedimentary rock.
☐ True
☐ False

Earth's surface features reflect its geologic history.

25 Tall, jagged mountains are older than rounded, smaller mountains.
☐ True
☐ False

Besides fossils, other materials give information about Earth's climate history.

26 Scientists study the width of tree rings to learn about past climate conditions.
☐ True
☐ False

Answers: 23 T; 24 T; 25 F; 26 T

27 **Explain** Describe three different materials that can be used to study Earth's history. What type of evidence does each give?

90 Unit 2 Earth's History

Lesson Review

Vocabulary

In your own words, define the following terms.

1 uniformitarianism

2 trace fossil

Key Concepts

3 **Identify** How old is Earth?

4 **Explain** How can sedimentary rock show Earth's history?

5 **List** Name three examples of trace fossils.

6 **Explain** Name five ways that organisms can be preserved as fossils, and explain what fossils can show about Earth's history.

7 **Describe** How do Earth's surface features indicate changes over time?

8 **Describe** What are two ways that scientists can study Earth's climate history?

Critical Thinking

9 **Justify** Is a piece of pottery an example of a fossil? Why or why not?

Use this photo to answer the following questions.

10 **Synthesize** How does the erosion of these mountains support the principle of uniformitarianism?

11 **Infer** The type and age of rocks found in this mountain range are also found on another continent. What might this mean?

Lesson 1 Geologic Change over Time 91

Visual Summary Answers

23. T
24. T
25. F
26. T
27. Three of the following materials: rock, fossils, trees, sea-floor sediment, and ice. The types of information that each material provides include environmental and climate changes, in addition to species adaptations.

Lesson Review Answers

1. Sample answer: The same geologic processes that happen now happened in the same way in the past.
2. Sample answer: marks of an animal's activity that are preserved
3. approximately 4.6 billion years old
4. It reflects the environment that the sediment was deposited in and the source of the sediment.
5. tracks, burrows, and coprolites
6. Trapped in amber, trapped in asphalt, buried in rock, frozen, petrification; they can show how the environment has changed and how organisms adapted over time.
7. Continents move and surfaces change by processes such as mountain building and erosion.
8. Students choose from two of the following: fossils, tree ring width, composition of sea-floor sediment, and width and composition of ice cores.
9. No, because it was not once a living organism and does not represent a trace of an organism's activity.
10. They look this way from erosion. Erosion has occurred the same way throughout Earth's history.
11. The two continents were once part of the same landmass.

Teacher Notes

Student Pages 90–91

Relative Dating

Essential Question How are the relative ages of rock measured?

For more detailed information about the topics in this lesson, refer to the Content Refresher in the Unit Opener pages.

Opening Your Lesson

Begin the lesson by assessing students' prerequisite and prior knowledge.

Prerequisite Knowledge

- Principle of uniformitarianism
- How sedimentary and igneous rocks form
- Definitions of *erosion* and *deposition*

Accessing Prior Knowledge

Ask: How can rocks tell scientists about the past? Sample answer: The composition and structure of rock units can tell scientists about the conditions of different time periods.

Ask: How can fossils tell scientists about the past? Sample answer: They can tell scientists about different plants and animals that lived during certain time periods.

Customize Your Opening

- ☐ **Accessing Prior Knowledge,** above
- ☐ **Print Path** Engage Your Brain, SE p. 93 #1–2
- ☐ **Print Path** Active Reading SE p. 93 #3–4
- ☐ **Digital Path** Lesson Opener

Key Topics/Learning Goals	Supporting Concepts
Dating Undisturbed Rock Layers 1 Define *relative dating.* 2 Describe deposition of sedimentary rock layers. 3 Summarize and apply the law of superposition.	• Relative dating is used to find if one object or event is older or younger than another. • Sedimentary rock forms in horizontal layers and will stay that way if not disturbed. • The law of superposition states that an undisturbed sedimentary rock layer is older than the layers above it and younger than the layers below it.
Dating Disturbed Rock Layers 1 Define *unconformity.* 2 Explain and apply the law of crosscutting relationships.	• An unconformity is a gap in the geologic record caused by erosion or a pause in deposition. • The law of crosscutting relationships states that a fault or body of rock is younger than any rock it cuts through.
Fossils and Relative Dating 1 Summarize how scientists can use fossils to determine the relative age of rock layers.	• A rock layer that contains a fossil of an earlier life form is relatively older than a rock layer that contains a fossil of a more recent life form.
Geologic Columns 1 Describe geologic columns and their use.	• A geologic column is an ordered arrangement of rock layers based on their relative ages that is used to identify the relative ages of rock layers that are located in different regions.

Options for Instruction

Two parallel paths provide coverage of the Essential Questions, with a strong **Inquiry** strand woven into each. Follow the **Print Path,** the **Digital Path,** or your customized combination of print, digital, and inquiry.

 Print Path *Teaching support for the Print Path appears with the Student Pages.*	 Inquiry Labs and Activities	Digital Path *Digital Path shortcut: TS671210*
Who's First?, SE pp. 94–95 **What is relative dating?** **How are undisturbed rock layers dated?** • Using Superposition	**Quick Lab** **Layers of Sedimentary Rock** **Daily Demo** **Line Up!**	**Geologic Time Scale** **Interactive Images**
How Disturbing! SE pp. 96–97 **How are sedimentary rock layers disturbed?** • By Titling and Folding • By Faults and Intrusions • By Unconformities	**Activity** **When Did It Happen?** **Quick Lab** **Ordering Rock Layers**	**Missing Layers** **Interactive Images** **Geologic Time Scale: Crosscutting** **Interactive Images**
I'm Cutting In!, SE p. 98 **How are rock layers ordered?**	**Activity** **Cheesy Rocks**	**Fossils** **Interactive Images** **The Age of Fossils** **Interactive Images**
So Far Away, SE pp. 100–101 **How are fossils used to determine relative ages of rocks?** **How are geologic columns used to compare relative ages of rocks?**	**Virtual Lab** **Ordering Rock Layers** **Exploration Lab** **Earth's History**	**Geologic Columns** **Interactive Images**

Options for Assessment

See the Evaluate page for options, including Formative Assessment, Summative Assessment, and Unit Review.

Engage and Explore

Activities and Discussion

Activity *When Did It Happen?*

Introducing Key Topics

 individuals, then pairs
25 min

Have students choose ten events or milestones from their life, such as learning to walk, losing their first tooth, learning to read, and starting middle school. Have them make a vertical timeline, listing the events in sequence from earliest to most recent, with the earliest event at the bottom of the timeline and the most recent at the top. Once the timelines are done, have each student partner with a classmate. One student should describe an event from his or her timeline in terms of the other events. For example, a student might say, "This event happened after I learned to ride a bike, but before I started second grade." The partner should then identify the event the first student describes based on the information in the timeline. Students can then reverse roles.

Probing Question *Detective Work*

Fossils and Relative Dating

 whole class
20 min

Analyze Scientists put together clues from Earth's geologic past piece by piece, taking various data into consideration. For example, scientists may find answers in how continents fit together, how rock has been layered and if it has been disturbed, and what organisms are fossilized in the rock. They need to see how the data fit together, figure out explanations for any disconnects, and look for answers. **Ask:** How is a scientist studying Earth's past like a detective?

Discussion *Rock Layers*

Synthesizing Key Topics

 whole class
20 min

Ask students to imagine they are using relative dating techniques. **Ask:** What problems might you face when using relative dating to date rock samples? List students' responses on chart paper or on the board, and encourage them to think about them during the lesson.

Labs and Demos

Quick Lab *Layers of Sedimentary Rock*

Dating of Undisturbed Rock Layers

 small groups
20 min
Inquiry **DIRECTED** inquiry

Students use a variety of sediments to model the process of deposition that forms sedimentary rock layers.

PURPOSE **To model deposition and formation of sedimentary rock layers**

MATERIALS

- coarse sand, 2 cups
- funnel
- gravel, 1 cup
- lab apron
- magnifying glass
- mixing bowl, large
- paper, blank
- plastic bottle, 2 L, with cap
- potting soil, 1 cup
- safety goggles
- water, 2 cups, or enough to fill bottle

Take It Home *Relative Age*

Dating Undisturbed Rock Layers

 adult-student pairs
30 min

Students work with adults to locate objects in their neighborhood of different ages. After taking pictures or sketching these objects, they arrange the pictures or sketches by their relative age. Sample answer: The fence that was just built around our neighbor's house last weekend is the newest; the plants that sprouted in our yard last spring are a few months older. The giant oak tree in the park is the oldest object of these three, since it takes many years for a tree to grow to that size.

Levels of Inquiry

DIRECTED inquiry introduces inquiry skills within a structured framework.

GUIDED inquiry develops inquiry skills within a supportive environment.

INDEPENDENT inquiry deepens inquiry skills with student-driven questions or procedures.

Quick Lab *Ordering Rock Layers*

Geologic Columns

individuals
20 min

DIRECTED inquiry

Students use the principle of superposition to make a geologic column.

PURPOSE **To apply the principle of superposition**

MATERIALS

- paper
- pencil
- ruler
- safety goggles
- scissors
- tape

Exploration Lab *Earth's History*

PURPOSE **To use climate and environmental data to make geologic columns**

See the Lab Manual or go Online for planning information.

Daily Demo *Line Up!*

Engage

Dating of Undisturbed Rock Layers

whole class

10 min

PURPOSE **To demonstrate relative dating**

MATERIALS

- **list of students' birthdays, written in order from oldest to youngest**

1. Call students' names according to the list.
2. Have them line up in the order called.
3. **Ask:** How are you all arranged? What is your age relative to the person in front of you? Behind you?
4. Reinforce the concept by selecting one group of three students and discussing their ages relative to each other; emphasize the youngest student in that group.
5. Have the two older students from the group return to the line, and make a new group by selecting the two students who lined up behind the student who was originally the youngest in the first group. Explain that although that student was younger than the other students, in this new group, his age, relative to the other two makes him the oldest.

Virtual Lab *Ordering Rock Layers*

Engage

Geologic Columns

flexible
15 min
GUIDED inquiry

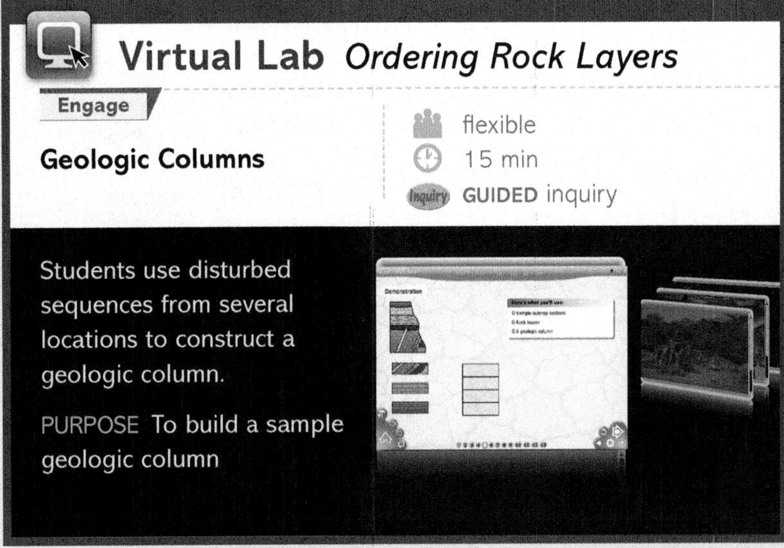

Students use disturbed sequences from several locations to construct a geologic column.

PURPOSE To build a sample geologic column

Customize Your Labs

See the Lab Manual for lab datasheets.

Go Online for editable lab datasheets.

Activities and Discussion

- ☐ **Activity** When Did it Happen?
- ☐ **Discussion** Rock Layers
- ☐ **Probing Question** Detective Work
- ☐ **Take It Home** Relative Age

Labs and Demos

- ☐ **Quick Lab** Layers of Sedimentary Rock
- ☐ **Quick Lab** Ordering Rock Layers
- ☐ **Daily Demo** Line Up!
- ☐ **Virtual Lab** Ordering Rock Layers
- ☐ **Exploration Lab** Earth's History

Your Resources

Explain Science Concepts

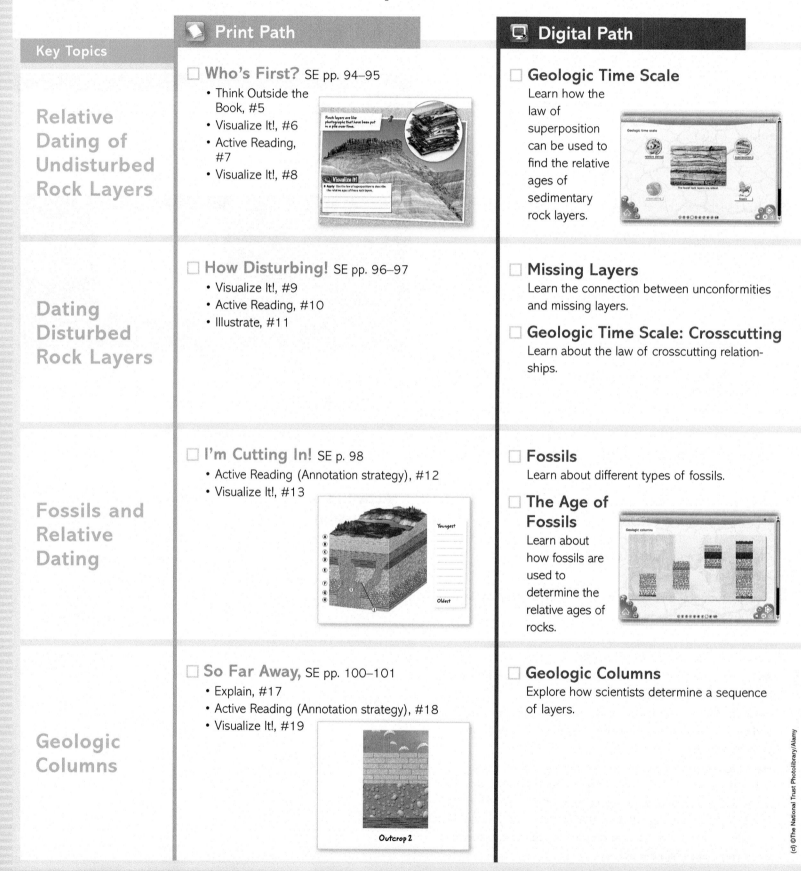

Key Topics	Print Path	Digital Path
Relative Dating of Undisturbed Rock Layers	☐ **Who's First?** SE pp. 94–95 • Think Outside the Book, #5 • Visualize It!, #6 • Active Reading, #7 • Visualize It!, #8 	☐ **Geologic Time Scale** Learn how the law of superposition can be used to find the relative ages of sedimentary rock layers. 
Dating Disturbed Rock Layers	☐ **How Disturbing!** SE pp. 96–97 • Visualize It!, #9 • Active Reading, #10 • Illustrate, #11	☐ **Missing Layers** Learn the connection between unconformities and missing layers. ☐ **Geologic Time Scale: Crosscutting** Learn about the law of crosscutting relationships.
Fossils and Relative Dating	☐ **I'm Cutting In!** SE p. 98 • Active Reading (Annotation strategy), #12 • Visualize It!, #13 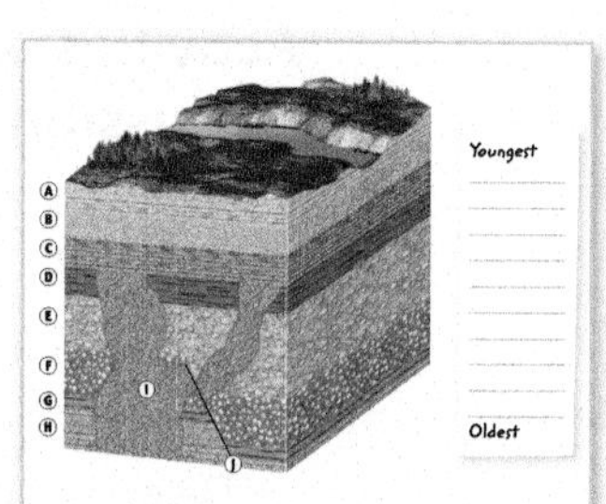	☐ **Fossils** Learn about different types of fossils. ☐ **The Age of Fossils** Learn about how fossils are used to determine the relative ages of rocks. 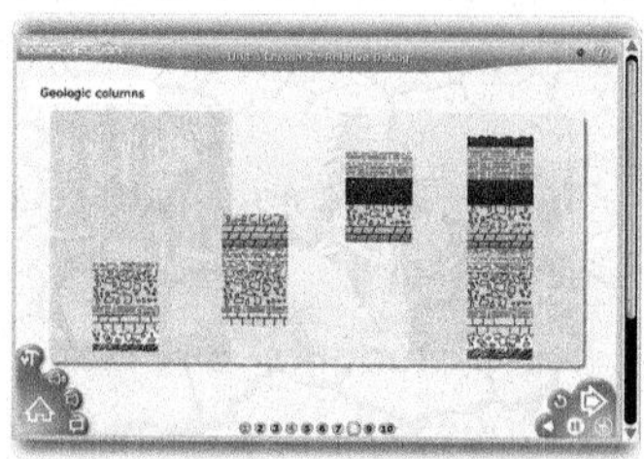
Geologic Columns	☐ **So Far Away,** SE pp. 100–101 • Explain, #17 • Active Reading (Annotation strategy), #18 • Visualize It!, #19 	☐ **Geologic Columns** Explore how scientists determine a sequence of layers.

Differentiated Instruction

Basic *Do Not Disturb*

Dating Disturbed Rock Layers

 individuals
 25 min

After students learn about the different ways sedimentary rock layers can be disturbed, ask them to develop a Layered Book FoldNote that contains a page and labeled drawing for each type of disturbance. Have them list details about each disturbance and how it is caused, along with their illustrations.

Online Resource: Layered Book FoldNote

Advanced *A History of Earth*

Synthesizing Key Topics

 individuals
varied

Quick Research Have students conduct research to learn more about Earth's history. Ask them to prepare a short written report addressing the following: *What are the major events (i.e., floods, earthquakes, heating, cooling) that scientists have discovered as a result of relative dating techniques? Have there been any surprising discoveries? Where have scientists in the United States focused their attention in recent years?*

 *Optional Online rubric: Written Pieces*

ELL *Concept Mapping*

Geologic Columns

 pairs
 40 min

Have students develop a Concept Map for the term ***geologic column***. Encourage them to use lots of details from the text. Encourage students to share their concept maps with a partner. Partners should review the maps and add any additional detail that has been left off of the map.

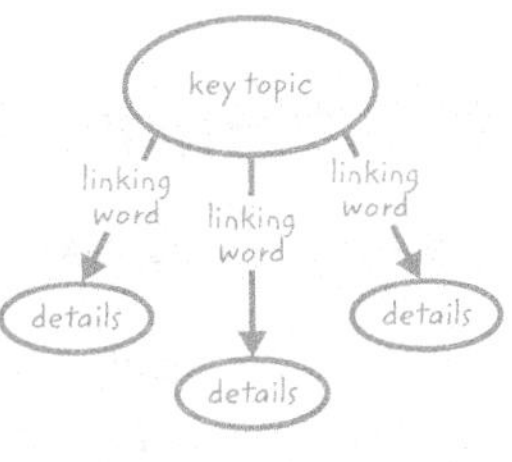

Online Resource: Layered Book FoldNote

Lesson Vocabulary

relative dating **superposition** **unconformity**
fossil **geologic column**

Previewing Vocabulary

 whole class, then pairs  25 min

Frame Game Have students use the Frame Game to learn their vocabulary words. Use a transparency of the blank frame available online to demonstrate the use of this vocabulary tool. Then allow students to work in pairs to complete a frame for each term.

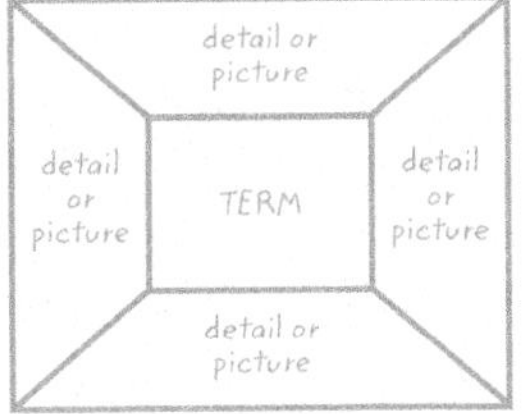

Online Resource: Frame Game

Reinforcing Vocabulary

 individuals 30 min

Four Square To help students remember the vocabulary words introduced in this lesson, have them complete a Four Square graphic organizer. Students place the term in the center. Then they fill the surrounding sections with the information shown.

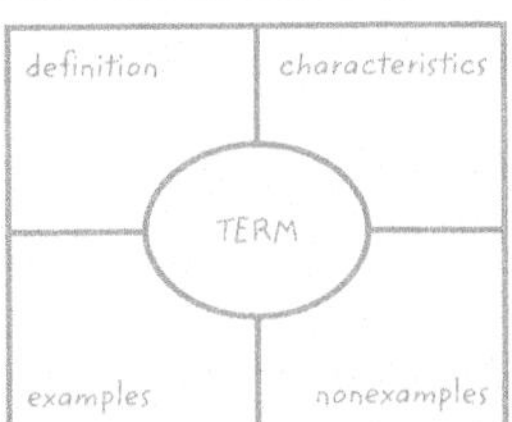

Online Resource: Four Square support

Customize Your Lesson

Core Instruction

☐ **Print Path** choices
☐ **Digital Path** choices

Vocabulary

☐ **Previewing Vocabulary** Frame Game
☐ **Reinforcing Vocabulary** Four Square

Differentiated Instruction

☐ **Basic** Do Not Disturb
☐ **Advanced** A History of Earth
☐ **ELL** Concept Mapping

Your Resources

Extend Science Concepts

Reinforce and Review

Activity *Cheesy Rocks*

Engage

Synthesizing Key Topics

small groups
40 min

Have each student sketch a cross section of a sandwich that consists of (from the bottom up) a slice of bread, cheese, lettuce, and another slice of bread (students may add other ingredients if they wish). Have students label each layer with the ingredient it represents. Tell students to imagine that their drawing represents an actual sandwich they have made. **Ask:** Applying the law of superposition to your sandwich, which layer is older, the lettuce or the cheese? the cheese How do you know? because the lettuce is on top of the cheese Have them label their drawing's layers from the oldest layer to the youngest layer. Finally, have them list the layers in the order in which they were laid down.

Graphic Organizer

Relative Dating

individuals
35 min

Main Idea Web After students have studied the lesson, ask them to create a Main Idea Web to show the different ways scientists use relative dating to date rock layers.

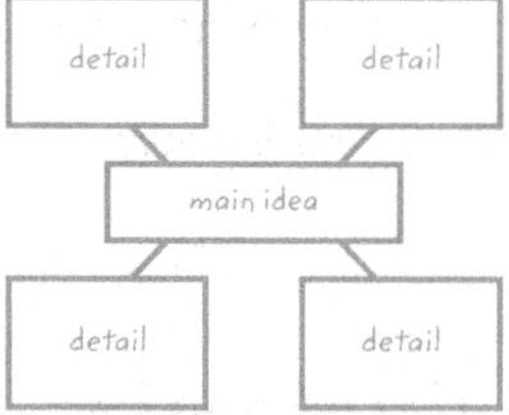

Optional Online resources: Main Idea Web Support

Going Further

Natural Resources Connection

Synthesizing Key Topics

individuals
varied

Research Project Scientists can use relative dating to determine where to drill for oil and other natural resources. Have students research this use of relative dating and prepare a report about it.

Optional Online rubric: Written Pieces

Social Studies Connection

Synthesizing Key Topics

pairs
35 min

Timeline Have students research major events that have happened in their community. Ask them to list the events in the order in which they occurred and develop a poster-sized timeline of the events. Then have them write descriptions of each event using relative dating to help them. Finally, have them draw conclusions: Did any of these events happen as a result of a previous event? How can one event affect another?

Customize Your Closing

See the Assessment Guide for quizzes and tests.

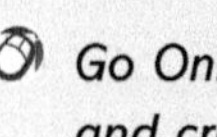
Go Online to edit and create quizzes and tests.

Reinforce and Review

- ☐ **Activity** Cheesy Rocks
- ☐ **Graphic Organizer** Main Idea Web
- ☐ **Print Path** Visual Summary, SE p. 102
- ☐ **Digital Path** Lesson Closer

Evaluate Student Mastery

Formative Assessment

See the teacher support below the Student Pages for additional Formative Assessment questions.

Describe or have students review the ways scientists use relative dating to date rock layers. **Ask:** How do scientists handle relative dating differently when rock layers are disturbed versus undisturbed? Sample answer: They use the law of crosscutting relationships in addition to the law of superposition to piece together a sequence of events.

Reteach

Formative assessment may show you that students need reinforcement for certain topics. The resources below are recommended for reteaching. If students were introduced to topics through the Print Path, you can also use the Digital Path for reteaching, and vice versa.

Can be assigned to individual students

Dating of Undisturbed Rock Layers

Quick Lab Layers of Sedimentary Rock

Daily Demo Line Up!

Dating Disturbed Rock Layers

Activity When Did It Happen?

Virtual Lab Ordering Rock Layers

Fossils and Relative Dating

Activity Cheesy Rocks

Geologic Columns

Quick Lab Ordering Rock Layers

Summative Assessment

Alternative Assessment

Relative Dating

Online resources: Student Worksheet; optional rubrics

Relative Dating

Choose Your Meal: ***Relative Dating***
Complete the activities to show what you've learned about relative dating.

1. Work on your own, with a partner, or with a small group.
2. Choose one item from each section of the menu, with an optional dessert. Check your choices.
3. Have your teacher approve your plan.
4. Submit or present your results.

Appetizers

____ **Sedimentary Summary** Design a pamphlet that describes the process in which sedimentary rock layers are formed. Include at least two illustrations of undisturbed sedimentary rock layers.

____ **This Just In!** Present a news report in which you identify and describe a section of sedimentary rock that has been disturbed. Include information about how the rock was disturbed and how scientists can use other clues to help them date the disturbed rock correctly.

Main Dish

____ **Relative Dating** Write a poem, report, or Website about relative dating. In your work, define relative dating, explain the methods scientists use to conduct relative dating, and add illustrations.

____ **Functional Fossils** Make a model of a plant or animal fossil. Describe what the fossil might tell about the age of the rock it was found in. Explain how scientists use fossils to determine relative ages.

____ **A Scientist's Story** Write a short story about a scientist who is researching the relative dates of sedimentary rocks in a town. The scientists should explain the law of superposition and talk about how that law helps date the rocks.

Side Dishes

____ **Explaining Geologic Columns** Imagine you are a scientist at a conference. Present a speech in which you explain the idea behind geologic columns. In your speech, include information about how scientists collect information about geologic columns and how scientists use geologic columns.

____ **Important Principles** Imagine you are working with scientists on a newly discovered island. Make a diagram or model of the island's geologic column. Explain the relative ages of rock layers.

Desserts (optional)

____ **Understanding Unconformities** Design a poster about the different ways that layers can be changed or disturbed. Include labels and brief descriptions on your poster.

Going Further

- ☐ Natural Resources Connection
- ☐ Social Studies Connection
- ☐ Why It Matters, SE p. 99

Formative Assessment

- ☐ Strategies Throughout TE
- ☐ Lesson Review SE

Summative Assessment

- ☐ Alternative Assessment Relative Dating
- ☐ Lesson Quiz
- ☐ Unit Review SE End-of-Unit
- ☐ Unit Tests A and B

Your Resources

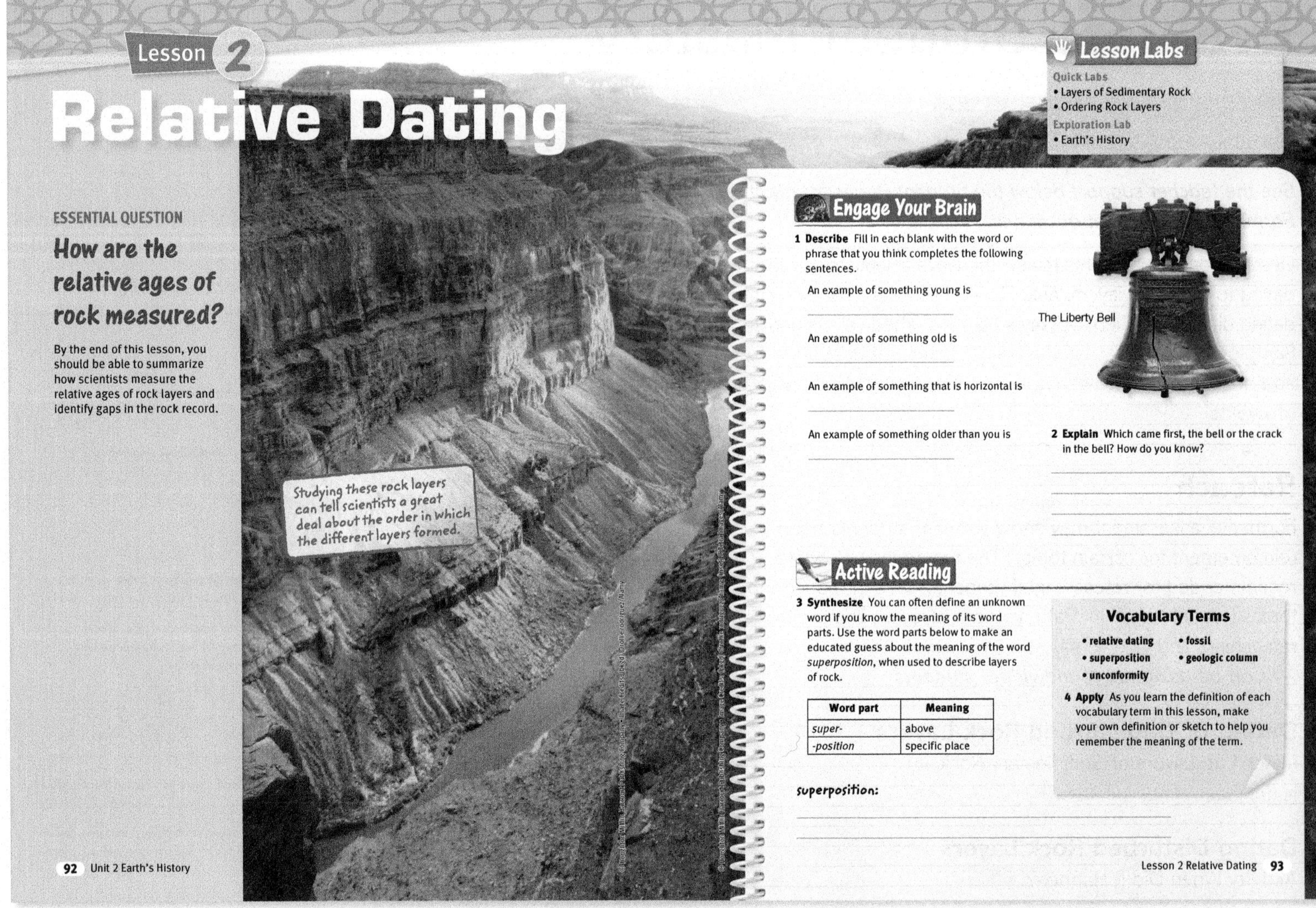

Lesson 2
Relative Dating
ESSENTIAL QUESTION
How are the relative ages of rock measured?
By the end of this lesson, you should be able to summarize how scientists measure the relative ages of rock layers and identify gaps in the rock record.
Studying these rock layers can tell scientists a great deal about the order in which the different layers formed.
92 Unit 2 Earth's History
Lesson Labs
Quick Labs
• Layers of Sedimentary Rock
• Ordering Rock Layers
Exploration Lab
• Earth's History
Engage Your Brain
1 Describe Fill in each blank with the word or phrase that you think completes the following sentences.
An example of something young is
An example of something old is
An example of something that is horizontal is
An example of something older than you is
The Liberty Bell
2 Explain Which came first, the bell or the crack in the bell? How do you know?
Active Reading
3 Synthesize You can often define an unknown word if you know the meaning of its word parts. Use the word parts below to make an educated guess about the meaning of the word superposition, when used to describe layers of rock.
Word part | Meaning
super- | above
-position | specific place
superposition:
Vocabulary Terms
• relative dating
• fossil
• superposition
• geologic column
• unconformity
4 Apply As you learn the definition of each vocabulary term in this lesson, make your own definition or sketch to help you remember the meaning of the term.
Lesson 2 Relative Dating 93

Answers

Answers for 1–3 should represent students' current thoughts, even if incorrect.

1. Sample answers: a baby, a grandmother, a book on a table, my older brother
2. Sample answer: The bell came before the crack. A crack could not form on something that had not yet been made.
3. Sample answer: One rock layer is placed on top of another.
4. Students should define or sketch each vocabulary term in the lesson.

Opening Your Lesson

Discuss student answers to item 2 to assess students' prerequisite knowledge and to estimate what they already know about key topics.

Preconception everyday meaning of *dating* as going out with or spending time with another person

Prerequisites Students should already know the principle of uniformitarianism; how igneous and sedimentary rocks form; and the definitions of *erosion* and *deposition,* and their roles in the formation of sedimentary rocks.

Accessing Prior Knowledge The SQ3R strategy asks students to think about what they are about to read by Surveying the material, Questioning it, Reading it, Reciting it, and then Reviewing it. Introduce the strategy by explaining what each letter stands for, and then allow students to work with a partner to employ the SQ3R strategy to preview this lesson.

Optional Online resource: SQ3R Strategy support

Who's First?

5 Model In groups of 6–10 people, form a line. Place the oldest person in the front of the line and the youngest person at the end of the line. What is your relative age compared to the person in front of you? Compared to the person behind you?

What is relative dating?

Imagine that you are a detective at a crime scene. You must figure out the order of events that took place before you arrived. Scientists have the same goal when studying Earth. They try to find out the order in which events happened during Earth's history. Instead of using fingerprints and witnesses, scientists use rocks and fossils. Determining whether an object or event is older or younger than other objects or events is called **relative dating**.

The telephones shown below show how technologies have changed over time. Layers of rock also show how certain things took place in the past. Using different pieces of information, scientists can find the order in which rock layers formed. Once they know the order, a relative age can be determined for each rock layer. Keep in mind, however, that this does not give scientists a rock's age in years. It only allows scientists to find out what rock layer is older or younger than another rock layer.

How are undisturbed rock layers dated?

To find the relative ages of rocks, scientists study the layers in sedimentary rocks. Sedimentary rocks form when new sediments are deposited on top of older rock. As more sediment is added, it is compressed and hardens into rock layers.

Scientists know that gravity causes sediment to be deposited in layers that are horizontal (hohr•ih•ZAHN•tuhl). Over time, different layers of sediment pile up on Earth's surface. Younger layers pile on top of older ones. If left undisturbed, the sediment will remain in horizontal layers. Scientists use the order of these layers to date the rock of each layer.

Active Reading **7 Explain** Why does gravity cause layers of sediment to be horizontal?

Using Superposition

Suppose that you have a brother who takes pictures of your family and piles them in a box. Over time, he adds new pictures to the top of the pile. Where are the oldest pictures—the ones taken when you were a baby? Where are the most recent pictures—the ones taken last week? The oldest pictures will be at the bottom of the pile. The youngest pictures will be at the top of the pile. Layers of rock are like the photographs shown below. As you go from top to bottom, the layers get older.

This approach is used to determine the relative age of sedimentary rock layers. The law of **superposition** (soo•per•puh•ZISH•uhn) is the principle that states that younger rocks lie above older rocks if the layers have not been disturbed.

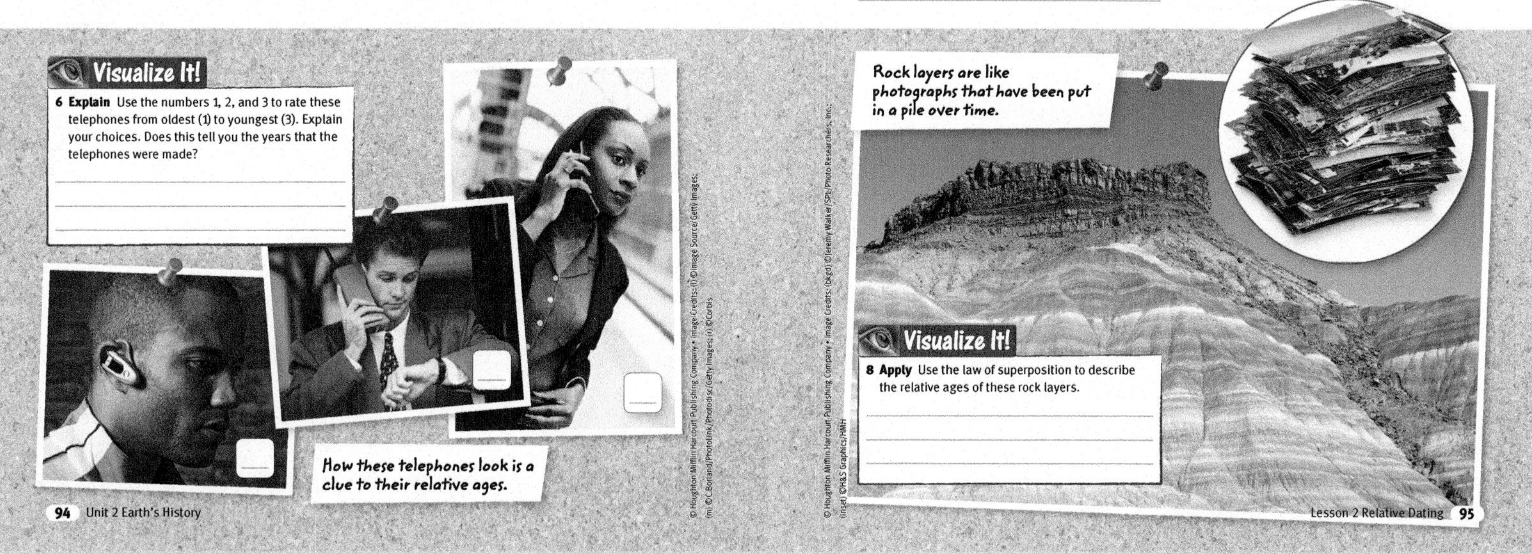

Visualize It!
6 Explain Use the numbers 1, 2, and 3 to rate these telephones from oldest (1) to youngest (3). Explain your choices. Does this tell you the years that the telephones were made?
How these telephones look is a clue to their relative ages.
Rock layers are like photographs that have been put in a pile over time.
Visualize It!
8 Apply Use the law of superposition to describe the relative ages of these rock layers.
94 Unit 2 Earth's History
Lesson 2 Relative Dating 95

Answers

5. Unless the student is the eldest or youngest, answers should reflect that they are younger than the person in front of them and older than the person behind them.
6. left to right: 3, 1, 2. Sample answer: The larger the telephone, the older it is. No, the year that each telephone was made is not known.
7. Gravity is acting from across Earth's surface. Sediment will deposit parallel to Earth's surface, which is horizontal.
8. Sample answer: According to the law of superposition, younger rocks lie above older rocks, if the layers are undisturbed.The oldest rock layer is at the bottom. As you move from bottom to top, each layer is younger than the one below it.

Interpreting Visuals

Have students look at the cell phone images to observe the differences among them. **Ask:** How has the technology used in the making of cell phones changed over the years? How are the cell phones in use now different from those that were used 10 years ago? Sample answer: The technology used in today's cell phones is more advanced than that in the past. In the past, cell phones could be used only when connected to a power source by a cord and were heavy and clunky. Now they are small, can do almost as much as a small computer, and have rechargeable batteries that last for hours.

Learning Alert

Explain that *dating* something means figuring out how old it is, or what era it came from. This word may be confusing for students, especially English language learners.

Probing Question GUIDED Inquiry

The law of superposition is like the ingredients in a sandwich: New layers are piled on top of older ones. Scientists study rock layers to gather data about the time period when each layer formed. **Ask:** Why is the law of superposition most easily applied to undisturbed rock layers? Sample answer: Undisturbed layers are in the order in which they formed.

How Disturbing!

How are sedimentary rock layers disturbed?

If rock layers are not horizontal, then something disturbed them after they formed. Forces in Earth can disturb rock layers so much that older layers end up on top of younger layers. Some of the ways that rock layers can be disturbed are shown below and on the next page.

By Tilting and Folding

Tilting happens when Earth's forces move rock layers up or down unevenly. The layers become slanted. *Folding* is the bending of rocks that can happen when rock layers are squeezed together. The bending is from stress on the rock. Folding can cause rock layers to be turned over by so much that older layers end up on top of younger layers.

By Faults and Intrusions

Scientists often find features that cut across existing layers of rock. A *fault* is a break or crack in Earth's crust where rocks can move. An *intrusion* (in•TROO•zhuhn) is igneous rock that forms when magma is injected into rock and then cools and becomes hard.

Folding, tilting, faults, and intrusions can make finding out the relative ages of rock layers difficult. This can be even more complicated when a layer of rock is missing. Scientists call this missing layer of rock an *unconformity*.

Visualize It!

9 Describe Write a caption for this group of images.

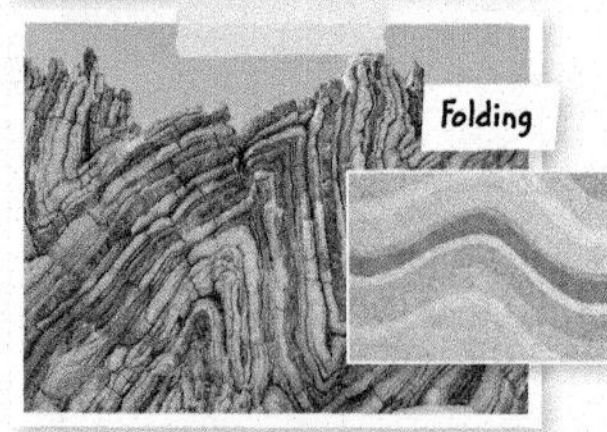

By Unconformities

A missing layer of rock forms a gap in Earth's geologic history, also called the geologic record. An **unconformity** (uhn•kuhn•FAWR•mih•tee) is a break in the geologic record that is made when rock layers are eroded or when sediment is not deposited for a long period of time. When scientists find an unconformity, they must question if the "missing layer" was simply never present or if it was removed. Two examples of unconformities are shown below.

Active Reading 10 Describe What are two ways that a rock layer can cause a gap in the geologic record?

An unconformity can happen between horizontal layers and layers that are tilted or folded. The older layers were tilted or folded and then eroded before horizontal layers formed above them.

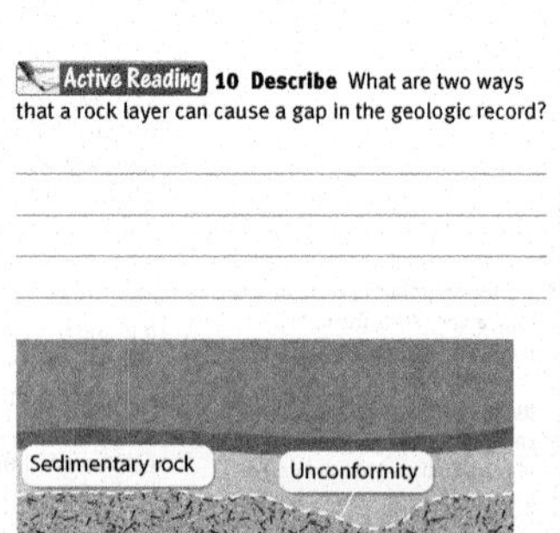

An unconformity can also happen when igneous or metamorphic rocks are exposed at Earth's surface and become eroded. Later, deposited sediment causes the eroded surface to become buried under sedimentary rock.

11 Illustrate Choose two of the following: tilting, folding, fault, intrusion, and an unconformity. Draw and label each one.

Answers

9. Sample answer: Rock layers can be disturbed by tilting, folding, faults, and intrusions.
10. When a rock layer is eroded or when sediment is not deposited for a very long time.
11. Accept all reasonable answers. Sketches should be similar to the illustrations provided, and include the key features of each.

Interpreting Visuals

Help students understand the differences among the four methods by which rock layers are disturbed by having them make sketches of rock layers on paper. They can then cut the sketch in half, and manipulate the paper to model the differences between tilting and faulting.

Formative Assessment

Ask: What is relative dating? determining an object's relative age by comparing it to other objects to find which is older or younger **Ask:** How accurate is relative dating? Relative dating can tell scientists which layers of rock came first, but not a rock's actual age in years. **Ask:** What is an unconformity? An unconformity is a gap in the geologic record that formed when rock layers were eroded or when sediment was not deposited for some time.

I'm Cutting In!

How are rock layers ordered?

Active Reading

12 Identify As you read, underline the law of crosscutting relationships.

Often, the order of rock layers is affected by more than one thing. Finding out what happened to form a group of rock layers is like piecing together a jigsaw puzzle. The law of superposition helps scientists to do this.

The idea that layers of rock have to be in place before anything can disturb them is also used. The law of crosscutting relationships states that a fault or a body of rock, such as an intrusion, must be younger than any feature or layer of rock that the fault or rock body cuts through. For example, if a fault has broken a rock layer, the fault is younger than the rock layer. If a fault has broken through igneous rock, the igneous rock must have been in place, and cool, before it could have been broken. The same is true for an unconformity. Look at the image below and use the laws of superposition and crosscutting relationships to figure out the relative ages of the rock layers and features.

Visualize It!

13 Analyze What is the order in which layers and features A through J formed? Fill in the lines according to the relative ages of the layers or features.

A B C D E F G H I J

Youngest

Oldest

98 Unit 2 Earth's History

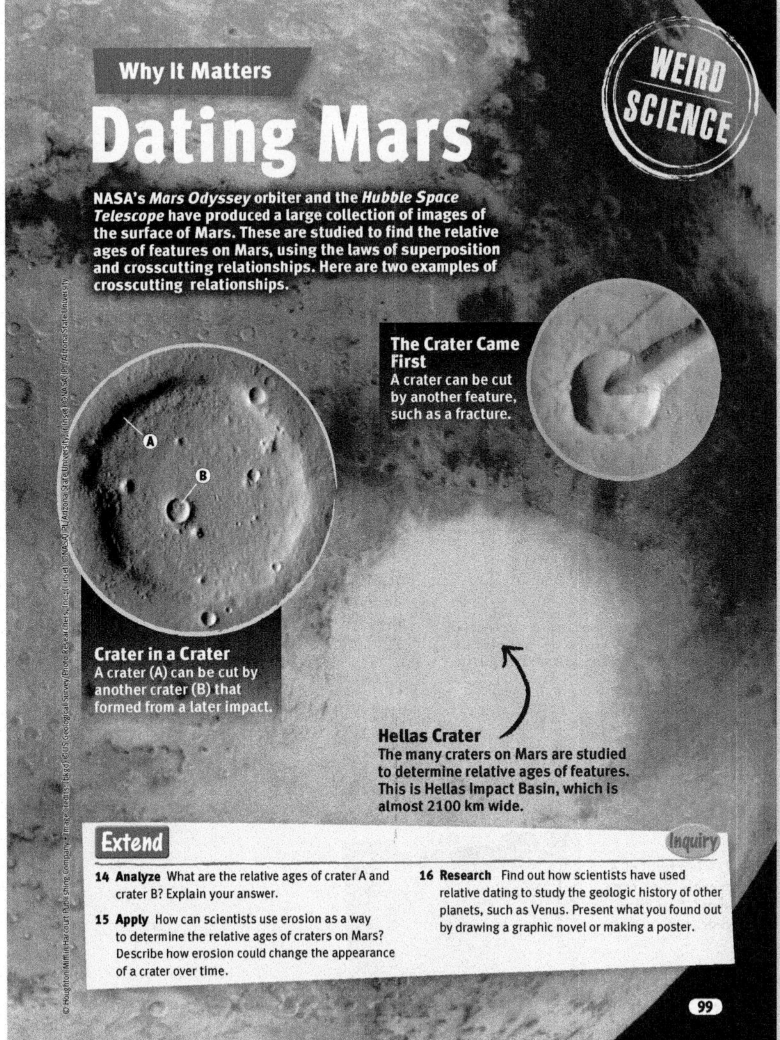

Why It Matters
Dating Mars
WEIRD SCIENCE
NASA's *Mars Odyssey* orbiter and the *Hubble Space Telescope* have produced a large collection of images of the surface of Mars. These are studied to find the relative ages of features on Mars, using the laws of superposition and crosscutting relationships. Here are two examples of crosscutting relationships.
The Crater Came First
A crater can be cut by another feature, such as a fracture.
A
B
Crater in a Crater
A crater (A) can be cut by another crater (B) that formed from a later impact.
Hellas Crater
The many craters on Mars are studied to determine relative ages of features. This is Hellas Impact Basin, which is almost 2100 km wide.
Extend
Inquiry
14 Analyze What are the relative ages of crater A and crater B? Explain your answer.
15 Apply How can scientists use erosion as a way to determine the relative ages of craters on Mars? Describe how erosion could change the appearance of a crater over time.
16 Research Find out how scientists have used relative dating to study the geologic history of other planets, such as Venus. Present what you found out by drawing a graphic novel or making a poster.
99

Answers

12. *See students' pages for annotations.*
13. From oldest to youngest: H, G, F, E, D, I, J, C, B, A
14. Crater A is older than crater B. Crater B is inside of crater A. Therefore, A had to be there before B.
15. Answers will vary. Students should apply their knowledge of erosion to what happens to craters. Sample answer: edges of older craters become more rounded with time.
16. Answers will vary. Students can take the opportunity to study another relative dating method that has been used for other planets.

Using Annotations

Text Structure: Summarize As students read about the law of crosscutting relationships, have them rewrite the law in their own words to help them internalize its meaning.

Building Reading Skills

Main Idea Web Have students develop a Main Idea Web to organize the information they learn about crosscutting relationships.

Optional Online resource: Main Idea Web support

Why It Matters

By applying the same principles they use to determine the relative ages of Earth features, scientists have used data gathered by space probes to study Mars. Discuss with students how dating features of other planets like Mars can help scientists understand more about Earth.

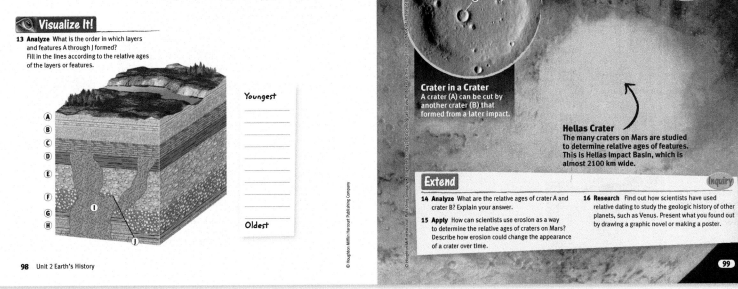

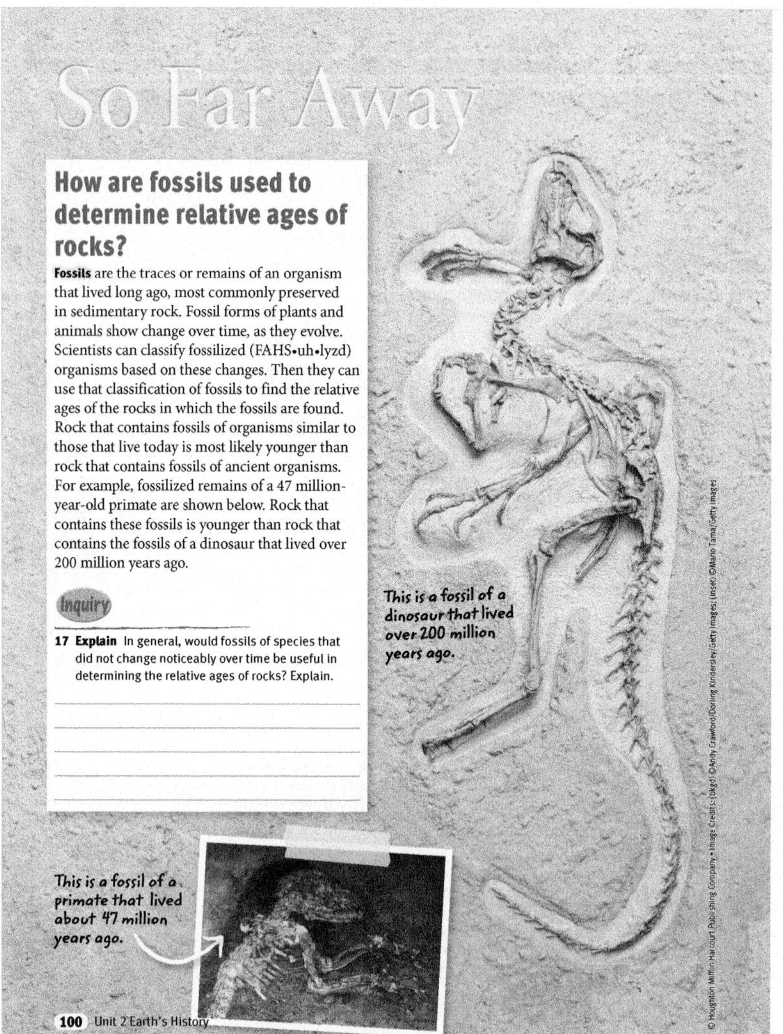

So Far Away
This is a fossil of a dinosaur that lived over 200 million years ago.
This is a fossil of a primate that lived about 47 million years ago.

How are fossils used to determine relative ages of rocks?

Fossils are the traces or remains of an organism that lived long ago, most commonly preserved in sedimentary rock. Fossil forms of plants and animals show change over time, as they evolve. Scientists can classify fossilized (FAHS•uh•lyzd) organisms based on these changes. Then they can use that classification of fossils to find the relative ages of the rocks in which the fossils are found. Rock that contains fossils of organisms similar to those that live today is most likely younger than rock that contains fossils of ancient organisms. For example, fossilized remains of a 47 million-year-old primate are shown below. Rock that contains these fossils is younger than rock that contains the fossils of a dinosaur that lived over 200 million years ago.

Inquiry

17 Explain In general, would fossils of species that did not change noticeably over time be useful in determining the relative ages of rocks? Explain.

How are geologic columns used to compare relative ages of rocks?

Relative dating can also be done by comparing the relative ages of rock layers in different areas. The comparison is done using a geologic column. A **geologic column** is an ordered arrangement of rock layers that is based on the relative ages of the rocks, with the oldest rocks at the bottom of the column. It is made by piecing together different rock sequences from different areas. A geologic column represents an ideal image of a rock layer sequence that doesn't actually exist in any one place on Earth.

The rock sequences shown below represent rock layers from different outcrops at different locations. Each has certain rock layers that are common to layers in the geologic column, shown in the middle. Scientists can compare a rock layer with a similar layer in a geologic column that has the same fossils or that has the same relative position. If the two layers match, then they probably formed around the same time.

Active Reading

18 Identify As you read, underline the description of how rock layers are ordered in a geologic column.

Visualize It!

19 Identify Draw lines from the top and bottom of each outcrop to their matching positions in the geologic column.

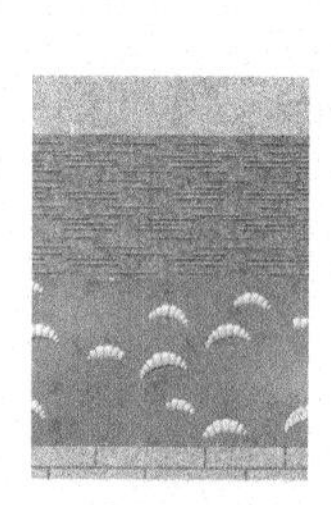
Outcrop 1

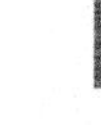

Rock layers from different outcrops can be compared to a geologic column.

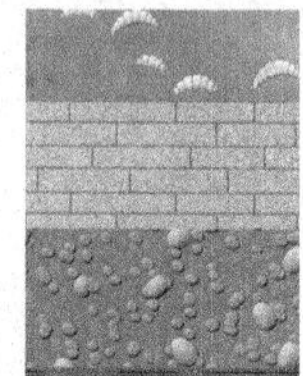
Outcrop 2

Answers

17. No, because it would be more difficult to accurately order their appearance over time, which is needed to determine the relative ages of the rocks they are found in.
18. *See students' pages for annotations.*
19. Students should draw lines from each outcrop to matching consecutive layers in the geologic column.

Learning Alert

Fossils Fossils exist in many locations throughout the world. Scientists use fossils to determine the relative ages of structures, what types of organisms were present during different time periods, and more.

Building Reading Skills

Text Structure: Summarize The ability to summarize a section of text is valuable to students. When they summarize the text in their own words, they synthesize the learning and show an understanding of what they read. Have students develop a summary of this key topic. Encourage them to share their summaries with a partner.

Formative Assessment

Have students look at the image of the geologic column. **Ask:** What is a geologic column? It is an ordered arrangement of rock layers that is based on the relative ages of the rocks from different outcrops and areas. **Ask:** How are geologic columns used by scientists? They apply the principles of superposition, crosscutting relationships, and information about fossils to compare the relative ages of rock layers that are located in different regions.

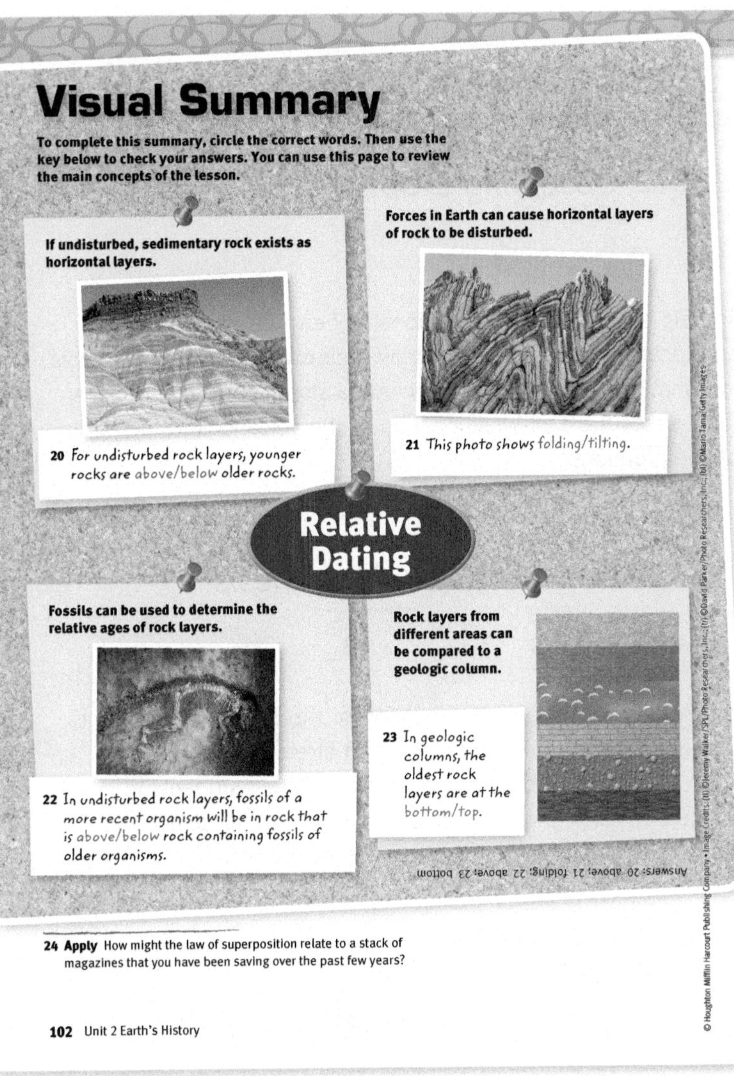
Visual Summary

To complete this summary, circle the correct words. Then use the key below to check your answers. You can use this page to review the main concepts of the lesson.

If undisturbed, sedimentary rock exists as horizontal layers.

20 For undisturbed rock layers, younger rocks are above/below older rocks.

Forces in Earth can cause horizontal layers of rock to be disturbed.

21 This photo shows folding/tilting.

Relative Dating

Fossils can be used to determine the relative ages of rock layers.

22 In undisturbed rock layers, fossils of a more recent organism will be in rock that is above/below rock containing fossils of older organisms.

Rock layers from different areas can be compared to a geologic column.

23 In geologic columns, the oldest rock layers are at the bottom/top.

Answers: 20 above; 21 folding; 22 above; 23 bottom

24 **Apply** How might the law of superposition relate to a stack of magazines that you have been saving over the past few years?

Lesson Review

Vocabulary

In your own words, define the following terms.

1 relative dating

2 unconformity

Key Concepts

3 **Describe** How are sedimentary rock layers deposited?

4 **List** Name five ways that the order of rock layers can be disturbed.

5 **Explain** How are the laws of superposition and crosscutting relationships used to determine the relative ages of rocks?

6 **Explain** How can fossils be used to determine the relative ages of rock layers?

7 **Describe** How is the geologic column used in relative dating?

Critical Thinking

8 **Justify** Does the law of crosscutting relationships involve sedimentary rock only? Why or why not?

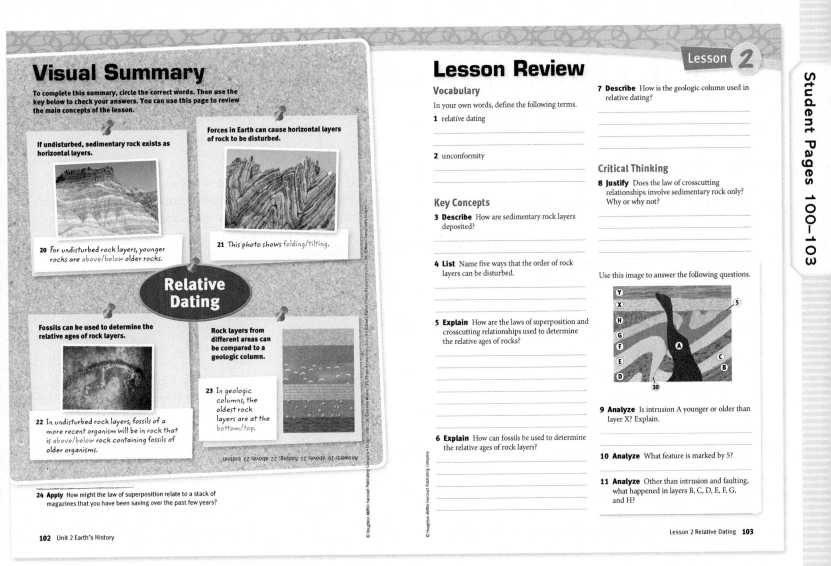

Use this image to answer the following questions.

9 **Analyze** Is intrusion A younger or older than layer X? Explain.

10 **Analyze** What feature is marked by 5?

11 **Analyze** Other than intrusion and faulting, what happened in layers B, C, D, E, F, G, and H?

Visual Summary Answers

20. above
21. folding
22. above
23. bottom
24. Sample answer: The magazines that are near the bottom of the pile on my shelf are older ones that I read a long time ago. The magazines near the top of the pile are newer ones that I read more recently.

Lesson Review Answers

1. Sample answer: A method to determine if something is younger or older than something else.
2. Sample answer: A missing rock layer in a rock bed.
3. in horizontal layers.
4. fault, intrusion, folding, tilting, unconformity
5. Superposition: An undisturbed rock layer is older than the layers above it. Crosscutting relationships: For disturbed rock layers, a feature or rock that causes the disruption is younger than the layer disrupted.
6. Arranging fossils based on which formed before others can be used to determine the relative ages of the rock layers the fossils are found in.
7. To compare and identify relative ages of rock layers that are in different areas. The oldest rock layer is at the bottom. The youngest rock layer is at the top.
8. No; for example, intrusions can be igneous rock.
9. It is younger, based on the law of crosscutting relationships.
10. An unconformity exists there.
11. Folding occurred in those layers.

Forming a Hypothesis

Purpose To learn how to form and test a hypothesis

Learning Goals

- Analyze data in tables and maps to form a hypothesis.
- Understand how to test and revise a hypothesis.

Informal Vocabulary

hypothesis, investigation, observation

Prerequisite Knowledge

- Plate tectonics
- Volcanoes

Discussion *Volcanoes*

 whole class

 10 min

 **GUIDED** inquiry

Have students think about what they already know about volcanoes. **Ask:** What is a volcano? Sample answer: A volcano is any place where gas, ash, and melted rock come out of the ground. **Ask:** What can cause volcanoes to form? Explain. Sample answers: Volcanoes can form where two tectonic plates move toward each other and one plate sinks beneath the other. Fluids that are squeezed out of the sinking plate make the rock above melt and form magma. This magma rises to the surface and erupts to form volcanoes. Volcanoes can form where columns of hot rock rise up through the mantle and crust. When the hot rock gets near the surface, it can melt, and then erupt to form a volcano.

 *Optional Online rubric: Class Discussion*

Differentiated Instruction

Basic *Observing Eruptions*

 pairs

 15 min

To help students see the relationship between eruption dates and locations, have students draw their own maps to display this information. Ask students to include a statement on their maps that relates the east-west location of the volcanoes to the dates of the eruptions.

Advanced *Testing a Hypothesis*

 individuals

 30 min

Have students research the location of the Emperor Seamounts, a chain of underwater mountains that stretches toward the northwest beyond the Hawaiian Islands. Direct students to suggest whether these seamounts provide any evidence to support or disprove the hypotheses they made.

ELL *Where Is Hawai'i?*

 pairs or small groups

10 min

Have students locate the Hawaiian Islands on a map or globe. Then review with students the names and meanings of the cardinal directions. Last, have students state where they live in relation to the Hawaiian Islands, using cardinal direction words.

To extend the activity, have students talk about where different volcanoes and islands in the Hawaiian Islands are located in relation to one another, using the map on these pages.

Customize Your Feature

- ☐ **Discussion** Volcanoes
- ☐ **Basic** Observing Eruptions
- ☐ **Advanced** Testing a Hypothesis
- ☐ **ELL** Where Is Hawai'i?

Think Science

Forming a Hypothesis

When conducting an investigation to test a hypothesis, a scientist must not let personal bias affect the results of the investigation. A scientist must be open to the fact that the results of an investigation may not completely support the hypothesis. They may even contradict it! Revising or forming a new hypothesis may lead a scientist to make a breakthrough that could be the basis of a new discovery.

Tutorial

The following procedure explains the steps that you will use to develop and evaluate a hypothesis.

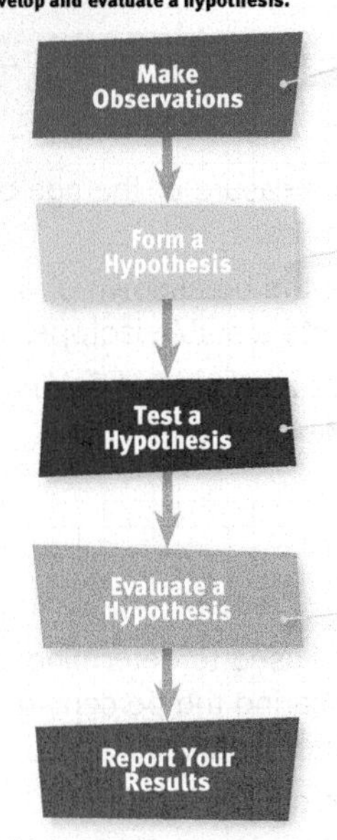

1 Making Observations Scientific investigations commonly begin with observations. Your observations may lead to a question. For example, you may wonder how, why, or when something happens.

2 Forming a Hypothesis To answer your question, you can start by forming a hypothesis. A hypothesis is a clear statement of what you expect will be the answer to your question. Start to form a hypothesis by stating the probable answer to your question based on your observations.

3 Testing a Hypothesis A useful hypothesis must be testable. To determine whether your hypothesis is testable, identify experiments that you can perform or observations that you can make to find out whether the hypothesis is supported or not.

4 Evaluating a Hypothesis After analyzing your data, you can determine if your results support your hypothesis. If your data support your hypothesis, you may want to repeat your observations or experiments to verify your results. If your data do not support your hypothesis, you may have to check your procedure for errors. You may even have to reject your hypothesis and form a new one.

You Try It!

The table provides observations about the latest eruptions of several volcanoes in Hawai'i.

Latest Eruption of Volcanoes in Hawai'i	
Volcano	**Year**
East Maui (Haleakala)	1460
Hualalai	1801
Mauna Loa	1984
Kilauea	still active

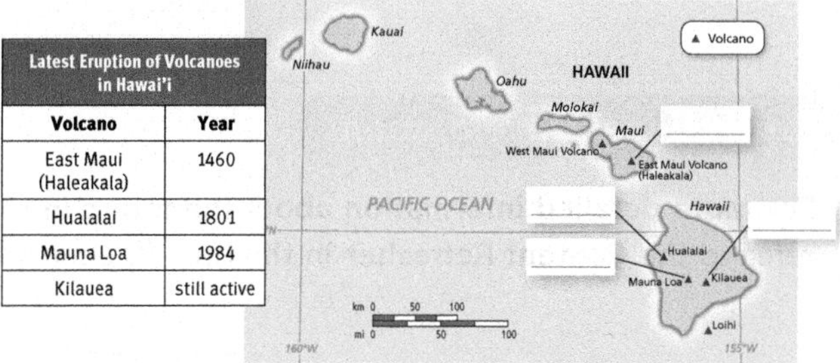

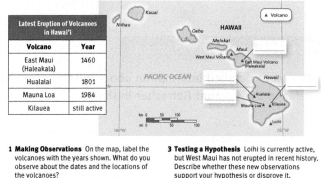

1 Making Observations On the map, label the volcanoes with the years shown. What do you observe about the dates and the locations of the volcanoes?

2 Forming a Hypothesis Use the observations above to form a hypothesis about the history of the area. Focus on the relationship between the activity of the volcanoes and the location of the volcanoes. Your hypothesis should be supported by all of your data. Summarize your completed hypothesis in a single paragraph.

3 Testing a Hypothesis Loihi is currently active, but West Maui has not erupted in recent history. Describe whether these new observations support your hypothesis or disprove it.

4 Revising a Hypothesis Share your hypothesis with your classmates. Rewrite your hypothesis so that it includes the changes suggested by your classmates.

Take It Home

While you already know the word *hypothesis*, you might not know the word *hypothetical*. Use the dictionary to look up the meaning of the suffix *-ical*. Combine the meanings of these two word parts, and write an original definition of *hypothetical* in your notebook.

Answers

1. From left to right based on volcano position:1460, 1801, 1984, still active. The volcanoes are ordered left to right (or top to bottom) according to when they last erupted.
2. Hypotheses should reflect that the southern islands of Hawaii are youngest and the northern islands are oldest.
3. These observations support students' hypotheses.
4. Students should have written down a hypothesis that combines the suggestions of their classmates as well as their own original hypothesis.

Take It Home

Sample answer: The suffix -ical is used to make adjectives. A situation or statement that describes a proposed explanation but has not been supported by evidence can be described as being hypothetical.

Absolute Dating

Essential Question How is the absolute age of rock measured?

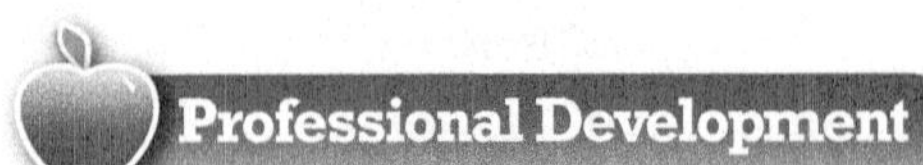

For more detailed information about the topics in this lesson, refer to the Content Refresher in the Unit Opener pages.

Opening Your Lesson

Begin the lesson by assessing students' prerequisite and prior knowledge.

Prerequisite Knowledge

- Scientists study rock and fossils to learn about Earth's history
- Some rock layers contain fossils
- Law of superposition

Accessing Prior Knowledge

Have students draw a picture of a fossil and list what they know about fossils. Ask them to share their ideas with the class. List their responses on the board. Revisit the list at the conclusion of the lesson and encourage students to revise their notes and drawings by adding new facts they learned and crossing out information that was incorrect.

Customize Your Opening

- ☐ **Accessing Prior Knowledge,** above
- ☐ **Print Path** Engage Your Brain, SE p. 107 #1–2
- ☐ **Print Path** Active Reading, SE p. 107 #3–4
- ☐ **Digital Path** Lesson Opener

Key Topics/Learning Goals	Supporting Concepts
Absolute Dating 1 Define *absolute dating.* 2 Define *radioactive decay.* 3 Apply the concept of half-life to problems of determining the age of a sample.	• Absolute dating is a measure of the age of an event or object in years. • Radioactive decay is the breakdown of a radioactive isotope into a stable isotope. • Radiometric dating is a method of finding the age of an object using half-life.
Radiometric Dating 1 Explain radiometric dating. 2 Identify radiometric dating methods.	• Radiometric dating is used to determine an object's age by comparing the percentages of parent and daughter isotopes. • Radiometric dating methods include radiocarbon dating, potassium–argon dating, and uranium–lead dating. Each method has a unique time range for which it is useful.
The Age of Earth 1 Identify approximately how old Earth is. 2 Explain how scientists have determined the age of Earth.	• Earth is approximately 4.6 billion years old. • Earth's age has been determined by using radiometric dating techniques on rocks from the moon and from other parts of the solar system, such as meteorites, that were formed when the solar system was forming.
Index Fossils 1 Define *index fossil.* 2 Explain how index fossils can be used to determine the age of rock.	• An index fossil is a fossil that is distinct, abundant, and widespread for only a short period of geologic time. • Because organisms that formed index fossils lived for short spans of geologic time, the rock layer in which the fossil was formed could have been formed only during that same time period.

Options for Instruction

Two parallel paths provide coverage of the Essential Questions, with a strong **Inquiry** strand woven into each. Follow the **Print Path,** the **Digital Path,** or your customized combination of print, digital, and inquiry.

Print Path

Teaching support for the Print Path appears with the Student Pages.

Inquiry Labs and Activities

Digital Path

Digital Path shortcut: TS671220

Print Path	Inquiry Labs and Activities	Digital Path
It's About Time, SE pp. 108–110 **How can the absolute age of rock be determined?** • Using Radioactive Isotopes • By Radiometric Dating **What is the best rock for radiometric dating?**	**Quick Lab** **Radioactive Decay** **Activity** **Absolute Dating Skit**	**Isotopes** **Animation** **Radioactive Decay** **Interactive Images**
Time for a Change, SE pp. 111–112 **What are some radiometric dating methods?** • Radiocarbon Dating • Potassium-Argon and Uranium-Lead	**Activity** **On the Clock**	**Radiometric Dating** **Interactive Images**
Time Will Tell, SE p. 113 **How is radiometric dating used to determine the age of Earth?**	**Daily Demo** **Penny Decay**	**Radiometric Dating** **Interactive Graphics**
Showing Your Age, SE pp. 114–115 **How can fossils help to determine the age of sedimentary rock?** • Using Index Fossils **How are index fossils used?**	**Activity** **Relative vs. Absolute Age** **Quick Lab** **Index Fossils**	**Index Fossils** **Diagram**

Options for Assessment

See the Evaluate page for options, including Formative Assessment, Summative Assessment, and Unit Review.

Engage and Explore

Activities and Discussion

Activity *Absolute Dating Skit*

Radiometric Dating

 whole class
 25 min

Have 28 students act as radioactive isotopes in a newly formed rock sample. Remaining students will play the role of geologists. Ask the isotopes to stand. Tell them that they have a half-life of 1 min. Have the geologists note the time and send them outside the classroom. After 1 min, have half of the isotopes sit. Repeat this step 1 min later (7 students remain standing). Call the geologists back. Ask them to determine the age of the rock sample based on the number of original isotopes, the time they waited, and the length of a half-life.

Discussion *Absolute Age*

Engage

Absolute Dating

 whole class
 20 min

When used to express the ages of very old rocks, absolute age may be off by millions of years. In the context of hundreds of billions of years, a million years is relatively insignificant. Use this example to clarify this concept. If a 12-year-old boy is asked, "How old are you?" the boy usually will answer, "12," not "12 years, 2 months, 3 weeks, and 4 days." Point out that in this example, the answer "12" is close enough to be useful as the boy's absolute age.

Activity *How Old Is It?*

Absolute Dating

 whole class; partners
 30 min

Students survey five classmates to find out how long ago they think an event happened. The student records each response and discusses with a partner to determine if the answers collected agree and are correct. Answers such as "11 years," "about 10 years," and "maybe a decade" can be different, but all still be accurate. Relate this to the idea that some forms of absolute dating give correct (accurate) answers, but not exact (precise) answers.

Activity *On the Clock*

Radiometric Dating

 individuals
 20 min
 GUIDED inquiry

Have students gather pencils in three colors. Direct them to draw the face of an analog clock on a sheet of paper. Have them draw arrows to represent the hour and minute hands as they would appear at 12:00. Remind students that radioactivity is like a clock in that elements break down at steady rates. Have students determine where on their clock the minute hand should appear after a radioactive isotope has undergone one half-life and draw the clock hand using a colored pencil. Then have them decide where the clock hand would appear after two-half lives, and draw this hand in a different color. Hand representing first half-life should appear at 6; hand for second half-life at 9.

Activity *Relative vs. Absolute Age*

Engage

Index Fossils

 small groups
 25 min
 GUIDED inquiry

Provide students with stacks of two different colored paper and two pieces of white paper that have sketches of fossils (*Tropites* or trilobites) and dates identifying how long ago the organisms that formed the fossils lived. Have one student in each group stack the colored paper in layers of alternating color. Then have a student place the fossil page representing the older fossil within a paper layer near the bottom of the stack and the younger fossil page in a layer nearer the top. Tell students that the colored papers represent rock layers. **Ask:** If the rock layers have remained undisturbed, what can you tell about their relative ages? Those nearest the bottom are older than those higher up. **Ask:** Find the location of the "index fossils." How does knowing when these organisms lived help you describe the ages of the rock layers? Sample answer: Now the absolute age of the rock layer can be determined.

DIRECTED inquiry introduces inquiry skills within a structured framework.

GUIDED inquiry develops inquiry skills within a supportive environment.

INDEPENDENT inquiry deepens inquiry skills with student-driven questions or procedures.

Labs and Demos

Daily Demo *Penny Decay*

Engage

Introducing Key Topics

 whole class

 20 min

GUIDED inquiry

PURPOSE **To show a concrete example of radiometric dating**

MATERIALS

- **quarters (25) (parent isotopes)**
- **pennies (25) (daughter isotopes)**
- **board and chalk or markers**

1 Create a three-column chart with the column heads *Time Step*, *Number of Quarters*, and *Number of Pennies*.

2 In the first row of your chart, write 1 in the first column, 25 in the second column, and 0 in the third column.

3 Drop the quarters on a flat surface.

4 Replace any quarters that are face up with pennies. These have decayed and are replaced by daughter isotopes.

5 Record the results in the second row of the chart: 2 in the first column, number of quarters left in the second column, and number of pennies in the third column.

6 Repeat until all of the quarters have been replaced by pennies.

7 Have students study the chart you have created.

8 **Observe** What is the half-life for the quarters in this demonstration? What changes to the outcome might adding quarters cause?

Quick Lab *Index Fossils*

PURPOSE **To illustrate how index fossils can be used as a method of absolute dating**

See the Lab Manual or go Online for planning information.

Quick Lab *Radioactive Decay*

Absolute Dating

 pairs

 25 min

DIRECTED inquiry

Students demonstrate how a sample of radioactive material decays over time using paper to represent the radioactive sample.

PURPOSE **To model radioactive decay**

MATERIALS

- **paper**
- **stopwatch**
- **scissors**

Customize Your Labs

See the Lab Manual for lab datasheets.

Go Online for editable lab datasheets.

Activities and Discussion

- ☐ **Activity** Absolute Dating Skit
- ☐ **Activity** On the Clock
- ☐ **Activity** Relative vs. Absolute Age
- ☐ **Activity** How Old Is It?
- ☐ **Discussion** Absolute Age

Labs and Demos

- ☐ **Daily Demo** Penny Decay
- ☐ **Quick Lab** Index Fossils
- ☐ **Quick Lab** Radioactive Decay

Your Resources

Explain Science Concepts

Key Topics	Print Path	Digital Path
Absolute Dating	☐ **It's About Time!,** SE pp. 108–110 • Active Reading, #5 • Visualize It!, #6 • Visualize It!, #7 • Do the Math, #8 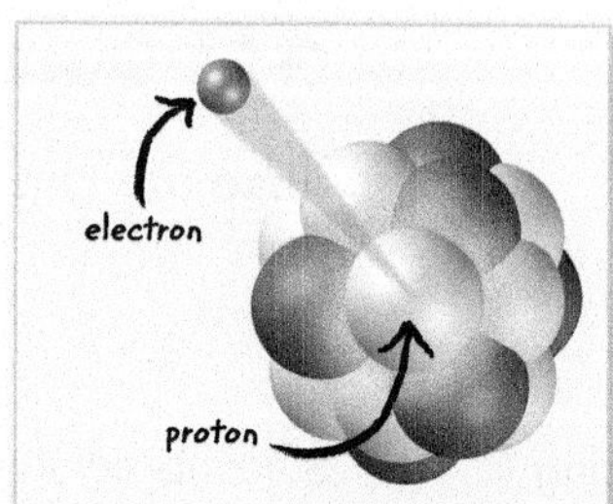 	☐ **Isotopes** Learn how some materials are unstable. ☐ **Radioactive Decay** See what happens to radioactive material over time.
Radiometric Dating	☐ **Time for a Change,** SE pp. 111–112 • Active Reading (Annotation Strategy) #9 • Active Reading, #10 • Active Reading (Annotation Strategy) #11 	☐ **Radiometric Dating** Learn how the age of rock can be found. 
The Age of the Earth	☐ **Time Will Tell,** SE p. 113 • Active Reading (Annotation Strategy) #12 • Think Outside the Book #13  	☐ **Radiometric Dating** Learn about how scientists have estimated the approximate age of Earth.
Index Fossils	☐ **Showing Your Age,** SE pp. 114–115 • Active Reading (Annotation Strategy) #14 • Active Reading (Annotation Strategy) #15 • Visualize It!, #16 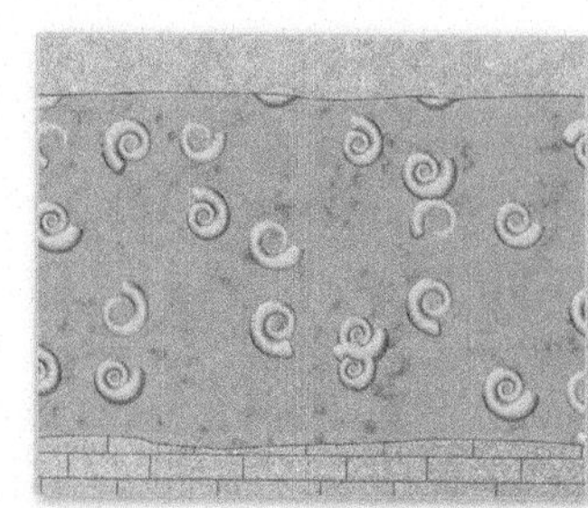	☐ **Index Fossils** Learn how fossils with certain qualities can be used to date layers. 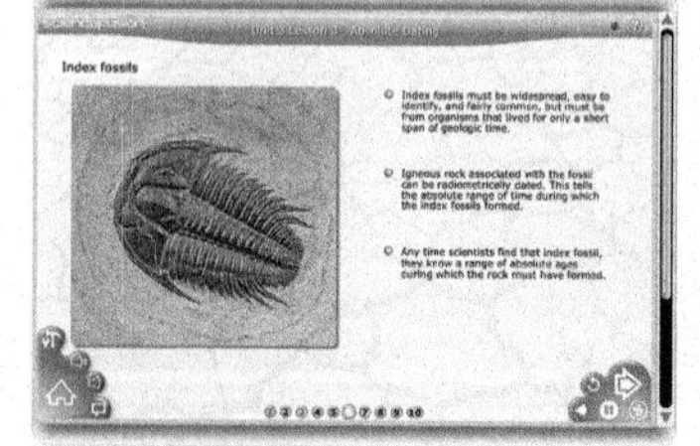

Differentiated Instruction

Basic *Jigsaw*

Synthesizing Key Topics

 small groups
 40 min

Have students gather in small groups composed of four students each. Assign one student in each group one section from this lesson for which they will become an expert. Have students regroup based on the section of the lesson they have been assigned so that experts in the same area are working together. Have the experts study their section, and any additional resources available in the classroom. Once students have been allowed time to master their section, have them rejoin their original group. Each expert should be provided time to teach the rest of the group members about their section. Group members should be encouraged to take notes and ask questions to make sure they know all there is to know about each section by the end of the lesson.

Advanced *Write It Out*

Synthesizing Key Topics

 individuals
 35 min

Written Pieces Ask students to synthesize their understanding of the differences between relative and absolute dating by writing a paragraph explaining why geologists use both absolute and relative dating to interpret the past. Direct students to include a description of how fossils and rock layers are used as part of each dating method. Ask students to share their ideas in the class by reading aloud their descriptions.

 *Optional Online rubric: Written Pieces*

ELL *Note Taking*

Synthesizing Key Topics

 pairs
40 min

Have students work in pairs to go back through the lesson content and take notes. Have them write down the question heads and then any other subheads. Then have them jot down important features from each of these subsections.

Lesson Vocabulary

absolute dating **radiometric dating** **radioactive decay**
half-life

Previewing Vocabulary

 whole class
 25 min

Pairing Up After students read the section, have them work together to define the terms and use each in a descriptive sentence.

Reinforcing Vocabulary

 individuals
 30 min

Three-Panel FlipChart To help students remember *absolute dating, radiometric dating* and *radioactive decay* have them make a Three-Panel FlipChart. On one panel, they should illustrate the term. On another, they should write the definition. On the third, they should write an example.

Optional Online resource: Three-Panel FlipChart support

Customize Your Core Lesson

Core Instruction

- ☐ Print Path choices
- ☐ Digital Path choices

Vocabulary

- ☐ Previewing Vocabulary Pairing Up
- ☐ Reinforcing Vocabulary Three-Panel FlipChart

Differentiated Instruction

- ☐ Basic Jigsaw
- ☐ Advanced Write It Out
- ☐ ELL Note Taking

Your Resources

Extend Science Concepts

Reinforce and Review

Activity *Review in the Round*

Synthesizing Key Topics

 small groups
45 min

Inside/Outside Circles Provide each student with an index card that contains a question about the topics in this lesson.

1 Have students write their answers on the back of the index cards. Check the answers to make sure they are correct. If incorrect, have students adjust incorrect answers.

2 Ask students to pair up to form two circles. One partner is in an inside circle; the other is in an outside circle. Students in the inside circle face out; those on the outside face in.

3 Have each student in the inside circle ask his or her partner the question on their index card. The partner answers. If the answer is incorrect, the student in the inside circle should teach the other student the correct answer. Repeat this step, having students in the outside circle ask the questions.

4 Have students on the outside circle rotate one person to the right. He or she faces a new partner and gets a new question. Students on the outside can continue to rotate after each question.

Graphic Organizer

Absolute Dating

 individuals
 35 min

Cluster Diagram After students have studied the lesson, ask them to develop a cluster diagram that includes the following terms: ***absolute dating, half-life, radioactive decay, radiometric dating.***

Optional Online resource: Cluster Diagram support

Going Further

Life Science Connection

Synthesizing Key Topics

 individuals or pairs
varied

Carbon-14 Carbon-14 is continuously created in the atmosphere by cosmic radiation. There is one atom of radioactive carbon-14 for every trillion atoms of carbon-12 in the atmosphere. Plants absorb carbon-14 directly through their leaves in the form of carbon dioxide. Animals take in carbon-14 indirectly when they eat plants. Although carbon-14 disintegrates at a constant rate, it is continuously renewed as long as an organism remains alive. When an organism dies, it stops absorbing carbon-14 and its radiocarbon "clock" is set. Have students draw a diagram of this process.

Math Connection

Radiometric Dating

 pairs
35 min

Calculating Half-Life Assess students' understanding by asking them to calculate how old the remains of an organism are when 1/4, 1/8, 1/32, and 1/64 of its carbon-14 remains. Remind students that the half-life for carbon-14 is 5,730 y. Answers: 11,460 y; 17,190 y; 28,650 y; 34,380 y Then have them calculate the age of a piece of volcanic igneous rock when samples of the rock show that 1/2, 1/8, and 1/64 of its potassium-40 remains. Remind students that potassium-40 decays to form argon and has a half-life of 1.25 billion years. Answers: 1.25 billion years; 3.75 billion years; 7.5 billion years

Customize Your Closing

See the Assessment Guide for quizzes and tests.

Go Online to edit and create quizzes and tests.

Reinforce and Review

- ☐ **Activity** Review in the Round
- ☐ **Graphic Organizer** Cluster Diagram
- ☐ **Print Path** Visual Summary, SE p. 116
- ☐ **Digital Path** Lesson Closer

Evaluate Student Mastery

Formative Assessment

See the teacher support below the Student Pages for additional Formative Assessment questions.

Ask students to describe how scientists are able to determine how long ago different events on Earth happened, such as when some rocks formed and when the Earth as a whole formed. Sample answers: Radiometric dating provides absolute ages for some rocks, mostly igneous rock. Index fossils provide age ranges for some sedimentary rock layers. These data with data about the relative ages of rock layers, can be used to deduce the ages of other layers. Radiometric dating from other parts of the solar system provide an approximate age for planet Earth.

Reteach

Formative assessment may show you that students need reinforcement for certain topics. The resources below are recommended for reteaching. If students were introduced to topics through the Print Path, you can also use the Digital Path for reteaching, and vice versa.

Can be assigned to individual students

Absolute Dating
Activity Absolute Dating Skit

Radiometric Dating
Activity On the Clock

The Age of Earth
Daily Demo Penny Decay

Index Fossils
Activity Relative vs. Absolute Age

Summative Assessment

Alternative Assessment

Create a Museum Exhibit

Online resources: student worksheet, optional rubrics

Absolute Dating

Tic-Tac-Toe: ***Create a Museum Exhibit***

Suppose you are an expert in absolute dating, and you have offered to help a local museum create an exhibit about Earth's age.

1. Work on your own, with a partner, or with a small group.
2. Choose three quick activities from the game. Check the boxes you plan to complete. They must form a straight line in any direction.
3. Have your teacher approve your plan.
4. Do each activity, and turn in your results.

__ **Half-Life Breakdown**	__ **You Ask the Questions**	__ **Which Is Best?**
Create a display for the museum exhibit that explains what half-life is. The poster should also discuss how scientists use half-life in radiometric dating.	The exhibit you're creating will have an interactive quiz for visitors to take. Write a quiz that contains at least four questions about index fossils and the ways scientists use them.	The museum's director wants a display showing radiometric dating of one rock sample. They have sedimentary, igneous, and metamorphic samples. Write a memo to the director, telling which sample to use and why.
__ **Decay Drama** Develop and put on a skit to show visitors how radioactive decay makes it possible for scientists to date objects.	__ **Dating Description** Create a multimedia presentation that lists and describes the different methods of radiometric dating. Include information about the best situations in which to use each method.	__ **Absolute Persuasion** Museum donors are unsure whether they want to pay you to develop the exhibit. They do not understand what absolute dating is. Give a persuasive speech in which you explain what absolute dating is and why the exhibit is needed.
__ **Meeting the Requirements** Design a Web page that will help bring people to the new exhibit. On the page, discuss the requirements fossils must meet to be considered index fossils.	__ **Come on Down!** To encourage press coverage of the exhibit, you must write a press release. Write a press release that explains what absolute dating is and why people should visit the exhibit.	__ **How Old Is Earth?** Create and perform a song that will play at the new museum exhibit. In your song, describe how scientists determine Earth's age.

Going Further
- ☐ Life Science Connection
- ☐ Math Connection

Formative Assessment
- ☐ Strategies Throughout TE
- ☐ Lesson Review SE

Summative Assessment
- ☐ Alternative Assessment Create a Museum Exhibit
- ☐ Lesson Quiz
- ☐ Unit Tests A and B
- ☐ Unit Review SE End-of-Unit

Your Resources

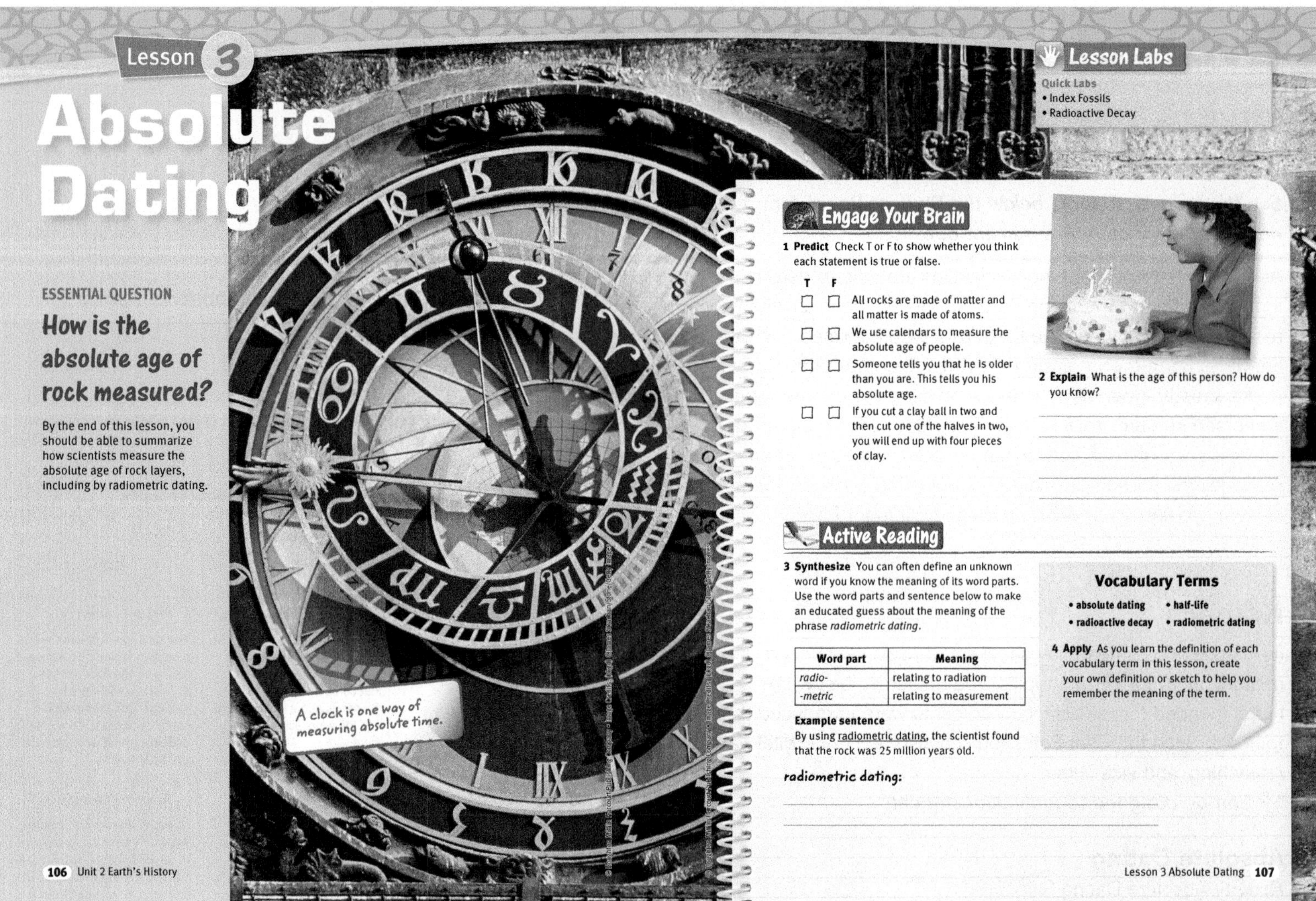

Lesson 3

Absolute Dating

ESSENTIAL QUESTION

How is the absolute age of rock measured?

By the end of this lesson, you should be able to summarize how scientists measure the absolute age of rock layers, including by radiometric dating.

A clock is one way of measuring absolute time.

Lesson Labs

Quick Labs
- Index Fossils
- Radioactive Decay

Engage Your Brain

1 Predict Check T or F to show whether you think each statement is true or false.

T	F	
☐	☐	All rocks are made of matter and all matter is made of atoms.
☐	☐	We use calendars to measure the absolute age of people.
☐	☐	Someone tells you that he is older than you are. This tells you his absolute age.
☐	☐	If you cut a clay ball in two and then cut one of the halves in two, you will end up with four pieces of clay.

2 Explain What is the age of this person? How do you know?

Active Reading

3 Synthesize You can often define an unknown word if you know the meaning of its word parts. Use the word parts and sentence below to make an educated guess about the meaning of the phrase *radiometric dating*.

Word part	Meaning
radio-	relating to radiation
-metric	relating to measurement

Example sentence

By using radiometric dating, the scientist found that the rock was 25 million years old.

radiometric dating:

Vocabulary Terms

- absolute dating
- half-life
- radioactive decay
- radiometric dating

4 Apply As you learn the definition of each vocabulary term in this lesson, create your own definition or sketch to help you remember the meaning of the term.

106 Unit 2 Earth's History

Lesson 3 Absolute Dating 107

Answers

Answers for 1–3 should represent students' current thoughts, even if incorrect.

1. T; T; F; F
2. Sample answer: She is 14 years old. The image is showing a birthday cake for the girl and the candles on it are shaped and positioned to form the number 14.
3. Sample answer: Measuring the age of something using radiation.
4. Students should define or sketch each vocabulary term in the lesson.

Opening Your Lesson

Have students share their thoughts about the age of the person shown in item 2. Discuss how the person's age might compare to theirs (e.g., Is the person older/younger than they are?) and how they might determine the person's actual age. Relate students' responses to the concepts of relative age and absolute age, which students will explore in this lesson.

Prerequisites: Scientists study rocks to learn more about Earth's history; some rock layers contain fossils; layers of rock are different ages, with older below younger if the layers are undisturbed.

Accessing Prior Knowledge: To assess students' prior knowledge about dating rock, have them conduct a Textbook DRTA. Begin by explaining that DRTA stands for directed reading/thinking activity. To complete the activity, students need to (1) preview the selection; (2) write what they know, what they think they know, and what they think they'll learn about dating rock; (3) read the selection; and (4) write what they learned. Discuss whether students' expectations were reasonable, and whether they learned additional information that they did not anticipate.

Optional Online resource: Textbook DRTA

It's About Time!

How can the absolute age of rock be determined?

Determining the actual age of an event or object in years is called **absolute dating**. Scientists use many different ways to find the absolute age of rock and other materials. One way is by using radioactive isotopes (ray•dee•oh•AK•tiv EYE•suh•tohpz).

Using Radioactive Isotopes

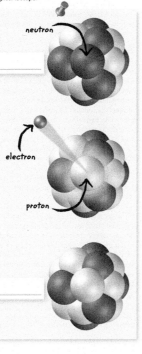

Atoms of the same element that have a different number of neutrons are called isotopes. Many isotopes are stable, meaning that they stay in their original form. But some isotopes are unstable, and break down to form different isotopes. The unstable isotopes are called *radioactive*. The breakdown of a radioactive isotope into a stable isotope of the same element or of another element is called **radioactive decay**. As shown on the right, radioactive decay for many isotopes happens when a neutron is converted to a proton, with the release of an electron. A radioactive isotope is called a *parent isotope*. The stable isotope formed by its breakdown is called the *daughter isotope*.

Each radioactive isotope decays at a specific, constant rate. **Half-life** is the time needed for half of a sample of a radioactive substance to undergo radioactive decay to form daughter isotopes. Half-life is always given in units of time.

Active Reading **5 Describe** How much of a radioactive parent isotope remains after one half-life has passed? Explain your answer.

Visualize It!

6 Identify Label the parent isotope and the daughter isotope.

neutron

electron

proton

By Radiometric Dating

Some radioactive isotopes in mineral crystals can act as clocks. These mineral crystals record the ages of the rocks in which the minerals formed. Scientists study the amounts of parent and daughter isotopes to date samples. If you know how fast a radioactive isotope decays, you can figure out the sample's absolute age. Finding the absolute age of a sample by determining the relative percentages of a radioactive parent isotope and a stable daughter isotope is called **radiometric dating** (ray•dee•oh•MET•rik DAYT•ing). The figure on the right shows how the relative percentages of a parent isotope and a daughter isotope change with the passing of each half-life.The following is an example of how radiometric dating can be used:

- You want to determine the age of a sample that contains a radioactive isotope that has a half-life of 10 million years.
- You analyze the sample and find equal amounts of parent and daughter isotopes.
- Because 50%, or ½, of the parent isotope has decayed, you know that 1 half-life has passed.
- So, the sample is 10 million years old.

What is the best rock for radiometric dating?

Igneous rock is often the best type of rock sample to use for radiometric dating. When igneous rock forms, elements are separated into different minerals in the rock. When they form, minerals in igneous rocks often contain only a parent isotope and none of the daughter isotope. This makes the isotope percentages easier to interpret and helps dating to be more accurate.

Visualize It!

7 Calculate Fill in the number of parent isotopes and daughter isotopes in the spaces beside the images below.

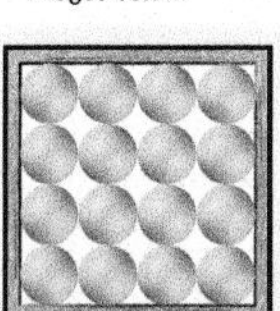

0 years
Parent isotope = 16
Daughter isotope = 0
100% of the sample is parent isotope.

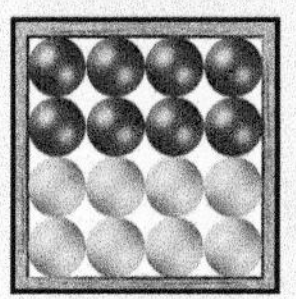

After 1 half-life
Parent isotope = 8
Daughter isotope = 8
50%, or $\frac{1}{2}$, of the sample is parent isotope.

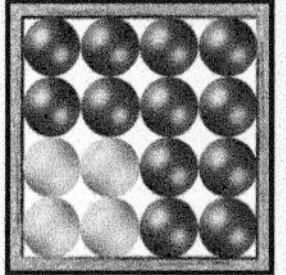

After 2 half-lives
Parent isotope = 4
Daughter isotope = ____
25%, or $\frac{1}{4}$, of the sample is parent isotope.

After 3 half-lives
Parent isotope = ____
Daughter isotope = ____
12.5%, or $\frac{1}{8}$, of the sample is parent isotope.

Answers

5. Half the original amount; half-life refers to the time it takes for half of a radioactive substance to undergo radioactive decay.
6. The parent isotope is the top image and the daughter isotope is the bottom image.
7. daughter isotope = 12; parent isotope = 2, daughter isotope = 14

Interpreting Visuals

Point out to students that the spheres in the diagram describing radioactive decay represent the subatomic particles that make up the isotope—protons, neutrons, and electrons. Point out that because the number of protons in the parent isotope changes, the daughter isotope represents a new element that has a different atomic number. Have students carry out the Visualize It! activity for the diagram that illustrates half-life. Use their responses to help point out that the spheres in the half-life diagram represent the amounts of the parent isotope and the daughter isotope present in a sample, not the subatomic particles making up each isotope.

Building Math Skills

Working with Fractions Help students recognize how fractions are manipulated to show the decrease in the total amount of the parent isotope remaining after each half-life cycle. To illustrate this point, explain that after 1 half-life, 50% or 1/2 of the parent isotope remains. After a second half-life, 1/2 of the parent isotope that was present after the first half-life remains, which is expressed mathematically as 1/2 × 1/2 = 1/4 (rather than 1/2 × 2). After a third half-life, 1/8 of the sample remains because 1/2 × 1/2 × 1/2 = 1/8. Have students calculate what fraction of the sample will remain after a fourth half-life. 1/2 × 1/2 × 1/2 × 1/2 = 1/16

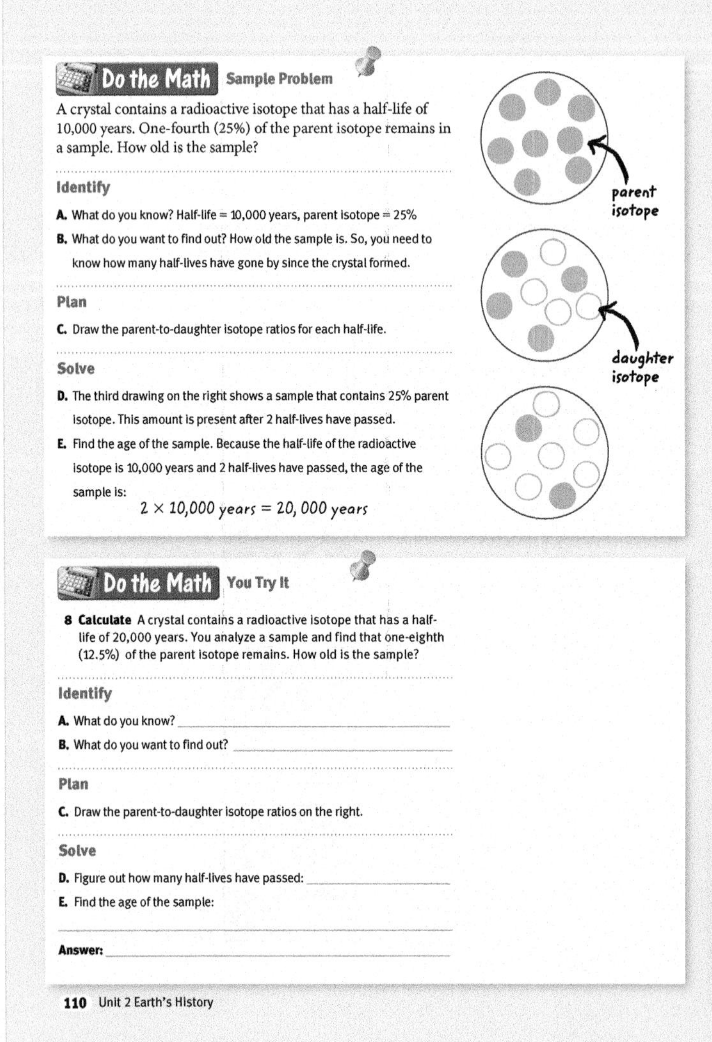

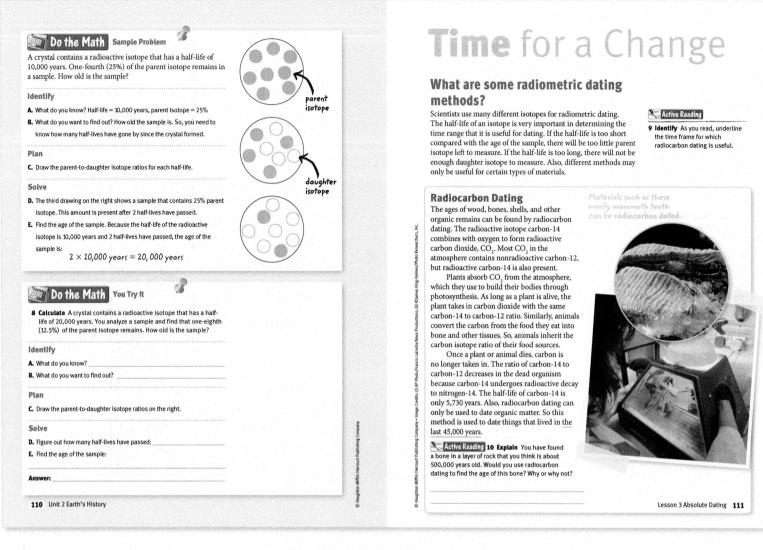

Do the Math Sample Problem

A crystal contains a radioactive isotope that has a half-life of 10,000 years. One-fourth (25%) of the parent isotope remains in a sample. How old is the sample?

Identify

A. What do you know? Half-life = 10,000 years, parent isotope = 25%

B. What do you want to find out? How old the sample is. So, you need to know how many half-lives have gone by since the crystal formed.

Plan

C. Draw the parent-to-daughter isotope ratios for each half-life.

Solve

D. The third drawing on the right shows a sample that contains 25% parent isotope. This amount is present after 2 half-lives have passed.

E. Find the age of the sample. Because the half-life of the radioactive isotope is 10,000 years and 2 half-lives have passed, the age of the sample is:

$2 \times 10{,}000\ years = 20{,}000\ years$

Do the Math You Try It

8 Calculate A crystal contains a radioactive isotope that has a half-life of 20,000 years. You analyze a sample and find that one-eighth (12.5%) of the parent isotope remains. How old is the sample?

Identify

A. What do you know? ____________

B. What do you want to find out? ____________

Plan

C. Draw the parent-to-daughter isotope ratios on the right.

Solve

D. Figure out how many half-lives have passed: ____________

E. Find the age of the sample: ____________

Answer: ____________

110 Unit 2 Earth's History

Time for a Change

What are some radiometric dating methods?

Scientists use many different isotopes for radiometric dating. The half-life of an isotope is very important in determining the time range that it is useful for dating. If the half-life is too short compared with the age of the sample, there will be too little parent isotope left to measure. If the half-life is too long, there will not be enough daughter isotope to measure. Also, different methods may only be useful for certain types of materials.

Active Reading

9 Identify As you read, underline the time frame for which radiocarbon dating is useful.

Radiocarbon Dating

The ages of wood, bones, shells, and other organic remains can be found by radiocarbon dating. The radioactive isotope carbon-14 combines with oxygen to form radioactive carbon dioxide, CO_2. Most CO_2 in the atmosphere contains nonradioactive carbon-12, but radioactive carbon-14 is also present.

Plants absorb CO_2 from the atmosphere, which they use to build their bodies through photosynthesis. As long as a plant is alive, the plant takes in carbon dioxide with the same carbon-14 to carbon-12 ratio. Similarly, animals convert the carbon from the food they eat into bone and other tissues. So, animals inherit the carbon isotope ratio of their food sources.

Once a plant or animal dies, carbon is no longer taken in. The ratio of carbon-14 to carbon-12 decreases in the dead organism because carbon-14 undergoes radioactive decay to nitrogen-14. The half-life of carbon-14 is only 5,730 years. Also, radiocarbon dating can only be used to date organic matter. So this method is used to date things that lived in the last 45,000 years.

Materials such as these woolly mammoth teeth can be radiocarbon dated.

Active Reading **10 Explain** You have found a bone in a layer of rock that you think is about 500,000 years old. Would you use radiocarbon dating to find the age of this bone? Why or why not?

____

Lesson 3 Absolute Dating 111

Answers

8. A: half-life = 20,000 years, parent isotope = 12.5%; B: How old the sample is. C: Student sketches should reflect the parent-to-daughter isotope ratio after each half-life has passed, until 12.5% of parent isotope is represented; D: 3; E: The age of the crystal is:

   3 × 20,000 years = 60,000 years old

9. *See students' pages for annotations.*

10. No, I would not use radiocarbon dating. The bone would be close to the age of the rock it is found in, which is about 500,000 years old. Radiocarbon dating is used for dating organic objects that are not older than about 45,000 years.

Do the Math

Remind students that the different colored spheres in the visuals represent the parent isotope and the daughter isotope. As students review the sample problem, review with them how to determine the number of half-lives represented by the fraction one-quarter (25%) parent isotope. Then explain that they need to multiply the number of half-lives represented by 1/4 parent isotope (2) by the length of the half-life (10,000 years) to determine that the age of the crystal is 20,000 years.

Have students work in small groups to solve the You Try It! portion of this feature. If needed, review how to calculate what fraction 12.5% represents (12.5/100 = 125/1,000). Students can reduce this fraction to its simplest form (1/8) by dividing the numerator and denominator by 125. Have them calculate how many times 2 is multiplied by itself to equal 8 (the denominator of the fraction) to find that the sample has undergone 3 half-lives. They can then multiply 3 by 20,000 y to determine the age of the crystal as 60,000 y.

Probing Question DIRECTED Inquiry

Synthesize What is the age of the crystal described above if 6.25% of the parent isotope remains? 6.25% represents 4 half-lives, so the age of the crystal is 4 × 20,000 = 80,000 y.

Radiometric dating has been done on Mammoth Mountain's volcanic rock.

Scientist and astronaut Harrison Schmitt collected samples of rock on the moon during the ***Apollo 17*** mission in 1972.

Active Reading 11 Identify As you read this page, underline the time frame for which each method is most useful.

Potassium-Argon Dating

The element potassium (puh•TAS•ee•uhm) occurs in two stable isotopes, potassium-41 and potassium-39, and one radioactive isotope that occurs naturally, potassium-40. Potassium-40 decays to argon and calcium. It has a half-life of 1.25 billion years. Scientists measure argon as the daughter isotope. Potassium-argon dating is often used to date igneous volcanic rocks. This method is used to date rocks that are between about 100,000 years and a few billion years old.

Uranium-Lead Dating

An isotope of uranium (yoo•RAY•nee•uhm), called uranium-238, is a radioactive isotope that decays to lead-206. Uranium-lead dating is based on measuring the amount of the lead-206 daughter isotope in a sample. Uranium-238 has a half-life of 4.5 billion years.

Uranium-lead dating can be used to determine the age of igneous rocks that are between 100 million years and billions of years old. Younger rocks do not have enough daughter isotope to be accurately measured by this method. Uranium-lead dating was used to find the earliest accurate age of Earth.

Time Will Tell

How is radiometric dating used to determine the age of Earth?

Radiometric dating can be used to find the age of Earth, though not by dating Earth rocks. The first rocks that formed on Earth have long ago been eroded or melted, or buried under younger rocks. So, there are no Earth rocks which can be directly studied that are as old as our planet. But other bodies in space do have rock that is as old as our solar system.

Meteorites (MEE•tee•uh•rytz) are small, rocky bodies that have traveled through space and fallen to Earth's surface. Scientists have found meteorites on Earth, such as the one shown below. Rocks from the moon have also been collected. Radiometric dating has been done on these rocks from other parts of our solar system. The absolute ages of these samples show that our solar system, including Earth, is about 4.6 billion years old.

Active Reading

12 Identify As you read, underline the reason why scientists cannot use rocks from Earth to measure the age of Earth.

Think Outside the Book Inquiry

13 Model Develop a way to help people understand how large the number 4.6 billion is.

This 4.5 billion-year-old rock is part of a meteorite that landed in Antarctica. It is thought to be from Mars.

Answers

11. *See students' pages for annotations.*
12. *See students' pages for annotations.*
13. Answers will vary. Students can use analogies for comparison. Encourage students to build models and to use common examples for analogies that people can easily relate to.

Building Reading Skills

Four-Column Chart This lesson contains difficult and sometimes confusing information about different types of radiometric dating methods. To help students keep all of the methods straight, encourage them to organize the information in a four-column chart. Students can begin by creating a chart that has four columns with the headings: ***Method of Radiometric Dating, Materials Involved, Types of Things Dated*** (rock or remains of organisms), and ***Useful Range of Age of Method***. Students can then fill in the cells of the chart with the applicable information for each of the radiometric dating methods discussed in the text as they read.

Formative Assessment

Ask: Why would radiocarbon dating not be useful for determining the ages of volcanic igneous rocks or rocks collected from the moon? Radiocarbon dating is used to date the remains of once-living things, not rocks. Also, this method of dating is not useful for objects that are more than 45,000 years old. **Ask:** On what types of organism remains is radiocarbon dating useful? Sample answer: only on remains that have not been altered by fossilization

Showing Your Age

How can fossils help to determine the age of sedimentary rock?

Active Reading

14 Identify As you read, underline the requirements for a fossil to be an index fossil.

Sedimentary rock layers and the fossils within these layers cannot be dated directly. But igneous rock layers on either side of a fossil layer can be dated radiometrically. Once the older and younger rock layers are dated, scientists can assign an absolute age range to the sedimentary rock layer that the fossils are found in.

Using Index Fossils

Scientists have found that particular types of fossils appear only in certain layers of rock. By dating igneous rock layers above and below these fossil layers, scientists can determine the time span in which the organisms lived. *Index fossils,* such as the ones shown below, are fossils that are used to estimate the absolute age of the rock layers in which they are found. Once the absolute age of an index fossil is known, it can be used to determine the age of rock layers that contain the same index fossil anywhere on Earth.

To be an index fossil, the organism from which the fossil formed must have lived during a relatively short geologic time span. The fossils of the organism must be relatively common and must be found over a large area. Index fossils must also have features that make them different from other fossils.

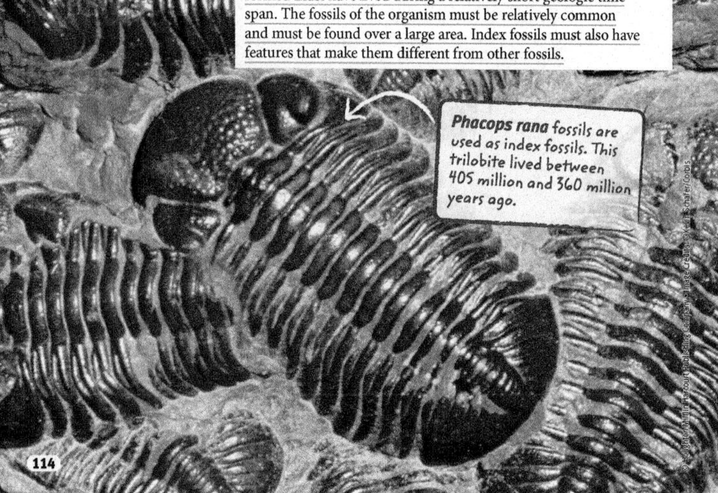

Phacops rana *fossils are used as index fossils. This trilobite lived between 405 million and 360 million years ago.*

How are index fossils used?

Index fossils act as markers for the time that the organisms lived on Earth. Organisms that formed index fossils lived during short periods of geologic time. So, the rock layer that an index fossil is found in can be dated accurately. For example, ammonites were marine mollusks, similar to a modern squid. They lived in coiled shells in ancient seas. The ammonite *Tropites* (troh•PY•teez) lived between 230 million and 208 million years ago. So, whenever scientists find a fossil of *Tropites*, they know that the rock layer the fossil was found in formed between 230 million and 208 million years ago. As shown below, this can also tell scientists something about the ages of surrounding rock layers.

Trilobite (TRY•luh•byt) fossils are another example of a good index fossil. The closest living relatives of trilobites are the horseshoe crab, spiders, and scorpions. *Phacops rana* is a trilobite that lived between 405 million and 360 million years ago. The *Phacops rana* fossil, shown on the previous page, is the state fossil of Pennsylvania.

Index fossils can also be used to date rock layers in separate areas. The appearance of the same index fossil in rock of different areas shows that the rock layers formed at about the same time.

Active Reading

15 Identify As you read, underline examples of organisms whose fossils are index fossils. Include the time frame for which they are used to date rock.

Visualize It!

16 Infer *Tropites* fossils are found in the middle rock layer shown below. Place each of the following ages beside the correct rock layer: 215 million/500 million/100 million.

Fossils of a genus of ammonites called ***Tropites*** *are good index fossils.*

Answers

14. *See students' pages for annotations.*
15. *See students' pages for annotations.*
16. top: 100 million ; middle: 215 million; bottom: 500 million

Formative Assessment

Ask: Why can't radiometric dating of Earth rocks be used to determine the age of Earth? Sample answer: Earth rocks are constantly changed through processes such as erosion and melting, so no rocks on Earth are as old as Earth itself. **Ask:** What are the characteristics of an index fossil? Sample answer: It must be present in rock found over a large region, have clearly distinguishing features, be from an organism that lived during only a short time period in Earth's history, and occur in large numbers within rock layers.

Using Annotations

Text Structure: Details Students are asked to underline the details contained in the description of how index fossils are used. Long descriptions can sometimes be difficult for students. Underlining is a great tool for drawing their attention to, and helping them remember, important details. Underline one or two items as a class, or review students' results as a class. Suggest that they underline only the important word or phrase.

For Greater Depth Have students put their underlined details into a mind map with *index fossil* in the center.

Optional Online resource: Mind Map support

Student Pages 114–117

Visual Summary

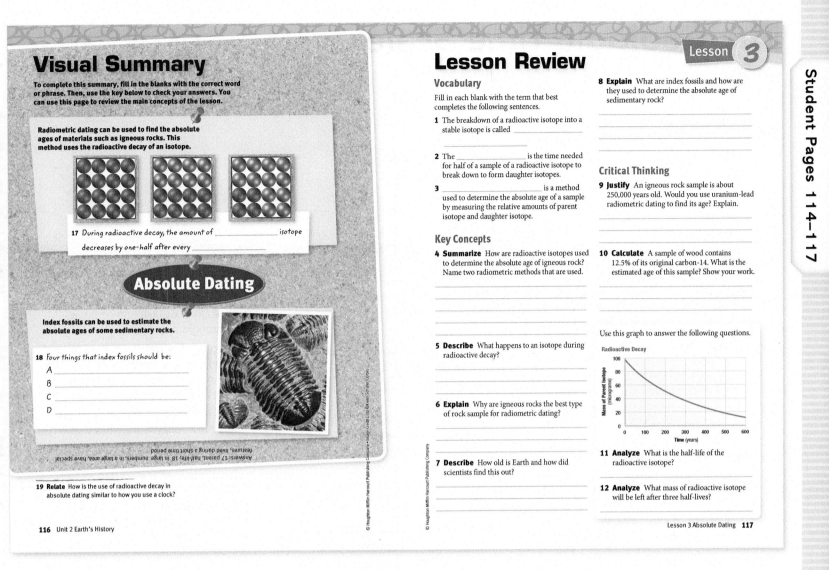

To complete this summary, fill in the blanks with the correct word or phrase. Then, use the key below to check your answers. You can use this page to review the main concepts of the lesson.

Radiometric dating can be used to find the absolute ages of materials such as igneous rocks. This method uses the radioactive decay of an isotope.

17 *During radioactive decay, the amount of ____________ isotope decreases by one-half after every ____________*

Absolute Dating

Index fossils can be used to estimate the absolute ages of some sedimentary rocks.

18 *Four things that index fossils should be:*

A ____________

B ____________

C ____________

D ____________

Answers: 17 parent, half-life; 18 in large numbers, in a large area, have special features, lived during a short time period

19 Relate How is the use of radioactive decay in absolute dating similar to how you use a clock?

Lesson 3

Lesson Review

Vocabulary

Fill in each blank with the term that best completes the following sentences.

1 The breakdown of a radioactive isotope into a stable isotope is called ____________

2 The ____________ is the time needed for half of a sample of a radioactive isotope to break down to form daughter isotopes.

3 ____________ is a method used to determine the absolute age of a sample by measuring the relative amounts of parent isotope and daughter isotope.

Key Concepts

4 Summarize How are radioactive isotopes used to determine the absolute age of igneous rock? Name two radiometric methods that are used.

5 Describe What happens to an isotope during radioactive decay?

6 Explain Why are igneous rocks the best type of rock sample for radiometric dating?

7 Describe How old is Earth and how did scientists find this out?

8 Explain What are index fossils and how are they used to determine the absolute age of sedimentary rock?

Critical Thinking

9 Justify An igneous rock sample is about 250,000 years old. Would you use uranium-lead radiometric dating to find its age? Explain.

10 Calculate A sample of wood contains 12.5% of its original carbon-14. What is the estimated age of this sample? Show your work.

Use this graph to answer the following questions.

Radioactive Decay

Mass of Parent Isotope (micrograms): 0, 20, 40, 60, 80, 100

Time (years): 0, 100, 200, 300, 400, 500, 600

11 Analyze What is the half-life of the radioactive isotope?

12 Analyze What mass of radioactive isotope will be left after three half-lives?

Visual Summary Answers

17. parent; half-life
18. in large numbers; in a large area; have distinct features; lived during a short time period
19. Sample answer: The amount of parent isotope left and daughter isotopes produced from radioactive decay is used as a measure of how much time has passed. A clock also measures how much time has passed.

Lesson Review Answers

1. radioactive decay
2. half-life
3. Radiometric dating
4. Radioactive isotopes decay at a particular rate. The relative amounts of parent and daughter isotopes indicate when the rock formed; radiocarbon and uranium-lead dating.
5. A parent isotope is converted to a daughter isotope, often by conversion of a proton to a neutron. Decay occurs at a constant and specific rate for each isotope.
6. They often contain only parent isotope and no daughter isotope when formed.
7. It is about 4.6 billion years; determined by radiometrically dating moon rocks and meteorite samples.
8. Index fossils can be used to determine the absolute age of rock layers they are found in. They are distinct and existed for a short period of time.
9. No; because of uranium's half-life, uranium-lead radiometric dating is used to date rocks that are more than 100 million years old.
10. Three half-lives have passed. The half-life of carbon-14 is 5,730 years. Therefore, the sample is approximately 17,190 years old.
11. 200 years
12. 12.5 μg

The Geologic Time Scale

Essential Question What is the geologic time scale?

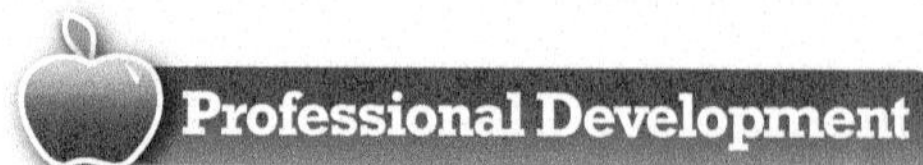

For more detailed information about the topics in this lesson, refer to the Content Refresher in the Unit Opener pages.

Opening Your Lesson

Begin the lesson by assessing students' prerequisite and prior knowledge.

Prerequisite Knowledge

- Fossils provide information about life forms and environments in Earth's past.
- Relative and absolute dating techniques are used to determine the ages of rocks.

Accessing Prior Knowledge

Use the KWL strategy to help students recognize what they already know about geologic time before they begin the lesson. They should write what they already know about geologic time in the *K* column, what they want to learn in the *W* column, and after they read about the topic, they should write what they learned in the *L* column.

Optional Online resource: KWL support

Customize Your Opening

- ☐ **Accessing Prior Knowledge,** above
- ☐ **Print Path** Engage Your Brain, SE p. 119
- ☐ **Print Path** Active Reading, SE p. 119
- ☐ **Digital Path** Lesson Opener

Key Topics/Learning Goals	Supporting Concepts
A Historical Perspective of Geologic Change 1 Describe the principle of catastrophism in terms of the rate of geologic change. 2 Describe the principle of uniformitarianism in terms of the rate of geologic change. 3 Explain what geologists mean today when they use the term *uniformitarianism*.	• Proponents of catastrophism thought that sudden, rapid, and devastating geologic processes brought about geologic change. • Proponents of uniformitarianism thought that the same geologic processes have occurred in a uniform manner throughout geologic time, and the rate of change was relatively slow and constant. • Uniformitarianism today recognizes that rates have varied and most geologic processes are uniform, yet catastrophic events play a role in shaping Earth as well.
The Geologic Time Scale 1 Explain how the age of Earth has been determined. 2 Describe the geologic time scale and explain how it is divided into different spans of time.	• Earth's age is estimated to be 4.6 billion years. This age was arrived at from dating of meteorites and rocks from the moon. • The geologic time scale is the standard method used to divide Earth's long history into parts. It is divided into different spans of time based on major events in the history of life on Earth. The major divisions of the scale are eons, eras, periods, and epochs.
Milestones in Earth History 1 List the four major divisions of Earth's history. 2 Describe major events in the geologic history of Earth during Precambrian time, the Paleozoic era, the Mesozoic era, and the Cenozoic era.	• The four major divisions of Earth's history are Precambrian time, the Paleozoic era, the Mesozoic era, and the Cenozoic era. • During the Precambrian time, continents formed and plate-tectonic processes began. During the Paleozoic era, continents collided to form Pangaea. Tectonic activity caused shallow seas to disappear. During the Mesozoic era, Pangaea broke up and the Atlantic Ocean opened up. During the Cenozoic era, which is the current era, the continents moved into their current positions.

Options for Instruction

Two parallel paths provide coverage of the Essential Questions, with a strong **Inquiry** strand woven into each. Follow the **Print Path,** the **Digital Path,** or your customized combination of print, digital, and inquiry.

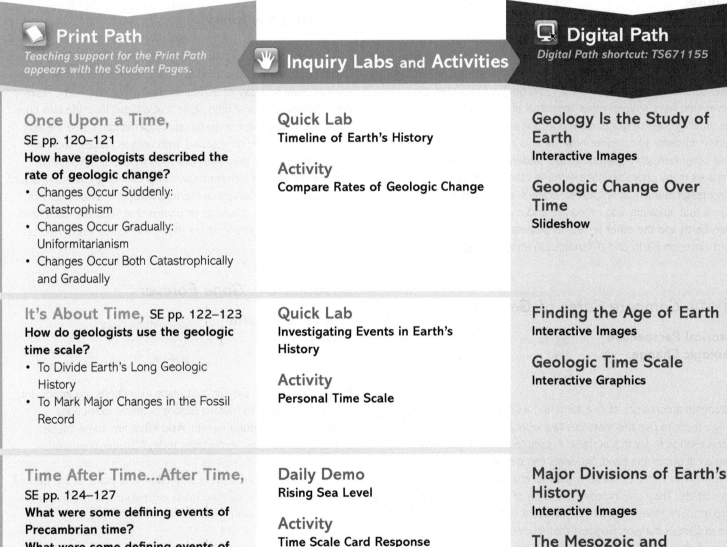

 Print Path *Teaching support for the Print Path appears with the Student Pages.*	 Inquiry Labs and Activities	 Digital Path *Digital Path shortcut: TS671155*
Once Upon a Time, SE pp. 120–121 **How have geologists described the rate of geologic change?** • Changes Occur Suddenly: Catastrophism • Changes Occur Gradually: Uniformitarianism • Changes Occur Both Catastrophically and Gradually	**Quick Lab** **Timeline of Earth's History** **Activity** **Compare Rates of Geologic Change**	**Geology Is the Study of Earth** **Interactive Images** **Geologic Change Over Time** **Slideshow**
It's About Time, SE pp. 122–123 **How do geologists use the geologic time scale?** • To Divide Earth's Long Geologic History • To Mark Major Changes in the Fossil Record	**Quick Lab** **Investigating Events in Earth's History** **Activity** **Personal Time Scale**	**Finding the Age of Earth** **Interactive Images** **Geologic Time Scale** **Interactive Graphics**
Time After Time...After Time, SE pp. 124–127 **What were some defining events of Precambrian time?** **What were some defining events of the Paleozoic Era?** **What were some defining events of the Mesozoic Era?** **What were some defining events of the Cenozoic Era?**	**Daily Demo** **Rising Sea Level** **Activity** **Time Scale Card Response** **Virtual Lab** **How Do We Divide Earth's History?**	**Major Divisions of Earth's History** **Interactive Images** **The Mesozoic and Cenozoic Eras** **Interactive Graphics**

Options for Assessment

See the Evaluate page for options, including Formative Assessment, Summative Assessment, and Unit Review.

Engage and Explore

Activities and Discussion

Probing Question *Planetary Geology*

A Historical Perspective of Geologic Change

 small groups
 30 min
 **GUIDED** inquiry

Analyzing Have students consider whether the principles of geology that help us understand Earth's history can be used to understand processes that have shaped other terrestrial planets. Have students work in small groups to discuss the question and draw a conclusion. Encourage students to consider how Earth is similar to and different from the other terrestrial planets. Guide students to recognize that Earth shares many characteristics with the other terrestrial planets, including features such as volcanoes, craters, mountains, and valleys. Make sure that students also recognize and consider key differences between Earth and the other terrestrial planets, such as the presence of liquid water on Earth and differences in atmospheres.

Activity *Compare Rates of Geologic Change*

A Historical Perspective of Geologic Change

 pairs
 40 min
 **DIRECTED** inquiry

Give students a container of fine sand and a spray bottle full of water. Challenge them to use the materials to model a gradual change and a sudden change to Earth's surface. A sample model might involve building a hill out of the sand. Students can gently mist the hill with water to model a gradual change to Earth's surface. They can increase the force of the spray to model a violent storm that causes a sudden change to Earth's surface. Suggest that students draw sketches of their models. Sketches should include labels and captions that describe students' results.

Activity *Personal Time Scale*

Engage

Introducing Key Topics

 individuals
 60 min
 **INDEPENDENT** inquiry

Direct students to make a list of major milestones in their lives, such as their first day of school or the birth of a sibling. Have them make a personal time scale that divides their life into time units defined by these milestones. Students can name the era, period, etc., of their time scales with unique names, such as "Babyozoic Era" or the "First-Grade-Ary Period." Encourage students to explore different ways of presenting this information. For example, they can place the information in a color-coded chart that includes drawings or photos that illustrate each time period. Invite students to share their time scales with the class.

Discussion *Gone Forever*

Milestones in Earth History

 whole class
 15 min
 **GUIDED** inquiry

Quick Discussion Explain that mass extinctions are important milestones in Earth's history. Before humans, extinctions were caused by natural events. **Ask:** What are some causes of individual species' extinctions today? Students should understand that extinctions are increasingly linked to human activities. **Ask:** Could a mass extinction take place in the future? Yes, the events that caused mass extinctions in the past may happen again in Earth's future.

Customize Your Labs

 *See the Lab Manual for lab datasheets.*

 *Go Online for editable lab datasheets.*

DIRECTED inquiry
introduces inquiry skills within a structured framework.

GUIDED inquiry
develops inquiry skills within a supportive environment.

INDEPENDENT inquiry
deepens inquiry skills with student-driven questions or procedures.

Labs and Demos

Daily Demo *Rising Sea Level*

Milestones in Earth History

 whole class
 20 min
 **GUIDED** inquiry

PURPOSE **To show that melting glaciers can affect sea levels**

MATERIALS

- **ice cubes**
- **lamp**
- **marker**
- **plastic container**
- **water**
- **wooden board**

1 Fill the container halfway with water. Rest the board on the edge of the container, and place about ten ice cubes on the board. Tilt the board so meltwater from the ice runs into the container, but the ice does not fall into the water.

2 **Hypothesizing** Mark the water level on the side of the container. Have students predict how much the water level will rise when the ice melts.

3 Put the lamp over the ice and set aside for 15 minutes to allow the ice to melt. After the ice has melted, have students observe whether their predictions were correct. **Ask:** How does this demonstration relate to sea levels over Earth's geologic past? When Earth's climate became warmer, glaciers and ice caps melted, causing a rise in sea level. **Ask:** What could cause a decrease in sea level? colder temperatures

Quick Lab *Timeline of Earth's History*

PURPOSE **To make a model of geologic time**

See the Lab Manual or go Online for planning information.

Quick Lab *Investigating Events in Earth's History*

The Geologic Time Scale

 small groups
 20 min
 **GUIDED** inquiry

Students will place events in Earth's history on a geologic timeline.

PURPOSE **To identify major events in Earth's history and the time period during which they occurred**

MATERIALS

- **index cards with events listed on them**
- **research materials**
- **transparent tape**

Virtual Lab *How Do We Divide Earth's History?*

Milestones in Earth History

flexible
 45 min
GUIDED inquiry

Students produce their own timeline of Earth's history.

PURPOSE To understand that different spans of time are based on major changes in Earth's biodiversity

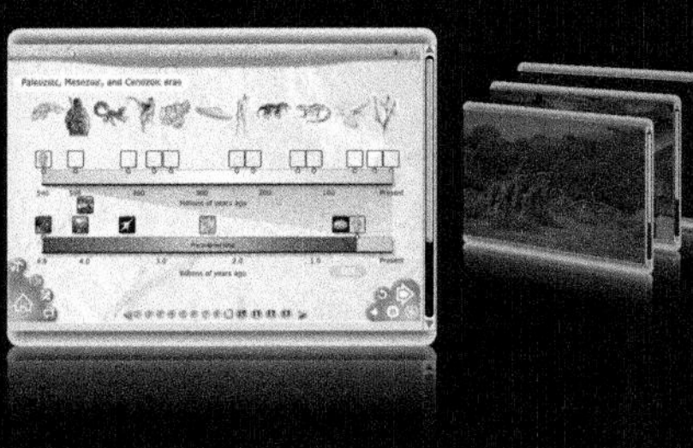

Activities and Discussion

- ☐ **Probing Question** Planetary Geology
- ☐ **Activity** Compare Rates of Geologic Change
- ☐ **Activity** Personal Time Scale
- ☐ **Discussion** Gone Forever

Labs and Demos

- ☐ **Daily Demo** Rising Sea Level
- ☐ **Quick Lab** Timeline of Earth's History
- ☐ **Quick Lab** Investigating Events in Earth's History
- ☐ **Virtual Lab** How Do We Divide Earth's History?

Your Resources

Explain Science Concepts

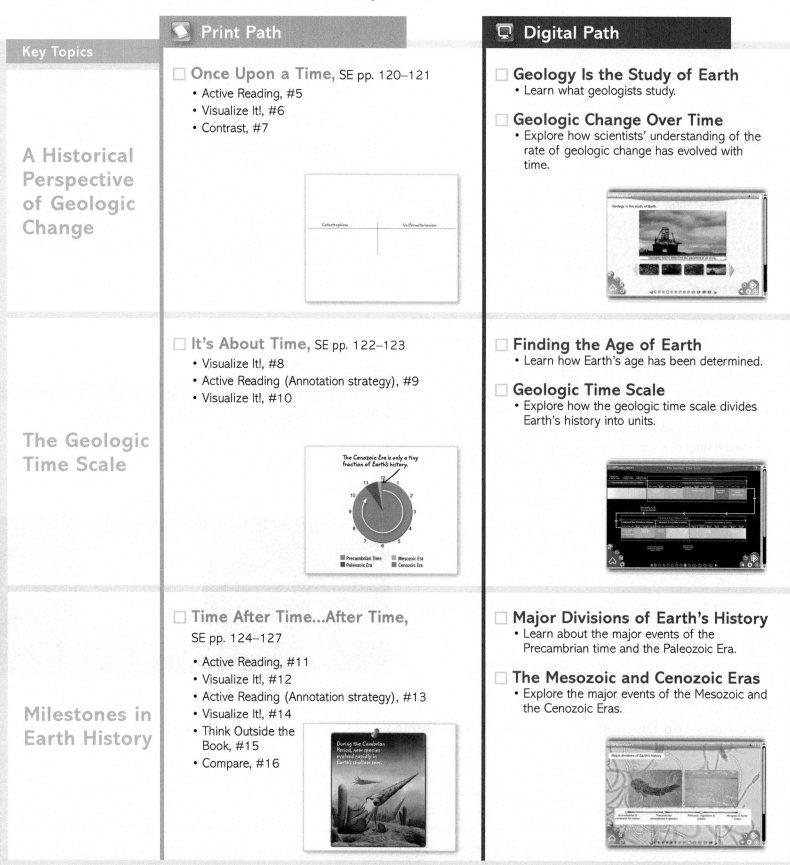

Key Topics	Print Path	Digital Path
A Historical Perspective of Geologic Change	☐ **Once Upon a Time,** SE pp. 120–121 • Active Reading, #5 • Visualize It!, #6 • Contrast, #7 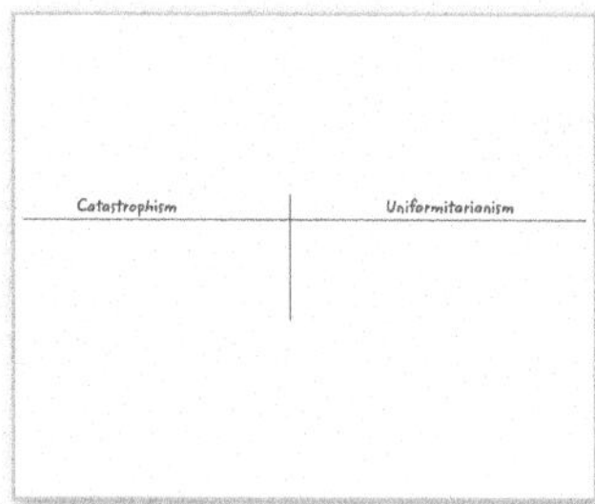 	☐ **Geology Is the Study of Earth** • Learn what geologists study. ☐ **Geologic Change Over Time** • Explore how scientists' understanding of the rate of geologic change has evolved with time. 
The Geologic Time Scale	☐ **It's About Time,** SE pp. 122–123 • Visualize It!, #8 • Active Reading (Annotation strategy), #9 • Visualize It!, #10 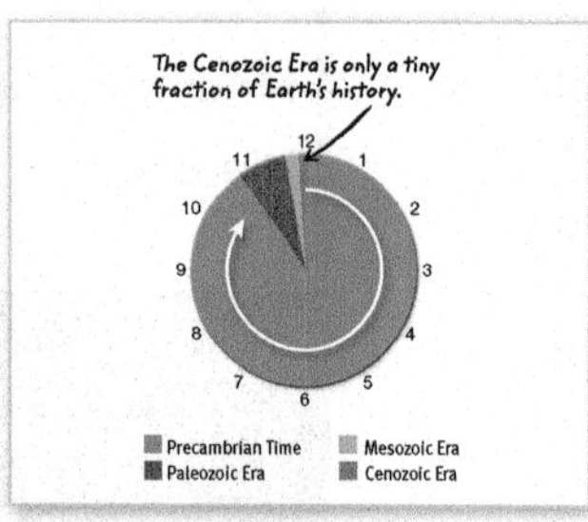 	☐ **Finding the Age of Earth** • Learn how Earth's age has been determined. ☐ **Geologic Time Scale** • Explore how the geologic time scale divides Earth's history into units. 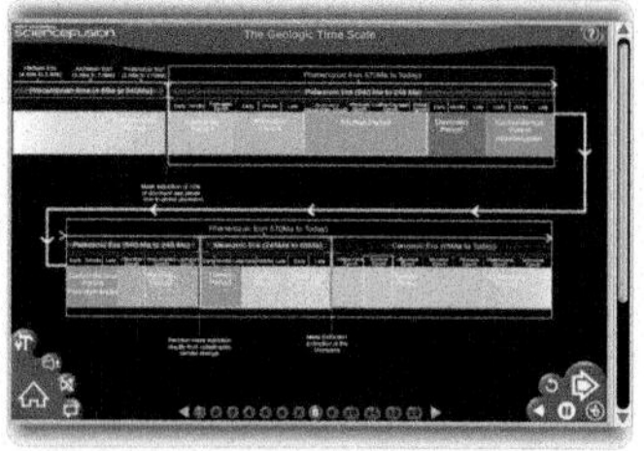
Milestones in Earth History	☐ **Time After Time...After Time,** SE pp. 124–127 • Active Reading, #11 • Visualize It!, #12 • Active Reading (Annotation strategy), #13 • Visualize It!, #14 • Think Outside the Book, #15 • Compare, #16  	☐ **Major Divisions of Earth's History** • Learn about the major events of the Precambrian time and the Paleozoic Era. ☐ **The Mesozoic and Cenozoic Eras** • Explore the major events of the Mesozoic and the Cenozoic Eras. 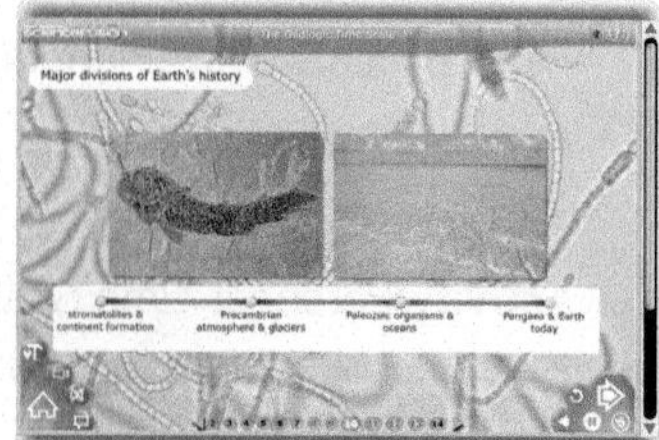

Differentiated Instruction

Basic *Sequence Time Divisions*

The Geologic Time Scale

 individuals
 10 min

Write the following terms on the board in random order: *eon, era, period,* and *epoch.* Give each student four pieces of paper of varying sizes. On the largest piece of paper, ask students to write the name of the largest geologic time division. On the next largest piece of paper, ask them to write the name of the next largest geologic time division, and so on. Students should write *eon, era, period,* and *epoch,* respectively. Point out that Precambrian time is a special time unit. **Ask:** Would a paper representing Precambrian time be bigger or smaller than your largest piece of paper? It would be bigger.

Advanced *Local Geologic Past*

A Historical Perspective of Geologic Change

 individuals or pairs
ongoing

Ask students to use video cameras or digital cameras to record evidence of changes to Earth's surface in their communities. Stress that they should look for evidence of both gradual changes and sudden changes. A gully formed by water erosion might be an example of a gradual change. A landslide might be an example of a sudden change. Ask students to share their results with the class.

ELL *Important Milestones*

Milestones in Earth History

 individuals
30–40 min

Description Wheel Show students how to make a Description Wheel. Direct them to write the name of each geologic era in the center circle of a wheel. They should write important milestones for that era on the spokes of the wheel. Encourage students to create Description Wheels for each era discussed in class. Students can use the wheels as study guides.

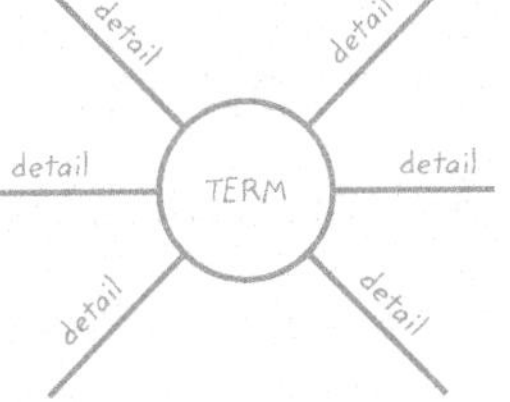

Lesson Vocabulary

geology **geologic time scale**

Previewing Vocabulary

 whole class
15 min

Etymology Tell students that good readers often use the etymology, or history, of a word to help determine or remember the word's meaning. For example, *geology* comes from the Greek words *geo-*, meaning "earth," and *logia,* meaning "study of." So geology is the study of Earth. The sequence of the eras in the most recent eon can be more easily remembered using their etymology. *Paleozoic* comes from Greek words meaning "old life." *Mesozoic* comes from Greek words meaning "middle life." And *Cenozoic* comes from Greek words meaning "recent life."

Reinforcing Vocabulary

whole class
15 min

Magnet Word Give students copies of the Magnet Word worksheet. Ask them to write the term *geologic time scale* in the magnet. Tell them to think of other terms and ideas that relate to this key vocabulary term. They should write the terms and ideas on the lines around the magnet.

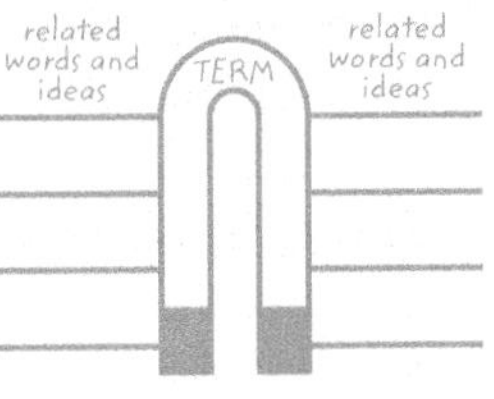

Customize Your Core Lesson

Core Instruction

- ☐ **Print Path** choices
- ☐ **Digital Path** choices

Vocabulary

- ☐ **Previewing Vocabulary** Etymology
- ☐ **Reinforcing Vocabulary** Magnet Word

Your Resources

Differentiated Instruction

- ☐ **Basic** Sequence Time Divisions
- ☐ **Advanced** Local Geologic Past
- ☐ **ELL** Important Milestones

Extend Science Concepts

Reinforce and Review

Activity *Time Scale Card Response*

Synthesizing Key Topics

 whole class
20 min

Card Responses Use this strategy to review content with students:

1. Give each student two index cards. Direct them to label one card "true" and the other "false."
2. Create a list of true/false statements about the geologic time scale. Use variations of questions in the lesson review or teacher pages.
3. Tell students that you are going to read a statement about the geologic time scale. Explain that on the count of three, they should hold up an answer card to indicate whether the statement is true or false. Read a statement. For example: *All eras in the geologic time scale are the same length.* (false) Assess whether students understand the directions and adjust accordingly.
4. As you teach, ask a question every ten minutes or so to assess students' understanding of content. Note the number of correct answers. If necessary, stop and reteach content in another way. Also, take the opportunity to identify any students who may need additional help.

FoldNote

Milestones in Earth History

 individuals
30 min

Four-Corner FoldNote Suggest that students use a Four-Corner FoldNote to take notes about milestones in Precambrian time, the Paleozoic Era, the Mesozoic Era, and the Cenozoic Era. Students can use the FoldNote as a study aid and to compare the characteristics of Earth during the four time periods.

Optional Online resource: Four-Corner FoldNote support

Going Further

Astrobiology Connection

Milestones in Earth History

 whole class
15 min

Discussion Remind students that the fossil record shows that Earth's first life forms appeared during Precambrian time. Ask students to think about the conditions that made life possible on Earth. **Ask:** Why do you think that life evolved as it did on Earth and not on other planets in our solar system? Sample answer: Earth was not too close or too far from the sun, and had the right climate for life to evolve. It also had liquid water and an atmosphere. Point out that astronomers are finding rocky planets in distant solar systems. As a class, discuss the possibility of finding life on extrasolar planets.

Language Arts Connection

Synthesizing Key Concepts

 individuals
varies

Going Back in Time Tell students to imagine they can travel back in time. Ask them to write a narrative about what they would see during Precambrian time, the Paleozoic Era, the Mesozoic Era, or the early Cenozoic Era. Students should write about environmental conditions and ancient life forms. Encourage them to share their stories with the class.

Customize Your Closing

See the Assessment Guide for quizzes and tests.

Go Online to edit and create quizzes and tests.

Reinforce and Review

- ☐ Activity Card Responses
- ☐ FoldNote Four-Corner FoldNote
- ☐ Print Path Visual Summary, SE p. 128
- ☐ Print Path Lesson Review, SE p. 129
- ☐ **Digital Path** Lesson Closer

Evaluate Student Mastery

Formative Assessment

See the teacher support below the Student Pages for additional Formative Assessment questions.

Ask the following questions to assess student mastery of the material. **Ask:** How does a modern geologist's view of geologic change most likely differ from that of James Hutton? Hutton thought geologic change happened gradually at a uniform rate over time. Modern geologists believe geologic change happens both gradually and suddenly. **Ask:** Why don't the divisions of the geologic time scale have fixed time lengths? The divisions are based on changes or events recorded in rocks and fossils, which did not take place at regular time intervals. **Ask:** Describe an example of a climate change that occurred in Earth's past. Sample answer: In the late Precambrian, Earth was nearly frozen, but the climate warmed during the Paleozoic era.

Reteach

Formative assessment may show that students need reinforcement for certain topics. The resources below are recommended for reteaching. If students were introduced to a topic through the Print Path, you can also use the Digital Path to reteach, and vice versa.
Can be assigned to individual students

A Historical Perspective of Geologic Change

Activity Compare Rates of Geologic Change

The Geologic Time Scale

Activity Personal Time Scale

Quick Lab Investigating Events in Earth's History

Milestones in Earth History

Virtual Lab How Do We Divide Earth's History?

Summative Assessment

Alternative Assessment

Earth's History

Online resources: student worksheet; optional rubrics

The Geologic Time Scale

Choose Your Meal: ***Earth's History***
Make a meal that shows what you know about Earth's geologic past.

1. Work on your own, with a partner, or with a small group.
2. Choose one item from each section of the menu, with an optional dessert. Check your choices.
3. Have your teacher approve your plan.
4. Submit or present your results.

Appetizers

____ **Big Change Coming** Draw a picture of a geologic event that could cause a sudden change to Earth's surface.

____ **Name Game** Research how geologists came up with the names of different periods in the geologic time scale. Share your results with the class in a presentation.

Main Dishes

____ **Earth Diary** Write a diary entry for each era of the Phanerozoic eon. In your entries, describe climate conditions and at least one major geologic event.

____ **Interview from the Past** Write a newspaper article about an interview with Scottish farmer and scientist James Hutton. Ask *how, what, why, where,* and *when* questions about geologic change over time.

Side Dishes

____ **Lights Out** Design a model that shows how a major volcanic eruption would affect plants and other producers. Use simple materials in your model, such as a lamp, plants, and a piece of cloth.

____ **On the Move** Plate tectonics results in the constant, slow movement of Earth's continents. Research the movement of the continents over Earth's history. Create a model of Earth's continents with moveable parts like a puzzle. Use it to demonstrate how the continents have moved at different times in Earth's history.

Dessert (optional)

____ **Geologic Time Puzzle** Make a crossword puzzle that uses milestones in geologic time as clues for identifying Precambrian time and the eras of the Phanerozoic eon.

Going Further

- ☐ Astrobiology Connection
- ☐ Language Arts Connection

Formative Assessment

- ☐ Strategies Throughout TE
- ☐ Lesson Review SE

Summative Assessment

- ☐ Alternative Assessment Earth's History
- ☐ Lesson Quiz
- ☐ Unit Tests A and B
- ☐ Unit Review SE End-of-Unit

Your Resources

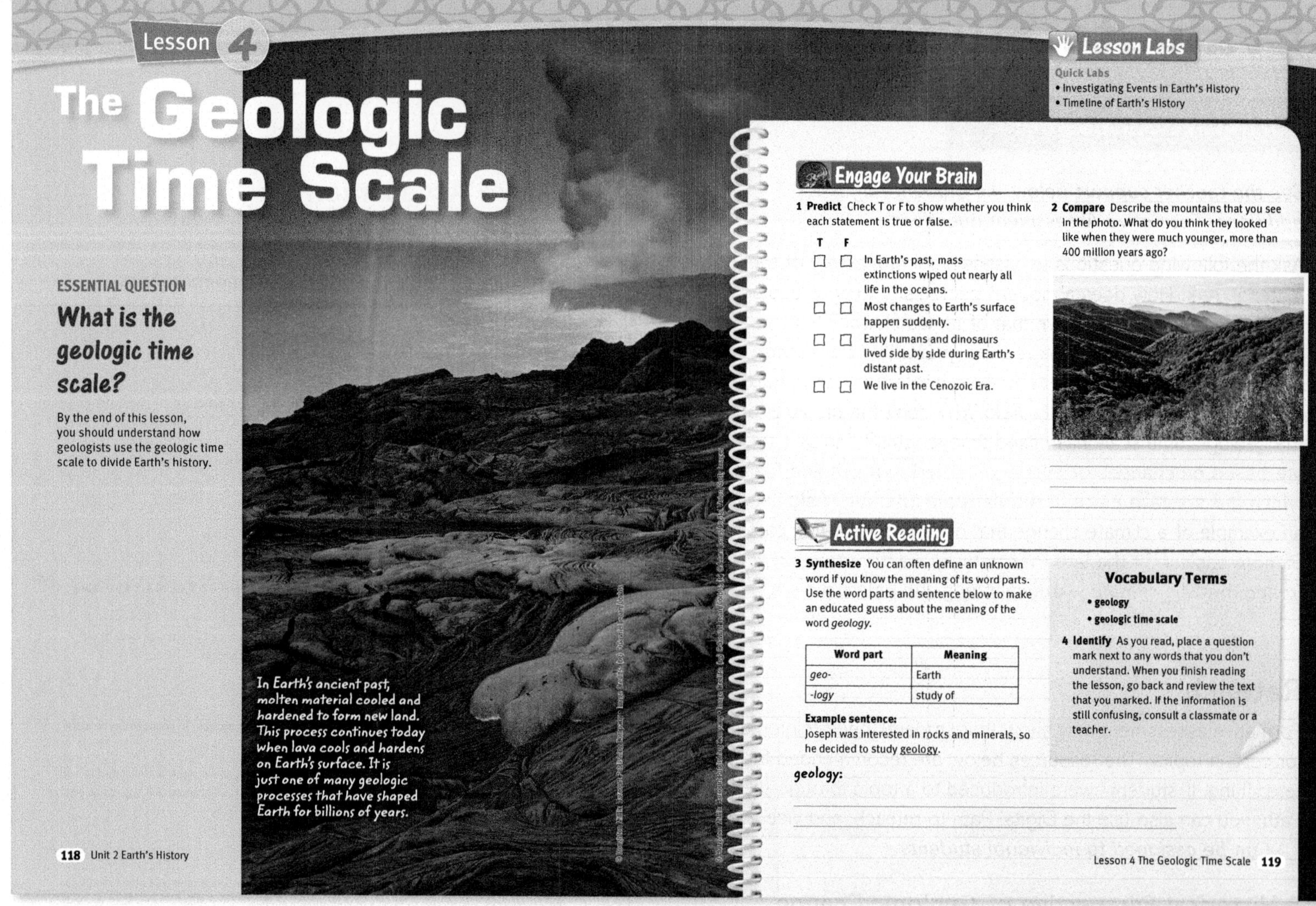

Lesson 4

The Geologic Time Scale

ESSENTIAL QUESTION

What is the geologic time scale?

By the end of this lesson, you should understand how geologists use the geologic time scale to divide Earth's history.

In Earth's ancient past, molten material cooled and hardened to form new land. This process continues today when lava cools and hardens on Earth's surface. It is just one of many geologic processes that have shaped Earth for billions of years.

118 Unit 2 Earth's History

Lesson Labs

Quick Labs
- Investigating Events in Earth's History
- Timeline of Earth's History

Engage Your Brain

1 Predict Check T or F to show whether you think each statement is true or false.

T	F	
☐	☐	In Earth's past, mass extinctions wiped out nearly all life in the oceans.
☐	☐	Most changes to Earth's surface happen suddenly.
☐	☐	Early humans and dinosaurs lived side by side during Earth's distant past.
☐	☐	We live in the Cenozoic Era.

2 Compare Describe the mountains that you see in the photo. What do you think they looked like when they were much younger, more than 400 million years ago?

Active Reading

3 Synthesize You can often define an unknown word if you know the meaning of its word parts. Use the word parts and sentence below to make an educated guess about the meaning of the word *geology*.

Word part	Meaning
geo-	Earth
-logy	study of

Example sentence:
Joseph was interested in rocks and minerals, so he decided to study geology.

geology:

Vocabulary Terms
- **geology**
- **geologic time scale**

4 Identify As you read, place a question mark next to any words that you don't understand. When you finish reading the lesson, go back and review the text that you marked. If the information is still confusing, consult a classmate or a teacher.

Lesson 4 The Geologic Time Scale 119

Answers

Answers for 1–3 should reflect students' current thoughts, even if incorrect.

1. T; F; F; T
2. Students should describe low, rounded mountains that were taller, less rounded, and less forested when they were younger.
3. the study of Earth
4. *Student's annotations will vary.*

Opening Your Lesson

Encourage students to review their answers to item 2 after they have read the lesson. Tell them to revise their answers, if necessary.

Accessing Prior Knowledge Introduce students to the Textbook DRTA strategy. Explain that DRTA stands for directed reading/thinking activity. Tell them they will preview the lesson, write what they know they know, what they think they know, and what they think they will learn. After they read the lesson, they will write what they know they have learned and address any misconceptions they previously held.

Encourage students to compare what they thought they would learn and what they actually did learn. If discrepancies exist, discuss whether students' expectations were reasonable and whether they learned information they did not anticipate.

Optional Online resource: Textbook DRTA support

Volcanic eruptions can cause sudden, drastic changes to Earth's surface.

How have geologists described the rate of geologic change?

How old is Earth? How does new rock form? How do mountains form? These are the types of questions asked by scientists who study geology. **Geology** is the scientific study of the origin, history, and structure of Earth and the processes that shape it. Early geologists proposed different ideas to explain how Earth changes over time.

Changes Occur Suddenly: Catastrophism

Some early scientists used catastrophism to explain geologic changes on Earth. *Catastrophism* (kuh•TAS•truh•fiz•uhm) is the principle that states that all geologic change occurs suddenly. Supporters of catastrophism thought that Earth's features, such as mountains and seas, formed during sudden events called *catastrophes* (kuh•TAS•truh•feez). These unpredictable events caused rapid change over large areas, sometimes even globally.

A volcanic eruption is just one example of a catastrophic event. In November 2010, the Merapi volcano in Indonesia erupted with violent explosions that could be heard 20 km away. Millions of cubic meters of ash, dust, and gases were released. Material reportedly fell in areas hundreds of kilometers from the volcano.

Active Reading **5 Identify** What is one example of a geologic catastrophe?

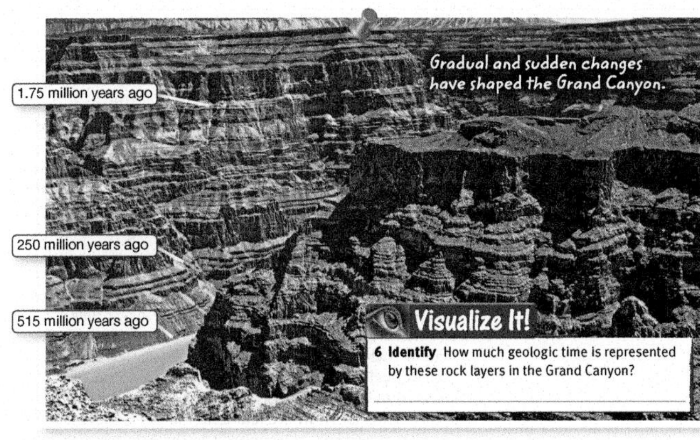

Gradual and sudden changes have shaped the Grand Canyon.

Visualize It!

6 Identify How much geologic time is represented by these rock layers in the Grand Canyon?

Changes Occur Gradually: Uniformitarianism

About 250 years ago, a Scottish farmer and scientist named James Hutton studied rock formations in Scotland. His years of observations challenged the principle of catastrophism and led to the foundation of modern geology.

Hutton believed that the key to understanding Earth's history is all around us. The processes that we observe today, such as erosion and deposition, do not change over time. They remain constant, or uniform. This principle is now called uniformitarianism (*yoo•nuh•fohr•mih•TAIR•ee•uh•niz•uhm*). *Uniformitarianism* is the idea that the same geologic processes that shape Earth today have been at work throughout Earth's history. The principle also states that the average rate of geologic change is slow and has remained relatively constant over time.

Changes Occur Both Catastrophically and Gradually

Today, geologists realize that neither uniformitarianism nor catastrophism accounts for all geologic change. While most geologic change is gradual and uniform, modern geologists recognize that catastrophes do cause some geologic change. For example, earthquakes, floods, volcanic eruptions, and asteroid impacts can cause sudden changes to Earth's surface.

Scientists have found huge craters caused by ancient asteroid impacts. About 65 million years ago, an asteroid hit Earth. Scientists think this led to the extinction of the dinosaurs. The impact would have thrown large amounts of debris into the atmosphere, which would have blocked the sun's rays. This likely limited photosynthesis, killing plants and causing the dinosaur food chain to collapse.

7 Contrast Compare catastrophism and uniformitarianism.

Catastrophism	Uniformitarianism

Answers

5. Sample answer: Earthquakes, tsunamis, floods, and mass movements can cause sudden changes to Earth's surface.
6. 515 million years
7. Sample anno: Catastrophism is the geologic principle that states that all geologic change occurs suddenly. Uniformitarianism is the idea that the same geologic processes shaping Earth today have been at work throughout Earth's history.

Learning Alert

Chain Reaction Make sure students understand that the asteroid collision itself did not kill off the dinosaurs. Instead, the collision sent up debris that blocked the sun's rays. This, in turn, drastically decreased rates of photosynthesis and killed off large populations of producers over time. **Ask:** What likely happened to the dinosaurs that ate plants and other producers? They starved when the producers died out. **Ask:** What likely happened to the dinosaurs that ate animals that ate producers? They starved, too, because the animals they ate had died from lack of food.

Interpreting Visuals

Remind students that the oldest rocks are found at the bottom of undisturbed rock layers; the youngest rocks are found at the top. **Ask:** What do you notice about the different rock layers in the Grand Canyon? Sample answer: They are different widths and different colors. **Ask:** Why do you think these differences exist? Sample answer: The layers contain different materials that were laid down at different rates.

It's About Time

How do geologists use the geologic time scale?

By using radiometric dating techniques on meteorites and moon rocks, geologists estimate that the solar system, and therefore Earth, is about 4.6 billion years old. To help make sense of this vast amount of time, geologists use the geologic time scale to organize Earth's history. The **geologic time scale** divides Earth's history into intervals of time defined by major events or changes on Earth.

To Divide Earth's Long Geologic History

The geologic time scale divides Earth's geologic history into eons, eras, periods, and epochs. The largest unit of geologic time is an *eon*. Earth's 4.6-billion-year history is divided into four eons: the Hadean, Archean, Proterozoic, and Phanerozoic. The Hadean, Archean, and Proterozoic eons together are called *Precambrian time*. Precambrian time makes up almost 90 percent of Earth's history. Eons may be divided into smaller units of time called *eras*. The Phanerozoic Eon is the present eon. This eon is divided into three eras: the Paleozoic, Mesozoic, and Cenozoic. Each era is subdivided into a number of *periods*. The periods of the Cenozoic, the present era, are further divided into *epochs*.

Visualize It!

8 List Use the diagram of the geologic time scale to list the different divisions of time, beginning with the largest division, the eon.

To Mark Major Changes in the Fossil Record

Active Reading **9 Identify** As you read, underline the factors used to determine the divisions of geologic time.

Unlike divisions of time such as days or minutes, the divisions of the geologic time scale have no fixed lengths. Many divisions are based on events in Earth's geologic history. Some divisions are based entirely on the fossil record.

At least five divisions of geologic time have ended in large mass extinction events. In mass extinction events, a larger than expected number of organisms "disappear" from the fossil record in rock layers worldwide. For example, the Paleozoic Era ended about 250 million years ago with the largest extinction event known. More than 90% of marine species and 70% of land species are thought to have become extinct. The Mesozoic Era ended with the extinction of dinosaurs and many other organisms about 65 million years ago. Causes of mass extinctions are varied. Movement of the continents, lowering of global sea level, rapid climate change, and asteroid impacts are all thought to be causes.

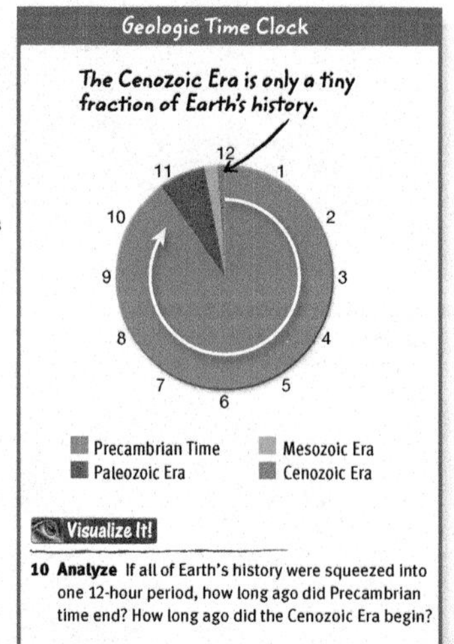

Visualize It!

10 Analyze If all of Earth's history were squeezed into one 12-hour period, how long ago did Precambrian time end? How long ago did the Cenozoic Era begin?

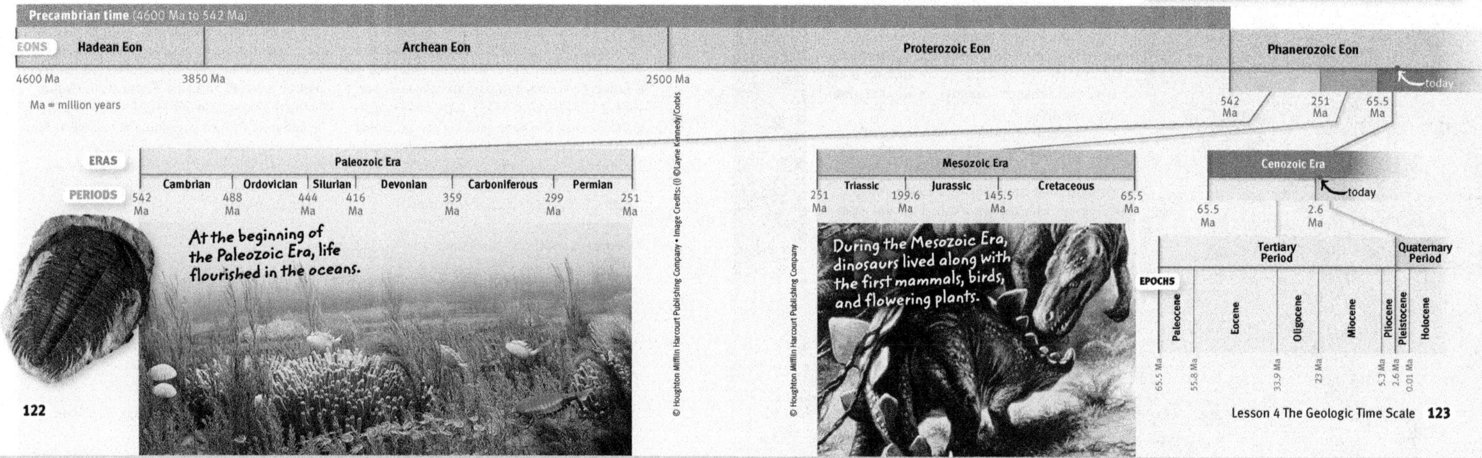

122

Lesson 4 The Geologic Time Scale 123

Answers

8. eon, era, period, epoch
9. Students should underline changes in Earth's geologic history and mass extinction events that are recorded in the fossil record.
10. Precambrian time ended about an hour ago. The Cenozoic Era started between 5 and 10 minutes ago.

Using Annotations

The annotation asks students to underline the factors used to determine the lengths of divisions of geologic time. As students complete this annotation, encourage them to read carefully so they do not miss any factors. If students struggle to identify factors, ask them guiding questions, and challenge them to look for answers in the text. For example, **ask:** Why is the Phanerozoic eon divided into smaller units of time than the eons in Precambrian time? The fossil record for the Phanerozoic is richer and records more changes. **Ask:** How did geologists decide on the lengths of the smaller time divisions in the Phanerozoic eon? The lengths of the divisions relate to how long certain conditions and life forms lasted on Earth.

Formative Assessment

Ask: What defines intervals of time on the geologic time scale? major events or changes on Earth **Ask:** Which is a larger unit of geologic time, an epoch or an era? an era **Ask:** Why don't we have many fossils from life forms during Precambrian time? Many life forms during Precambrian time had soft bodies that rarely formed into fossils. **Ask:** Why does more information exist for later geologic time divisions? The fossil record is more intact and thus richer.

Time After Time...

What were some defining events of Precambrian time?

Precambrian time began with the formation of Earth about 4.6 billion years ago. Many changes occurred during this time. From about 4.5 to 3.8 billion years ago, early Earth formed into a spherical planet, and its molten rocks cooled. Continents began to form, and tectonic activity occurred along continental margins. The oldest fossils, life forms in the oceans, date from this time.

Massive supercontinents formed and broke up at least twice during Precambrian time. Earth's early atmosphere was made mainly of gases released by volcanic eruptions. During the Archean Eon, water vapor was added to the atmosphere by almost constant volcanic activity. This water fell as rain and collected in basins to form the first oceans. The atmosphere had no free oxygen until the Proterozoic Eon, when cyanobacteria released oxygen into the air during the process of photosynthesis.

Toward the end of Precambrian time, much of Earth's land surfaces were located near the poles and covered in ice. Land on Earth was largely frozen and lifeless.

The first continents, oceans, and atmosphere formed during Precambrian time.

Active Reading **11 Identify** What was the first source of oxygen for Earth's atmosphere?

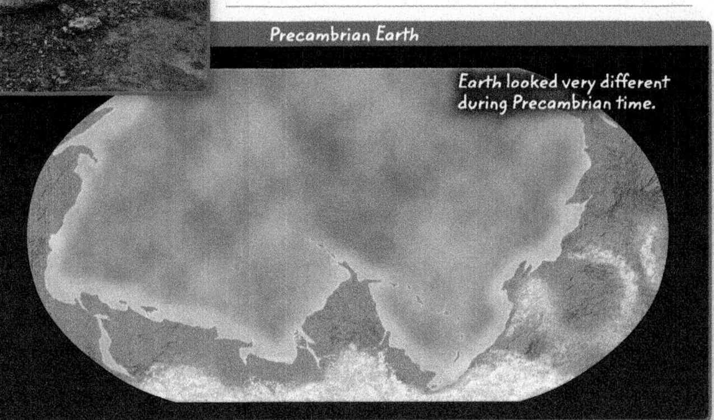

Precambrian Earth
Earth looked very different during Precambrian time.

...After Time

What were some defining events of the Paleozoic Era?

The Paleozoic Era began about 540 million years ago as the global supercontinent Pannotia was breaking up. Sea level rose and fell, at times covering much of the continents in shallow seas. Vast mountain ranges built up along the margins of the continents.

The formation of a new supercontinent, Pangaea, began during the Paleozoic. Sea level slowly dropped, and the shallow inland seas retreated. The climate during the late Paleozoic varied as Pangaea drifted toward and away from the South Pole. Conditions were warmer and drier farther from the pole.

At the start of the Paleozoic, all life was found in the ocean. Life diversified quickly and dramatically during the Cambrian Explosion, during which most major groups of organisms first evolved. The era ended about 250 million years ago with a huge mass extinction event. Between 90 and 95 percent of marine species and approximately 70 percent of land species disappeared.

During the Cambrian Period, new species evolved rapidly in Earth's shallow seas.

Visualize It!

12 Analyze Compare the two maps. What changes do you notice in the Paleozoic map?

Paleozoic Earth
Life began to flourish in the seas and on land during the Paleozoic Era.

Answers

11. cyanobacteria
12. There is more water and less land. Some land has moved away from the South Pole. The land is greener with less ice.

Formative Assessment

Ask: How did cyanobacteria affect Earth's atmosphere during the Proterozoic eon? They released oxygen into the air by photosynthesis. **Ask:** How did Earth's oceans form? During the Archean eon, water vapor produced by almost constant volcanic activity collected in basins to form the first oceans. **Ask:** What is the "Cambrian Explosion"? a period during the Paleozoic era when life diversified quickly and dramatically

Learning Alert

Difficult Concepts You may need to review the concept of plate tectonics with students. Be sure they understand that Pangaea, like modern continents, slowly moved over time due to convection currents in Earth's asthenosphere, or upper mantle. **Ask:** What made Pangaea drift toward and away from the South Pole? convection of Earth's mantle, causing tectonic plates **Ask:** Is this an example of a process that supports catastrophism or uniformitarianism? Explain. It is a process that supports uniformitarianism because it has occurred at the same relative rate over time and has been shaping Earth throughout its geologic history.

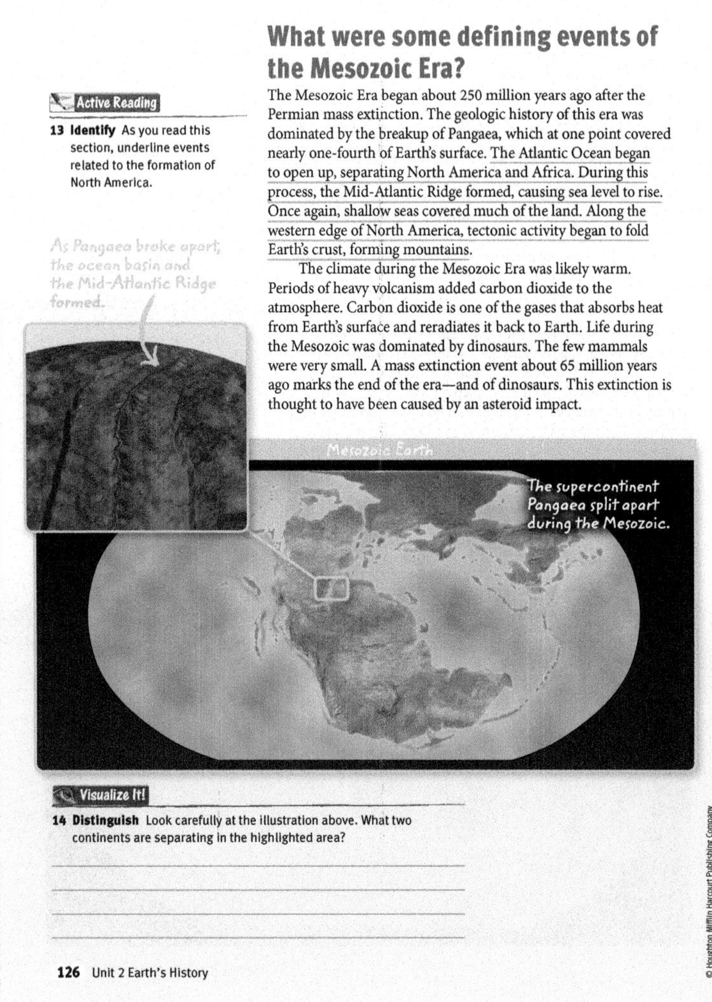

Mesozoic Earth
The supercontinent Pangaea split apart during the Mesozoic.
As Pangaea broke apart, the ocean basin and the Mid-Atlantic Ridge formed.

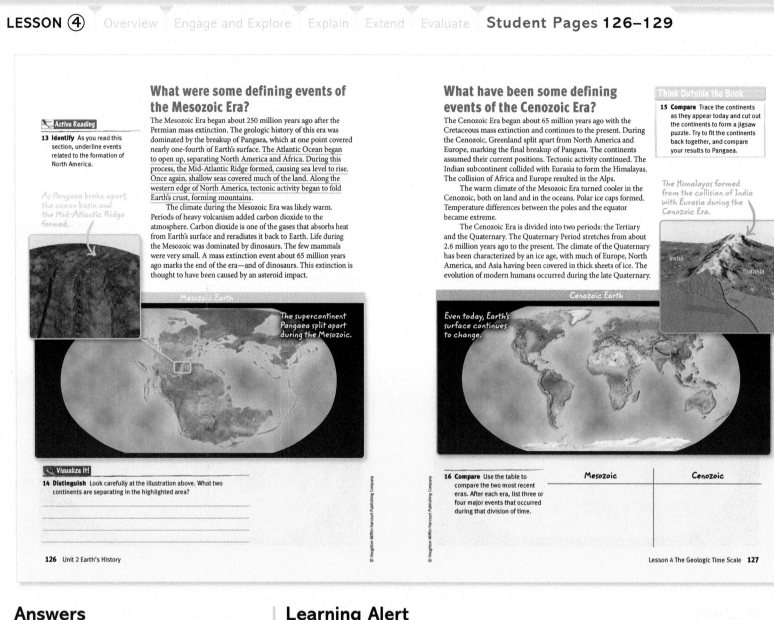

What were some defining events of the Mesozoic Era?

Active Reading

13 Identify As you read this section, underline events related to the formation of North America.

The Mesozoic Era began about 250 million years ago after the Permian mass extinction. The geologic history of this era was dominated by the breakup of Pangaea, which at one point covered nearly one-fourth of Earth's surface. The Atlantic Ocean began to open up, separating North America and Africa. During this process, the Mid-Atlantic Ridge formed, causing sea level to rise. Once again, shallow seas covered much of the land. Along the western edge of North America, tectonic activity began to fold Earth's crust, forming mountains.

The climate during the Mesozoic Era was likely warm. Periods of heavy volcanism added carbon dioxide to the atmosphere. Carbon dioxide is one of the gases that absorbs heat from Earth's surface and reradiates it back to Earth. Life during the Mesozoic was dominated by dinosaurs. The few mammals were very small. A mass extinction event about 65 million years ago marks the end of the era—and of dinosaurs. This extinction is thought to have been caused by an asteroid impact.

Visualize It!

14 Distinguish Look carefully at the illustration above. What two continents are separating in the highlighted area?

What have been some defining events of the Cenozoic Era?

The Cenozoic Era began about 65 million years ago with the Cretaceous mass extinction and continues to the present. During the Cenozoic, Greenland split apart from North America and Europe, marking the final breakup of Pangaea. The continents assumed their current positions. Tectonic activity continued. The Indian subcontinent collided with Eurasia to form the Himalayas. The collision of Africa and Europe resulted in the Alps.

The warm climate of the Mesozoic Era turned cooler in the Cenozoic, both on land and in the oceans. Polar ice caps formed. Temperature differences between the poles and the equator became extreme.

The Cenozoic Era is divided into two periods: the Tertiary and the Quaternary. The Quaternary Period stretches from about 2.6 million years ago to the present. The climate of the Quaternary has been characterized by an ice age, with much of Europe, North America, and Asia having been covered in thick sheets of ice. The evolution of modern humans occurred during the late Quaternary.

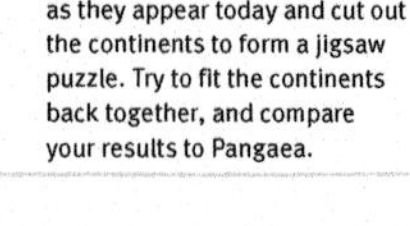

Think Outside the Book

15 Compare Trace the continents as they appear today and cut out the continents to form a jigsaw puzzle. Try to fit the continents back together, and compare your results to Pangaea.

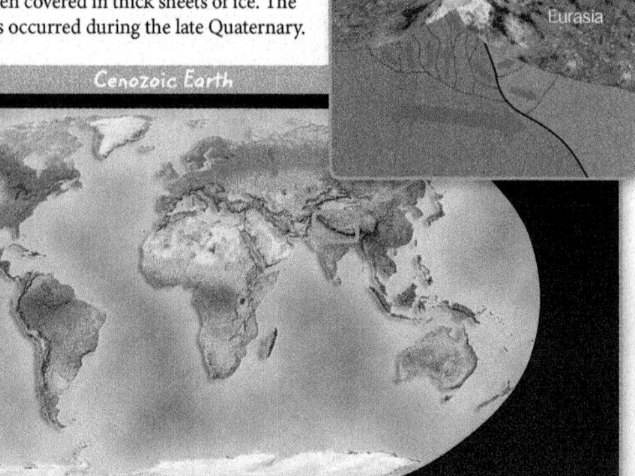

16 Compare Use the table to compare the two most recent eras. After each era, list three or four major events that occurred during that division of time.

Mesozoic	Cenozoic

Answers

13. *See students' pages for annotations.*
14. North America and Africa
15. Students' jigsaw puzzles should place North America and South America against western Africa. Australia should be placed against eastern Africa.
16. Sample answer: Mesozoic Era: breakup of Pangaea, Atlantic Ocean formed; climate warmed; mountains formed in western North America; Cenozoic Era: continents moved to current positions, Himalayas and Alps formed, climate cooled, ice age during Quaternary Period

Learning Alert

Humans and Dinosaurs Some students mistakenly believe that humans and dinosaurs walked Earth at the same time. Have them conduct research to find information about the appearance of the first human ancestors. **Ask:** When did dinosaurs become extinct? about 65 million years ago **Ask:** When did the first human ancestors appear in the fossil record? several million years ago **Ask:** When did humans begin their rise to become the dominant species? not until the late Quaternary period, or less than a million years ago

Probing Questions GUIDED Inquiry

Comparing What changes in Earth's atmosphere are occurring today that are similar to those that occurred during the Mesozoic era? Sample answer: Today, human activities are adding carbon dioxide to the atmosphere. In the Mesozoic era, volcanism added carbon dioxide to the atmosphere.

Analyzing What are the consequences of these changes? They can cause Earth's climate to change.

Proposing What can be done to slow this trend? Sample answer: People can conserve energy or use clean energy that does not add carbon dioxide to the atmosphere.

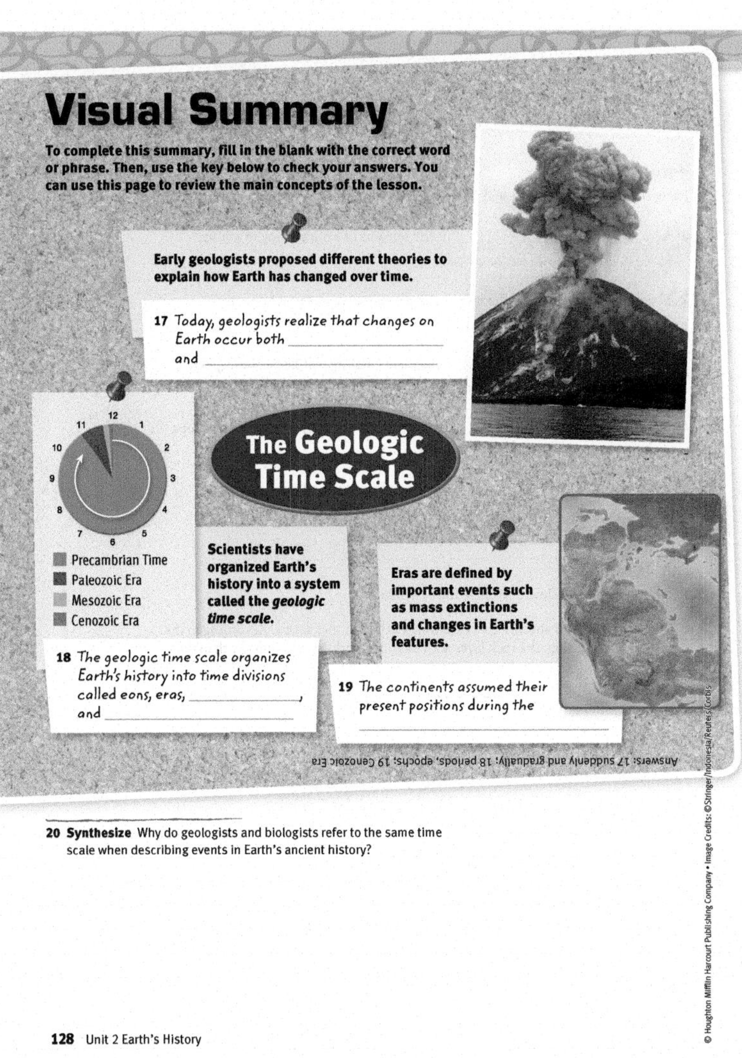

Visual Summary

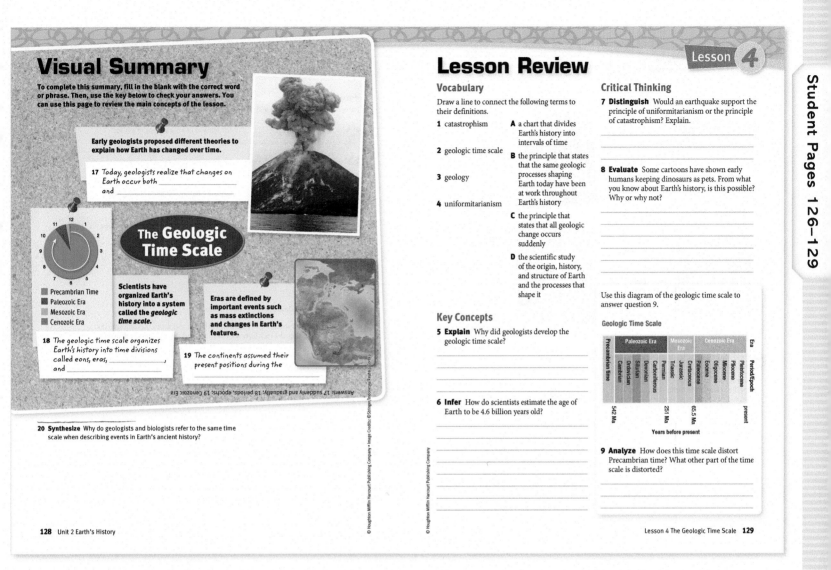

To complete this summary, fill in the blank with the correct word or phrase. Then, use the key below to check your answers. You can use this page to review the main concepts of the lesson.

Early geologists proposed different theories to explain how Earth has changed over time.

17 Today, geologists realize that changes on Earth occur both ______ and ______

The Geologic Time Scale

- Precambrian Time
- Paleozoic Era
- Mesozoic Era
- Cenozoic Era

Scientists have organized Earth's history into a system called the *geologic time scale.*

Eras are defined by important events such as mass extinctions and changes in Earth's features.

18 The geologic time scale organizes Earth's history into time divisions called eons, eras, ______, and ______

19 The continents assumed their present positions during the ______

Answers: 17 suddenly and gradually; 18 periods, epochs; 19 Cenozoic Era

20 **Synthesize** Why do geologists and biologists refer to the same time scale when describing events in Earth's ancient history?

128 Unit 2 Earth's History

Lesson Review

Lesson 4

Vocabulary

Draw a line to connect the following terms to their definitions.

1 catastrophism
2 geologic time scale
3 geology
4 uniformitarianism

A a chart that divides Earth's history into intervals of time

B the principle that states that the same geologic processes shaping Earth today have been at work throughout Earth's history

C the principle that states that all geologic change occurs suddenly

D the scientific study of the origin, history, and structure of Earth and the processes that shape it

Key Concepts

5 Explain Why did geologists develop the geologic time scale?

6 Infer How do scientists estimate the age of Earth to be 4.6 billion years old?

Critical Thinking

7 Distinguish Would an earthquake support the principle of uniformitarianism or the principle of catastrophism? Explain.

8 Evaluate Some cartoons have shown early humans keeping dinosaurs as pets. From what you know about Earth's history, is this possible? Why or why not?

Use this diagram of the geologic time scale to answer question 9.

Geologic Time Scale

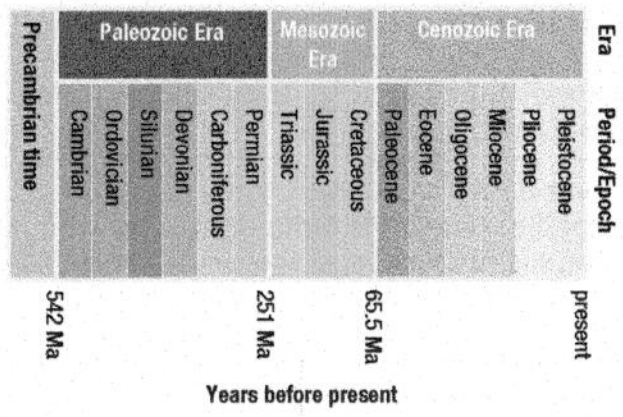

9 Analyze How does this time scale distort Precambrian time? What other part of the time scale is distorted?

Lesson 4 The Geologic Time Scale 129

Student Pages 126–129

Visual Summary Answers

17. suddenly and gradually
18. periods, epochs
19. Cenozoic Era
20. The geologic time scale is based largely on events in the history of life on Earth as recorded by fossils in beds of sedimentary rock.

Lesson Review Answers

1. C
2. A
3. D
4. B
5. to help them make sense of Earth's long geologic history
6. Scientists have found the age of moon rocks and meteorites using radiometric dating. Since these rocks are 4.6 billion years old, scientists infer that the Earth formed at the same time and is also 4.6 billion years old.
7. An earthquake would support the principle of catastrophism because it causes a sudden change to Earth's surface.
8. This is not possible, because the mass extinction of dinosaurs happened at the end of the Mesozoic Era. Humans evolved more than 60 million years later, during the Quaternary Period of the Cenozoic Era.
9. Precambrian time looks much shorter than it was. The Cenozoic Era looks longer than it should be. The time scale also mixes periods and epochs on the same line.

Student Pages 132–135

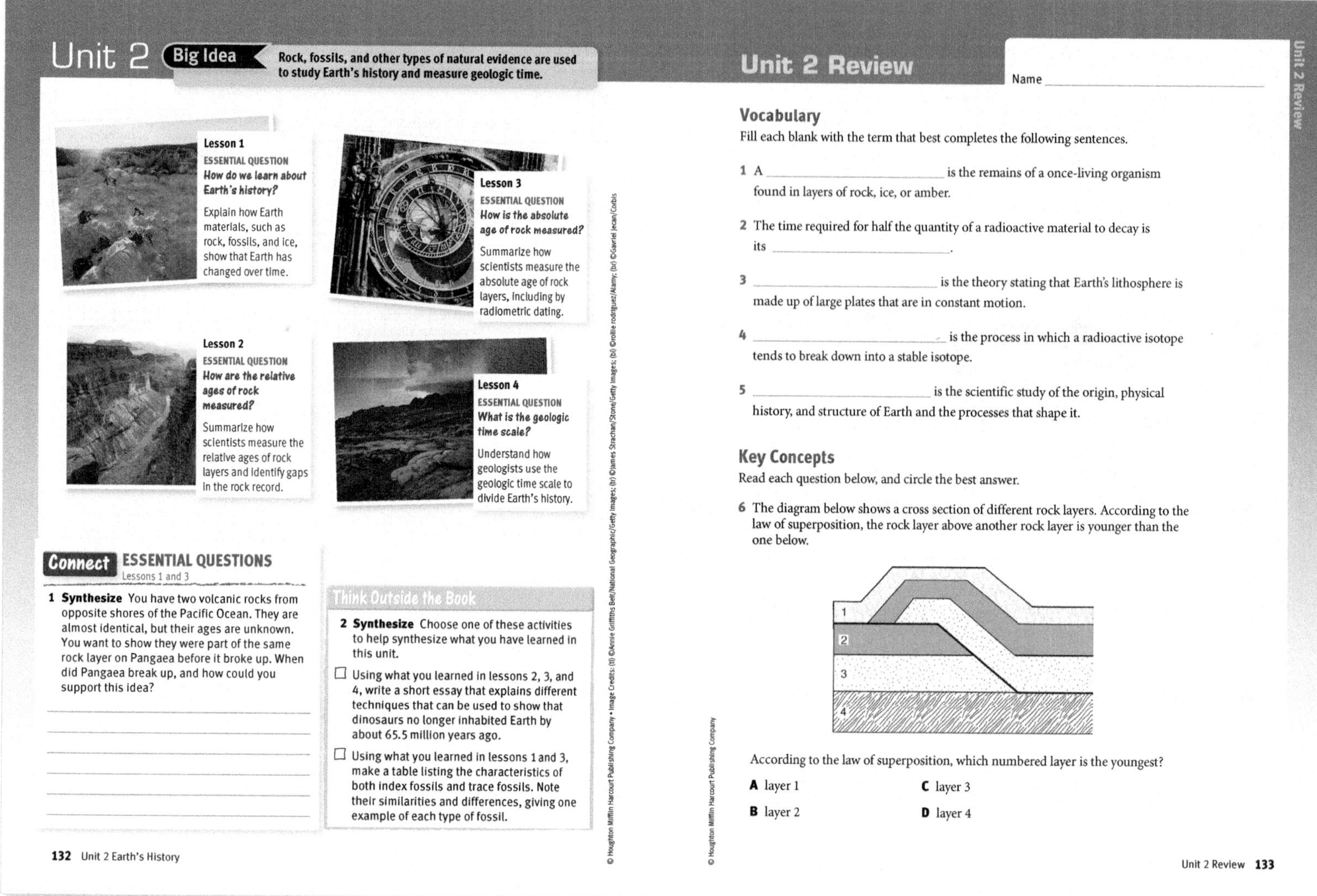

Unit 2 Big Idea Rock, fossils, and other types of natural evidence are used to study Earth's history and measure geologic time.

Lesson 1
ESSENTIAL QUESTION
How do we learn about Earth's history?
Explain how Earth materials, such as rock, fossils, and ice, show that Earth has changed over time.

Lesson 3
ESSENTIAL QUESTION
How is the absolute age of rock measured?
Summarize how scientists measure the absolute age of rock layers, including by radiometric dating.

Lesson 2
ESSENTIAL QUESTION
How are the relative ages of rock measured?
Summarize how scientists measure the relative ages of rock layers and identify gaps in the rock record.

Lesson 4
ESSENTIAL QUESTION
What is the geologic time scale?
Understand how geologists use the geologic time scale to divide Earth's history.

Connect ESSENTIAL QUESTIONS
Lessons 1 and 3

1 **Synthesize** You have two volcanic rocks from opposite shores of the Pacific Ocean. They are almost identical, but their ages are unknown. You want to show they were part of the same rock layer on Pangaea before it broke up. When did Pangaea break up, and how could you support this idea?

Think Outside the Book

2 **Synthesize** Choose one of these activities to help synthesize what you have learned in this unit.

☐ Using what you learned in lessons 2, 3, and 4, write a short essay that explains different techniques that can be used to show that dinosaurs no longer inhabited Earth by about 65.5 million years ago.

☐ Using what you learned in lessons 1 and 3, make a table listing the characteristics of both index fossils and trace fossils. Note their similarities and differences, giving one example of each type of fossil.

132 Unit 2 Earth's History

© Houghton Mifflin Harcourt Publishing Company • Image Credits: (t) ©Annie Griffiths Belt/National Geographic/Getty Images; (b) ©James Strachan/Stone/Getty Images; (b) ©Cecilie rodriguez/Alamy; (b) ©Gavriel Jecan/Corbis

Unit 2 Review

Name ______

Vocabulary
Fill each blank with the term that best completes the following sentences.

1 A ______ is the remains of a once-living organism found in layers of rock, ice, or amber.

2 The time required for half the quantity of a radioactive material to decay is its ______.

3 ______ is the theory stating that Earth's lithosphere is made up of large plates that are in constant motion.

4 ______ is the process in which a radioactive isotope tends to break down into a stable isotope.

5 ______ is the scientific study of the origin, physical history, and structure of Earth and the processes that shape it.

Key Concepts
Read each question below, and circle the best answer.

6 The diagram below shows a cross section of different rock layers. According to the law of superposition, the rock layer above another rock layer is younger than the one below.

According to the law of superposition, which numbered layer is the youngest?

A layer 1
B layer 2
C layer 3
D layer 4

© Houghton Mifflin Harcourt Publishing Company

Unit 2 Review 133

Unit Summary Answers

1. Pangaea started to break apart about 200 million years ago. Radiometric dating, such as Potassium-Argon or Uranium-Lead, could be used to find the age of each volcanic rock to support that they are from the same rock layer on Pangaea.
2. Option 1: No dinosaur fossils appear in sedimentary strata younger than about 65.5 million years. Both relative dating and absolute dating techniques can show this. The geologic column shows that no dinosaur fossils are found in rock younger than about 65.5 million years. Radiometric dating could be used to date rock layers above the rock layers containing the last remains of dinosaurs.

   Option 2: Index fossils must have distinct features, be found over a large area, and the time span of their existence must be known (from dating layers above and below). Index fossils found in the same rock units worldwide can be assigned an age range. Trilobites are one example. A trace fossil is a fossilized structure formed by animal activity, such as tracks or burrows.

Unit Review Response to Intervention

A Quick Grading Chart follows the Answers. See the Assessment Guide for more detail about correct and incorrect answer choices. Refer back to the Lesson Planning pages for activities and assignments that can be used as remediation for students who answer questions incorrectly.

Answers

1. fossil Fossils preserve the remains of organisms up to billions of years before present time and are commonly found in sedimentary rock. (Lesson 1)
2. half-life Knowing the half-life of certain radioactive materials makes it possible to date very old rocks. (Lesson 3)
3. Continental drift The theory of plate tectonics explains large-scale movements of Earth's lithosphere on top of the asthenosphere. It also explains continental drift, mountain building, rifting, and events such as earthquakes. (Lesson 1)

Name ______

7 Earth is approximately 4.6 billion years old. How do scientists determine this?

A by measuring the age of the oldest glaciers

B by using radiometric dating techniques on meteorites

C by measuring the age of the oldest fossils

D by determining the chemical composition of sea-floor sediments

8 Which best describes a fossil that was discovered in rock at the base of a cliff?

A It is likely younger than a fossil discovered in rock at the top of the cliff.

B It is likely older than a fossil discovered in rock at the top of the cliff.

C It is likely younger than a fossil discovered halfway up the cliff.

D It is most likely an index fossil.

9 The law of crosscutting relationships states that a rock unit or geologic feature (such as a fault) is younger than any other rock unit it cuts through. A fault has shifted the rocks in the diagram below.

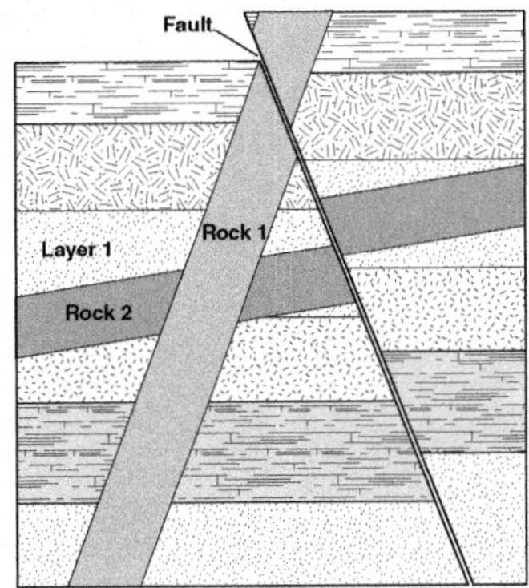

Which of the following is the oldest feature in this rock column?

A Fault

B Rock 1

C Rock 2

D Layer 1

10 Which of these choices names two kinds of trace fossils?

A tracks and burrows

B shells and bones

C bee and beetle in amber

D petrified and mummified fossils

11 Earth's surface features slowly change over time. For example, sharp, jagged mountain ranges become lower and more rounded over time. What is responsible for this change in their shape?

A weathering and erosion

B deposition

C movement of continents

D collisions between continental plates

12 The figure below shows an arch, a geologic formation made over a long period of time by a process that supports the principle of uniformitarianism.

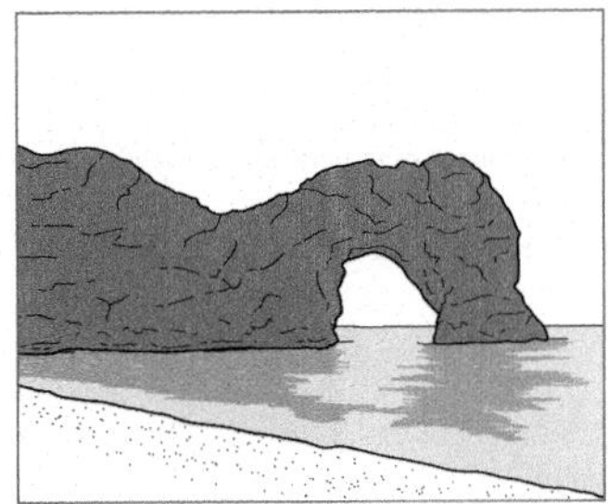

Which process below formed the arch shown in the figure?

A precipitation

B deposition

C erosion

D volcanism

13 Which statement best describes an index fossil?

A a fossil that can be used to establish the absolute age of a rock layer

B a fossil which is formed in soft sediment by the movement of an animal

C a fossil of an insect captured in amber

D a fossil of an animal captured in ice

Answers *(continued)*

4. Radioactive decay Radioactive decay involves unstable isotopes that emit particles and energy, changing the parent atom into a daughter atom. (Lesson 3)
5. geology Geologists study the physical history of Earth and the processes that have shaped Earth (and that are shaping it today). (Lesson 1)
6. Answer A is correct because the top layer, layer 1, is the youngest. (Lesson 2)
7. Answer B is correct because this is how the age of Earth is determined—by dating meteorites. (Lesson 3)
8. Answer B is correct because the fossil at the base of the cliff is likely older than any fossil found above it. (Lesson 2)
9. Answer D is correct because the Fault, Rock 1, and Rock 2 cut through Layer 1, so they formed after Layer 1 formed. (Lesson 2)
10. Answer A is correct because both tracks and burrows form in soft sediment as a result of animal activities, and then may harden over time to form trace fossils. (Lesson 1)
11. Answer A is correct because weathering and erosion break down, remove, and smooth bedrock in mountains over time. (Lesson 1)
12. Answer C is correct because wave action gradually eroded the rock to form an arch. (Lesson 1)
13. Answer A is correct because an index fossil is one of a known age range, so when found in a certain rock layer (or any rock unit) it can give a close estimate of the age. (Lesson 2)
14. Key Elements:
    - Precambrian; Paleozoic; Mesozoic; Cenozoic
    - These divisions are based on major changes that occurred in Earth's history, such as the rise of mammals or mass extinctions. These divisions help to organize the study of Earth's history. (Lesson 4)

Unit 2 Review continued

Critical Thinking

Answer the following questions in the space provided.

14 List the four major divisions of Earth's history. Explain how these divisions were made and why they are useful.

15 Scientists study how radioactive isotopes in rocks, such as Carbon-14, decay to tell the age of the rock.

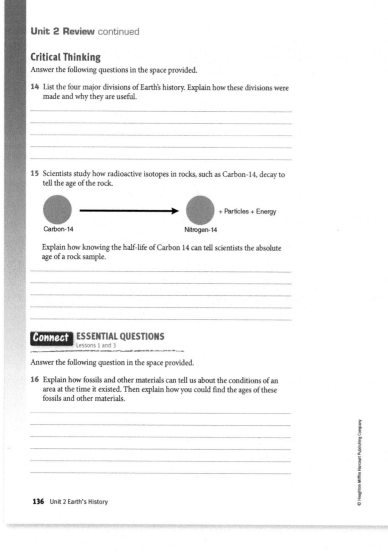

Carbon-14 → Nitrogen-14 + Particles + Energy

Explain how knowing the half-life of Carbon 14 can tell scientists the absolute age of a rock sample.

Connect ESSENTIAL QUESTIONS
Lessons 1 and 3

Answer the following question in the space provided.

16 Explain how fossils and other materials can tell us about the conditions of an area at the time it existed. Then explain how you could find the ages of these fossils and other materials.

Answers *(continued)*

15. Key Elements:
    - Radioactive decay is the process in which a radioactive isotope decays to a different isotope.
    - Half-life is the time required for half of a quantity of radioactive isotope to decay. Rate of decay is predictable.
    - Comparing the relative percentages of a radioactive (parent) isotope and a stable (daughter) isotope allows scientists to determine how long ago the rock formed. (Lesson 3)
16. Key Elements:
    - Fossils can show what the environment was like.
    - Other materials, such as tree rings, can tell about past growing conditions. Sea-floor sediments and ice cores can tell us past chemical compositions. Ages of these can be found by radiometric dating techniques.
    - For organic materials, radiocarbon dating could be used (45,000 years to present). (Lessons 1, 3)

Quick Grading Chart

Use the chart below for quick test grading. The lesson correlations can help you target reteaching for missed items.

Item	Answer	Cognitive Complexity	Lesson
1.	—	Low	1
2.	—	Low	3
3.	—	Low	1
4.	—	Low	3
5.	—	Low	1
6.	A	Moderate	2
7.	B	Moderate	3
8.	B	Moderate	2
9.	D	Moderate	2
10.	A	Moderate	1
11.	A	Moderate	1
12.	C	Moderate	1
13.	A	Moderate	2
14.	—	Moderate	4
15.	—	Moderate	3
16.	—	Moderate	1, 3

Cognitive Complexity refers to the demand on thinking associated with an item, and may vary with the answer choices, the number of steps required to arrive at an answer, and other factors, but not the ability level of the student.

UNIT 3 Minerals and Rocks

The Big Idea and Essential Questions

This Unit was designed to focus on this Big Idea and Essential Questions.

Big Idea **Minerals and rocks are basic building blocks of Earth and can change over time from one type of mineral or rock to another.**

Lesson	ESSENTIAL QUESTION	Student Mastery	PD Professional Development	Lesson Overview
LESSON 1 Minerals	*What are minerals, how do they form, and how can they be identified?*	To describe the basic structure of minerals and identify different minerals by using their physical properties	Content Refresher, TE p. 172	TE p. 178
LESSON 2 The Rock Cycle	*What is the rock cycle?*	To describe the series of processes and classes of rocks that make up the rock cycle	Content Refresher, TE p. 173	TE p. 194
LESSON 3 Three Classes of Rock	*How do rocks form?*	To describe the formation and classification of the three classes of rocks	Content Refresher, TE p. 174	TE p. 212

Science Background

Use the keywords at right to access

- Professional Development from **The NSTA Learning Center**
- **SciLinks** for additional online content appropriate for students and teachers

Keywords

minerals
rocks
rock cycle

Options for Instruction

Two parallel paths provide coverage of the Essential Questions, with a strong **Inquiry** strand woven into each. Follow the **Print Path,** the **Digital Path,** or your customized combination of print, digital, and inquiry.

	LESSON 1 Minerals	LESSON 2 The Rock Cycle	LESSON 3 Three Classes of Rock
Essential Questions	***What are minerals, how do they form, and how can they be identified?***	***What is the rock cycle?***	***How do rocks form?***
Key Topics	• Matter and Minerals • Formation of Minerals • Types of Minerals • Properties of Minerals	• Weathering, Erosion, and Deposition • Three Classes of Rock • Rock Cycle • Tectonic Plate Motion and the Rock Cycle	• Rocks and Their Classification • Igneous Rock • Sedimentary Rock • Metamorphic Rock
Print Path	Teacher Edition pp. 178–192 Student Edition pp. 140–153	Teacher Edition pp. 194–207 Student Edition pp. 154–165	Teacher Edition pp. 212–225 Student Edition pp. 170–181
Inquiry Labs	Lab Manual **Quick Lab** Cooling Rate and Crystal Size **Quick Lab** Scratch Test **Exploration Lab** Intrinsic Identification of Minerals	Lab Manual **Quick Lab** Crayon Rock Cycle **Quick Lab** Modeling Weathering	Lab Manual **Quick Lab** Stretching Out **S.T.E.M. Lab** Modeling Rock Formation Virtual Lab Rock Test Kitchen
Digital Path	Digital Path TS691010	Digital Path TS671010	Digital Path TS671015

UNIT 3
Unit Projects

Citizen Science Project
Mineral Resources

Teacher Edition p. 177

Student Edition
pp. 138–139

Teacher Notes

Unit Assessment

Formative Assessment

Strategies RTI
Throughout TE

Lesson Reviews SE

Unit PreTest

Summative Assessment

Alternative Assessment
(1 per lesson) RTI

Lesson Quizzes

Unit Tests A and B

Unit Review RTI
(with answer remediation)

Practice Tests
(end of module)

Project-Based Assessment

See the Assessment Guide for quizzes and tests.

Go Online to edit and create quizzes and tests.

Response to Intervention

See RTI teacher support materials on p. PD6.

Differentiated Instruction

English Language Proficiency

Strategies for **English Language Learners (ELL)** are provided for each lesson, under the Explain tabs.

LESSON 1 *Comparing Minerals,* TE p. 183

LESSON 2 *Notetaking,* TE p. 199

LESSON 3 *Notetaking,* TE p. 217

Vocabulary strategies provided for all students can also be a particular help for ELL. Use different strategies for each lesson or choose one or two to use throughout the unit. Vocabulary strategies can be found under the Explain tab for each lesson (TE pp. 183, 199, and 217).

Leveled Inquiry

Inquiry labs, activities, probing questions, and daily demos provide a range of inquiry levels. Preview them under the Engage and Explore tabs starting on TE pp. 180, 196, and 214.

Levels of Inquiry	**DIRECTED** inquiry	**GUIDED** inquiry	**INDEPENDENT** inquiry
	introduces inquiry skills within a structured framework.	develops inquiry skills within a supportive environment.	deepens inquiry skills with student-driven questions or procedures.

Each long lab has two inquiry options:

LESSON 1 **Exploration Lab** *Intrinsic Identification of Minerals*

LESSON 3 **S.T.E.M. Lab** *Modeling Rock Formation*

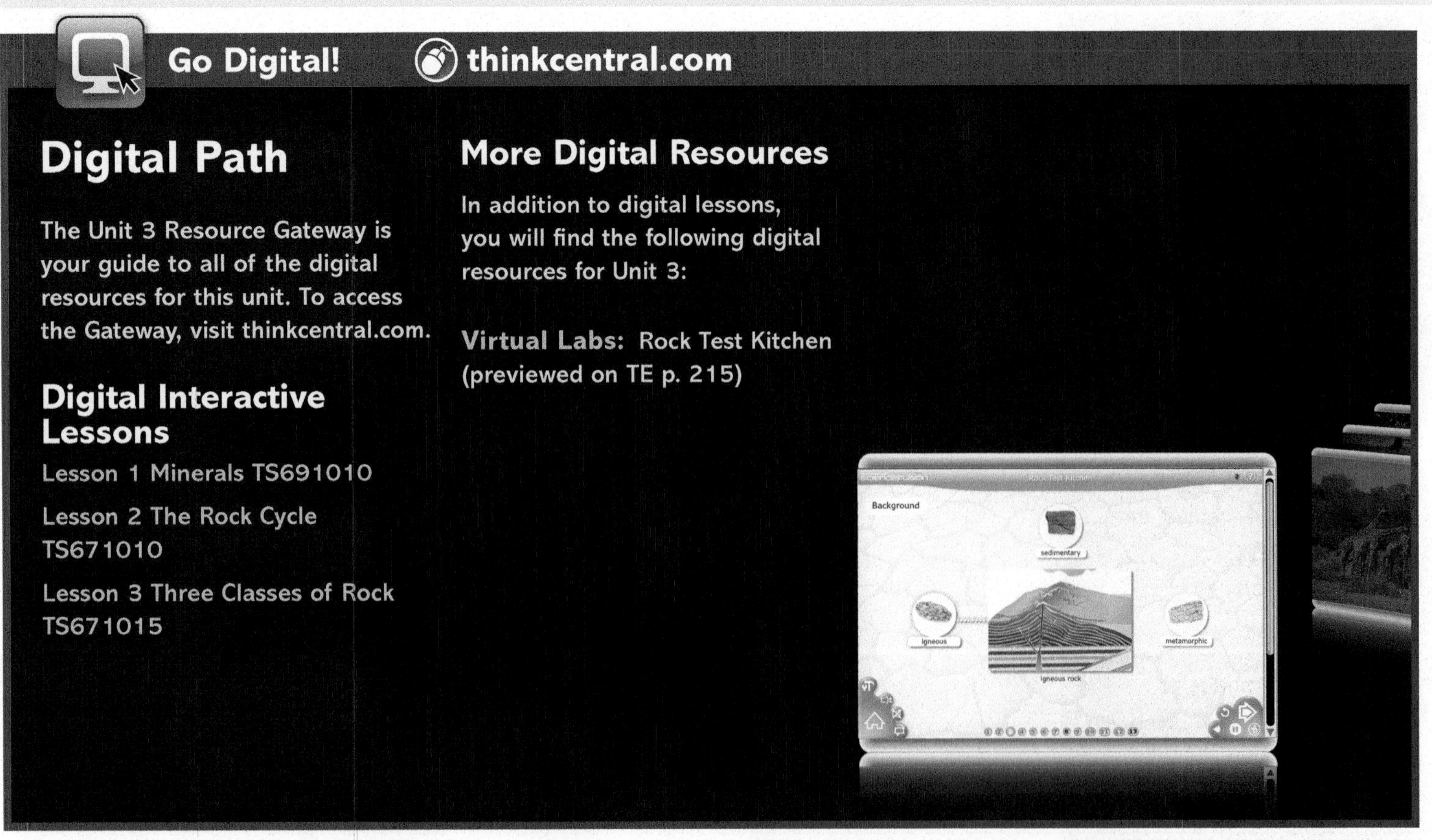

Go Digital! thinkcentral.com

Digital Path

The Unit 3 Resource Gateway is your guide to all of the digital resources for this unit. To access the Gateway, visit thinkcentral.com.

Digital Interactive Lessons

Lesson 1 Minerals TS691010

Lesson 2 The Rock Cycle TS671010

Lesson 3 Three Classes of Rock TS671015

More Digital Resources

In addition to digital lessons, you will find the following digital resources for Unit 3:

Virtual Labs: Rock Test Kitchen (previewed on TE p. 215)

RTI Response to Intervention

Response to Intervention (RTI) is a process for identifying and supporting students who are not making expected progress toward essential learning goals. The following *ScienceFusion* components can be used to provide strategic and intensive intervention.

Component	Location	Strategies and Benefits
STUDENT EDITION Active Reading prompts, Visualize It!, Think Outside the Book	**Throughout each lesson**	Student responses can be used as screening tools to assess whether intervention is needed.
TEACHER EDITION Formative Assessment, Probing Questions, Learning Alerts	**Throughout each lesson**	Opportunities are provided to assess and remediate student understanding of lesson concepts.
TEACHER EDITION Extend Science Concepts	**Reinforce and Review, TE pp. 184, 200, 218** **Going Further, TE pp. 184, 200, 218**	Additional activities allow students to reinforce and extend their understanding of lesson concepts.
TEACHER EDITION Evaluate Student Mastery	**Formative Assessment, TE pp. 185, 201, 219** **Alternative Assessment, TE pp. 185, 201, 219**	These assessments allow for greater flexibility in assessing students with differing physical, mental, and language abilities as well as varying learning and communication modes.
TEACHER EDITION Unit Review Remediation	**Unit Review, TE pp. 226–228**	Includes reference back to Lesson Planning pages for remediation activities and assignments.
INTERACTIVE DIGITAL LESSONS and VIRTUAL LABS	**thinkcentral.com** **Unit 3 Gateway** **Lesson 1 TS691010** **Lesson 2 TS671010** **Lesson 3 TS671015**	Lessons and labs make content accessible through simulations, animations, videos, audio, and integrated assessment. Useful for review and reteaching of lesson concepts.

Content Refresher

Lesson 1

Minerals

ESSENTIAL QUESTION

What are minerals, how do they form, and how can they be identified?

1. Matter and Minerals

Minerals are matter.

Matter comprises everything that has mass. Matter exists in five states: solid, liquid, gas, plasmas, and Bose-Einstein condensates (discovered in 1995). An atom is the smallest part of an element that retains the element's properties. Compounds are substances that are made up of two or more elements that are chemically bonded as molecules. Minerals are solids and are composed of elements.

Minerals are naturally formed, usually inorganic solids that have crystalline arrangements of repeating patterns of atoms or molecules. The shape of the crystal is determined by the arrangement of atoms within the crystal. Minerals are grouped into classes according to the shape of their crystals.

2. Formation of Minerals

Minerals form in several different ways.

Many minerals form when magma solidifies. Magma contains all of the atoms present in minerals. Magma cools and solidifies at different rates. If magma cools quickly, the crystals that form are small. If magma cools slowly over time, the crystals grow larger.

Temperature and pressure changes within Earth also lead to mineral formation. Temperature and pressure can break bonds between atoms and allow them to rejoin to form new crystalline solids. Minerals can grow and replace other minerals during metamorphism. For example, graphite (a mineral composed entirely of carbon) transforms into diamond (a different mineral also composed of carbon) at high pressure.

Minerals also form from solutions. Water generally has many different substances dissolved in it. These substances can develop into minerals by precipitating out of solution or when water evaporates.

3. Types of Minerals

Minerals are classified in two large groups.

Silicate minerals are the largest group of minerals on Earth. Geologists estimate that up to 90% of Earth's crust is made of silicates. Silicates are made up of repeating tetrahedron-shaped units. Silicate minerals (with examples) include quartz and olivine, and the mineral groups known as the pyroxenes (augite, pigeonite), amphiboles (hornblende), micas (biotite, muscovite), and feldspars (orthoclase, plagioclase).

Nonsilicate minerals are those that do not contain the silicate tetrahedron unit. These minerals are made up of elements such as carbon, fluorine, iron, and sulfur. The nonsilicate mineral groups (with examples) include: oxides (hematite, magnetite), sulfides (pyrite), sulfates (gypsum), halides (halite), carbonates (calcite), and native elements (sulfur, copper, gold).

4. Properties of Minerals

Minerals are identified by their properties.

Although minerals are only absolutely identified by x-ray and chemical analysis, there are methods that scientists and collectors can use in the field without specialized equipment. Minerals have several defining physical properties that can be used to identify them.

Most minerals have a distinct color. However, this can change in the presence of other elements or under certain physical conditions. Therefore, color is not an accurate characteristic by which to identify minerals. By contrast, streak, a mineral's color in powdered form, shows the true color of a mineral.

Hardness is a measure of a mineral's resistance to scratching; it is described on Mohs hardness scale. The ways in which a mineral breaks are described as ***cleavage*** and ***fracture***. Crystal habit (shape) and cleavage patterns are usually good diagnostic tools for identifying mineral types. Luster is the way that light is reflected by a mineral's surface.

Teacher to Teacher

Pamela Sweeney
Smith-Hale Middle School
Kansas City, MO

Lesson 3 Three Classes of Rock Give each student 3 unidentified rock samples, one from each class of rock. Ask students to divide a paper into 3 columns, and place each rock sample into one of the columns. In each column, have the student list the characteristics of that rock that sets it apart from the other two. Students can then use the listed characteristics to determine which class each rock belongs in.

Lesson 2

The Rock Cycle

ESSENTIAL QUESTION
What is the rock cycle?

1. Weathering, Erosion, and Deposition

Rock is changed by weathering and erosion.

Rock has been important to humans throughout history. It has been used to build shelters and as weapons and tools. It is defined as a naturally occurring, solid mixture of minerals, which may also include organic matter. Rock can have a crystalline makeup or be crystal free. Rock can give scientists glimpses into Earth's past.

Over time, rock changes due to weathering and erosion. Weathering is the breakdown of rock by temperature changes, water, wind, and ice; the activity of chemicals and plant roots can cause rock to break down, too. The particles of broken rock (sediments) are transported by water, wind, ice, and gravity in a process called erosion. The sediments are carried for a distance and then dropped in another area, such as in the bed of a stream or on the ocean floor. This is called ***deposition***.

2. Three Classes of Rock

There are three classes of rock.

The classes of rock are grouped based on their formation. Igneous rock, such as granite, forms from cooling magma or lava. As the molten rock cools, minerals crystallize and grow, forming various types of rocks depending on the local temperature and pressure, the composition of the molten rock, and how long it took for molten rock to cool. Sedimentary rock, such as sandstone, forms when fragments of older rocks, the shells and skeletons of marine organisms, and fossils that break down through weathering and erosion, become cemented together.

Finally, metamorphic rock, such as marble, is formed when temperature and pressure change the texture and mineral content of rock within Earth. Usually, metamorphic rock is formed by a combination of temperature and pressure changes, although it can be formed by temperature changes alone.

3. Rock Cycle

Rock is formed and changed through the rock cycle.

The rock cycle is the process by which rock is formed or changed. Each class of rock can be changed into another class by the action of temperature, pressure, weathering, and erosion.

4. Tectonic Plate Motion and the Rock Cycle

Tectonic plates form mountains and ocean basins.

Earth's tectonic plates have different thicknesses and densities; the oceanic basins with thin, dense, basalt-rich ocean crust ride lower on the mantle than do the continental plates, with thick and less-dense, granite-rich crust. When plates move apart, cracks appear in Earth's surface, forming ***rift zones***. Iceland, which is partly on the North American plate and partly on the Eurasian plate, straddles an active rift zone. Rift zones can also occur within plates, as is the case in east Africa. Scientists expect an ocean will form at this location as pieces of the African plate and the Arabian plate move apart from each other.

When plates collide, mountain ranges can rise as the pressure of the moving plates causes folding in the crust and uplift of the area. ***Uplift*** is the raising up of Earth's crust due to pressure or stress relief. Earthquakes are often a result of the plate motion associated with uplift and can also occur when mountains wear down or massive ice sheets retreat, exerting less downward pressure, and the crust rebounds. Uplift can also occur slowly and without earthquake activity, as happens in the continuously rising Himalayas.

The sinking of the crust is called ***subsidence***; it can be the result of many factors, including the removal of groundwater. When the groundwater recharges (as in an ongoing project in California), the area can experience uplift.

Content Refresher (continued)

Lesson 3

Three Classes of Rock

ESSENTIAL QUESTION

How do rocks form?

1. Rocks and Their Classification

Students will learn that rocks are classified not only by how they form, but also by texture and composition.

Rock is composed of minerals and nonminerals such as organic matter. Rock is divided into three main classes: igneous, sedimentary, and metamorphic. It is further classified by texture, which is the size and shape of the grains in the rock, and by composition, which is the chemical makeup of the rock.

2. Igneous Rock

Students will learn that igneous rock can be intrusive or extrusive.

Extrusive igneous rock forms when magma reaches Earth's surface and becomes lava. Eruptions include lava, escaping gas, and pyroclastic materials, such as ash and cinder.

As lava cools it may crystallize and form extrusive igneous rock with tiny crystals and a fine-grained texture. If lava cools very quickly, there is no time for crystallization and volcanic glass forms. Pyroclastic materials settle, and may be compacted to form rocks such as volcanic tuff.

Intrusive igneous rock forms when magma cools and solidifies beneath Earth's surface. Beneath Earth's surface, magma cools slowly in intrusions that range from dikes that fill fissures to batholiths, which may cover areas as large as 100 km^2.

Intrusive igneous rock contains minerals which form large, visible crystals. These rocks generally have a coarse-grained texture. Examples include granite and diorite.

3. Sedimentary Rock

Students will learn that sedimentary rock is compressed and cemented into layers.

Sedimentary rock forms from deposited materials, which can include clay, organic remains, silt, sand, and gravel.

Sedimentary rock may also form by mineral precipitation.

Over long periods of time, sediments are compressed and compacted into layers. Each layer may contain completely different material. This difference in material creates the distinct layering commonly seen in sedimentary rock.

Sedimentary rock can be chemical, formed from precipitation of dissolved minerals out of bodies of water; clastic, formed from fragments of rock cemented together; or organic, containing remains of plants and animals.

Fossils are commonly found in sedimentary rock. Fossilization is the process by which an organism's remains are entombed rapidly in sediment. The sediment may preserve the organism's hard parts, such as bone, shell, or wood. However, imprints, molds, and casts are more common.

4. Metamorphic Rock

Students will learn that metamorphic rock can be foliated or nonfoliated.

Large increases in temperature, pressure, or both may form metamorphic rocks. Metamorphism causes changes in mineralogy, texture, and/or chemical composition.

Hydrothermal activity can dissolve minerals and then precipitate new minerals, chemically changing the rock. Intrusion of magma bodies causes contact metamorphism by greatly increasing the temperature of the surrounding country rock. Burial can increase both temperature and pressure on rock, resulting in regional metamorphism.

Foliated metamorphic rocks, such as gneiss, result from extensive deformation by regional metamorphism. They contain aligned, planar arrangements of minerals grains. Nonfoliated metamorphic rocks, such as marble, result from minimal deformation of rocks containing one or few minerals.

Teacher Notes

Advance Planning

These activities may take extended time or special conditions.

Unit 3

Project Mineral Resources, p. 177
research and analysis

Graphic Organizers and Vocabulary pp. 183, 184, 199, 200, 217, 218
ongoing with reading

Lesson 1

Activity Making Crystals, p. 184
requires observations over multiple days

Lesson 2

Daily Demo Igneous Rock Formation, p. 196
powdered sulfur

Lesson 3

Activity Making Sedimentary Rocks, p. 214
fish bones, shell pieces, plaster of Paris, various sediments

What Do You Think?

Encourage students to consider how people use minerals and rocks.

Ask: What are some ways in which people use rocks? Sample answers: as building materials, on roads, in fish tanks, cut into floor tiles

Ask: What are some products made using minerals such as metals and gems? Sample answer: building materials, cars, jewelry, computers, cookware

Ask: Where do you think rocks and minerals that we use come from? They are mostly mined from the ground.

Learning Alert

Mining Jobs Along with considering the environmental impacts of mining, students can also research the benefits and dangers associated with working in mines. Mining provides jobs for thousands of people in the United States. In 2008, more than 717,000 people worked in the U.S. mining industry. Of these, 80,000 people worked in coal mining, and almost 150,000 worked mining metals and nonmetallic minerals. However, some mining jobs (such as underground coal mining) are among the most dangerous jobs in the United States. Have interested students research health hazards associated with mining.

Unit 3
Minerals and Rocks

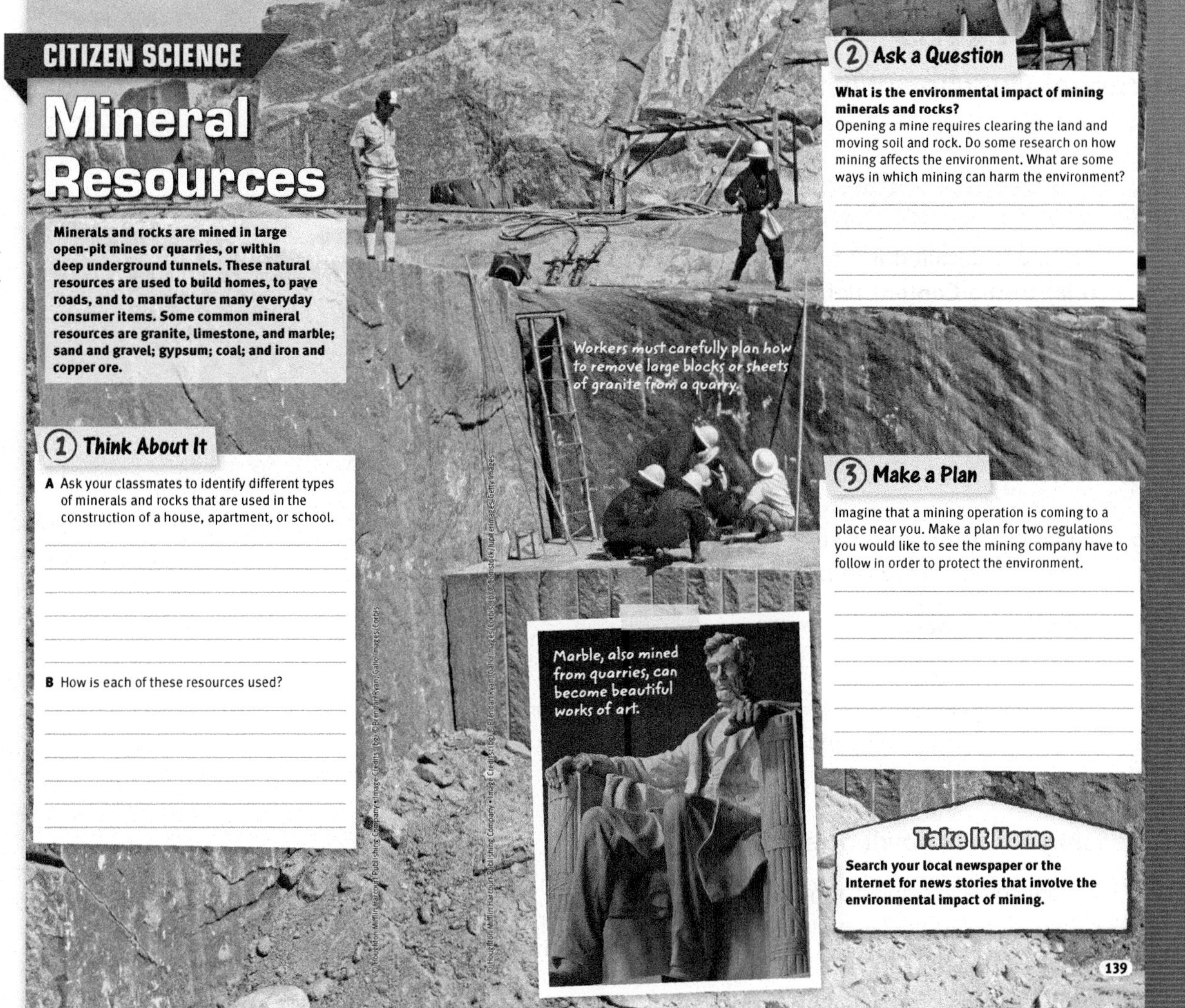

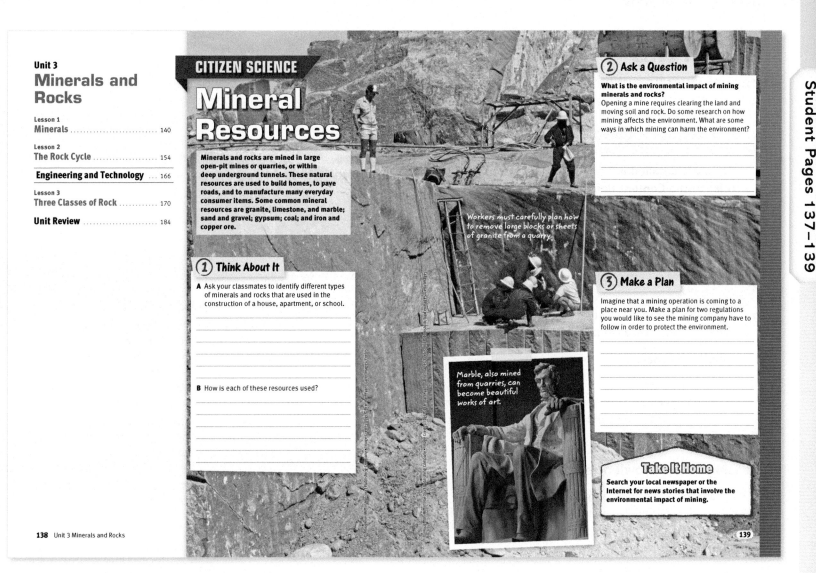

CITIZEN SCIENCE

Unit Project Mineral Resources

1. Think About It

Encourage students to brainstorm several examples of minerals and rocks used in the construction of a building. If students struggle, prompt them with questions, such as *What can the foundation of a house be made from? How might metal be used in a building?*

2. Ask a Question

Allow students time to research the environmental impacts of mining using the Internet or library resources. Students may identify impacts such as removing trees and other plants, eliminating animal habitats, altering the flow of water, releasing chemicals into water, burning fossil fuels, and polluting the air.

3. Make a Plan

Sample answer: The mining company should have to replant as many trees as it removes. The company should also be required to test the water that leaves the mine area for dangerous chemicals.

Take It Home

Ask students to bring in copies of Internet or newspaper stories that they found while working with an adult. Encourage students to share the stories with the class and to summarize what they learned.

Optional Online rubric: Class Discussion

Minerals

Essential Question What are minerals, how do they form, and how can they be identified?

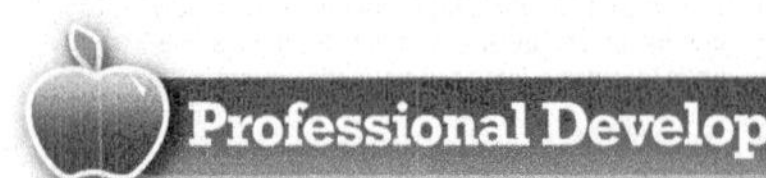

For more detailed information about the topics in this lesson, refer to the Content Refresher in the Unit Opener pages.

Opening Your Lesson

Begin the lesson by assessing students' prerequisite and prior knowledge.

Prerequisite Knowledge

- Minerals form naturally.
- Many different types of minerals can be extracted from Earth's crust and used by people.

Accessing Prior Knowledge

Ask: What are some examples of minerals? Answers will vary, and may include incorrect examples. Help students separate correct and incorrect responses.

Ask: What do these examples have in common? Sample answer: They are all crystals.

Ask: Where are minerals found? Sample answer: in Earth's crust; on other planets or bodies in space

Customize Your Opening

- ☐ **Accessing Prior Knowledge,** above
- ☐ **Print Path** Engage Your Brain, SE p. 141 #1–2
- ☐ **Print Path** Active Reading, SE p. 141 #3–4
- ☐ **Digital Path** Lesson Opener

Key Topics/Learning Goals	Supporting Concepts
Matter and Minerals 1 Define *matter*. 2 Compare elements and compounds. 3 List the characteristics of minerals.	• Matter is anything having mass and volume. • Elements are pure substances that cannot be broken down by chemical means into simpler substances. Elements consist of atoms. Two or more atoms that bonded to each other form a molecule. A molecule that consists of two or more elements is a compound. • A mineral is a natural, usually inorganic solid with a definite crystalline structure and chemical composition.
Formation of Minerals 1 Summarize three ways that minerals form.	• Minerals can form when magma or lava cool, by metamorphism, or from solutions.
Types of Minerals 1 Describe silicate minerals and name some common silicate minerals. 2 Identify the main classes of nonsilicate minerals.	• Silicate minerals contain silicon-oxygen compounds; examples are quartz, feldspars, and micas. • The main classes of nonsilicate minerals are carbonates, halides, native elements, oxides, sulfates, and sulfides.
Properties of Minerals 1 Identify physical properties that are used to identify minerals.	• Physical properties that can be used to identify minerals are color, streak, luster, hardness, fracture and cleavage, and density.

Options for Instruction

Two parallel paths provide coverage of the Essential Questions, with a strong **Inquiry** strand woven into each. Follow the **Print Path,** the **Digital Path,** or your customized combination of print, digital, and inquiry.

 Print Path *Teaching support for the Print Path appears with the Student Pages.*	 Inquiry Labs and Activities	 Digital Path *Digital Path shortcut: TS691010*
Animal, Vegetable, or Mineral?, SE pp. 142–143 **What do minerals have in common?** • Definite Chemical Composition • Solid • Usually Inorganic • Crystalline Structure • Naturally Occurring	**Activity** **Making Crystals** **Exploration Lab** **Intrinsic Identification of Minerals**	**Matter and Minerals** **Interactive Images**
Crystal Clear!, SE pp. 144–145 **How are minerals formed?** • As Magma and Lava Cool • By Metamorphism • From Solutions	**Quick Lab** **Cooling Rate and Crystal Size**	**How Minerals Form** **Interactive Graphics**
Sort It Out, SE pp. 146–147 **How are minerals classified?** • Silicate Minerals • Nonsilicate Minerals	**Activity** **Mineral Display**	**Types of Minerals** **Interactive Graphics**
Name That Mineral!, SE pp. 148–150 **What properties can be used to identify minerals?** • Color, Streak, Luster • Cleavage and Fracture, Density • Hardness, Special Properties	**Quick Lab** **Scratch Test** **Daily Demo** **Common Streaks**	**Identifying Minerals** **Interactive Graphics**

Options for Assessment

See the Evaluate page for options, including Formative Assessment, Summative Assessment, and Unit Review.

Engage and Explore

Activities and Discussion

Activity *Mineral Display*

Engage

Types of Minerals

 small groups
 varied

Assign each student a mineral and have them research the mineral and its uses. Have individuals report on their findings. Then have all students combine the information they gathered to make a bulletin board display. The display should include details about each mineral researched, its uses, its properties, and an illustration or photo of the mineral. Leave the display up for use as a reference throughout the lesson.

Probing Question *Finding Gold*

Formation of Minerals

 whole class
20 min

Apply Some minerals form quickly; others take thousands of years to form. Some are more prized than others because of their rarity, while others are overlooked because they are so common. **Ask:** Why are some minerals such as gold and silver hard to find?

Discussion *Planetary Mineral Differences*

Introducing Key Topics

 whole class
20 min

The matter that makes up Earth has been around since Earth formed 4.6 billion years ago. Since then, many different kinds of minerals have formed in different ways and over different periods of time. Discuss how different minerals have formed in relation to the characteristics of Earth's atmosphere and lithosphere. Discuss how these characteristics differ from those of other planets. Then ask students to explain whether they think minerals formed on other planets are the same or different from those that form on Earth.

Labs and Demos

Quick Lab *Cooling Rate and Crystal Size*

Engage

Formation of Minerals

 large groups
 15 min
Inquiry **DIRECTED** inquiry

Students role-play atoms (individuals) and crystal size (groups) to model mineral crystal formation as it relates to time.

PURPOSE **To model mineral crystal formation to study how cooling time affects crystal size**

MATERIALS

- **index cards**
- **stopwatch**

Exploration Lab *Intrinsic Identification of Minerals*

Properties of Minerals

 small groups
45 min
 **DIRECTED/GUIDED** inquiry

Students will determine the identity of two minerals based on their densities.

PURPOSE **To calculate density and then use density to identify minerals**

MATERIALS

- **balance**
- **clamp**
- **graduated cylinder**
- **graphite sample**
- **pyrite sample**
- **ring stand**
- **spring scale**
- **string**
- **water (400 mL)**

Levels of 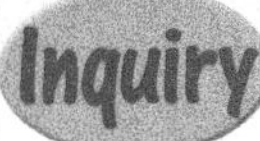

DIRECTED inquiry introduces inquiry skills within a structured framework.

GUIDED inquiry develops inquiry skills within a supportive environment.

INDEPENDENT inquiry deepens inquiry skills with student-driven questions or procedures.

Daily Demo *Common Streaks*

Engage

Properties of Minerals

 whole class

 15 min

 **GUIDED** inquiry

PURPOSE **To demonstrate the mineral property streak**

MATERIALS

- piece of paper
- tape
- pencil
- artist's charcoal (stick or pencil)
- chalk

1 Use the tape to attach a piece of paper to a wall where it can be seen by all students.

2 **Describing** Show students the pencil. Pressing firmly, use the pencil to draw a dark line across the paper. **Ask:** How did the pencil make the line? Sample answer: The graphite in the pencil left a dark streak as it was moved across the paper.

3 Repeat the process with the chalk and with the artist's charcoal. Pass the paper around so students can see up close the differences between the three streaks. Invite them to speculate what causes the similarities and differences among the three.

Quick Lab *Scratch Test*

Engage

Properties of Minerals

 small groups

 15 min

 **DIRECTED** inquiry

Students test the hardness of common materials and compare the hardness of two unknown minerals to determine their identity.

PURPOSE **To identify the hardness of minerals**

MATERIALS

- calcite sample, labeled *A*
- quartz sample, labeled *B*
- penny
- steel nail
- pencil
- safety goggles

Customize Your Labs

See the Lab Manual for lab datasheets.

Go Online for editable lab datasheets.

Activities and Discussion

- ☐ **Activity** Mineral Display
- ☐ **Probing Question** Finding Gold
- ☐ **Discussion** Planetary Mineral Differences

Labs and Demos

- ☐ **Quick Lab** Cooling Rate and Crystal Size
- ☐ **Exploration Lab** Intrinsic Identification of Minerals
- ☐ **Daily Demo** Common Streaks
- ☐ **Quick Lab** Scratch Test

Your Resources

Explain Science Concepts

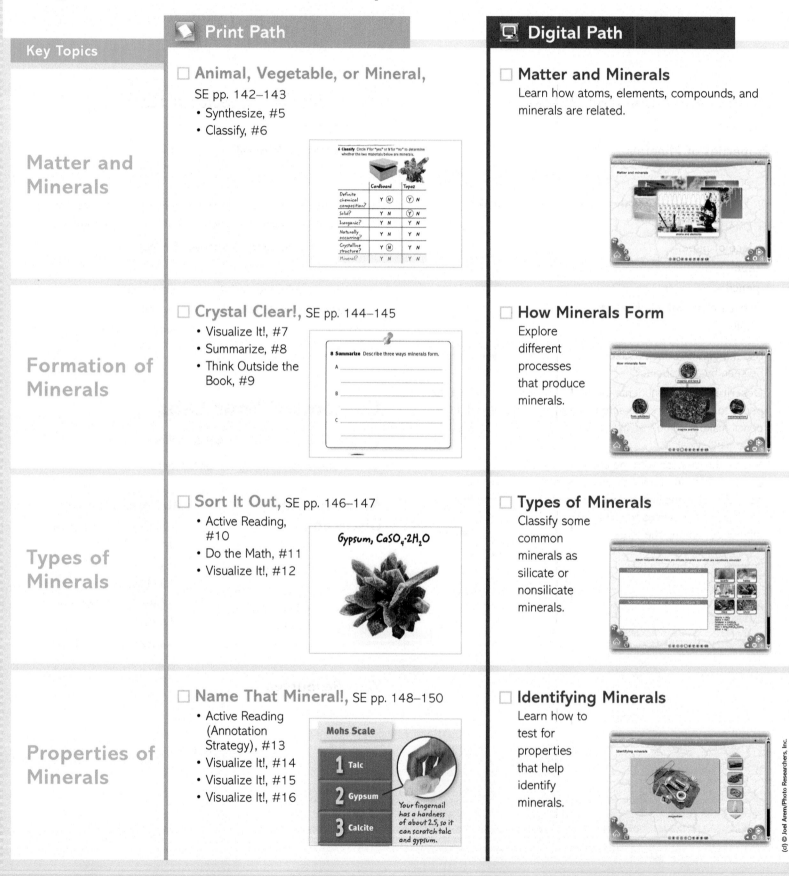

Key Topics	Print Path	Digital Path

Matter and Minerals

Print Path

☐ **Animal, Vegetable, or Mineral,** SE pp. 142–143
- Synthesize, #5
- Classify, #6

6 Classify Circle Y for "yes" or N for "no" to determine whether the two materials below are minerals.

	Cardboard	Topaz
Definite chemical composition?	Y (N)	(Y) N
Solid?	Y N	(Y) N
Inorganic?	Y N	Y N
Naturally occurring?	Y N	Y N
Crystalline structure?	Y (N)	Y N
Mineral?	Y N	Y N

Digital Path

☐ **Matter and Minerals**
Learn how atoms, elements, compounds, and minerals are related.

Formation of Minerals

Print Path

☐ **Crystal Clear!,** SE pp. 144–145
- Visualize It!, #7
- Summarize, #8
- Think Outside the Book, #9

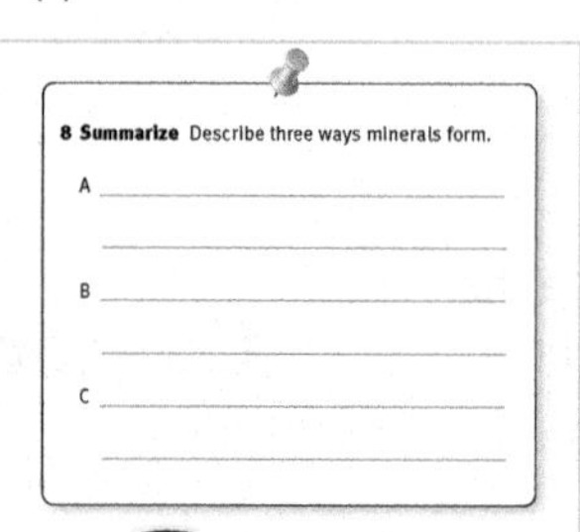

8 Summarize Describe three ways minerals form.
A
B
C

Digital Path

☐ **How Minerals Form**
Explore different processes that produce minerals.

Types of Minerals

Print Path

☐ **Sort It Out,** SE pp. 146–147
- Active Reading, #10
- Do the Math, #11
- Visualize It!, #12

Digital Path

☐ **Types of Minerals**
Classify some common minerals as silicate or nonsilicate minerals.

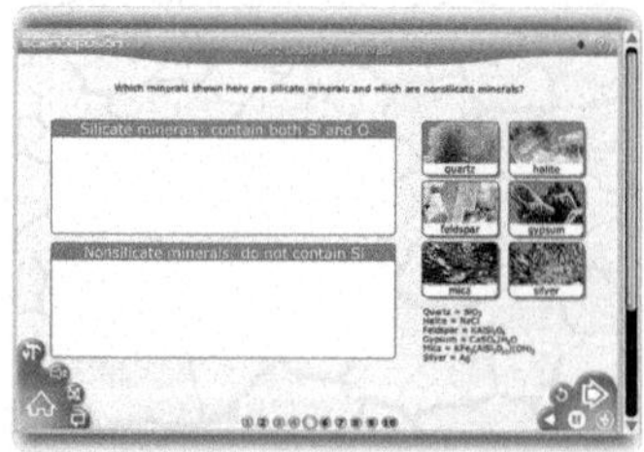

Properties of Minerals

Print Path

☐ **Name That Mineral!,** SE pp. 148–150
- Active Reading (Annotation Strategy), #13
- Visualize It!, #14
- Visualize It!, #15
- Visualize It!, #16

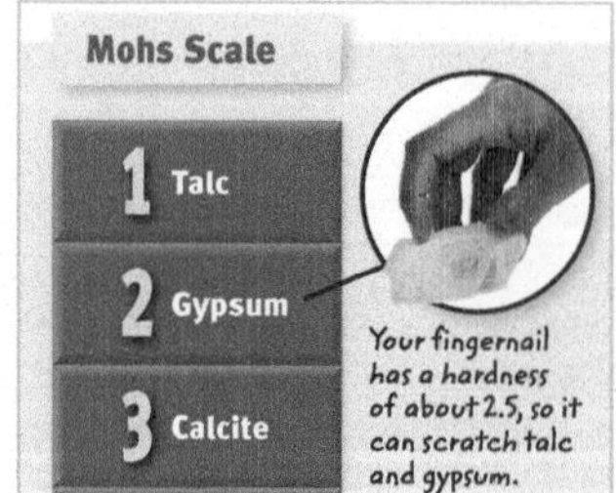

Mohs Scale
1 Talc
2 Gypsum
3 Calcite
Your fingernail has a hardness of about 2.5, so it can scratch talc and gypsum.

Digital Path

☐ **Identifying Minerals**
Learn how to test for properties that help identify minerals.

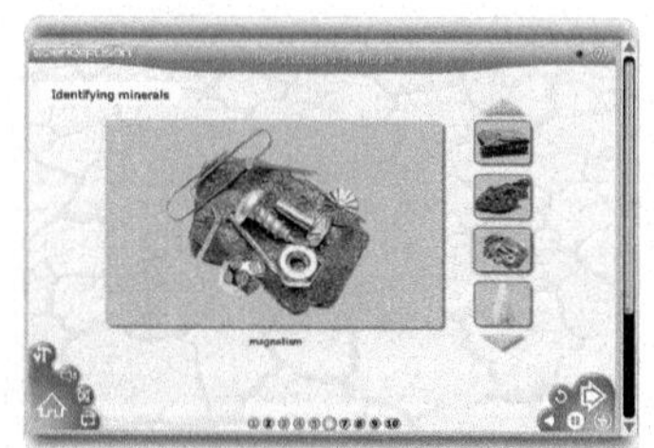

Differentiated Instruction

Basic *Mineral or Not?*

Synthesizing Key Topics

 small groups
 35 min

Display ten pictures of common objects around the room. Post clues about each object beneath its photo. Allow students 10 min to walk around the room and use the clues to identify which objects are minerals and which are not minerals. The student who correctly classifies the most items wins.

Basic *Home Minerals*

Synthesizing Key Topics

 individuals
varied

Have students find products at home that are made from minerals. Ask them to research the characteristics of the minerals and how the products are made, and then present their findings in a poster.

Advanced *Mineral Search*

Synthesizing Key Topics

 individuals
 varied

Display samples of five to ten minerals or materials made from minerals, such as copper wire, a silver ring, water softener (halite), drywall (gypsum), glass (quartz), and chalk (gypsum if chalkboard; calcite if rock). Have students match each mineral or mineral product to cards on which you have written the mineral name and several of its characteristics.

ELL *Comparing Minerals*

Synthesizing Key Topics

 pairs
 40 min

Have pairs of students compare silicates and nonsilicates. Have them list properties, examples, and products made from both groups of minerals in a Two-Panel Flip Chart FoldNote.

Online resource: Two-Panel Flip Chart FoldNote support

Lesson Vocabulary

mineral	**element**	**atom**
compound	**matter**	**crystal**
streak	**luster**	**cleavage**

Previewing Vocabulary

 whole class, then pairs
 25 min

Frame Game Have students make frame game diagrams to learn vocabulary terms. Use a blank frame to demonstrate the use of the diagram. Then have students work in pairs to develop a frame for each term.

Online resource: Frame Game support

Reinforcing Vocabulary

individuals
30 min

Paragraphs To help students remember the vocabulary words introduced in this lesson, have them write a descriptive paragraph or two about minerals. Encourage students to use at least five of the vocabulary words in their paragraphs. Stress that as they write, they should develop descriptive paragraphs, not merely list each term and its definition.

Customize Your Core Lesson

Core Instruction

- ☐ **Print Path** choices
- ☐ **Digital Path** choices

Vocabulary

- ☐ **Previewing Vocabulary** Frame Game
- ☐ **Reinforcing Vocabulary** Paragraphs

Differentiated Instruction

- ☐ **Basic** Mineral or Not?
- ☐ **Basic** Home Minerals
- ☐ **Advanced** Mineral Search
- ☐ **ELL** Comparing Minerals

Your Resources

Extend Science Concepts

Reinforce and Review

Activity *Making Crystals*

Formation of Minerals

 small groups
 25 min

Gather the following materials for each group of students: a glass jar, pencil, thread, salt, and water.

1. Fill the jar about halfway with warm water.
2. Stir salt in the water until it is completely dissolved.
3. Keep adding and dissolving salt until no more will dissolve.
4. Attach the thread to the pencil.
5. Lay the pencil across the jar's mouth so that the thread falls into the water. Adjust the thread length so that the free end of the thread stops just above the bottom of the jar.
6. Place the setup in an area where it will remain undisturbed.
7. Observe the thread each day through the jar. As the water evaporates, salt crystals will form on the thread.

Graphic Organizer

Synthesizing Key Topics

 individual
35 min

Cluster Diagram After students have studied the lesson, ask them to make a cluster diagram that includes the following terms: *matter, element, atom, compound, mineral.*

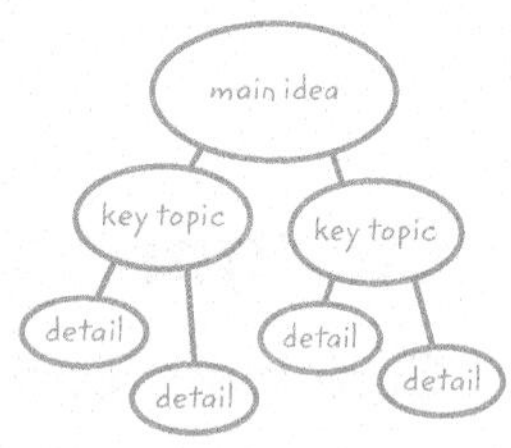

Optional Online resource: Cluster Diagram Support

Going Further

Social Studies Connection

Synthesizing Key Topics

 individual
varied

The History of Mining Communities Have each student create a scrapbook of a mining community. Students should research the history of the community from the discovery of ore to the present. They may include photographs and drawings that show changes in the community, as well as written descriptions of events. Ask students to focus on the type of ore mined, the ore's uses, and the effect of the mine on the people and the environment. Possible communities include Bodie, Calico, Johannesburg, and Randsburg in California; Bullfrog, Goldfield, Manhattan, Rhyolite, and Tonoph in Nevada; Silver City, Utah; and Leadville, Colorado.

Optional Online rubric: Written Pieces

Ecology Connection

Properties of Minerals

 individuals
varied

Aluminum Explain that aluminum is refined from bauxite ore and takes a great deal of electrical energy to produce. Recycling one aluminum can saves enough energy to run a television for 3 h. Aluminum can be recycled over and over again without affecting the metal's basic properties. Have students research and report on aluminum recycling in the United States. They can present their findings in written or verbal form.

Customize Your Closing

 *See the Assessment Guide for quizzes and tests.*

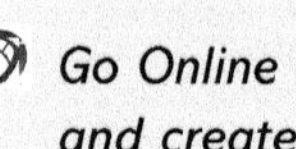

Go Online to edit and create quizzes and tests.

Reinforce and Review

- ☐ **Activity** Making Crystals
- ☐ **Graphic Organizer** Cluster Diagram
- ☐ **Print Path** Visual Summary, SE p. 152
- ☐ **Digital Path** Lesson Closer

Evaluate Student Mastery

Formative Assessment

See the teacher support below the Student Pages for additional Formative Assessment questions.

Describe or have students review the different ways to identify minerals. **Ask:** Which is a more reliable test for identifying a mineral: color or streak? Explain. The streak test is more reliable than color, because a mineral's color can change depending on the conditions in which it is found. Also, some minerals have more than one color. Streak, on the other hand, is not affected by environmental conditions such as air or water.

Reteach

Formative assessment may show you that students need reinforcement for certain topics. The resources below are recommended for reteaching. If students were introduced to topics through the Print Path, you can also use the Digital Path for reteaching, and vice versa.

Can be assigned to individual students

Matter and Minerals

Discussion Planetary Mineral Difference

Formation of Minerals

Activity Making Crystals

Quick Lab Cooling Rate and Crystal Size

Types of Minerals

Activity Mineral Display

Properties of Minerals

Quick Lab Scratch Test

Exploration Lab Intrinsic Identification of Minerals

Summative Assessment

Alternative Assessment

Matter and Minerals

Online resources: student worksheet; optional rubrics

Minerals

Tic-Tac-Toe: *Matter and Minerals*
Complete the activities to show what you've learned about matter and minerals.

1. Work on your own, with a partner, or with a small group.
2. Choose three quick activities from the game. Check the boxes you plan to complete. They must form a straight line in any direction.
3. Have your teacher approve your plan.
4. Do each activity, and turn in your results.

__ **You Ask the Questions**	__ **Trading Definitions**	__ **Distinguished Work**
Compose a quiz that contains at least six questions. Write about the ways minerals form. Include different types of questions such as multiple choice, true/false, and short answer.	Design trading cards for the terms *elements, atoms,* and *compounds.* Give each term its own card. On each card, draw an example of the item, label it, define the term, and, if appropriate, list a few examples.	Design a collage distinguishing between minerals and nonminerals. Illustrate your collage with pictures from the Internet or old magazines. Include the characteristics of minerals and nonminerals.
__ **Presenting Properties** Make a PowerPoint presentation in which you compare and contrast properties of common minerals. Include illustrations or diagrams.	__ **You Decide** On a small sheet of paper or an index card, answer these questions: *What did you know about minerals before reviewing this lesson? What did you learn about minerals that you did not know before?*	__ **Picturing Minerals** Design a poster that shows minerals and describes their characteristics. Include illustrations or pictures of common minerals. Also list characteristics that all minerals share.
__ **Pair Match Up** Make cards about minerals' physical properties (for example, *color, streak, luster, hardness, density, cleavage,* and *fracture*). Then make another card that will pair with each property (for example, word definitions, an illustration, and so on). Play a matching game. See who can match the most pairs.	__ **What Am I?** Present a skit in which two actors are different minerals who compare their properties. For example, one actor might be a silicate mineral and another actor a nonsilicate mineral. The actors can talk about their properties and the things that make them different from each other. Then have the class guess who is the silicate mineral and who is the nonsilicate mineral.	__ **Guess the Mineral** Design a game that shows you know the ways to identify minerals. On index cards, write the name of some minerals and how to identify them. To play, draw a card and describe how to identify the mineral. Other players try to guess the mineral.

Going Further

- ☐ Social Studies Connection
- ☐ Ecology Connection
- ☐ Print Path Why It Matters, SE p. 151

Formative Assessment

- ☐ Strategies Throughout TE
- ☐ Lesson Review SE

Summative Assessment

- ☐ Alternative Assessment Matter and Minerals
- ☐ Lesson Quiz
- ☐ Unit Tests A and B
- ☐ Unit Review SE End-of-Unit

Your Resources

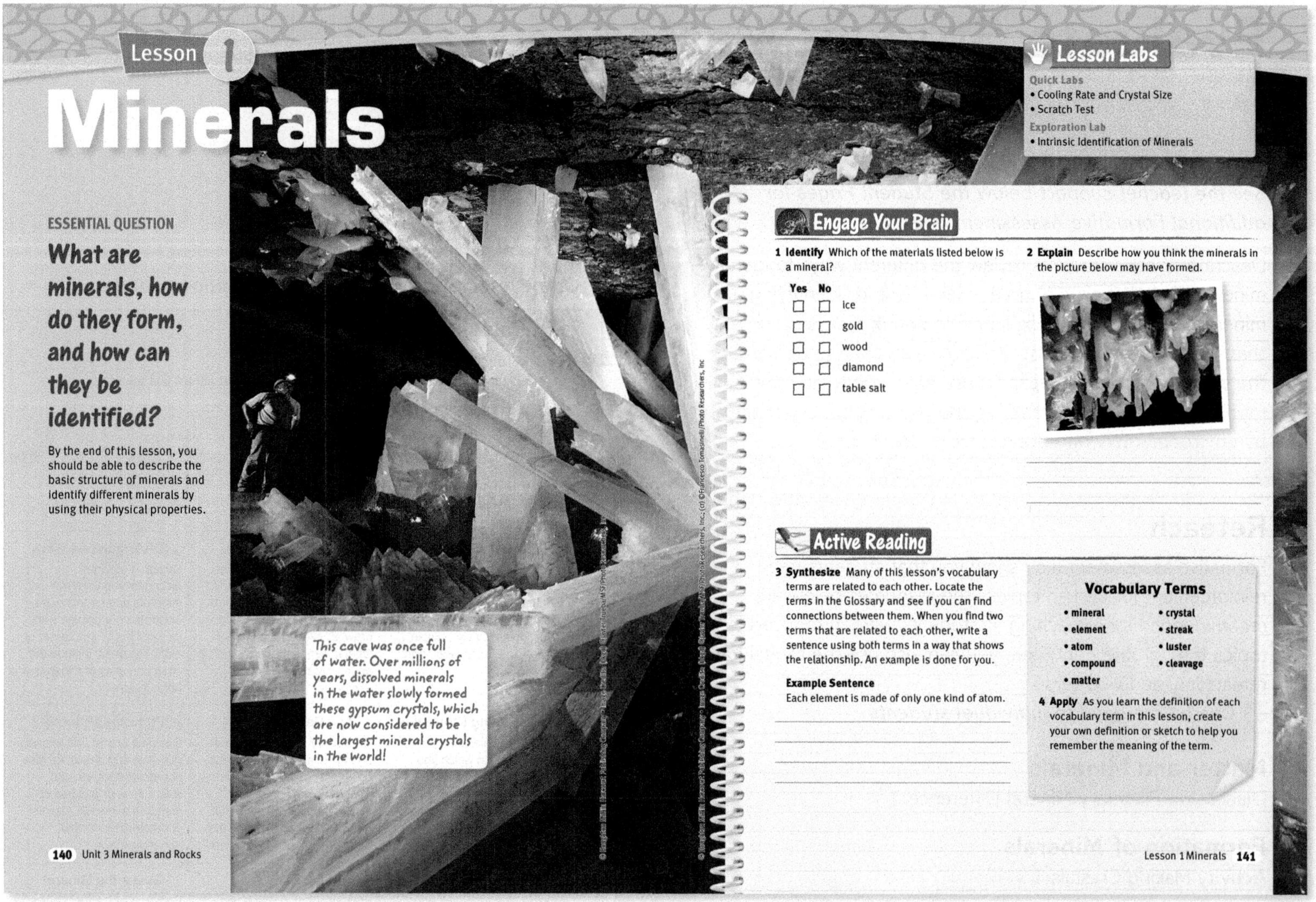

Lesson 1

Minerals

ESSENTIAL QUESTION

What are minerals, how do they form, and how can they be identified?

By the end of this lesson, you should be able to describe the basic structure of minerals and identify different minerals by using their physical properties.

This cave was once full of water. Over millions of years, dissolved minerals in the water slowly formed these gypsum crystals, which are now considered to be the largest mineral crystals in the world!

140 Unit 3 Minerals and Rocks

Lesson Labs

Quick Labs
- Cooling Rate and Crystal Size
- Scratch Test

Exploration Lab
- Intrinsic Identification of Minerals

Engage Your Brain

1 Identify Which of the materials listed below is a mineral?

Yes	No	
☐	☐	ice
☐	☐	gold
☐	☐	wood
☐	☐	diamond
☐	☐	table salt

2 Explain Describe how you think the minerals in the picture below may have formed.

Active Reading

3 Synthesize Many of this lesson's vocabulary terms are related to each other. Locate the terms in the Glossary and see if you can find connections between them. When you find two terms that are related to each other, write a sentence using both terms in a way that shows the relationship. An example is done for you.

Example Sentence
Each element is made of only one kind of atom.

Vocabulary Terms
- mineral
- element
- atom
- compound
- matter
- crystal
- streak
- luster
- cleavage

4 Apply As you learn the definition of each vocabulary term in this lesson, create your own definition or sketch to help you remember the meaning of the term.

Lesson 1 Minerals 141

Answers

Answers for 1–3 should represent students' current thoughts, even if incorrect.

1. Yes; Yes; No; Yes; Yes
2. Many crystals in caves form as dissolved particles organize into crystals as they solidify.
3. The example sentence given on the student page can be used as a guide.
4. Students should define or sketch each vocabulary term in the lesson.

Opening Your Lesson

Have students share their ideas about how the minerals in the photograph formed (item 2) to assess their prior knowledge of the key topics.

Prerequisites: Many everyday objects are made of minerals; minerals can be removed from the ground and used by people; minerals form naturally.

Accessing Prior Knowledge: Develop an Anticipation Guide for the content in this lesson to assess student's prior knowledge about the key topics.

Online resource: Anticipation Guide support

Learning Alert MISCONCEPTION

Is It a Gem? Some students may confuse the words ***minerals*** and ***gems***. Explain that gems are precious or semiprecious materials that are valued for their aesthetic beauty. Point out that while many gems are, in fact, minerals, others are not. Gems often are cut and polished for use in the making of jewelry and other displays.

Animal, Vegetable, or Mineral?

What do minerals have in common?

When you hear the word *mineral*, you may think of sparkling gems. But, in fact, most minerals are found in groups that make up rocks. So what is a mineral? A **mineral** is a naturally occurring, usually inorganic solid that has a definite crystalline structure and chemical composition.

Definite Chemical Composition

To understand what a definite chemical composition is, you need to know a little about elements. **Elements** are pure substances that cannot be broken down into simpler substances by ordinary chemical means. Each element is made of only one kind of atom. All substances are made up of atoms, so **atoms** can be thought of as the building blocks of matter. Stable particles that are made up of strongly bonded atoms are called *molecules*. And, if a substance is made up of molecules of two or more elements, the substance is called a **compound.**

The chemical composition of a mineral is determined by the element or compound that makes up the mineral. For example, minerals such as gold and silver are composed of only one element. Such a mineral is called a *native element*. The mineral quartz is a compound in which silicon atoms can each bond with up to four oxygen atoms in a repeating pattern.

5 Synthesize What is the relationship between elements, atoms, and compounds?

Solid

Matter is anything that has volume and mass. *Volume* refers to the amount of space an object takes up. For example, a golf ball has a smaller volume than a baseball does. Matter is generally found in one of three states: solid, liquid, or gas. A mineral is a solid—that is, it has a definite volume and shape. A substance that is a liquid or a gas is not a mineral. However, in some cases its solid form is a mineral. For instance, liquid water is not a mineral, but ice is because it is solid and has all of the other mineral characteristics also.

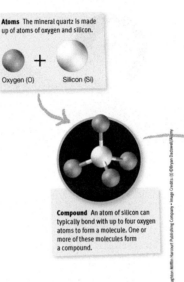

Atoms The mineral quartz is made up of atoms of oxygen and silicon.

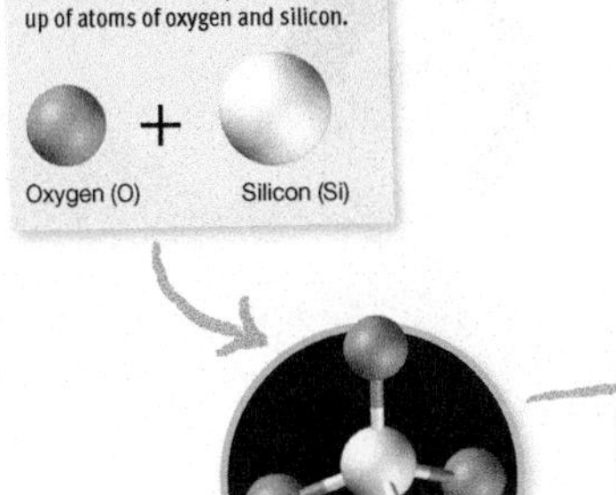

Compound An atom of silicon can typically bond with up to four oxygen atoms to form a molecule. One or more of these molecules form a compound.

Usually Inorganic

Most substances made by living things are categorized as organic substances, such as kidney stones and wood. However, a few substances made by animals, such as clam shells, are categorized as inorganic. An inorganic substance is usually one that is not made up of living things or the remains of living things. And, although a few organic substances such as kidney stones are categorized as minerals, most minerals are inorganic. And, unlike clam shells, most of the processes that form minerals usually take place in the non-living environment.

Crystalline Structure

Minerals have a crystalline structure because they are composed of crystals. A **crystal** is a solid, geometric form that results from a repeating pattern of atoms or molecules. A crystal's shape is produced by the arrangement of the atoms or molecules within the crystal. This arrangement is determined by the kinds of atoms or molecules that make up the mineral and the conditions under which it forms. All minerals can be placed into crystal classes according to their specific crystal shape. This diagram shows how silica compounds can be arranged in quartz crystals.

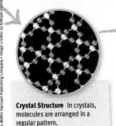

Crystal Structure In crystals, molecules are arranged in a regular pattern.

Mineral Crystal Billions of molecules arranged in a crystalline structure form these quartz crystals.

Naturally Occurring

Minerals are formed by many different natural processes that occur on Earth and throughout the universe. On Earth, the mineral halite, which is used for table salt, forms as water evaporates and leaves behind the salt it contained. Some minerals form as molten rock cools. Talc, a mineral that can be used to make baby powder, forms deep in Earth as high temperature and pressure change the rock. Some of the other ways in which minerals form are on the next page.

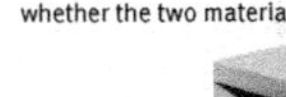

6 Classify Circle *Y* for "yes" or *N* for "no" to determine whether the two materials below are minerals.

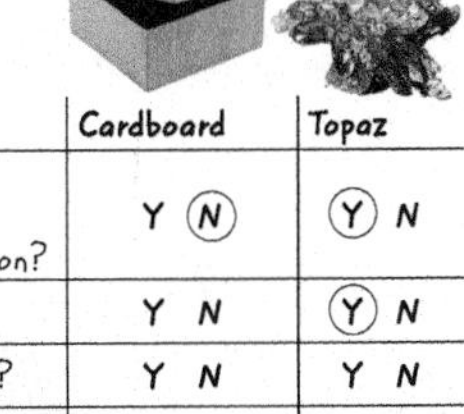

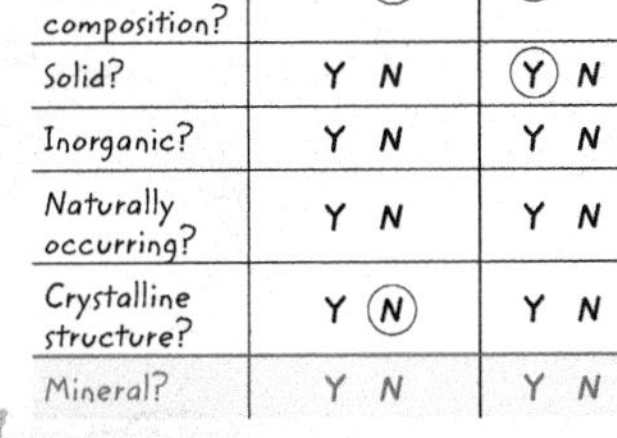

	Cardboard	Topaz
Definite chemical composition?	Y (N)	(Y) N
Solid?	Y N	(Y) N
Inorganic?	Y N	Y N
Naturally occurring?	Y N	Y N
Crystalline structure?	Y (N)	Y N
Mineral?	Y N	Y N

Answers

5. Each element is made up of one kind of atom, and a compound is made up of molecules that are themselves made up of the atoms of two or more elements.
6. (Cardboard) N; Y; N; N; N; N; (Topaz) Y; Y; Y; Y; Y; Y

Probing Questions GUIDED Inquiry

Apply Minerals are mined and used by people in a variety of ways. Think of the household products your family uses on a regular basis. Which products are made up of only a single mineral? Which products are made up of combinations of minerals?

Building Reading Skills

Concept Map Students can use a Concept Map to organize the information they are learning as they read. Ask them to draw and complete a concept map about the relationship between elements, atoms, molecules, and compounds.

Online resource: Concept Map Support

Learning Alert MISCONCEPTION

Mass vs. Weight Students may confuse mass and weight. Explain that mass is the amount of matter in an object. By contrast, weight is a measure of the force of gravity that is exerted on an object. An object's weight will change in response to gravity, while an object's mass will not. Thus, if a boulder is carried from Earth to Mars, the mass of the boulder will remain the same in both locations. The weight of the boulder will differ in both locations, because the force of gravity exerted by each planet on the boulder differs.

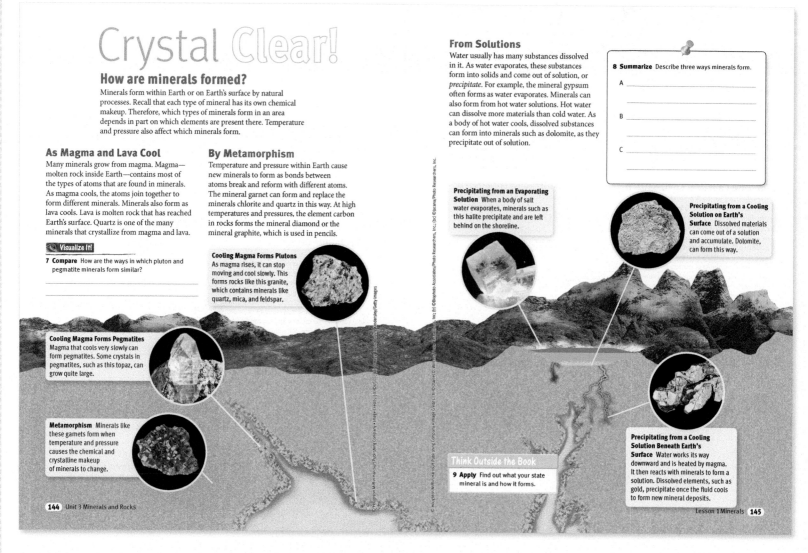

Crystal Clear!

How are minerals formed?

Minerals form within Earth or on Earth's surface by natural processes. Recall that each type of mineral has its own chemical makeup. Therefore, which types of minerals form in an area depends in part on which elements are present there. Temperature and pressure also affect which minerals form.

As Magma and Lava Cool

Many minerals grow from magma. Magma—molten rock inside Earth—contains most of the types of atoms that are found in minerals. As magma cools, the atoms join together to form different minerals. Minerals also form as lava cools. Lava is molten rock that has reached Earth's surface. Quartz is one of the many minerals that crystallize from magma and lava.

Visualize It!

7 Compare How are the ways in which pluton and pegmatite minerals form similar?

By Metamorphism

Temperature and pressure within Earth cause new minerals to form as bonds between atoms break and reform with different atoms. The mineral garnet can form and replace the minerals chlorite and quartz in this way. At high temperatures and pressures, the element carbon in rocks forms the mineral diamond or the mineral graphite, which is used in pencils.

Cooling Magma Forms Plutons As magma rises, it can stop moving and cool slowly. This forms rocks like this granite, which contains minerals like quartz, mica, and feldspar.

Cooling Magma Forms Pegmatites Magma that cools very slowly can form pegmatites. Some crystals in pegmatites, such as this topaz, can grow quite large.

Metamorphism Minerals like these garnets form when temperature and pressure causes the chemical and crystalline makeup of minerals to change.

From Solutions

Water usually has many substances dissolved in it. As water evaporates, these substances form into solids and come out of solution, or *precipitate.* For example, the mineral gypsum often forms as water evaporates. Minerals can also form from hot water solutions. Hot water can dissolve more materials than cold water. As a body of hot water cools, dissolved substances can form into minerals such as dolomite, as they precipitate out of solution.

8 Summarize Describe three ways minerals form.

A

B

C

Precipitating from an Evaporating Solution When a body of salt water evaporates, minerals such as this halite precipitate and are left behind on the shoreline.

Precipitating from a Cooling Solution on Earth's Surface Dissolved materials can come out of a solution and accumulate. Dolomite, can form this way.

Precipitating from a Cooling Solution Beneath Earth's Surface Water works its way downward and is heated by magma. It then reacts with minerals to form a solution. Dissolved elements, such as gold, precipitate once the fluid cools to form new mineral deposits.

Think Outside the Book

9 Apply Find out what your state mineral is and how it forms.

Answers

7. Both pluton and pegmatite minerals form from cooling magma.
8. A. in reponse to the temperatures and pressures below Earth's surface; B. as magma rising upward cools; C. as minerals precipitate out of solutions
9. Answers will vary depending on the state students live in.

Formative Assessment

Ask: What are some of the ways that minerals are formed? Sample answer: They form within Earth from cooling magma and in response to the temperatures and pressures below Earth's surface. **Ask:** What is a solution? Sample answer: A solution is a mixture in which one substance is dissolved in another. **Prompt:** Think about how minerals can form from a solution.

Learning Alert

Synthetic Minerals? Students may be surprised to learn that a new crystalline material synthesized in the laboratory cannot be a mineral. In fact, part of the definition of a *mineral* is that it can be found in nature. However, naturally occurring minerals can also be synthesized in the laboratory and may be indistinguishable from their natural counterparts.

Student Pages 144–147

Sort It Out

How are minerals classified?

The most common classification of minerals is based on chemical composition. Minerals are divided into two groups based on their composition. These groups are the silicate (SIL'ih•kayt) minerals and the nonsilicate (nawn•SIL'ih•kayt) minerals.

Silicate Minerals

Silicon and oxygen are the two most common elements in Earth's crust. Minerals that contain a combination of these two elements are called *silicate minerals.* Silicate minerals make up most of Earth's crust. The most common silicate minerals in Earth's crust are feldspar and quartz. Most silicate minerals are formed from basic building blocks called *silicate tetrahedrons.* Silicate tetrahedrons are made of one silicon atom bonded to four oxygen atoms. Most silicate minerals, including mica and olivine, are composed of silicate tetrahedrons combined with other elements, such as aluminum or iron.

Active Reading **10 Explain** Why is Earth's crust made up mostly of silicate minerals?

Nonsilicate Minerals

Minerals that do not contain the silicate tetrahedron building block form a group called the *nonsilicate minerals.* Some of these minerals are made up of elements such as carbon, oxygen, fluorine, iron, and sulfur. The table on the next page shows the most important classes of nonsilicate minerals. A nonsilicate mineral's chemical composition determines its class.

Do the Math — You Try It

11 Calculate Calculate the percent of non-silicates in Earth's crust to complete the graph's key.

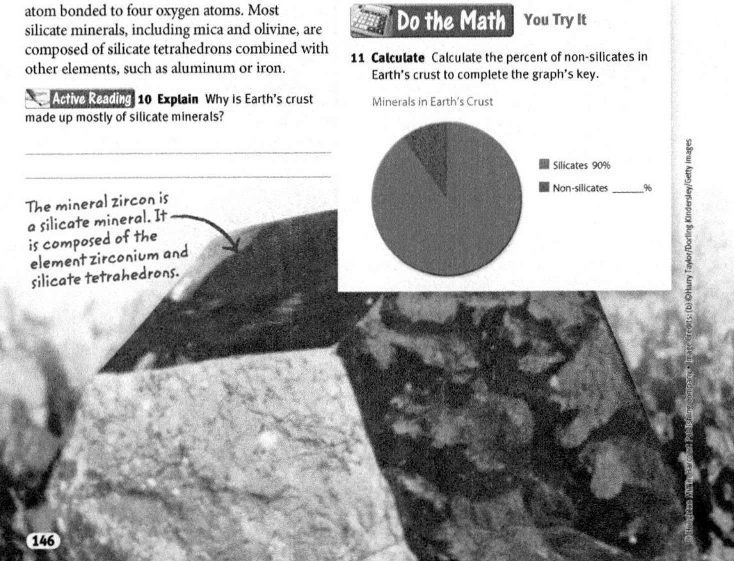

The mineral zircon is a silicate mineral. It is composed of the element zirconium and silicate tetrahedrons.

Classes of Nonsilicate Minerals

Native elements are minerals that are composed of only one element. Copper (Cu) and silver (Ag) are two examples. Native elements are often used to make electronics.

Silver, Ag

Carbonates are minerals that contain carbon (C) and oxygen (O) in the form of the carbonate ion CO_3^{2-}. We use carbonate minerals in cement, building stones, and fireworks.

Calcite, $CaCO_3$

Halides are compounds that form when elements such as fluorine (F) and chlorine (Cl), combine with elements such as calcium (Ca). Halides are used in the chemical industry and in detergents.

Fluorite, CaF_2

Oxides are compounds that form when an element, such as aluminum (Al) or iron (Fe), combines with oxygen. Oxide minerals are used to make abrasives, aircraft parts, and paint.

Corundum, Al_2O_3

Sulfates are minerals that contain sulfur (S) and oxygen (O) in the form of the sulfate ion SO_4^{2-}. Sulfates are used in cosmetics, toothpaste, cement, and paint.

Barite, $BaSO_4$

Sulfides are minerals that contain one or more elements, such as lead (Pb), or iron (Fe), combined with sulfur (S). Sulfide minerals are used to make batteries and medicines.

Pyrite, FeS_2

Visualize It!

12 Classify Examine the chemical formulas for the two minerals at right. Classify the minerals as a silicate or nonsilicate. If it is a nonsilicate, also write its class.

Gypsum, $CaSO_4 \cdot 2H_2O$

Kyanite, Al_2SiO_5

Answers

10. Because, silicon and oxygen are the two most common elements in Earth's crust.
11. 10%
12. (Under Gypsum, $CaSO_4$) nonsilicate, sulfate; (under Kyanite, Al_2SiO_5) silicate

Using Annotations

Text Structure: Main Ideas/Details Students are asked why silicate minerals are the most common in Earth's crust. Have them expand on this knowledge by researching the names of several common silicates not discussed in the lesson. Ask them to compare them to each other and describe their attributes.

Interpreting Visuals

Have students look at the images of the silicate mineral structure and the structures of the different classes of nonsilicate minerals. **Ask:** How are they different? Sample answer: Silicate minerals are made up of silicate tetrahedra; nonsilicate materials are not. What are some examples of silicate and nonsilicate minerals? Sample answer: Quartz is the most common silicate mineral; zircon is also a silicate mineral. Halite, sulfur, pyrite, silver, fluorite, barite, calcite, and corundum are examples of nonsilicate minerals.

Name That Mineral!

What properties can be used to identify minerals?

If you closed your eyes and tasted different foods, you could probably determine what the foods are by noting properties such as saltiness or sweetness. You can also determine the identity of a mineral by noting different properties. In this section, you will learn about the properties that will help you identify minerals.

Color

Active Reading

13 Identify Underline the name of the property on this page that is most reliable for identifying a mineral.

The same mineral can come in different colors. For example, pure quartz is colorless. However, impurities can make quartz pink, orange, or many other colors. Other factors can also change a mineral's color. Pyrite is normally golden, but turns black or brown if exposed to air and water. The same mineral can be different colors, and different minerals can be the same color. So, color is helpful but usually not the best way to identify a mineral.

Streak

The color of the powdered form of a mineral is its **streak**. A mineral's streak is found by rubbing the mineral against a white tile called a *streak plate*. The mark left is the streak. A mineral's streak is not always the same as the color of the mineral, but all samples of the same mineral have the same streak color. Unlike the surface of a mineral, the streak is not affected by air or water. For this reason, streak is more reliable than color in identifying a mineral.

Visualize It!

14 Evaluate Look at these two mineral samples. What property indicates that they may be the same mineral?

Mineral Lusters

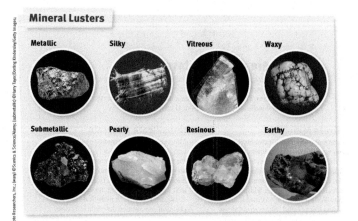

Metallic | Silky | Vitreous | Waxy

Submetallic | Pearly | Resinous | Earthy

Luster

The way a surface reflects light is called **luster**. When you say an object is shiny or dull, you are describing its luster. The two major types of luster are metallic and nonmetallic. Pyrite has a metallic luster. It looks as if it is made of metal. A mineral with a nonmetallic luster can be shiny, but it does not appear to be made of metal. Different types of lusters are shown above.

Cleavage and Fracture

The tendency of a mineral to split along specific planes of weakness to form smooth, flat surfaces is called **cleavage**. When a mineral has cleavage, it breaks along flat surfaces that generally run parallel to planes of weakness in the crystal structure. For example, mica tends to split into parallel sheets. Many minerals, however, do not break along cleavage planes. Instead, they fracture, or break unevenly, into pieces that have curved or irregular surfaces. Scientists describe a fracture according to the appearance of the broken surface. For example, a rough surface has an irregular fracture, and a curved surfaces has a conchoidal (kahn•KOY•duhl) fracture.

Visualize It!

15 Identify Write the correct description, either *cleavage* or *fracture*, under the two broken mineral crystals shown here.

Answers

13. *See students' pages for annotations.*
14. The two minerals have the same streak color.
15. The top mineral shows an example of cleavage, and the bottom mineral shows an example of fracture.

Probing Questions GUIDED Inquiry

Applying How does defining and identifying physical properties of minerals help people use minerals? Sample answer: Knowing the properties of a mineral can help to determine how the mineral might best be used. For example, knowing that copper is ductile and conducts electricity makes it a useful material in wiring.

Building Reading Skills

Combination Notes Have students use the Combination Notes strategy as they work through the ideas of this key topic.

Optional Online resource: Combination Notes support

Formative Assessment

Ask: How can minerals be identified? Minerals can be identified by their color, streak, luster, cleavage/fracture, hardness, and density. **Ask:** What is a streak plate and how is it used? A streak plate is a white tile that minerals are rubbed against. Minerals can be identified by the streak left behind. **For greater depth:** Have students try to identify minerals in the classroom.

Mohs Scale

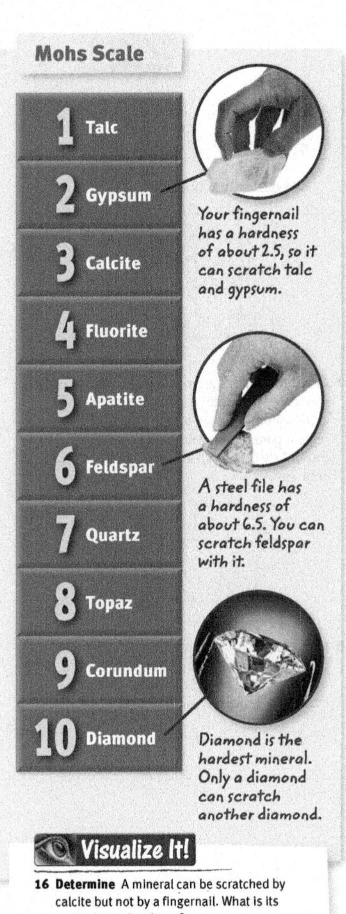

1 Talc
2 Gypsum
3 Calcite
4 Fluorite
5 Apatite
6 Feldspar
7 Quartz
8 Topaz
9 Corundum
10 Diamond
Your fingernail has a hardness of about 2.5, so it can scratch talc and gypsum.
A steel file has a hardness of about 6.5. You can scratch feldspar with it.
Diamond is the hardest mineral. Only a diamond can scratch another diamond.

Density

If you pick up a golf ball and a table-tennis ball, which will feel heavier? Although the balls are of similar size, the golf ball will feel heavier because it is denser. *Density* is the measure of how much matter is in a given amount of space. Density is usually measured in grams per cubic centimeter. Gold has a density of 19 g/cm^3. The mineral pyrite looks very similar to gold, but its density is only 5 g/cm^3. Because of this, density can be used to tell gold from pyrite. Density can also be used to tell many other similar-looking minerals apart.

Hardness

A mineral's resistance to being scratched is called its *hardness*. To determine the hardness of minerals, scientists use the Mohs hardness scale, shown at left. Notice that talc has a rating of 1 and diamond has a rating of 10. The greater a mineral's resistance to being scratched, the higher its hardness rating. To identify a mineral by using the Mohs scale, try to scratch the surface of a mineral with the edge of one of the 10 reference minerals. If the reference mineral scratches your mineral, the reference mineral is as hard as or harder than your mineral.

Special Properties

All minerals exhibit the properties that were described earlier in this section. However, a few minerals have some additional, special properties that can help identify those minerals. For example, the mineral magnetite is a natural magnet. The mineral calcite is usually white in ordinary light, but in ultraviolet light, it often appears red. Another special property of calcite is shown below.

A clear piece of calcite placed over an image will cause a double image.

Visualize It!

16 Determine A mineral can be scratched by calcite but not by a fingernail. What is its approximate hardness?

Why It Matters

Made from Minerals

Many minerals contain useful substances. Rutile and several other minerals contain the metal titanium. Titanium can resist corrosion and is about as strong as steel, but it is 47% lighter than steel. These properties make titanium very valuable.

Devices for Doctors
Surgical procedures like joint replacements require metal implantations. Titanium is used because it can resist body fluid corrosion and its low density and elasticity is similar to human bone.

Marvels for Mechanics
Motorcycle exhaust pipes are often made out of titanium, which dissipates heat better than stainless steel.

An Aid to Architects
Titanium doesn't just serve practical purposes. Architect Frank Gehry used titanium panels to cover the outside of the Guggenheim Museum in Bilbao, Spain. He chose titanium because of its luster.

Extend

17 Infer How do you think the density of titanium-containing minerals would compare to the density of minerals used to make steel? Explain.

18 List Research some other products made from minerals. Make a list summarizing your research.

19 Determine Choose one of the products you researched. How do the properties of the minerals used to make the product contribute to the product's characteristics or usefulness?

Answers

16. 3
17. The density of titanium-containing minerals would be less than the density of minerals used to make steel because titanium is less dense than steel.

Interpreting Visuals

Have students look at the images regarding the Mohs scale. Help them to understand that materials can have hardness values that fall between the whole numbers represented on the scale. As an example, **ask:** Where would a mineral fall on the scale if it can scratch apatite but cannot be scratched by feldspar? Sample answer: greater than 5 but less than 6

Formative Assessment

Ask: What properties do all minerals have? All minerals have a hardness level, density, cleavage and fracture, luster, streak, and color. **Ask:** What are some properties that are unique to some minerals? magnetism, and response to ultraviolet light **For greater depth:** Have students create a chart depicting the properties of some common minerals. Have them include a photograph or illustration of each mineral.

Why It Matters

Have students review the various uses of titanium discussed in the feature. **Ask:** Besides luster, what property of titanium might make it useful as an exterior cover for buildings? Sample answer: its ability to resist corrosion; its lighter than steel

Visual Summary

To complete this summary, fill in the blanks with the correct words or phrase. Then use the key below to check your answers. You can use this page to review the main concepts of the lesson.

Minerals make up Earth's crust.

20 A mineral:

- has a definite chemical composition
- is a solid
- is usually inorganic
- is formed in nature
- ____________

Minerals are classified by composition.

21 Minerals are classified in two groups as:

Quartz, SiO_2 ____________

Calcite, $CaCO_3$ ____________

Minerals

Minerals form by natural processes.

22 Minerals form by:

- metamorphism
- the cooling of magma and lava
- ____________

Minerals are identified by their properties.

23 Properties used to identify minerals include:

- color and luster
- ____________
- cleavage or fracture
- density and hardness
- special properties

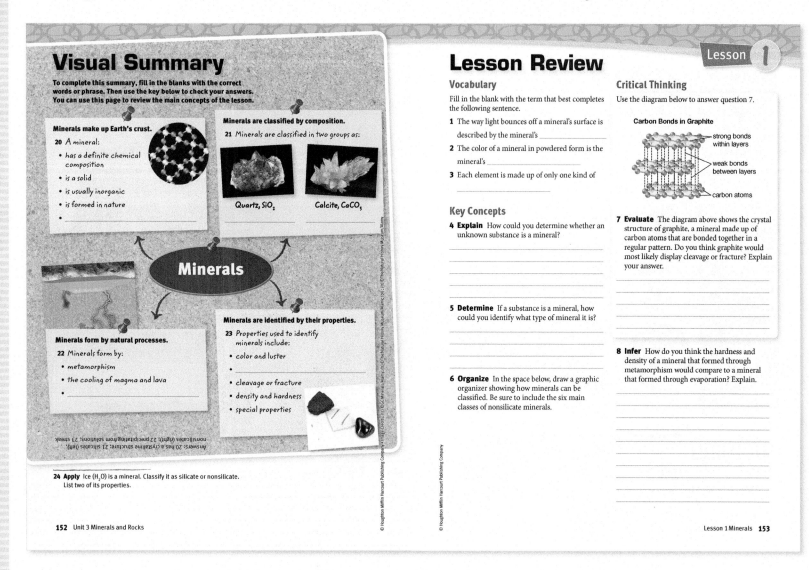

Answers: 20 has a crystalline structure; 21 silicates (left), nonsilicates (right); 22 precipitating from solutions; 23 streak

24 Apply Ice (H_2O) is a mineral. Classify it as silicate or nonsilicate. List two of its properties.

Lesson Review

Lesson 1

Vocabulary

Fill in the blank with the term that best completes the following sentence.

1 The way light bounces off a mineral's surface is described by the mineral's ____________

2 The color of a mineral in powdered form is the mineral's ____________

3 Each element is made up of only one kind of ____________

Key Concepts

4 **Explain** How could you determine whether an unknown substance is a mineral?

5 **Determine** If a substance is a mineral, how could you identify what type of mineral it is?

6 **Organize** In the space below, draw a graphic organizer showing how minerals can be classified. Be sure to include the six main classes of nonsilicate minerals.

Critical Thinking

Use the diagram below to answer question 7.

Carbon Bonds in Graphite

7 **Evaluate** The diagram above shows the crystal structure of graphite, a mineral made up of carbon atoms that are bonded together in a regular pattern. Do you think graphite would most likely display cleavage or fracture? Explain your answer.

8 **Infer** How do you think the hardness and density of a mineral that formed through metamorphism would compare to a mineral that formed through evaporation? Explain.

Visual Summary Answers

20. has a crystalline structure
21. silicate (left), nonsilicate (right)
22. precipitating from solutions
23. streak
24. Ice is a nonsilicate mineral. Two possible properties students may list are its color (colorless), its fracture (irregular), or a special property, such as the fact that it melts at temperatures above 0 degrees Celsius.

Lesson Review Answers

1. luster
2. streak
3. atom
4. Identify whether the substance had a definite chemical composition, was solid, was naturally occurring, and was crystalline.
5. Determine the mineral's color, luster, streak, cleavage or fracture, density, and hardness.
6. Students' graphic organizers should show minerals being classified into two groups: silicate and nonsilicate. The nonsilicate minerals can be further classified as native elements, carbonates, halides, oxides, sulfates, and sulfides.
7. Graphite displays cleavage along the planes where there are weak bonds between the atoms.
8. Minerals formed by metamorphism most likely are harder and denser than minerals formed through evaporation because the temperatures and pressures that caused the metamorphism would have compacted the atoms making up the minerals tightly together.

Teacher Notes

The Rock Cycle

Essential Question What is the rock cycle?

For more detailed information about the topics in this lesson, refer to the Content Refresher in the Unit Opener pages.

Opening Your Lesson

Begin the lesson by assessing students' prerequisite and prior knowledge.

Prerequisite Knowledge

- There are different types of rocks.
- Earth's rocks are constantly moving and changing.
- Studying rock changes helps scientists learn about Earth.

Accessing Prior Knowledge

Have students draw a rock. Ask them to write words and phrases describing what they know about rocks around their drawing, including why scientists study rocks. Have volunteers share their ideas with the class as their classmates add new details to their sketches. At the end of the lesson, have students use what they learned to review and update their notes and drawings.

Customize Your Opening

- ☐ **Accessing Prior Knowledge,** above
- ☐ **Print Path** Engage Your Brain, SE p. 155 #1–2
- ☐ **Print Path** Active Reading, SE p. 155 #3–4
- ☐ **Digital Path** Lesson Opener

Key Topics/Learning Goals	Supporting Concepts
Weathering, Erosion, and Deposition 1 Define *weathering*. 2 Define *erosion*. 3 Define *deposition*.	• Weathering is the process by which atmospheric and environmental agents, such as wind, rain, and temperature change, disintegrate and decompose rock. • Erosion is the process by which wind, water, ice, or gravity moves soil and sediment from place to place. • Deposition is the process in which Earth materials are laid down.
Three Classes of Rock 1 Describe sedimentary rock formation. 2 Describe igneous rock formation. 3 Describe metamorphic rock formation.	• Sedimentary rock forms when rock pieces become cemented together. • Igneous rock forms when hot, liquid rock cools and hardens. • Metamorphic rock forms when chemical processes or temperature and pressure change rock.
Rock Cycle 1 Discuss how rock changes as it goes through the rock cycle.	• The rock cycle is a series of processes in which rocks form, change from one type to another, melt, and form again by geologic processes. • Rocks follow various pathways in the rock cycle.
Tectonic Plate Motion and the Rock Cycle 1 Define *uplift*. 2 Define *subsidence*. 3 Define *rift zone*.	• Uplift is the rising of regions of Earth's crust to higher elevations. • Subsidence is the sinking of regions of Earth's crust to lower elevations. • A rift zone is an area of deep cracks that form in a plate or between tectonic plates that are moving apart.

Options for Instruction

Two parallel paths provide coverage of the Essential Questions, with a strong **Inquiry** strand woven into each. Follow the **Print Path**, the **Digital Path**, or your customized combination of print, digital, and inquiry.

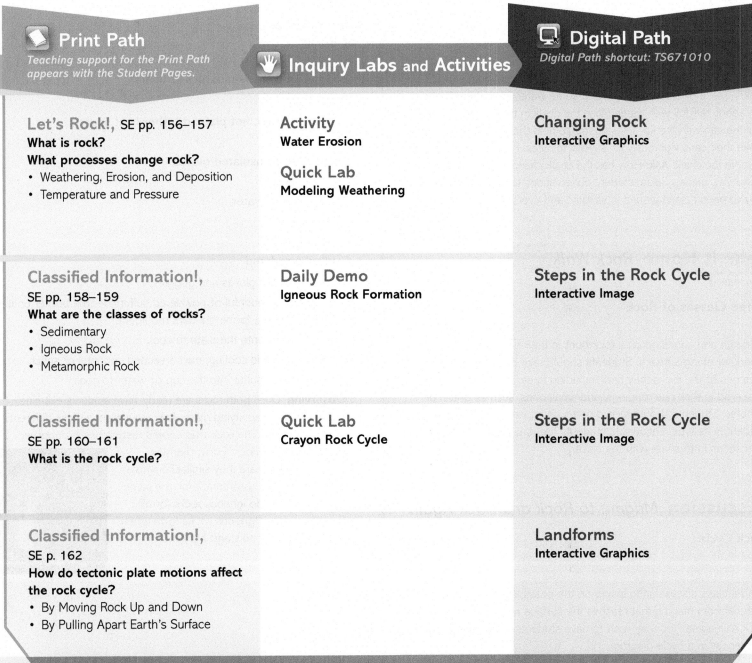

 Print Path *Teaching support for the Print Path appears with the Student Pages.*	 Inquiry Labs and Activities	 Digital Path *Digital Path shortcut: TS671010*
Let's Rock!, SE pp. 156–157 **What is rock?** **What processes change rock?** • Weathering, Erosion, and Deposition • Temperature and Pressure	**Activity** **Water Erosion** **Quick Lab** **Modeling Weathering**	**Changing Rock** **Interactive Graphics**
Classified Information!, SE pp. 158–159 **What are the classes of rocks?** • Sedimentary • Igneous Rock • Metamorphic Rock	**Daily Demo** **Igneous Rock Formation**	**Steps in the Rock Cycle** **Interactive Image**
Classified Information!, SE pp. 160–161 **What is the rock cycle?**	**Quick Lab** **Crayon Rock Cycle**	**Steps in the Rock Cycle** **Interactive Image**
Classified Information!, SE p. 162 **How do tectonic plate motions affect the rock cycle?** • By Moving Rock Up and Down • By Pulling Apart Earth's Surface		**Landforms** **Interactive Graphics**

Options for Assessment

See the Evaluate page for options, including Formative Assessment, Summative Assessment, and Unit Review.

Engage and Explore

Activities and Discussion

Activity *Water Erosion*

Engage

Weathering, Erosion, and Deposition

 pairs
 15 min
 DIRECTED inquiry

Give pairs of students a metal coffee can with a tight-fitting lid, a broken piece of sidewalk chalk, and some water. Have them fill their can about half full with water, place the chalk in the can, and then seal the can with the lid. Tell students to hold the lids in place as they shake their cans vigorously for several minutes. Have them remove and observe the chalk. **Ask:** How has the chalk changed in appearance? It broke into pieces. Relate student observations to how rocks look after they've been tossed around in streams and rivers for a period of time.

Take It Home *Rock Walk*

Engage

Three Classes of Rock

 adult–student pairs
 30 min

Students and adults go on a rock hunt in their neighborhood, in a park, or along a beach. Students should take pictures or make sketches of the rocks they find, including large ones, such as those observed in rock outcroppings, and small ones, such as gravel or pebbles. Students should record notes about each rock and try to identify its type. Encourage students to bring small, interesting specimens in to share with the class.

Discussion *Magma to Rock and Back Again*

Rock Cycle

 whole class
 20–25 min

Lead a class discussion focusing on the possible journey of rock material from magma that reaches the surface as lava all the way back to magma. You may wish to have students record the possible sequences in a cycle diagram.

Optional Online resource: Cycle Diagram support

Labs and Demos

Daily Demo *Igneous Rock Formation*

Engage

Three Classes of Rocks

 whole class
20 min
 DIRECTED inquiry

PURPOSE **To demonstrate rock formation**

MATERIALS

- **Bunsen burner, hot plate, or other heat source**
- **hand lens**
- **oven mitt or insulated gloves**
- **spoon, metal**
- **paper cup of water**
- **plate, paper**
- **safety goggles**
- **sulfur, powdered**

1 Put on insulated gloves and goggles.
2 Slowly heat a spoonful of powdered sulfur over the burner until it melts completely, forming a dark red liquid.
3 Pour the liquid onto the plate to cool.
4 While the liquid is cooling, melt a second spoonful of sulfur.
5 Pour this liquid sulfur into the cup of water to cool.
6 **Observing** Once both rocks are ready, have students examine them with the magnifying glass. **Ask:** How are the rocks different? Sample answer: The rock that cooled fastest has a smoother texture and smaller crystals than the other rock. How are they similar? Sample answer: They are both made of the same materials. How do igneous rocks form? Sample answer: Igneous rocks form when magma or lava cools and hardens.

DIRECTED inquiry
introduces inquiry skills within a structured framework.

GUIDED inquiry
develops inquiry skills within a supportive environment.

INDEPENDENT inquiry
deepens inquiry skills with student-driven questions or procedures.

Quick Lab *Crayon Rock Cycle*

Rock Cycle

 small groups
 30 min
 **DIRECTED** inquiry

Students use wax shavings from crayons to model processes that occur during the rock cycle.

PURPOSE **To model the rock cycle**

MATERIALS

- **aluminum foil, 15 cm × 15 cm sheet**
- **crayons, multicolored (3)**
- **hot plate**
- **knife, plastic**
- **oven mitt**
- **tongs**

Quick Lab *Modeling Weathering*

Weathering, Erosion, and Deposition

 individuals
 30 min
 **DIRECTED** inquiry

Students will explore mechanical weathering and chemical weathering.

PURPOSE **To design an experiment to model weathering**

MATERIALS

- **clear plastic bowl with lid**
- **eyedropper**
- **paper plate**
- **rocks**
- **sugar cubes (6)**
- **vinegar**

Customize Your Labs

See the Lab Manual for lab datasheets.

Go Online for editable lab datasheets.

Activities and Discussion

- ☐ **Activity** Water Erosion
- ☐ **Take It Home** Rock Walk
- ☐ **Discussion** Magma to Rock and Back Again

Labs and Demos

- ☐ **Daily Demo** Igneous Rock Formation
- ☐ **Quick Lab** Crayon Rock Cycle
- ☐ **Quick Lab** Modeling Weathering

Your Resources

Explain Science Concepts

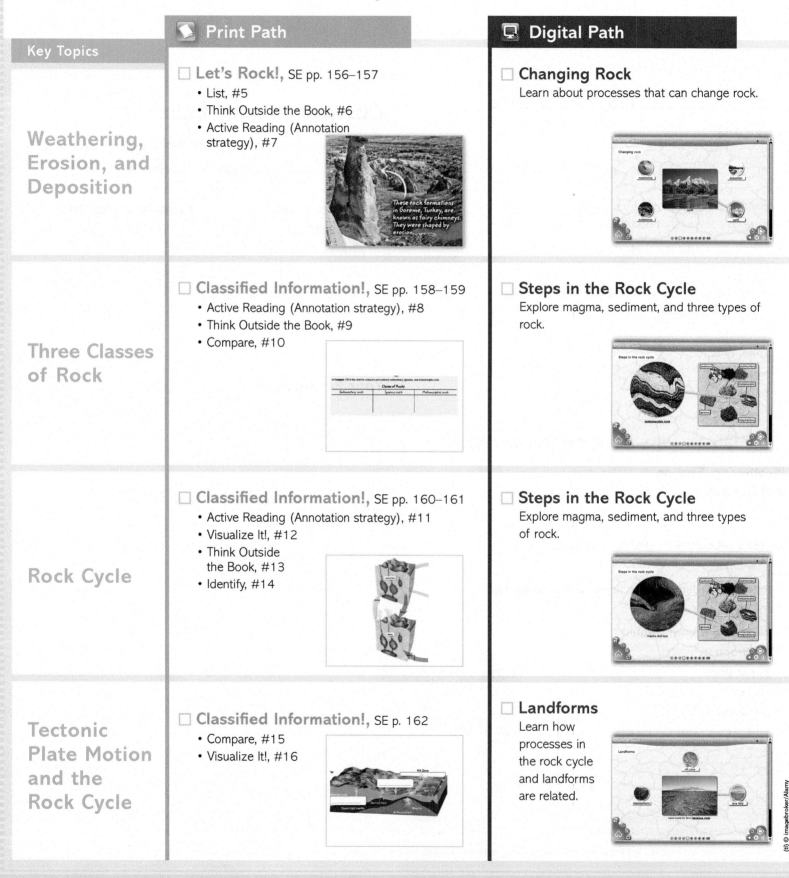

Key Topics	Print Path	Digital Path
Weathering, Erosion, and Deposition	☐ **Let's Rock!,** SE pp. 156–157 • List, #5 • Think Outside the Book, #6 • Active Reading (Annotation strategy), #7  These rock formations in Goreme, Turkey, are known as fairy chimneys. They were shaped by erosion.	☐ **Changing Rock** Learn about processes that can change rock. 
Three Classes of Rock	☐ **Classified Information!,** SE pp. 158–159 • Active Reading (Annotation strategy), #8 • Think Outside the Book, #9 • Compare, #10 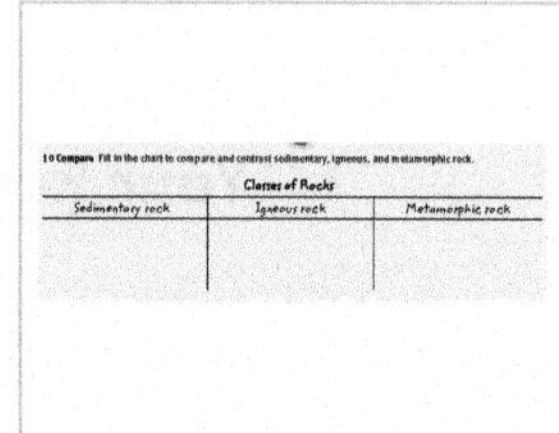	☐ **Steps in the Rock Cycle** Explore magma, sediment, and three types of rock. 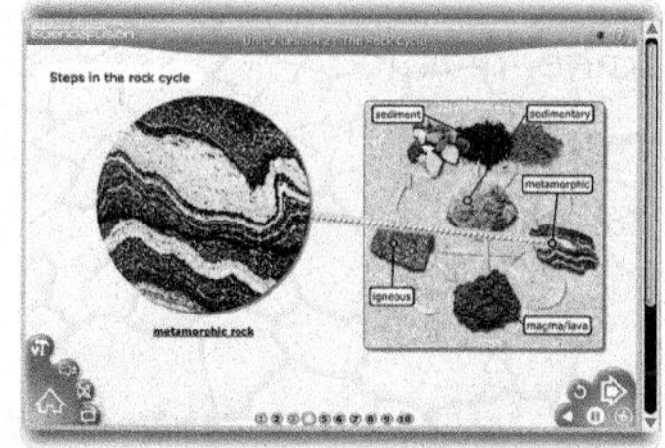
Rock Cycle	☐ **Classified Information!,** SE pp. 160–161 • Active Reading (Annotation strategy), #11 • Visualize It!, #12 • Think Outside the Book, #13 • Identify, #14 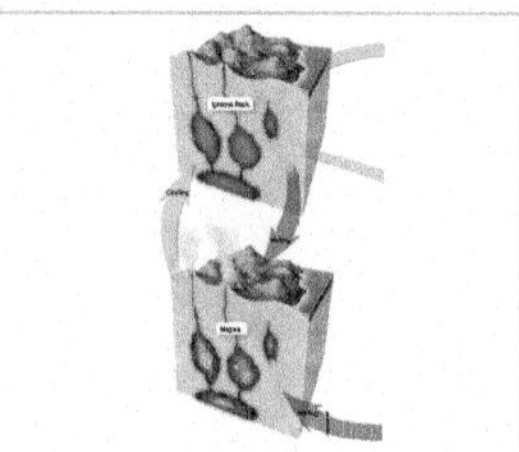	☐ **Steps in the Rock Cycle** Explore magma, sediment, and three types of rock. 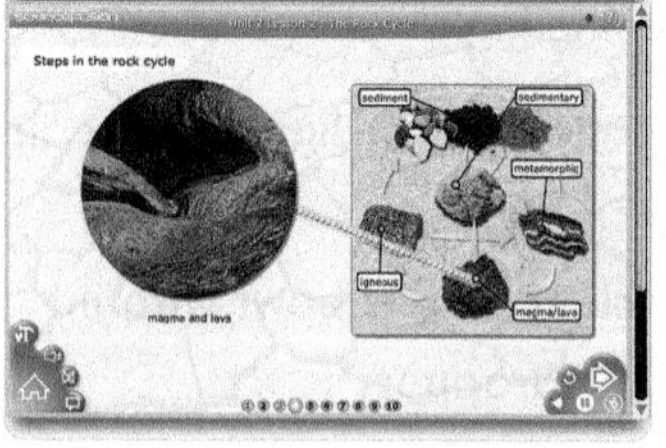
Tectonic Plate Motion and the Rock Cycle	☐ **Classified Information!,** SE p. 162 • Compare, #15 • Visualize It!, #16 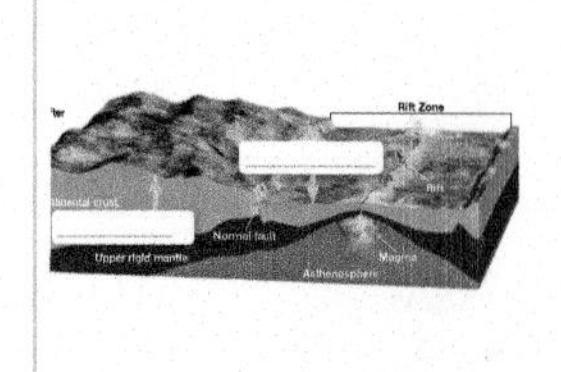	☐ **Landforms** Learn how processes in the rock cycle and landforms are related. 

Differentiated Instruction

Basic *Write It Out*

Synthesizing Key Topics

 individuals
 10–15 min

Ask students to synthesize their understanding of the rock cycle by writing a paragraph explaining how rocks can form and change.

Basic *Jigsaw*

Synthesizing Key Topics

 small groups
 varied

Form small groups of four students each. Assign each student a key topic in this lesson to become an expert about. Have them study the key topic, and any additional resources available in the classroom, and teach the rest of their group about their key topic. Encourage group members to take notes and ask questions to make sure they know all there is to know about each section by the end of the lesson. Students can serve as section experts throughout the lesson, and other students can seek out these experts when they need additional information about a key topic.

Advanced *Making Models*

Ocean Basins and Mountain Building

 small groups
 30–40 min

Modeling Have students in groups use modeling clay to model one of these processes: uplift and mountain formation, subsidence, or rift zone formation. Students should use different colors of clay to represent different sections of rock.

ELL *Notetaking*

Synthesizing Key Topics

 pairs
 30 min

Have students work in pairs to go back through the lesson content and take notes. Have them write the titles of each section, the question heads, and any other subheads. Then have them record important details from each subsection.

Lesson Vocabulary

weathering	**erosion**	**deposition**
igneous rock	**sedimentary rock**	**metamorphic rock**
rock cycle	**uplift**	**subsidence**
rift zone		

Previewing Vocabulary

 whole class  25 min

Pairing Up After students read the lesson, have them work together to define the terms and come up with examples of each.

Reinforcing Vocabulary

 individuals 30 min

Diagramming To help students remember each of the vocabulary words introduced in this lesson, have them draw a diagram of each word. Then have them write the word underneath the diagram, define it, and use it in a sentence.

Customize Your Core Lesson

Core Instruction

- ☐ **Print Path** choices
- ☐ **Digital Path** choices

Vocabulary

- ☐ **Previewing Vocabulary** Pairing Up
- ☐ **Reinforcing Vocabulary** Diagramming

Differentiated Instruction

- ☐ **Basic** Write It Out
- ☐ **Basic** Jigsaw
- ☐ **Advanced** Making Models
- ☐ **ELL** Notetaking

Your Resources

Extend Science Concepts

Reinforce and Review

Activity *Model the Rock Cycle*

Rock Cycle

small groups
20 min

Divide students into three groups: Igneous Rocks, Sedimentary Rocks, and Metamorphic Rocks. Explain that you're going to call on each group and tell them what is "happening" to their group: weathering and erosion, extreme pressure and temperature, or melting. After you announce the action, students should move from their current group to the group of rock they become. For example, if you tell the Sedimentary Rocks that they experience extreme pressure, they should move to the Metamorphic Rock group.

Graphic Organizer

Plate Tectonics and the Rock Cycle

individuals
varied

Concept Map After students have studied the lesson, ask them to develop Concept Maps about uplift, subsidence, and rift zones so they understand the differences among them.

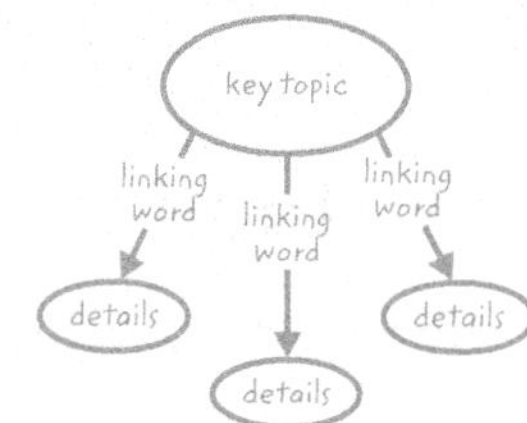

Optional Online resources: Concept Map support

Going Further

Ecology Connection

Weathering and Erosion

individuals
varied

Beach Erosion Beach erosion can cause problems for humans living in coastal communities. Houses can be destroyed when water erodes bluffs and cliffs that the houses are built on. The ocean moves inland as beaches are eroded, causing habitat loss for coastal wildlife dependent on the beaches for food and shelter. Have students research coastal erosion and prepare a short report or project describing the actions that governments and activist groups are taking to reverse and stop environmental damage from beach erosion.

Optional Online rubric: Written Pieces

Art Connection

Three Classes of Rocks

individuals
30 min

Mosaics Using bits of rock, colored plastics, beads, and other hard colored objects, have students make a mosaic of one of the rock types. First, have them draw a rock on a small piece of cardboard. Then, have them fill it in with pieces of the colored materials you have gathered by gluing the pieces down to cover the drawing. Have them try to replicate the type of rock they chose. For example, a student may choose to create a mosaic of the igneous rock, basalt, by gluing down different black and gray pieces. Display the mosaics and have other students try to identify the rock type.

Customize Your Closing

See the Assessment Guide for quizzes and tests.

Go Online to edit and create quizzes and tests.

Reinforce and Review

- ☐ **Activity** Model the Rock Cycle
- ☐ **Graphic Organizer** Concept Map
- ☐ **Print Path** Visual Summary, SE p. 164
- ☐ **Digital Path** Lesson Closer

Evaluate Student Mastery

Formative Assessment

See the teacher support below the Student Pages for additional Formative Assessment questions.

Describe or have students review the types of rocks and how they form. **Ask:** How are the different types of rocks interrelated? Sample answer: Each type of rock can form and reform; each can also change into different types of rock as a result of the rock cycle.

Reteach

Formative assessment may show you that students need reinforcement for certain topics. The resources below are recommended for reteaching. If students were introduced to topics through the Print Path, you can also use the Digital Path for reteaching, and vice versa.

Can be assigned to individual students

Weathering, Erosion, and Deposition

Activity Water Erosion

Three Classes of Rock

Daily Demo Igneous Rock Formation

Rock Cycle

Discussion Magma to Rock and Back Again

Plate Tectonics and the Rock Cycle

Graphic Organizer Concept Map

Summative Assessment

Alternative Assessment

Changes to Rock Types

Online resources: student worksheet; optional rubrics

The Rock Cycle

Mix and Match: ***Changes to Rock Types***

Mix and match ideas to show what you've learned about the rock cycle and the ways rock types change.

1. Work on your own, with a partner, or with a small group.
2. Choose one information source from Column A, two topics from Column B, and one option from Column C. Check your choices.
3. Have your teacher approve your plan.
4. Submit or present your results.

A. Choose Two Rock Types and Processes	B. Choose Two Things to Analyze	C. Choose One Way to Communicate Analysis
___ igneous rock	___ observable properties and characteristics	___ news report or news article
___ sedimentary rock	___ details	___ fictional story or monologue
___ metamorphic rock	___ causes or formation	___ poster or illustration
___ weathering	___ types and variations	___ game
___ erosion		___ questionnaire or worksheet
___ deposition		___ invented dialogue or interview
		___ model or diorama
		___ commercial or video
		___ PowerPoint presentation
		___ a skit or performance

Going Further

- ☐ Ecology Connection
- ☐ Art Connection
- ☐ Print Path Why It Matters, SE p. 163

Formative Assessment

- ☐ Strategies Throughout TE
- ☐ Lesson Review SE

Summative Assessment

- ☐ Alternative Assessment Changes to Rock Types
- ☐ Lesson Quiz
- ☐ Unit Tests A and B
- ☐ Unit Review SE End-of-Unit

Your Resources

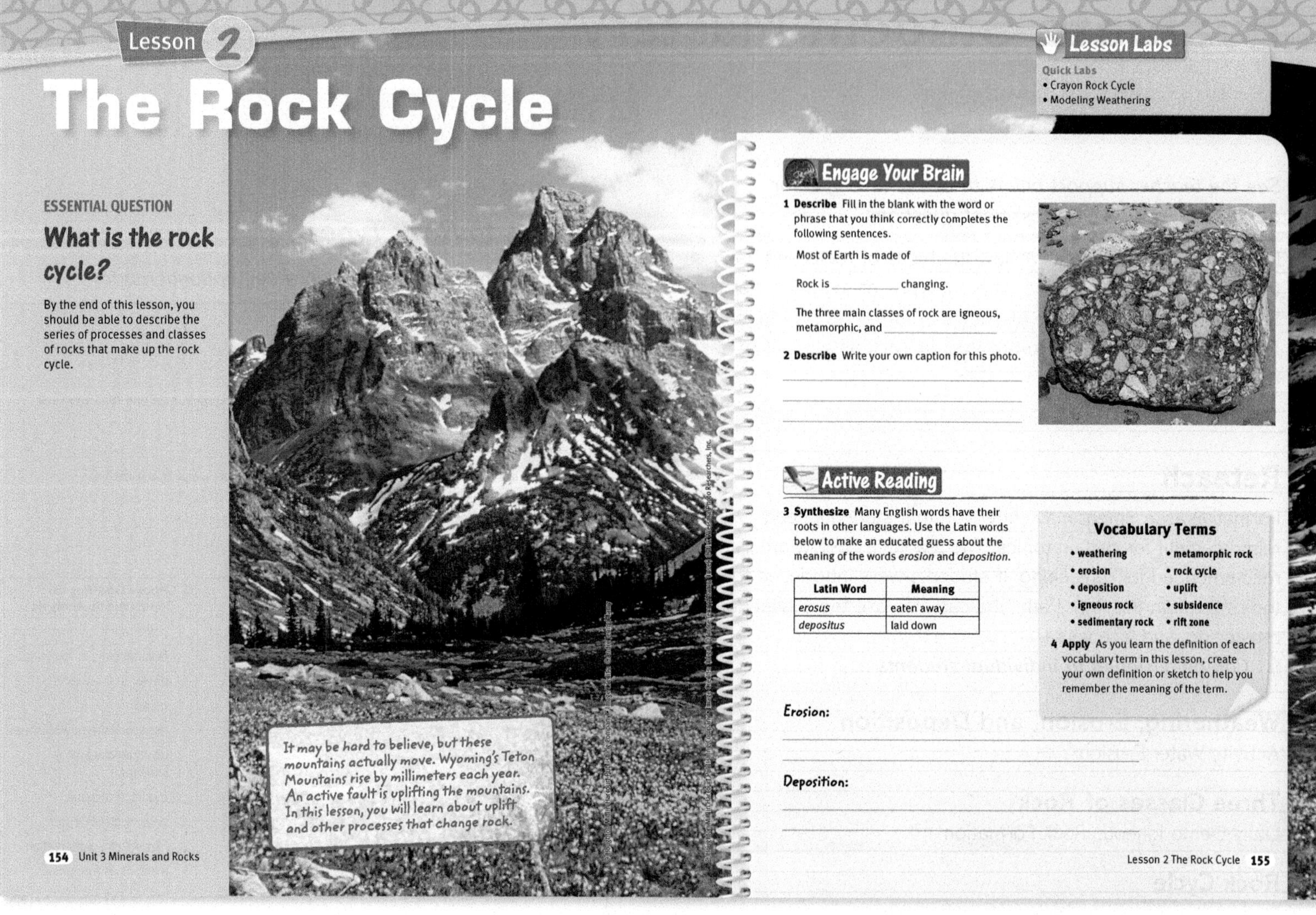

Lesson 2

The Rock Cycle

ESSENTIAL QUESTION

What is the rock cycle?

By the end of this lesson, you should be able to describe the series of processes and classes of rocks that make up the rock cycle.

154 Unit 3 Minerals and Rocks

Lesson Labs

Quick Labs
- Crayon Rock Cycle
- Modeling Weathering

Engage Your Brain

1 Describe Fill in the blank with the word or phrase that you think correctly completes the following sentences.

Most of Earth is made of ______

Rock is ______ changing.

The three main classes of rock are igneous, metamorphic, and ______

2 Describe Write your own caption for this photo.

Active Reading

3 Synthesize Many English words have their roots in other languages. Use the Latin words below to make an educated guess about the meaning of the words *erosion* and *deposition*.

Latin Word	Meaning
erosus	eaten away
depositus	laid down

Erosion:

Deposition:

Vocabulary Terms
- weathering
- erosion
- deposition
- igneous rock
- sedimentary rock
- metamorphic rock
- rock cycle
- uplift
- subsidence
- rift zone

4 Apply As you learn the definition of each vocabulary term in this lesson, create your own definition or sketch to help you remember the meaning of the term.

Lesson 2 The Rock Cycle 155

Answers

Answers 1–3 should represent students' current thoughts, even if incorrect.

1. rock; always; sedimentary
2. Sample answer: This rock is made of smaller rock pieces.
3. Erosion: the process by which sediment is moved from one place to another

   Deposition: the process by which sediment comes to rest
4. Students should define or sketch each vocabulary term in the lesson.

Opening Your Lesson

Have students share their captions about the photo (item 2) to assess their working knowledge of the key topics.

Prerequisites: Students should already know the following: rocks are made by natural processes; scientists can study rocks to learn about Earth's past conditions; different types of rock form in different ways.

Accessing Prior Knowledge: To assess students' prior knowledge about rocks and their formation, have them conduct a Textbook DRTA. Explain that DRTA stands for Directed Reading/Thinking Activity. Once students complete the DRTA, discuss whether their expectations were reasonable and if they learned additional information that they did not anticipate.

Online resource: DRTA support

Learning Alert

Everyday Definitions The word *cycle* means a "circular pattern." The rock cycle is used to describe the sequence of events in the "life" of a rock's formation: alteration, destruction, and reformation. The three types of rock—igneous, sedimentary, and metamorphic—form, change, melt, and re-form in different ways.

Let's Rock!

What is rock?

The solid parts of Earth are made almost entirely of rock. Scientists define rock as a naturally occurring solid mixture of one or more minerals that may also include organic matter. Most rock is made of minerals, but some rock is made of nonmineral material that is not organic, such as glass. Rock has been an important natural resource as long as humans have existed. Early humans used rocks as hammers to make other tools. For centuries, people have used different types of rock, including granite, marble, sandstone, and slate, to make buildings, such as the pyramids shown below.

It may be hard to believe, but rocks are always changing. People study rocks to learn how areas have changed through time.

5 List How is rock used today?

The ancient Egyptians used a rock called limestone to construct the Great Sphinx and the pyramids at Giza.

156

These rock formations in Goreme, Turkey, are known as fairy chimneys. They were shaped by erosion.

Think Outside the Book

6 Design Create a travel brochure for Goreme, Turkey.

What processes change rock?

Natural processes make and destroy rock. They change each type of rock into other types of rock and shape the features of our planet. These processes also influence the type of rock that is found in each area of Earth's surface.

Active Reading **7 Identify** As you read, underline the processes and factors that can change rock.

Weathering, Erosion, and Deposition

The process by which water, wind, ice, and changes in temperature break down rock is called **weathering**. Weathering breaks down rock into fragments called *sediment*. The process by which sediment is moved from one place to another is called **erosion**. Water, wind, ice, and gravity can erode sediments. These sediments are eventually deposited, or laid down, in bodies of water and other low-lying areas. The process by which sediment comes to rest is called **deposition**.

Temperature and Pressure

Rock that is buried can be squeezed by the weight of the rock or the layers of sediment on top of it. As pressure increases with depth beneath Earth's surface, so does temperature. If the temperature and pressure are high enough, the buried rock can change into metamorphic rock. In some cases, the rock gets hot enough to melt and forms *magma*, or molten rock. If magma reaches Earth's surface, it is called *lava*. The magma or lava eventually cool and solidify to form new rock.

Lesson 2 The Rock Cycle 157

Answers

5. Rock is used to construct buildings, monuments, roads, and bridges; to make machines and tools; minerals from rock are used to make everyday items, such as computers, cooking pots, toothpaste, and jewelry; rock is also used for decorations.
6. Students' brochures should highlight the fairy chimney rock formations. Sample answer: On a visit to Goreme, Turkey, you will see unique rock formations shaped by erosion.
7. *See students' pages for annotations.*

Interpreting Visuals

Ask students to look closely at the photo of the ancient Egyptian pyramid. Ask them to imagine what the process may have been like to build such impressive structures before the invention of modern technology such as cranes and power drills. Discuss how ancient people may have worked with rocks such as limestone.

Using Annotations

Text Structure: Main Ideas/Details Actively reading a text helps students gain more from its contents. Underlining key points or steps in a process reminds students that the information is important when they go back to study. In addition, by underlining, they are kinesthetically learning. By adding the notetaking, reading becomes interactive, and students increase the likelihood that they will retain the information.

Building Reading Skills

Concept Map Have students develop a Concept Map to explain the word *weathering*. Give them time to share their maps with the class or small groups.

Optional Online resource: Concept Map support

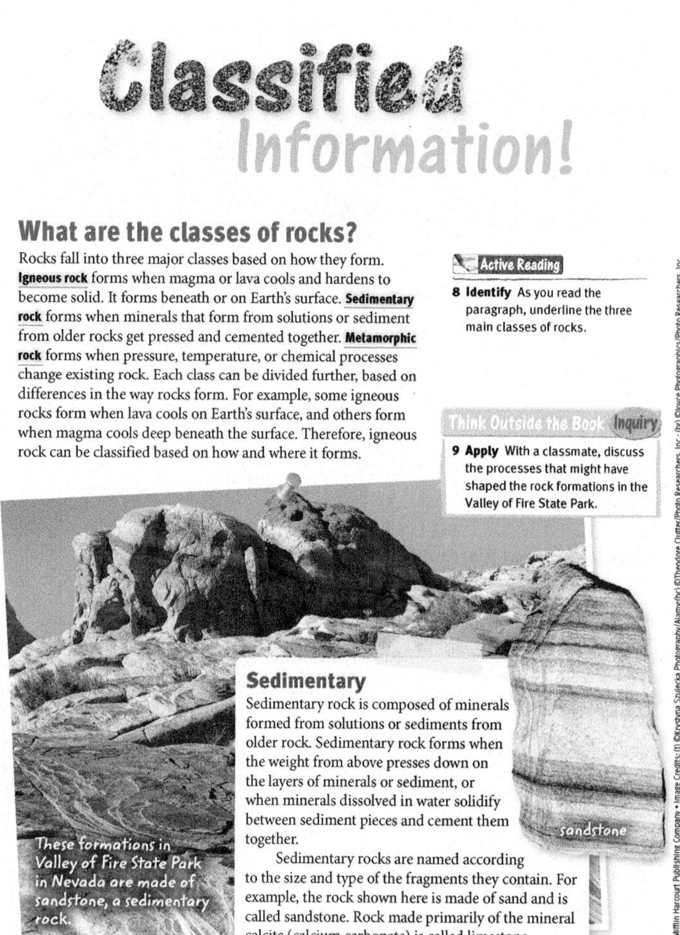

Classified Information!

What are the classes of rocks?

Rocks fall into three major classes based on how they form. **Igneous rock** forms when magma or lava cools and hardens to become solid. It forms beneath or on Earth's surface. **Sedimentary rock** forms when minerals that form from solutions or sediment from older rocks get pressed and cemented together. **Metamorphic rock** forms when pressure, temperature, or chemical processes change existing rock. Each class can be divided further, based on differences in the way rocks form. For example, some igneous rocks form when lava cools on Earth's surface, and others form when magma cools deep beneath the surface. Therefore, igneous rock can be classified based on how and where it forms.

Active Reading

8 Identify As you read the paragraph, underline the three main classes of rocks.

Think Outside the Book Inquiry

9 Apply With a classmate, discuss the processes that might have shaped the rock formations in the Valley of Fire State Park.

Sedimentary

Sedimentary rock is composed of minerals formed from solutions or sediments from older rock. Sedimentary rock forms when the weight from above presses down on the layers of minerals or sediment, or when minerals dissolved in water solidify between sediment pieces and cement them together.

Sedimentary rocks are named according to the size and type of the fragments they contain. For example, the rock shown here is made of sand and is called sandstone. Rock made primarily of the mineral calcite (calcium carbonate) is called limestone.

These formations in Valley of Fire State Park in Nevada are made of sandstone, a sedimentary rock.

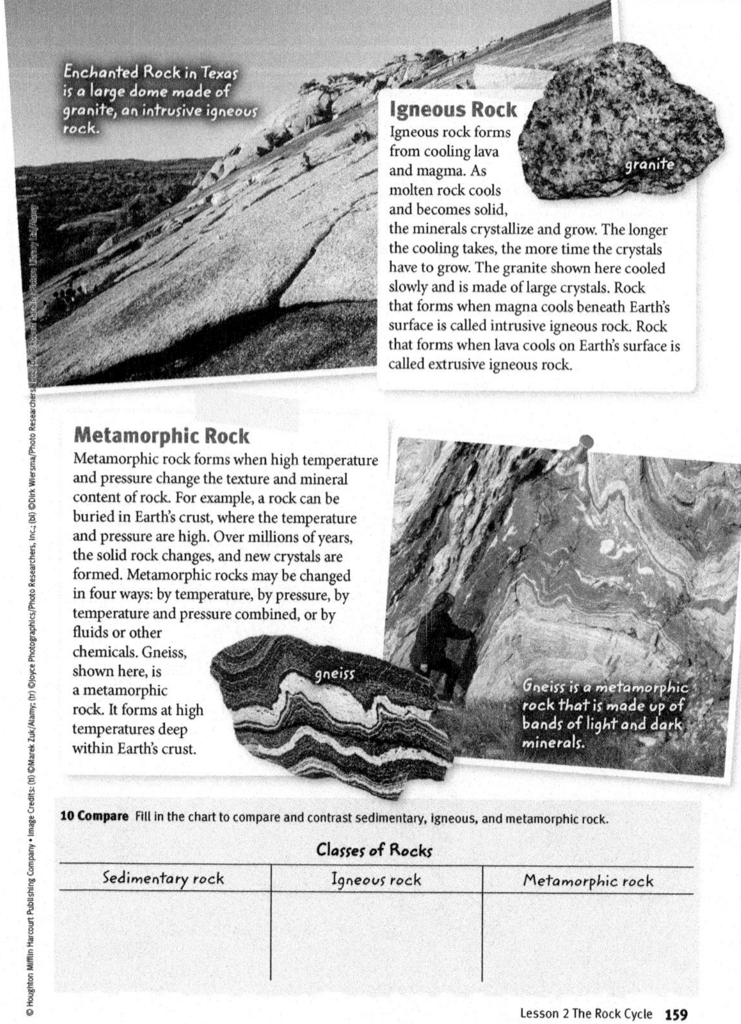

Enchanted Rock in Texas is a large dome made of granite, an intrusive igneous rock.

Igneous Rock

Igneous rock forms from cooling lava and magma. As molten rock cools and becomes solid, the minerals crystallize and grow. The longer the cooling takes, the more time the crystals have to grow. The granite shown here cooled slowly and is made of large crystals. Rock that forms when magma cools beneath Earth's surface is called intrusive igneous rock. Rock that forms when lava cools on Earth's surface is called extrusive igneous rock.

Metamorphic Rock

Metamorphic rock forms when high temperature and pressure change the texture and mineral content of rock. For example, a rock can be buried in Earth's crust, where the temperature and pressure are high. Over millions of years, the solid rock changes, and new crystals are formed. Metamorphic rocks may be changed in four ways: by temperature, by pressure, by temperature and pressure combined, or by fluids or other chemicals. Gneiss, shown here, is a metamorphic rock. It forms at high temperatures deep within Earth's crust.

Gneiss is a metamorphic rock that is made up of bands of light and dark minerals.

10 Compare Fill in the chart to compare and contrast sedimentary, igneous, and metamorphic rock.

Classes of Rocks

Sedimentary rock	Igneous rock	Metamorphic rock

Answers

8. *See students' pages for annotations.*
9. Sample answer: weathering may have created sediment; deposition may have led to settling of sediment, which may have then been compressed and cemented to form rocks; erosion could have shaped formations by moving sediment
10. Sample answer: Sedimentary: composed of sediments; minerals or sediments are compressed, cemented, hardened; named according to size of fragments

Igneous: forms when molten rock cools, hardens either below or on Earth's surface; can be instrusive or extrusive.

Metamorphic: forms when existing rock is altered by high pressure, high temperature, or chemical processes

Using Annotations

Students are asked to underline as they read this section. Have students build on this information by drawing and labeling each type of rock in their notebooks. Then have them list the characteristics of each rock type beneath its drawing.

Probing Question DIRECTED Inquiry

Application How were the rock formations in the Valley of Fire State Park in Nevada formed? What other types of rocks are found in this park? Sample answer: They were formed when sediment was compacted and cemented together to form sedimentary rock that was later uplifted. Once at the surface, the rocks were shaped by weathering processes that broke them down and by the removal of particles through erosion. The park also has limestone, shale, and conglomerate rocks.

Build Reading Skills

Text Structure: Main Idea/Details As students complete the chart in this section, have them find photographs of each rock type on the Internet. Ask them to print their photos and include them with their chart as a visual reminder of each type of rock and its characteristics.

Student Pages 158–161

What is the rock cycle?

Active Reading 11 Apply As you read, underline the rock types that metamorphic rock can change into.

Rocks may seem very permanent, solid, and unchanging. But over millions of years, any of the three rock types can be changed into another of the three types. For example, igneous rock can change into sedimentary or metamorphic rock, or back into another kind of igneous rock. This series of processes in which rock changes from one type to another is called the **rock cycle**. Rocks may follow different pathways in the cycle. Examples of these pathways are shown here. Factors, including temperature, pressure, weathering, and erosion, may change a rock's identity. Where rock is located on a tectonic plate and whether the rock is at Earth's surface also influence how it forms and changes.

When igneous rock is exposed at Earth's surface, it may break down into sediment. Igneous rock may also change directly into metamorphic rock while still beneath Earth's surface. It may also melt to form magma that becomes another type of igneous rock.

When sediment is pressed together and cemented, the sediment becomes sedimentary rock. With temperature and pressure changes, sedimentary rocks may become metamorphic rocks, or they may melt and become igneous rock. Sedimentary rock may also be broken down at Earth's surface and become sediment that forms another sedimentary rock.

Under certain temperature and pressure conditions, metamorphic rock will melt and form magma. Metamorphic rock can also be altered by heat and pressure to form a different type of metamorphic rock. Metamorphic rock can also be broken down by weathering and erosion to form sediment that forms sedimentary rock.

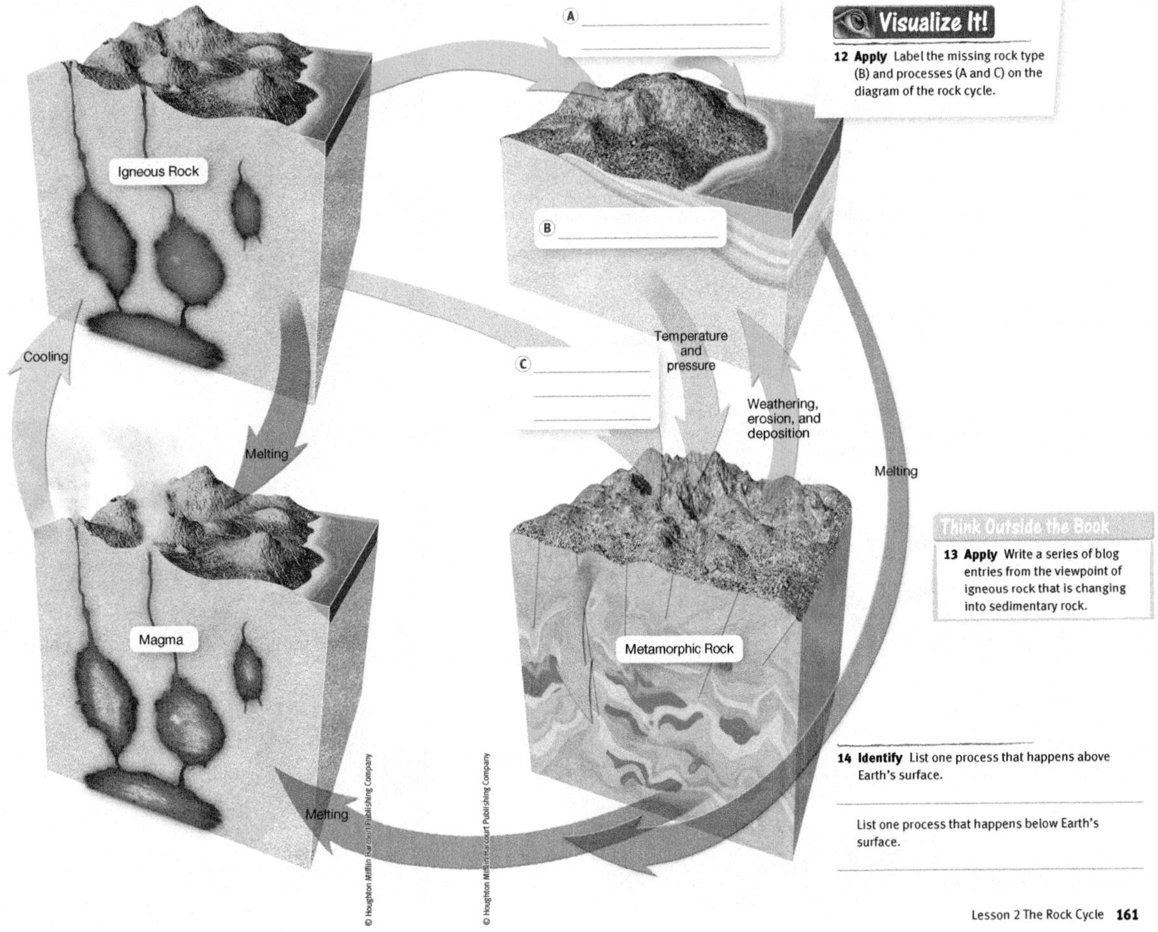

Igneous Rock
Cooling
Melting
Magma
Melting
A
B
C
Temperature and pressure
Weathering, erosion, and deposition
Melting
Metamorphic Rock
Visualize It!
12 Apply Label the missing rock type (B) and processes (A and C) on the diagram of the rock cycle.
Think Outside the Book
13 Apply Write a series of blog entries from the viewpoint of igneous rock that is changing into sedimentary rock.
14 Identify List one process that happens above Earth's surface.
List one process that happens below Earth's surface.
© Houghton Mifflin Harcourt Publishing Company
Lesson 2 The Rock Cycle 161

Answers

11. *See students' pages for annotations.*
12. A: weathering, erosion, and deposition; B: sedimentary rock; C: temperature and pressure
13. Students should include information about being exposed at Earth's surface before breaking down into sediment and then as sediment being compressed, cemented, and hardened to become sedimentary rock.
14. erosion; melting

Building Reading Skills

Combination Notes This lesson contains difficult and sometimes confusing information about different types of rock and their formation. Help students keep all of it straight by teaching them to take combination notes as they read. Encourage students to include labeled diagrams showing how each type of rock forms and the steps in their rock cycles in their notes. This activity provides a good study tool to help them remember each type of rock formation.

Online resource: Combination Notes support

Formative Assessment

Ask: What is the difference between the three types of rock? Sample answer: Sedimentary rocks form when minerals or sediments are cemented together or pressed together with pressure. Igneous rocks form when molten rock cools. Metamorphic rocks form when high temperature or pressure changes sedimentary, metamorphic, or igneous rocks. **Ask:** How are they similar? Sample answer: All three types of rock can be changed into other types of rock through natural processes.

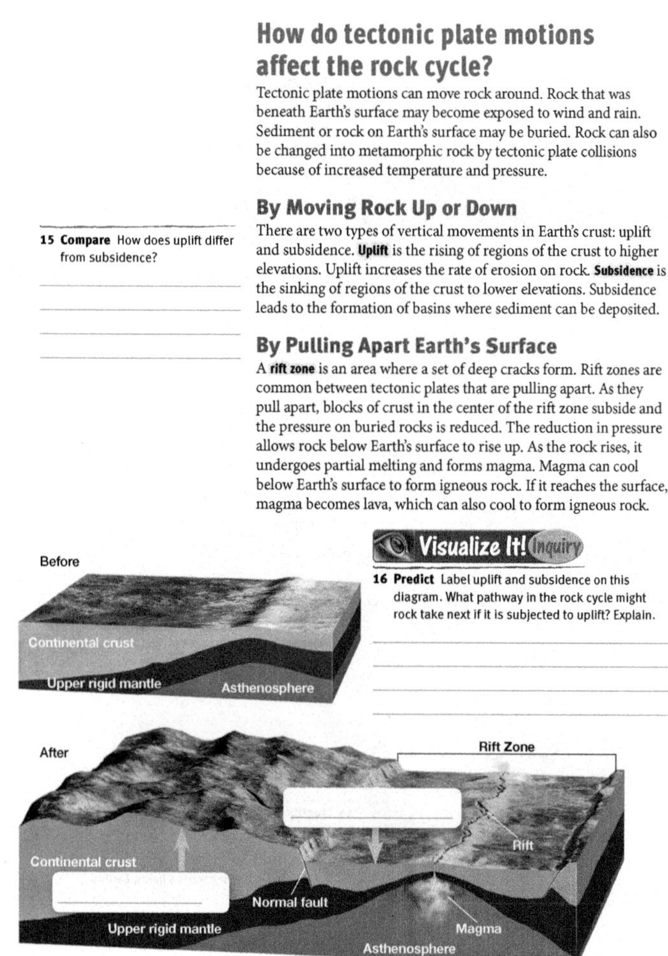

How do tectonic plate motions affect the rock cycle?
Tectonic plate motions can move rock around. Rock that was beneath Earth's surface may become exposed to wind and rain. Sediment or rock on Earth's surface may be buried. Rock can also be changed into metamorphic rock by tectonic plate collisions because of increased temperature and pressure.
By Moving Rock Up or Down
There are two types of vertical movements in Earth's crust: uplift and subsidence. Uplift is the rising of regions of the crust to higher elevations. Uplift increases the rate of erosion on rock. Subsidence is the sinking of regions of the crust to lower elevations. Subsidence leads to the formation of basins where sediment can be deposited.
15 Compare How does uplift differ from subsidence?
By Pulling Apart Earth's Surface
A rift zone is an area where a set of deep cracks form. Rift zones are common between tectonic plates that are pulling apart. As they pull apart, blocks of crust in the center of the rift zone subside and the pressure on buried rocks is reduced. The reduction in pressure allows rock below Earth's surface to rise up. As the rock rises, it undergoes partial melting and forms magma. Magma can cool below Earth's surface to form igneous rock. If it reaches the surface, magma becomes lava, which can also cool to form igneous rock.
Visualize It! Inquiry
16 Predict Label uplift and subsidence on this diagram. What pathway in the rock cycle might rock take next if it is subjected to uplift? Explain.
Before
Continental crust
Upper rigid mantle
Asthenosphere
After
Rift Zone
Rift
Continental crust
Normal fault
Upper rigid mantle
Magma
Asthenosphere
162 Unit 3 Minerals and Rocks

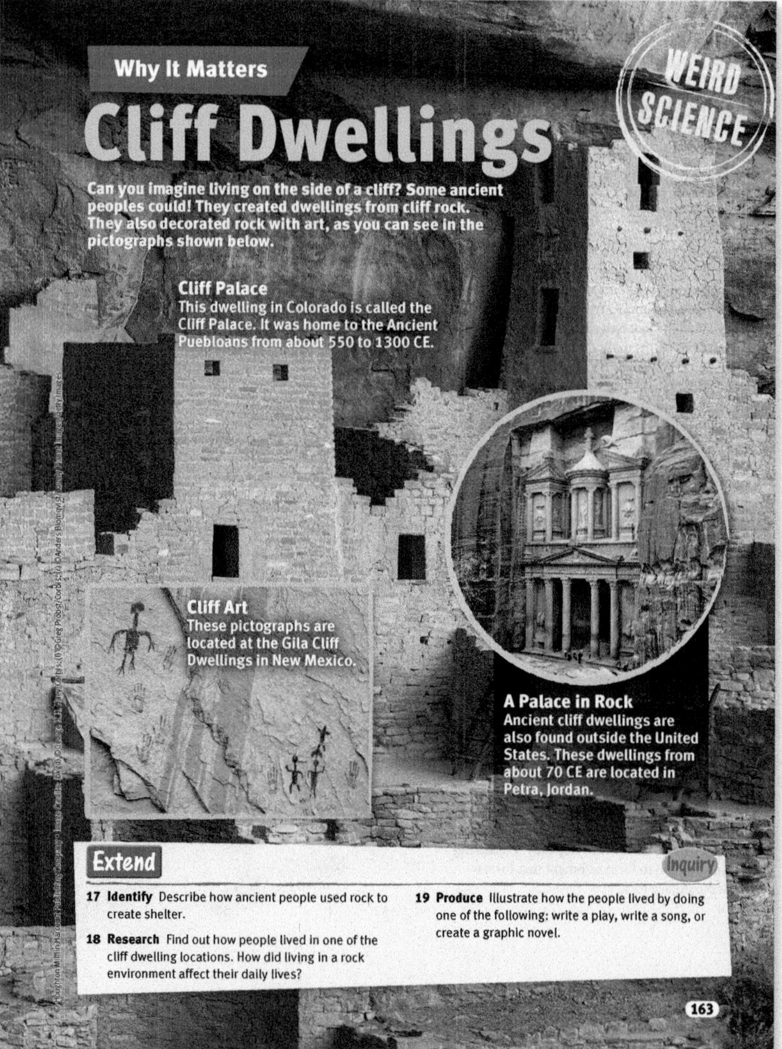

Why It Matters
WEIRD SCIENCE
Cliff Dwellings
Can you imagine living on the side of a cliff? Some ancient peoples could! They created dwellings from cliff rock. They also decorated rock with art, as you can see in the pictographs shown below.
Cliff Palace
This dwelling in Colorado is called the Cliff Palace. It was home to the Ancient Puebloans from about 550 to 1300 CE.
Cliff Art
These pictographs are located at the Gila Cliff Dwellings in New Mexico.
A Palace in Rock
Ancient cliff dwellings are also found outside the United States. These dwellings from about 70 CE are located in Petra, Jordan.
Extend
Inquiry
17 Identify Describe how ancient people used rock to create shelter.
18 Research Find out how people lived in one of the cliff dwelling locations. How did living in a rock environment affect their daily lives?
19 Produce Illustrate how the people lived by doing one of the following: write a play, write a song, or create a graphic novel.
163

Answers

15. Uplift is the rising of parts of the crust to higher elevations. Subsidence is the sinking of parts of the crust to lower elevations. Uplift increases erosion rates. Subsidence leads to basin formation, where sediment can be deposited.
16. *See students' pages for annotations.* If igneous rock is uplifted, it may reach Earth's surface,be broken down into sediment, and form sedimentary rock.

Extend

17. Dwellings were created from sides of cliffs.
18. Answers could include specifics about shelter types, tools used or art created.
19. Productions should include information about shelter, tools, and daily life.

Learning Alert

Rift Zones and Igneous Rock Formation Igneous rocks that form in rift zones located in the ocean are an example of extrusive igneous rock. Extrusive igneous rock forms when lava erupts onto Earth's surface. Lava that flows from fissures onto the ocean floor in rift zones is cooled by water to form new ocean floor. By contrast, igneous rock that forms from magma that hardens beneath Earth's crust is classified as intrusive igneous rock. Intrusive igneous rock typically has large crystals that result from cooling at a slower rate.

Why It Matters

Have students look at images of the cliff dwellings. **Ask:** What is a cliff dwelling? Sample answer: A cliff dwelling is a home that has been chiseled out of the side of a cliff. **Ask:** Why do you think that some ancient people chose this way to live? Sample answer: They may have chosen to live on the sides of cliffs to stay protected and sheltered.

For Greater Depth, Have students research cliff dwellings. Ask them to find out if there are modern people living in cliffs anywhere. Ask them to think about the practicalities and impracticalities of this type of living.

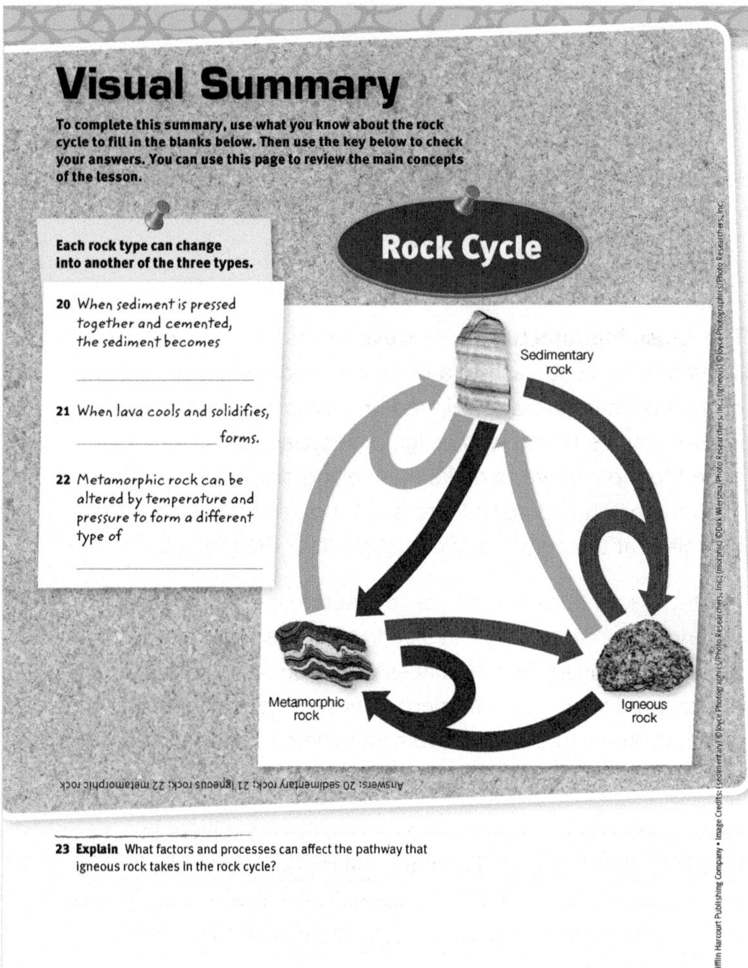

164 Unit 3 Minerals and Rocks

Lesson Review

Lesson 2

Vocabulary

In your own words, define the following terms.

1 Rock cycle

2 Weathering

3 Rift zone

Key Concepts

Use these photos to classify the rock as sedimentary, igneous, or metamorphic.

Example	Type of rock
4 **Classify** This rock is made up of the mineral calcite, and it formed from the remains of organisms that lived in water.	
5 **Classify** Through high temperature and pressure, this rock formed from a sedimentary rock.	
6 **Classify** This rock is made of tiny crystals that formed quickly when molten rock cooled at Earth's surface.	

7 **Describe** How can sedimentary rock become metamorphic rock?

8 **Explain** How can subsidence lead to the formation of sedimentary rock?

9 **Explain** Why are rift zones common places for igneous rock to form?

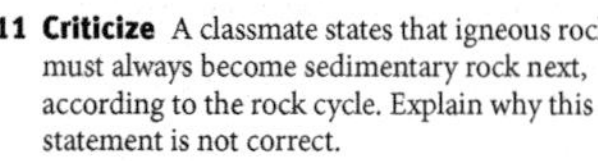

Critical Thinking

10 **Hypothesize** What would happen to the rock cycle if erosion did not occur?

11 **Criticize** A classmate states that igneous rock must always become sedimentary rock next, according to the rock cycle. Explain why this statement is not correct.

12 **Predict** Granite is an igneous rock that forms from magma cooled below Earth's surface. Why would granite have larger crystals than igneous rocks formed from lava cooled above Earth's surface?

Lesson 2 The Rock Cycle 165

Student Pages 162–165

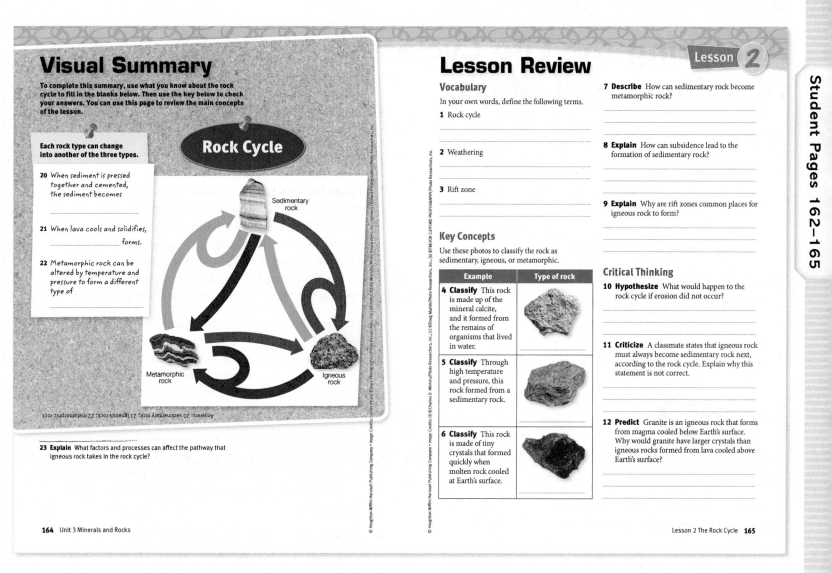

Visual Summary Answers

20. sedimentary rock
21. igneous rock
22. metamorphic rock
23. whether it is below or above Earth's surface (erosion, weathering); the temperatures and pressures it is subjected to

Lesson Review Answers

1. The processes that form, change, and re-form rock.
2. Occurs when water, wind, ice, or heat break down rock into fragments.
3. Cracks that form between two tectonic plates that are pulling away from each other.
4. sedimentary
5. metamorphic
6. igneous
7. Sedimentary rock can become metamorphic rock if it is subjected to changes in temperature and pressure.
8. When regions of the crust sink to lower elevations, basins form where sediment can be deposited. This sediment may then be compressed and cemented to form sedimentary rock.
9. Rift zones are common places for igneous rock to form because the pulling apart of rocks decreases the pressure on buried rocks. Magma can then form and solidify.
10. sediment would not be created; sedimentary rock would not form
11. All three types of rock can become any of the other three types.
12. The longer magma takes to cool, the more time the crystals have to grow in size.

Student Pages 166–167

Analyzing the Life Cycles of Aluminum and Glass

Purpose To analyze the life cycle of a glass bottle

Learning Goals

- Analyze the life cycles of two recyclable consumer products.
- Evaluate the financial and environmental costs of technology.
- Propose life cycle improvements for a consumer product that reduce the financial and environmental cost of the product.

Informal Vocabulary

life cycle analysis bauxite, smelting, silica

Prerequisite Knowledge

- Basic understanding of renewable and nonrenewable resources
- Familiarity with the flow of energy in systems

21st Century SKILLS **Theme: Environmental Literacy**

Activities focusing on 21st Century Skills are included for this feature and can be found on the following pages.

These activities focus on the following skills:

- **Critical Thinking and Problem Solving**
- **Information Literacy**
- **Initiative and Self-Direction**

You can learn more about the 21st Century Skills in the front matter of this Teacher's Edition.

Content Refresher

The Glass Manufacturing Process Trains or trucks deliver sand, limestone, and soda ash to a glass manufacturing plant. Batches of the raw materials are weighed on scales and sent to a mixer, where they are mixed with cullet, or recycled glass. Water is added to the mixture to make the melting process more efficient. Then the batch is dropped into a hot furnace, where it is melted into glass at temperatures from 2,600 to 2,800 °F.

Most furnaces burn natural gas, but some use oil, propane, or electricity. Furnaces range in size from 450 square feet to more than 1,400 square feet. Furnaces use about 4 million BTUs of energy per ton of glass. Modern furnaces inject oxygen into the combustion mixture to improve flame control and to increase the efficiency of the production process.

Gobs of molten glass are formed into glass containers in machines that shape and cool the glass. As glass cools, it becomes more viscous. A 7-ounce gob is typically used to make a 12-ounce glass bottle. One machine can make 700 glass bottles per minute.

Glass Facts Glass can be recycled forever with no loss of quality. In 2008, 36% of glass beverage bottles in the United States were recycled. In California, about 80% of glass bottles were recycled.

It takes about 30 days for a glass container to go from a recycling bin to a store shelf. Recycling one glass bottle saves enough energy to light a 100-watt light bulb for four hours or to run a computer for 30 minutes.

Using 50% recycled glass to make new containers would remove 180,000 tons of waste from landfills every month and save enough energy to power about 22,000 homes in the United States for one year.

S.T.E.M. Engineering & Technology

Analyzing Technology

Skills
Identify risks
Identify benefits
✓ Evaluate cost of technology
✓ Evaluate environmental impact
✓ Propose improvements
Propose risk reduction
✓ Compare technology
✓ Communicate results

Objectives
• Analyze the life cycle of an aluminum can.
• Analyze the life cycle of a glass bottle.
• Evaluate the cost of recycling versus disposal of technology.
• Analyze the environmental impact of technology.

Analyzing the Life Cycles of Aluminum and Glass

A life cycle analysis is a way to evaluate the real cost of a product. The analysis considers how much money an item costs to make. It also examines how making the product affects the economy and the environment through the life of the product. Engineers, scientists, and technologists use this information to improve processes and to compare products.

Costs of Production

Have you ever wondered where an aluminum soda can comes from? Have you wondered where the can goes when you are done with it? If so, you have started a life cycle analysis by asking the right questions. Aluminum is a metal found in a type of rock called *bauxite*. To get aluminum, first bauxite must be mined. The mined ore is then shipped to a processing plant. There, the bauxite is melted to get aluminum in a process called *smelting*. After smelting, the aluminum is processed. It may be shaped into bicycle parts or rolled into sheets to make cans. Every step in the production involves both financial costs and environmental costs that must be considered in a life cycle analysis.

Many bicycles are made of aluminum because it is lightweight and strong.

Costs of Disposal

After an aluminum can is used it can travel either to a landfill or to a recycling plant. The process of recycling an aluminum can does require the use of some energy. However, the financial and environmental costs of disposing of a can and mining ore are much greater than the cost of recycling a can. Additionally, smelting bauxite produces harmful wastes. A life cycle analysis of an aluminum can must include the cost and environmental effects of mining, smelting, and disposing of the aluminum can.

1 Analyze After a can is recycled, which steps are no longer part of the life cycle?

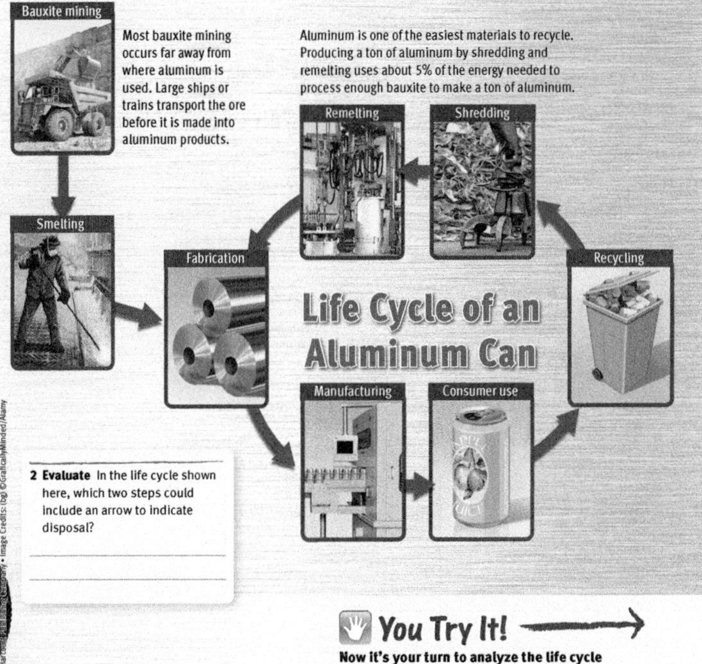

Most bauxite mining occurs far away from where aluminum is used. Large ships or trains transport the ore before it is made into aluminum products.

Aluminum is one of the easiest materials to recycle. Producing a ton of aluminum by shredding and remelting uses about 5% of the energy needed to process enough bauxite to make a ton of aluminum.

2 Evaluate In the life cycle shown here, which two steps could include an arrow to indicate disposal?

You Try It!
Now it's your turn to analyze the life cycle of a product.

Answers

1. bauxite mining and smelting
2. smelting and consumer use

Analyzing Technology

You Try It!

Now, apply what you have learned about the life cycle of aluminum to analyze the life cycle of a glass bottle. Glass is made by melting silica from sand or from mineral deposits mined from the Earth. A kiln heats the silica until it melts to form a red-hot glob. Then, the glass is shaped and cooled to form useful items.

(1) Evaluate Cost of Technology

As a group, discuss the steps that would be involved in making a glass bottle. List the steps in the space below. Start with mining and end at a landfill. Include as many steps in the process as you can think of. Beside each step, tell whether there would be financial costs, environmental costs, or both.

Life Cycle of a Glass Bottle

(2) Evaluate Environmental Impact

Use the table below to indicate which of the steps listed above would have environmental costs, and what type of cost would be involved. A step can appear in more than one column.

Cause pollution	Consume energy	Damage habitat

S.T.E.M. Engineering & Technology

(3) Propose Improvements

In your group, discuss how you might improve the life cycle of a glass bottle and reduce the impact on the environment. Draw a life cycle that includes your suggestions for improvement.

(4) Compare Technology

How does your improved process decrease the environmental effects of making and using glass bottles?

(5) Communicate Results

Imagine that you are an accountant for a company that produces glass bottles. In the space below, write an argument for using recycled glass that is based on financial savings for your company.

Answers

1. Answers will vary. Sample answer: mining quartz or sand, shipping to a processing center, melting silica, shaping into a bottle, shipping to a store, consumer use, shipping to landfill.
2. Answers will vary. Sample answer: Cause pollution: shipping quartz or sand, melting, shipping product; Consume energy: mining, melting silica, forming bottles, shipping product; Damage habitat: removing sand, mining silica, disposing of wastes from melting, disposing of glass bottles in landfill
3. Students' diagrams will vary but should include recycling used bottles back to the melting stage.
4. Sample answer: By recycling glass, the improved process reduces damage to habitats by reducing the amount of mining. It reduces pollution by using less energy to ship sand or mined quartz. It also reduces the amount of garbage in the landfill.
5. Students' answers will vary, but should recognize that costs are reduced when less energy is used to produce glass bottles and less fuel is spent shipping sand or mined quartz.

21st Century SKILLS

Learning and Innovation Skills

small groups | 15 min

Critical Thinking and Problem Solving After students have proposed improvements to the life cycle of glass, have them meet in small groups to analyze and evaluate each other's evidence and arguments. Challenge students to consider alternative points of view, make connections between information and arguments, and draw conclusions based on the best ideas. Have students ask each other questions to clarify points of view and strive for better solutions. Finally, have students present their ideas to the class, reflecting critically on what they learned and the process they used to reach their conclusions.

Information, Media, and Technology Skills

 pairs or small groups | 20 min

Information Literacy Invite pairs or small groups of students to use publicly available sources of information to compare their ideas about the life cycle of glass with what happens in the real world. Students should consult several sources, including a glass industry source and an environmental source. If the sources provide conflicting ideas, students should evaluate the information critically and competently based on what they know about the reliability and biases of each source. Encourage students to share their research findings with the class.

Life and Career Skills

 individuals | ongoing

Initiative and Self-Direction Invite students to compare the environmental impacts of glass, aluminum cans, and plastic bottles. Have them set a time-table for their research and decide how to present their findings. Students can then complete their short-term and long-term goals without direct oversight. Encourage students to go beyond what they already know to become an expert on the topic. Invite students to share their projects with the class.

Differentiated Instruction

Basic *Life Cycles*

 individuals |  10 min

Invite students to think about the life cycles of glass, aluminum, and paper. Based on what they know, have them draw a sequence diagram that shows the general life cycle of raw materials. For example, where do raw materials come from? How do they get to a manufacturing plant? What happens at the plant? How does the product get to a consumer? What happens after the product has been used? Encourage students to explain their diagram to a partner.

Advanced *Benefits of Recycling*

 individuals or pairs |  20 min

Invite students to select a common item, such as aluminum cans, newspaper, paper cups, or plastic bottles. Encourage students to research the recycling rate for the item, and how much energy could be saved if 50 or 75% of the items were recycled. Challenge students to develop a plan to communicate the benefits of recycling this item to the school population.

ELL *Comparing Life Cycles*

 individuals or pairs | 10 min

Have students use a Venn diagram to compare the life cycles of aluminum and glass. Then have students use their own words to explain orally how the two cycles are alike and different.

Customize Your Feature

- ☐ **21st Century Skills** Learning and Innovation Skills
- ☐ **21st Century Skills** Information, Media, and Technology Skills
- ☐ **21st Century Skills** Life and Career Skills
- ☐ **Basic** Life Cycles
- ☐ **Advanced** Benefits of Recycling
- ☐ **ELL** Comparing Life Cycles

Three Classes of Rock

Essential Question How do rocks form?

For more detailed information about the topics in this lesson, refer to the Content Refresher in the Unit Opener pages.

Opening Your Lesson

Begin the lesson by assessing students' prerequisite and prior knowledge.

Prerequisite Knowledge

- A general understanding of the rock cycle
- A general understanding that Earth's surface continually changes because of the cycling of rock.

Accessing Prior Knowledge

Ask: How do rocks change over time? They change form through the rock cycle.

Ask: How can rocks form? They can form from the heating and cooling of molten rock, the accumulation of sediment, and the alteration of existing rocks by pressure and heat.

Customize Your Opening

- ☐ **Accessing Prior Knowledge,** above
- ☐ **Print Path** Engage Your Brain, SE p. 171, #1–2
- ☐ **Print Path** Active Reading, SE p. 171, # 3–4
- ☐ **Digital Path** Lesson Opener

Key Topics/Learning Goals	Supporting Concepts
Rocks and Their Classification 1 Describe the components of rock. 2 Describe two properties that are used to classify rock. 3 Identify the three major classes of rock.	• Rock is a naturally occurring, solid combination of minerals or organic matter. • Composition is the chemical makeup of a rock. It describes the minerals or other materials in the rock. • Texture is the quality of a rock based on the sizes, shapes, and positions of its grains. • The three major classes of rock are igneous, sedimentary, and metamorphic.
Igneous Rock 1 Describe the process by which igneous rock forms. 2 Explain where intrusive igneous rock forms. 3 Explain where extrusive igneous rock forms.	• Igneous rock forms when *magma* beneath Earth's surface and *lava* flowing across Earth's surface cools and solidifies. • Intrusive igneous rock forms when magma cools and solidifies beneath Earth's surface. • Extrusive igneous rock forms from when lava cools and solidifies at Earth's surface.
Sedimentary Rock 1 Describe the process by which sedimentary rock forms. 2 Identify the three major types of sedimentary rock and explain how they form.	• Sedimentary rock forms when sediment is deposited and compressed. • Clastic sedimentary rock forms when sediment is compacted and cemented. • Chemical sedimentary rock forms when minerals precipitate out of a solution. • Organic sedimentary rock forms from the remains of plants or animals.
Metamorphic Rock 1 Describe the process by which metamorphic rock forms. 2 Describe the two types of metamorphic rock.	• Metamorphic rock forms when temperature and pressure change the composition and texture of an existing rock. • In foliated metamorphic rock, mineral grains are arranged in planes or bands; in nonfoliated metamorphic rock, they are not.

Options for Instruction

Two parallel paths provide coverage of the Essential Questions, with a strong **Inquiry** strand woven into each. Follow the **Print Path,** the **Digital Path,** or your customized combination of print, digital, and inquiry.

 Print Path *Teaching support for the Print Path appears with the Student Pages.*	 Inquiry Labs and Activities	 Digital Path *Digital Path shortcut: TS671015*
A Rocky World, SE pp. 172–173 **How are rocks classified?** • By Mineral Composition • By Texture	**Quick Lab** **Observing Rocks** **Activity** **Types of Rocks** **Virtual Lab** **Rock Test Kitchen**	**Classifying Rocks** **Interactive Graphics**
The Furnace Below, SE pp. 174–175 **What are two kinds of igneous rock?** • Intrusive Igneous Rock • Extrusive Igneous Rock	**S.T.E.M. Lab** **Modeling Rock Formation** **Activity** **Rockin' Review Game**	**Igneous Rock Formations** **Interactive Images** **Igneous Rock Texture** **Interactive Images**
Lay It On!, SE pp. 176–177 **What are three types of sedimentary rock?** • Clastic Sedimentary Rock • Chemical Sedimentary Rock • Organic Sedimentary Rock	**Activity** **Making Sedimentary Rocks**	**Clastic Sedimentary Rocks** **Interactive Images** **Chemical/Organic Sedimentary Rock** **Video Clips**
The Heat Is On!, SE pp. 178–179 **What are two types of metamorphic rock?** • Foliated Metamorphic Rock • Nonfoliated Metamorphic Rock	**Quick Lab** **Stretching Out** **Daily Demo** **Metamorphic Candy Bar**	**Types of Metamorphism** **Interactive Images** **Nonfoliated versus Foliated Rocks** **Interactive Images**

Options for Assessment

See the Evaluate page for options, including Formative Assessment, Summative Assessment, and Unit Review.

Engage and Explore

Activities and Discussion

Activity *Types of Rocks*

Rocks and Their Classification

 individuals or pairs
 20 min
 **DIRECTED** inquiry

Display pairs of rocks without telling students what they are; for igneous rocks: basalt (extrusive) and granite (intrusive); for sedimentary rocks: sandstone (clastic) and limestone (organic); and for metamorphic rocks: gniess (foliated) and slate (nonfoliated). Give each rock a number to identify it. Ask students to record observations for each rock. Remind them to look at texture, grain size, color, banding, and anything else they notice. Encourage students to share their observations with the class. Compile students' observations on the board, then lead a discussion in which students try to identify each type of rock.

Activity *Making Sedimentary Rocks*

Engage

Sedimentary Rock

 small groups
 varied
 **GUIDED** inquiry

Give each group a clean, half-gallon cardboard milk carton with the top cut off and several small cups. Have students measure out about ¾ cup of gravel and small pieces of fish bone. This material represents a river environment. Direct them to then mix plaster of Paris in a small cup with water according to the manufacturer's instructions, then to stir in the gravel and fish bones. This mixture should then be poured from the cup into the milk carton and patted down to form a relatively flat layer. This process should be repeated to make additional layers. One layer should have sand and shell pieces to represent a beach environment; another, dirt and shell pieces to represent a shallow, marshy ocean environment; and a final, fourth layer with crushed white chalk, fish bones, and shells to represent the deep ocean. After their sedimentary rock layer models have dried, about an hour, have students peel the carton off the plaster and sand the sides to show the layers clearly. If possible, have them compare their models to pictures of places with sedimentary rock layers such as the Grand Canyon.

Labs and Demos

Daily Demo *Metamorphic Candy Bar*

Engage

Metamorphic Rock

 whole class
 10 min
 **GUIDED** inquiry

PURPOSE **To help students visualize the process of metamorphic rock formation**

MATERIALS

- **boards, small (2)**
- **candy bar, with layers such as caramel, peanuts, and chocolate**
- **clamps (2)**
- **knife**

1 Cut the candy bar in half, and show students the layers apparent in the cross section. If possible, draw a diagram of the layers on the board or on a transparency that you project with an overhead projector.
2 Place half of the candy bar between the two boards and clamp them together, with the clamps on opposite sides.
3 Have one or two volunteers slowly tighten the clamps until the candy bar is completely crushed.
4 Hold the candy bar up for students to see.
5 **Observe Ask:** What do you see? Sample answer: The candy bar is squished together; the layers are pressed together.
6 **Apply Ask:** How is this like the process that creates metamorphic rock from sedimentary rock? Sample answer: The pressure caused the original layers to be pressed together.
7 Draw a new diagram next to the first to show this difference more clearly.

Customize Your Labs

 *See the Lab Manual for lab datasheets.*

 *Go Online for editable lab datasheets.*

Levels of 

DIRECTED inquiry introduces inquiry skills within a structured framework.

GUIDED inquiry develops inquiry skills within a supportive environment.

INDEPENDENT inquiry deepens inquiry skills with student-driven questions or procedures.

Quick Lab *Stretching Out*

Metamorphic Rock

 individuals
 15 min
 **DIRECTED** inquiry

Students sketch a rock, use putty to model changes, then sketch the rock again.

PURPOSE **To demonstrate the effects of metamorphism on granite**

MATERIALS

- granite
- lab apron
- paper
- pencil
- plastic play putty
- safety goggles

Quick Lab *Observing Rocks*

Rocks and Their Classification

 individuals
 30 min
 **DIRECTED** inquiry

Students observe and classify igneous, sedimentary, and metamorphic rocks.

PURPOSE **To analyze rock characteristics and develop hypotheses**

MATERIALS

- colored pencils
- hand lens
- Key of Rock Characteristics
- labeling stickers
- rock samples, 5

S.T.E.M. Lab *Modeling Rock Formation*

Synthesizing Key Topics

 pairs
 45 min
  **GUIDED/INDEPENDENT** inquiry

Students model the formation of different types of rocks.

PURPOSE **To observe how different types of rocks form**

MATERIALS

- beads
- beaker, 400 mL
- candles, small, 20
- clay, modeling
- craft sticks, 2
- cups, paper
- glue, white
- gravel, pea
- pans, aluminum, pie, 3
- paper, wax
- rolling pin
- salt
- sand
- tongs
- water, cold

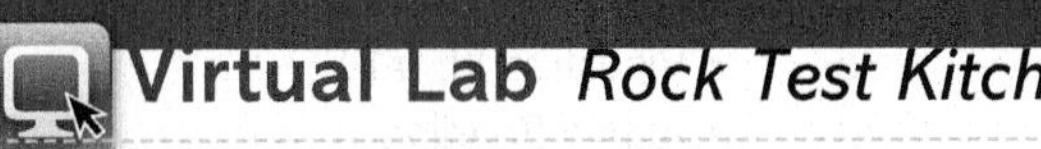

Virtual Lab *Rock Test Kitchen*

Rocks and Their Classification

 flexible
 45 min
 **GUIDED** inquiry

Students apply processes to sediment, magma, and types of rock.

PURPOSE To explore connections among types of rock

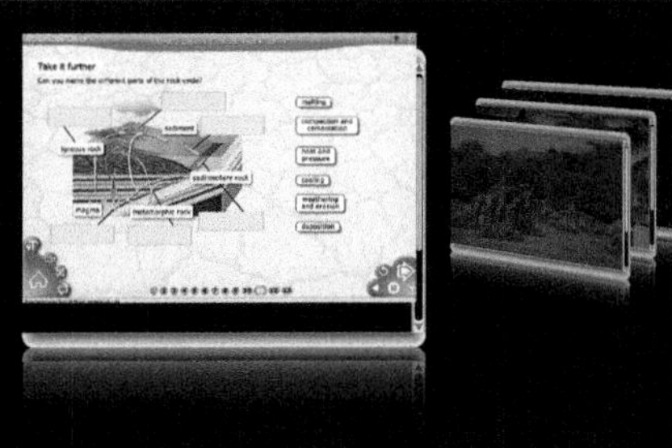

Activities and Discussion

☐ **Activity** Types of Rocks
☐ **Activity** Making Sedimentary Rocks

Labs and Demos

☐ **Daily Demo** Metamorphic Candy Bar
☐ **Quick Lab** Stretching Out
☐ **Quick Lab** Observing Rocks
☐ **S.T.E.M. Lab** Modeling Rock Formation
☐ **Virtual Lab** Rock Test Kitchen

Your Resources

Explain Science Concepts

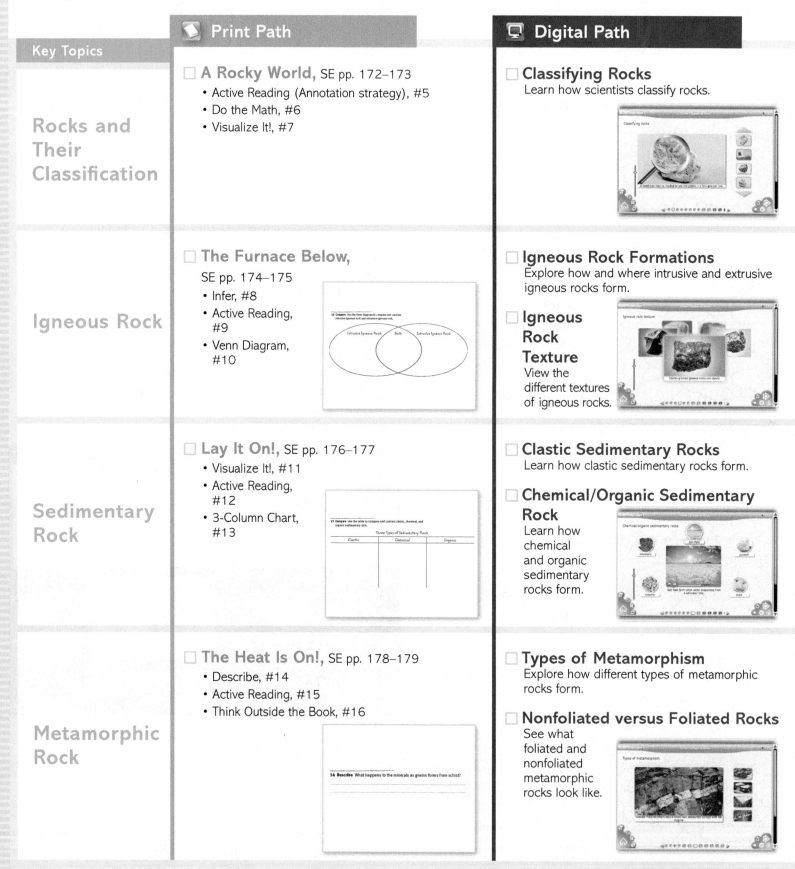

Key Topics	Print Path	Digital Path
Rocks and Their Classification	☐ **A Rocky World,** SE pp. 172–173 • Active Reading (Annotation strategy), #5 • Do the Math, #6 • Visualize It!, #7	☐ **Classifying Rocks** Learn how scientists classify rocks. 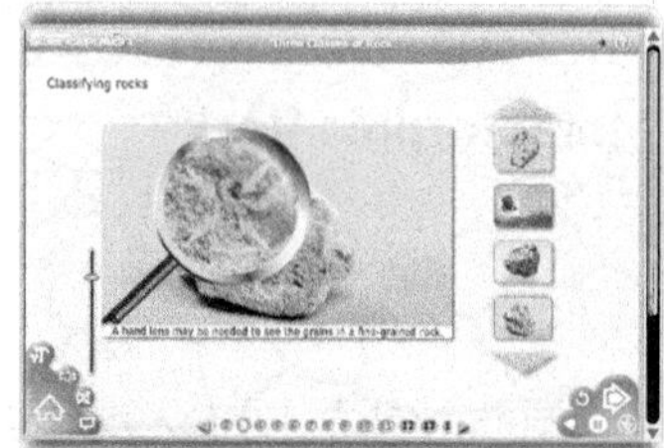
Igneous Rock	☐ **The Furnace Below,** SE pp. 174–175 • Infer, #8 • Active Reading, #9 • Venn Diagram, #10 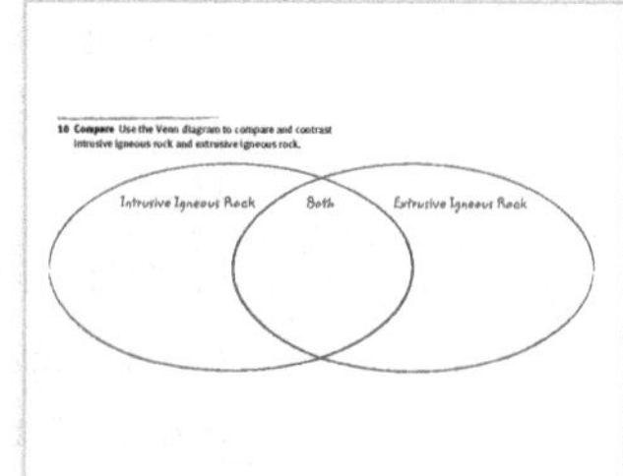	☐ **Igneous Rock Formations** Explore how and where intrusive and extrusive igneous rocks form. ☐ **Igneous Rock Texture** View the different textures of igneous rocks. 
Sedimentary Rock	☐ **Lay It On!,** SE pp. 176–177 • Visualize It!, #11 • Active Reading, #12 • 3-Column Chart, #13 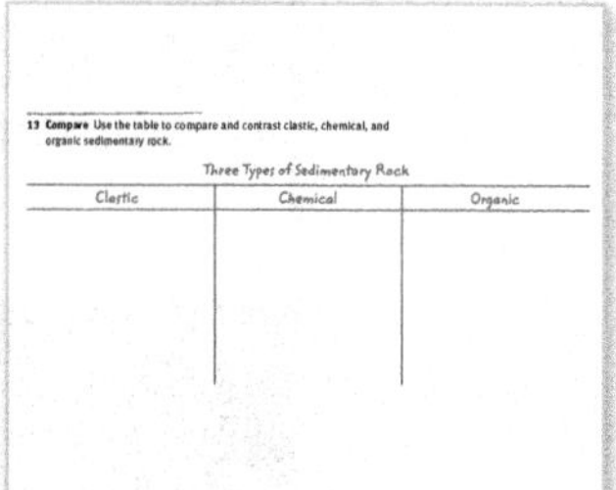	☐ **Clastic Sedimentary Rocks** Learn how clastic sedimentary rocks form. ☐ **Chemical/Organic Sedimentary Rock** Learn how chemical and organic sedimentary rocks form. 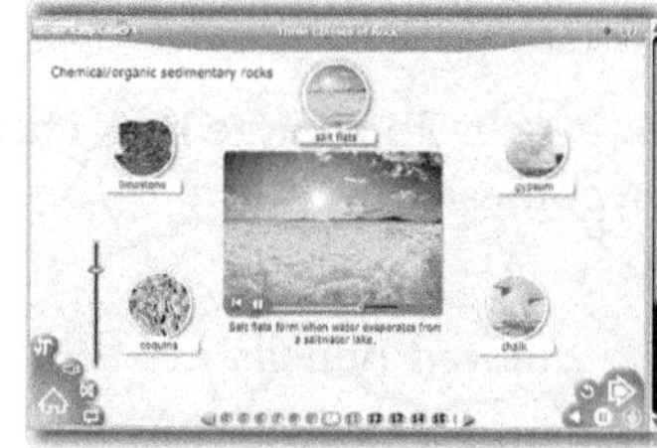
Metamorphic Rock	☐ **The Heat Is On!,** SE pp. 178–179 • Describe, #14 • Active Reading, #15 • Think Outside the Book, #16 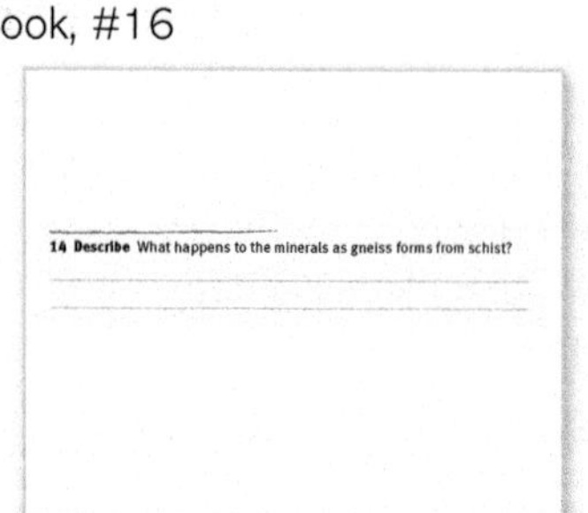	☐ **Types of Metamorphism** Explore how different types of metamorphic rocks form. ☐ **Nonfoliated versus Foliated Rocks** See what foliated and nonfoliated metamorphic rocks look like. 

Differentiated Instruction

Basic *Recipe for Igneous Rocks*

Igneous Rock

 individuals
35 min

Have students write a “recipe” for igneous rocks. Students should choose either extrusive or intrusive igneous rock and write a step-by-step guide that details each step in the formation process. Remind students to include information on where the rock is formed, how quickly the magma cools, and how the crystals form.

Advanced *Chemical Sedimentary Rock*

Sedimentary Rock

 small groups
 40 min

Invite students to research different types of chemical sedimentary rock, Students can research carbonate precipitates, such as calcite, evaporates, such as borax, and different halides, such as sylvite and halite. Remind students to include details about composition and other physical properties. Students should identify locations where these rock types can actually be found, such as Death Valley National Park, White Sands National Monument, and Boron, California. Students can also research what these minerals are used for. For example, halite is used for table salt. Students can present their research in a written report or a visual display.

ELL *Note-Taking*

Synthesizing Key Topics

 pairs
40 min

Tell students that taking notes on what they read can help them better understand and remember the information. Encourage students to work in pairs to go back through the lesson content and take notes. Have them write down the topic of each section, such as igneous rock. Remind them to look at the question heads and subheads for clues about what information they will find in a section and then write down important information they find in each section.

Lesson Vocabulary

rock **composition** **texture**

Previewing Vocabulary

 individuals then pairs  35 min

Word Triangles Have students create a word triangle for each vocabulary term. In the bottom of the triangle, they should write the term and its definition, in the middle, a sentence using the term, and at the top draw a picture illustrating the term. Have them share their word triangles with a partner.

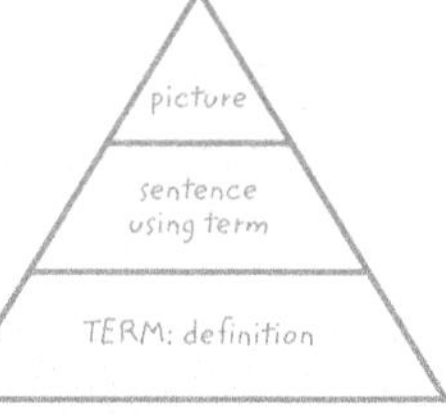

Optional Online resource: Word Triangle support

Reinforcing Vocabulary

 individuals  30 minutes

Paragraphs To help students remember each of the vocabulary words introduced in this lesson, have them write a paragraph or two that describes the ways scientists classify different types of rock. Explain that they are to come up with descriptive paragraphs, not merely list each term and its definition. Tell students to use all three vocabulary words and to include as much detail as they can about how and why composition and texture are so important in the classification of rock.

Customize Your Core Lesson

Core Instruction

- ☐ **Print Path** choices
- ☐ **Digital Path** choices

Vocabulary

- ☐ **Previewing Vocabulary** Word Triangles
- ☐ **Reinforcing Vocabulary** Paragraphs

Differentiated Instruction

- ☐ **Basic** Recipe for Igneous Rocks
- ☐ **Advanced** Chemical Sedimentary Rock
- ☐ **ELL** Note-Taking

Your Resources

Extend Science Concepts

Reinforce and Review

Activity *Rockin' Review Game*

Synthesizing Key Topics

 small groups
25 minutes

Sticky Note Review Divide the board into four numbered sections. Write each of the following four questions on the board, one in each section:

1. How are rocks classified?
2. How can igneous rocks form?
3. How can sedimentary rocks form?
4. How can metamorphic rocks form?

Split the class into groups of four. Groups should write each question on a separate piece of paper. Then, each student in each group will answer one of the questions. When students are finished, they should trade questions, and each student should answer a new question. Have students continue until all students have answered all four questions. Have each group read all the answers to each question, then collaborate to come up with the best answer for each one. Tell students that they can combine answers or parts of answers to create a final answer. When they are finished, direct groups to write their group name, the question number, and their collaborative answer on a sticky note. Each group can then stick their answers to the appropriately numbered section on the board. Finally, check each group's answer by reviewing the material as a class.

Graphic Organizer

Synthesizing Key Topics

 individual
35 minutes

Mind Map After students have studied the lesson, ask them to create a mind map for the following terms: *Rock, Composition,* and *Texture.*

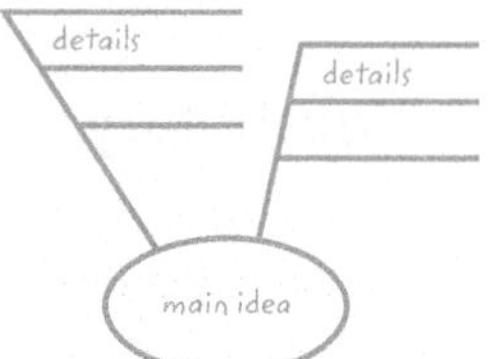

Optional Online resource: Mind Map support

Going Further

Chemistry Connection

Synthesizing Key Topics

 individuals or pairs
varied

Short Research Tell students that corundum is a very useful mineral. It is exceptionally hard, and can be used for a variety of industrial applications. Some specimens of corundum have exceptional transparency, color, and purity, and are highly valued as gemstones. Invite students to research corundum, the gemstones that are members of the corundum group, and the chemical properties that differentiate one gemstone type, such as a blue sapphire, from another, such as a pink sapphire. Students should present their findings in a short written report. If they like, students can include photographs of different types of corundum.

Optional Online rubric: Written Pieces

Architecture Connection

Synthesizing Key Topics

 individuals
varied

Research and Presentation Rock has been used through the ages to construct buildings. Invite students to research types of rock used in buildings. Make sure they find at least one example of a building that uses sedimentary rock, one that uses metamorphic rock, and one that uses igneous rock. Encourage them to find out exactly what type of rock was used—for example, intrusive igneous rock—and why this particular type of rock was chosen. Students can create presentations that include photographs, diagrams, rock samples, and written material.

Customize Your Closing

 *See the Assessment Guide for quizzes and tests.*

Go Online to edit and create quizzes and tests.

Reinforce and Review

- ☐ Activity Rockin' Review Game
- ☐ Graphic Organizer Mind Map
- ☐ Print Path Visual Summary, SE p. 180
- ☐ Print Path Lesson Review, SE p. 181
- ☐ **Digital Path** Lesson Closer

Evaluate Student Mastery

Formative Assessment

See the teacher support below the Student Pages for additional Formative Assessment questions.

Describe or have students review the three classes of rock and how each forms. **Ask:** What are the three classes of rock? Describe how one class of rock forms, and explain different types of rock that belong to that class. Sample answer: igneous, sedimentary, and metamorphic. Igneous rock forms when magma cools and solidifies. If it solidifies beneath Earth's surface, it is intrusive igneous rock. If it cools rapidly above Earth's surface, it is extrusive igneous rock.

Reteach

Formative assessment may show that students need reinforcement for certain topics. The resources below are recommended for reteaching. If students were introduced to a topic through the Print Path, you can also use the Digital Path to reteach, and vice versa.

Can be assigned to individual students

Rocks and Their Classification
Activity Types of Rocks

Igneous Rock
Quick Lab Modeling Rock Formation

Sedimentary Rock
Activity Making Sedimentary Rocks

Metamorphic Rock
Daily Demo Metamorphic Candy Bar

Summative Assessment

Alternative Assessment

It Rocks!

Online resources: student worksheet, optional rubrics

Three Classes of Rock

Take Your Pick: *It Rocks!*
Complete the activities to show what you've learned about the three classes of rock.

1. Work on your own, with a partner, or with a small group.
2. Choose items below for a minimum total of 10 points. Check your choices.
3. Have your teacher approve your plan.
4. Submit or present your results.

2 Points

____ **Rock and Roll** Create an original song that explains how rock is classified and describes the three classes of rock. Record your song, and play it or sing it for the class.

____ **Rockin' Art** Design a poster or other art project that shows the three classes of rock and how each forms. Include details and examples of each type of rock.

5 Points

____ **Pet Rock** Find a rock of any type. Decorate your new pet to personalize it, but leave some of the original rock surface visible. Figure out whether your rock is igneous, sedimentary, or metamorphic. Write a short paper explaining what type of rock it is and how you know.

____ **Rock Models** Create a model for each class of rock: sedimentary, igneous, and metamorphic. Label each model, and include a place of origin and a story about how it formed.

____ **Take a Hike** Go on a rock hunt. Gather at least 10 varied rock samples. Afterwards, classify them as to type. Place each rock in a plastic bag. Attach labels, and tell how you made identifications.

____ **Floating Rock** Pumice is an extrusive igneous rock that has a surprising characteristic… it floats! Research this rock type. Write a report or draw a diagram detailing how pumice forms and why it floats. If possible, find a sample of pumice to share with the class.

8 Points

____ **Rock Puzzle** Design a crossword puzzle about rocks. First, make a list of a minimum of 15 terms you want to use. Next, put these words into puzzle format. Finally, write clues that give details and information about each term. Test your puzzle on classmates or your teacher.

____ **Movie Rocks** Write a script describing how each of the three rock types and their subtypes (intrusive and extrusive igneous; clastic, chemical, and organic sedimentary; foliated and nonfoliated metamorphic) are formed. Film your movie, and share it with your class.

Going Further

- ☐ Chemistry Connection
- ☐ Architecture Connection

Formative Assessment

- ☐ Strategies Throughout TE
- ☐ Lesson Review SE

Summative Assessment

- ☐ Alternative Assessment *It Rocks!*
- ☐ Lesson Quiz
- ☐ Unit Tests A and B
- ☐ Unit Review SE End-of-Unit

Your Resources

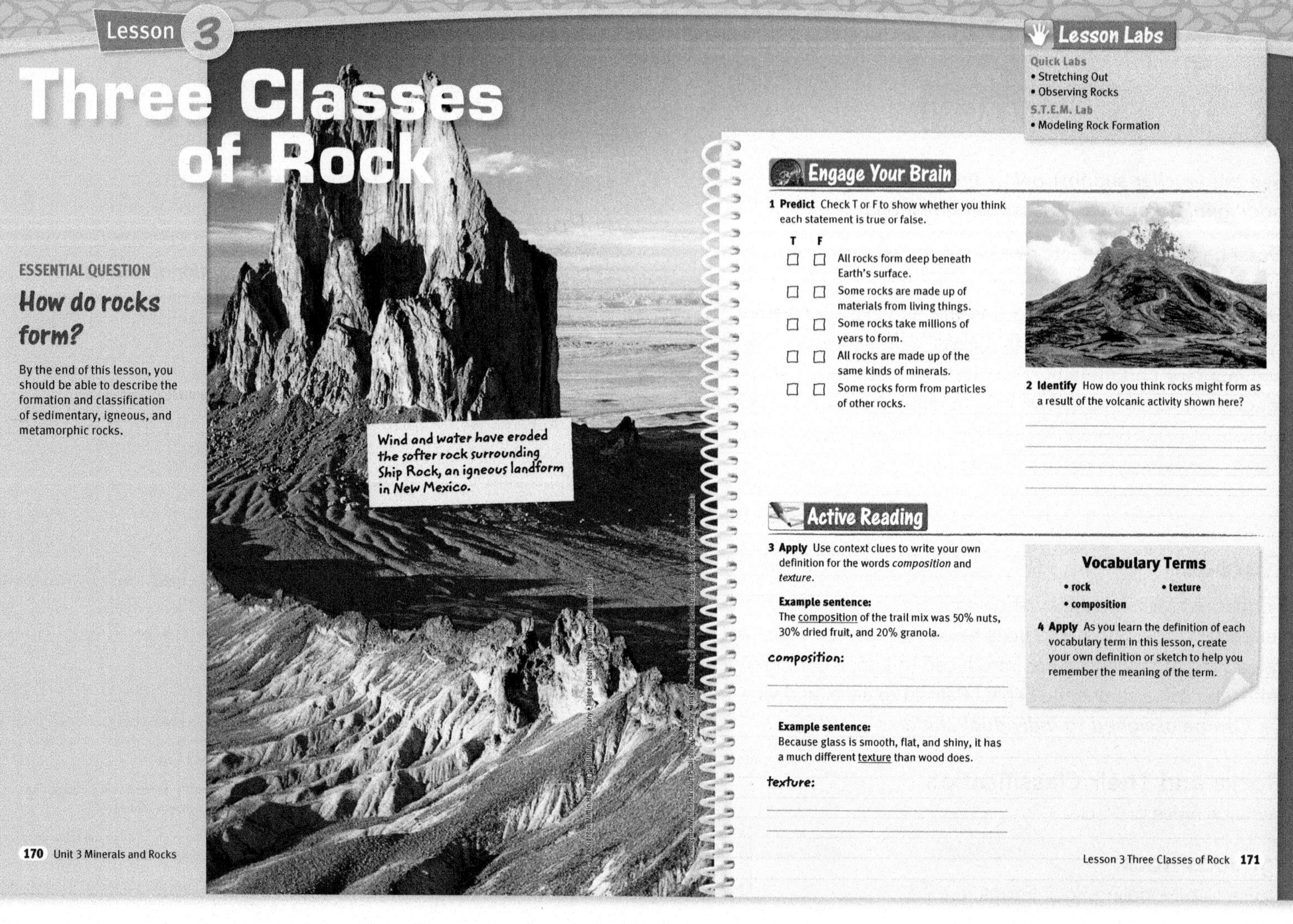
Lesson 3

Three Classes of Rock

ESSENTIAL QUESTION

How do rocks form?

By the end of this lesson, you should be able to describe the formation and classification of sedimentary, igneous, and metamorphic rocks.

Wind and water have eroded the softer rock surrounding Ship Rock, an igneous landform in New Mexico.

170 Unit 3 Minerals and Rocks

Lesson Labs

Quick Labs
- Stretching Out
- Observing Rocks

S.T.E.M. Lab
- Modeling Rock Formation

Engage Your Brain

1 Predict Check T or F to show whether you think each statement is true or false.

T	F	
☐	☐	All rocks form deep beneath Earth's surface.
☐	☐	Some rocks are made up of materials from living things.
☐	☐	Some rocks take millions of years to form.
☐	☐	All rocks are made up of the same kinds of minerals.
☐	☐	Some rocks form from particles of other rocks.

2 Identify How do you think rocks might form as a result of the volcanic activity shown here?

Active Reading

3 Apply Use context clues to write your own definition for the words *composition* and *texture*.

Example sentence:
The composition of the trail mix was 50% nuts, 30% dried fruit, and 20% granola.

composition:

Example sentence:
Because glass is smooth, flat, and shiny, it has a much different texture than wood does.

texture:

Vocabulary Terms
- rock
- texture
- composition

4 Apply As you learn the definition of each vocabulary term in this lesson, create your own definition or sketch to help you remember the meaning of the term.

Lesson 3 Three Classes of Rock 171

Answers

Answers for 1–3 should represent students' current thoughts, even if incorrect.

1. F; T; T; F; T
2. Sample answer: The lava flows down the side of the volcano. When the lava hardens, rock is formed.
3. Sample answer: *Composition* is what something is made up of.

   Sample answer: *Texture* is how smooth or bumpy an object is.
4. Students should define or sketch each vocabulary term in the lesson.

Opening Your Lesson

Have students share their ideas about rock materials in their everyday lives (item 2) to assess their working knowledge of the Key Topics.

Prerequisites Students should have a working knowledge of the rock cycle and how rocks move through it. They should understand that Earth's surface continually changes from the cycling of rock.

Accessing Prior Knowledge Have students create an Anticipation Guide for the content in this lesson. Direct students to make a three-column chart, and label the first column "Statement," the second column "My Answer," and the third column "Text Answer." Then help students list statements about the three classes of rocks in the first column. Under the second column, students should write whether they agree or disagree with each statement. Finally, as they read, they should write under the third column whether the text agrees or disagrees with each statement.

Learning Alert

Minerals In a previous section, minerals were introduced. It is important for students to understand that all rocks contain minerals.

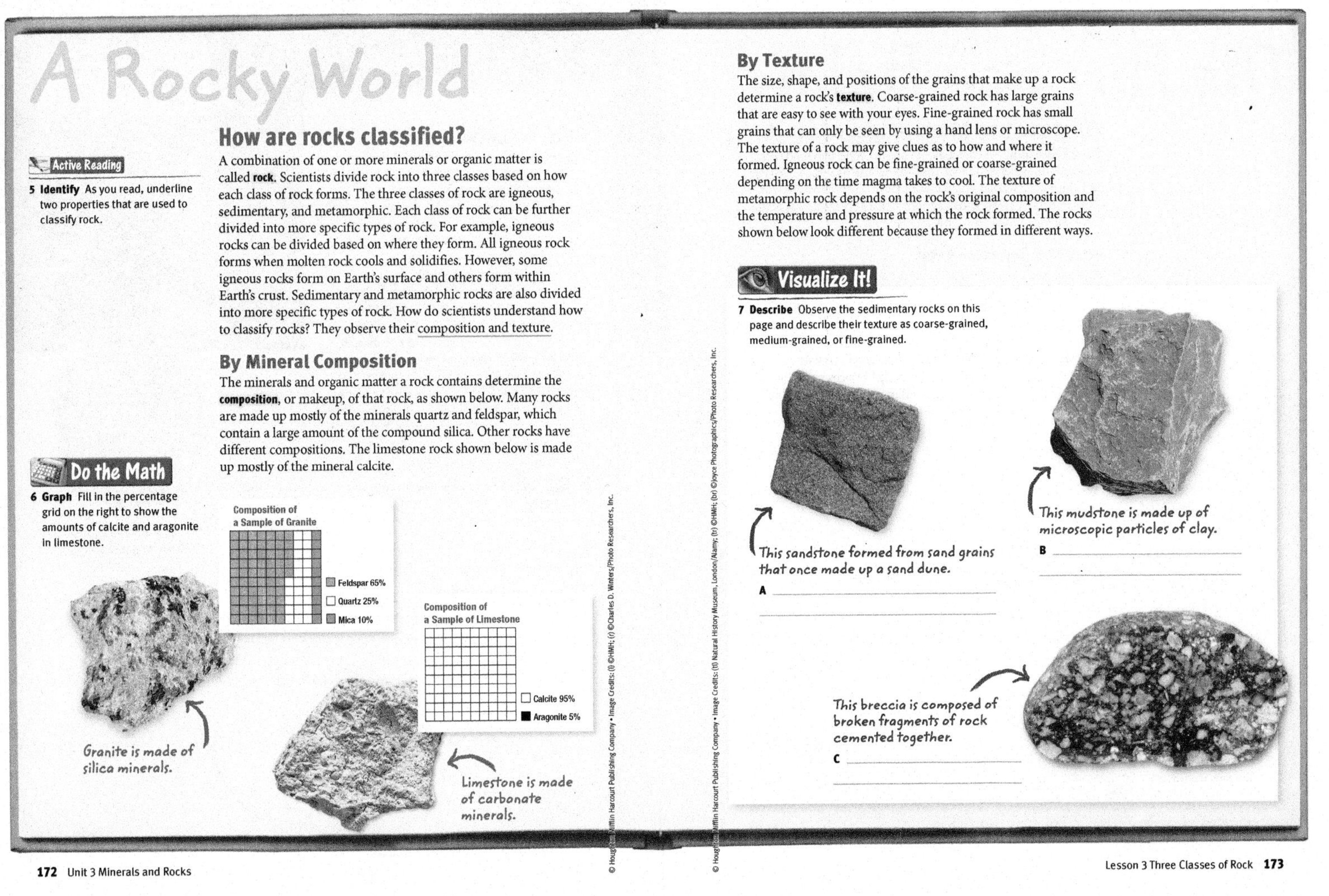

A Rocky World

How are rocks classified?

Active Reading

5 Identify As you read, underline two properties that are used to classify rock.

A combination of one or more minerals or organic matter is called **rock**. Scientists divide rock into three classes based on how each class of rock forms. The three classes of rock are igneous, sedimentary, and metamorphic. Each class of rock can be further divided into more specific types of rock. For example, igneous rocks can be divided based on where they form. All igneous rock forms when molten rock cools and solidifies. However, some igneous rocks form on Earth's surface and others form within Earth's crust. Sedimentary and metamorphic rocks are also divided into more specific types of rock. How do scientists understand how to classify rocks? They observe their composition and texture.

By Mineral Composition

The minerals and organic matter a rock contains determine the **composition**, or makeup, of that rock, as shown below. Many rocks are made up mostly of the minerals quartz and feldspar, which contain a large amount of the compound silica. Other rocks have different compositions. The limestone rock shown below is made up mostly of the mineral calcite.

Do the Math

6 Graph Fill in the percentage grid on the right to show the amounts of calcite and aragonite in limestone.

Granite is made of silica minerals.

Limestone is made of carbonate minerals.

By Texture

The size, shape, and positions of the grains that make up a rock determine a rock's **texture**. Coarse-grained rock has large grains that are easy to see with your eyes. Fine-grained rock has small grains that can only be seen by using a hand lens or microscope. The texture of a rock may give clues as to how and where it formed. Igneous rock can be fine-grained or coarse-grained depending on the time magma takes to cool. The texture of metamorphic rock depends on the rock's original composition and the temperature and pressure at which the rock formed. The rocks shown below look different because they formed in different ways.

Visualize It!

7 Describe Observe the sedimentary rocks on this page and describe their texture as coarse-grained, medium-grained, or fine-grained.

This sandstone formed from sand grains that once made up a sand dune.
A ______

This mudstone is made up of microscopic particles of clay.
B ______

This breccia is composed of broken fragments of rock cemented together.
C ______

Answers

5. *See students' pages for annotations.*
6. Students should color 5 boxes to represent aragonite. The 95 uncolored boxes represent calcite.
7. A: medium-grained; B: fine-grained; C: coarse-grained

Interpreting Visuals

Have students look at the images of the rocks and what they are composed of. Ask them to compare and contrast them. **Ask:** How do you think different mineral compositions contribute to differences in each rock? Sample answer: Different mineral compositions could affect the hardness, color, shape, or texture of a rock. They might also determine whether or not a rock is a useful human resource.

Building Reading Skills

Idea Wheel Have students draw a large circle with a smaller circle inside. Have them divide the outer ring into three sections. In the smaller, central ring, have them write the main idea, *types of rocks*. Ask students to label the sections with the different types of rocks: *igneous, sedimentary,* and *metamorphic*. As they read, have them write details about each type of rock and the different ways each type can form.

Do the Math

Students may be confused as to how to color in the percentage grid for limestone. Have students look at the grid for granite. **Ask:** How many squares are in the grid? 100 **Ask:** What percent does each square represent? 1% **Ask:** How many squares would you color for 10%? 10

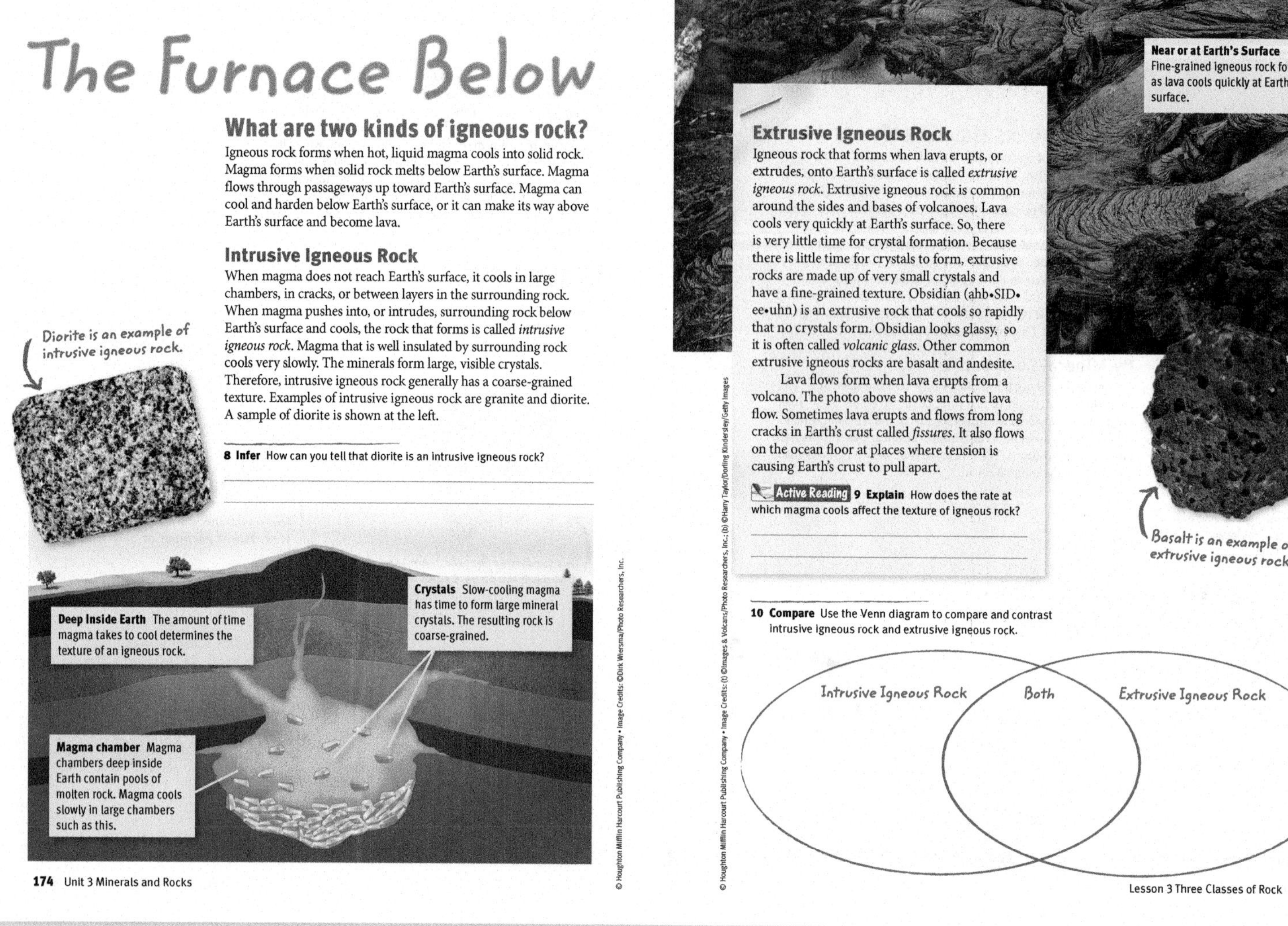

The Furnace Below

What are two kinds of igneous rock?

Igneous rock forms when hot, liquid magma cools into solid rock. Magma forms when solid rock melts below Earth's surface. Magma flows through passageways up toward Earth's surface. Magma can cool and harden below Earth's surface, or it can make its way above Earth's surface and become lava.

Intrusive Igneous Rock

When magma does not reach Earth's surface, it cools in large chambers, in cracks, or between layers in the surrounding rock. When magma pushes into, or intrudes, surrounding rock below Earth's surface and cools, the rock that forms is called *intrusive igneous rock.* Magma that is well insulated by surrounding rock cools very slowly. The minerals form large, visible crystals. Therefore, intrusive igneous rock generally has a coarse-grained texture. Examples of intrusive igneous rock are granite and diorite. A sample of diorite is shown at the left.

Diorite is an example of intrusive igneous rock.

8 Infer How can you tell that diorite is an intrusive igneous rock?

Deep Inside Earth The amount of time magma takes to cool determines the texture of an igneous rock.

Crystals Slow-cooling magma has time to form large mineral crystals. The resulting rock is coarse-grained.

Magma chamber Magma chambers deep inside Earth contain pools of molten rock. Magma cools slowly in large chambers such as this.

174 Unit 3 Minerals and Rocks

Extrusive Igneous Rock

Igneous rock that forms when lava erupts, or extrudes, onto Earth's surface is called *extrusive igneous rock.* Extrusive igneous rock is common around the sides and bases of volcanoes. Lava cools very quickly at Earth's surface. So, there is very little time for crystal formation. Because there is little time for crystals to form, extrusive rocks are made up of very small crystals and have a fine-grained texture. Obsidian (ahb•SID•ee•uhn) is an extrusive rock that cools so rapidly that no crystals form. Obsidian looks glassy, so it is often called *volcanic glass.* Other common extrusive igneous rocks are basalt and andesite.

Lava flows form when lava erupts from a volcano. The photo above shows an active lava flow. Sometimes lava erupts and flows from long cracks in Earth's crust called *fissures.* It also flows on the ocean floor at places where tension is causing Earth's crust to pull apart.

Active Reading **9 Explain** How does the rate at which magma cools affect the texture of igneous rock?

Near or at Earth's Surface Fine-grained igneous rock forms as lava cools quickly at Earth's surface.

Basalt is an example of extrusive igneous rock.

10 Compare Use the Venn diagram to compare and contrast intrusive igneous rock and extrusive igneous rock.

Lesson 3 Three Classes of Rock 175

Answers

8. Diorite has crystals that I can see without having to use a hand lens. So, diorite has a coarse-grained texture, which shows that it cooled beneath Earth's surface surrounded by other rock.
9. The less time that magma has to cool, the smaller the crystals will grow. The resulting rock will be fine-grained.
10. Intrusive Igneous Rock: forms within Earth's crust; crystal growth is slow; coarse-grained texture; Both: form when molten rock (either magma or lava) cools and solidifies; Extrusive Igneous Rock: forms at or near Earth's surface; crystal growth is rapid; fine-grained texture

Learning Alert

Types of Magma Students may think all magmas and lavas are the same. Point out that they have different compositions. For example, a magma with at least 65% silica that cools underground may form granite. A magma with 45-55% silica and high in iron, magnesium, and calcium, may form basalt after erupting as lava and cooling.

Interpreting Visuals

Direct students to study the image of the magma chamber, which is slowly cooling and forming large crystals. Ask: What would happen if this magma chamber cooled more quickly. Sample answer: The mineral crystals would be smaller since they would have less time to form.

Formative Assessment

Ask: Explain how intrusive igneous rock forms. Sample answer: Magma cools slowly in large magma chambers and has time to form large mineral crystals. This creates coarse-grained rock. **Ask:** How does extrusive igneous rock form? Sample answer: Lava either erupts from a volcano or flows from fissures. It cools quickly, so crystals have very little time to form. The rock that forms is fine grained.

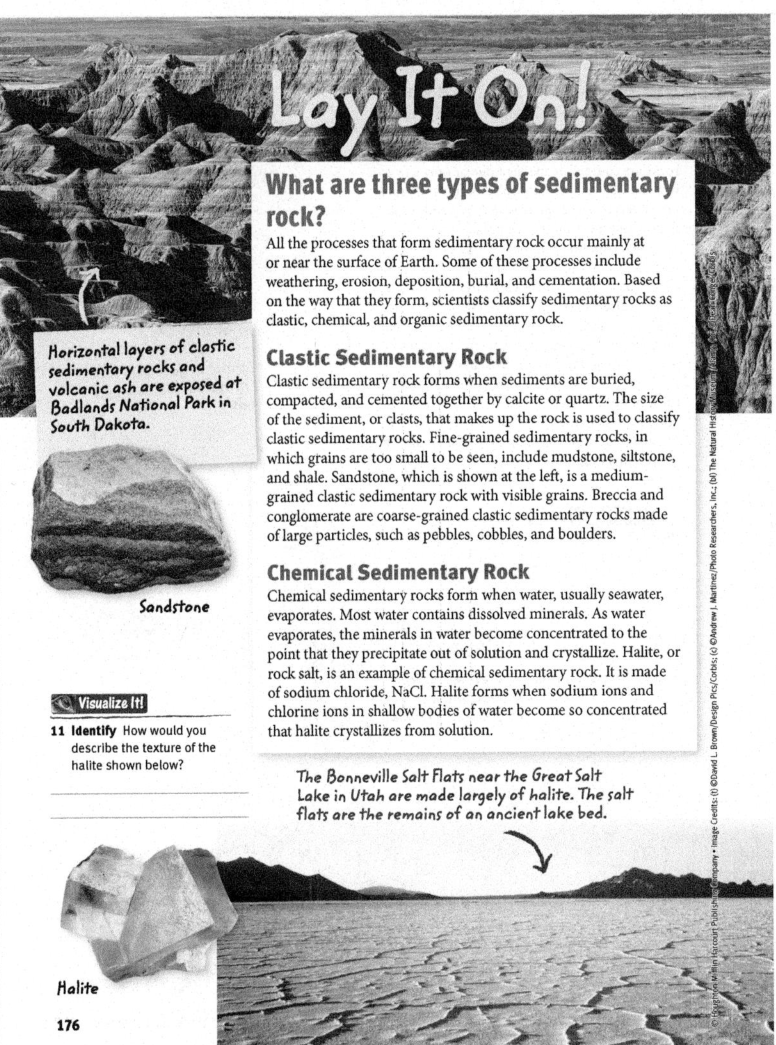

Lay It On!

What are three types of sedimentary rock?

All the processes that form sedimentary rock occur mainly at or near the surface of Earth. Some of these processes include weathering, erosion, deposition, burial, and cementation. Based on the way that they form, scientists classify sedimentary rocks as clastic, chemical, and organic sedimentary rock.

Clastic Sedimentary Rock

Clastic sedimentary rock forms when sediments are buried, compacted, and cemented together by calcite or quartz. The size of the sediment, or clasts, that makes up the rock is used to classify clastic sedimentary rocks. Fine-grained sedimentary rocks, in which grains are too small to be seen, include mudstone, siltstone, and shale. Sandstone, which is shown at the left, is a medium-grained clastic sedimentary rock with visible grains. Breccia and conglomerate are coarse-grained clastic sedimentary rocks made of large particles, such as pebbles, cobbles, and boulders.

Chemical Sedimentary Rock

Chemical sedimentary rocks form when water, usually seawater, evaporates. Most water contains dissolved minerals. As water evaporates, the minerals in water become concentrated to the point that they precipitate out of solution and crystallize. Halite, or rock salt, is an example of chemical sedimentary rock. It is made of sodium chloride, NaCl. Halite forms when sodium ions and chlorine ions in shallow bodies of water become so concentrated that halite crystallizes from solution.

Horizontal layers of clastic sedimentary rocks and volcanic ash are exposed at Badlands National Park in South Dakota.

Sandstone

Visualize It!

11 Identify How would you describe the texture of the halite shown below?

The Bonneville Salt Flats near the Great Salt Lake in Utah are made largely of halite. The salt flats are the remains of an ancient lake bed.

Halite

176

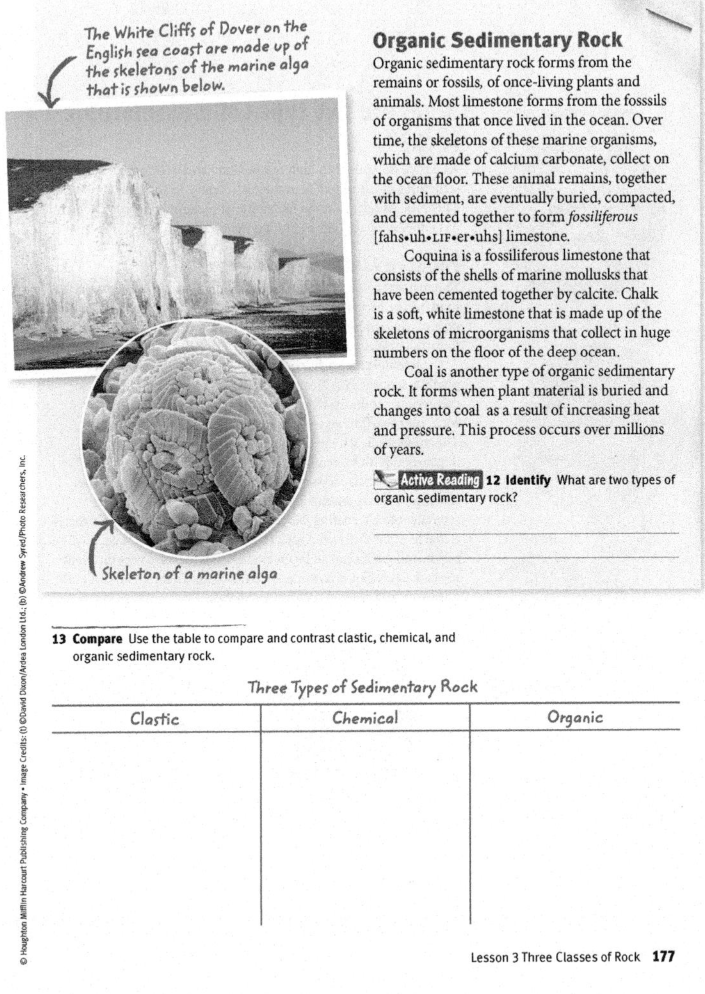

The White Cliffs of Dover on the English sea coast are made up of the skeletons of the marine alga that is shown below.

Skeleton of a marine alga

Organic Sedimentary Rock

Organic sedimentary rock forms from the remains or fossils, of once-living plants and animals. Most limestone forms from the fosssils of organisms that once lived in the ocean. Over time, the skeletons of these marine organisms, which are made of calcium carbonate, collect on the ocean floor. These animal remains, together with sediment, are eventually buried, compacted, and cemented together to form *fossiliferous* [fahs•uh•LIF•er•uhs] limestone.

Coquina is a fossiliferous limestone that consists of the shells of marine mollusks that have been cemented together by calcite. Chalk is a soft, white limestone that is made up of the skeletons of microorganisms that collect in huge numbers on the floor of the deep ocean.

Coal is another type of organic sedimentary rock. It forms when plant material is buried and changes into coal as a result of increasing heat and pressure. This process occurs over millions of years.

Active Reading 12 Identify What are two types of organic sedimentary rock?

13 Compare Use the table to compare and contrast clastic, chemical, and organic sedimentary rock.

Three Types of Sedimentary Rock

Clastic	Chemical	Organic

Lesson 3 Three Classes of Rock 177

Student Pages 174–177

Answers

11. It has a crystalline or medium- to coarse- grained texture.
12. Sample answer: chalk and coal
13. Clastic: forms from sediment, or clasts, cemented together; classified as fine-grained, medium-grained, and coarse-grained; Chemical: forms from solutions of dissolved minerals; Organic: forms from the remains of animals or plants

Interpreting Visuals

Have students look at the photographs of halite and sandstone and compare them. **Ask:** How are they different in appearance? Sample answer: The halite is in the form of large, visible crystals, giving it a crystalline texture. It has defined planes which look smooth. The sandstone appears to be made of many grains of sand cemented together. It looks like it has a coarse-grained texture. **Ask:** Ask: What might this tell you about the rocks? Sample answer: That they formed in different ways and have different compositions.

Building Reading Skills

Context Clues: Inference Students are to define the term *organic* based on the context surrounding it. **Ask:** What words give you the best clue as to the meaning of *organic*? Sample answer: I think the phrase "from the remains or fossils of once-living plants and animals" gives the best clue; *organic* has to do with living things, both plant and animal.

Probing Questions GUIDED Inquiry

Analyzing Ask: What role do streams play in the formation of sedimentary rock? Sample answer: Streams erode rock into sediments, then transport and deposit it. It accumulates and becomes buried and cemented. Over time, these processes form sedimentary rock.

The Heat Is On!

Sedimentary shale

Slate

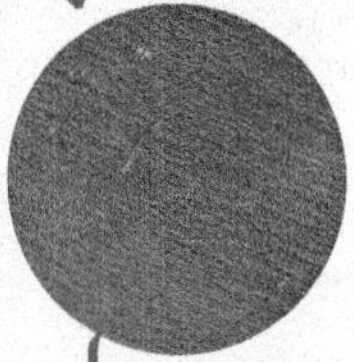

Phyllite

When shale is exposed to increasing temperature and pressure, different foliated metamorphic rocks form.

What are two types of metamorphic rock?

As a rock is exposed to high temperature and pressure, the crystal structures of the minerals in the rock change to form new minerals. This process results in the formation of metamorphic rock, which has either a foliated texture or a nonfoliated texture.

Foliated Metamorphic Rock

The metamorphic process in which mineral grains are arranged in planes or bands is called *foliation* (foh•lee•AY•shuhn). Foliation occurs when pressure causes the mineral grains in a rock to realign to form parallel bands.

Metamorphic rocks with a foliated texture include slate, phyllite, schist (SHIST), and gneiss (NYS). Slate and phyllite are commonly produced when shale, a fine-grained sedimentary rock, is exposed to an increase in temperature and pressure. The minerals in slate and phyllite are squeezed into flat, sheet-like layers. With increasing temperature and pressure, phyllite may become schist, a coarse-grained foliated rock. With further increases in temperature and pressure, the minerals in schist separate into alternating bands of light and dark minerals. Gneiss is a coarse-grained, foliated rock that forms from schist. Slate, phyllite, schist, and gneiss can all begin as shale, but they are very different rocks. Each rock forms under a certain range of temperatures and pressures, and contains different minerals.

Schist

Gneiss

14 Describe What happens to the minerals as gneiss forms from schist?

Nonfoliated Metamorphic Rock

Metamorphic rocks that do not have mineral grains that are aligned in planes or bands are called *nonfoliated*. Nonfoliated metamorphic rocks are commonly made of one or only a few minerals. During metamorphism, mineral grains or crystals may change size or shape, and some may change into another mineral.

Two common nonfoliated metamorphic rocks are quartzite and marble. Quartzite forms when quartz sandstone is exposed to high temperature and pressure. This causes the sand grains to grow larger and the spaces between the sand grains disappear. For that reason, quartzite is very hard and not easily broken down.

When limestone undergoes metamorphism, the limestone becomes marble. During the process of metamorphism, the calcite crystals in the marble grow larger than the calcite grains in the original limestone.

The mineral grains in quartzite (top) and crystals in marble (bottom) do not form bands.

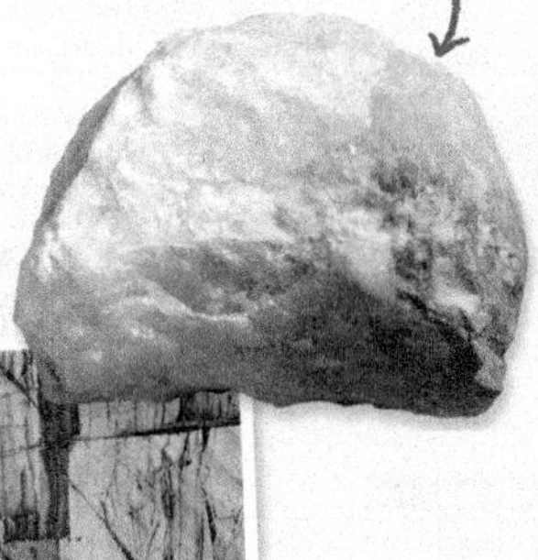

Active Reading **15 Apply** What are two characteristics of nonfoliated metamorphic rocks?

Marble is a nonfoliated metamorphic rock that forms when limestone is metamorphosed. Marble is used to build monuments and statues.

Think Outside the Book | Inquiry

16 Apply With a classmate, discuss how different types of rocks can be used as building or construction materials.

Answers

14. The minerals recrystallize and separate into distinct bands of dark and light minerals.
15. Nonfoliated rocks do not have bands or aligned mineral planes.
16. Students' answers should demonstrate knowledge of the characteristics of certain rock types used in building and construction, and how these characteristics are related to the rock's formation. For example, marble is compact due to metamorphism, but soft enough to carve detailed statues or monuments.

Formative Assessment

Ask: What do scientists base their classifications of rock on? They classify rock by composition and texture, which give clues as to how it was formed. **Ask:** Why does grain size vary so much in sedimentary rock? because the texture and size of the original material that was cemented together to form the rock varies; for example, larger pebbles or microscopic particles **Ask:** What determines grain size in metamorphic rock? the original rock type and the temperature and pressure it is subjected to **Ask:** What is the difference between foliated and nonfoliated metamorphic rock? In foliated metamorphic rock, minerals are arranged in bands or planes. In nonfoliated metamorphic rock, they are not. **Ask:** What characteristics do most nonfoliated metamorphic rocks have in common? The original rock that was changed into metamorphic rock was made mostly of one type of mineral and contained smaller mineral grains or crystals.

Building Reading Skills

Concept Map Learning about the different types of rocks and how they can form can be confusing for some students. Have your students create concept maps for each of the three main classes of rocks. Direct students to write ***igneous*** in the center of one concept map, ***sedimentary*** in another, and ***metamorphic*** in a third. Encourage them to fill in details about each type of rock as they read.

Visual Summary

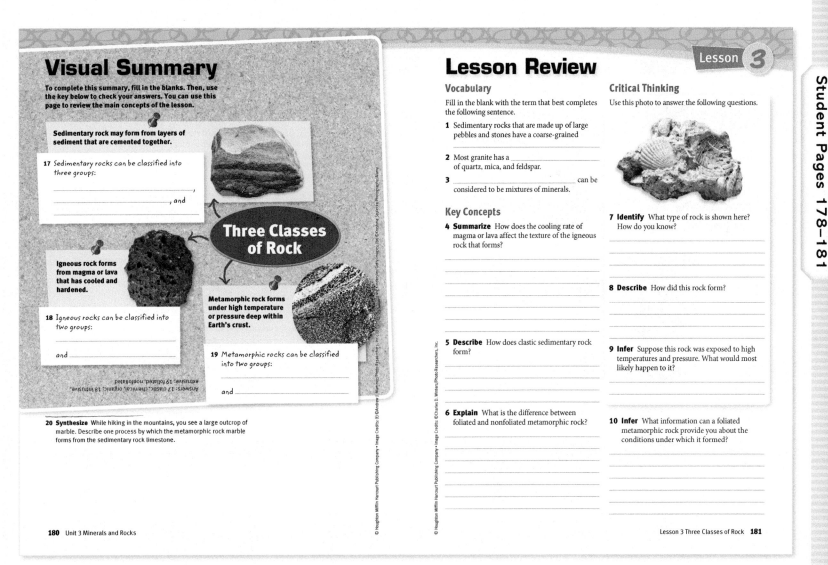

To complete this summary, fill in the blanks. Then, use the key below to check your answers. You can use this page to review the main concepts of the lesson.

Three Classes of Rock

Sedimentary rock may form from layers of sediment that are cemented together.

17 Sedimentary rocks can be classified into three groups: ________, ________, and ________

Igneous rock forms from magma or lava that has cooled and hardened.

18 Igneous rocks can be classified into two groups: ________ and ________

Metamorphic rock forms under high temperature or pressure deep within Earth's crust.

19 Metamorphic rocks can be classified into two groups: ________ and ________

Answers: 17 clastic, chemical, organic; 18 intrusive, extrusive; 19 foliated, nonfoliated

20 **Synthesize** While hiking in the mountains, you see a large outcrop of marble. Describe one process by which the metamorphic rock marble forms from the sedimentary rock limestone.

Lesson Review

Lesson 3

Vocabulary

Fill in the blank with the term that best completes the following sentence.

1 Sedimentary rocks that are made up of large pebbles and stones have a coarse-grained ________

2 Most granite has a ________ of quartz, mica, and feldspar.

3 ________ can be considered to be mixtures of minerals.

Key Concepts

4 **Summarize** How does the cooling rate of magma or lava affect the texture of the igneous rock that forms?

5 **Describe** How does clastic sedimentary rock form?

6 **Explain** What is the difference between foliated and nonfoliated metamorphic rock?

Critical Thinking

Use this photo to answer the following questions.

7 **Identify** What type of rock is shown here? How do you know?

8 **Describe** How did this rock form?

9 **Infer** Suppose this rock was exposed to high temperatures and pressure. What would most likely happen to it?

10 **Infer** What information can a foliated metamorphic rock provide you about the conditions under which it formed?

Visual Summary Answers

17. clastic, chemical, organic
18. intrusive, extrusive
19. foliated, nonfoliated
20. First, sediment and the remains of organisms had to build up in layers on the ocean floor. Then, over time these layers were buried and compressed, and then hardened into limestone. The limestone was buried deeper within Earth's crust, where high temperatures or pressure caused the limestone to change into the marble, a nonfoliated metamorphic rock.

Lesson Review Answers

1. texture
2. composition
3. Rock
4. When magma cools slowly, crystals have a long time to form and can grow to a large size. The resulting rock has a coarse-grained texture. Lava on Earth's surface cools rapidly, so crystals have only a short time to grow. Therefore, the crystals are small. The resulting extrusive igneous rock has a fine-grained texture.
5. Clastic sedimentary rock forms when sediments that are buried are compacted and cemented together.
6. Foliated rocks have minerals that are arranged in layers or bands. In nonfoliated rocks there is no regular arrangement of the minerals.
7. Sample answer: It is an organic sedimentary rock. I can tell because it is made up of marine fossils.
8. Marine organisms died, and their remains built up in layers. Over time, these layers were buried and compressed, and then hardened to form fossiliferous limestone, an organic sedimentary rock.
9. The rock would most likely change into marble, a nonfoliated metamorphic rock.
10. A foliated metamorphic rock can provide some information about the composition of the rock that was metamorphosed and the pressure under which it metamorphosed.

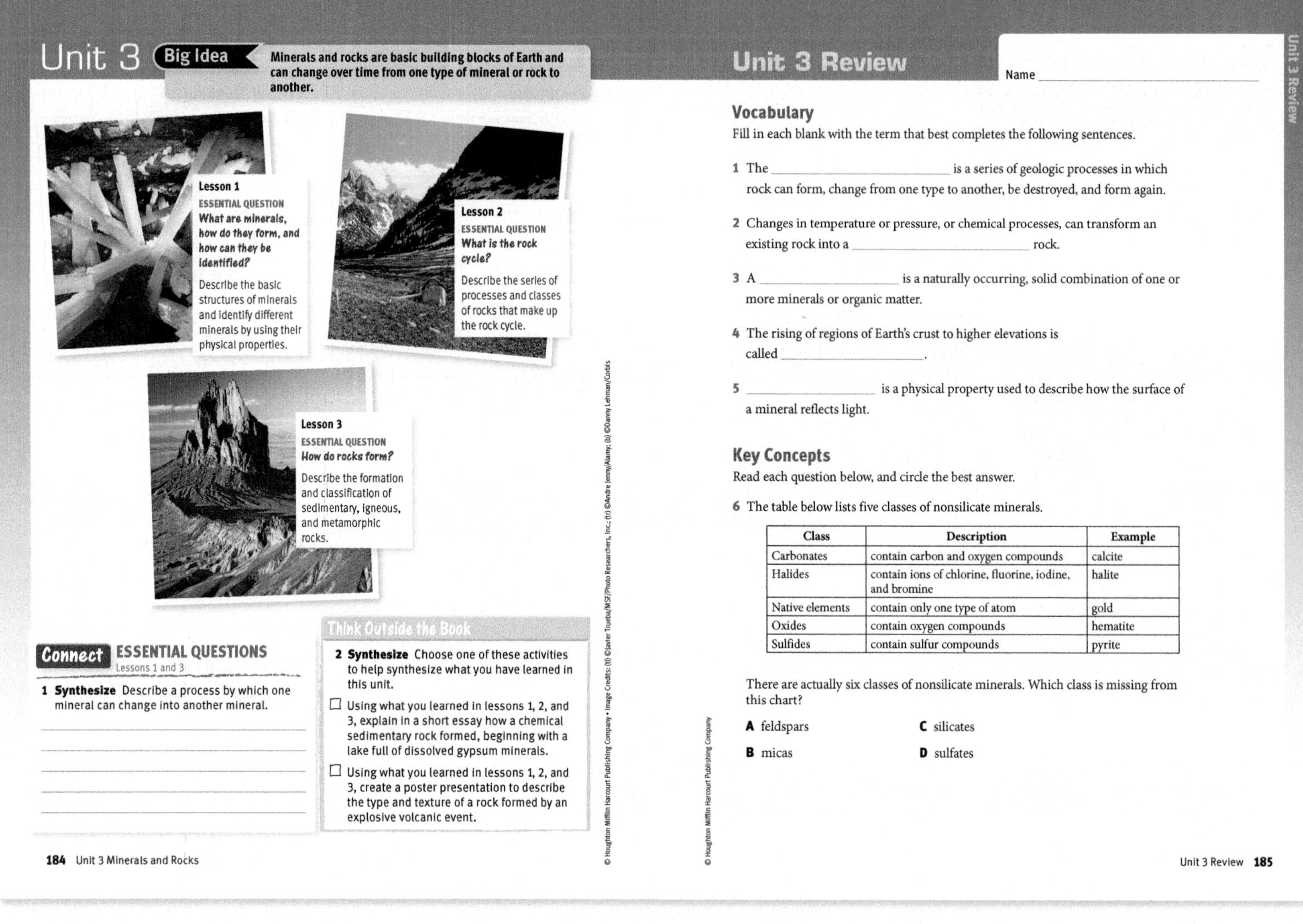

Unit 3 **Big Idea** Minerals and rocks are basic building blocks of Earth and can change over time from one type of mineral or rock to another.

Lesson 1
ESSENTIAL QUESTION
What are minerals, how do they form, and how can they be identified?
Describe the basic structures of minerals and identify different minerals by using their physical properties.

Lesson 2
ESSENTIAL QUESTION
What is the rock cycle?
Describe the series of processes and classes of rocks that make up the rock cycle.

Lesson 3
ESSENTIAL QUESTION
How do rocks form?
Describe the formation and classification of sedimentary, igneous, and metamorphic rocks.

Connect ESSENTIAL QUESTIONS
Lessons 1 and 3

1 **Synthesize** Describe a process by which one mineral can change into another mineral.

Think Outside the Book

2 **Synthesize** Choose one of these activities to help synthesize what you have learned in this unit.

☐ Using what you learned in lessons 1, 2, and 3, explain in a short essay how a chemical sedimentary rock formed, beginning with a lake full of dissolved gypsum minerals.

☐ Using what you learned in lessons 1, 2, and 3, create a poster presentation to describe the type and texture of a rock formed by an explosive volcanic event.

© Houghton Mifflin Harcourt Publishing Company • Image Credits: (tl) ©Javier Trueba/MSF/Photo Researchers, Inc.; (tr) ©Andre Jenny/Alamy; (b) ©Danny Lehman/Corbis

184 Unit 3 Minerals and Rocks

Unit 3 Review Name ____________

Unit 3 Review

Vocabulary
Fill in each blank with the term that best completes the following sentences.

1 The ____________ is a series of geologic processes in which rock can form, change from one type to another, be destroyed, and form again.

2 Changes in temperature or pressure, or chemical processes, can transform an existing rock into a ____________ rock.

3 A ____________ is a naturally occurring, solid combination of one or more minerals or organic matter.

4 The rising of regions of Earth's crust to higher elevations is called ____________.

5 ____________ is a physical property used to describe how the surface of a mineral reflects light.

Key Concepts
Read each question below, and circle the best answer.

6 The table below lists five classes of nonsilicate minerals.

Class	Description	Example
Carbonates	contain carbon and oxygen compounds	calcite
Halides	contain ions of chlorine, fluorine, iodine, and bromine	halite
Native elements	contain only one type of atom	gold
Oxides	contain oxygen compounds	hematite
Sulfides	contain sulfur compounds	pyrite

There are actually six classes of nonsilicate minerals. Which class is missing from this chart?

A feldspars **C** silicates

B micas **D** sulfates

© Houghton Mifflin Harcourt Publishing Company

Unit 3 Review 185

Unit Summary Answers

1. One mineral can be changed into another by the process of metamorphism. As a rock is exposed to high temperature and pressure, the crystal structures of the minerals in the rock change to form new minerals.
2. Option 1: Chemical sedimentary rock forms when dissolved minerals come out of solution as water evaporates. A large body of water containing dissolved gypsum minerals evaporated over time and the gypsum came out of solution, depositing layer after layer until it completely dried up.

   Option 2: Rock from any volcanic eruption, explosive or not, is an extrusive igneous rock. Since the lava cooled quickly at Earth's surface, it has very small crystals and a fine-grained texture. If the lava cooled very quickly, no crystals formed at all, giving the rock a glassy texture (obsidian, for example).

Unit Review **Response to Intervention**

A Quick Grading Chart follows the Answers. See the Assessment Guide for more detail about correct and incorrect answer choices. Refer back to the Lesson Planning pages for activities and assignments that can be used as remediation for students who answer questions incorrectly.

Answers

1. rock cycle Rocks may follow various pathways in the rock cycle. (Lesson 2)
2. metamorphic Metamorphic rocks are formed from any of the three main types of rocks due to a change in pressure and/or temperature or chemical processes. (Lesson 3)
3. rock There are three major classes of rock: sedimentary, igneous and metamorphic. (Lesson 2)
4. uplift Uplift is the rising of Earth's crust, subsidence is the sinking of regions of Earth's crust. (Lesson 2)

Unit 3 Review continued

Name ______________________

7 Granite can form when magma cools within Earth. Basalt can form when lava cools on Earth's surface. What do granite and basalt have in common?

A They are igneous.

B They are old.

C They are fossils.

D They are intrusive.

8 A student is trying to identify a mineral in science class.

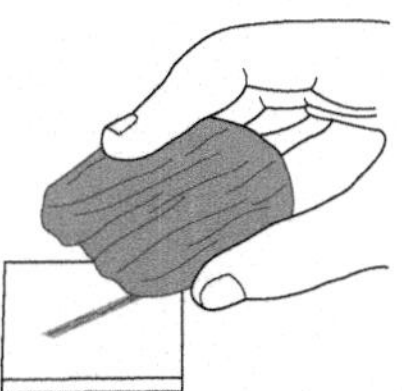

What property of the mineral is the student testing?

A cleavage **C** luster

B color **D** streak

9 Which one of the following statements about elements, atoms, and compounds is not true?

A Elements consist of one type of atom and can combine to form compounds.

B Compounds are smaller than atoms.

C Elements and compounds form the basis of all materials on Earth.

D Atoms cannot be broken down into smaller substances.

10 Which of the following best describes how sedimentary rock forms?

A Molten rock beneath the surface of Earth cools and becomes solid.

B Layers of sediment become compressed over time to form rock.

C Chemical processes or changes in pressure or temperature change a rock.

D Molten rock reaches the surface and cools to become solid rock.

11 Study the diagram below.

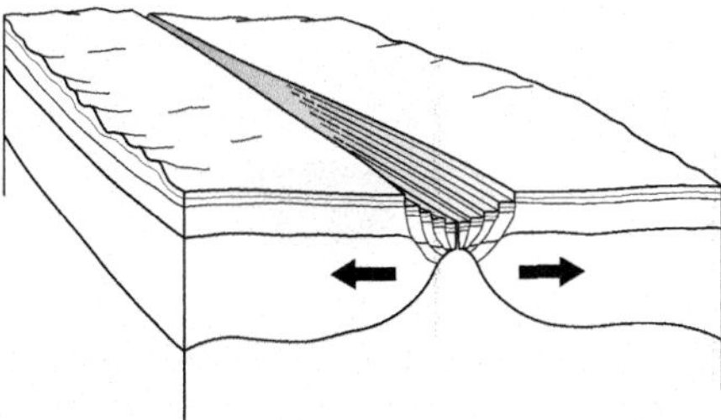

What process is occurring in this image?

A Two tectonic plates are moving toward each other, creating a syncline.

B Two tectonic plates are pulling away from each other, creating a rift zone.

C Two tectonic plates are moving toward each other, creating an anticline.

D Two tectonic plates are moving away from each other, creating a new mountain range.

12 Over time, repeated temperature changes can cause a rock to break down into smaller pieces. What is this an example of?

A subsidence **C** deposition

B weathering **D** erosion

Critical Thinking

Answer the following questions in the space provided.

13 You are standing by a cliff far away from the ocean. You see a sedimentary layer with shells in it. You are told the shells are from oceanic organisms. How do you think this layer formed?

____

____

____

____

Answers *(continued)*

5. Luster Luster is a physical property used to identify minerals. Examples of describing luster include things such as metallic, nonmetallic, and pearly. (Lesson 1)
6. Answer D is correct because sulfates contain compounds of sulfur and oxygen and so are nonsilicate minerals. (Lesson 1)
7. Answer A is correct because granite and basalt are both igneous rock; both form when molten rock cools and forms a solid. (Lesson 3)
8. Answer D is correct because streak is the color of a mineral in a powdered form. Streak is observed by rubbing the mineral across a porcelain plate, called a streak plate. (Lesson 1)
9. Answer B is correct because compounds are not smaller than atoms. (Lesson 1)
10. Answer B is correct because most sedimentary rock is formed when materials are deposited in layers and compacted over time due to accumulating pressure. (Lessons 2, 3)
11. Answer B is correct because a rift zone is an area where two plates move away from each other and form a landform such as the one shown in the diagram. (Lesson 2)
12. Answer B is correct because weathering, such as freeze-thaw, causes rocks to break down. (Lesson 2)
13. Key Elements:
    - The area was covered by an inland sea or ocean. Shells and sediment accumulated over time. The sea either retreated or evaporated. The shells and sediment were compacted and cemented, eventually forming this sedimentary rock unit. (Lesson 3)
14. Key Elements:
    - Sedimentary and igneous rock must undergo chemical changes due to heat (for example, contact metamorphism) or heat and pressure (for example, burial) to turn into metamorphic rock.
    - This could occur by contact metamorphism, where a magma body heats the rock around it and changes this rock.

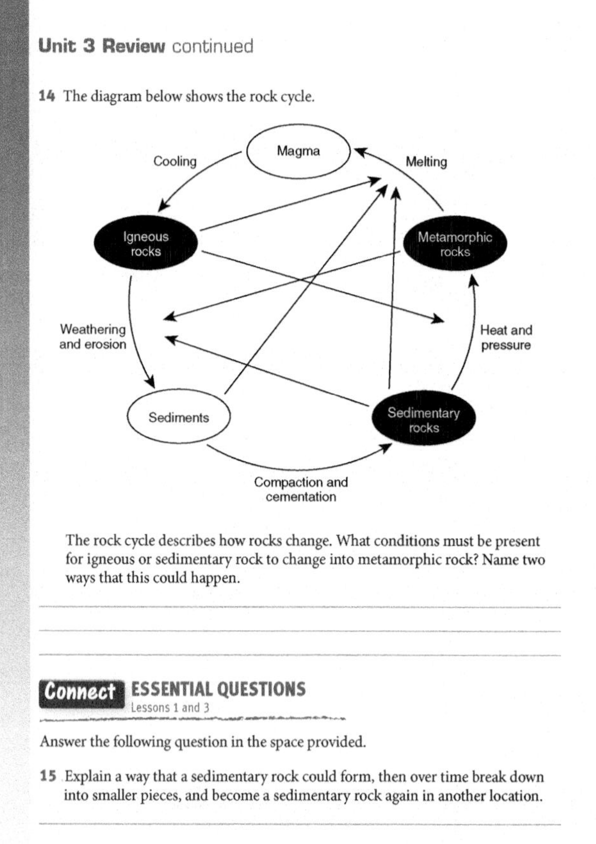

Unit 3 Review continued

14 The diagram below shows the rock cycle.

The rock cycle describes how rocks change. What conditions must be present for igneous or sedimentary rock to change into metamorphic rock? Name two ways that this could happen.

Connect ESSENTIAL QUESTIONS
Lessons 1 and 3

Answer the following question in the space provided.

15 Explain a way that a sedimentary rock could form, then over time break down into smaller pieces, and become a sedimentary rock again in another location.

188 Unit 3 Minerals and Rocks

Answers *(continued)*

- It could occur by repeated deposition on top of a rock unit, burying it over time. This layer experiences heat and pressure of varying degrees throughout this process, slowly changing into a metamorphic rock. (Lessons 2, 3)

15. Key Elements:

- Sedimentary rocks form when rock is broken down into smaller pieces by the process of weathering.
- This sedimentary rock is weathered and eroded by wind, precipitation, and temperature changes over a very long period of time.
- The sediment can be eroded and transported to another location by a river or glacier (accept any reasonable), where it is eventually deposited.
- This deposit is compacted over time due to accumulating pressure of sediments deposited on top of it. The layers of sediment can become sedimentary rocks again if subjected to compression. (Lessons 1, 3)

Quick Grading Chart

Use the chart below for quick test grading. The lesson correlations can help you target reteaching for missed items.

Item	Answer	Cognitive Complexity	Lesson
1.	—	Low	2
2.	—	Low	3
3.	—	Low	2
4.	—	Low	2
5.	—	Low	1
6.	D	High	1
7.	A	Moderate	3
8.	D	Moderate	1
9.	B	Moderate	1
10.	B	Moderate	2, 3
11.	B	Moderate	2
12.	B	Moderate	2
13.	—	Moderate	3
14.	—	Moderate	2, 3
15.	—	Moderate	1, 3

Cognitive Complexity refers to the demand on thinking associated with an item, and may vary with the answer choices, the number of steps required to arrive at an answer, and other factors, but not the ability level of the student.

UNIT 4 The Restless Earth

The Big Idea and Essential Questions

This Unit was designed to focus on this Big Idea and Essential Questions.

Big Idea **The movement of tectonic plates accounts for important features of Earth's surface and major geologic events.**

Lesson	ESSENTIAL QUESTION	Student Mastery	Professional Development	Lesson Overview
LESSON 1 Earth's Layers	*What are Earth's layers?*	To identify Earth's compositional and physical layers and describe their properties	Content Refresher, TE p. 236	TE p. 244
LESSON 2 Plate Tectonics	*What is plate tectonics?*	To explain the theory of plate tectonics and plate movement, and identify the geologic events caused by this	Content Refresher, TE p. 237	TE p. 256
LESSON 3 Mountain Building	*How do mountains form?*	To describe how the movement of Earth's tectonic plates causes mountain building	Content Refresher, TE p. 238	TE p. 274
LESSON 4 Volcanoes	*How do volcanoes change Earth's surface?*	To describe various kinds of volcanoes and eruptions, including where they occur and how they change Earth's surface	Content Refresher, TE p. 239	TE p. 288
LESSON 5 Earthquakes	*Why do earthquakes happen?*	To describe the causes of earthquakes and identify where earthquakes happen	Content Refresher, TE p. 240	TE p. 302
LESSON 6 Measuring Earthquake Waves	*How are seismic waves used to study earthquakes?*	To understand how seismic waves are useful in determining the strength, location, and effects of an earthquake	Content Refresher, TE p. 241	TE p. 320

Science Background

Use the keywords at right to access

- Professional Development from **The NSTA Learning Center**
- **SciLinks** for additional online content appropriate for students and teachers

Keywords
earthquakes
mountains
plate tectonics
volcanoes

Options for Instruction

Two parallel paths provide coverage of the Essential Questions, with a strong **Inquiry** strand woven into each. Follow the **Print Path,** the **Digital Path,** or your customized combination of print, digital, and inquiry.

	LESSON 1 Earth's Layers	LESSON 2 Plate Tectonics	LESSON 3 Mountain Building
Essential Questions	***What are Earth's layers?***	***What is plate tectonics?***	***How do mountains form?***
Key Topics	• Earth's Compositional Layers • Earth's Physical Layers	• Theory of Plate Tectonics • Tectonic Plates • Types of Plate Boundaries • Causes of Tectonic Plate Motion	• Deformation and Folding • Faulting • Mountains
Print Path	Teacher Edition pp. 244–255 Student Edition pp. 192–199	Teacher Edition pp. 256–270 Student Edition pp. 200–213	Teacher Edition pp. 274–286 Student Edition pp. 216–225
Inquiry Labs	Lab Manual **Quick Lab** Layers of Earth **Quick Lab** Ordering Earth's Layers **S.T.E.M. Lab** Models of Earth	Lab Manual **Quick Lab** Tectonic Ice Cubes **Exploration Lab** Seafloor Spreading Virtual Lab Plate Boundaries	Lab Manual **Quick Lab** What Happens When Objects Collide? **Quick Lab** Modeling Mountains **Quick Lab** Geologic Processes
Digital Path	Digital Path TS671030	Digital Path TS671040	Digital Path TS671050

LESSON 4 Volcanoes	LESSON 5 Earthquakes	LESSON 6 and UNIT 4 Unit Projects
How do volcanoes change Earth's surface?	***Why do earthquakes happen?***	*See the next page*
• Volcanoes • Volcanic Landforms • Where Volcanoes Form	• What Earthquakes Are and Why They Happen • Where Earthquakes Happen • Effects of Earthquakes	
Teacher Edition pp. 288–301 Student Edition pp. 226–237	Teacher Edition pp. 302–314 Student Edition pp. 238–247	**Unit Assessment** *See the next page*
Lab Manual **Quick Lab** Modeling an Explosive Eruption **Quick Lab** Volcano Mapping **Exploration Lab** Modeling Lava Viscosity	Lab Manual **Quick Lab** Modeling Strike-Slip Faults **Quick Lab** Earthquake Vibrations **Quick Lab** Elastic Rebound	
Digital Path TS671310	Digital Path TS671320	

Options for Instruction

Two parallel paths provide coverage of the Essential Questions, with a strong **Inquiry** strand woven into each. Follow the **Print Path,** the **Digital Path,** or your customized combination of print, digital, and inquiry.

	LESSON 6 Measuring Earthquake Waves	UNIT 4 Unit Projects
Essential Questions	***How are seismic waves used to study earthquakes?***	 Citizen Science Project Stable Structures Teacher Edition p. 243 Student Edition pp. 190–191
Key Topics	• The Causes of Earthquakes • Seismic Waves and Their Measurement • Earthquake Magnitude and Intensity • Factors Determining the Effects of Earthquakes	 Seismic Monitoring
  Print Path	Teacher Edition pp. 320–334 Student Edition pp. 252–265	
Inquiry Labs	Lab Manual **Quick Lab** Earthquakes and Buildings **S.T.E.M. Lab** Seismograph **Virtual Lab** How Can We Study Earthquakes?	
 Digital Path	Digital Path TS671325 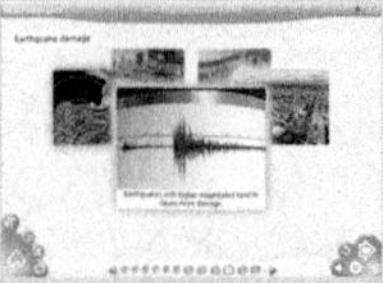	

Unit Assessment

Formative Assessment

Strategies RTI
Throughout TE

Lesson Reviews SE

Unit PreTest

Summative Assessment

Alternative Assessment
(1 per lesson) RTI

Lesson Quizzes

Unit Tests A and B

Unit Review RTI
(with answer remediation)

Practice Tests
(end of module)

Project-Based Assessment

See the Assessment Guide for quizzes and tests.

Go Online to edit and create quizzes and tests.

Response to Intervention

See RTI teacher support materials on p. PD6. 

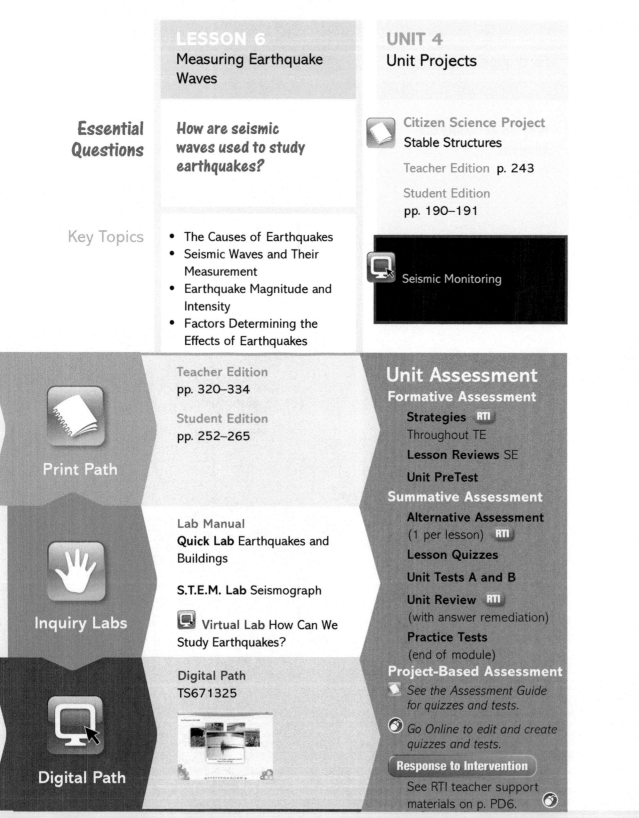

Teacher Notes

Differentiated Instruction

English Language Proficiency

Strategies for **English Language Learners (ELL)** are provided for each lesson, under the Explain tabs.

LESSON 1 *Avocado Earth,* TE p. 249

LESSON 2 *Taking Combination Notes,* TE p. 261

LESSON 3 *Previewing,* TE p. 279

LESSON 4 *Handy Vocabulary,* TE p. 293

LESSON 5 *Studying Faults,* TE p. 307

LESSON 6 *Whose Fault Is It?,* TE p. 325

Vocabulary strategies provided for all students can also be a particular help for ELL. Use different strategies for each lesson or choose one or two to use throughout the unit. Vocabulary strategies can be found under the Explain tab for each lesson (TE pp. 249, 261, 279, 293, 307, and 325).

Leveled Inquiry

Inquiry labs, activities, probing questions, and daily demos provide a range of inquiry levels. Preview them under the Engage and Explore tabs starting on TE pp. 246, 258, 276, 290, 304, and 322.

Levels of Inquiry

DIRECTED inquiry	**GUIDED** inquiry	**INDEPENDENT** inquiry
introduces inquiry skills within a structured framework.	develops inquiry skills within a supportive environment.	deepens inquiry skills with student-driven questions or procedures.

Each long lab has two inquiry options:

LESSON 1 **S.T.E.M. Lab** *Models of Earth*

LESSON 2 **Exploration Lab** *Seafloor Spreading*

LESSON 4 **Exploration Lab** *Modeling Lava Viscosity*

LESSON 6 **S.T.E.M. Lab** *Use a Seismograph to Determine the Amount of Energy in an Earthquake*

Go Digital!

thinkcentral.com

Digital Path

The Unit 4 Resource Gateway is your guide to all of the digital resources for this unit. To access the Gateway, visit thinkcentral.com.

Digital Interactive Lessons

Lesson 1 Earth's Layers TS671030

Lesson 2 Plate Tectonics TS671040

Lesson 3 Mountain Building TS671050

Lesson 4 Volcanoes TS671310

Lesson 5 Earthquakes TS671320

Lesson 6 Measuring Earthquake Waves TS671325

More Digital Resources

In addition to digital lessons, you will find the following digital resources for Unit 4:

Video-Based Project: Seismic Monitoring (previewed on TE p. 242)

People in Science: Estella Atekwana

Virtual Labs: Plate Boundaries (previewed on TE p. 259), How Can We Study Earthquakes? (previewed on TE p. 323)

RTI Response to Intervention

Response to Intervention (RTI) is a process for identifying and supporting students who are not making expected progress toward essential learning goals. The following *ScienceFusion* components can be used to provide strategic and intensive intervention.

Component	Location	Strategies and Benefits
STUDENT EDITION Active Reading prompts, Visualize It!, Think Outside the Book	**Throughout each lesson**	Student responses can be used as screening tools to assess whether intervention is needed.
TEACHER EDITION Formative Assessment, Probing Questions, Learning Alerts	**Throughout each lesson**	Opportunities are provided to assess and remediate student understanding of lesson concepts.
TEACHER EDITION Extend Science Concepts	**Reinforce and Review, TE pp. 250, 262, 280, 294, 308, 326** **Going Further, TE p. 250, 262, 280, 294, 308, 326**	Additional activities allow students to reinforce and extend their understanding of lesson concepts.
TEACHER EDITION Evaluate Student Mastery	**Formative Assessment, TE pp. 251, 263, 281, 295, 309, 327** **Alternative Assessment, TE pp. 251, 263, 281, 295, 309, 327**	These assessments allow for greater flexibility in assessing students with differing physical, mental, and language abilities as well as varying learning and communication modes.
TEACHER EDITION Unit Review Remediation	**Unit Review, TE pp. 336–339**	Includes reference back to Lesson Planning pages for remediation activities and assignments.
INTERACTIVE DIGITAL LESSONS and VIRTUAL LABS	**thinkcentral.com** **Unit 4 Gateway** **Lesson 1 TS671030** **Lesson 2 TS671040** **Lesson 3 TS671050** **Lesson 4 TS671310** **Lesson 5 TS671320** **Lesson 6 TS671325**	Lessons and labs make content accessible through simulations, animations, videos, audio, and integrated assessment. Useful for review and reteaching of lesson concepts.

Content Refresher

Lesson 1

Earth's Layers

ESSENTIAL QUESTION

What are Earth's layers?

1. Earth's Compositional Layers

Different parts of Earth have different compositions.

Earth can be divided into different types of layers. One type is based on the composition, or chemical makeup, of the layers. When Earth is divided compositionally, it has three layers: the crust, the mantle, and the core.

The crust is the thinnest layer. Continental crust is about 10–50 km thick, and oceanic crust 5–10 km thick. The crust is made up mostly of oxygen, silicon, and aluminum. The most abundant minerals found in the crust are silicates such as quartz.

The mantle is second of Earth's compositional layers. It is about 2,900 km thick and is made up mostly of oxygen, silicon, magnesium, and iron. The mantle is extremely hot—more than 1,000 °C. Although the mantle is solid (that is, made up of crystalline minerals), it is able to flow slowly like a fluid or plastic material because of its high temperature. Under certain circumstances, it can also undergo melting to supply magma to volcanoes.

At the center of Earth is the core. The core is made up of a liquid outer core and a solid inner core. The liquid of the outer core is predominantly iron and nickel, plus about 10% of light elements whose identity is not known, but could be oxygen, sulfur, silicon, or a mix of these. The inner core is nearly pure iron-nickel alloy. Together, the two layers of the core are about 3,430 km thick.

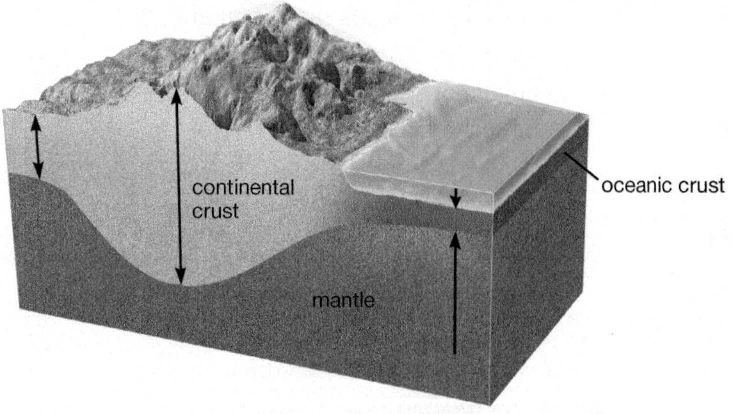

2. Earth's Physical Layers

Earth can be divided into five physical layers.

Earth's physical layers differ from its compositional layers in that the physical layers are grouped by distinct physical characteristics. The density of these layers increases inward from Earth's surface. Earth's five physical layers are the lithosphere, the asthenosphere, the mesosphere, the outer core, and the inner core.

The lithosphere ("rock sphere") is the outer layer of Earth, and is made up of the crust and the rigid, upper part of the mantle. Below the lithosphere is the asthenosphere ("weak sphere"). The lower part of the mantle is the mesosphere ("middle sphere"). Scientists have observed differences in the velocity of seismic waves as they cross from the asthenosphere into the mesosphere, and surmise that pressure and temperature differences, partial melting, or traces of water, and variations in chemistry, lead to these changes in velocity. The outer core and inner core are the final two physical layers.

Karen Cavalluzzi
Sunny Vale Middle School
Blue Springs, MO

Lesson 5 Earthquakes A great way to help your students make a connection between Earth Science and current events is to access the Earthquake Hazards Program provided by the U.S. Geological Survey. (This program can be found easily through any Internet search engine.) The Earthquake Hazards Program, through its web site, shows the data, intensity, and placement of earthquakes on a world map—as they happen!

Lesson 2

Plate Tectonics

ESSENTIAL QUESTION

What is plate tectonics?

1. Theory of Plate Tectonics

Geologic evidence supports plate tectonics.

Plate tectonics is the theory that Earth's lithosphere is broken into large plates that move atop the asthenosphere. A lot of evidence supports the theory of plate tectonics. Magnetic reversal patterns, which are mirrored on each side of mid-ocean ridges suggest that the magnetic south poles and magnetic north poles have "flipped" many times over Earth's history. The age of the sea floor, sea-floor spreading at mid-ocean ridges, and the formation of ocean trenches also support the theory.

Continent shape helped Alfred Wegener (VAY-guh-nuhr) develop his continental drift hypothesis, which stated that the continents were once a single landmass that broke apart and moved over the years. Wegener observed that the shapes of the continents appear complementary and resemble puzzle pieces that could fit together, most obviously South America and Africa. Evidence supporting the idea of a "supercontinent" called Pangaea suggests that the landmass broke apart about 200 million years ago, forming Laurasia to the north and Gondwana to the south. About 65 million years ago, the fragments of Pangaea separated, with the continents gradually taking the configuration we recognize today.

2. Tectonic Plates

Tectonic plates are in motion.

Tectonic plates fit together with the boundaries of neighboring plates. The continents and oceans rest on top of the moving tectonic plates. Some plates carry only continental crust and some carry only oceanic crust; others carry both types of crust.

3. Types of Plate Boundaries

Tectonic plates meet at plate boundaries.

Plates come together at convergent boundaries. At a convergent boundary of a continental plate and oceanic plate, the denser oceanic plate is forced down into the mantle in a process known as ***subduction***. Volcanic mountains form in areas where subduction occurs. When two continental plates collide, they fold, forming mountain ranges. At a collision of two oceanic plates, the denser plate subducts and volcanic islands form parallel to the plate boundary.

Plates move away from each other at divergent boundaries. At divergent boundaries, the asthenosphere rises to fill the space between diverging plates. The pressure release causes partial melting and the resulting magma rises, erupts onto Earth's surface as lava and then cools to form new crust.

Transform plate boundaries are locations where two plates slide past each other, parallel to Earth's surface. Transform faults also form beneath the ocean, perpendicular to the ridge where plates pull apart. These faults give the ridges a zig-zag pattern.

4. Causes of Tectonic Plate Motion

Processes drive tectonic plate motion.

Today, most scientists think that ***slab pull*** is the primary force that drives plate motion. As the edge of a subducting plate responds to gravity and sinks into the mantle, it pulls the rest of the plate along with it. This is called slab pull.

Another force that is used to explain plate motion is called ***ridge push***. Newly formed rock is hotter and less dense than older rock and therefore, rides higher on the asthenosphere than older, denser, cooler rock. As the new rock cools, it becomes denser and flows down the slope of the asthenosphere. This movement pushes the rest of the plate away from the mid-ocean ridge. This is called ridge push.

Scientists used to think that convection currents in Earth's mantle were the primary cause of plate motion. Today, most scientists think that these convection currents could not provide the force needed to explain plate motion and are therefore, much less important than slab pull and ridge push.

Content Refresher (continued)

Lesson 3

Mountain Building

ESSENTIAL QUESTION
How do mountains form?

1. Deformation and Folding

Rock undergoes constant stress from plate movement.

Stress from plate movement can cause changes in the shape of rocks. ***Deformation*** is the process in which rock changes shape due to stress. The largest component of stress on rock beneath Earth's surface is pressure due to the weight of overlying rock. This stress is equal on all sides of the rock and does not promote deformation. There can also be a component of differential stress that is not equal in all directions that does promote deformation. The differential component can take the form of horizontal stretching (tension), horizontal squeezing (compression), or side-to-side shearing. When enough stress is placed on rocks, they may bend or even break.

Folding occurs when rocks bend as a result of stress. Sediment that can be compacted into rock is normally deposited in horizontal layers. When scientists see a fold in a layer of rocks, they know a deformation has occurred. Folds are composed of two main parts: a hinge and two limbs. The limbs are the sloping sides of a fold. The hinge is where the two limbs meet.

The most common types of folds are anticlines and synclines. An ***anticline*** is a fold in which the oldest layers of rock are located in the center of the fold. In many anticlines, the rock limbs slope down from a hinge to form an arch. In contrast to an anticline, the youngest layers of a ***syncline*** are located at the center of the fold. The limbs generally slope upward from the hinge to form a U shape.

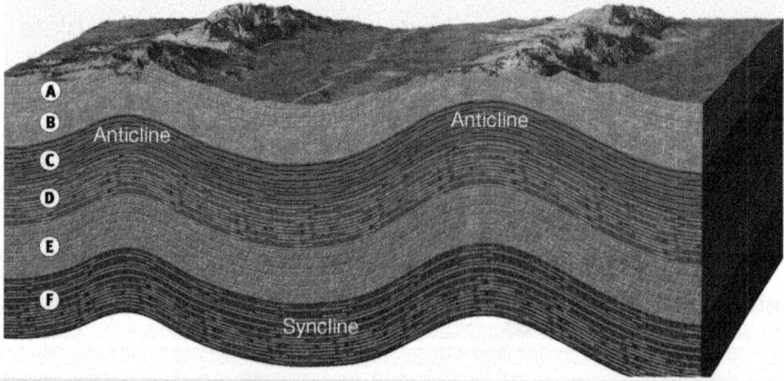

2. Faulting

Faulting is the breaking of rock.

Continued stress may eventually cause rock to break. When a rock breaks, a fracture forms. If the rock moves, a fault is formed. In a fault there is a hanging wall and a footwall. The hanging wall is the fault block that is above the fault plane, the nonvertical surface between the two moving pieces. The footwall is below the fault plane.

Faults are classified according to how the hanging wall and footwall move in relation to each other. In a normal fault, the hanging wall moves down in relation to the footwall. These faults commonly form because of tension.

In a reverse fault, the hanging wall moves up in relation to the footwall. This is the reverse of a normal fault. These faults commonly form because of compression.

In a strike-slip fault, two blocks move past each other horizontally. These faults commonly form where tectonic plates cause shear stress parallel to Earth's surface and are therefore common along transform boundaries.

3. Mountains

Three types of mountains form, either by forces from tectonic plate movement or by volcanism.

When rock layers are squeezed and pushed upwards, folded mountains form at convergent boundaries. Compression folds and then uplifts rock.

Fault-block mountains form when tension in Earth's surface causes the crust to break. Large blocks of crust drop downward in relation to other blocks.

Volcanic mountains may form when magma erupts onto the surface of Earth as lava. Many of Earth's volcanic mountains are located at convergent boundaries. In these regions, convergent margin processes generate magma within Earth, which may rise to the surface and erupt as lava, forming volcanic mountains. Volcanic mountains form both on land and on the ocean floor. The hot spot that formed the Hawaiian Islands is an example of volcanism that began on the ocean floor. Over time, many volcanic mountains increase in size due to recurring eruptions.

Lesson 4

Volcanoes

ESSENTIAL QUESTION

How do volcanoes change Earth's surface?

1. Volcanoes

Volcanoes form on land and under the sea.

A volcano is a vent or crack in Earth's surface where gas, ash, and melted rock, comes out of the ground. Magma is generated below Earth's surface by temperature, pressure, and exposure to substances such as water. These processes most often occur at tectonic plate boundaries. At divergent boundaries, magma rises and erupts onto Earth's surface as lava. Lava that flows smoothly and has a ropey surface is called ***pahoehoe***. Lava that has a blocky, jagged surface as it cools is called *aa*. Pahoehoe can transition into aa along a given lava flow. Lava that cools underwater takes on a distinctive puffy shape that gives it the name ***pillow lava***.

Besides lava, volcanoes produce solid fragments called ***pyroclastic material***—ash and rock. Round rocks greater than 64 mm across, called volcanic bombs, and large angular rocks, called blocks, can be thrown hundreds of kilometers. Most eruptions include lava and pyroclastic material. In particularly violent eruptions, pyroclastic materials and hot gases can combine to form ***pyroclastic flow***, a hot and deadly cloud that can move at speeds of more than 100 km/h. Pyroclastic flow buried the ancient city of Pompeii in 79 CE.

2. Volcanic Landforms

Volcanoes have different forms.

The shape of a volcanic landform depends largely on the qualities of the materials it expels. Lava of basaltic composition has low viscosity, and tends to flow a long way before it hardens. This type of lava forms a broad-based volcano called a ***shield volcano***. Mauna Loa in Hawaii is a shield volcano.

When magma and gases spray out of small vents, they form cinder cones. The magma cools and hardens in the air to form volcanic cinders that rain down to the ground, building up the cone. Cinder cones often form on the sides of larger volcanoes. An example is Capulin, a cinder cone located in New Mexico.

Composite volcanoes are made up of both hardened lava and volcanic ash. During nonexplosive eruptions, lava flows over and down the sides of the cone. When an explosion occurs, lava and volcanic ash are deposited around the vent. Then, eruptions quiet down again. These volcanoes can become very large. California's Mount Shasta is a composite volcano.

Sometimes, the magma chamber below a volcano empties, and the cone collapses. This leaves a huge basin called a *caldera*. Calderas may eventually fill with water to form lakes; Oregon's Crater Lake is a water-filled caldera.

3. Where Volcanoes Form

Most volcanoes form at the edge of tectonic plates.

Many volcanoes make up the Ring of Fire, which surrounds the Pacific plate. Some form in the middle of plates over hot spots. A ***mantle plume*** is a column of hot, rising mantle rock that undergoes partial melting as it nears the surface, even when it ascends under the thick lithosphere. A hot spot is a place where the material carried by the plume breaks through the crust to reach the surface. The Hawaiian Islands formed from a hot spot under the Pacific Plate.

Volcanic activity also occurs at divergent boundaries. Because the magma that forms at such a boundary is less dense than the surrounding rock, it rises and then cools to form new crust. This process occurs most frequently along mid-ocean ridges.

Content Refresher (continued)

Lesson 5

Earthquakes

Essential Question

Why do earthquakes happen?

1. What Earthquakes Are and Why They Happen

Energy released by rock under stress causes earthquakes.

Earthquakes are sudden tremors in Earth that occur because of a sudden release of energy as rocks move along a fault. Most earthquakes occur in areas near tectonic plate boundaries. Stress builds up on rock near the edges of the plates as the plates move in different directions, and the sudden release of stress results in an earthquake.

Seismic waves begin at the earthquake's focus, its point of origin within Earth. Directly above the focus, on Earth's surface, is the epicenter.

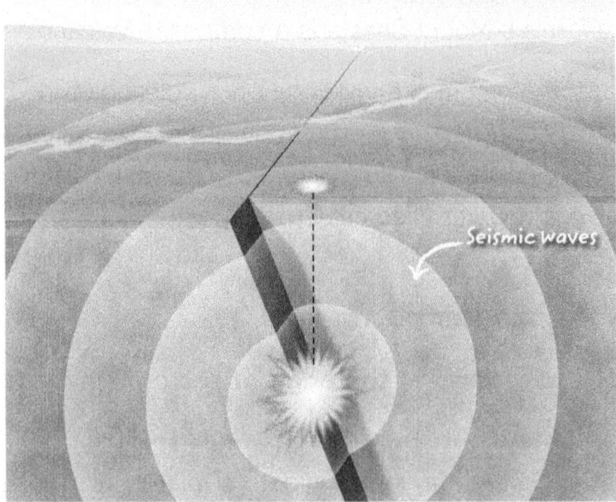

Deformation is the process by which rocks bend and break due to stress. For example, deformation takes place when rocks bend under stress but then return to their normal shape once the stress is released. Earthquakes happen when rocks break under stress. As the rock breaks, the stress on the rock is reduced and energy is released in the form of seismic waves. Once the energy is released, the new pieces of rock return to almost the same shape each piece had prior to the break, in a process called ***elastic rebound***.

2. Where Earthquakes Happen

Most earthquakes happen near tectonic plate boundaries.

As tectonic plates move, large forces alter Earth's crust. These forces cause faulting. Rocks along a fault or between plates may become locked as plates continue to move. These rocks will eventually slip and the potential energy that was stored up is released, causing an earthquake.

At divergent boundaries, Earth's crust may stretch out until it eventually breaks into fault blocks. The earthquakes associated with divergent plates are usually minor. The focal points tend to be shallow, usually occurring at less than 20 km below the surface.

At convergent boundaries, two plates may collide and form folded or fault-block mountains. On the other hand, one plate may subduct beneath another. In both cases, earthquakes may result due to the immense stress on these rocks. Subduction zone earthquakes can be major and very damaging. The focal points can be as deep at 700 km, although most are less than 400 km below the surface.

When two tectonic plates slide past each other, parallel to Earth's surface at transform boundaries, stress builds up on the rocks and they may become locked. This shear stress usually forms strike-slip faults.

3. Effects of Earthquakes

Earthquakes cause rapid changes to Earth's surface.

Earthquakes can cause a great deal of destruction to human-made structures and result in billions of dollars in damage each year. Scientists are looking for ways to make buildings more earthquake-proof and for ways to predict earthquakes.

When an earthquake happens under the ocean, it can generate a series of giant waves called a ***tsunami***. These deadly waves cause death and destruction as they wash away anything in their paths.

Lesson 6

Measuring Earthquake Waves

ESSENTIAL QUESTION

How are seismic waves used to study earthquakes?

1. The Causes of Earthquakes

Students will learn that earthquakes occur when rocks break or slip beneath Earth's surface.

Earthquakes occur every day in places all over the world, but most earthquakes are not strong enough for people to feel on Earth's surface.

Most earthquakes result from the division of Earth's lithosphere into giant slabs called ***tectonic plates***. These plates are constantly moving, albeit quite slowly. Their movement causes stress to build up in rocks along *faults*, which are breaks in the crust along which movement occurs. Faults are concentrated at or near plate boundaries. When the stress on the rock along a fault becomes too great, the rock breaks and moves suddenly. This sends *seismic waves* into the surrounding rock, which are felt on the surface as an earthquake.

2. Seismic Waves and Their Measurement

Students will learn that there are different types of seismic waves.

Seismic waves include two types of body waves, which are waves that travel through Earth's interior. P waves are the fastest waves, and are first to arrive at a given point on the surface. P waves can travel through any material. S waves travel through solids only. They arrive after P waves.

Surface waves, which include Love waves and Rayleigh waves, move only across Earth's surface. Surface waves are the slowest waves, yet they cause the most damage.

Seismic waves are measured with a seismometer. The lines from the pen or stylus show the seismic waves and the time they arrive. Scientists use the difference in the waves' arrival times to calculate the distance to the epicenter of the earthquake. By measuring the distance to the epicenter from three separate seismometers (a process called *triangulation*), scientists can determine the exact location of the epicenter.

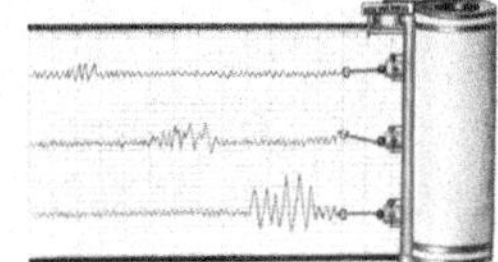

3. Earthquake Magnitude and Intensity

Students will learn that there are different scales used to measure earthquake magnitude and intensity.

The magnitude of an earthquake is a measure of the energy it releases. The Richter scale measures earthquake magnitude by the extent of ground shaking an earthquake causes.

The Moment Magnitude scale is a more accurate measurement of earthquake magnitude and reflects the strength and movement of the rocks that caused the earthquake.

The intensity of an earthquake is a measure of its effects on Earth's surface. The Modified Mercalli scale measures intensity. Unlike magnitude, intensity varies with distance from the epicenter.

4. Factors Determining the Effects of Earthquakes

Students will learn that four factors determine how much damage an earthquake causes.

Earthquakes cannot be predicted, nor can they be prevented. Yet scientists can predict how a severe earthquake will affect an area, and they can help people prepare for earthquakes.

In any area, the damage caused by an earthquake tends to increase with the earthquake's magnitude and the area's proximity to the epicenter. Geologic factors, such as loose soil and porous sediments, can increase earthquake damage due to a process called ***liquefaction***, which causes the ground to act like a liquid and to shift dramatically.

A variety of construction techniques can help buildings become more earthquake resistant. Many of these techniques involve electronic sensors and computerized control mechanisms.

Advance Planning

These activities may take extended time or special conditions.

Unit 4

Video-Based Project Seismic Monitoring, p. 242
multiple activities spanning several lessons

Project Stable Structures, p. 243
research and writing time

Graphic Organizers and Vocabulary pp. 249, 250, 261, 262, 279, 280, 293, 294, 307, 308, 325, 326
ongoing with reading

Lesson 1

S.T.E.M. Lab Models of Earth, p. 247
requires two 45-min periods; prepare illustration of Earth layers

Lesson 2

Activity Map Puzzle, p. 258
world map photocopies (2 per student)

Quick Lab Reconstructing Land Masses, p. 259
map of continents (1 per student)

Lesson 4

Quick Lab Modeling an Explosive Eruption, p. 291
conduct lab outdoors; gather materials in advance

Quick Lab Volcano Mapping, p. 291
world map photocopies (1 per group)

Differentiated Instruction (Basic) Volcanoes of the World, p. 293
world map photocopies (1 per student)

Lesson 5

Daily Demo Must Be Jelly, p. 305
prepare gelatin tray with magnet in advance

Lesson 6

S.T.E.M. Lab Use a Seismograph, p. 323
roll of adding machine paper (1 per group)

What Do You Think?

Have students describe some features of the surrounding landscape, such as mountains, valleys, or coastlines. Ask students to share ideas about how these features formed. Then have students look at the image of the volcano. **Ask:** How is this volcano causing the land to change? Sample answer: The volcano is putting lava on the outer surface of Earth, which will harden to form new layers on Earth's crust.

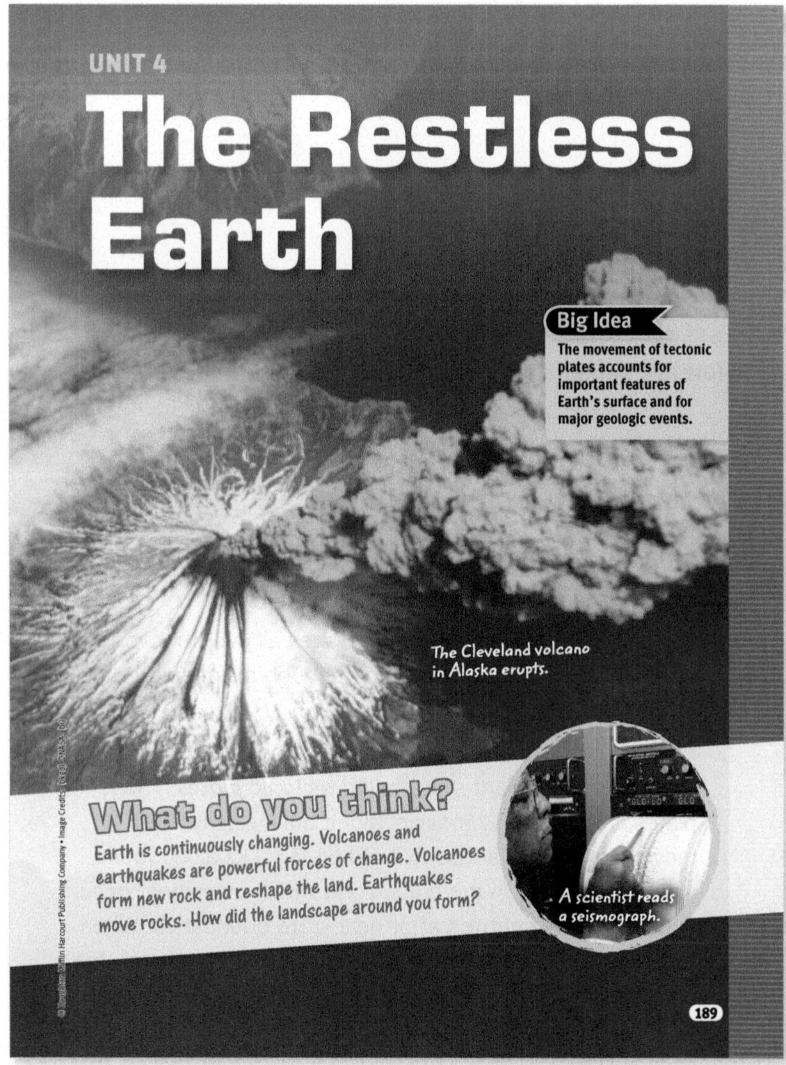

UNIT 4
The Restless Earth
Big Idea
The movement of tectonic plates accounts for important features of Earth's surface and for major geologic events.
The Cleveland volcano in Alaska erupts.
What do you think?
Earth is continuously changing. Volcanoes and earthquakes are powerful forces of change. Volcanoes form new rock and reshape the land. Earthquakes move rocks. How did the landscape around you form?
A scientist reads a seismograph.
189

Video-Based Project

Seismic Monitoring

Host Michael DiSpezio visits NOAA's Pacific Marine Environmental Laboratory in Seattle, WA, to explore the science and technology of seismic monitoring buoys and tsunami models.

Activities

See the print resources that accompany this video-based project for student activities.

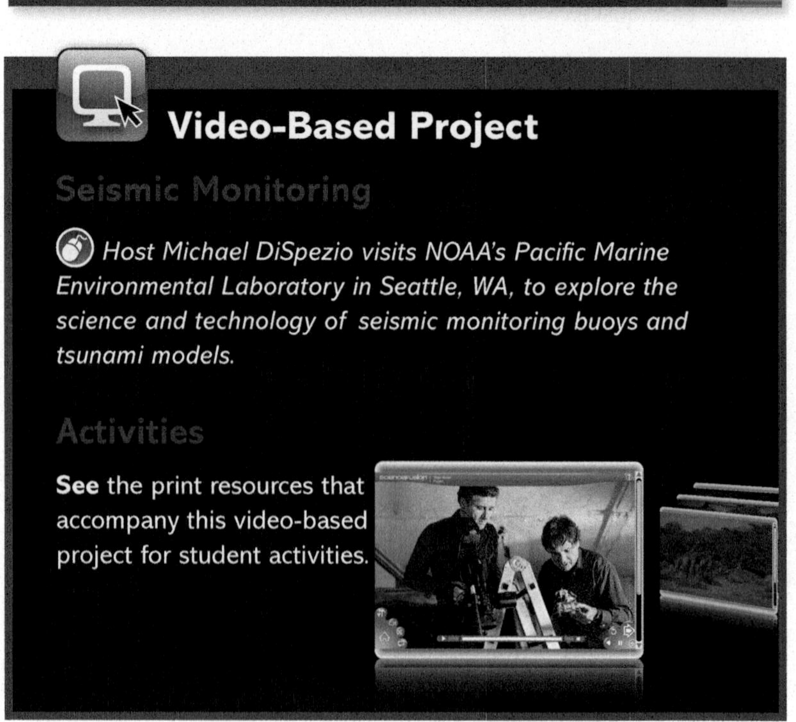

Unit 4
The Restless Earth

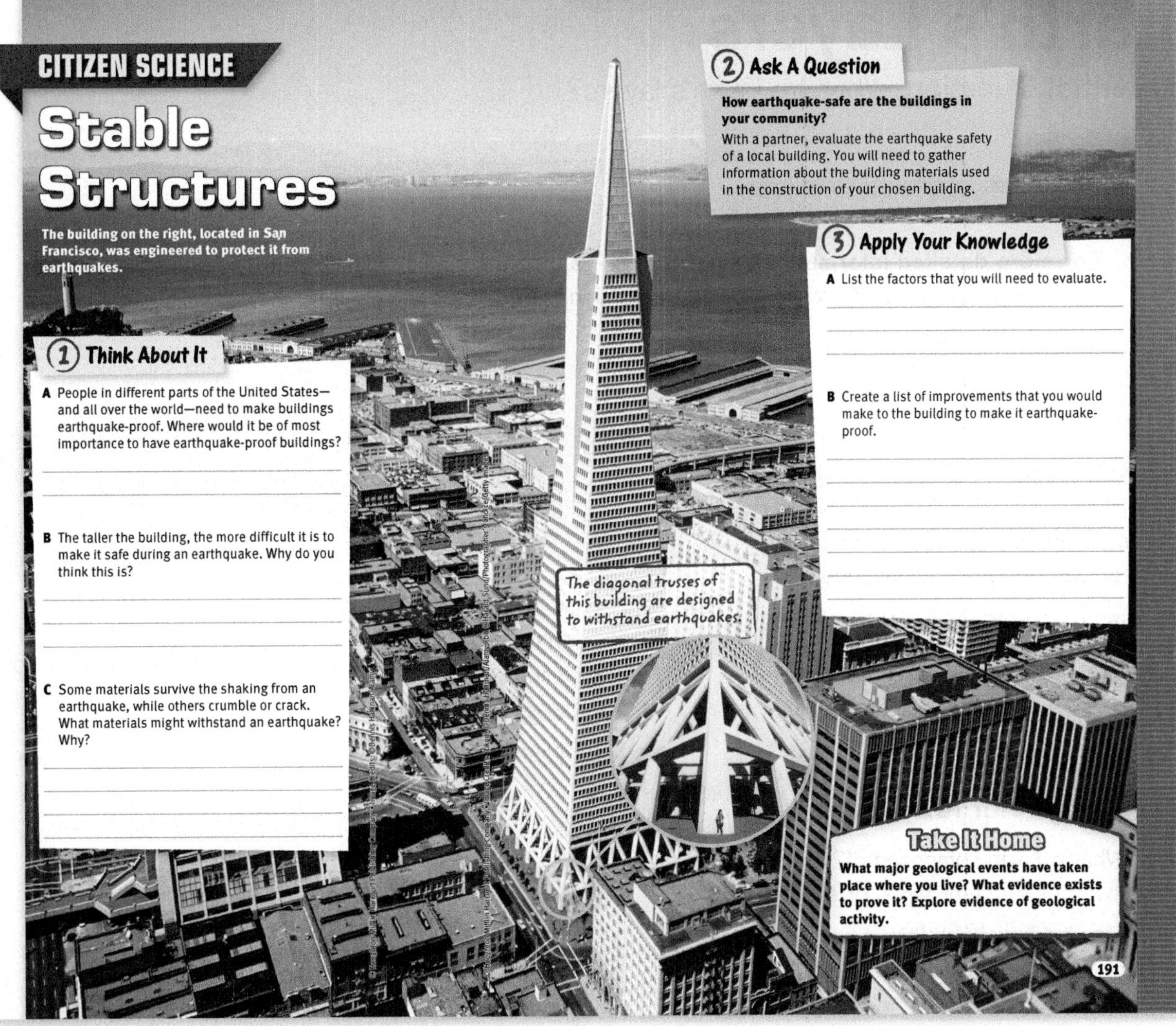

CITIZEN SCIENCE
Stable Structures
The building on the right, located in San Francisco, was engineered to protect it from earthquakes.
(1) Think About It
A People in different parts of the United States—and all over the world—need to make buildings earthquake-proof. Where would it be of most importance to have earthquake-proof buildings?
B The taller the building, the more difficult it is to make it safe during an earthquake. Why do you think this is?
C Some materials survive the shaking from an earthquake, while others crumble or crack. What materials might withstand an earthquake? Why?
(2) Ask A Question
How earthquake-safe are the buildings in your community?
With a partner, evaluate the earthquake safety of a local building. You will need to gather information about the building materials used in the construction of your chosen building.
(3) Apply Your Knowledge
A List the factors that you will need to evaluate.
B Create a list of improvements that you would make to the building to make it earthquake-proof.
The diagonal trusses of this building are designed to withstand earthquakes.
Take It Home
What major geological events have taken place where you live? What evidence exists to prove it? Explore evidence of geological activity.
191

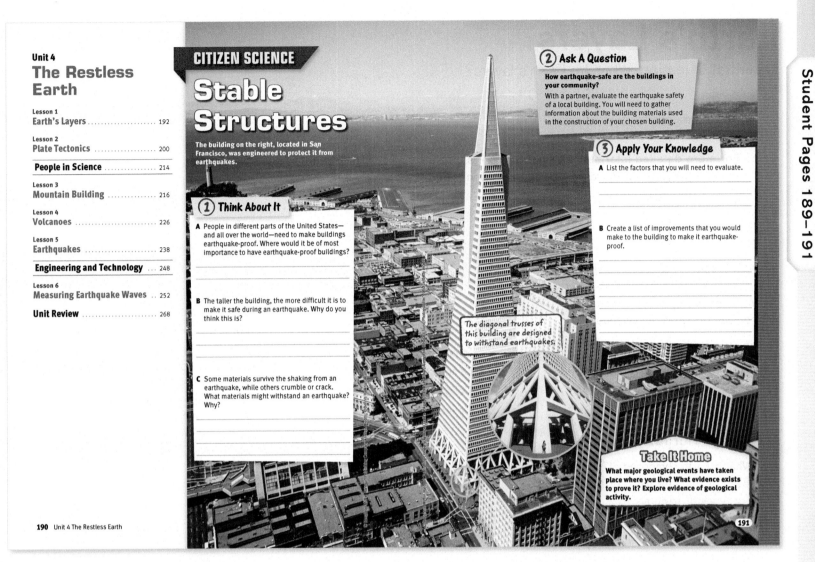

CITIZEN SCIENCE

Unit Project Stable Structures

1. Think About It

A. Students should identify populated areas that experience a great deal of tectonic activity, such as cities in California, Haiti, and the east coast of Japan.

B. Taller buildings are not as stable as shorter ones, unless they have been constructed to be earthquake-proof.

C. Materials that can bend and then return to their shape are more likely to survive an earthquake. They can bounce back from all the shaking. Steel, for example, is more likely to survive an earthquake than unreinforced concrete.

3. Apply Your Knowledge

A. Factors to evaluate include building materials, height and footprint of the building, earthquake-proofing that may already exist (like certain trusses), whether the building is built on bedrock or fill, and building methods.

B. Students should not feel limited to making small improvements to the existing structure. Encourage them to consider improvements that they would make if they were to rebuild the building or design another building of similar size. Improvements could take the form of different materials, different designs, and different construction techniques.

Take It Home

Students may be able to find some information about local geological activity at a museum or park. Direct students to resources that can help them investigate local geological activity.

Earth's Layers

Essential Question What are Earth's layers?

Professional Development

For more detailed information about the topics in this lesson, refer to the Content Refresher in the Unit Opener pages.

Opening Your Lesson

Begin the lesson by assessing students' prerequisite and prior knowledge.

Prerequisite Knowledge

- Earth is made up of rocks and minerals.
- Earth is made up of rocky and liquid layers.

Accessing Prior Knowledge

Ask: What is Earth composed of? Earth is composed of different types of rocks and different types of minerals.

Ask: How can scientists learn about the different layers of Earth? They can study the rocks and lava from volcanoes to learn about molten rock from within Earth.

Customize Your Opening

- ☐ **Accessing Prior Knowledge,** above
- ☐ **Print Path** Engage Your Brain, SE p. 193 #1–2
- ☐ **Print Path** Active Reading, SE p. 193 #3–4
- ☐ **Digital Path** Lesson Opener

Key Topics/Learning Goals	Supporting Concepts
Earth's Compositional Layers 1 Describe the compositional layers of Earth. 2 Define *core.* 3 Define *crust.* 4 Define *mantle.*	• Earth is divided into three layers based on chemical composition. • The core is the central part of Earth that is below the mantle. • The crust is the solid, outermost layer of Earth above the mantle. • The hot, convecting mantle is the layer of rock between Earth's crust and core.
Earth's Physical Layers 1 Describe the physical structure of Earth. 2 Define *lithosphere.* 3 Define *asthenosphere.* 4 Define *mesosphere.* 5 Compare the inner and outer cores.	• Earth is divided into five layers based on physical properties. • The lithosphere is the solid, outer layer of Earth that consists of the crust and the rigid part of the mantle. • The asthenosphere is the soft layer of the mantle on which the tectonic plates move. • The mesosphere is the lower, slow-flowing part of the mantle. • Both the outer core and the inner core are made up of mostly iron and nickel. • The outer core is liquid and the inner core is solid.

Options for Instruction

Two parallel paths provide coverage of the Essential Questions, with a strong **Inquiry** strand woven into each. Follow the **Print Path,** the **Digital Path,** or your customized combination of print, digital, and inquiry.

Print Path

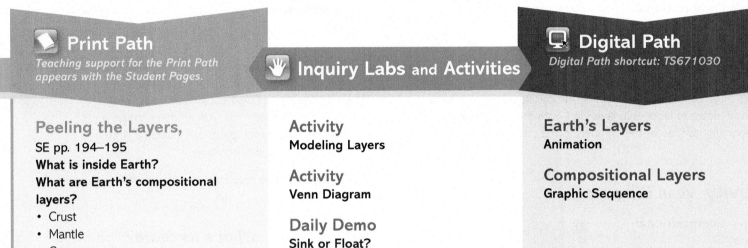

Teaching support for the Print Path appears with the Student Pages.

Inquiry Labs and Activities

Digital Path

Digital Path shortcut: TS671030

Print Path	Inquiry Labs and Activities	Digital Path
Peeling the Layers, SE pp. 194–195 **What is inside Earth?** **What are Earth's compositional layers?** • Crust • Mantle • Core	**Activity** **Modeling Layers** **Activity** **Venn Diagram** **Daily Demo** **Sink or Float?**	**Earth's Layers** **Animation** **Compositional Layers** **Graphic Sequence**
Peeling the Layers, SE pp. 196–197 **What are Earth's physical layers?** • Lithosphere • Asthenosphere • Mesosphere • Outer Core • Inner Core	**Activity** **Book It!** **Quick Lab** **Ordering Earth's Layers** **Quick Lab** **Layers of Earth** **Activity** **Carousel Review** **S.T.E.M. Lab** **Models of Earth**	**Physical Layers** **Graphic Sequence** **How Layers Correspond** **Animation**

Options for Assessment

See the Evaluate page for options, including Formative Assessment, Summative Assessment, and Unit Review.

Engage and Explore

Activities and Discussion

Activity *Modeling Layers*

Earth's Compositional Layers

 individuals
 45 min

Give each student modeling clay in three colors, a piece of cardboard, and sticky notes. Ask students to use the clay to create a model of Earth's three compositional layers on the cardboard. Have them use the sticky notes to label each layer and write one fact about it. Allow students time to present their models to the class.

Activity *Venn Diagram*

Earth's Compositional Layers

 individuals
 varied

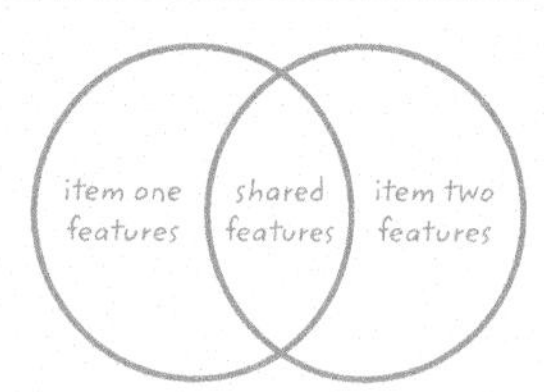

Have students make Venn diagrams to compare the two types of crust—continental crust and oceanic crust. Instruct students how to set up and label their Venn diagrams. Then have them work individually to list characteristics unique to each type of crust in the appropriate circles and characteristics shared by both types of crust in the overlapping section of the circles. Students should retain their completed diagrams for use as a study tool.

 ***Optional Online resource: Venn Diagram support***

Discussion *Earth's Layers*

Introducing Key Topics

 whole class
 20 min

Have students study the two diagrams of Earth's different layers. Ask them to explain how the five physical layers relate to the three compositional layers. Discuss the significance of recognizing both organizations of Earth's layers.

Activity *Book It!*

Earth's Physical Layers

 individuals
varied

Have each student make a Booklet FoldNote that includes one page for each of the physical layers of Earth (lithosphere, asthenosphere, mesosphere, outer core, and inner core). Ask students to use a sketch to illustrate each page and include a written paragraph to describe each layer.

Optional Online resource: Booklet FoldNote support

Discussion *What's Its State?*

Earth's Physical Layers

 whole class
20 min

Students often have difficulty understanding the composition of the asthenosphere. Explain to students that the upper part of the mantle gets cooler and less plastic as it nears the crust. The asthenosphere, upon which tectonic plates of the lithosphere float, is a solid that deforms plastically. Challenge students to identify another solid that displays plastic flow. Sample answers: In large glaciers, the ice below a certain depth will flow in response to the stress exerted by the weight of the ice above that layer. Other examples can include candies such as toffees that become more plastic as their temperatures increase.

DIRECTED inquiry
introduces inquiry skills within a structured framework.

GUIDED inquiry
develops inquiry skills within a supportive environment.

INDEPENDENT inquiry
deepens inquiry skills with student-driven questions or procedures.

Labs and Demos

Daily Demo *Sink or Float?*

Earth's Compositional Layers

 whole class
20 min
 **GUIDED** inquiry

PURPOSE **To demonstrate how a dense material sinks when combined with a less dense material**

MATERIALS
- cups, clear plastic (2)
- food coloring
- plastic spoon
- table salt
- tap water

1 Add equal amounts of water to 2 cups. As students observe, add 3 teaspoonfuls of salt to one of the cups and stir until the salt is dissolved. **Ask:** How does the addition of the salt affect the density of the water? It makes the water denser.

2 Add 10 drops of food coloring to the cup containing salt water, and stir until the food coloring is evenly distributed in the water.

3 **Observe** As students observe, gently pour about one-third of the colored water into the cup containing the fresh water. Do not shake or stir the water. **Ask:** What do you observe? The salt water sinks down below the fresh water. **Ask:** Why? A more dense material sinks through a less dense material.

4 Relate students' observations to the role of convection in the mantle.

S.T.E.M. Lab *Models of Earth*

Earth's Compositional and Physical Layers

 small groups
 45 min, on 2 days
 **GUIDED/INDEPENDENT** inquiry

PURPOSE **To construct models of Earth's layers**

MATERIALS
- aluminum foil
- clay
- corks
- glue
- marbles
- newspaper
- pipe cleaners
- plastic wrap
- foam balls and sheets
- potatoes
- rock salt
- sand
- sponge
- washers

Quick Lab *Ordering Earth's Layers*

PURPOSE **To make a 3-D model of Earth's layers**

See the Lab Manual or go Online for planning information.

Quick Lab *Layers of Earth*

Earth's Compositional and Physical Layers

 individuals
 30 min
DIRECTED inquiry

PURPOSE **To model Earth's compositional and physical layers**

MATERIALS
- markers
- scissors or plastic knife
- styrene ball

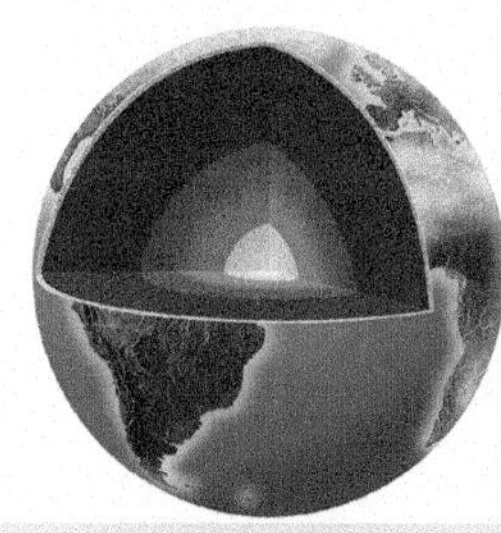

Customize Your Labs

See the Lab Manual for lab datasheets.

Go Online for editable lab datasheets.

Activities and Discussion
- ☐ **Activity** Modeling Layers
- ☐ **Activity** Venn Diagram
- ☐ **Discussion** Earth's Layers
- ☐ **Activity** Book It!
- ☐ **Discussion** What's Its State?

Labs and Demos
- ☐ **Daily Demo** Sink or Float?
- ☐ **S.T.E.M. Lab** Models of Earth
- ☐ **Quick Lab** Layers of Earth
- ☐ **Quick Lab** Ordering Earth's Layers

Your Resources

Explain Science Concepts

Key Topics	Print Path	Digital Path
Earth's Compositional Layers	☐ **Peeling the Layers,** SE pp. 194–195 • Think Outside the Book, #5 • Active Reading, #6 • Active Reading, #7	☐ **Earth's Layers** See two ways that Earth's internal layers can be classified. ☐ **Compositional Layers** Explore the core, mantle, and crust of Earth and the composition of the layers.
Earth's Physical Layers	☐ **Peeling the Layers,** SE pp. 196–197 • Active Reading, #8 • Visualize It!, #9 • Do the Math, #10	☐ **Physical Layers** Explore the inner and outer cores, convective mantle, asthenosphere, and lithosphere of Earth and the behavior of the layers. ☐ **How Layers Correspond** Match and compare the physical layers with the compositional layers.

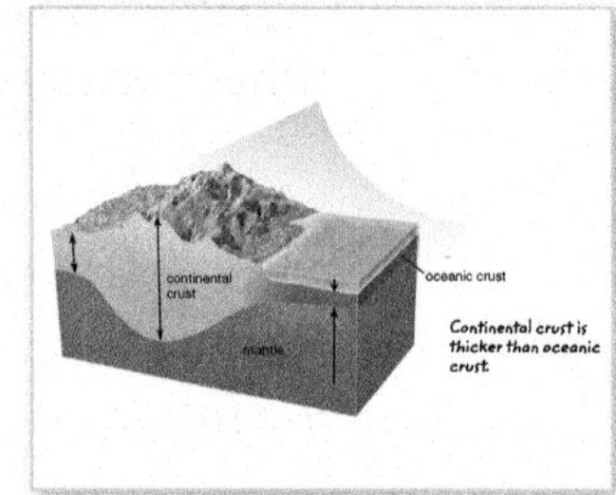

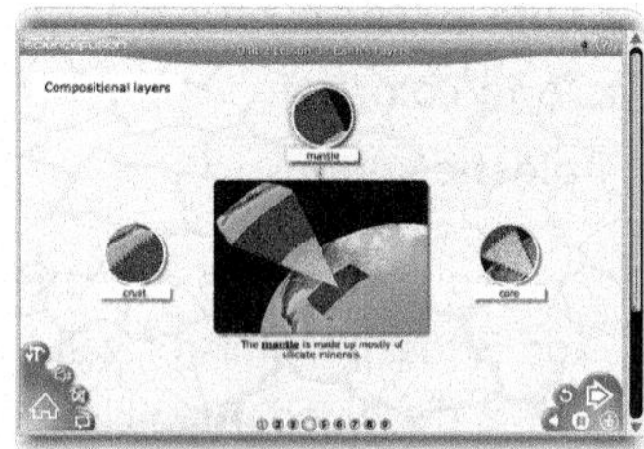

Do the Math Sample Problem

Here's an example of how to find the percentage thickness of the core that is the outer core.

Physical	Compositional
Continental lithosphere (150 km)	Continental crust (30 km)
Asthenosphere (250 km)	Mantle (2,900 km)
Mesosphere (2,550 km)	
Outer core (2,200 km)	Core (3,430 km)
Inner core (1,230 km)	

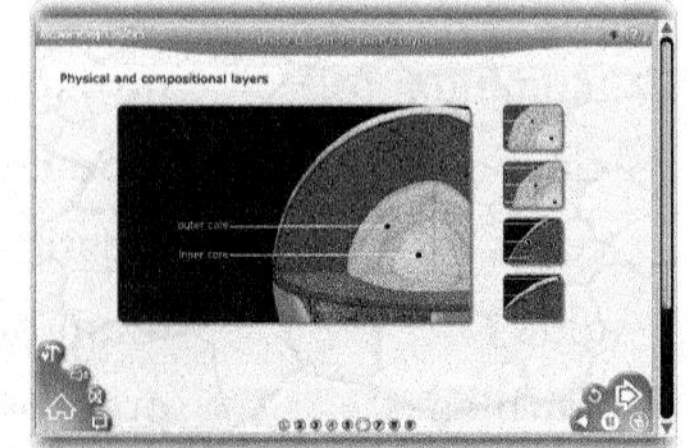

Differentiated Instruction

Basic *Diagram Earth*

Earth's Physical Layers

 individuals
35 min

Have students draw a diagram of Earth's physical layers. Then, have them color each layer a different color, create a key for their diagram, and write a sentence describing each layer. Display diagrams in the classroom.

Advanced *Getting on the Scale*

Earth's Compositional Layers

 small groups
varied

Write the following on the board: "Crust: 5 to 50 km thick"; "Mantle: 2,900 km thick"; and "Core: 3,500 km radius." Have students use this information to draw a scale diagram by using a scale of 1 cm = 100 km. Have students compare their drawings to the illustration in the book. Discuss why diagrams and other scientific illustrations use scales.

Advanced *Planet Composition Comparison*

Earth's Compositional Layers

 pairs
varied

Ask students to select another planet in our solar system. Have them find out about that planet's layers and the composition of each of those layers. Then, have them draw a diagram that compares the compositional layers of their chosen planet with Earth's compositional layers.

ELL *Avocado Earth*

Earth's Compositional Layers

 individuals
30 min

Using an avocado, help students understand the composition of Earth. Cut a wedge so that the intact part looks like a cutaway of Earth with the pit of the avocado whole to represent the core. Explain that the thickness of the skin is comparable to the thickness of Earth's crust. The flesh is similar to the thickness of the mantle. The pit is similar to Earth's core.

Lesson Vocabulary

core	**crust**	**mantle**
convection	**lithosphere**	**asthenosphere**
mesosphere		

Previewing Vocabulary

small groups
35 min

Word Triangles Have students create Word Triangles for each vocabulary term. Have them share their completed Word Triangles with a partner.

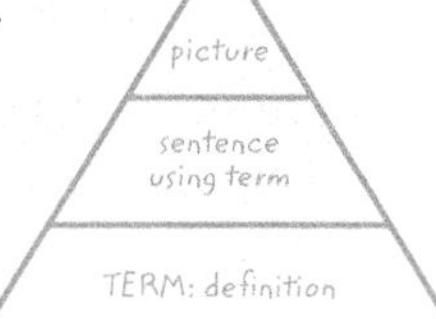

 *Optional Online resource: Word Triangle support*

Reinforcing Vocabulary

individuals
30 min

Paragraphs To help students remember each of the vocabulary words introduced in this lesson, have them write a paragraph or two, describing the differences between Earth's compositional and physical layers. Encourage them to use at least five of the vocabulary words in their paragraphs. Explain that they are to come up with descriptive paragraphs, not merely to list each term and its definition. Give bonus points to students who create a well-written paragraph or two using all of the terms.

Customize Your Lesson

Core Instruction

- ☐ **Print Path** choices
- ☐ **Digital Path** choices

Vocabulary

- ☐ **Previewing Vocabulary** Word Triangles
- ☐ **Reinforcing Vocabulary** Paragraphs

Your Resources

Differentiated Instruction

- ☐ **Basic** Diagram Earth
- ☐ **Advanced** Getting on the Scale
- ☐ **Advanced** Planet Composition Comparison
- ☐ **ELL** Avocado Earth

Extend Science Concepts

Reinforce and Review

Activity *Carousel Review*

Synthesizing Key Topics

 small groups
25 min

1 Arrange chart paper in different parts of the room. On each paper, write a question to review content.
2 Divide students into small groups and assign each group a chart. Give each group a different colored marker.
3 Groups discuss their question, discuss their answer, and write a response.
4 After 5 to 10 min, each group rotates to the next station. Groups put a check by each answer they agree with, comment on answers they don't agree with, and add their own answers. Continue until all groups have reviewed all charts.
5 Invite each group to share information with the class.

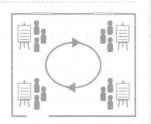

Graphic Organizer

Synthesizing Key Topics

 individuals
 35 min

Cluster Diagram After students have studied the lesson, ask them to develop a cluster diagram that uses the following terms: *core, crust, mantle, lithosphere, asthenosphere,* and *mesosphere.*

Optional Online resources: Cluster Diagram Support

Going Further

Physics Connection

Synthesizing Key Topics

 individuals
varied

Waves and Energy Explain to students that a wave is a disturbance that transfers energy. Matter through which waves pass is called a *medium*. Waves that require a medium, such as seismic waves, cause particles of the medium to vibrate, which passes along the wave energy. The speed of waves through a medium is affected by the medium's elasticity (the amount of force required to displace particles a certain distance from their original positions). The stiffer an elastic medium is, the faster the waves travel through it. Ask students to write a few sentences about how scientists might use waves to learn about Earth's inner layers. Sample answer: Scientists can compare the speed at which waves pass through different layers of Earth to learn about the elasticity of the layers.

Optional Online rubric: Written Pieces

Language Arts Connection

Synthesizing Key Topics

individuals
varied

Key Word Scan Test students' ability to find definitions of key terms by playing this game. Tell students that they will have to come up with a question based on a definition you give. For example, if you say, "The softer layer on which the lithosphere moves," students would say, "What is the asthenosphere?"

Customize Your Closing

See the Assessment Guide for quizzes and tests.

Go Online to edit and create quizzes and tests.

Reinforce and Review

- ☐ **Activity** Carousel Review
- ☐ **Graphic Organizer** Cluster Diagram
- ☐ **Print Path** Visual Summary, SE p. 198
- ☐ **Digital Path** Lesson Closer

Evaluate Student Mastery

Formative Assessment

See the teacher support below the Student Pages for additional Formative Assessment questions.

Describe or have students review the differences between the compositional layers and the physical layers of Earth. **Ask:** How are the inner and outer cores similar? How are they different? Sample answer: They are both made up of iron and nickel. The inner core is solid, whereas the outer core is liquid.

Reteach

Formative assessment may show you that students need reinforcement for certain topics. The resources below are recommended for reteaching. If students were introduced to topics through the Print Path, you can also use the Digital Path for reteaching, and vice versa.
Can be assigned to individual students

Earth's Compositional Layers

Activity Modeling Layers
Activity Venn Diagram
Daily Demo Sink or Float?

Earth's Physical Layers

Discussion Earth's Layers
Discussion What's Its State?
Activity Book It!
Quick Lab Ordering Earth's Layers
Quick Lab Layers of Earth

Summative Assessment

Alternative Assessment

Earth's Physical and Compositional Layers

Online resources: student worksheet; optional rubrics

Earth's Layers

Take Your Pick: *Earth's Physical and Compositional Layers*
Complete the activities to show what you've learned about Earth's structure.

1. Work on your own, with a partner, or with a small group.
2. Choose items below for a total of 10 points. Check your choices.
3. Have your teacher approve your plan.
4. Submit or present your results.

2 Points

____ **Picturing Earth's Layers** Create a poster that shows Earth's compositional layers. On the poster, label and briefly describe the three layers.

____ **What Are Your Thoughts?** Make a card that answers the following questions: What did you know about Earth's compositional layers before completing this lesson? What was the most interesting thing you learned about Earth's compositional layers during this lesson?

____ **Down to the Core** Make a Venn diagram in which you compare and contrast Earth's inner and outer cores. Label one circle *Outer Core*, the other circle *Inner Core*, and the overlapping section *Both*. Complete the diagram with details about the cores.

5 Points

____ **The Layer Quiz** Make a quiz that deals with Earth's physical layers. Write the names of Earth's layers on note cards. Then write some of the properties of the layers on the back of the cards. Shuffle the cards and choose one from the pile. With a partner, take turns quizzing each other about the layers.

____ **Seeing Inside** How do scientists know about Earth's interior? Find out more about how seismic waves and their speed help scientists learn about the inside of Earth. Present your findings in a visual presentation.

____ **Your Turn to Teach** Suppose you are a teacher. Your task is to prepare a lesson about the layers of Earth. Gather information from your studies. Present your lesson to another student.

8 Points

____ **Blast from the Past** Scientific understanding is constantly changing. Find out what scientists thought Earth was made of in the past. Make a timeline showing some past theories about Earth's internal structure.

____ **What's in a Layer?** Make a multimedia presentation in which you compare and contrast the two ways of looking at Earth's internal structure.

Going Further

- [ ] Physics Connection
- [ ] Language Arts Connection

Formative Assessment

- [ ] Strategies Throughout TE
- [ ] Lesson Review SE

Summative Assessment

- [ ] Alternative Assessment Earth's Physical and Compositional Layers
- [ ] Lesson Quiz
- [ ] Unit Tests A and B
- [ ] Unit Review SE End-of-Unit

Your Resources

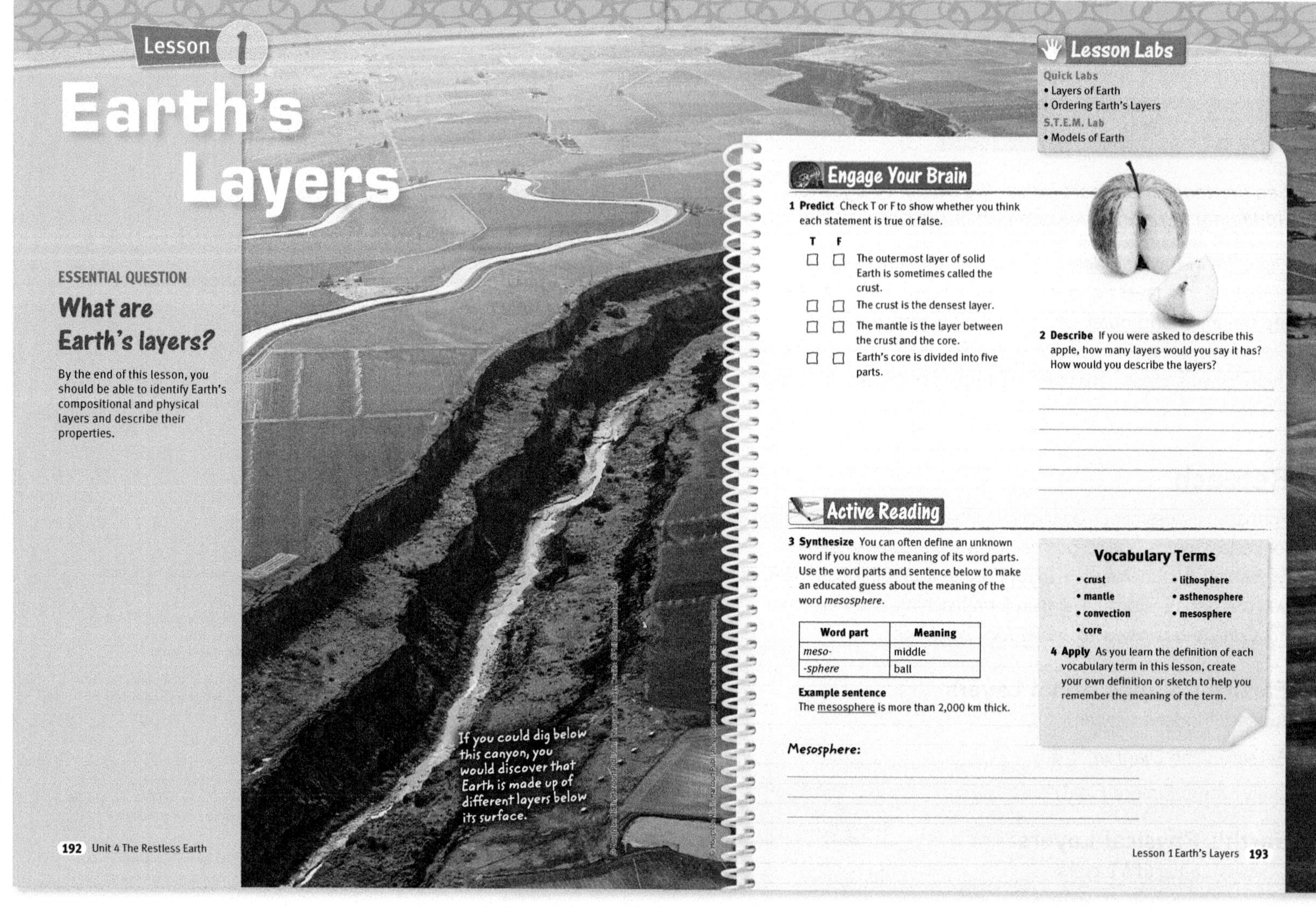
Lesson 1

Earth's Layers

ESSENTIAL QUESTION

What are Earth's layers?

By the end of this lesson, you should be able to identify Earth's compositional and physical layers and describe their properties.

If you could dig below this canyon, you would discover that Earth is made up of different layers below its surface.

192 Unit 4 The Restless Earth

Lesson Labs

Quick Labs
- Layers of Earth
- Ordering Earth's Layers

S.T.E.M. Lab
- Models of Earth

Engage Your Brain

1 **Predict** Check T or F to show whether you think each statement is true or false.

T	F	
☐	☐	The outermost layer of solid Earth is sometimes called the crust.
☐	☐	The crust is the densest layer.
☐	☐	The mantle is the layer between the crust and the core.
☐	☐	Earth's core is divided into five parts.

2 **Describe** If you were asked to describe this apple, how many layers would you say it has? How would you describe the layers?

Active Reading

3 **Synthesize** You can often define an unknown word if you know the meaning of its word parts. Use the word parts and sentence below to make an educated guess about the meaning of the word *mesosphere*.

Word part	Meaning
meso-	middle
-sphere	ball

Example sentence
The mesosphere is more than 2,000 km thick.

Mesosphere:

Vocabulary Terms
- crust
- mantle
- convection
- core
- lithosphere
- asthenosphere
- mesosphere

4 **Apply** As you learn the definition of each vocabulary term in this lesson, create your own definition or sketch to help you remember the meaning of the term.

Lesson 1 Earth's Layers 193

Answers

Answers for 1–3 should represent students' current thoughts, even if incorrect.

1. T; F; T; F
2. Student answers may vary. Sample answer: three layers; a thin outer layer (the skin); a fleshy, thick middle layer; and a denser core
3. Sample answer: The middle layer of Earth.

Opening Your Lesson

Have students share their ideas about the number of layers an apple has (item 2) to assess their working knowledge of the key kopics.

Prerequisites Earth's crust is made up of rock; molten rock, or magma, is located in many areas beneath Earth's crust; each part of Earth contains different minerals.

Accessing Prior Knowledge Develop an Anticipation Guide for the content in this lesson with your students. Anticipation guides prompt students to review what they know about a topic before reading about it, alerting them to the key concepts they will encounter. The key to anticipation guides is to choose some statements that sound plausible but that students will discover to be untrue after they read the material.

Optional Online resource: Anticipation Guide support

Learning Alert

Layers A layer is a thickness of matter that covers or forms an underlayment of another thickness. In the apple example on this page, the apple's top or outer layer is the skin. The next layer is the flesh of the apple. Finally, the inner layer is the apple core that contains the seeds. Help students use this as an analogy for Earth's layers; it can help them understand the layers of Earth and internalize the differences more quickly.

Peeling the Layers

What is inside Earth?

If you tried to dig to the center of Earth, what do you think you would find? Would Earth be solid or hollow? Would it be made of the same material throughout? Actually, Earth is made of several layers. The materials that make up each layer have characteristic properties that vary from layer to layer. Scientists think about Earth's layers in two ways—in terms of their chemical composition and in terms of their physical properties.

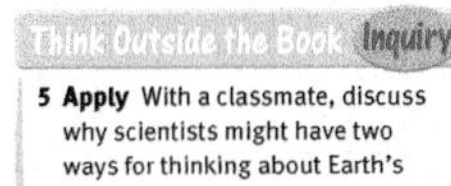

Think Outside the Book Inquiry

5 Apply With a classmate, discuss why scientists might have two ways for thinking about Earth's layers.

What are Earth's compositional layers?

Earth can be divided into three layers based on chemical composition. These layers are called the *crust*, the *mantle*, and the *core*. Each compositional layer is made up of a different mixture of chemicals.

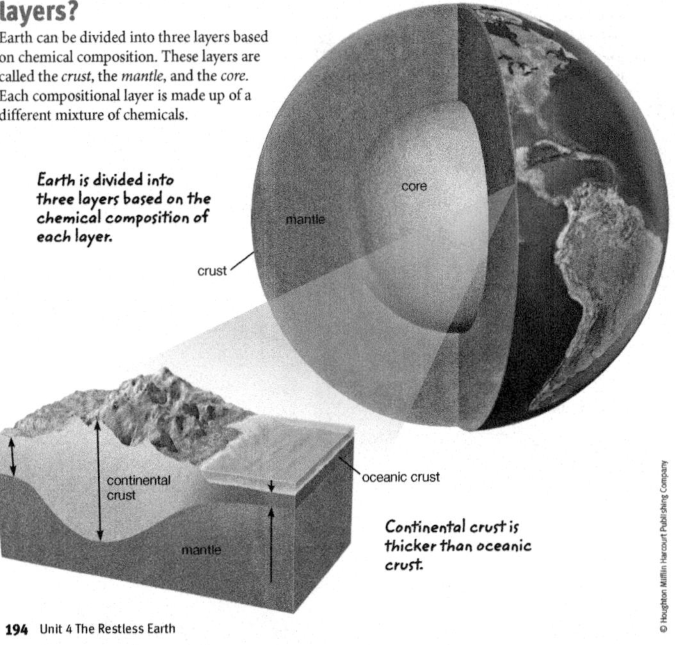

Earth is divided into three layers based on the chemical composition of each layer.

Continental crust is thicker than oceanic crust.

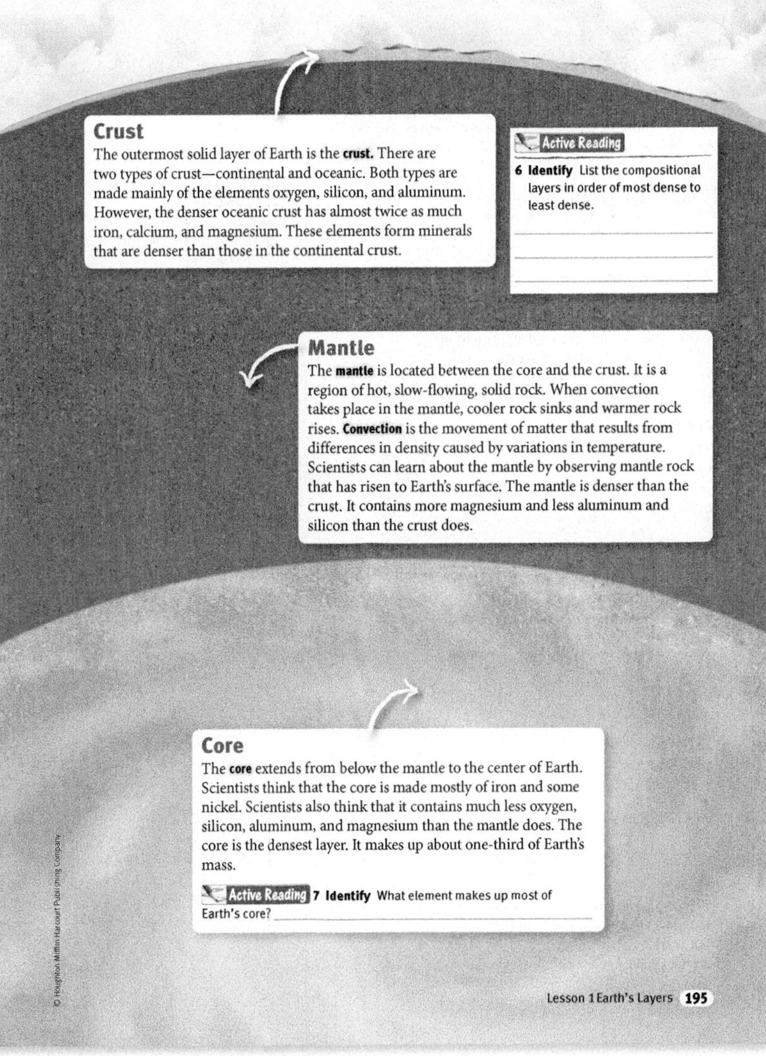

Crust

The outermost solid layer of Earth is the **crust.** There are two types of crust—continental and oceanic. Both types are made mainly of the elements oxygen, silicon, and aluminum. However, the denser oceanic crust has almost twice as much iron, calcium, and magnesium. These elements form minerals that are denser than those in the continental crust.

Active Reading

6 Identify List the compositional layers in order of most dense to least dense.

Mantle

The **mantle** is located between the core and the crust. It is a region of hot, slow-flowing, solid rock. When convection takes place in the mantle, cooler rock sinks and warmer rock rises. **Convection** is the movement of matter that results from differences in density caused by variations in temperature. Scientists can learn about the mantle by observing mantle rock that has risen to Earth's surface. The mantle is denser than the crust. It contains more magnesium and less aluminum and silicon than the crust does.

Core

The **core** extends from below the mantle to the center of Earth. Scientists think that the core is made mostly of iron and some nickel. Scientists also think that it contains much less oxygen, silicon, aluminum, and magnesium than the mantle does. The core is the densest layer. It makes up about one-third of Earth's mass.

Active Reading **7 Identify** What element makes up most of Earth's core? ____

Answers

5. Sample answer: Different layers of Earth differ in chemical composition and physical properties. Thinking about Earth's layers in different ways allows scientists to compare and contrast different parts of Earth.
6. core, mantle, crust
7. iron

Probing Questions GUIDED Inquiry

Evaluating Understanding the structure of Earth can help scientists understand natural events such as earthquakes and volcanoes. How do you think knowledge of Earth's structure provides insight into how and why these natural events happen? Explain your thoughts.

Building Reading Skills

Concept Map Have students develop a Concept Map to organize information about the different layers of Earth.

Optional Online resource: Concept Map support

Learning Alert MISCONCEPTION

Liquid Throughout Students may hold the misconception that the mantle or all of Earth's interior is entirely liquid. Explain that very small portions of the mantle are liquid while most of the rest is solid. Also point out that the centermost part of Earth, the inner core, is actually solid and composed mostly of iron and nickel.

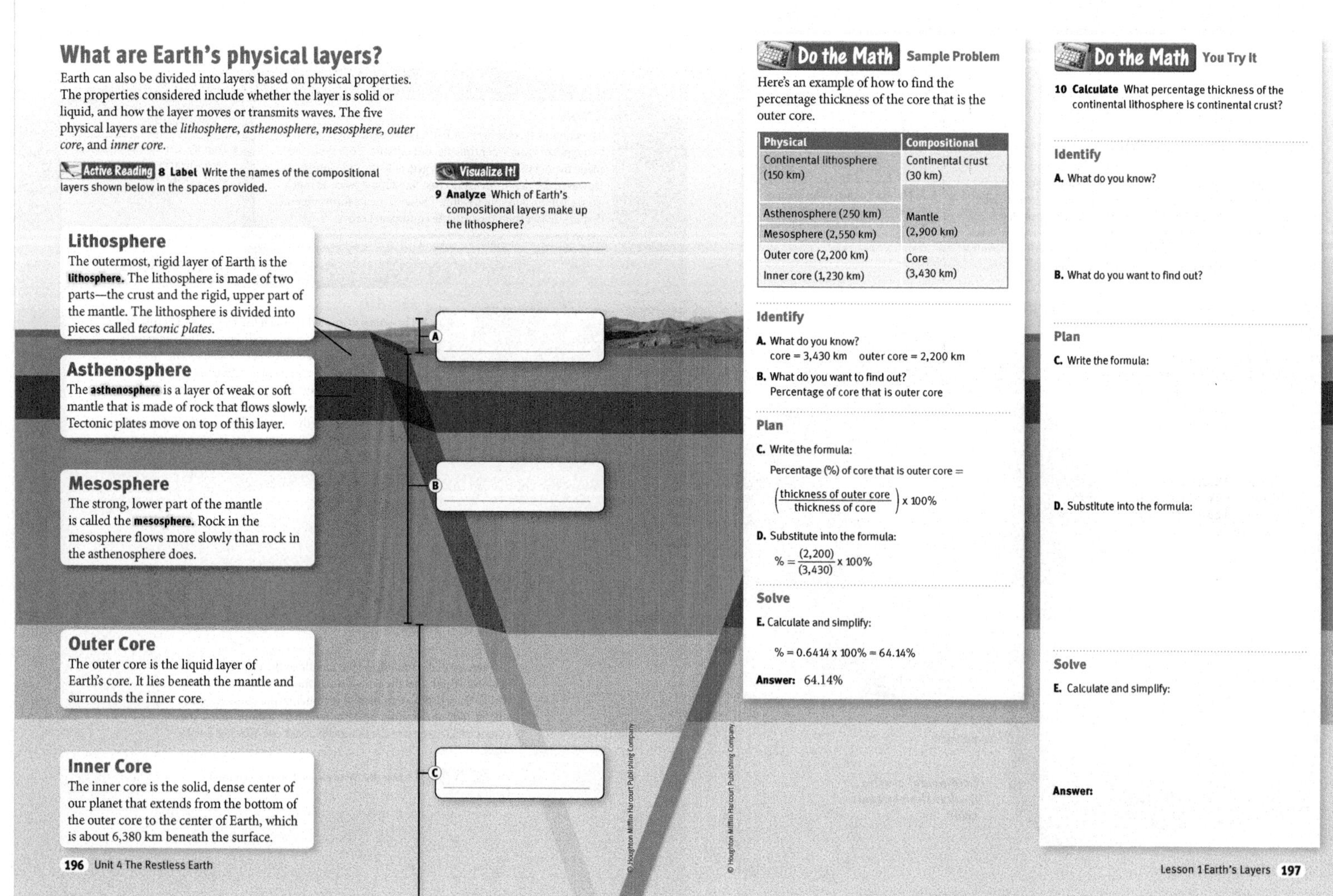

What are Earth's physical layers?
Earth can also be divided into layers based on physical properties. The properties considered include whether the layer is solid or liquid, and how the layer moves or transmits waves. The five physical layers are the lithosphere, asthenosphere, mesosphere, outer core, and inner core.
Active Reading 8 Label Write the names of the compositional layers shown below in the spaces provided.
Visualize It! 9 Analyze Which of Earth's compositional layers make up the lithosphere?
Lithosphere
The outermost, rigid layer of Earth is the lithosphere. The lithosphere is made of two parts—the crust and the rigid, upper part of the mantle. The lithosphere is divided into pieces called tectonic plates.
Asthenosphere
The asthenosphere is a layer of weak or soft mantle that is made of rock that flows slowly. Tectonic plates move on top of this layer.
Mesosphere
The strong, lower part of the mantle is called the mesosphere. Rock in the mesosphere flows more slowly than rock in the asthenosphere does.
Outer Core
The outer core is the liquid layer of Earth's core. It lies beneath the mantle and surrounds the inner core.
Inner Core
The inner core is the solid, dense center of our planet that extends from the bottom of the outer core to the center of Earth, which is about 6,380 km beneath the surface.
A
B
C
196 Unit 4 The Restless Earth
Do the Math Sample Problem
Here's an example of how to find the percentage thickness of the core that is the outer core.
Physical | Compositional
Continental lithosphere (150 km) | Continental crust (30 km)
Asthenosphere (250 km) | Mantle (2,900 km)
Mesosphere (2,550 km)
Outer core (2,200 km) | Core (3,430 km)
Inner core (1,230 km)
Identify
A. What do you know?
core = 3,430 km outer core = 2,200 km
B. What do you want to find out?
Percentage of core that is outer core
Plan
C. Write the formula:
Percentage (%) of core that is outer core =
(thickness of outer core / thickness of core) x 100%
D. Substitute into the formula:
% = (2,200) / (3,430) x 100%
Solve
E. Calculate and simplify:
% = 0.6414 x 100% = 64.14%
Answer: 64.14%
Do the Math You Try It
10 Calculate What percentage thickness of the continental lithosphere is continental crust?
Identify
A. What do you know?
B. What do you want to find out?
Plan
C. Write the formula:
D. Substitute into the formula:
Solve
E. Calculate and simplify:
Answer:
© Houghton Mifflin Harcourt Publishing Company
Lesson 1 Earth's Layers 197

Answers

8. A. Crust B. Mantle C. Core
9. crust and upper rigid part of the mantle
10. 20.0%

Formative Assessment

Have students look at the image of Earth's layers here and on the previous spread. **Ask:** What is the difference between the chemical (or compositional) layers of Earth and the physical layers of Earth? Sample answer: Physical layers are based on physical properties, not position; compositional layers are based on chemical composition.

Building Reading Skills

FoldNote Booklet Have students create a FoldNote Booklet titled *Earth's Physical Layers*. They should include pages on the lithosphere, asthenosphere, mesosphere, outer core, and inner core. On each page, have them write a description of the layer. One page should include a diagram showing the location of each layer.

Optional Online resource: FoldNote Booklet support

Probing Question DIRECTED Inquiry

Analyzing In this lesson, students learn about rock flow in Earth's layers. They find out that denser materials are found closer to Earth's center. Ask them to discuss, in their own words, why this occurs. Sample answer: Denser materials are heavier, so they sink down toward Earth's center.

Visual Summary

To complete this summary, fill in the blanks with the correct word or phrase. Then, use the key below to check your answers. You can use this page to review the main concepts of the lesson.

Earth is divided into three compositional layers.

11 The outermost compositional layer of the Earth is the __________.

12 The __________ is denser than the crust and contains more magnesium.

Earth is divided into five physical layers.

13 The __________ is divided into pieces called tectonic plates.

14 The __________ core is the liquid layer of Earth's core.

Earth's Layers

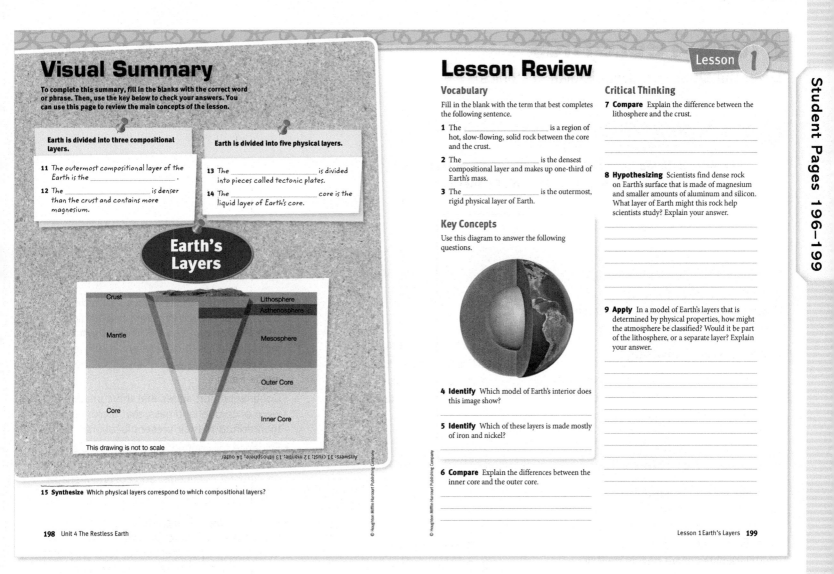

Crust
Mantle
Core
Lithosphere
Asthenosphere
Mesosphere
Outer Core
Inner Core

This drawing is not to scale

Answers: 11 crust; 12 mantle; 13 lithosphere; 14 outer

15 Synthesize Which physical layers correspond to which compositional layers?

Lesson Review

Lesson 1

Vocabulary

Fill in the blank with the term that best completes the following sentence.

1 The __________ is a region of hot, slow-flowing, solid rock between the core and the crust.

2 The __________ is the densest compositional layer and makes up one-third of Earth's mass.

3 The __________ is the outermost, rigid physical layer of Earth.

Key Concepts

Use this diagram to answer the following questions.

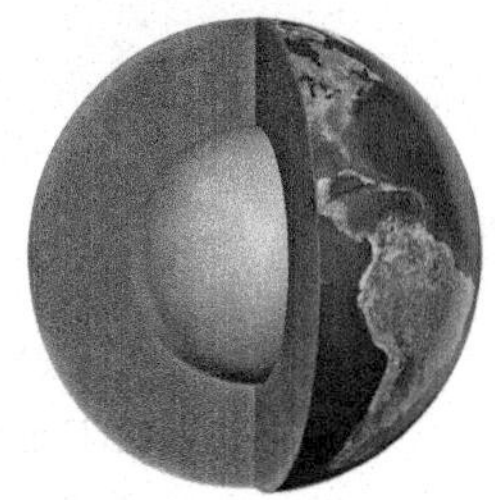

4 Identify Which model of Earth's interior does this image show?

5 Identify Which of these layers is made mostly of iron and nickel?

6 Compare Explain the differences between the inner core and the outer core.

Critical Thinking

7 Compare Explain the difference between the lithosphere and the crust.

8 Hypothesizing Scientists find dense rock on Earth's surface that is made of magnesium and smaller amounts of aluminum and silicon. What layer of Earth might this rock help scientists study? Explain your answer.

9 Apply In a model of Earth's layers that is determined by physical properties, how might the atmosphere be classified? Would it be part of the lithosphere, or a separate layer? Explain your answer.

Visual Summary Answers

11. crust
12. mantle
13. lithosphere
14. outer
15. lithosphere: crust and upper part of mantle
    asthenosphere: mantle
    mesosphere: mantle
    outer core: core
    inner core: core

Lesson Review Answers

1. mantle
2. core
3. lithosphere
4. Earth's compositional layers
5. core
6. The inner core is solid and dense and is at the center of Earth. The outer core is liquid, less dense than the inner core, and surrounds the inner core.
7. The lithosphere is a physical layer and includes the crust and the upper rigid part of the mantle.
8. mantle; Scientists know the mantle contains more magnesium, and less aluminum and silicon than the crust does.
9. It would be a separate layer. The lithosphere is physically rigid and divided into tectonic plates. The atmosphere is not.

Plate Tectonics

Essential Question What is plate tectonics?

For more detailed information about the topics in this lesson, refer to the Content Refresher in the Unit Opener pages.

Opening Your Lesson

Begin the lesson by assessing students' prerequisite and prior knowledge.

Prerequisite Knowledge

- Earth is made up of compositional layers.
- Earth is made up of physical layers.
- Some of these layers are solid and some are liquid.

Accessing Prior Knowledge:

Have students draw a picture of Earth. Ask them to share some of the things they know already about plate tectonics with the class. Encourage students to list the ideas their classmates share beside their drawings. At the conclusion of the lesson, have students revisit their drawings and cross out any information they now know is incorrect. They should also add new information learned throughout the lesson.

Customize Your Opening

- ☐ **Accessing Prior Knowledge,** above
- ☐ **Print Path** Engage Your Brain, SE p. 201 #1–2
- ☐ **Print Path** Active Reading, SE p. 201 #3–4
- ☐ **Digital Path** Lesson Opener

Key Topics/Learning Goals	Supporting Concepts
Theory of Plate Tectonics 1 Define *plate tectonics.* 2 Define *continental drift.* 3 Discuss scientific evidence supporting continental drift.	• The theory of plate tectonics states that Earth's lithosphere is made of large pieces called tectonic plates that are in constant motion as a result of density differences caused by the transfer of energy as heat inside Earth. • Continental drift states that the continents were once one landmass, that broke up and then drifted to their present locations. • Evidence for continental drift includes similar fossils, rock formations, and mountain ranges on different continents, and continent shape.
Tectonic Plates 1 Define *tectonic plate.* 2 Compare continental and oceanic crust.	• A tectonic plate is a block of lithosphere that consists of the crust and the rigid, outermost part of the mantle. Tectonic plates move around on top of the asthenosphere. • Continental crust is thicker, and less dense than oceanic crust is.
Types of Plate Boundaries 1 Define *convergent boundary.* 2 Define *divergent boundary.* 3 Define *transform boundary.*	• A convergent boundary occurs between tectonic plates that are colliding. • A divergent boundary occurs between tectonic plates that are moving away from each other. • A transform boundary occurs between plates that are sliding past each other.
Causes of Tectonic Plate Motion 1 List three possible causes for the movement of tectonic plates.	• Three possible mechanisms for tectonic plate motion are mantle convection, ridge push, and slab pull.

Options for Instruction

Two parallel paths provide coverage of the Essential Questions, with a strong **Inquiry** strand woven into each. Follow the **Print Path**, the **Digital Path**, or your customized combination of print, digital, and inquiry.

 Print Path *Teaching support for the Print Path appears with the Student Pages.*	 Inquiry Labs and Activities	 Digital Path *Digital Path shortcut: TS671040*
Puzzling Evidence, SE pp. 202–205 **What evidence suggests that continents move?** **What is Pangaea?** **What discoveries support the idea of continental drift?** • Age and Magnetic Properties of the Sea Floor • Sea-Floor Spreading • Ocean Trenches	**Activity** Map Puzzle **Quick Lab** Reconstructing Land Masses	**Continental Drift** Diagram **Sea-Floor Spreading** Interactive Image **Pangaea** Animation
A Giant Jigsaw, SE pp. 206–207 **What is the theory of plate tectonics?** **What is a tectonic plate?**	**Daily Demo** Continental Collisions **Quick Lab** Tectonic Ice Cubes	**Theory of Plate Tectonics** Diagram **Sea-Floor Spreading** Interactive Image
Boundaries, SE pp. 208–209 **What are the three types of plate boundaries?** • Convergent Boundaries • Divergent Boundaries • Transform Boundaries	**Activity** What Boundary Is It? **Virtual Lab** Plate Boundaries	**Plate Boundary Types** Interactive Graphics **Boundary Types** Interactive Image
Hot Plates, SE pp. 210–211 **What causes tectonic plates to move?** • Mantle Convection • Ridge Push • Slab Pull	**Exploration Lab** Sea-Floor Spreading **Quick Lab** Mantle Convection	**Mantle Convection** Diagram

Options for Assessment

See the Evaluate page for options, including Formative Assessment, Summative Assessment, and Unit Review.

Engage and Explore

Activities and Discussion

Activity *What Boundary Is It?*

Types of Plate Boundaries

 small groups
 35 min

Assign each group one of the boundary types. Have students use the Internet to research the boundary, finding out what happens along it and finding examples of places on Earth where it occurs. Groups should then create a visual display showing the information they learned about that type of boundary. Encourage groups to be creative in their depiction of their topic. Have them share their work with their classmates.

Discussion *Fossil Locations*

Engage

Theory of Plate Tectonics

 whole class
 20 min

Explain to students that scientists have discovered fossils of the same plants and animals on different continents that are separated by large oceans. Lead a discussion with students about how this is possible and what it suggests about the continents.

Discussion *Evaluating Evidence*

Theory of Plate Tectonics

 whole class
 60 min

Students must read carefully in order to evaluate evidence. Ask students what a hypothesis is and why an idea about how the continents move would be called a hypothesis. Tell students to read about the theory of continental drift in their texts and/or research it on the Internet. Ask them to weigh the evidence against the way it is able to be tested. Have them share their conclusions and opinions about how the hypothesis became accepted as a theory.

Activity *Map Puzzle*

Engage

Exploring Key Topics

 individuals
25 min

Give each student two copies of a world map. Have them cut out the continents from one map, and treat them like puzzle pieces to see how they best fit together. By referring to the complete map and the altered map, students can explain and demonstrate how continents moved from their original locations as part of Pangaea to their present locations.

Activity *Modeling Sea-Floor Spreading*

Causes of Plate Motion

 pairs
30 min

Have students model sea-floor spreading. Place a 6-ft length of tape on the floor to represent the rift through which molten rock rises. (If space is limited in your classroom, you may wish to carry out this activity in the gymnasium, cafeteria, or outdoors.) Have some students lie lengthwise along each side of the tape to represent newly formed rock. To demonstrate the formation of more new rock, have students roll away from the tape on your cue. Select other students to lie between the tape and the students on the floor, facing in the same direction. Instruct students on the floor to again roll away from the tape on your cue. Explain that these students represent a new layer, "band of rock," that forms the sea floor and the students on the outer edge represent rock that has been pushed apart as new sea floor was added. Continue until several "bands of rock" are added.

Customize Your Labs

 *See the Lab Manual for lab datasheets.*

 *Go Online for editable lab datasheets.*

Levels of **Inquiry**

DIRECTED inquiry introduces inquiry skills within a structured framework.

GUIDED inquiry develops inquiry skills within a supportive environment.

INDEPENDENT inquiry deepens inquiry skills with student-driven questions or procedures.

Labs and Demos

Daily Demo *Continental Collisions*

Engage

Introducing Key Topics

 whole class
 15 min
 **GUIDED** inquiry

PURPOSE **To model tectonic plate movement and collisions at plate boundaries**

MATERIALS

- **stacks of paper, 1 cm thick (2)**

1 Place the two stacks of paper, with their shorter ends facing each other, side-by-side, on a flat surface.

2 **Observing** Have students observe as you slowly push the two stacks toward each other until the stacks collide. **Ask:** What happens when the stacks collide? Sample answer: They fold and build upward. Relate this to how tectonic plates interact at a convergent boundary.

3 **Observing** Grasp the outer edges of each stack of paper. Pull the stacks in opposite directions. **Ask:** How does plate motion differ in this example? Sample answer: They are moving away from each other. Relate this to how tectonic plates move at a divergent boundary.

4 **Observing** Slowly slide the stacks in opposite directions so that their edges slide along one another. Relate this to movement at transform boundaries.

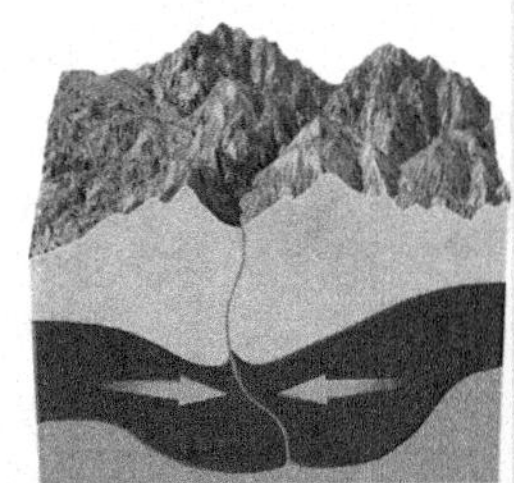

Quick Lab *Mantle Convection*

PURPOSE **To model differences in density that, in part, cause mantle convection**

See the Lab Manual or go Online for planning information.

Quick Lab *Tectonic Ice Cubes*

PURPOSE **To model tectonic plates**

See the Lab Manual or go Online for planning information.

Quick Lab *Reconstructing Land Masses*

PURPOSE **To model the formation of a supercontinent**

See the Lab Manual or go Online for planning information.

Exploration Lab *Seafloor Spreading*

PURPOSE **To explore seafloor spreading**

See the Lab Manual or go Online for planning information.

Virtual Lab *Plate Boundaries*

Theory of Plate Tectonics

 flexible
 45 min
GUIDED inquiry

Students explore Earth's tectonic plate boundaries.

PURPOSE To investigate how the locations of earthquakes and volcanoes correlate to locations and types of plate boundaries.

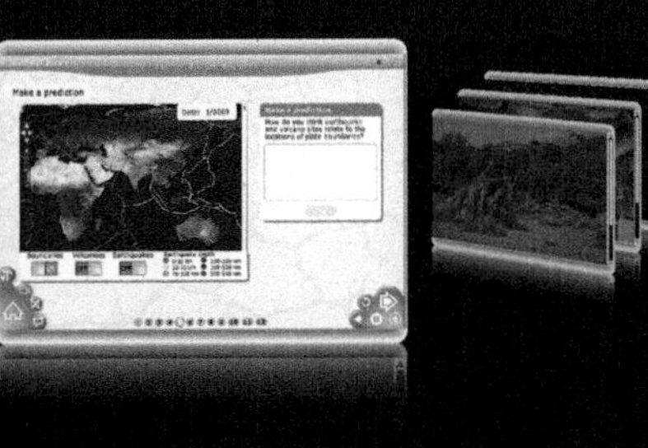

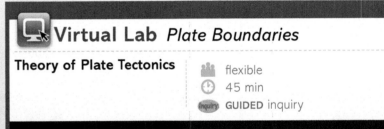

Activities and Discussion

- ☐ **Activity** Map Puzzle
- ☐ **Activity** Modeling Sea-Floor Spreading
- ☐ **Activity** What Boundary Is It?
- ☐ **Discussion** Fossil Locations
- ☐ **Discussion** Evaluating Evidence

Labs and Demos

- ☐ **Daily Demo** Continental Collisions
- ☐ **Quick Lab** Mantle Convection
- ☐ **Quick Lab** Tectonic Ice Cubes
- ☐ **Quick Lab** Reconstructing Land Masses
- ☐ **Exploration Lab** Seafloor Spreading
- ☐ **Virtual Lab** Plate Boundaries

Your Resources

Explain Science Concepts

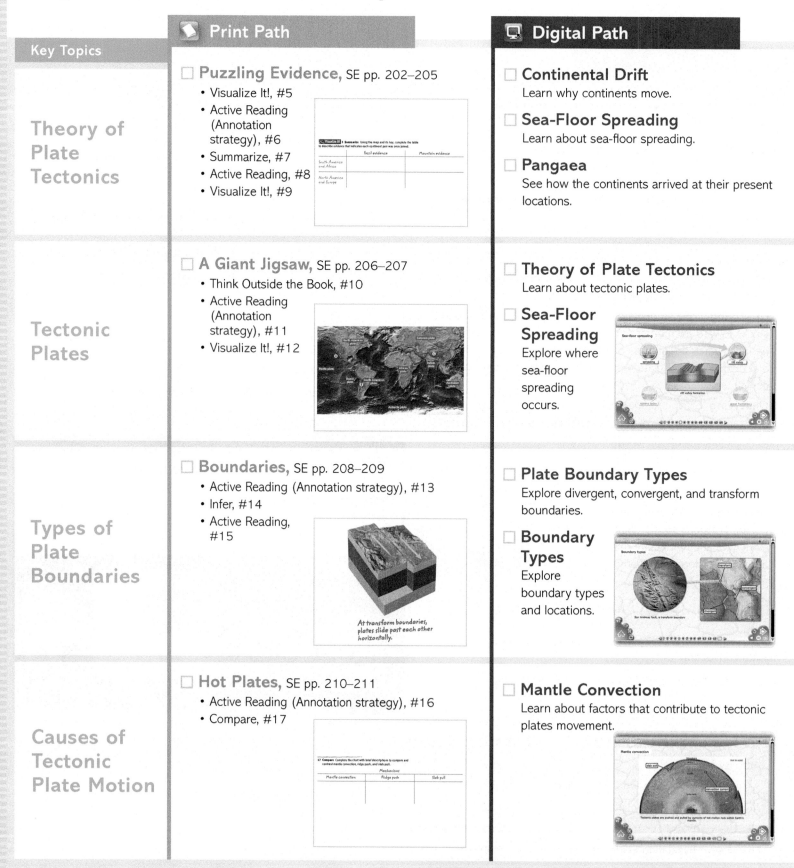

Key Topics	Print Path	Digital Path
Theory of Plate Tectonics	☐ **Puzzling Evidence,** SE pp. 202–205 • Visualize It!, #5 • Active Reading (Annotation strategy), #6 • Summarize, #7 • Active Reading, #8 • Visualize It!, #9	☐ **Continental Drift** Learn why continents move. ☐ **Sea-Floor Spreading** Learn about sea-floor spreading. ☐ **Pangaea** See how the continents arrived at their present locations.
Tectonic Plates	☐ **A Giant Jigsaw,** SE pp. 206–207 • Think Outside the Book, #10 • Active Reading (Annotation strategy), #11 • Visualize It!, #12 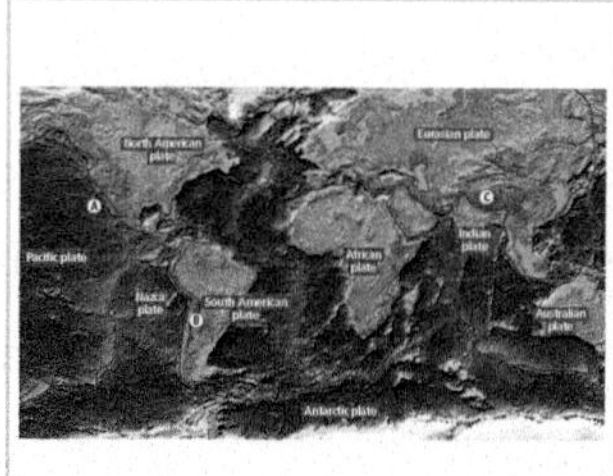	☐ **Theory of Plate Tectonics** Learn about tectonic plates. ☐ **Sea-Floor Spreading** Explore where sea-floor spreading occurs. 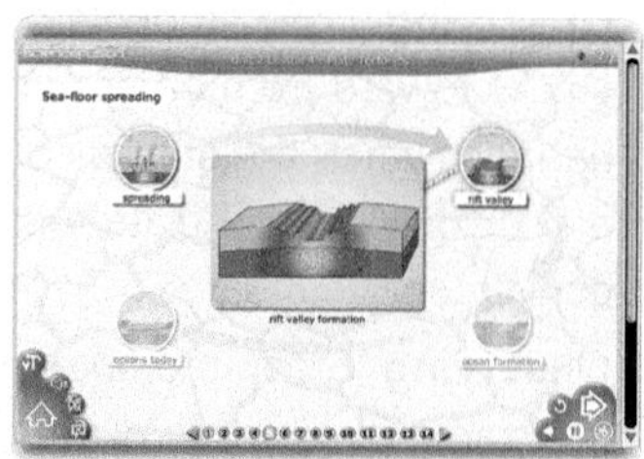
Types of Plate Boundaries	☐ **Boundaries,** SE pp. 208–209 • Active Reading (Annotation strategy), #13 • Infer, #14 • Active Reading, #15  At transform boundaries, plates slide past each other horizontally.	☐ **Plate Boundary Types** Explore divergent, convergent, and transform boundaries. ☐ **Boundary Types** Explore boundary types and locations. 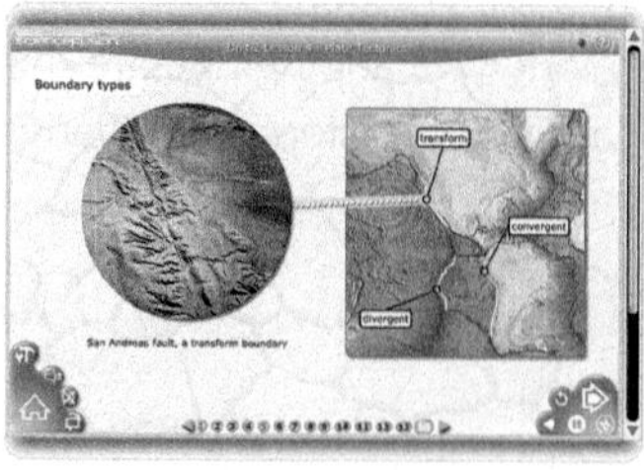
Causes of Tectonic Plate Motion	☐ **Hot Plates,** SE pp. 210–211 • Active Reading (Annotation strategy), #16 • Compare, #17	☐ **Mantle Convection** Learn about factors that contribute to tectonic plates movement. 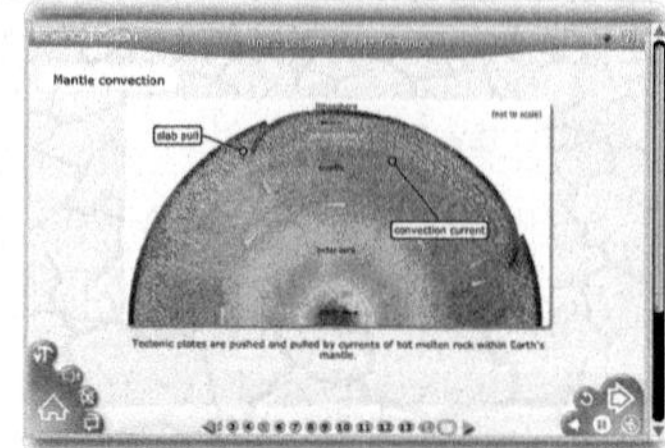

Differentiated Instruction

Basic *Cause and Effect*

Types of Plate Boundaries

 individuals
35 minutes

Have students develop a cause-and-effect organizer on a piece of paper or in their science notebook. Have them draw a simple T Chart with the left column labeled *Cause* and the right column labeled *Effect.* Provide the following example: *Cause:* Continental lithosphere collides with continental lithosphere. *Effect:* Plates crumple, forming a mountain range. Have students complete an organizer for each type of boundary.

Basic *Illustrating Plate Movements*

Causes of Tectonic Plate Motion

 pairs
40 min

Have students work in pairs to make an illustrated chart of plate movements. Students should show the different types of motion and write captions that explain how the plates move. Encourage students to use vocabulary words from the lesson.

Advanced *A Dynamic Tectonic Plate Map*

Synthesizing Key Topics

 individuals
 varied

Have students work individually to research a different type of plate boundary using online or library resources. Then have them work in groups to make a tectonic map of Earth that uses arrows that show the directions of plate movements. Each member of the group should explain what is happening at a different boundary.

ELL *Taking Combination Notes*

Synthesizing Key Topics

 pairs
 40 min

Have students take Combination Notes as they read each section. These notes will help students better understand tectonic plates, tectonic plate boundaries, and tectonic plate motion.

Online resource: Combination Notes support

Lesson Vocabulary

Pangaea	**convection**
sea-floor spreading	**divergent boundary**
convergent boundary	**transform boundary**
plate tectonics	**tectonic plate**

Previewing Vocabulary

whole class  25 min

Prefixes Use the prefixes of the words to help students understand the word meanings. To teach this skill, use the transparency available online. Then, explain the meanings of the prefixes ***con-*** and ***div-*** to help students understand the difference between convergent and divergent boundaries.

 *Online resource: Prefixes*

Reinforcing Vocabulary

individuals 30 min

Drawing To help students remember each vocabulary word introduced in this lesson, have them draw an illustration of each word. Then, have them write the word beneath the illustration, define it, and use it in a sentence.

Customize Your Lesson

Core Instruction

- ☐ **Print Path** choices
- ☐ **Digital Path** choices

Vocabulary

- ☐ **Previewing Vocabulary** Prefixes
- ☐ **Reinforcing Vocabulary** Drawing

Differentiated Instruction

- ☐ **Basic** Cause and Effect
- ☐ **Basic** Illustrating Plate Movements
- ☐ **Advanced** A Dynamic Tectonic Plate Map
- ☐ **ELL** Taking Combination Notes

Your Resources

Extend Science Concepts

Reinforce and Review

Activity *What Was This All About?*

Synthesizing Key Topics

small groups
45 min

Think, Pair, Share Have students use the Think, Pair, Share strategy to reinforce their learning. Ask them to form groups of four. Each group member should select a section from the lesson to summarize. Students can then form pairs, with each student explaining the key points of their section to their partner. Students can then reform their complete group and exchange ideas about their topic with the group. Students may find it helpful to use the reproducible available online to help them organize their ideas.

Online resource: Think, Pair, Share worksheet.

Graphic Organizer

Theory of Plate Tectonics

individuals
35 min

Concept Map After students have studied the lesson, ask them to create a Concept Map to summarize the main ideas of the theory of plate tectonics.

Optional Online resources: Concept Map support

Going Further

Life Science Connection

Synthesizing Key Topics

individuals
varied

Pangaea and Dinosaur Evolution Explain that prior to the breakup of Pangaea, many species of dinosaurs roamed Pangaea. As Pangaea broke up, dinosaur populations became fragmented and isolated on the new continents. These populations evolved into new species in response to their new environments. Have groups of students research some species of dinosaurs that lived after the breakup of Pangaea and speculate why these dinosaurs evolved in the manner they did.

Physical Science Connection

Synthesizing Key Topics

small groups
varied

Sonar In the 1950s, scientists began using sonar to map the ocean floor. This technology works by sending out a sound wave from a ship and then measuring the amount of time it takes for the wave to bounce off the ocean floor and return to the ship. Because sound waves travel at a specific rate, the time required for the echo to return can be used to measure distance. The echoes revealed an ocean floor with a complex topography. Scientists were amazed to find a chain of undersea mountains that snaked thousands of kilometers around the globe. These mountains are the mid-ocean ridges. Have students explain and diagram what echoes are and how they can be used by scientists to map areas that can't be seen.

Customize Your Closing

See the Assessment Guide for quizzes and tests.

Go Online to edit and create quizzes and tests.

Reinforce and Review

- ☐ **Activity** What Was This All About?
- ☐ **Graphic Organizer** Concept Map
- ☐ **Print Path** Visual Summary, SE p. 212
- ☐ **Digital Path** Lesson Closer

Evaluate Student Mastery

Formative Assessment

See the teacher support below the Student Pages for additional Formative Assessment questions.

Describe or have students review the differences between the different types of plate boundaries. **Ask:** What types of landforms can form at convergent and divergent boundaries? Sample answer: Mountains and trenches can form at convergent boundaries and valleys and mid-ocean ridges can form at divergent boundaries.

Reteach

Formative assessment may show you that students need reinforcement for certain topics. The resources below are recommended for reteaching. If students were introduced to topics through the Print Path, you can also use the Digital Path for reteaching, and vice versa.

Can be assigned to individual students

Theory of Plate Tectonics

Activity Map Puzzle

Discussion Evaluating Evidence

Tectonic Plates

Daily Demo Continental Collisions

Types of Plate Boundaries

Activity What Boundary Is It?

Causes of Tectonic Plate Motion

Activity Modeling Sea-Floor Spreading

Virtual Lab Plate Boundaries

Summative Assessment

Alternative Assessment

Exploring Tectonic Plates

Online resources: student worksheet; optional rubrics

Plate Tectonics

Climb the Pyramid: ***Exploring Tectonic Plates***
Complete the activities to show what you have learned about plate tectonics.

1. Work on your own, with a partner, or with a small group.
2. Choose one item from each layer of the pyramid. Check your choices.
3. Have your teacher approve your plan.
4. Submit or present your results.

__ A Puzzling Picture
Create a drawing of the continents as they once fit together. Each continent should be a labeled and drawn in a different color. Carefully cut out each continent to create a puzzle. Then demonstrate the hypothesis of plate tectonics by moving the puzzle pieces and explaining the hypothesis and evidence to support it.

__ Plate Interview	__ Sea-floor Spreading
Imagine that you are a newspaper reporter in 1912 who has heard about Alfred Wegener's astonishing new idea called continental drift. You are going to interview the scientist about his theory. List 10 questions to ask Wegener.	Write a description of the process of sea-floor spreading, using the Mid-Atlantic Ridge as an example. Be sure to tell about how material reaches the surface and why the ridge is higher than the surrounding oceanic plates.

__ Density Differences	__ Flipbook	__ Collision Diorama
Write a poem or song that explains how density differences below Earth's plates causes the plates to move and change shape.	Draw a flipbook to show what happens at plate boundaries. Show a convergent boundary, a divergent boundary, and a transform boundary.	Make a diorama showing convergent boundaries formed between (1) two continental plates, (2) a continental plate and an oceanic plate, or (3) two oceanic plates. Create labels for your diorama.

Going Further

- ☐ Life Science Connection
- ☐ Physical Science Connection

Formative Assessment

- ☐ Strategies Throughout TE
- ☐ Lesson Review SE

Summative Assessment

- ☐ Alternative Assessment Exploring Tectonic Plates
- ☐ Lesson Quiz
- ☐ Unit Tests A and B
- ☐ Unit Review SE End-of-Unit

Your Resources

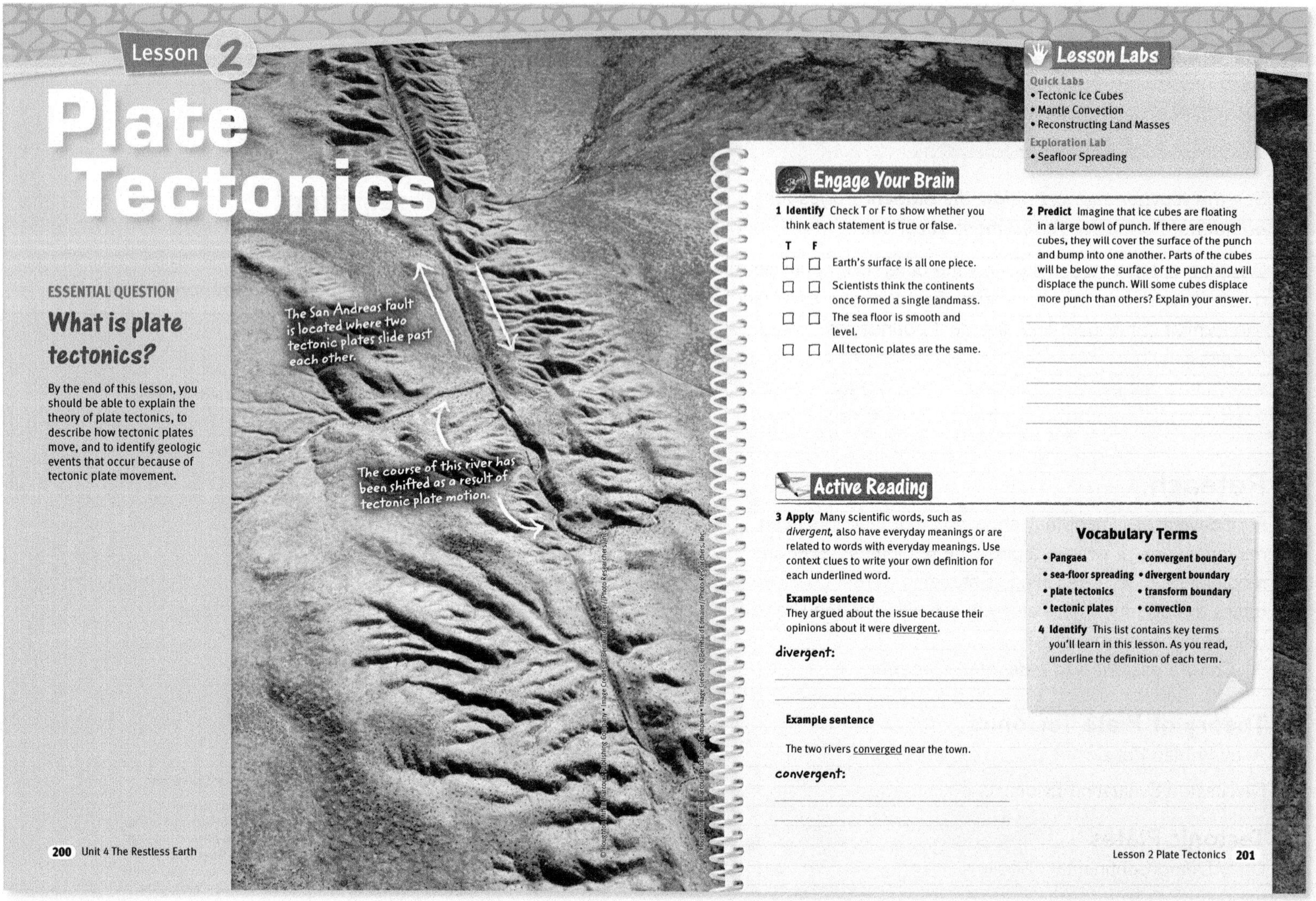

Lesson 2

Plate Tectonics

ESSENTIAL QUESTION

What is plate tectonics?

By the end of this lesson, you should be able to explain the theory of plate tectonics, to describe how tectonic plates move, and to identify geologic events that occur because of tectonic plate movement.

The San Andreas Fault is located where two tectonic plates slide past each other.

The course of this river has been shifted as a result of tectonic plate motion.

Lesson Labs

Quick Labs
- Tectonic Ice Cubes
- Mantle Convection
- Reconstructing Land Masses

Exploration Lab
- Seafloor Spreading

Engage Your Brain

1 Identify Check T or F to show whether you think each statement is true or false.

T	F	
☐	☐	Earth's surface is all one piece.
☐	☐	Scientists think the continents once formed a single landmass.
☐	☐	The sea floor is smooth and level.
☐	☐	All tectonic plates are the same.

2 Predict Imagine that ice cubes are floating in a large bowl of punch. If there are enough cubes, they will cover the surface of the punch and bump into one another. Parts of the cubes will be below the surface of the punch and will displace the punch. Will some cubes displace more punch than others? Explain your answer.

Active Reading

3 Apply Many scientific words, such as *divergent*, also have everyday meanings or are related to words with everyday meanings. Use context clues to write your own definition for each underlined word.

Example sentence

They argued about the issue because their opinions about it were divergent.

divergent:

Example sentence

The two rivers converged near the town.

convergent:

Vocabulary Terms

- Pangaea
- sea-floor spreading
- plate tectonics
- tectonic plates
- convergent boundary
- divergent boundary
- transform boundary
- convection

4 Identify This list contains key terms you'll learn in this lesson. As you read, underline the definition of each term.

200 Unit 4 The Restless Earth

Lesson 2 Plate Tectonics 201

Answers

Answers for 1–3 should represent students' current thoughts, even if incorrect.

1. F; T; F; F
2. Sample answer: Larger cubes will displace more punch than smaller cubes. Cubes that are more submerged will displace more punch than others that are floating on top.
3. Sample answer: Divergent means differing. It also means moving away from a common point. Convergent means meeting or coming together.
4. Students' annotations will vary.

Opening Your Lesson

Have students share their predictions about how much punch would be displaced by ice cubes (item 2) to assess their working knowledge of the key topics.

Prerequisites Earth is made up of different physical and compositional layers.

Accessing Prior Knowledge To assess students' prior knowledge about tectonic plates, you may wish to have them conduct a Textbook DRTA. Begin by explaining that DRTA stands for Directed Reading/Thinking Activity. To complete the activity, students need to (1) preview the selection; (2) write what they know, what they think they know, and what they think they'll learn about tectonic plates; (3) read the selection; and (4) write what they learned. Discuss whether students' expectations were reasonable, and whether they learned additional information that they did not anticipate.

Optional Online resource: Textbook DRTA support

Learning Alert

Plate Motion Tectonic plates are in constant motion. Although imperceptible to humans, the motion can be detected and measured by GPS receivers and seismographs. The lithosphere is made up of more than a dozen plates that move in relation to one another and cause both slow and rapid changes to Earth's crust.

Puzzling Evidence

What evidence suggests that continents move?

Have you ever looked at a map and noticed that the continents look like they could fit together like puzzle pieces? In the late 1800s, Alfred Wegener proposed his hypothesis of continental drift. He proposed that the continents once formed a single landmass, broke up, and drifted. This idea is supported by several lines of evidence. For example, fossils of the same species are found on continents on different sides of the Atlantic Ocean. These species could not have crossed the ocean. The hypothesis is also supported by the locations of mountain ranges and rock formations and by evidence of the same ancient climatic conditions on several continents.

Geologic evidence supports the hypothesis of continental drift.

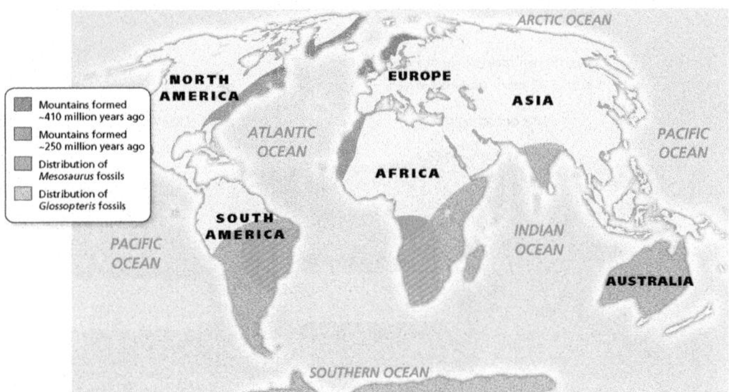

Visualize It! 5 Summarize Using the map and its key, complete the table to describe evidence that indicates each continent pair was once joined.

	Fossil evidence	Mountain evidence
South America and Africa		
North America and Europe		

What is Pangaea?

Active Reading 6 Identify As you read, underline the description of how North America formed from Pangaea.

Using evidence from many scientific fields, scientists can construct a picture of continental change throughout time. Scientists think that about 245 million years ago, the continents were joined in a single large landmass they call **Pangaea** (pan•JEE•uh). As the continents collided to form Pangaea, mountains formed. A single, large ocean called Panthalassa surrounded Pangaea.

About 200 million years ago, a large rift formed and Pangaea began to break into two continents—*Laurasia* and *Gondwana*. Then, Laurasia began to drift northward and rotate slowly, and a new rift formed. This rift separated Laurasia into the continents of North America and Eurasia. The rift eventually formed the North Atlantic Ocean. At the same time, Gondwana also broke into two continents. One continent contained land that is now the continents of South America and Africa. The other continent contained land that is now Antarctica, Australia, and India.

About 150 million years ago, a rift between Africa and South America opened to form the South Atlantic Ocean. India, Australia, and Antarctica also began to separate from each other. As India broke away from Australia and Antarctica, it started moving northward, toward Eurasia.

As India and the other continents moved into their present positions, new oceans formed while others disappeared. In some cases, continents collided with other continents. About 50 million years ago, India collided with Eurasia, and the Himalaya Mountains began to form. Mountain ranges form as a result of these collisions, because a collision welds new crust onto the continents and uplifts some of the land.

The Breakup of Pangaea

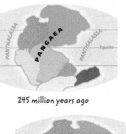

245 million years ago

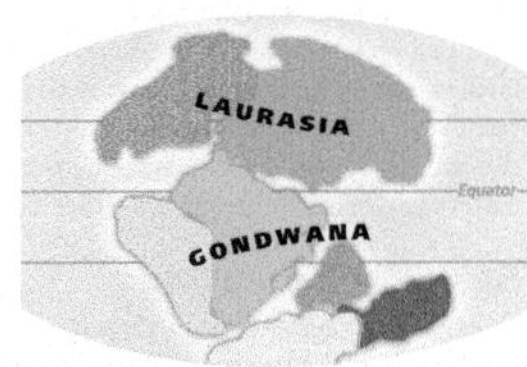

200 million years ago

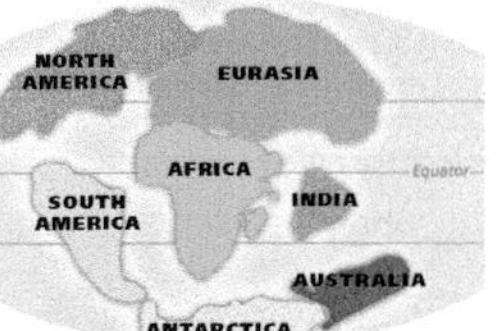

65 million years ago

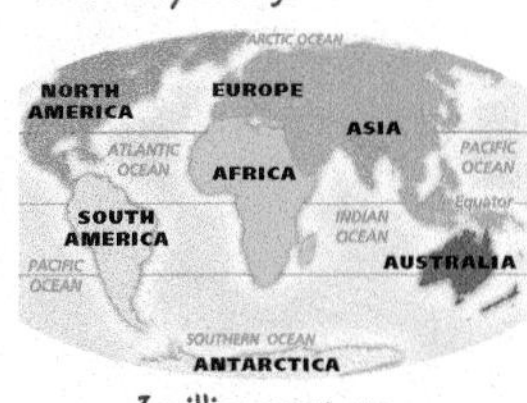

3 million years ago

Answers

5. South America and Africa

   Fossil evidence: have corresponding distribution of both types of fossils

   Mountain evidence: no evidence shown on map

   North America and Europe

   Fossil evidence: no evidence shown on map

   Mountain evidence: have corresponding distribution of mountains

6. *See students' pages for annotations.*

Interpreting Visuals

Have students look closely at the maps on these pages. Ask them to use the map key and other information to explain how scientists have come to the conclusion that the continents were once one, and have drifted apart. Sample answer: The shapes of continents appear to fit together like puzzle pieces; similar fossils and mountain ranges exist on different continents that appear to have once been joined.

Using Annotations

Text Structure: Main Ideas/Details Actively reading a text helps students gain more from its contents. When students complete this annotation, give them a chance to share the words they underlined with a partner. They may have found descriptions their partner missed and vice versa.

Probing Question DIRECTED Inquiry

Evaluate Scientists use different pieces of evidence to support the conclusion that the continents were once joined together to form one large continent called *Pangaea*. Have students read through the evidence presented in this lesson and in other sources and decide if they agree or disagree. Have them support their stance with evidence.

What discoveries support the idea of continental drift?

Wegener's ideas of continental drift were pushed aside for many years because scientists could not determine how continents moved. Then, in the mid-1900s, scientists began mapping the sea floor. They expected the floor to be smooth and level. Instead, they found huge under-water mountain ranges called *mid-ocean ridges*. The discovery of mid-ocean ridges eventually led to the theory of plate tectonics, which built on some of Wegener's ideas.

7 Summarize Why would many scientists not accept the hypothesis of continental drift?

Age and Magnetic Properties of the Sea Floor

Scientists learned that the mid-ocean ridges form along cracks in the crust. Rock samples from the sea floor revealed that the youngest rock is closest to the ridge, while the oldest rock is farthest away. The samples also showed that even the oldest ocean crust is young compared to continental crust. Scientists also discovered that sea-floor rock contains magnetic patterns. These patterns form mirror images on either side of a mid-ocean ridge.

Sea-Floor Spreading

To explain the age and magnetic patterns of sea-floor rocks, scientists proposed a process called **sea-floor spreading**. In this process, molten rock from inside Earth rises through the cracks in the ridges, cools, and forms new oceanic crust. The old crust breaks along the mid-point of the ridge and the two pieces of crust move away in opposite directions from each other. In this way, the sea floor slowly spreads apart. As the sea floor moves, so do the continents on the same piece of crust.

This map shows where mid-ocean ridges are located.

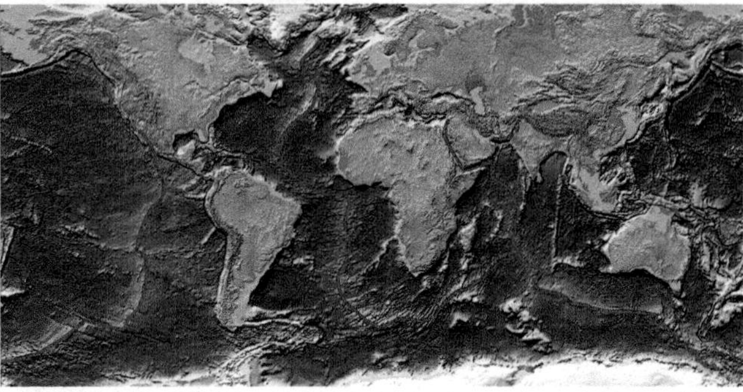

Ocean Trenches

If the sea floor has been spreading for millions of years, why is Earth not getting larger? Scientists discovered the answer when they found huge trenches, like deep canyons, in the sea floor. At these sites, dense oceanic crust is sinking into the asthenosphere as shown in the diagram below. Older crust is being destroyed at the same rate new crust is forming. Thus, Earth remains the same size.

With this new information about the sea floor, sea-floor spreading, and ocean trenches, scientists could begin to understand how continents were able to move.

Active Reading

8 Identify Why is Earth not getting larger if the sea floor is spreading?

Visualize It!

9 Provide Label the youngest rock and the oldest rock on this diagram of sea-floor spreading.

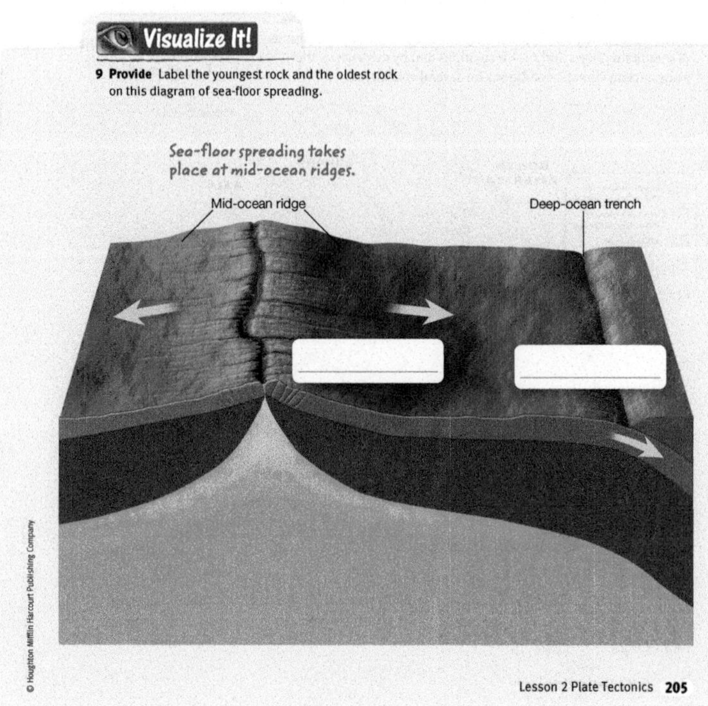
Sea-floor spreading takes place at mid-ocean ridges.
Mid-ocean ridge
Deep-ocean trench

Answers

7. They did not have evidence of how continents could move.
8. Old crust is destroyed at the same rate as new crust forms.
9. youngest rock: closest to mid-ocean ridge; oldest rock: furthest from ridge

Learning Alert

Magnetic reversals show that new lithosphere forms at mid-ocean ridges. At the same time, older lithosphere is being pushed away from mid-ocean ridges. Magnetic reversals are a record of past events, which occur periodically, although not at regular intervals, over millions of years. The last magnetic reversal occurred nearly 780,000 years ago.

Formative Assessment

Ask: What magnetic pattern occurs in the rocks located on either side of a mid-ocean ridge? Sample answer: Rocks show a magnetic pattern that forms mirror images of each other on each side of a mid-ocean ridge. **Ask:** What is true about the ages of rocks on either side of a mid-ocean ridge? Sample answer: Rock samples indicate that those samples nearest the ridge are younger than those farther away. **Ask:** What process explains the magnetic patterns and age variations in rock along a mid-ocean ridge? sea-floor spreading

Student Pages 204–207

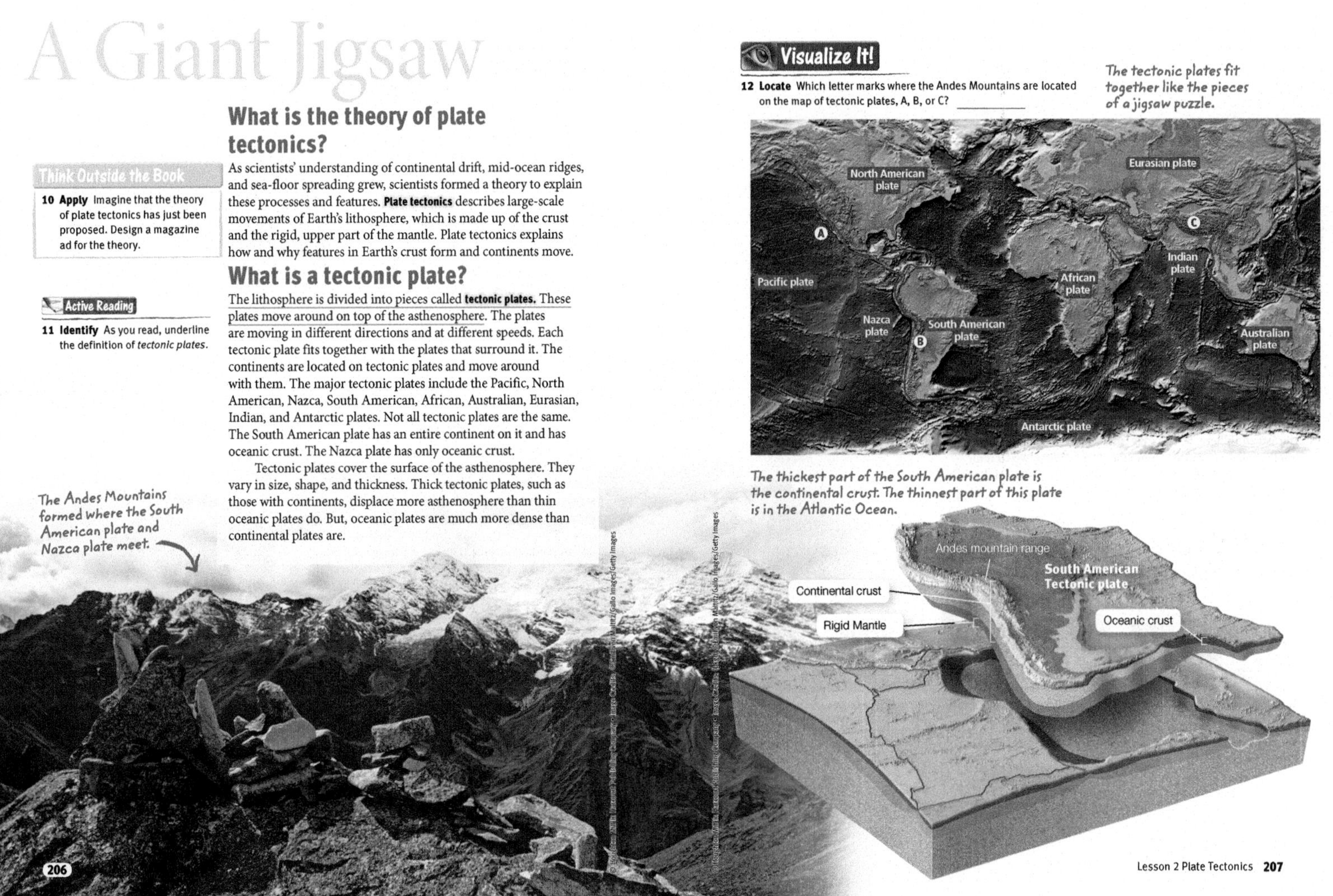

A Giant Jigsaw

What is the theory of plate tectonics?

As scientists' understanding of continental drift, mid-ocean ridges, and sea-floor spreading grew, scientists formed a theory to explain these processes and features. **Plate tectonics** describes large-scale movements of Earth's lithosphere, which is made up of the crust and the rigid, upper part of the mantle. Plate tectonics explains how and why features in Earth's crust form and continents move.

Think Outside the Book

10 Apply Imagine that the theory of plate tectonics has just been proposed. Design a magazine ad for the theory.

What is a tectonic plate?

The lithosphere is divided into pieces called **tectonic plates.** These plates move around on top of the asthenosphere. The plates are moving in different directions and at different speeds. Each tectonic plate fits together with the plates that surround it. The continents are located on tectonic plates and move around with them. The major tectonic plates include the Pacific, North American, Nazca, South American, African, Australian, Eurasian, Indian, and Antarctic plates. Not all tectonic plates are the same. The South American plate has an entire continent on it and has oceanic crust. The Nazca plate has only oceanic crust.

Tectonic plates cover the surface of the asthenosphere. They vary in size, shape, and thickness. Thick tectonic plates, such as those with continents, displace more asthenosphere than thin oceanic plates do. But, oceanic plates are much more dense than continental plates are.

Active Reading

11 Identify As you read, underline the definition of *tectonic plates.*

The Andes Mountains formed where the South American plate and Nazca plate meet.

Visualize It!

12 Locate Which letter marks where the Andes Mountains are located on the map of tectonic plates, A, B, or C? ________

The tectonic plates fit together like the pieces of a jigsaw puzzle.

The thickest part of the South American plate is the continental crust. The thinnest part of this plate is in the Atlantic Ocean.

206

Lesson 2 Plate Tectonics 207

Answers

10. Students should include information on what the theory is and the evidence scientists have found to support the theory.
11. *See students' pages for annotations.*
12. B

Interpreting Visuals

Have students compare the map showing the locations of tectonic plates above with that showing the locations of mid-ocean ridges earlier in the lesson. Ask: What similarities do you observe in the two maps? Sample answer: Many mid-ocean ridges are located along the edges of tectonic plates.

Building Reading Skills

Outline This lesson contains a great deal of information about plate tectonics. Students may find it helpful to outline the text as they read. Instructions for helping to teach students outlining skills are available online.

Online resource: Outline support

Formative Assessment

Ask: What evidence has contributed to the theory of plate tectonics? Sample answer: continental drift, the formation of mid-ocean ridges, and sea-floor spreading **Ask:** What is a tectonic plate? Sample answer: A tectonic plate is a piece of the lithosphere that moves as it floats on top of the asthenosphere.

Boundaries

What are the three types of plate boundaries?

The most dramatic changes in Earth's crust occur along plate boundaries. Plate boundaries may be on the ocean floor, around the edges of continents, or even within continents. There are three types of plate boundaries: divergent boundaries, convergent boundaries, and transform boundaries. Each type of plate boundary is associated with characteristic landforms.

13 Identify As you read, underline the locations where plate boundaries may be found.

Convergent Boundaries

Convergent boundaries form where two plates collide. Three types of collisions can happen at convergent boundaries. When two tectonic plates of continental lithosphere collide, they buckle and thicken, which pushes some of the continental crust upward. When a plate of oceanic lithosphere collides with a plate of continental lithosphere, the denser oceanic lithosphere sinks into the asthenosphere. Boundaries where one plate sinks beneath another plate are called subduction zones. When two tectonic plates of oceanic lithosphere collide, one of the plates subducts, or sinks, under the other plate.

Inquiry

14 Infer Why do you think the denser plate subducts in a collision?

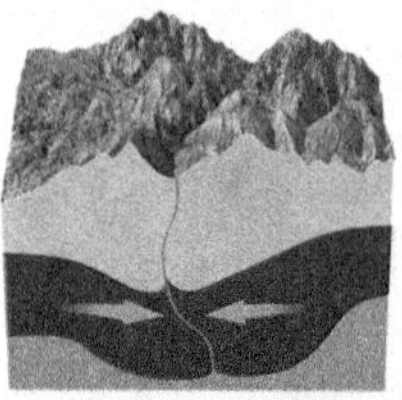

Continent-Continent Collisions
When two plates of continental lithosphere collide, they buckle and thicken. This causes mountains to form.

Continent-Ocean Collisions
When a plate of oceanic lithosphere collides with a plate of continental lithosphere, the oceanic lithosphere subducts because it is denser.

Ocean-Ocean Collisions
When two plates of oceanic lithosphere collide, the older, denser plate subducts under the other plate.

Divergent Boundaries

At a **divergent boundary**, two plates move away from each other. This separation allows the asthenosphere to rise toward the surface and partially melt. This melting creates magma, which erupts as lava. The lava cools and hardens to form new rock on the ocean floor.

As the crust and the upper part of the asthenosphere cool and become rigid, they form new lithosphere. This lithosphere is thin, warm, and light. This warm, light rock sits higher than the surrounding sea floor because it is less dense. It forms mid-ocean ridges. Most divergent boundaries are located on the ocean floor. However, rift valleys may also form where continents are separated by plate movement.

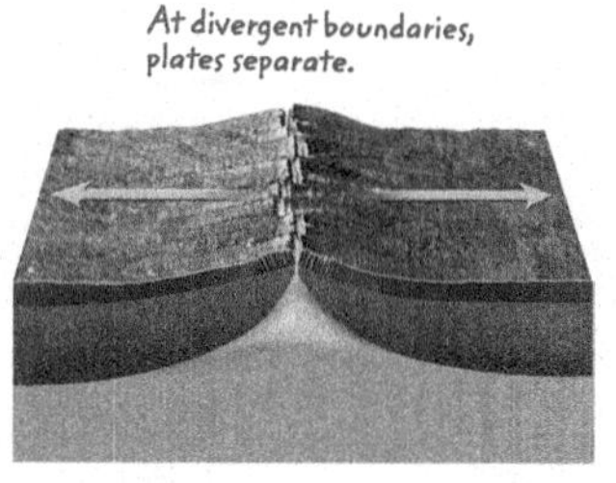

At divergent boundaries, plates separate.

Transform Boundaries

A boundary at which two plates move past each other horizontally is called a **transform boundary**. However, the plate edges do not slide along smoothly. Instead, they scrape against each other in a series of sudden slippages of crustal rock that are felt as earthquakes. Unlike other types of boundaries, transform boundaries generally do not produce magma. The San Andreas Fault in California is a major transform boundary between the North American plate and the Pacific plate. Transform motion also occurs at divergent boundaries. Short segments of mid-ocean ridges are connected by transform faults called fracture zones.

Active Reading

15 Contrast How are transform boundaries different from convergent and divergent boundaries?

At transform boundaries, plates slide past each other horizontally.

Answers

13. *See students' pages for annotations.*
14. The denser plate subducts because it is heavier. It sinks below the less dense plate.
15. Transform boundaries are different because the plates slide past each other parallel to Earth's surface, they do not move closer or farther apart from each other.

Interpreting Visuals

Have students compare the images of the different plate boundaries. **Ask:** What are the differences among the three? Convergent boundaries occur where two plates collide. Divergent boundaries occur where two plates move away from each other. Transform boundaries occur where two plates slide past each other parallel to Earth's surface.

Using Annotations

Text Structure: Contrast Students are asked to contrast transform, convergent, and divergent boundaries. This is an effective way to think more deeply about a topic. Encourage students to locate and record all of the characteristics of each type of boundary. Have them keep their notes in their science folder or notebook so it is easy to refer to as they complete the lesson.

Hot Plates

What causes tectonic plates to move?

Scientists have proposed three mechanisms to explain how tectonic plates move over Earth's surface. Mantle convection drags plates along as mantle material moves beneath tectonic plates. Ridge push moves plates away from mid-ocean ridges as rock cools and becomes more dense. Slab pull tugs plates along as the dense edge of a plate sinks beneath Earth's surface.

Active Reading

16 Identify As you read, underline three mechanisms scientists have proposed to explain plate motion.

Ridge Push

Newly formed rock at a mid-ocean ridge is warm and less dense than older, adjacent rock. Because of its lower density, the new rock rests at a higher elevation than the older rock. The older rock slopes downward away from the ridge. As the newer, warmer rock cools, it also becomes more dense. These cooling and increasingly dense rocks respond to gravity by moving down the slope of the asthenosphere, away from the ridge. This force, called ridge push, pushes the rest of the plate away from the mid-ocean ridge.

Slab Pull

At subduction zones, a denser tectonic plate sinks, or subducts, beneath another, less dense plate. The leading edge of the subducting plate is colder and denser than the mantle. As it sinks, the leading edge of the plate pulls the rest of the plate with it. This process is called slab pull. In general, subducting plates move faster than other plates do. This evidence leads many scientists to think that slab pull may be the most important mechanism driving tectonic plate motion.

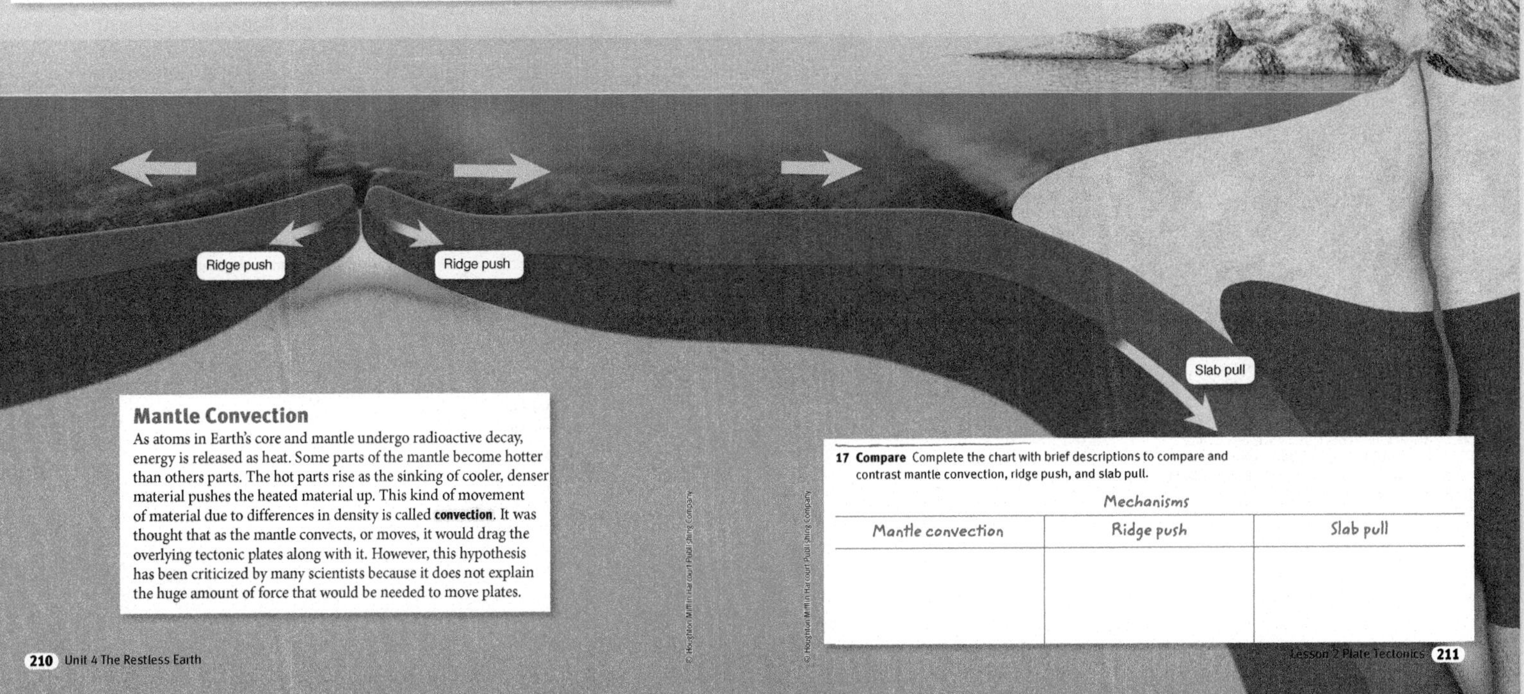

Mantle Convection

As atoms in Earth's core and mantle undergo radioactive decay, energy is released as heat. Some parts of the mantle become hotter than others parts. The hot parts rise as the sinking of cooler, denser material pushes the heated material up. This kind of movement of material due to differences in density is called **convection**. It was thought that as the mantle convects, or moves, it would drag the overlying tectonic plates along with it. However, this hypothesis has been criticized by many scientists because it does not explain the huge amount of force that would be needed to move plates.

17 Compare Complete the chart with brief descriptions to compare and contrast mantle convection, ridge push, and slab pull.

Mechanisms		
Mantle convection	Ridge push	Slab pull

Answers

16. *See students' pages for annotations.*
17. Mantle convection: Convection currents drag the overlying tectonic plates with them. However, many scientists don't think that this force is large enough to explain plate motion.

    Ridge push: New rock is elevated at the mid-ocean ridge because it warmer and less dense than older rock. As the newer rock cools, it becomes denser and flows down the slope of the asthenosphere, pushing the rest of the plate away from the mid-ocean ridge.

    Slab pull: As part of a plate sinks into the asthnosphere, it's weight pulls the rest of the plate along with it. This force is thought to be the most important force behind tectonic plate motion.

Learning Alert MISCONCEPTION

Earthquake Activity Some students may think that geologic activity, such as earthquakes, occurs only at plate boundaries. Explain that, although active margins experience the greatest amount of geologic activity, earthquakes can happen anywhere. Three of the largest earthquakes in U.S. history happened in New Madrid, Missouri, during the winter of 1811–1812. The quakes were so strong that they made church bells ring in Boston, more than 1,000 miles away!

Probing Questions DIRECTED Inquiry

Apply What pattern of seismic and volcanic activity can be seen on Earth? Most of this activity occurs at plate boundaries.

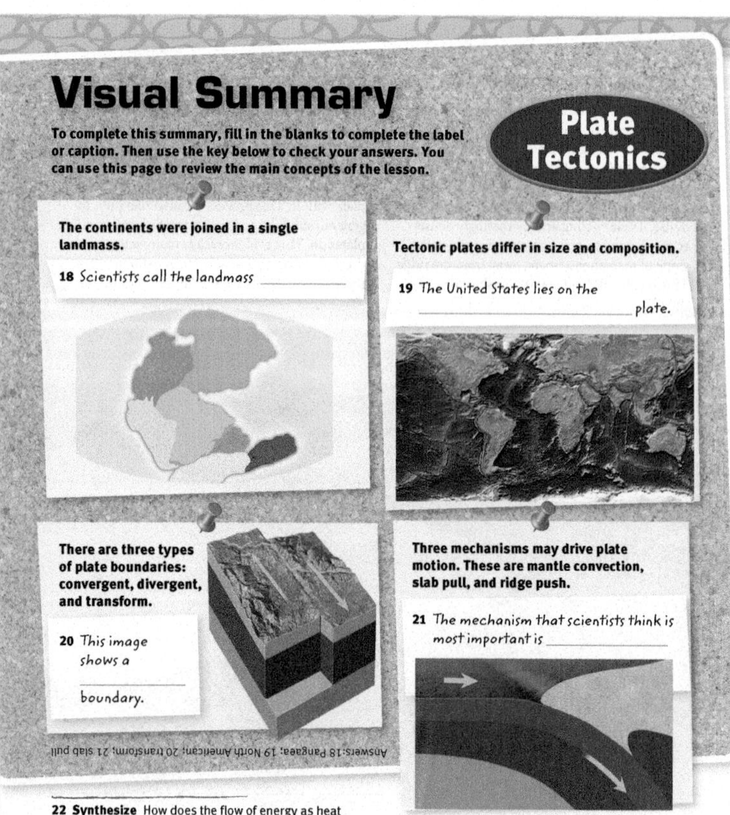

Visual Summary

To complete this summary, fill in the blanks to complete the label or caption. Then use the key below to check your answers. You can use this page to review the main concepts of the lesson.

Plate Tectonics

The continents were joined in a single landmass.

18 Scientists call the landmass ________

Tectonic plates differ in size and composition.

19 The United States lies on the ________ plate.

There are three types of plate boundaries: convergent, divergent, and transform.

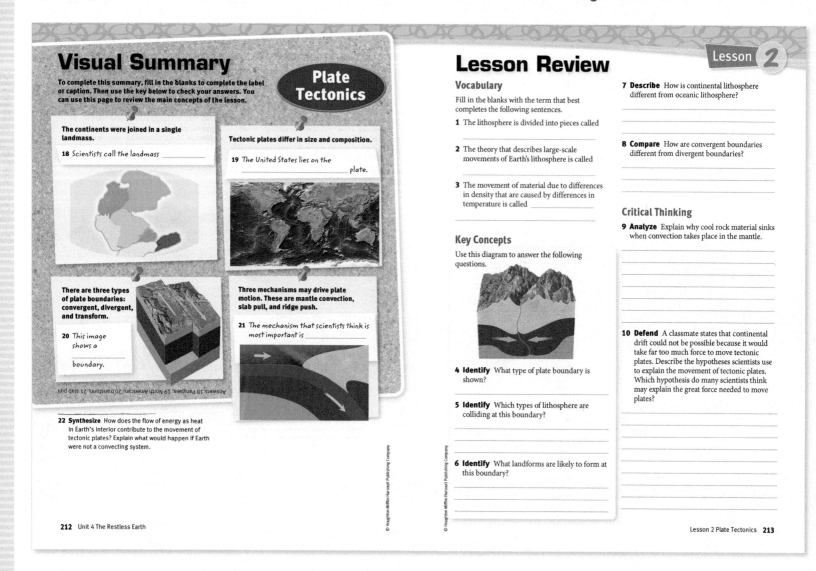

20 This image shows a ________ boundary.

Three mechanisms may drive plate motion. These are mantle convection, slab pull, and ridge push.

21 The mechanism that scientists think is most important is ________

Answers: 18 Pangaea; 19 North American; 20 transform; 21 slab pull

22 **Synthesize** How does the flow of energy as heat in Earth's interior contribute to the movement of tectonic plates? Explain what would happen if Earth were not a convecting system.

212 Unit 4 The Restless Earth

Lesson Review

Lesson 2

Vocabulary

Fill in the blanks with the term that best completes the following sentences.

1 The lithosphere is divided into pieces called ________

2 The theory that describes large-scale movements of Earth's lithosphere is called ________

3 The movement of material due to differences in density that are caused by differences in temperature is called ________

Key Concepts

Use this diagram to answer the following questions.

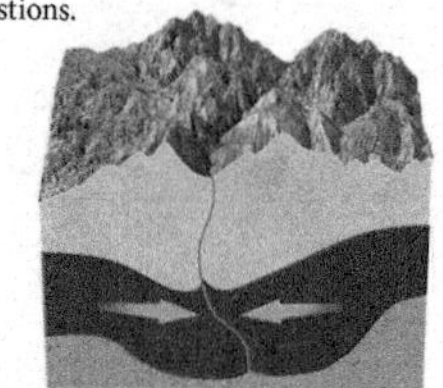

4 **Identify** What type of plate boundary is shown?

5 **Identify** Which types of lithosphere are colliding at this boundary?

6 **Identify** What landforms are likely to form at this boundary?

7 **Describe** How is continental lithosphere different from oceanic lithosphere?

8 **Compare** How are convergent boundaries different from divergent boundaries?

Critical Thinking

9 **Analyze** Explain why cool rock material sinks when convection takes place in the mantle.

10 **Defend** A classmate states that continental drift could not be possible because it would take far too much force to move tectonic plates. Describe the hypotheses scientists use to explain the movement of tectonic plates. Which hypothesis do many scientists think may explain the great force needed to move plates?

Lesson 2 Plate Tectonics 213

Visual Summary Answers

18. Pangaea
19. North American
20. transform
21. slab pull
22. Tectonic plates move mainly because of slab pull, then ridge push, and least of all, due to convection currents. In the mantle, cooler materials sink, displacing warmer materials. This motion sets up convection currents. Some of the tectonic plate motion we observe today is due to these currents. Without these currents, the rate of motion would likely be slower.

Lesson Review Answers

1. tectonic plates
2. plate tectonics
3. convection
4. convergent
5. continental
6. mountains
7. Continental lithosphere is thicker and less dense than oceanic lithosphere.
8. Convergent: two plates collide, three types of collisions can occur

   Divergent: two plates move away from each other, most on ocean floor
9. Cool rock material sinks because it is denser and heavier than warm rock is.
10. Mantle convection: As mantle convects, it drags tectonic plates with it; not likely to create the amount of force needed to explain plate motion.

    Ridge push: New warm, light rock at mid-ocean ridges is elevated relative to the older, adjacent rock, which is denser and colder. As the new rock cools, it becomes denser and flows down the slope of the asthenosphere, away from the mid-ocean ridge. At the same time, it also pushes the rest of the plate away from the mid-ocean ridge.

    Slab pull: At subduction zones, denser plates subduct beneath less dense plates. The leading edge of a subducting plate is colder than the mantle and sinks, pulling the rest of the plate with it.

    Scientists think slab pull explains the force needed to explain plate motion.

Teacher Notes

Estella Atekwana

Purpose To learn about Estella Atekwana and the work that geologists do

Learning Goals

- Understand what geologists can tell us about how Earth has changed over time.
- State how studying changes in rocks on Earth might help us detect the existence of life on other planets.

Informal Vocabulary

rift valley, biogeophysics, paleontological

Prerequisite Knowledge

- Earth's crust
- Plate tectonics
- Microorganisms

Activity *Career Quiz*

 small groups |  15 min |  **GUIDED** inquiry

Have students write on separate index cards the following phrases: *What You'll Do, Where You Might Work, Education, and Other Job Requirements.* Then have students use these phrases to quiz each other on what survey and mapping technicians, petroleum technicians, and geologists do.

Variation: Students can make up questions based on the job descriptions on these pages, such as, Which professional might work on the slope of a volcano? Then they can use their questions to quiz each other about these jobs.

Differentiated Instruction

Basic *Botswana and Zambia*

 pairs |  30 min

Mapping Have pairs of students draw a map that shows the region of Africa containing Botswana and Zambia. Then have students mark the location of the rift valley that Dr. Atekwana studies. Last, have students draw and label other physical features on their maps, such as deserts, rivers, and lakes.

Advanced *Microorganisms and Rocks*

pairs |  30 min

Oral Presentations Have student pairs conduct research and prepare an oral presentation about how microorganisms can change rocks. What tools and techniques do biogeophysicists use to detect such changes? How might what they learn be used to search for life on other planets? Encourage students to include visuals with their presentations.

Optional Online rubric: Oral Presentations

ELL *Role-Play a Profession*

 pairs or small groups | 15 min

Have pairs or small groups role-play to show what the people in the jobs described on these pages do. For example, they could act out taking measurements to show what a surveying technician does or pretend to take water samples to demonstrate something a geologist might do.

Customize Your Feature

- ☐ **Activity** Career Quiz
- ☐ **People in Science** Online
- ☐ **Basic** Botswana and Zambia
- ☐ **Advanced** Microorganisms and Rocks
- ☐ **ELL** Role-Play a Profession
- ☐ **Social Studies Connection**
- ☐ **Building Reading Skills**

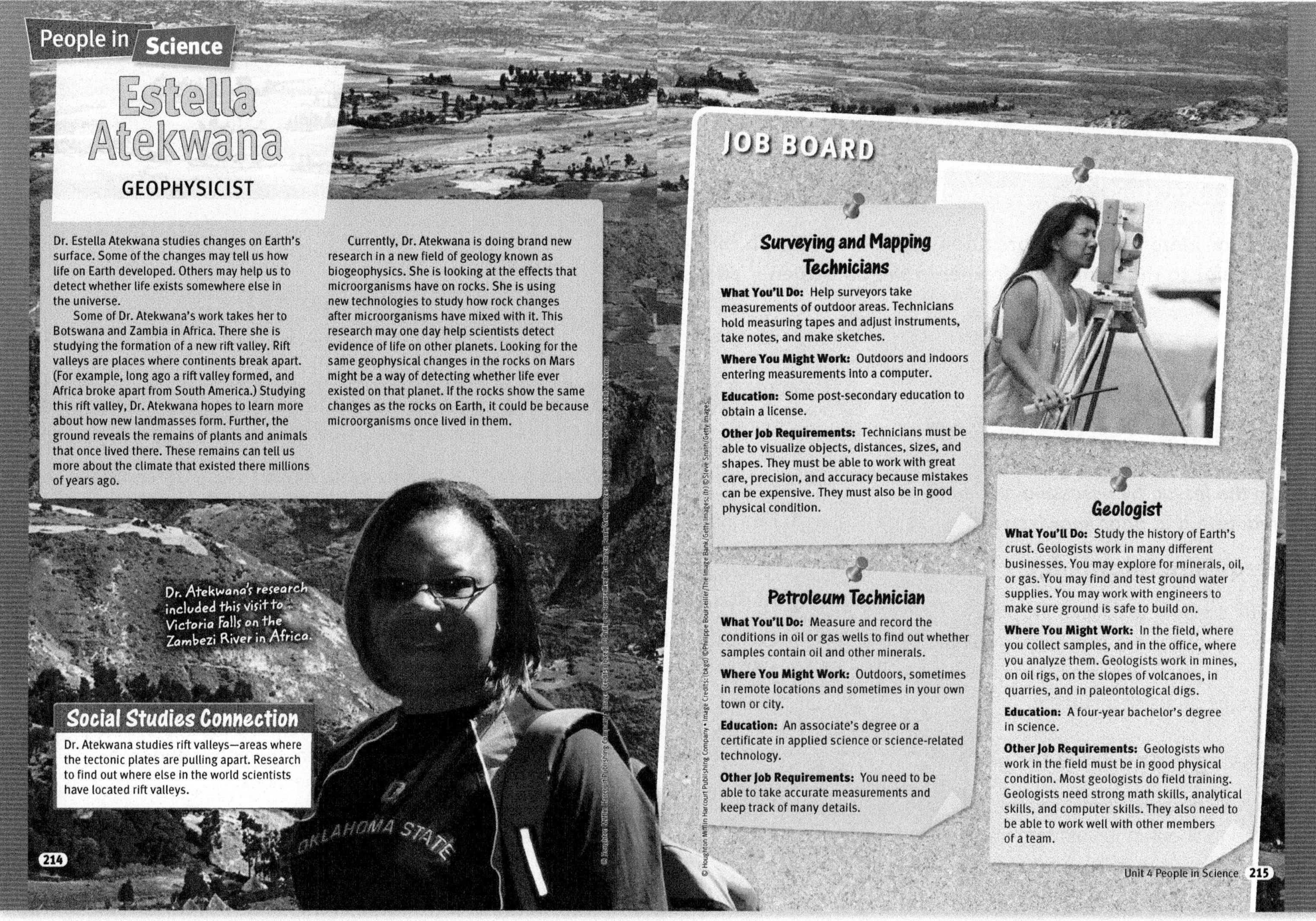

People in Science

Estella Atekwana

GEOPHYSICIST

Dr. Estella Atekwana studies changes on Earth's surface. Some of the changes may tell us how life on Earth developed. Others may help us to detect whether life exists somewhere else in the universe.

Some of Dr. Atekwana's work takes her to Botswana and Zambia in Africa. There she is studying the formation of a new rift valley. Rift valleys are places where continents break apart. (For example, long ago a rift valley formed, and Africa broke apart from South America.) Studying this rift valley, Dr. Atekwana hopes to learn more about how new landmasses form. Further, the ground reveals the remains of plants and animals that once lived there. These remains can tell us more about the climate that existed there millions of years ago.

Currently, Dr. Atekwana is doing brand new research in a new field of geology known as biogeophysics. She is looking at the effects that microorganisms have on rocks. She is using new technologies to study how rock changes after microorganisms have mixed with it. This research may one day help scientists detect evidence of life on other planets. Looking for the same geophysical changes in the rocks on Mars might be a way of detecting whether life ever existed on that planet. If the rocks show the same changes as the rocks on Earth, it could be because microorganisms once lived in them.

Dr. Atekwana's research included this visit to Victoria Falls on the Zambezi River in Africa.

Social Studies Connection

Dr. Atekwana studies rift valleys—areas where the tectonic plates are pulling apart. Research to find out where else in the world scientists have located rift valleys.

214

JOB BOARD

Surveying and Mapping Technicians

What You'll Do: Help surveyors take measurements of outdoor areas. Technicians hold measuring tapes and adjust instruments, take notes, and make sketches.

Where You Might Work: Outdoors and indoors entering measurements into a computer.

Education: Some post-secondary education to obtain a license.

Other Job Requirements: Technicians must be able to visualize objects, distances, sizes, and shapes. They must be able to work with great care, precision, and accuracy because mistakes can be expensive. They must also be in good physical condition.

Petroleum Technician

What You'll Do: Measure and record the conditions in oil or gas wells to find out whether samples contain oil and other minerals.

Where You Might Work: Outdoors, sometimes in remote locations and sometimes in your own town or city.

Education: An associate's degree or a certificate in applied science or science-related technology.

Other Job Requirements: You need to be able to take accurate measurements and keep track of many details.

Geologist

What You'll Do: Study the history of Earth's crust. Geologists work in many different businesses. You may explore for minerals, oil, or gas. You may find and test ground water supplies. You may work with engineers to make sure ground is safe to build on.

Where You Might Work: In the field, where you collect samples, and in the office, where you analyze them. Geologists work in mines, on oil rigs, on the slopes of volcanoes, in quarries, and in paleontological digs.

Education: A four-year bachelor's degree in science.

Other Job Requirements: Geologists who work in the field must be in good physical condition. Most geologists do field training. Geologists need strong math skills, analytical skills, and computer skills. They also need to be able to work well with other members of a team.

Unit 4 People in Science 215

Social Studies Connection

Rift valleys include the Mid-Atlantic Ridge, the East African Rift, and the Baikal Rift Zone in Siberia. They can also be found near Quilotoa, Ecuador, and Ontario, Canada.

Building Reading Skills

Prefixes Ask: What does the prefix geo- mean? Earth **Ask:** Using what you know about the meaning of the prefix *geo-*, what do you think *geology* and *geologist* mean? Sample answer: Geology is the study of the history and structure of Earth. A geologist is a person who studies the history and structure of Earth, including rocks, minerals, and plate tectonics. **Ask:** What do you think a biogeologist might do? Sample answer: I know bio- is a prefix that refers to living organisms. So a biogeologist might be a person who studies how living organisms interact with rocks, minerals, or other nonliving parts of Earth.

Optional Online resource: Prefixes support

Mountain Building

Essential Question How do mountains form?

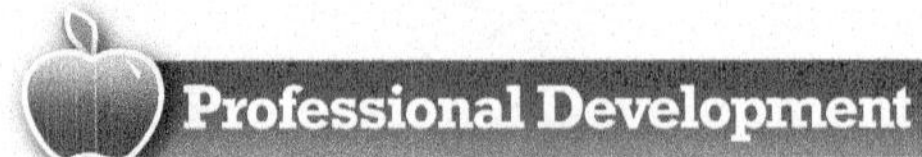

For more detailed information about the topics in this lesson, refer to the Content Refresher in the Unit Opener pages.

Opening Your Lesson

Begin the lesson by assessing students' prerequisite and prior knowledge.

Prerequisite Knowledge

- Earth is made up of tectonic plates.
- Tectonic plates are constantly moving.
- Tectonic plate movement can cause changes on Earth's surface.

Accessing Prior Knowledge

Use a KWL chart to access students' prior knowledge about mountain formation. Have them work in pairs to fill out the *K* portion of the organizer with what they know about mountain formation. Then, ask them to write at least three questions about mountain formation in the *W* section of the organizer. Have them complete the *L* section at the end of the lesson.

Online resource: KWL support

Customize Your Opening

- ☐ **Accessing Prior Knowledge,** above
- ☐ **Print Path** Engage Your Brain, SE p. 217 #1–2
- ☐ **Print Path** Engage Your Brain, SE p. 217 #3–4
- ☐ **Digital Path** Lesson Opener

Key Topics/Learning Goals	Supporting Concepts
Deformation and Folding 1 Describe how tectonic plate motion can cause deformation. 2 Define *folding*. 3 Compare anticline and syncline folds.	• Tectonic plate motion causes three kinds of stress that make rocks deform: compression (squeezing and shortening), tension (stretching and pulling apart), and shear stress (twisting). • *Folding* is the bending of rock layers due to stress. • An anticline is a fold in which the oldest rock layers are at the fold's center and the youngest layers are outside the fold; anticlines peak at the center and arch downward at the sides. • A syncline is a fold in which the youngest rock layers are at the fold's center and the oldest layers are outside the fold; in synclines, rock layers form a bowl shape.
Faulting 1 Define *faults*. 2 Compare the three kinds of faults.	• A *fault* is a break in a body of rock along which one block slides in relation to another. • In a strike-slip fault, the two fault blocks move past each other horizontally. In a normal fault, the hanging wall moves down in relation to the footwall. In a reverse fault, the hanging wall moves up in relation to the footwall.
Mountains 1 Compare the three kinds of mountains.	• Folded mountains form when compression folds and uplifts rock layers. • Fault-block mountains form when tension causes blocks of rock to drop down relative to other blocks. • Volcanic mountains form where molten rock erupts onto Earth's surface.

Options for Instruction

Two parallel paths provide coverage of the Essential Questions, with a strong **Inquiry** strand woven into each. Follow the **Print Path**, the **Digital Path**, or your customized combination of print, digital, and inquiry.

Print Path

Teaching support for the Print Path appears with the Student Pages.

Inquiry Labs and Activities

Digital Path

Digital Path shortcut: TS671050

Print Path	Inquiry Labs and Activities	Digital Path
Stressed Out, SE pp. 218–219 **How can tectonic plate motion cause deformation?** **What are two kinds of folds?** • Synclines and Anticlines	**Daily Demo** **Spaghetti Rocks** **Activity** **Bend and Stretch** **Quick Lab** **Modeling Geologic Processes** **Quick Lab** **What Happens When Objects Collide?**	**Types of Stresses** **Interactive Graphics** **Anticline and Syncline** **Interactive Image**
Faulted, SE pp. 220–221 **What are the three kinds of faults?** • Strike-Slip Faults • Normal Faults • Reverse Faults	**Activity** **Hanging Walls vs. Footwalls**	**Types of Faults** **Interactive Graphics**
Moving On Up, SE pp. 222–223 **What are the three kinds of mountains?** • Folded Mountains • Volcanic Mountains • Fault-Block Mountains	**Activity** **Making (Delicious) Mountains** **Quick Lab** **Modeling Mountains**	**Types of Mountains** **Interactive Graphics** **Erosion and Weathering** **Animation**

Options for Assessment

See the Evaluate page for options, including Formative Assessment, Summative Assessment, and Unit Review.

Engage and Explore

Activities and Discussion

Activity *Modeling Tectonic Plates*

Engage

Introducing Key Topics

 small groups
 35 min

Have students work in small groups to plan and build a three-dimensional model of a tectonic plate. Suggest they use two or more materials. Instruct them to label the continental lithosphere, oceanic lithosphere, and any topographical features they include. Have each group display and give a brief presentation of their completed model.

Activity *Bend and Stretch*

Engage

Deformation and Folding

 small groups
 20 min

Provide groups with modeling clay in three or more colors. Have students form rectangular blocks of similar size and thickness for each color of clay. Then have them stack the rectangles to form layers. Provide groups with plastic knives and direct them to cut the clay rectangle into three sections. Have a student place his or her hands at each end of one of the sections. Direct the student to push his or her hands together to model compression. Have a second student grasp the ends of another section and pull the pieces in opposite directions to model tension. Direct a third student to grasp the ends of the remaining section and push each end in opposite, sideways directions. Explain that this models shear stress. Have students sketch each model and label it with the type of stress it illustrates.

Activity *Hanging Walls vs. Footwalls*

Faulting

pairs
 35 min

Have students work with a partner to locate and print photos of hanging walls and footwalls on the Internet. Create a large classroom display and hang the photos in two groups to show the differences.

Activity *Modeling Fault Motion*

Faulting

 individuals
30 min

Have students use two blocks of wood to model the three types of fault motion. Tell students to sand one side of each block until it is smooth and to score the other side of each block until it is rough. Point out that the San Andreas fault is a strike-slip fault. As students demonstrate strike-slip motion, have them compare and describe the amounts of resistance they observe as they first slide the smooth surfaces together and then slide the rough surfaces together.

Activity *Making (Delicious) Mountains*

Mountains

 pairs
30 min

Provide students with one slice of white bread, two slices of wheat bread, grape jelly, strawberry jam, a plastic knife, and a paper plate. **Caution** students not to eat the materials. Have students assemble the materials as follows: Place the white bread on the plate, cover the bread with jam, add a slice of wheat bread, add a layer of jelly, and add the final slice of wheat bread. Point out that the ingredients (rock layers) are in their original positions. Have students model folding by pushing inward on their sandwich from the sides. Then have them cut the sandwich in half across the fold and draw what they see. Discuss how this activity models the formation of folded mountains.

DIRECTED inquiry introduces inquiry skills within a structured framework.

GUIDED inquiry develops inquiry skills within a supportive environment.

INDEPENDENT inquiry deepens inquiry skills with student-driven questions or procedures.

Labs and Demos

Daily Demo *Spaghetti Rocks*

Engage

Deformation and Folding

 whole class
 15 min
 **GUIDED** inquiry

Use this short demo as an introduction to deformation and folds, or to introduce the lesson.

PURPOSE **To show how stress affects rock layers**

MATERIALS

- **safety goggles**
- **large bowl**
- **dry spaghetti noodles, 1 bunch**

1 Put the safety goggles on.
2 Hold the spaghetti noodles in a bunch over the bowl.
3 **Observing** Slowly apply downward pressure on each end of the bunch of spaghetti so they bend without breaking. **Ask:** What do you observe? Sample answer: The spaghetti bends when a small amount of stress is applied.
4 **Observing** Repeat the previous step, but apply enough pressure to cause the spaghetti to break. **Ask:** What do you observe? Sample answer: Additional stress causes the spaghetti to break.

Quick Lab *Modeling Mountains*

Mountains

 individuals
 25 min
 **GUIDED** inquiry

PURPOSE **To make models of different types of mountains**

See the Lab Manual or go Online for planning information.

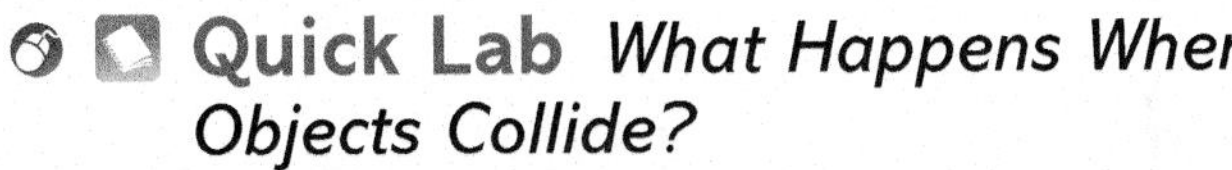

Quick Lab *What Happens When Objects Collide?*

PURPOSE **To demonstrate how collisions can cause deformation**

See the Lab Manual or go Online for planning information.

Quick Lab *Modeling Geologic Processes*

Engage

Deformation and Folding

 small groups
 20 min
DIRECTED inquiry

Students use modeling clay and paper plates to observe how compression and tension result in deformation.

PURPOSE **To model deformation caused by compression and tension**

MATERIALS

- **clay, several colors**
- **paper plates**
- **scissors**
- **safety goggles**
- **lab apron**

Customize Your Labs

See the Lab Manual for lab datasheets.

Go Online for editable lab datasheets.

Activities and Discussion

- ☐ **Activity** Modeling Tectonic Plates
- ☐ **Activity** Bend and Stretch
- ☐ **Activity** Hanging Walls vs. Footwalls
- ☐ **Activity** Modeling Fault Motion
- ☐ **Activity** Making (Delicious) Mountains

Labs and Demos

- ☐ **Daily Demo** Spaghetti Rocks
- ☐ **Quick Lab** Modeling Mountains
- ☐ **Quick Lab** What Happens When Objects Collide?
- ☐ **Quick Lab** Modeling Geologic Processes

Your Resources

Explain Science Concepts

Key Topics	Print Path	Digital Path
Deformation and Folding	☐ **Stressed Out!,** SE pp. 218–219 • Active Reading, #5 • Visualize It!, #6 • Think Outside the Book, #7 • Visualize It!, #8 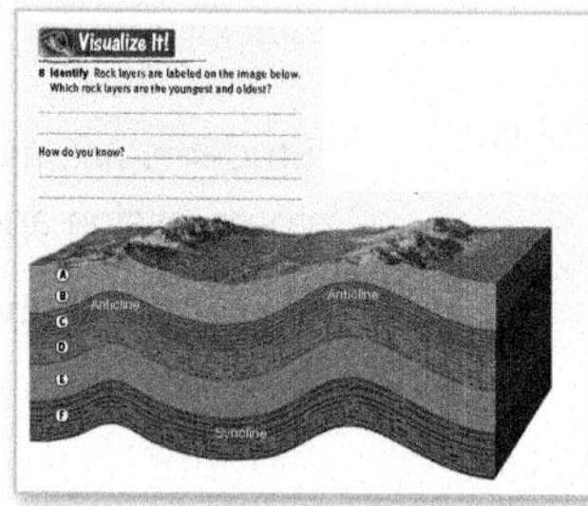	☐ **Types of Stresses** View how compression, tension, and sheer stress work. ☐ **Anticline and Syncline** Learn the different parts of folded layers. 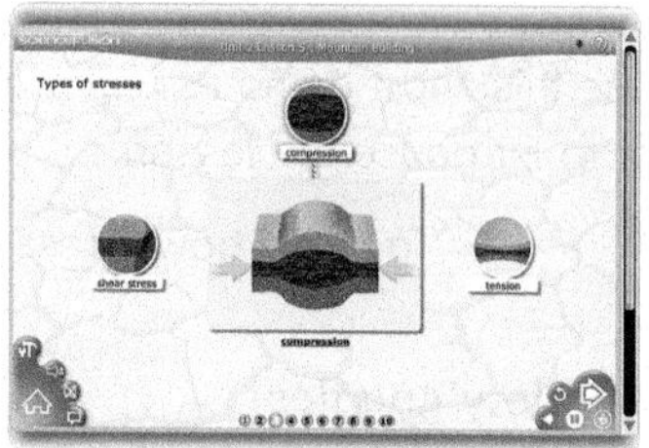
Faulting	☐ **Faulted,** SE pp. 220–221 • Active Reading (Annotation Strategy) #9 • Visualize It!, #10 • Think Outside the Book, #11 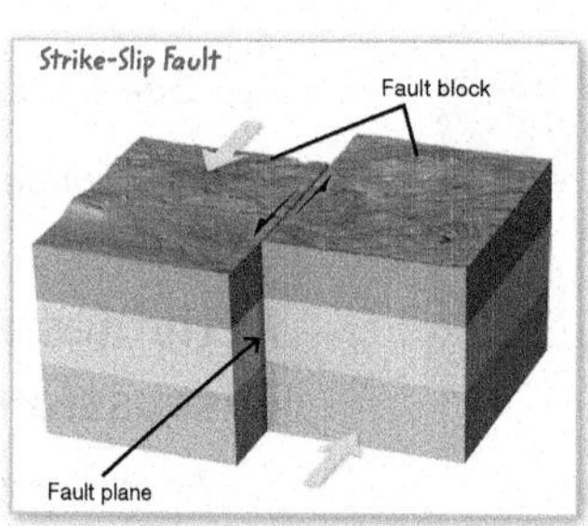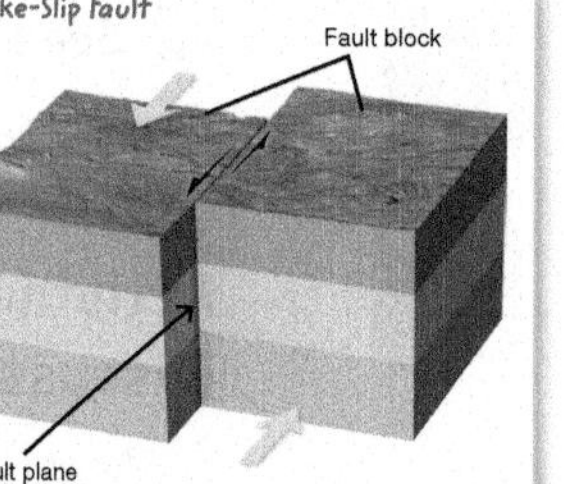	☐ **Types of Faults** Explore how the three types of motion produce faults with different properties. 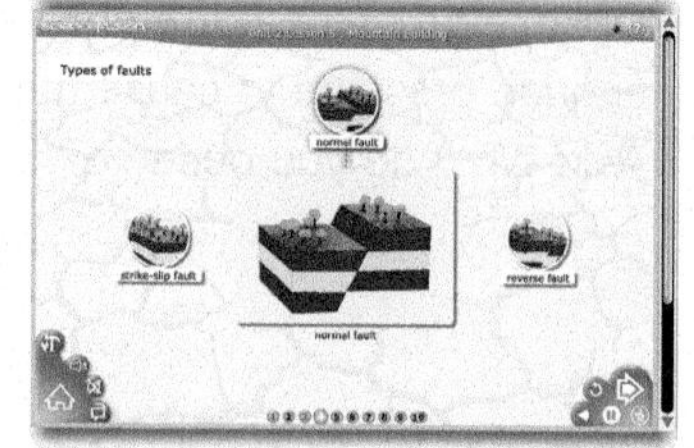
Mountains	☐ **Moving On Up,** SE pp. 222–223 • Active Reading (Annotation Strategy) #12 • Visualize It!, #13 • Identify, #14 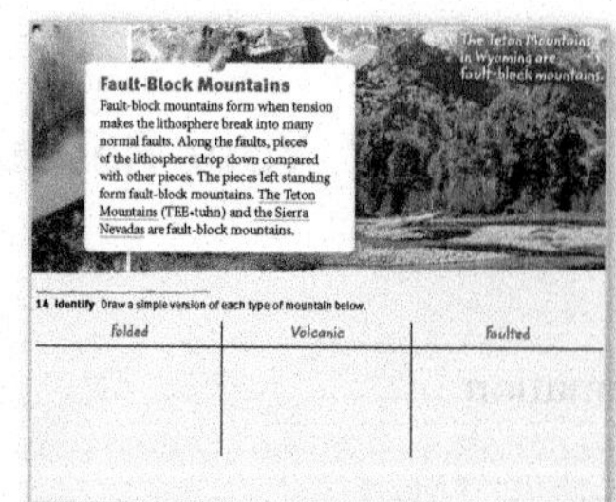	☐ **Types of Mountains** Compare mountains produced by folding, faults, and volcanoes. ☐ **Erosion and Weathering** See how erosion can shape a mountain. 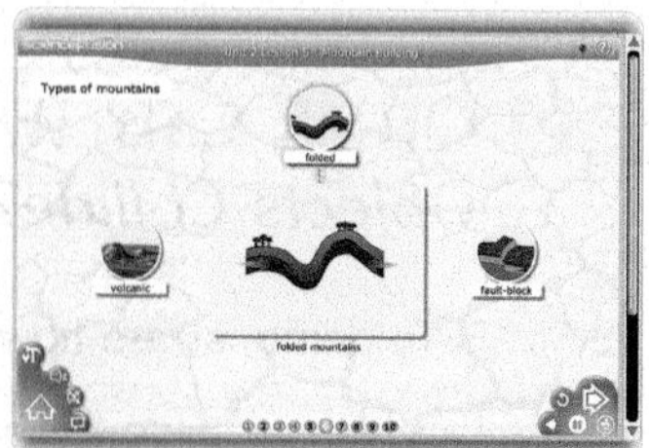

Fault-Block Mountains

Fault-block mountains form when tension makes the lithosphere break into many normal faults. Along the faults, pieces of the lithosphere drop down compared with other pieces. The pieces left standing form fault-block mountains. The Teton Mountains (TEE•tuhn) and the Sierra Nevadas are fault-block mountains.

The Teton Mountains in Wyoming are fault-block mountains.

14 Identify Draw a simple version of each type of mountain below.

Folded	Volcanic	Faulted

Differentiated Instruction

Basic *Mountain Models*

Mountains

 individuals
 35 min

Have pairs of students make models of folded, fault-block, and volcanic mountains from modeling clay. Tell students that their models should suggest the processes that caused each kind of mountain to form.

Basic *Changing Topography*

Synthesizing Key Topics

 pairs
 40 min

Have students research a topographic feature that resulted from the deformation of Earth's crust. Have them find out how and when the feature formed. Students should create a poster that documents their research. They should use key vocabulary words from this lesson on their posters. Have students present their posters to the class.

Advanced *Short Story*

Synthesizing Key Topics

 pairs
 varied

Ask students to write a short story that describes how faults and mountains form. Suggest that they use what they have learned about plate tectonics and deformation to create realistic stories.

ELL *Previewing*

Synthesizing Key Topics

pairs
40 min

Previewing can help students predict what type of structural pattern the author will use before they read. Ask for volunteers to read the first sentences in each subsection. Ask students to predict what the subsection will be about. Then, tell them to read to see if they were correct.

Lesson Vocabulary

deformation	compression	tension
shear stress	folding	fault

Previewing Vocabulary

 whole class
25 min

Description Wheel The meanings of the terms *shear stress* and *tension* are difficult to represent through drawing. Have students create a description wheel for each of these terms.

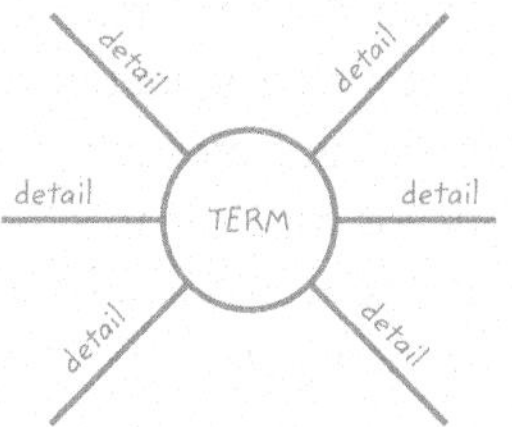

Reinforcing Vocabulary

 individuals
30 min

Analogies Have students develop an analogy for each of the vocabulary terms. Then ask students to share their analogies with the class.

Customize Your Lesson

Core Instruction

- ☐ Print Path choices
- ☐ Digital Path choices

Vocabulary

- ☐ Previewing Vocabulary Description Wheel
- ☐ Reinforcing Vocabulary Analogies

Your Resources

Differentiated Instruction

- ☐ Basic Mountain Models
- ☐ Basic Changing Topography
- ☐ Advanced Short Story
- ☐ ELL Previewing

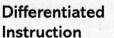

Extend Science Concepts

Reinforce and Review

Activity *Plate Boundaries*

Synthesizing Key Topics

 whole class
 30 min

Have students describe the three types of tectonic plate boundaries. Then, have students use their hands to demonstrate the direction in which plates move at each boundary. Students should push their hands together to show a convergent boundary, pull them apart to show a divergent boundary, and slide them past each other to demonstrate a transform boundary.

FoldNote Organizer

Synthesizing Key Topics

 individual
 35 min

Layered Book FoldNote After students have studied the lesson, ask them to make a Layered Book FoldNote that details the different types of faults and mountains. Have them share their books with a partner.

Optional Online resources: Layered Book FoldNote support

Going Further

Fine Arts Connection

Synthesizing Key Topics

 individual
varied

Collage Project Have students develop a collage that illustrates various examples of mountains, faults, and folds. They might clip photographs from brochures or magazines, print them from the Internet, or create their own. Suggest that they surround a map of the United States with the photos and draw a line or use yarn to connect each geologic feature with its actual location on the map. Have them share their collages with the class.

Social Studies Connection

Synthesizing Key Topics

small groups
 varied

A Tectonic History Review with students how slab pull, ridge push and convection currents in Earth's mantel drive the motion of tectonic plates, which results in mountain building and other geologic features. Direct groups of students to research past geologic forces that shaped the geologic features of different regions thoughout their state. Have them work cooperatively to make a poster that uses a relief map and labels to explain the geologic history of each region.

Customize Your Closing

 *See the Assessment Guide for quizzes and tests*

Go Online to edit and create quizzes and tests

Reinforce and Review

- ☐ Activity Plate Boundaries
- ☐ Graphic Organizer Layered Book
- ☐ Print Path Visual Summary, SE p. 224
- ☐ **Digital Path** Lesson Closer

Evaluate Student Mastery

Formative Assessment

See the teacher support below the Student Pages for additional Formative Assessment questions.

Have student volunteers review the differences between each type of fault and mountain. **Ask:** How are the different mountain types formed? Sample answer: Folded mountains form when rock layers are squeezed together and pushed up. Volcanic mountains form when melted rock (magma) erupts onto Earth's surface as lava. Fault-block mountains form when tension pulls the lithosphere apart allowing the formation of normal faults.

Reteach

Formative assessment may show you that students need reinforcement for certain topics. The resources below are recommended for reteaching. If students were introduced to topics through the Print Path, you can also use the Digital Path for reteaching, and vice versa.

Can be assigned to individual students

Deformation and Folding

Activity Modeling Tectonic Plates

Activity Bend and Stretch

Daily Demo Spaghetti Rocks

Faulting

Activity Modeling Fault Motion

Mountains

Activity Making (Delicious) Mountains

Quick Lab Modeling Mountains

Summative Assessment

Alternative Assessment

Faults, Folds, and Mountains

Online resources: student worksheet, optional rubrics

Mountain Building

Climb the Ladder: ***Faults, Folds, and Mountains***

Complete the activities to show what you've learned about mountain building.

1. Work on your own, with a partner, or with a small group.
2. Choose one item from each rung of the ladder. Check your choices.
3. Have your teacher approve your plan.
4. Submit or present your results.

__ **Quiz Cards** On three separate cards, write the terms *compression, tension,* and *shear stress.* Then write their definitions on three other cards. Finally, mix up the cards and use them to quiz your friends about the terms.	__ **To a Fault** Make a poster that describes the three types of faults. Then draw a sketch of each type under the appropriate heading.
__ **Flipping Forward** Imagine that one of your classmates needs help understanding how folded mountains form. To help your classmate, create a flipbook that shows the process of a folded mountain forming.	__ **On the Range** Find out about a famous mountain range located anywhere in the world. Then share with the class what type of mountain range it is and the way it formed.
__ **Plate Talk** Imagine that you are a tectonic plate that is slowly pushing against another tectonic plate. Present a skit in which you describe what might happen to you and the other plate and why.	__ **You're the Expert!** Imagine you are a geologist who has examined a syncline fold. Write a report about what you observed in the field. In your report, note where the oldest rock is located in the fold and describe the shape of fold. Also discuss how the syncline occurred.

Going Further

- ☐ Fine Arts Connection
- ☐ Social Studies Connection

Formative Assessment

- ☐ Strategies Throughout TE
- ☐ Lesson Review SE

Summative Assessment

- ☐ Alternative Assessment Faults, Folds, and Mountains
- ☐ Lesson Quiz
- ☐ Unit Tests A and B
- ☐ Unit Review SE End-of-Unit

Your Resources

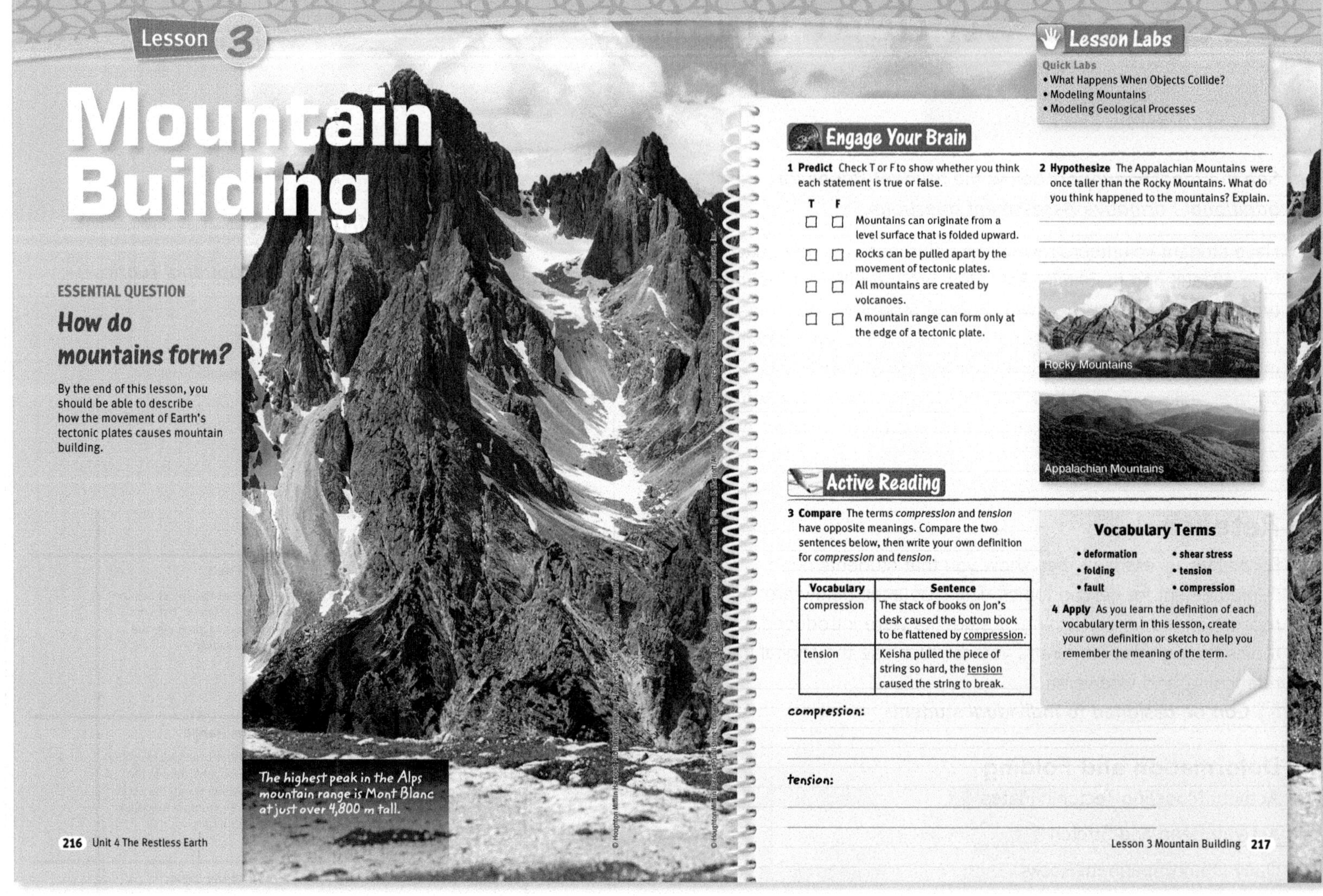

Lesson 3
Mountain Building
ESSENTIAL QUESTION
How do mountains form?
By the end of this lesson, you should be able to describe how the movement of Earth's tectonic plates causes mountain building.
The highest peak in the Alps mountain range is Mont Blanc at just over 4,800 m tall.
216 Unit 4 The Restless Earth
Lesson Labs
Quick Labs
• What Happens When Objects Collide?
• Modeling Mountains
• Modeling Geological Processes
Engage Your Brain
1 Predict Check T or F to show whether you think each statement is true or false.
T F
Mountains can originate from a level surface that is folded upward.
Rocks can be pulled apart by the movement of tectonic plates.
All mountains are created by volcanoes.
A mountain range can form only at the edge of a tectonic plate.
2 Hypothesize The Appalachian Mountains were once taller than the Rocky Mountains. What do you think happened to the mountains? Explain.
Rocky Mountains
Appalachian Mountains
Active Reading
3 Compare The terms compression and tension have opposite meanings. Compare the two sentences below, then write your own definition for compression and tension.
Vocabulary | Sentence
compression | The stack of books on Jon's desk caused the bottom book to be flattened by compression.
tension | Keisha pulled the piece of string so hard, the tension caused the string to break.
compression:
tension:
Vocabulary Terms
• deformation • shear stress
• folding • tension
• fault • compression
4 Apply As you learn the definition of each vocabulary term in this lesson, create your own definition or sketch to help you remember the meaning of the term.
Lesson 3 Mountain Building 217

Answers

Answers for 1–3 should represents students' current thoughts, even if incorrect.

1. T; T; F; F
2. The mountains were worn down over time. The Rocky Mountains have sharper peaks. The Appalachian Mountains are more rounded.
3. Compression: Rocks that get pushed together; Tension: Rocks that get pulled apart.
4. Students should define or sketch each vocabulary term in the lesson.

Opening Your Lesson

Have students share their ideas about the change in height of the Appalachian Mountains (item 2) to assess their prior knowledge of the key topics.

Prerequisites Earth's lithosphere is broken into tectonic plates; these plates move in response to slab pull, ridge push, and convection currents in Earth's mantle; when tectonic plates move apart or collide with one another, they cause changes to Earth's surface.

Accessing Prior Knowledge Use this question to assess students' prior knowledge about how movement of tectonic plates takes place.

- What causes movement of tectonic plates? Sample answer: Slab pull is the main force causing tectonic plate motion, followed by ridge push. The release of energy as heat deep inside Earth causes the movement of Earth materials in convection currents. As material within the mantle moves, it drags tectonic plates along with it, contributing to tectonic plate motion as well.

Learning Alert

Everyday Definitions Mountains are landmasses that have a higher elevation than areas surrounding them. Formation of mountains results from folding, faulting, and volcanic activity. There are mountain ranges all over the world.

Stressed Out

How can tectonic plate motion cause deformation?

The movement of tectonic plates places stress on rocks. A tectonic plate is a block of lithosphere that consists of crust and the rigid outermost part of the mantle. *Stress* is the amount of force per unit area that is placed on an object. Rocks can bend or break under stress. In addition, low temperatures make materials more brittle, or easily broken. High temperatures can allow rock to bend.

When a rock is placed under stress, it deforms, or changes shape. **Deformation** (dee•fohr•MAY•shuhn) is the process by which rocks change shape when under stress. Rock can bend if it is placed under high temperature and pressure for long periods of time. If the stress becomes too great, or is applied quickly, rock can break. When rocks bend, folds form. When rocks break, faults form.

Active Reading

5 Identify As you read, list some objects near you that can bend or break from deformation.

By applying stress, the boy is causing the spaghetti to deform. Similarly, stress over a long period of time can cause rock to bend.

Like the spaghetti, stress over a short period of time or great amounts of stress can cause rock to break.

Visualize It!

6 Correlate How can the same material bend in one situation but break in another?

What are two kinds of folds?

Folded rock layers appear bent or buckled. **Folding** occurs when rock layers bend under stress. The bends are called *folds*. Scientists assume that all rock layers start out as horizontal layers deposited on top of each other over time. Sometimes, different layers of rocks can still be seen even after the rocks have been folded. When scientists see a fold, they know that deformation has happened. Two common types of folds are synclines and anticlines.

Think Outside the Book

7 Model Stack several sheets of paper together. Apply stress to the sides of the paper to create a model of a syncline and an anticline. Share your model with your teacher.

Synclines and Anticlines

Folds are classified based on the age of the rock layers. In a *syncline* (SIN•klyn), the youngest layers of rock are found at the core of a fold. The oldest layers are found on the outside of the fold. Synclines usually look like rock layers that are arched upward, like a bowl. In an *anticline* (AN•tih•klyn), the oldest layers of rock are found at the core of the fold. The youngest layers are found on the outside of the fold. Anticlines often look like rock layers that are arched downwards and high in the middle. Often, both types of folds will be visible in the same rock layers, as shown below.

The hinge is the middle point of the bend in a syncline or anticline.

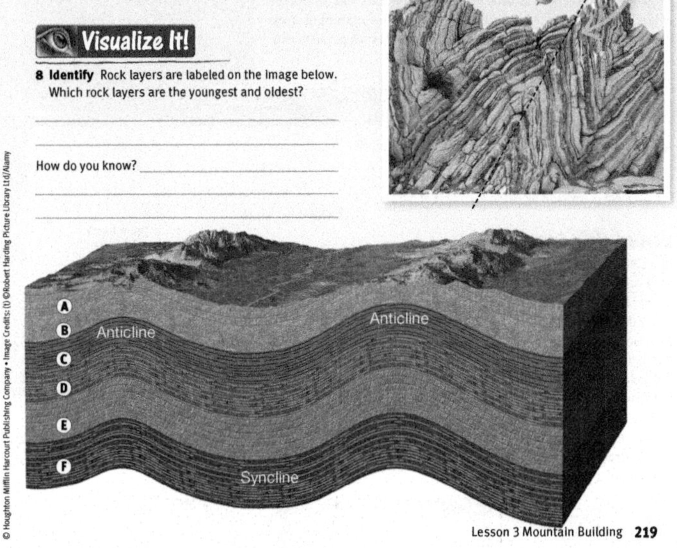
Visualize It!
8 Identify Rock layers are labeled on the image below. Which rock layers are the youngest and oldest?
How do you know?
A
B
C
D
E
F
Anticline
Anticline
Syncline

Answers

5. Sample answers: Pencils, books, rulers, and even desks can be bent or broken from deformation if enough stress is applied.
6. The speed with which a force is applied and the amount of force determine whether materials will bend or break under stress.
7. Students should show stress applied to the edges of the paper to form a syncline and anticline. Students should also be able to discuss the relative ages of the rock layers.
8. Rock layer A is youngest; Rock layer F is oldest; Rock layers are deposited on existing layers over time making the youngest layers at the top and oldest layers at the bottom.

Interpreting Visuals

Ask students to look at the photographs of bent and broken rocks. Ask them to explain why these rocks reacted in this way. They reacted to the force, or stress, that was placed on them.

Formative Assessment

Ask: What is deformation? It is when rocks break or bend under stress. **Ask:** How do differences in stress result in the bending or breaking of rocks? When stress is great, rocks will break. If stress is not that great, they will just bend to form folds.

Learning Alert MISCONCEPTION

Bendable Rock Students may have difficulty believing that massive blocks of rock can bend. Explain that different kinds of rocks are composed of different combinations of minerals. These rocks vary in their plasticity. One of the factors that affects the plasticity of a rock is based on the kinds of chemical bonds between the atoms and molecules that make up the rock. To help students understand how rocks bend, have students bend different kinds of wire (which consist of different elements) and compare the ease with which each type of wire bends.

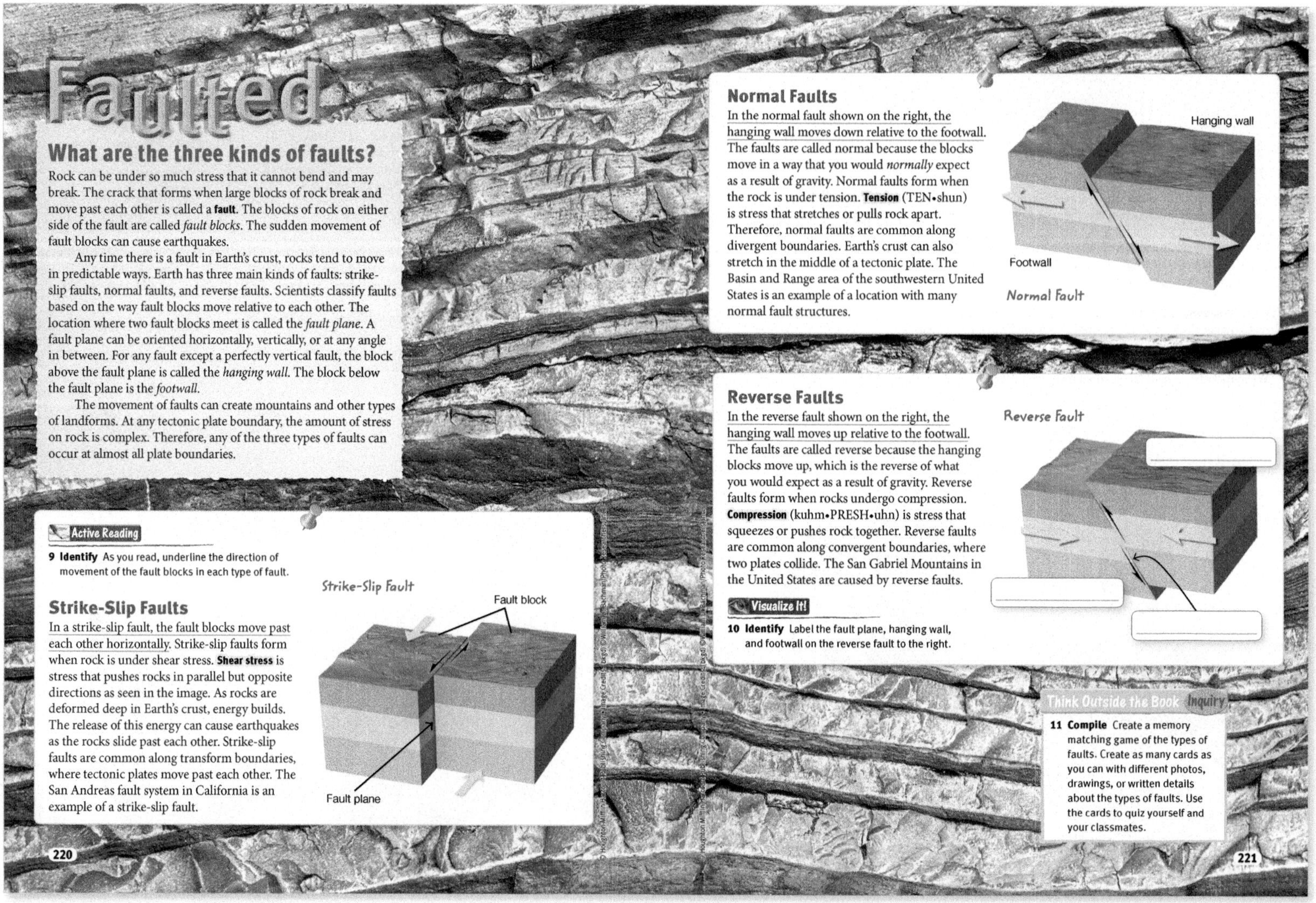

Faulted

What are the three kinds of faults?

Rock can be under so much stress that it cannot bend and may break. The crack that forms when large blocks of rock break and move past each other is called a **fault**. The blocks of rock on either side of the fault are called *fault blocks*. The sudden movement of fault blocks can cause earthquakes.

Any time there is a fault in Earth's crust, rocks tend to move in predictable ways. Earth has three main kinds of faults: strike-slip faults, normal faults, and reverse faults. Scientists classify faults based on the way fault blocks move relative to each other. The location where two fault blocks meet is called the *fault plane*. A fault plane can be oriented horizontally, vertically, or at any angle in between. For any fault except a perfectly vertical fault, the block above the fault plane is called the *hanging wall*. The block below the fault plane is the *footwall*.

The movement of faults can create mountains and other types of landforms. At any tectonic plate boundary, the amount of stress on rock is complex. Therefore, any of the three types of faults can occur at almost all plate boundaries.

Active Reading

9 Identify As you read, underline the direction of movement of the fault blocks in each type of fault.

Strike-Slip Faults

In a strike-slip fault, the fault blocks move past each other horizontally. Strike-slip faults form when rock is under shear stress. **Shear stress** is stress that pushes rocks in parallel but opposite directions as seen in the image. As rocks are deformed deep in Earth's crust, energy builds. The release of this energy can cause earthquakes as the rocks slide past each other. Strike-slip faults are common along transform boundaries, where tectonic plates move past each other. The San Andreas fault system in California is an example of a strike-slip fault.

Normal Faults

In the normal fault shown on the right, the hanging wall moves down relative to the footwall. The faults are called normal because the blocks move in a way that you would *normally* expect as a result of gravity. Normal faults form when the rock is under tension. **Tension** (TEN•shun) is stress that stretches or pulls rock apart. Therefore, normal faults are common along divergent boundaries. Earth's crust can also stretch in the middle of a tectonic plate. The Basin and Range area of the southwestern United States is an example of a location with many normal fault structures.

Reverse Faults

In the reverse fault shown on the right, the hanging wall moves up relative to the footwall. The faults are called reverse because the hanging blocks move up, which is the reverse of what you would expect as a result of gravity. Reverse faults form when rocks undergo compression. **Compression** (kuhm•PRESH•uhn) is stress that squeezes or pushes rock together. Reverse faults are common along convergent boundaries, where two plates collide. The San Gabriel Mountains in the United States are caused by reverse faults.

Visualize It!

10 Identify Label the fault plane, hanging wall, and footwall on the reverse fault to the right.

Think Outside the Book Inquiry

11 Compile Create a memory matching game of the types of faults. Create as many cards as you can with different photos, drawings, or written details about the types of faults. Use the cards to quiz yourself and your classmates.

220 221

Answers

9. *See students' pages for annotations.*
10. Fault plane separates the two blocks; Footwall on left below the fault plane; hanging wall on right above the fault plane.
11. Students create separate memory cards with information on faults; Students use the cards to quiz each other.

Formative Assessment

Ask: What are the three types of faults? How do they differ from one another and how does each form? Sample answer: The three types of faults are strike-slip faults, normal faults, and reverse faults. A strike-slip fault forms when fault blocks on opposite sides of the fault move past each other horizontally. Strike-slip faults form when the dominant stresses push the fault blocks in different directions. Normal faults form when a hanging wall moves downward as a result of tension. Reverse faults form when a hanging wall moves up. These are caused when rock is being compressed.

Using Annotations

Text Structure: Main Idea and Details As students complete this annotation, have them add notes to their memory cards. Ask them to clearly differentiate between the fault types on their cards so they can use them as a study tool. Have them label their illustrations. Encourage students to use this strategy when they read a text, and to use these cards as study guides.

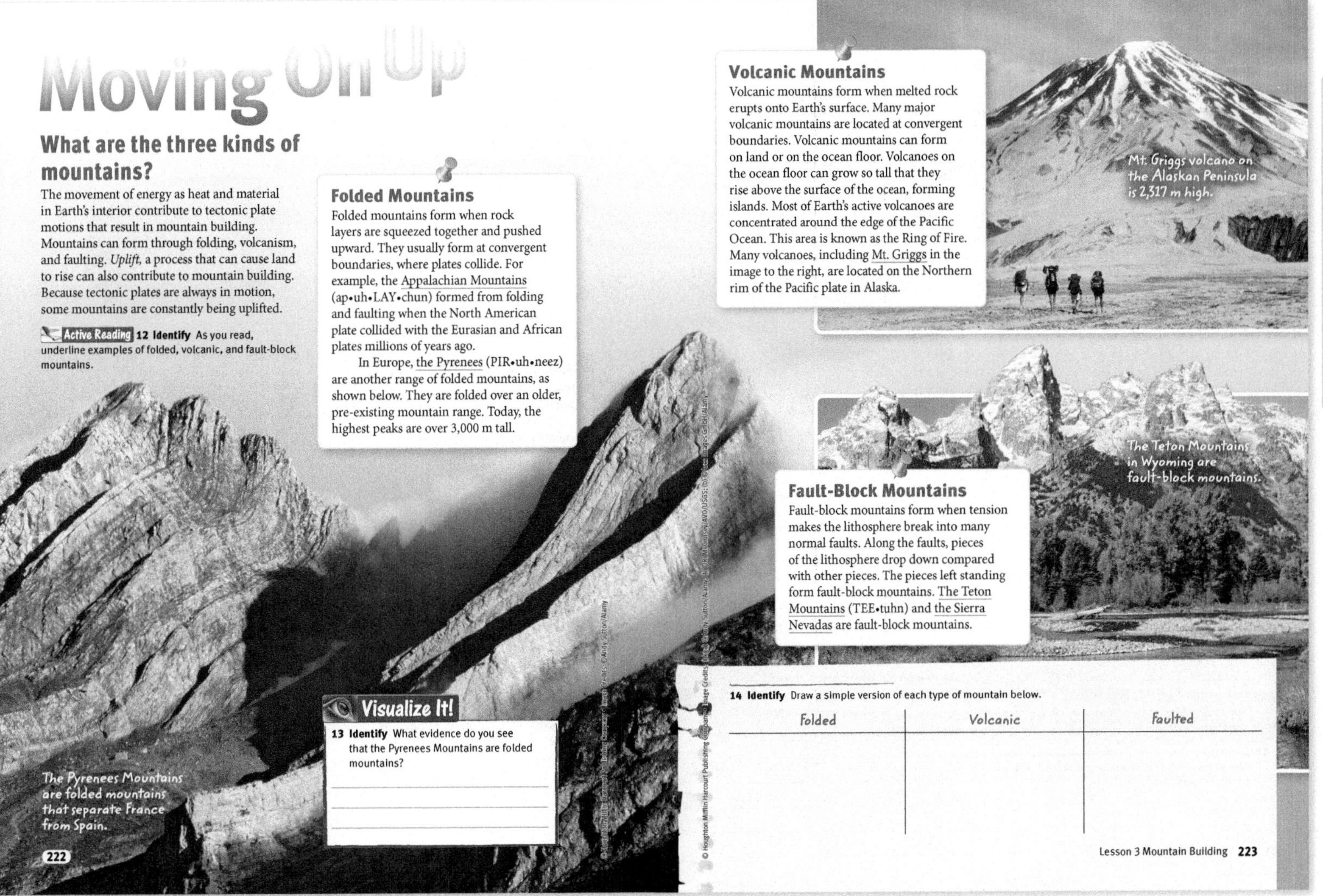

Moving On Up

What are the three kinds of mountains?

The movement of energy as heat and material in Earth's interior contribute to tectonic plate motions that result in mountain building. Mountains can form through folding, volcanism, and faulting. *Uplift*, a process that can cause land to rise can also contribute to mountain building. Because tectonic plates are always in motion, some mountains are constantly being uplifted.

Active Reading **12 Identify** As you read, underline examples of folded, volcanic, and fault-block mountains.

Folded Mountains

Folded mountains form when rock layers are squeezed together and pushed upward. They usually form at convergent boundaries, where plates collide. For example, the Appalachian Mountains (ap•uh•LAY•chun) formed from folding and faulting when the North American plate collided with the Eurasian and African plates millions of years ago.

In Europe, the Pyrenees (PIR•uh•neez) are another range of folded mountains, as shown below. They are folded over an older, pre-existing mountain range. Today, the highest peaks are over 3,000 m tall.

Volcanic Mountains

Volcanic mountains form when melted rock erupts onto Earth's surface. Many major volcanic mountains are located at convergent boundaries. Volcanic mountains can form on land or on the ocean floor. Volcanoes on the ocean floor can grow so tall that they rise above the surface of the ocean, forming islands. Most of Earth's active volcanoes are concentrated around the edge of the Pacific Ocean. This area is known as the Ring of Fire. Many volcanoes, including Mt. Griggs in the image to the right, are located on the Northern rim of the Pacific plate in Alaska.

Mt. Griggs volcano on the Alaskan Peninsula is 2,317 m high.

Fault-Block Mountains

Fault-block mountains form when tension makes the lithosphere break into many normal faults. Along the faults, pieces of the lithosphere drop down compared with other pieces. The pieces left standing form fault-block mountains. The Teton Mountains (TEE•tuhn) and the Sierra Nevadas are fault-block mountains.

The Teton Mountains in Wyoming are fault-block mountains.

Visualize It!

13 Identify What evidence do you see that the Pyrenees Mountains are folded mountains?

The Pyrenees Mountains are folded mountains that separate France from Spain.

14 Identify Draw a simple version of each type of mountain below.

Folded	Volcanic	Faulted

222

Lesson 3 Mountain Building 223

Answers

12. *See students' pages for annotations.*
13. Layers of rock and evidence of older synclines and anticlines can be seen.
14. Students should draw models of the three types of mountains.

Learning Alert

Faults and Earthquakes Earthquakes commonly, although not always, occur at strike-slip faults. The San Andreas Fault in California is one example of a strike-slip fault that has produced major earthquakes. The 1989 Loma Prieta earthquake, sometimes called the World Series earthquake, is an example. Provide students with news clippings and videos (available on the Internet) to illustate the damage and effects resulting from such earthquakes. Another example is the 2004 Sumatra-Andaman earthquake and resulting tsunami, which occurred at a reverse fault.

Interpreting Visuals

Direct students attention to the different mountain types. Ask them to think how each is formed. **For greater depth**, have them work with a partner to research a mountain range and describe its formation and history.

Probing Questions GUIDED Inquiry

Apply How are mountains related to plate tectonics? Mountains form as a result of plate movement.

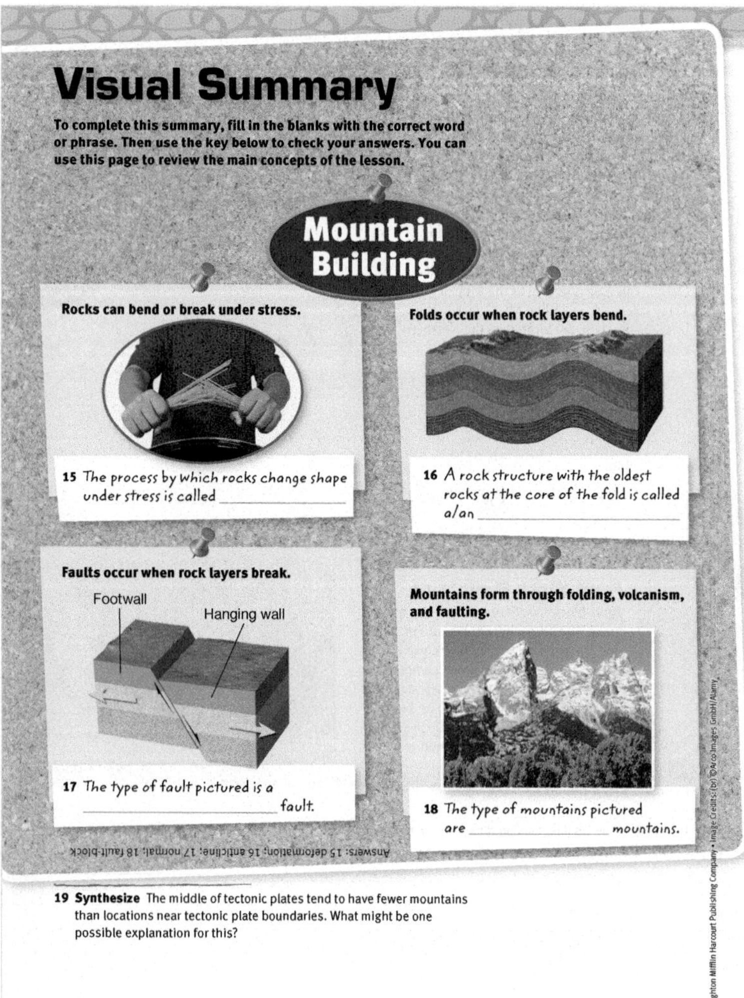

Visual Summary
To complete this summary, fill in the blanks with the correct word or phrase. Then use the key below to check your answers. You can use this page to review the main concepts of the lesson.
Mountain Building
Rocks can bend or break under stress.
15 The process by which rocks change shape under stress is called ________
Folds occur when rock layers bend.
16 A rock structure with the oldest rocks at the core of the fold is called a/an ________
Faults occur when rock layers break.
Footwall
Hanging wall
17 The type of fault pictured is a ________ fault.
Mountains form through folding, volcanism, and faulting.
18 The type of mountains pictured are ________ mountains.
Answers: 15 deformation; 16 anticline; 17 normal; 18 fault-block

19 **Synthesize** The middle of tectonic plates tend to have fewer mountains than locations near tectonic plate boundaries. What might be one possible explanation for this?

224 Unit 4 The Restless Earth

Lesson Review

Lesson 3

Vocabulary

Fill in the blank with the term that best completes the following sentences.

1 A normal fault is a result of a type of stress known as ________

2 A strike-slip fault is a result of ________ stress.

3 A reverse fault is caused by a type of stress known as ________

Key Concepts

Fill in the table below by identifying the type of mountain described in the example question.

Example	Type of Mountain
4 Identify The Basin and Range province is characterized by many normal faults.	
5 Identify The Cascade Range in the United States has many eruptive mountains.	
6 Identify The Pyrenees Mountains have many syncline and anticline structures.	

7 Describe How does the movement of tectonic plates cause deformation in rock?

8 Compare How do folded, volcanic, and fault-block mountains differ?

Critical Thinking

Use the diagram below to answer the following questions.

9 Correlate What type of stress caused the fault shown in the image?

10 Apply Along which type of tectonic plate boundary would this fault be common? How do you know?

11 Analyze Can rock undergo compression, tension, and shear stress all at once? Explain.

12 Conclude Imagine you are walking along a roadway and see a syncline. What can you conclude about the formation of that fold?

Lesson 3 Mountain Building 225

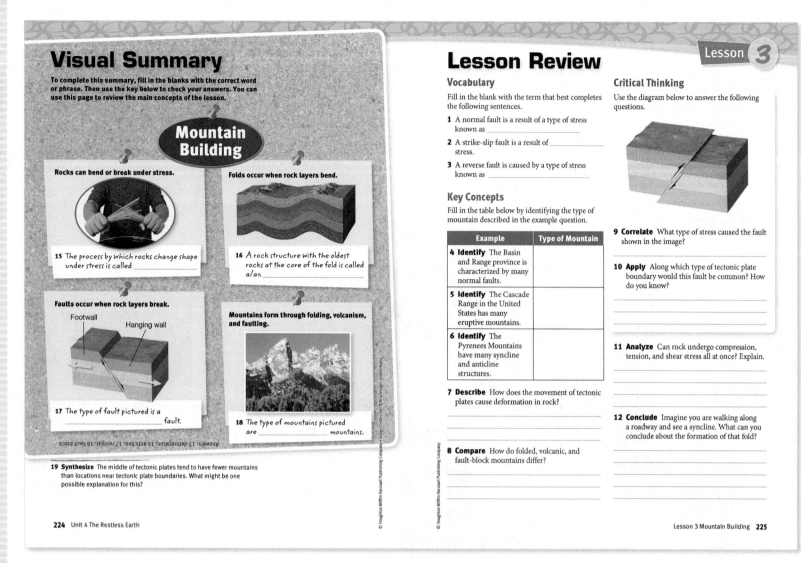

Visual Summary Answers

15. deformation
16. anticline
17. normal
18. fault-block
19. Sample answer: There are more mountain building processes that occur near tectonic boundaries than in the middle of plates.

Lesson Review Answers

1. tension
2. shear
3. compression
4. fault-block
5. volcanic
6. folded
7. The movement of tectonic plates causes stress in rock structures. Deformation results from stress.
8. Each type of mountain results from the motion of tectonic plates. Folded mountains commonly have visible layers of folded rock; Volcanic mountains are often eruptive; Fault-block mountains have large blocks of rock that form peaks when rocks move because of tensional stress.
9. Compression is seen in this reverse fault.
10. Reverse faults are common along convergent plate boundaries where rock is pushed together.
11. No. Compression=together; tension=apart; shear=opposing directions. Rock cannot move in three ways at once.
12. Before folding, the rock layers would be deposited with the oldest layers on the bottom; Now the youngest layers are in the core of the fold and the oldest layers are on the outside. Some form of compressional stress was applied to the rock.

Teacher Notes

Student Pages 224–225

Volcanoes

Essential Question How do volcanoes change Earth's surface?

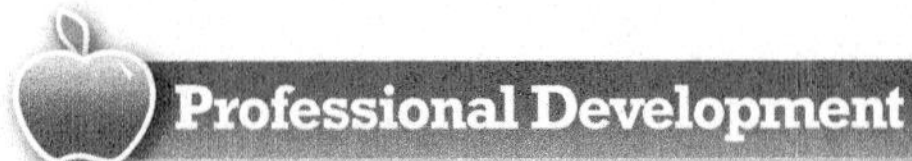

For more detailed information about the topics in this lesson, refer to the Content Refresher in the Unit Opener pages.

Opening Your Lesson

Begin the lesson by assessing students' prerequisite and prior knowledge.

Prerequisite Knowledge

- Earth's lithosphere is made up of tectonic plates that are always moving.
- Plate movement can cause changes to occur on Earth's surface.

Accessing Prior Knowledge

Ask: Do surface changes resulting from movement of tectonic plates happen quickly or slowly? Some changes happen quickly; others take thousands or millions of years.

Ask: With a partner, brainstorm all you know about volcanoes. How does plate movement cause volcanoes to form? It causes magma generation followed by eruption.

Customize Your Opening

- ☐ **Accessing Prior Knowledge,** above
- ☐ **Print Path** Engage Your Brain, SE p. 227 #1–2
- ☐ **Print Path** Active Reading, SE p. 227 #3–4
- ☐ **Digital Path** Lesson Opener

Key Topics/Learning Goals	Supporting Concepts
Volcanoes 1 Define *volcano*. 2 Define *magma* and *lava*. 3 Define *vent*. 4 Describe the kinds of materials that erupt from volcanoes.	• A volcano is a vent or fissure in Earth's surface where molten rock and gases are expelled. • Magma is molten rock produced in the high temperature and pressure conditions within Earth's mantle; lava is magma that flows onto Earth's surface. • A vent is an opening at the surface of Earth through which volcanic material passes. • Volcanoes release gases, pyroclastic material, and lava. Pyroclastic material forms when magma explodes from a volcano and solidifies in the air. Lava flows from volcanoes onto Earth's surface, often in nonexplosive eruptions.
Volcanic Landforms 1 Describe the landforms formed by volcanoes. 2 Identify three kinds of volcanic mountains.	• Volcanic landforms include volcanic mountains, craters, calderas, fissures, and lava plateaus. • There are three kinds of volcanic mountains: cinder cones, shield volcanoes, and composite volcanoes.
Where Volcanoes Form 1 Discuss the occurrence of volcanoes at plate boundaries and at hot spots.	• Volcanoes form at convergent and divergent boundaries and at hot spots. • Divergent boundaries display volcanism as plates separate, forming rifts. At convergent boundaries, volcanoes form as a result of a subducting plate. • Volcanoes form at hot spots as hot plumes of mantle rise through convection.

Options for Instruction

Two parallel paths provide coverage of the Essential Questions, with a strong **Inquiry** strand woven into each. Follow the **Print Path,** the **Digital Path,** or your customized combination of print, digital, and inquiry.

 Print Path *Teaching support for the Print Path appears with the Student Pages.*	 Inquiry Labs and Activities	 Digital Path *Digital Path shortcut: TS671310*
Magma Magic, SE p. 228 **What is a volcano?**	**Activity** **A Look Within** **Exploration Lab** **Modeling Lava Viscosity**	**Volcano Formation** **Video Clip**
Magma Magic, SE pp. 229–230 **What are the kinds of volcanic landforms?** • Volcanic Mountains • Fissures and Lava Plateaus • Craters and Calderas	**Activity** **Volcanic Mountain Models** **Quick Lab** **Modeling an Explosive Eruption** **Daily Demo** **On the Move**	**Volcanic Landforms** **Interactive Images**
ERUPTION!, SE pp. 231–234 **Where do volcanoes form?** • At Divergent Boundaries • At Convergent Boundaries • At Hot Spots	**Activity** **Divergent Boundary Volcanoes** **Activity** **Volcano Field Guide** **Quick Lab** **Volcano Mapping**	**Volcanoes and Tectonics** **Interactive Image** **The Ring of Fire** **Diagram** **Hot Spots** **Animation**

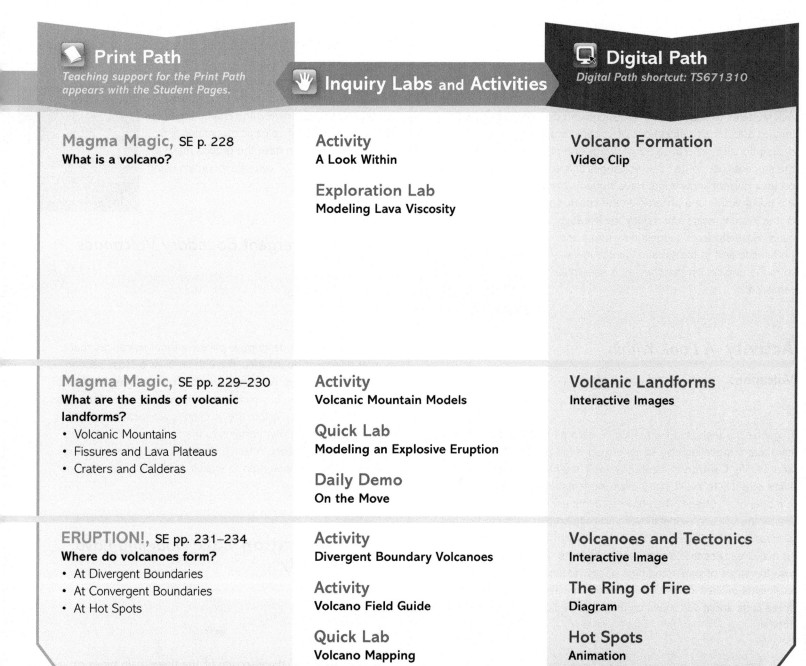

Options for Assessment

See the Evaluate page for options, including Formative Assessment, Summative Assessment, and Unit Review.

Engage and Explore

Activities and Discussion

Discussion *Volcanic Impressions*

Engage

Introducing Key Topics

 whole class
 20 min

Student Impressions of Eruptions Encourage students to discuss images of volcanoes that they have seen in movies and on television. Ask students to share their impressions and describe how these images affect their perceptions of volcanic eruptions. Use student descriptions to generate a list of words and phrases on the board that the students use to describe volcanoes and volcanic eruptions based on their current knowledge. Have students copy the list of words and phrases. At the conclusion of the lesson, revisit and modify the list as a class. Have students suggest new terms and phrases to add to the list and identify ideas from the original list that they think should be removed.

Activity *A Look Within*

Volcanoes

 pairs
 40 min

Organize students into pairs. Provide each pair with two pieces of cardboard, modeling clay, strips of paper, hat pins or thumbtacks, and a knife. **Caution** students to handle the hat pins (tacks) and knife carefully to avoid injury. Have students use the clay to construct a model of a volcano. Then have students use the knife to carefully divide the volcano model in half vertically, so that each student has a cross section. Have each student work with one half of the model to make features that clearly represent vents. Then have the students use the strips of paper and pins (tacks) to label the magma chamber and vents of their volcano cross section. Finally, have students write three facts about volcanoes on the cardboard at the base of their model.

Labs and Demos

Activity *Volcanic Mountain Models*

Engage

Volcanic Landforms

 small groups
30 min

Organize students into small groups. Provide each group with several colors of modeling clay. Have students review the characteristics of the three kinds of volcanic mountains and how they form. Then have the groups make a model of each type of volcanic mountain using modeling clay.

Activity *Divergent Boundary Volcanoes*

Engage

Where Volcanoes Form

 whole class
35 min

Have students write descriptive phrases about volcanoes that form at divergent boundaries. Have them draw a cross section of a mid-ocean ridge. Ask them to add arrows to the drawing to indicate the direction in which plates are moving. They should also add labels to identify where the volcanoes are located and other relevant information that pertains to the formation of volanoes at a divergent boundary. After students complete their drawings, have them write a paragraph to explain how volcanoes form at divergent boundaries.

Exploration Lab *Modeling Lava Viscosity*

Volcanoes

 small groups
 25 min
Inquiry **DIRECTED** inquiry

PURPOSE **To model the viscosity of the three main types of lava**

See the Lab Manual or go Online for planning information.

Levels of **Inquiry**

DIRECTED inquiry introduces inquiry skills within a structured framework.

GUIDED inquiry develops inquiry skills within a supportive environment.

INDEPENDENT inquiry deepens inquiry skills with student-driven questions or procedures.

Daily Demo *On the Move*

Engage

Volcanic Landforms

 whole class
 15 min
 **GUIDED** inquiry

PURPOSE **To demonstrate the concept of viscosity**

MATERIALS
- **molasses or honey**
- **vegetable oil**
- **water**
- **cookie sheet**
- **book**

1 Use the book to elevate one end of the cookie sheet.

2 **Observing** Have students observe as you pour a small amount of each liquid onto the cookie sheet. **Ask:** What do you observe about the rate at which the liquids flow? Sample answer: The molasses moved most slowly, then the oil; the water flowed fastest. **Ask:** Why do you think the liquids flowed at the rates they did? Sample answer: The thickness of the liquid affected its rate of flow. Explain that viscosity is a liquid's resistance to flow. Molasses has a high viscosity so it flows very slowly. Water has a low viscosity so it flows quickly. Relate the concept of viscosity to the rate of magma flow and how this rate affects the type of volcano that will form.

For greater depth: Lava viscosity is greatly influenced by temperature and is an important aspect of volcano morphology. To help students visualize how temperature affects viscosity, repeat the demonstration using molasses that has been refrigerated, molasses at room temperature, and molasses that has been heated in a hot-water bath.

Quick Lab *Modeling an Explosive Eruption*

PURPOSE **To model the effects and landforms resulting from an explosive volcanic eruption**

See the Lab Manual or go Online for planning information.

Quick Lab *Volcano Mapping*

Where Volcanoes Form

 small groups
 25 min
 **DIRECTED** inquiry

PURPOSE **To illustrate the relationship between tectonic plate boundaries and volcanic eruptions**

MATERIALS
- **clear transparency film**
- **dry-erase marker**
- **photocopy of world map**
- **world map or transparency overlay that shows tectonic plate boundaries**

Customize Your Labs

See the Lab Manual for lab datasheets.

Go Online for editable lab datasheets.

Activities and Discussion

- ☐ **Discussion** Volcanic Impressions
- ☐ **Activity** A Look Within
- ☐ **Activity** Volcanic Mountain Models
- ☐ **Activity** Divergent Boundary Volcanoes

Labs and Demos

- ☐ **Exploration Lab** Modeling Lava Viscosity
- ☐ **Daily Demo** On the Move
- ☐ **Quick Lab** Modeling an Explosive Eruption
- ☐ **Quick Lab** Volcano Mapping

Your Resources

Explain Science Concepts

Key Topics

Volcanoes

Print Path

☐ **Magma Magic,** SE p. 228
- Visualize It!, #5

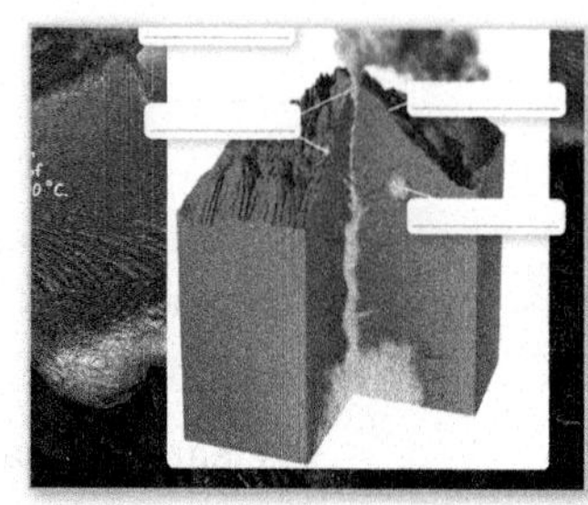

Digital Path

☐ **Volcano Formation**
Learn about volcanoes, magma, and lava.

Volcanic Landforms

Print Path

☐ **Magma Magic,** SE pp. 229–230
- Think Outside the Book, #6
- Active Reading (Annotation strategy), #7
- Visualize It!, #8

Digital Path

☐ **Volcanic Landforms**
Explore three types of volcanic mountains.

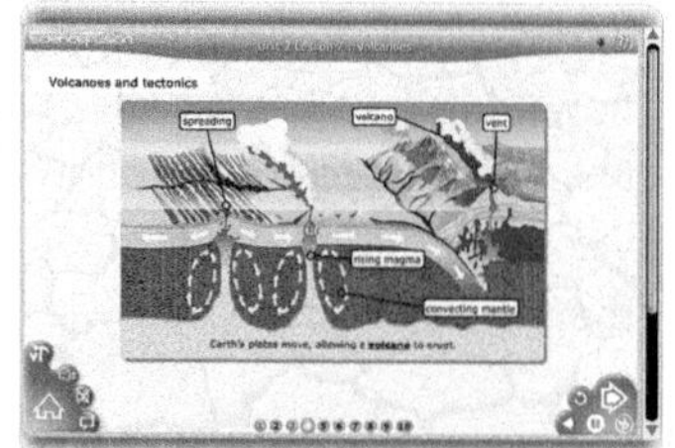

Where Volcanoes Form

Print Path

☐ **ERUPTION!,** SE pp. 231–234
- Active Reading (Annotation strategy), #9
- Visualize It!, #10
- Active Reading, #11
- Visualize It!, #12
- Summarize, #13
- Visualize It!, #14

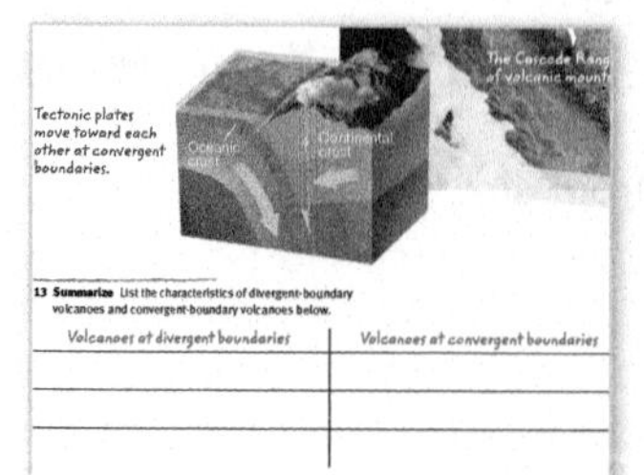

Digital Path

☐ **Volcanoes and tectonics**
Explore how volcanoes can form at tectonic plate boundaries.

☐ **The Ring of Fire**
See how volcanoes are found around the Pacific Ocean at plate boundaries.

☐ **Hot Spots**
Learn how a series of volcanoes can form as a tectonic plate changes position.

Differentiated Instruction

Basic *Volcanoes of the World*

Synthesizing Key Topics

 individuals
 25 min

Show students a large world map and a map identifying the locations and names of Earth's tectonic plates. Ask volunteers to use the tectonic plate map to identify locations on the world map where volcanoes are likely to form. Then have students locate areas of major volcanic activity. Distribute a blank world map to each student. Have students use markers or colored pencils to draw red lines on their maps to identify areas of strong volcanic activity. For a Quick Lab version of this activity, see the Quick Lab titled, Volcano Mapping.

Advanced *Volcano Pen Pals*

Synthesizing Key Topics

 individuals
 varied

Have students write a letter to a friend. Students should write the letter as if they are survivors of a volcanic eruption. Have students describe the volcano before the eruption, during the eruption, and after the eruption. Students can then exchange and read the letters to the class. Based on the description of the eruption, have the class identify whether the volcano described resulted from interactions at a particular type of plate boundary (and identify the type of boundary) or at a hot spot.

ELL *Handy Vocabulary*

Where Volcanoes Form

 whole class
 10 min

Remind students that *divergent* means pulling apart. Move your hands away from each other to physically demonstrate the meaning of the word. Ask students to say "divergent" as they move their hands away from each other. Repeat the process for the word *convergent*. Finally, have students draw pairs of arrows on paper to illustrate the meaning of each term.

Lesson Vocabulary

volcano	magma	lava
vent	tectonic plate	hot spot

Previewing Vocabulary

 whole class, then pairs
 25 min

Frame Game Have students make Frame Game diagrams to learn vocabulary terms. Use a blank frame (available online) to demonstrate the use of the diagram. Then have students work in pairs to develop a frame for each term.

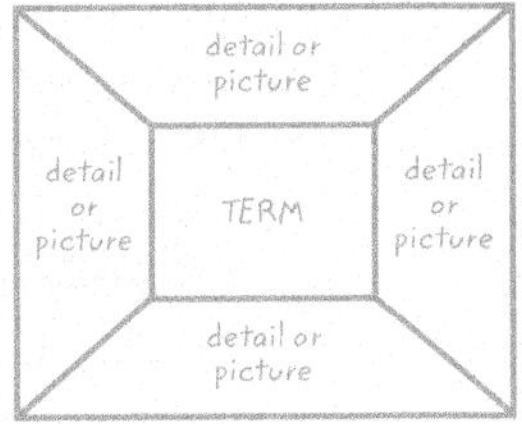

Online resource: Frame Game Support

Reinforcing Vocabulary

 individuals
 30 min

Four Square To help students remember each of the vocabulary terms introduced in this lesson, have them complete a Four Square graphic organizer for each term.

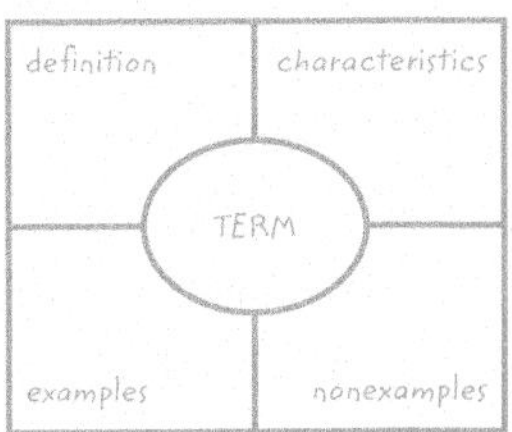

Online resource: Four Square support

Customize Your Core Lesson

Core Instruction

- ☐ Print Path choices
- ☐ Digital Path choices

Vocabulary

- ☐ Previewing Vocabulary Frame Game
- ☐ Reinforcing Vocabulary Four Square

Differentiated Instruction

- ☐ Basic Volcanoes of the World
- ☐ Advanced Volcano Pen Pals
- ☐ ELL Handy Vocabulary

Your Resources

Extend Science Concepts

Reinforce and Review

Activity *Match It Up Game*

Synthesizing Key Topics

 small groups
25 min

Before playing the game, make several decks of game cards. Game cards consist of question cards and corresponding answer cards. You may find it helpful to use a different colored index card for each deck of cards. Each deck of game cards should include about 50 cards (25 question/25 answer). Choose questions about key topics and other material you found important in this lesson. Make a complete set of cards for each group of four or five students.

1 Give each group one deck of cards.
2 Assign a dealer to deal each player five cards and then spread the rest face down between the players.
3 Have players take turns asking each other for matches. For example, if a player has a question card that reads, "Where are most volcanoes located?" then the player should ask another player, "Do you have a 'Ring of Fire' card?" The request would be reversed if the player had the answer card and was looking for the question.
4 If yes, the other player hands over the match and play moves on. If no, the requestor must choose from the "pool" before play moves on.
5 The player with the most matches at the end of the game wins.

Graphic Organizer

Volcanic Landforms

individuals
35 min

Concept Map After students have studied the lesson, ask them to develop a Concept Map that identifies the different types of volcanic landforms. Have students share their Concept Maps with a partner.

Optional Online resources: Concept Map support

Going Further

Math Connection

Volcanic Eruptions

 individuals
varied

Kilauea Kilauea, in Hawaii, is one of the youngest and one of the most studied volcanoes in the world. It has been erupting regularly since 1983. Each day, enough lava to pave a two-lane road 32 km long pours out from the volcano. Have students calculate how long this "road" will be if the volcano continues to erupt at the same rate for 40 years. 365 days × 32 km/day = 11,680 km/y; 11,680 km/y × 40 y = 467,200 km; 467,200 km. Have advanced students make the additional calculation to account for the 10 leap days that occur during the 40-year period. 0.25 days × 32 km/day = 320 km, so 467,200 km + 320 km = 467,520 km. You may wish to point out to students that after 40 years, the road would be more than 11 times Earth's circumference!

Language Arts Connection

Synthesizing Key Topics

 whole class
15 min

Word Connections Write the word ***pyroclastic*** on the board. Ask students to define it. Explain that this word is derived from the Greek words ***pyros*** and ***klastos***. ***Pyros*** means "fire," and ***klastos*** means "broken." Challenge students to develop a list of other words that contain the word part ***pyro-***. Ask them to provide a definition for each word they list.

Customize Your Closing

See the Assessment Guide for quizzes and tests.

Go Online to edit and create quizzes and tests.

Reinforce and Review

- ☐ **Activity** Match It Up Game
- ☐ **Graphic Organizer** Concept Map
- ☐ **Print Path** Visual Summary, SE p. 236
- ☐ **Digital Path** Lesson Closer

Evaluate Student Mastery

Formative Assessment

See the teacher support below the Student Pages for additional Formative Assessment questions.

Describe or have students review how volcanoes form. **Ask:** What are some volcanic landforms? Sample answer: lava plateaus, craters, calderas, and volcanic mountains (shield volcanoes, cinder cones, and composite volcanoes)

Reteach

Formative assessment may show you that students need reinforcement for certain topics. The resources below are recommended for reteaching. If students were introduced to topics through the Print Path, you can also use the Digital Path for reteaching, and vice versa.

Can be assigned to individual students

Volcanoes

Discussion Volcanic Impressions

Activity A Look Within

Volcanic Landforms

Activity Volcanic Mountain Models

Quick Lab Modeling an Explosive Eruption

Daily Demo On the Move

Where Volcanoes Form

Quick Lab Volcano Mapping

Activity Divergent Boundary Volcanoes

Summative Assessment

Alternative Assessment
Volcanoes and Volcanic Activity

Online resources: student worksheet, optional rubrics

Volcanoes

Points of View: ***Volcanoes and Volcanic Activity***
Your class will work together to show what you've learned about volcanoes from several different viewpoints.

1. Work in groups as assigned by your teacher. Each group will be assigned to one or two viewpoints.
2. Complete your assignment, and present your perspective to the class.

Vocabulary Look up the root of the word *volcano*. Then find other words in the lesson that contain the same root. List these words, and write a definition for each.

Illustrations Design trading cards for each type of volcano. On the cards draw images of and label all the types of volcanoes. Then describe how each type is different from or similar to other types of volcanoes.

Analysis When volcanoes erupt, they release a number of different materials and change the landforms around them. Volcanoes can also change landforms by collapsing or exploding. How might Earth's surface be different if volcanoes did not exist? Which landforms and landmasses might not exist if it weren't for volcanoes? Create a PowerPoint presentation in which you describe your answers and ideas.

Details Imagine that you have just watched a news report that stated that all volcanoes form at the boundaries of tectonic plates. Write a letter to the news station explaining that volcanoes can also form in other areas. Describe the other areas in which volcanoes form and explain how these volcanoes occur.

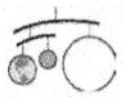

Models Make a model of a shield volcano. Label the vent, the lava flow, and the magma chamber. Describe how a shield volcano is different from and similar to other types of volcanoes.

Going Further

- ☐ Math Connection
- ☐ Language Arts Connection
- ☐ Print Path Why It Matters, SE p. 235

Formative Assessment

- ☐ Strategies Throughout TE
- ☐ Lesson Review SE

Summative Assessment

- ☐ Alternative Assessment Volcanoes and Volcanic Activity
- ☐ Lesson Quiz
- ☐ Unit Tests A and B
- ☐ Unit Review SE End-of-Unit

Your Resources

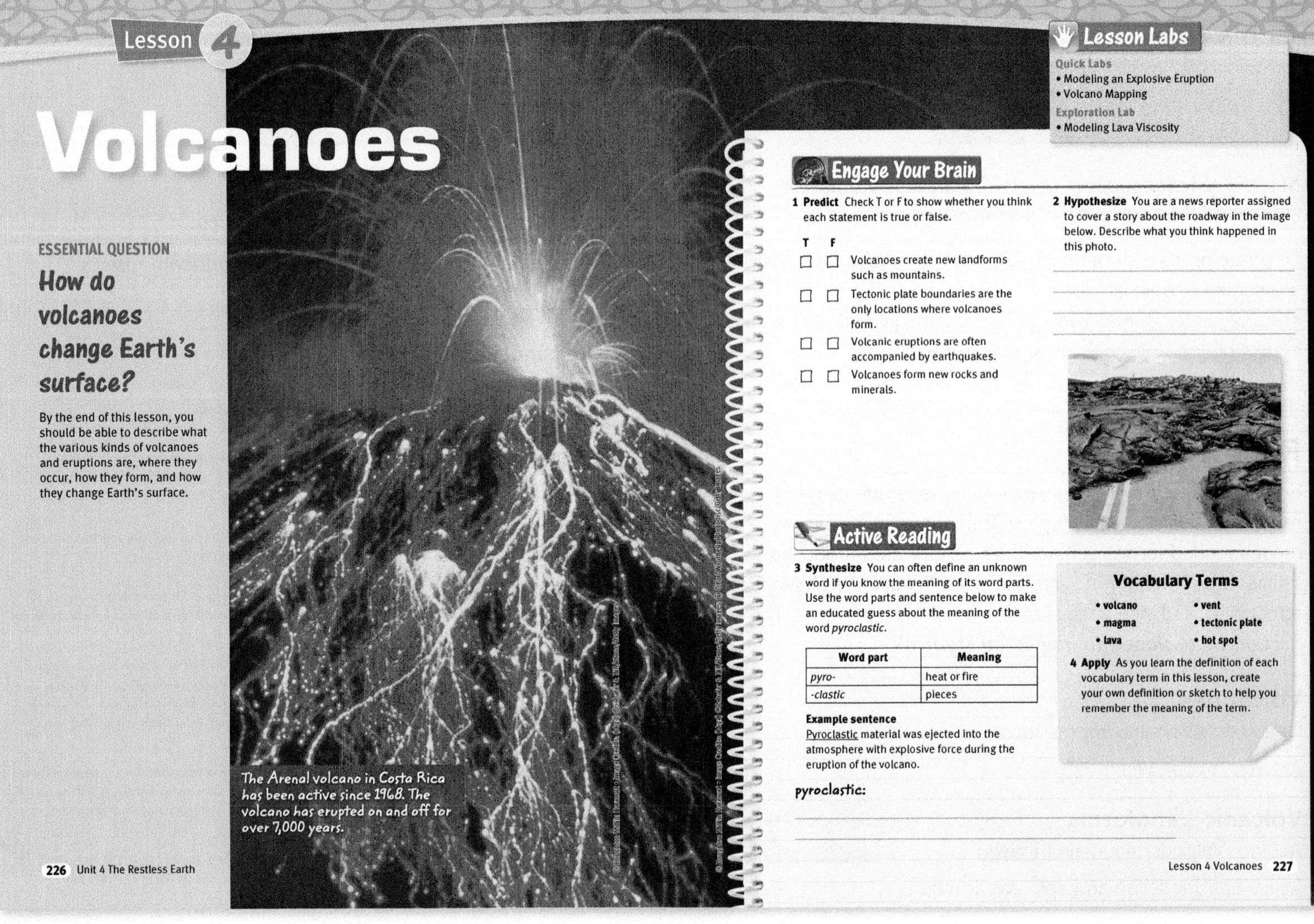

Answers

Answers for 1–3 should represent students' current thoughts, even if incorrect.

1. T; F; T; T
2. Sample answer: The roadway was covered in a lava flow that later cooled and hardened into rock.
3. Pyroclastic - materials formed by the fragmentation of lava and rock by explosive volcanic activity.
4. Students should define or sketch each vocabulary term in the lesson.

Opening Your Lesson

Discuss student interpretations of the image (item 2) to assess students' prerequisite knowledge and to estimate what they already know about key topics.

Prerequisites: Earth's crust is broken into tectonic plates that are in constant motion; movements of tectonic plates cause changes to Earth's surface.

Accessing Prior Knowledge: Use the SQ3R support materials to explain and demonstrate the strategy for students. Then, allow them to work with partners as they employ the SQ3R strategy to preview the lesson.

Online resources: SQ3R support

Learning Alert MISCONCEPTION

Nonexplosive Volcanoes Students may think that all volcanic eruptions are explosive and destructive. Ask students to describe volcanoes and volcanic eruptions and see if they mention nonexplosive eruptions. Point out that volcanic activity may be nonexplosive. Show students a world map and point out locations such as Hawaii where volcanoes are adding crust to Earth's surface through nonexplosive eruptions. Volcanoes are erupting all the time—some right on the ocean floor!

Magma MAGIC

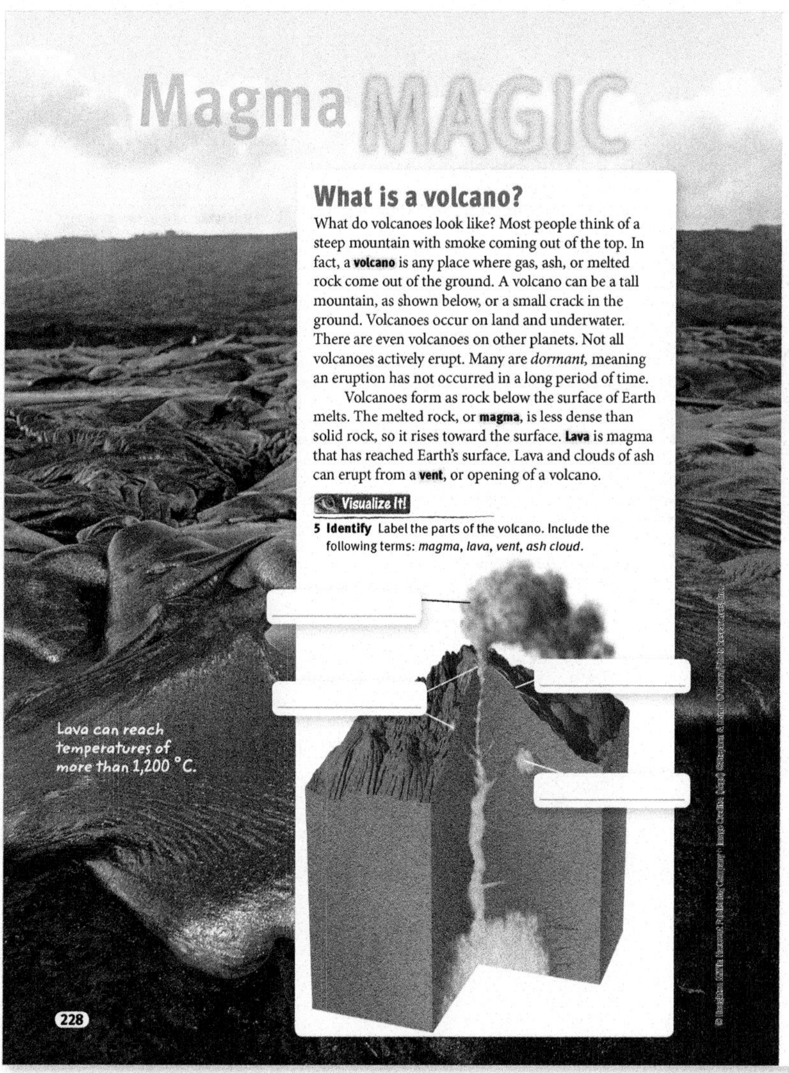

Lava can reach temperatures of more than 1,200 °C.

What is a volcano?

What do volcanoes look like? Most people think of a steep mountain with smoke coming out of the top. In fact, a **volcano** is any place where gas, ash, or melted rock come out of the ground. A volcano can be a tall mountain, as shown below, or a small crack in the ground. Volcanoes occur on land and underwater. There are even volcanoes on other planets. Not all volcanoes actively erupt. Many are *dormant*, meaning an eruption has not occurred in a long period of time.

Volcanoes form as rock below the surface of Earth melts. The melted rock, or **magma**, is less dense than solid rock, so it rises toward the surface. **Lava** is magma that has reached Earth's surface. Lava and clouds of ash can erupt from a **vent**, or opening of a volcano.

Visualize It!

5 Identify Label the parts of the volcano. Include the following terms: *magma, lava, vent, ash cloud.*

What are the kinds of volcanic landforms?

The location of a volcano and the composition of magma determine the type of volcanic landforms created. Shield volcanoes, cinder cones, composite volcanoes, lava plateaus, craters, and calderas are all types of volcanic landforms.

Volcanic Mountains

Materials ejected from a volcano may build up around a vent to create volcanic mountains. *Viscosity* (vyz•SKAHZ•ih•tee) is the resistance of a liquid material, such as lava, to flow. The viscosity of lava determines the explosiveness of an eruption and the shape of the resulting volcanic mountain. Low-viscosity lava flows easily, forms low slopes, and erupts without large explosions. High-viscosity lava does not flow easily, forms steep slopes, and can erupt explosively. *Pyroclastic materials* (py•roh•KLAHZ•tyk), or hot ash and bits of rock, may also be ejected into the atmosphere.

Think Outside the Book **Inquiry**

6 Apply Small fragments of rock material that are ejected from a volcano are known as *volcanic ash*. Volcanic ash is a form of pyroclastic material. The material does not dissolve in water and is very abrasive, meaning it can scratch surfaces. Ash can build up to great depths in locations around a volcano. Write a cleanup plan for a town that explains how you might safely remove and dispose of volcanic ash.

Active Reading

7 Identify As you read, underline the main features of each type of volcanic mountain.

- **Shield Volcanoes** Volcanoes with a broad base and gently sloping sides are *shield volcanoes*. Shield volcanoes cover a wide area and generally form from mild eruptions. Layers of lava flow out from the vent, harden, and slowly build up to form the cone. The Hawaiian Islands are shield volcanoes.

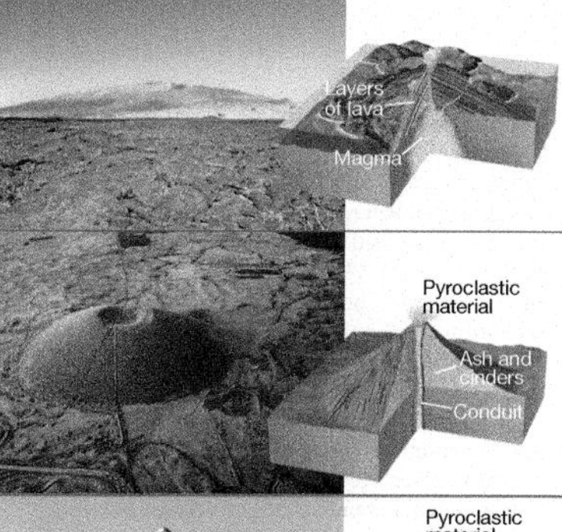

- **Cinder Cones** Sometimes, ash and pieces of lava harden in the air and can fall to the ground around a small vent. The hardened pieces of lava are called cinders. The cinders and ash build up around the vent and form a steep volcano called a *cinder cone*. A cinder cone can also form at a side vent on other volcanic mountains, such as on shield or composite volcanoes.

- **Composite Volcanoes** Alternating layers of hardened lava flows and pyroclastic material create *composite volcanoes* (kuhm•PAHZ•iht). During a mild eruption, lava flows cover the sides of the cone. During an explosive eruption, pyroclastic material is deposited around the vent. Composite volcanoes commonly develop into large and steep volcanic mountains.

Pyroclastic material

Lava and ash layers

Answers

5. Students should fill in the diagram with ash cloud (top left), vent (bottom left), lava (top right), and magma (bottom right).
6. Sample answer: Wear dust masks and use equipment that is not easily scratched from the abrasive material. Be careful of hot ashes.
7. *See students' pages for annotations.*

Learning Alert

Students may have trouble remembering that high temperature alone is not always sufficient to melt rock. The melting point of rocks rises with increasing pressure, so that most of the mantle is in a solid state even though the temperature is quite high. It takes a suitable combination of increasing temperature, decreasing pressure, or the addition of materials that have low boiling points and evaporate easily to generate magma in Earth's mantle.

Using Annotations

Text Structure: Details Once students have labeled the parts of a volcano in the text, have them go back and think about each. Are there any parts that were new to them? Were any of the details in this section a surprise to them? Why? Encourage them to become better readers by reflecting on what they read.

Fissures and Lava Plateaus

Fissure eruptions (FIH•shohr ee•RUHP•shuhnz) happen when lava flows from giant cracks, or *fissures*, in Earth's surface. The fissures are found on land and on the ocean floor. A fissure eruption has no central opening. Lava flows out of the entire length of the fissure, which can be many kilometers long. As a result, a thick and mostly flattened layer of cooled lava, called a *lava plateau* (plah•TOH), can form. One example of a lava plateau is the Columbia Plateau Province in Washington, Oregon, and Idaho, as shown to the right.

The Palouse Falls in Washington plunge deep into exposed layers of the Columbia lava plateau.

Craters and Calderas

A *volcanic crater* is an opening or depression at the top of a volcano caused by eruptions. Inside the volcano, molten rock can form an expanded area of magma called a *magma chamber*, as shown to the right. When the magma chamber below a volcano empties, the roof of the magma chamber may collapse and leave an even larger, basin-shaped depression called a *caldera* (kahl•DAHR•uh). Calderas can form from the sudden drain of a magma chamber during an explosive eruption or from a slowly emptied magma chamber. More than 7,000 years ago, the cone of Mount Mazama in Oregon collapsed to form a caldera. The caldera later filled with water and is now called Crater Lake.

A caldera can be more than 100 km in diameter.

Visualize It!

8 Describe How does the appearance of land surfaces change before and after a caldera forms?

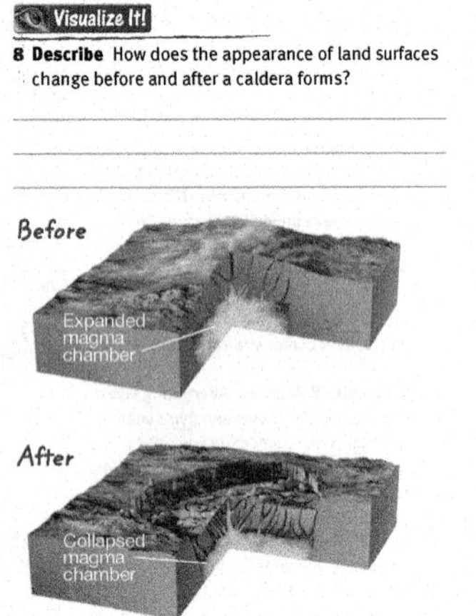

ERUPTION!

Where do volcanoes form?

Volcanoes can form at plate boundaries or within the middle of a plate. Recall that **tectonic plates** are giant sections of lithosphere on Earth's surface. Volcanoes can form at *divergent plate boundaries* where two plates are moving away from each other. Most fissure eruptions occur at divergent boundaries. Shield volcanoes, fissure eruptions, and cinder cones can also occur away from plate boundaries within a plate at *hot spots*. The type of lava normally associated with these volcanoes has a relatively low viscosity, few trapped gases, and is usually not explosive.

Composite volcanoes are most common along *convergent plate boundaries* where oceanic plates subduct. In order for the rock to melt, it must be hot and the pressure on it must drop, or water and other fluids must be added to it. Extra fluids from ocean water form magma of higher viscosity with more trapped gases. Thus, composite volcanoes produce the most violent eruptions. The *Ring of Fire* is a name used to describe the numerous explosive volcanoes that form on convergent plate boundaries surrounding the Pacific Ocean.

Active Reading

9 Identify As you read, underline three locations where volcanoes can form.

Plate Tectonic Boundaries and Volcano Locations Worldwide

Visualize It!

10 Describe How do the locations of volcanoes relate to tectonic plate boundaries?

Answers

8. A large hole or depression can be made in the ground after the collapse of a magma chamber.
9. *See students' pages for annotations.*
10. Most volcanoes occur near plate tectonic boundaries. Some volcanoes occur away from the edges of tectonic plates at hot spots.

Interpreting Visuals

Have students look at the images of a caldera before and after formation. **Ask:** What occurs to allow the caldera to form? A caldera forms when an underground magma chamber empties and the land above collapses into the empty chamber, forming a cauldron-shaped depression on Earth's surface. This often occurs following volcanic eruptions.

Building Reading Skills

Main Idea Web Students can use a Main Idea Web to organize the information they are learning as they read about the different places volcanoes form.

Interpreting Visuals

Have students look at the map of the Ring of Fire. Discuss how a volcano forms. **Ask:** What is important about the Ring of Fire? Why do so many volcanoes form in this region? The Ring of Fire is a place where many volcanoes form because of plate tectonic activity surrounding the Pacific Plate.

At Divergent Boundaries

At divergent boundaries, plates move away from each other. The lithosphere stretches and gets thinner, so the pressure on the mantle rock below decreases. As a result, the asthenosphere bulges upward and magma forms. This magma rises through fissures in the lithosphere, out onto the land or the ocean floor.

Most divergent boundaries are on the ocean floor. When eruptions occur in these areas, undersea volcanoes develop. These volcanoes and other processes lead to the formation of a long, underwater mountain range known as a *mid-ocean ridge.* Two examples of mid-ocean ridges are the East Pacific Rise in the Pacific Ocean and the Mid-Atlantic Ridge in the Atlantic Ocean. The youngest rocks in the ocean are located at mid-ocean ridges.

Shield volcanoes and cinder cones are common in Iceland, where the Mid-Atlantic Ridge runs through the country. As the plates move away from each other, new crust forms. When a divergent boundary is located in the middle of a continent, the crust stretches until a rift valley is formed, as shown below.

Active Reading 11 Identify What types of volcanic landforms occur at divergent plate boundaries?

Divergent plate boundaries create fissure eruptions and shield volcanoes.

Fissure

The Great Rift Valley in Africa is a location where the crust is stretching and separating.

Tectonic plates move away from each other at divergent boundaries.

At Convergent Boundaries

At convergent boundaries, two plates move toward each other. In most cases, one plate sinks beneath the other plate. As the sinking plate dives into the mantle, fluids in the sinking plate become super heated and escape. These escaping fluids cause the rock above the sinking plate to melt and form magma. This magma rises to the surface and erupts to form volcanoes.

The magma that forms at convergent boundaries has a high concentration of fluids. As the magma rises, decreasing pressure causes the fluid trapped in the magma to form gas bubbles. But, because the magma has a high viscosity, these bubbles cannot escape easily. As the bubbles expand, the magma rises faster. Eventually, the magma can erupt explosively, forming calderas or composite volcanoes. Gas, ash, and large chunks of rock can be blown out of the volcanoes. The Cascade Range is a chain of active composite volcanoes in the northwestern United States, as shown to the right. In 1980, Mt. St. Helens erupted so violently that the entire top of the mountain was blown away.

Visualize It!

12 Identify Draw two arrows in the white boxes to indicate the direction of motion of the plates that formed the Cascade volcanoes.

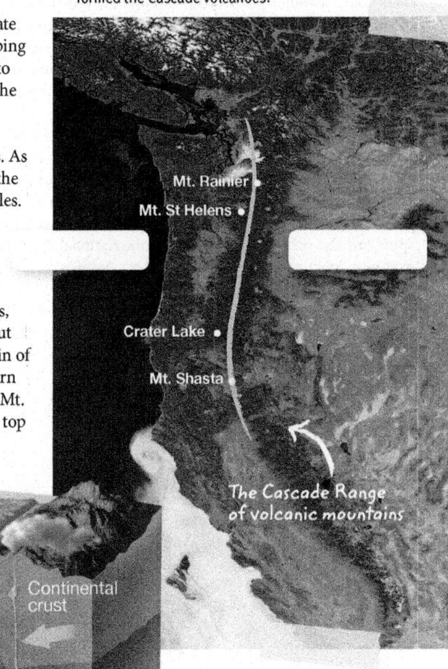

The Cascade Range of volcanic mountains

Tectonic plates move toward each other at convergent boundaries.

Oceanic crust

Continental crust

13 Summarize List the characteristics of divergent-boundary volcanoes and convergent-boundary volcanoes below.

Volcanoes at divergent boundaries	Volcanoes at convergent boundaries

Answers

11. rift valleys, shield vocanoes, fissure eruptions, mid-ocean ridges.
12. Arrows drawn by the student should be pointing towards each other.
13. Sample answers:

    Divergent - mild eruptions, caused by pressure changes, low-viscosity lava

    Convergent - explosive, more trapped gases, high-viscosity lava

Using Annotations

Text Structure: Details As students underline the characteristics of divergent plate boundary volcanoes, encourage them to think about how these characteristics make these volcanoes different from volcanoes that form at other plate boundaries.

Formative Assessment

Ask: How do pressure and temperature help to form magma? When hot rock is under high pressure in the mantle, it tends to remain solid. When pressure is released by rocks moving upward in the mantle, the rock melts partially (if the temperature remains high enough). **Ask:** How does new crust form at divergent boundaries? As tectonic plates spread apart, older, thicker crust moves away from the plate boundary. In the area of thinner crust, the pressure drops and partial melting generates magma, which rises up from the mantle. Some of this magma may erupt through cracks onto the sea floor to make new crust.

At Hot Spots

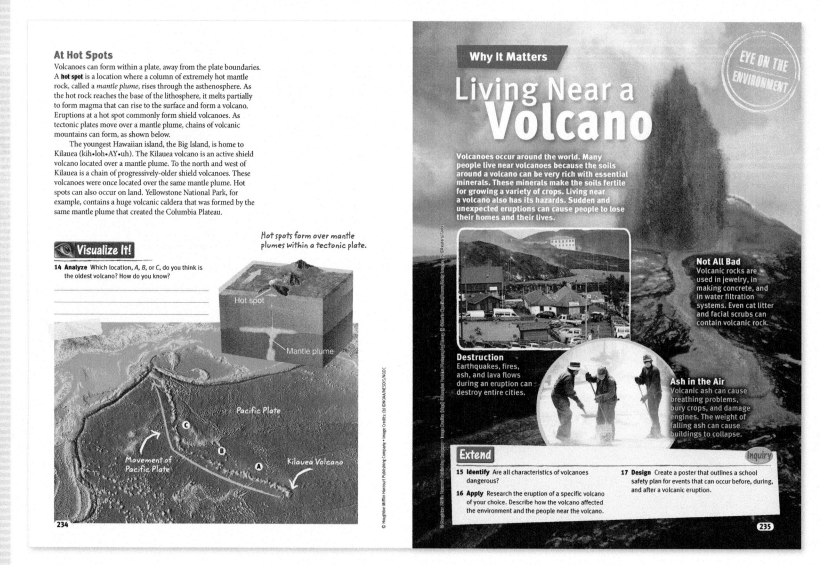

Volcanoes can form within a plate, away from the plate boundaries. A **hot spot** is a location where a column of extremely hot mantle rock, called a *mantle plume*, rises through the asthenosphere. As the hot rock reaches the base of the lithosphere, it melts partially to form magma that can rise to the surface and form a volcano. Eruptions at a hot spot commonly form shield volcanoes. As tectonic plates move over a mantle plume, chains of volcanic mountains can form, as shown below.

The youngest Hawaiian island, the Big Island, is home to Kilauea (kih•loh•AY•uh). The Kilauea volcano is an active shield volcano located over a mantle plume. To the north and west of Kilauea is a chain of progressively-older shield volcanoes. These volcanoes were once located over the same mantle plume. Hot spots can also occur on land. Yellowstone National Park, for example, contains a huge volcanic caldera that was formed by the same mantle plume that created the Columbia Plateau.

Visualize It!

14 Analyze Which location, *A, B,* or *C*, do you think is the oldest volcano? How do you know?

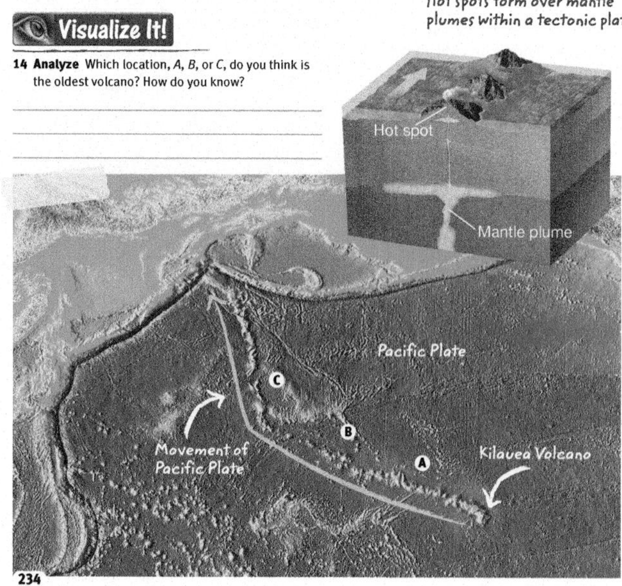

Hot spots form over mantle plumes within a tectonic plate.

Why It Matters

EYE ON THE ENVIRONMENT

Living Near a Volcano

Volcanoes occur around the world. Many people live near volcanoes because the soils around a volcano can be very rich with essential minerals. These minerals make the soils fertile for growing a variety of crops. Living near a volcano also has its hazards. Sudden and unexpected eruptions can cause people to lose their homes and their lives.

Not All Bad
Volcanic rocks are used in jewelry, in making concrete, and in water filtration systems. Even cat litter and facial scrubs can contain volcanic rock.

Destruction
Earthquakes, fires, ash, and lava flows during an eruption can destroy entire cities.

Ash in the Air
Volcanic ash can cause breathing problems, bury crops, and damage engines. The weight of falling ash can cause buildings to collapse.

Extend Inquiry

15 Identify Are all characteristics of volcanoes dangerous?

16 Apply Research the eruption of a specific volcano of your choice. Describe how the volcano affected the environment and the people near the volcano.

17 Design Create a poster that outlines a school safety plan for events that can occur before, during, and after a volcanic eruption.

235

Answers

14. Answer C would be the oldest because it is farthest from the hot spot.
15. Sample answers: Not all volcanic characteristics are dangerous. Rocks and minerals are necessary for life and are created by volcanoes. Volcanic soils can be very fertile. Volcanic rock can be used in a variety of products.
16. Student answers should include details on a specific volcano. Environmental problems and benefits should be outlined in the description.
17. Accept all reasonable answers.

Formative Assessment

Ask: How do mantle plumes generate volcanic activity at hot spots? Mantle plumes are columns of hot rock that rise through Earth's mantle. As the top of a mantle plume approaches the base of the lithosphere, it undergoes partial melting and spreads out. Magma is released onto Earth's surface as lava, creating volcanic landforms, such as volcanic cones.

Why It Matters

Most students will not have a clear understanding of exactly what materials erupt from a volcano. Explain that eruptions include volcanic ash, rocks, lava, and gases. Large rocks called volcanic bombs are expelled from a volcano in a molten state and cool while in the air. Volcanic blocks are "preformed" rocks that are solid when thrown from the volcano. Have students use the information in the "Living Near a Volcano" feature to identify some positive and negative aspects of volcanic eruptions.

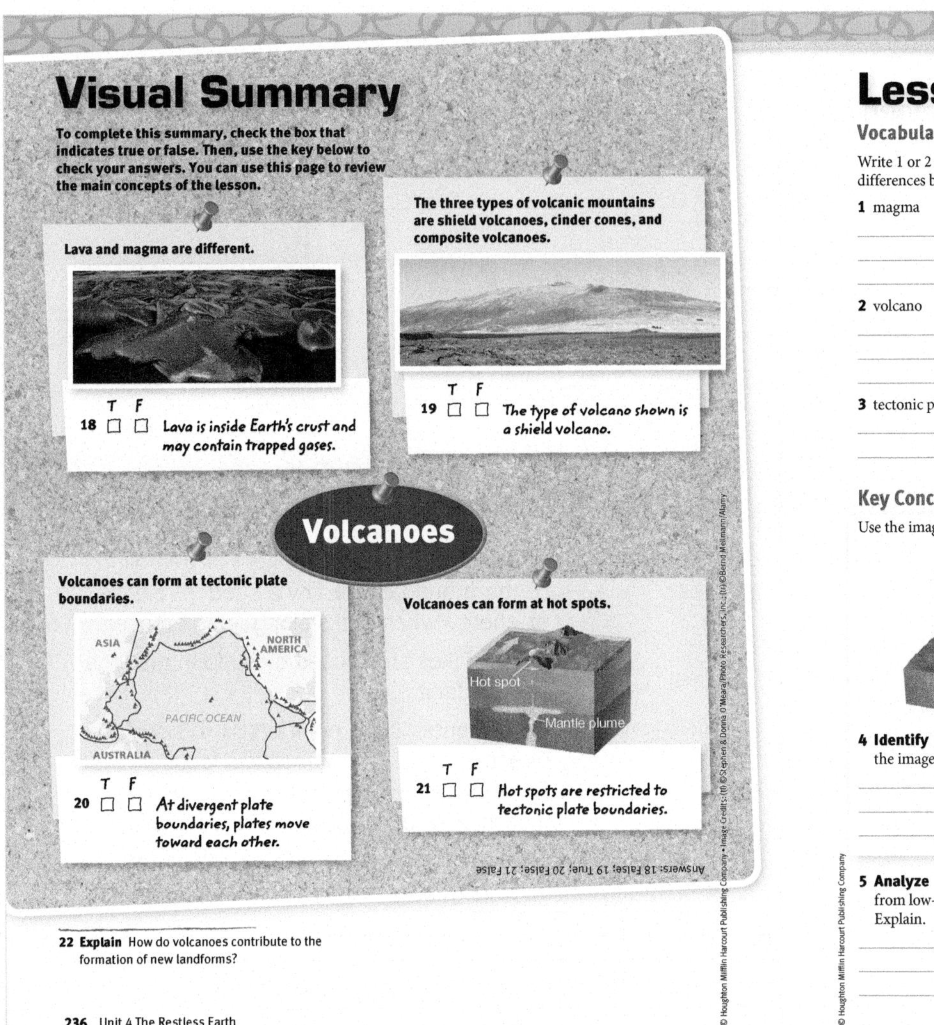

Visual Summary

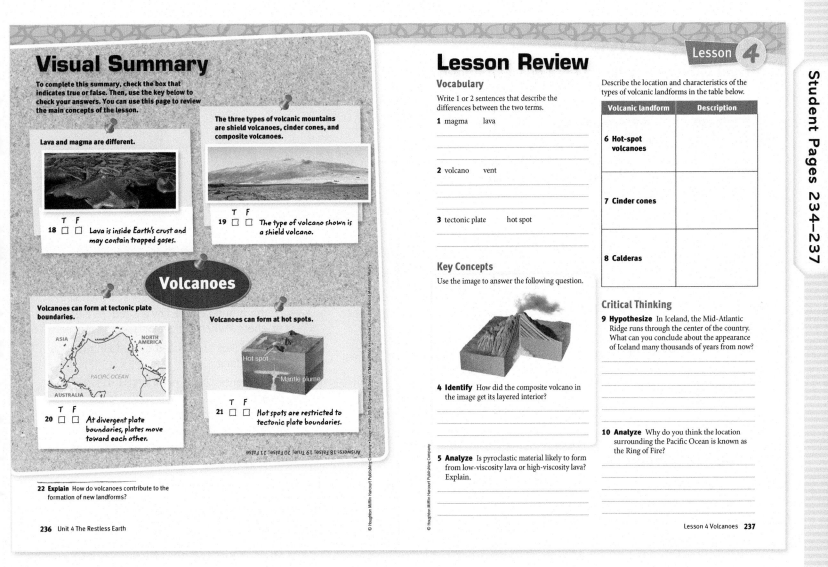

To complete this summary, check the box that indicates true or false. Then, use the key below to check your answers. You can use this page to review the main concepts of the lesson.

Volcanoes

Lava and magma are different.

T F
18 ☐ ☐ *Lava is inside Earth's crust and may contain trapped gases.*

The three types of volcanic mountains are shield volcanoes, cinder cones, and composite volcanoes.

T F
19 ☐ ☐ *The type of volcano shown is a shield volcano.*

Volcanoes can form at tectonic plate boundaries.

T F
20 ☐ ☐ *At divergent plate boundaries, plates move toward each other.*

Volcanoes can form at hot spots.

T F
21 ☐ ☐ *Hot spots are restricted to tectonic plate boundaries.*

Answers: 18 False; 19 True; 20 False; 21 False

22 **Explain** How do volcanoes contribute to the formation of new landforms?

Lesson Review

Vocabulary

Write 1 or 2 sentences that describe the differences between the two terms.

1 magma lava

2 volcano vent

3 tectonic plate hot spot

Key Concepts

Use the image to answer the following question.

4 **Identify** How did the composite volcano in the image get its layered interior?

5 **Analyze** Is pyroclastic material likely to form from low-viscosity lava or high-viscosity lava? Explain.

Describe the location and characteristics of the types of volcanic landforms in the table below.

Volcanic landform	Description
6 Hot-spot volcanoes	
7 Cinder cones	
8 Calderas	

Critical Thinking

9 **Hypothesize** In Iceland, the Mid-Atlantic Ridge runs through the center of the country. What can you conclude about the appearance of Iceland many thousands of years from now?

10 **Analyze** Why do you think the location surrounding the Pacific Ocean is known as the Ring of Fire?

Student Pages 234–237

Visual Summary Answers

18. False
19. True
20. False
21. False
22. As volcanoes erupt, volcanic mountains can form. Lava can harden to form new rocks. Ash and other pyroclastic materials can be deposited.

Lesson Review Answers

1. Magma is under Earth's surface, lava is on Earth's surface.
2. A vent is just one part of a volcano. A volcano is any location where gas, ash, or melted rock come out of the ground.
3. A tectonic plate is a giant section of Earth's lithosphere. A hot spot can occur at the boundary or within the boundaries of a plate.
4. Composite volcanoes have cycles of lava flows and explosive eruptions that deposit different layers over time.
5. from high-viscosity lava because it does not flow as easily as low-viscosity lava and erupts explosively
6. Hot-spot volcanoes form over mantle plumes and can create chains of shield vocanoes or lava plateaus.
7. Cinder cones are sometimes explosive and are made of layers of pyroclastic material. They can form individually or as a side vent on other volcanic mountains.
8. Calderas are large depressions made from the collapse of a magma chamber. Large volcanic mountains become calderas.
9. Iceland will grow or become divided as the lithosphere on either side of the Mid-Atlantic Ridge separates.
10. Many of Earth's volcanoes are located in a ring shape around the Pacific Ocean.

Earthquakes

Essential Question Why do earthquakes happen?

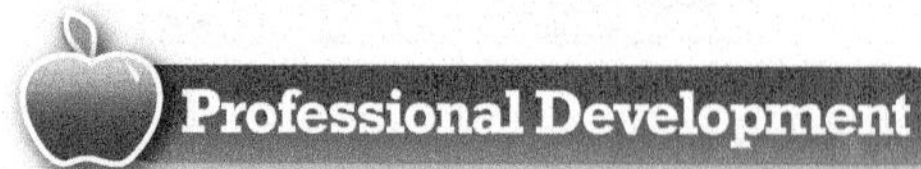

For more detailed information about the topics in this lesson, refer to the Content Refresher in the Unit Opener pages.

Opening Your Lesson

Begin the lesson by assessing students' prerequisite and prior knowledge.

Prerequisite Knowledge

- Earth's lithosphere is made up of tectonic plates that are always moving.
- Plate movement can cause changes in Earth's surface.

Accessing Prior Knowledge

Ask: What is an earthquake? Sample answer: a shaking of the ground caused by a sudden release of energy within Earth

Ask: How do earthquakes occur? Sample answer: Earthquakes occur when plates move along fault lines.

Customize Your Opening

- ☐ **Accessing Prior Knowledge,** above
- ☐ **Print Path** Engage Your Brain, SE p. 239 #1–2
- ☐ **Print Path** Active Reading, SE p. 239 #3–4
- ☐ **Digital Path** Lesson Opener

Key Topics/Learning Goals	Supporting Concepts
What Earthquakes Are and Why They Happen 1 Define *earthquake*. 2 Explain why earthquakes occur. 3 Define *epicenter* and *focus*. 4 Define *elastic rebound*. 5 Define *deformation*.	• An earthquake is a movement or trembling of the ground caused by a sudden release of energy when rocks along a fault move. • Earthquakes are caused by sudden motions along a fault. • An epicenter is the point on Earth's surface directly above an earthquake's focus. A focus is the location within Earth at which the first motion of an earthquake occurs along a fault. • Elastic rebound is the sudden return of elastically deformed rock to its undeformed shape. • Deformation is the bending, tilting, and breaking of Earth's crust in response to stress.
Where Earthquakes Happen 1 Describe where earthquakes happen. 2 Define *tectonic plate boundary*.	• Most earthquakes happen along faults near tectonic plate boundaries. • A tectonic plate boundary is the place where two or more tectonic plates interact. Earthquakes happen at divergent boundaries, at convergent boundaries, and at transform boundaries.
Effects of Earthquakes 1 Describe what can happen at Earth's surface during an earthquake. 2 Describe how earthquakes can affect people and structures.	• The ground and structures shake during an earthquake. Earth's surface can change during an earthquake. Tsunamis can happen as the result of an earthquake. • Earthquakes can cause structures to collapse, causing great danger to people. Earthquakes can also cause tsunamis, extremely large waves, that destroy everything in their path.

Options for Instruction

Two parallel paths provide coverage of the Essential Questions, with a strong **Inquiry** strand woven into each. Follow the **Print Path,** the **Digital Path,** or your customized combination of print, digital, and inquiry.

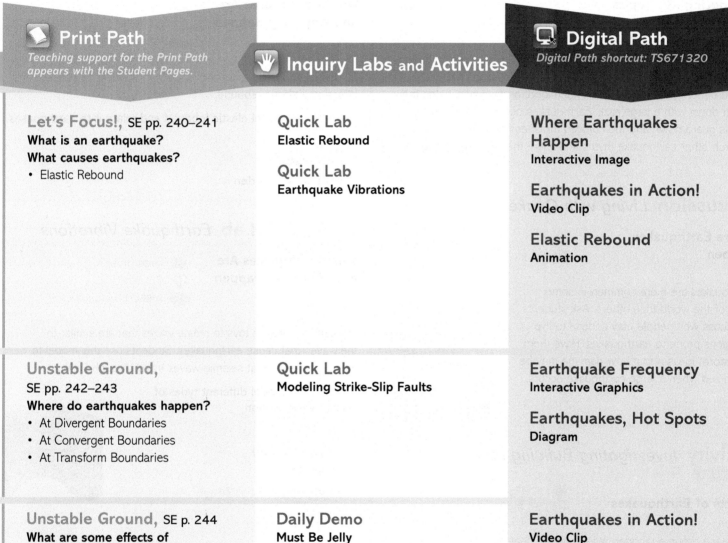

 **Print Path** *Teaching support for the Print Path appears with the Student Pages.*	 **Inquiry Labs and Activities**	 **Digital Path** *Digital Path shortcut: TS671320*
Let's Focus!, SE pp. 240–241 **What is an earthquake?** **What causes earthquakes?** • Elastic Rebound	**Quick Lab** **Elastic Rebound** **Quick Lab** **Earthquake Vibrations**	**Where Earthquakes Happen** **Interactive Image** **Earthquakes in Action!** **Video Clip** **Elastic Rebound** **Animation**
Unstable Ground, SE pp. 242–243 **Where do earthquakes happen?** • At Divergent Boundaries • At Convergent Boundaries • At Transform Boundaries	**Quick Lab** **Modeling Strike-Slip Faults**	**Earthquake Frequency** **Interactive Graphics** **Earthquakes, Hot Spots** **Diagram**
Unstable Ground, SE p. 244 **What are some effects of earthquakes?** • Danger to People and Structures • Tsunamis	**Daily Demo** **Must Be Jelly** **Activity** **Investigating Building Materials** **Activity** **Earthquake Review Game**	**Earthquakes in Action!** **Video Clip**

Options for Assessment

See the Evaluate page for options, including Formative Assessment, Summative Assessment, and Unit Review.

Engage and Explore

Activities and Discussion

Discussion *Mythical Earth Shaking*

Introducing Key Topics

 whole class
 20 min

Many cultures have myths about earthquakes. In Japanese mythology, earthquakes are caused by a giant catfish, the *namazu*, that lives in mud beneath Earth's surface. A demigod, or *daimyojin*, holds the catfish down with a large rock. Earthquakes occur when the *daimyojin* lets his guard down and the *namazu* thrashes free. Ask students to research other earthquake myths and share them with the class.

Discussion *Living with Quakes*

Where Earthquakes Happen

 whole class
20 min

Earthquakes are more common in some parts of the world than others. Ask students to discuss why people may choose to live in regions prone to earthquakes. Have them brainstorm ideas about how damage may be minimized when a large earthquake occurs.

Activity *Investigating Building Materials*

Engage

Effects of Earthquakes

 small groups
 35 min

Give each group a wooden twig, a plastic coat hanger, and a wire coat hanger. Have students draw a straight line on a piece of paper. Then, have them use a protractor to draw the following angles emerging from the center of the line: 20 degrees, 45 degrees, and 90 degrees. Have students wear safety goggles as they try bending each item 20, 45, and then 90 degrees. After each attempt, have them release the item slowly. Ask them the following: Does the item bend? Does it return to normal when released? Does it break? Explain that in areas where earthquakes occur, engineers make use of building materials that bend but don't break.

Labs and Demos

Quick Lab *Elastic Rebound*

What Earthquakes Are and Why They Happen

 individuals
 15 min
 GUIDED inquiry

Students use plastic forks and wooden craft sticks to observe and investigate elastic rebound.

PURPOSE **To model elastic rebound and relate it to earthquakes**

MATERIALS

- fork, plastic
- craft stick, wooden

Quick Lab *Earthquake Vibrations*

What Earthquakes Are and Why They Happen

 large groups
 30 min
 DIRECTED inquiry

Students use spring toys to create waves that are similar to the waves that cause earthquakes. Students use this model to investigate ways that seismic waves travel through Earth.

PURPOSE **To model different types of seismic wave motion**

MATERIALS

- stopwatches (6)
- spring toys (6)
- safety goggles

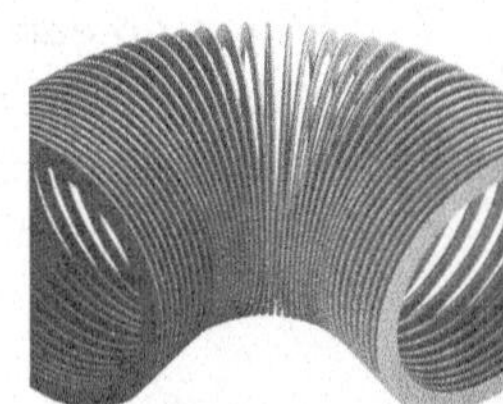

Customize Your Labs

 *See the Lab Manual for lab datasheets.*

 *Go Online for editable lab datasheets.*

Levels of Inquiry

DIRECTED inquiry introduces inquiry skills within a structured framework.

GUIDED inquiry develops inquiry skills within a supportive environment.

INDEPENDENT inquiry deepens inquiry skills with student-driven questions or procedures.

Daily Demo *Must Be Jelly*

Engage

Effects of Earthquakes

 whole class
 15 min
 **GUIDED** inquiry

PURPOSE **To demonstrate an earthquake's effects**

MATERIALS

- **pan of gelatin with a magnet inside**
- **second magnet**
- **toothpick**

1 Prepare the gelatin the night before the demonstration, placing a strong magnet inside the gelatin before it has set.

2 Display the gelatin so it is visible to all students.

3 **Observing** Move the free magnet across the surface of the gelatin without touching it. **Ask:** What do you observe? Sample response: The gelatin moves.

4 Stand a toothpick in the gelatin above the magnet.

5 **Observing** Move the free magnet across the surface of the gelatin as in step 3. **Ask:** What do you observe? Sample response: Movement within the gelatin causes the toothpick to move a bit as well. **Ask:** What do the toothpick and magnet in the gelatin represent? The magnet inside the gelatin is the focus of the earthquake, and the toothpick marks the epicenter.

Quick Lab *Modeling Strike-Slip Faults*

Engage

Where Earthquakes Happen

 small groups
 15 min
 **DIRECTED** inquiry

Students model the movement of plates along a strike-slip fault and observe how this movement affects objects on the surface of Earth.

PURPOSE **To demonstrate how the movement of material within Earth causes earthquakes**

MATERIALS

- **modeling clay (enough to construct a 10 cm × 10 cm × 8 cm block)**
- **index cards, 4 in. × 6 in. (4)**
- **paper, lined notebook**
- **scissors**
- **tape**

Activities and Discussion

- ☐ **Activity** Investigating Building Materials
- ☐ **Discussion** Living with Quakes
- ☐ **Discussion** Mythical Earth Shaking

Labs and Demos

- ☐ **Quick Lab** Modeling Strike-Slip Faults
- ☐ **Quick Lab** Earthquake Vibrations
- ☐ **Quick Lab** Elastic Rebound
- ☐ **Daily Demo** Must Be Jelly

Your Resources

Explain Science Concepts

Key Topics	Print Path	Digital Path
What Earthquakes Are and Why They Happen	☐ **Let's Focus!,** SE pp. 240–241 • Active Reading (Annotation Strategy) #5 • Visualize It!, #6 • Visualize It!, #7 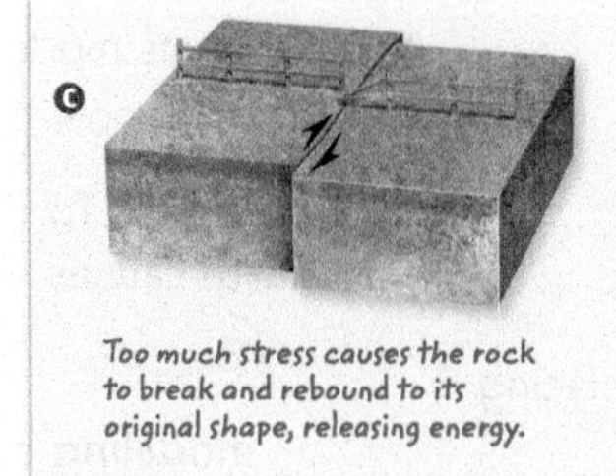 Too much stress causes the rock to break and rebound to its original shape, releasing energy.	☐ **Where Earthquakes Happen** Explore the surface and underground locations important for earthquakes, including the focus and epicenter. ☐ **Earthquakes in Action!** See what happens during an earthquake. ☐ **Elastic Rebound** Learn how energy builds up and is released." 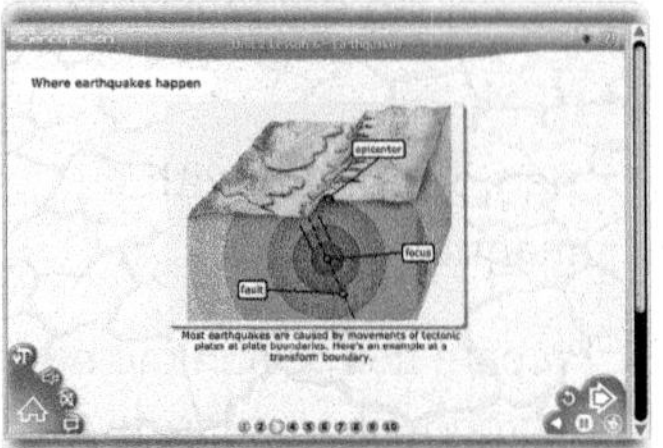
Where Earthquakes Happen	☐ **Unstable Ground,** SE pp. 242–243 • Active Reading (Annotation Strategy) #8 • Visualize It!, #9 • Correlate, #10 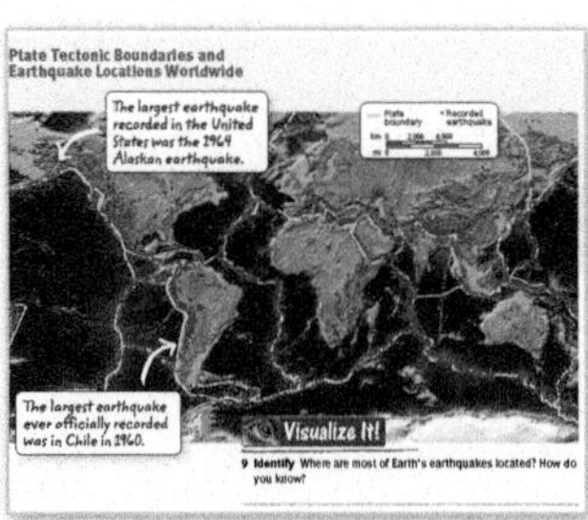	☐ **Earthquake Frequency** Explore the connection of earthquakes to tectonic plate boundaries. ☐ **Earthquakes, Hot Spots** Learn how volcanic activity can lead to earthquakes. 
Effects of Earthquakes	☐ **Unstable Ground,** SE p. 244 • Think Outside the Book, #11 • Identify, #12 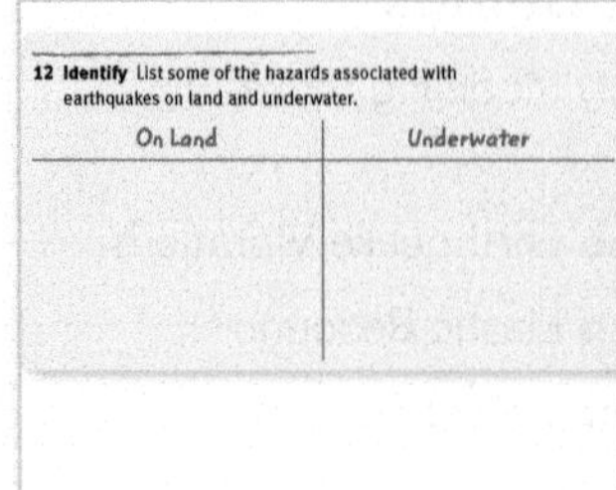 12 **Identify** List some of the hazards associated with earthquakes on land and underwater. On Land / Underwater	☐ **Earthquakes in Action!** See what happens during an earthquake. 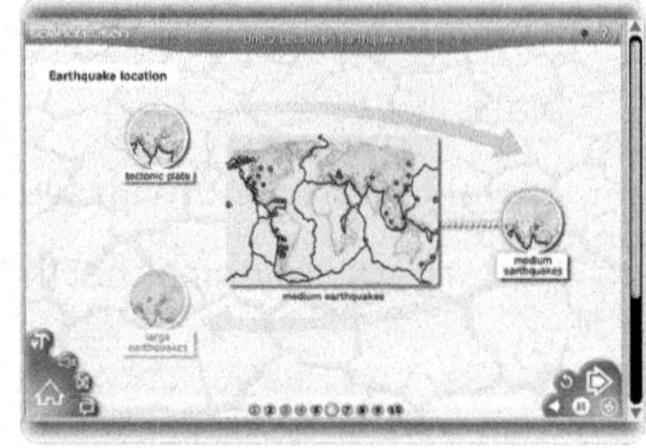

Differentiated Instruction

Basic *Plate Boundaries*

Where Earthquakes Happen

 small groups
 35 min

Layered Book FoldNote Have students make a Layered Book FoldNote to help them remember the characteristics of earthquakes at each type of plate boundary. The book should include a page for each type of plate boundary along with a drawing. Students should label each drawing with the name of the type of boundary it represents and add arrows to show the direction of plate motion. Encourage students to include information that details the type of fault likely to occur at the boundary, the depth of earthquakes occurring there, and a list of the types of topographic features that result from motion along the boundary.

 *Optional Online resource: Layered Book FoldNote support*

Advanced *Mapping Earthquakes*

Where Earthquakes Happen

 individuals
varied

Have students make an earthquake map using data from webpages that include data about the times and locations of earthquakes around the world. This activity will help students understand that earthquakes happen every day, largely near plate boundaries. This activity can be used as an ongoing investigation in which students keep records of earthquakes throughout the school year.

ELL *Studying Faults*

Synthesizing Key Topics

 pairs
40 min

Organize students into pairs. Instruct them to make labeled drawings of the three types of faults. Remind them to label the faults with the type of plate boundary (motion) that occurs there. Have students locate an example of each type of tectonic fault boundary on a map.

Lesson Vocabulary

earthquake	**epicenter**	**focus**
fault	**elastic rebound**	**deformation**
tectonic plate boundary		

Previewing Vocabulary

 small groups   35 min

Mnemonic Devices Mnemonic devices can help students remember the meanings of similar words. On the board, write the words *epicenter, focus,* and *fault*. Divide the class into groups. Have each group create a mnemonic device to help them remember the definitions of each term. For example, students might come up with the sentence, *The focus is found within Earth.* Give each group a chance to share their mnemonic devices with the rest of the class.

Reinforcing Vocabulary

 individuals   30 min

Paragraphs To help students remember each of the vocabulary words introduced in this lesson, have them write a paragraph or two describing how earthquakes happen. Encourage them to use at least five of the vocabulary words in their paragraphs. Explain that they are to come up with descriptive paragraphs, not merely list each term and its definition. Give bonus points to students who develop one or more well-written paragraphs that use all of the terms.

Customize Your Lesson

Core Instruction

- ☐ Print Path choices
- ☐ Digital Path choices

Vocabulary

- ☐ Previewing Vocabulary Mnemonic Devices
- ☐ Reinforcing Vocabulary Paragraphs

Differentiated Instruction

- ☐ Basic Plate Boundaries
- ☐ Advanced Mapping Earthquakes
- ☐ ELL Studying Faults

Your Resources

Extend Science Concepts

Reinforce and Review

Activity *Earthquake Review Game*

Synthesizing Key Topics

 small groups
 25 min

Sticky Note Review Divide the board into four numbered sections. Divide the class into groups of four. Provide each group with a sheet of paper that includes the following four questions, clearly numbered:

1 What is an earthquake? An earthquake is a sudden trembling or jolting of Earth.

2 Why do earthquakes happen? Earthquakes happen as a result of motion along a fault, which is caused by tectonic plate movement.

3 Where do earthquakes happen? Earthquakes usually happen along faults located near tectonic plate boundaries.

4 What are some effects of earthquakes? They can cause structures to move or break, and they can cause tsunamis.

Have each group sit together around a table or on the floor. Have students cut apart their question papers, forming strips of one question each. Each student in each group should choose one question and answer it on their own. Then have students switch questions with another group member and answer that question. Continue until all students have answered each question. Once all the questions have been answered individually, have students share their answers to each question with the other students in their group. Ask them to collaborate to come up with the best answer for each question, then write their answer, group name, and question number on a sticky note. Each group should attach their answers to the appropriately numbered section on the board. Finally, take some time to check each group's answer by reviewing the material as a class.

Graphic Organizer

Synthesizing Key Topics

 individuals
35 min

Mind Map After students have studied the lesson, ask them to develop a Mind Map using these terms: *earthquake, fault, epicenter, focus, elastic rebound*

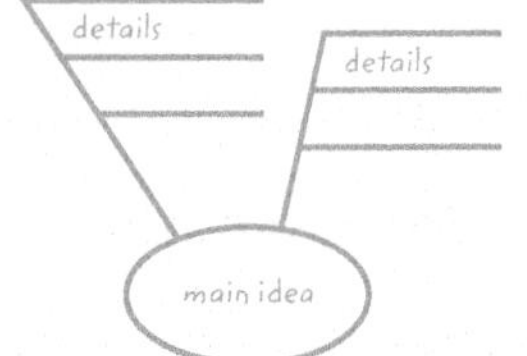

Optional Online resource: Mind Map support

Going Further

Geography Connection

Synthesizing Key Topics

 individuals
varied

Earthquake History Display Direct students to identify an area of the United States or another country that has experienced repeated earthquake activity over time. Have students plot the location on a map. Have students use their map as a central piece of art for a poster display. Then have them do library or Internet research to find when earthquakes occurred in the area they are interested in and suggest that they list the dates beside their maps in a timeline fashion. Finally, have them choose one or two earthquakes to report on in greater detail. Have them provide written descriptions of the number of people affected by the earthquake or damage caused by the earthquake. Students may choose to include this information as captions for photographs, if they are available.

Fine Arts Connection

Synthesizing Key Topics

 individuals
varied

The Protection of Art Treasures Have students find out what has been done to protect sculptures from earthquake damage at an art museum such as the J. Paul Getty Museum, located in a frequent-earthquake zone in California. Ask them to report their findings in an oral report.

Customize Your Closing

See the Assessment Guide for quizzes and tests

Go Online to edit and create quizzes and tests

Reinforce and Review

- ☐ **Activity** Earthquake Review Game
- ☐ **Graphic Organizer** Mind Map
- ☐ **Print Path** Visual Summary, SE p. 246
- ☐ **Digital Path** Lesson Closer

Evaluate Student Mastery

Formative Assessment

See the teacher support below the Student Pages for additional Formative Assessment questions.

Describe or have students review how earthquakes happen.
Ask: How do earthquakes happen along a transform fault? Fault blocks become locked together. Over time, movements of tectonic plates cause stress to build slowly on each side of the fault. Eventually, the fault blocks break free from each other and release the energy stored up from being locked up, causing an earthquake.

Reteach

Formative assessment may show you that students need reinforcement for certain topics. The resources below are recommended for reteaching. If students were introduced to topics through the Print Path, you can also use the Digital Path for reteaching, and vice versa.

Can be assigned to individual students

What Earthquakes Are and Why They Happen

Quick Lab Elastic Rebound

Quick Lab Earthquake Vibrations

Where Earthquakes Happen

Discussion Living with Quakes

Effects of Earthquakes

Daily Demo Must Be Jelly

Activity Investigating Building Materials

Summative Assessment

Alternative Assessment
Earthquake Exercises

Online resources: student worksheet; optional rubrics

Earthquakes

Climb the Ladder: *Earthquake Exercises*
Complete the activities to show what you've learned about earthquakes.

1. Work on your own, with a partner, or with a small group.
2. Choose one item from each rung of the ladder. Check your choices.
3. Have your teacher approve your plan.
4. Submit or present your results.

__ **Earthquake Poster** Make a poster that shows how an earthquake occurs. Label the focus, epicenter, and fault. Show how deformation can take place.	__ **Word Swap** Choose one vocabulary word from this lesson. Write it at the bottom of a sheet of paper. Number each letter. Above the word, write a paragraph that tells something about the word. Then underline letters in your paragraph that are used in the word. Number these letters. Give your puzzle to partner. Have the partner use the numbers to figure out the word.
__ **Earthquake Events** Create a flipchart that animates the sequence of events that causes an earthquake. Arrange you images into a book, so that when you flip the pages of the book, the earthquake causes the ground to move.	__ **Earthquake Article** Suppose you are a reporter who experiences an earthquake. Write a magazine article about your experience. Describe what caused the quake, when it hit, what the aftermath was like, and how people's lives were affected.
__ **Shaky Story** Write a short story in which an earthquake occurs. What do your characters do? How do they react? What caused the earthquake?	__ **Boundary Action** Make models of a divergent boundary, a convergent boundary, and a transform plate boundary. Label the direction of plate movement.

Going Further

- ☐ Geography Connection
- ☐ Fine Arts Connection
- ☐ Print Path Why It Matters, SE p. 245

Formative Assessment

- ☐ Strategies Throughout TE
- ☐ Lesson Review SE

Summative Assessment

- ☐ Alternative Assessment Earthquake Exercises
- ☐ Lesson Quiz
- ☐ Unit Tests A and B
- ☐ Unit Review SE End-of-Unit

Your Resources

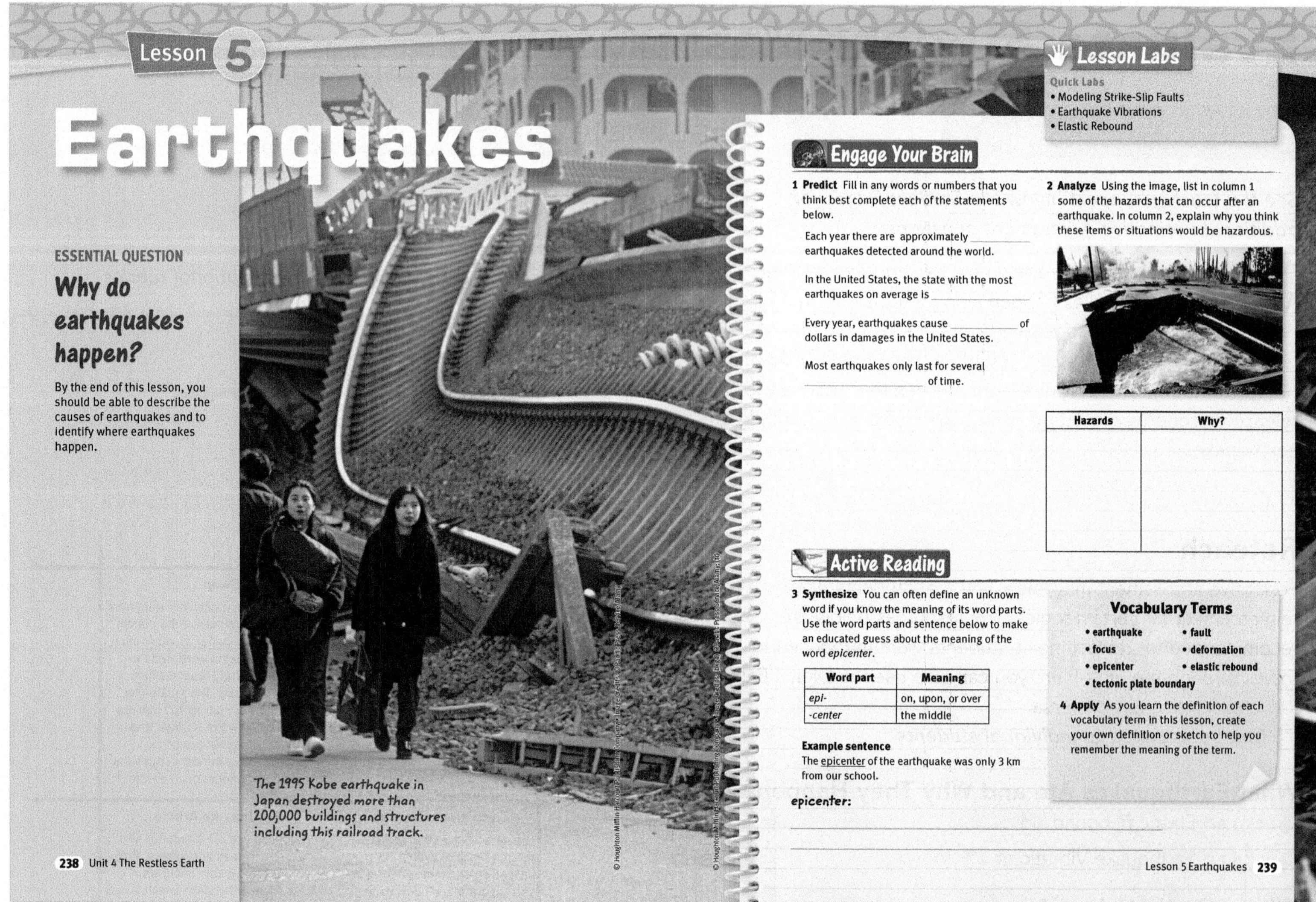

Lesson 5

Earthquakes

ESSENTIAL QUESTION

Why do earthquakes happen?

By the end of this lesson, you should be able to describe the causes of earthquakes and to identify where earthquakes happen.

The 1995 Kobe earthquake in Japan destroyed more than 200,000 buildings and structures including this railroad track.

238 Unit 4 The Restless Earth

Lesson Labs

Quick Labs
- Modeling Strike-Slip Faults
- Earthquake Vibrations
- Elastic Rebound

Engage Your Brain

1 Predict Fill in any words or numbers that you think best complete each of the statements below.

Each year there are approximately ________ earthquakes detected around the world.

In the United States, the state with the most earthquakes on average is ________

Every year, earthquakes cause ________ of dollars in damages in the United States.

Most earthquakes only last for several ________ of time.

2 Analyze Using the image, list in column 1 some of the hazards that can occur after an earthquake. In column 2, explain why you think these items or situations would be hazardous.

Hazards	Why?

Active Reading

3 Synthesize You can often define an unknown word if you know the meaning of its word parts. Use the word parts and sentence below to make an educated guess about the meaning of the word *epicenter*.

Word part	Meaning
epi-	on, upon, or over
-center	the middle

Example sentence
The epicenter of the earthquake was only 3 km from our school.

epicenter:

Vocabulary Terms
- earthquake
- fault
- focus
- deformation
- epicenter
- elastic rebound
- tectonic plate boundary

4 Apply As you learn the definition of each vocabulary term in this lesson, create your own definition or sketch to help you remember the meaning of the term.

Lesson 5 Earthquakes 239

Answers

Answers for 1–3 should represent students' current thoughts, even if incorrect.

1. 500,000; Alaska; billions; seconds
2. Sample answers: Fire: homes and businesses can be destroyed; floods: water lines can break, destroying homes and polluting water supplies; gas leaks: underground lines can break, causing fires and polluted air.
3. The epicenter is the location on Earth's surface from which the earthquake seems to radiate. It is the point directly above the focus.
4. Students should define or sketch each vocabulary term in the lesson.

Opening Your Lesson

Have students share their thoughts about what might be dangerous in the classroom during an earthquake (item 2) to assess their prior knowledge of the key topics.

Prerequisites: Earth's surface is divided into tectonic plates that are in constant motion primarily as a result of slab pull, followed by ridge push, and to a lesser extent by convection within Earth; movements of tectonic plates cause changes to Earth's surface.

Accessing Prior Knowledge: Develop an Anticipation Guide to preview the content of the lesson and to assess students' prior knowledge about earthquakes.

Online Resource: Anticipation Guide support

Learning Alert MISCONCEPTION

Earthquake Frequency Students may think that earthquakes are rare events that always cause large scale damage. Ask students when the last earthquake occurred. Students may describe the last major earthquake that received media coverage. Point out that more than 3 million earthquakes with Richter magnitudes of 1 or more occur each year. Find and share a map that shows recent earthquake activity and ask students to tally the number of earthquakes in each magnitude range. Students will see that small magnitude earthquakes happen many times each day—about one every 10 s!

Let's Focus

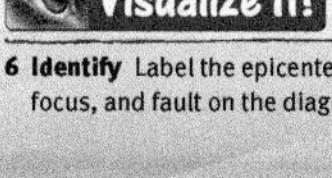

5 Identify As you read, underline the definitions of *focus* and *epicenter*.

What is an earthquake?

Earthquakes can cause extreme damage and loss of life. **Earthquakes** are ground movements that occur when blocks of rock in Earth move suddenly and release energy. The energy is released as seismic waves which cause the ground to shake and tremble.

Earthquake waves can be tracked to a point below Earth's surface known as the focus. The **focus** is a place within Earth along a fault at which the first motion of an earthquake occurs. Motion along a fault causes stress. When the stress on the rock is too great, the rock will rupture and cause an earthquake. The earthquake releases the stress. Directly above the focus on Earth's surface is the **epicenter** (EP•i•sen•ter). Seismic waves flow outward from the focus in all directions.

Visualize It!

6 Identify Label the epicenter, focus, and fault on the diagram.

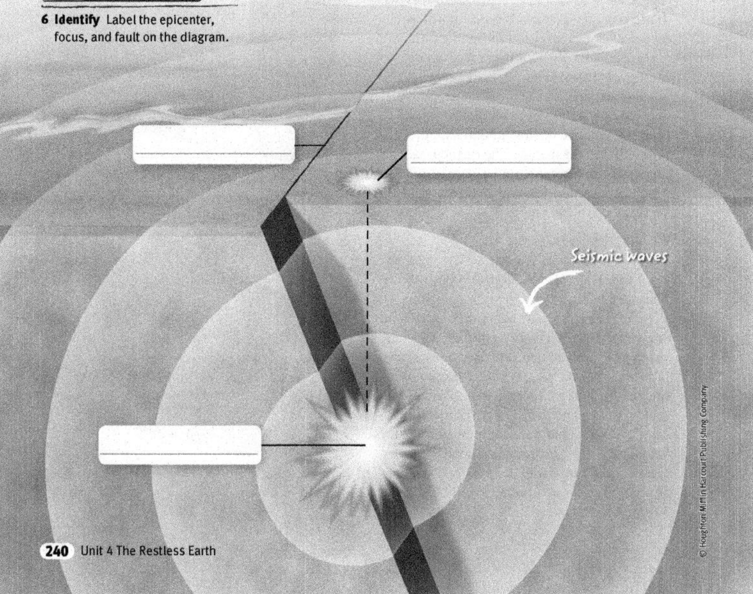

What causes earthquakes?

Most earthquakes occur near the boundaries of tectonic plates. A **tectonic plate boundary** is where two or more tectonic plates meet. As tectonic plates move, pressure builds up near the edges of the plates. These movements break Earth's crust into a series of faults. A **fault** is a break in Earth's crust along which blocks of rock move. The release of energy that accompanies the movement of the rock along a fault causes an earthquake.

Elastic Rebound

When rock is put under tremendous pressure, stress may deform, or change the shape of, the rock. **Deformation** (dee•for•MAY•shun) is the process by which rock becomes deformed and changes shape due to stress. As stress increases, the amount of energy that is stored in the rock increases, as seen in image B to the right.

Stress can change the shape of rock along a fault. Once the stress is released, rock may return to its original shape. When rock returns to nearly the same shape after the stress is removed, the process is known as *elastic deformation*. Imagine an elastic band that is pulled tight under stress. Once stress on the elastic band is removed, there is a *snap!* The elastic band returns to its original shape. A similar process occurs during earthquakes.

Similar to an elastic band, rock along tectonic plate boundaries can suddenly return to nearly its original shape when the stress is removed. The sudden *snap* is an earthquake. The return of rock to its original shape after elastic deformation is called **elastic rebound**. Earthquakes accompany the release of energy during elastic rebound. When the rock breaks and rebounds, it releases energy as seismic waves. The seismic wave energy radiates from the focus of the earthquake in all directions. This energy causes the ground to shake for a short time. Most earthquakes last for just a few seconds.

7 Compare Did an earthquake occur between images A and B or between images B and C? How do you know?

A

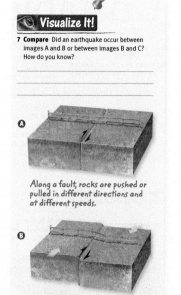

Along a fault, rocks are pushed or pulled in different directions and at different speeds.

B

As stress increases and energy builds within the rock, the rock deforms but remains locked in place.

C

Too much stress causes the rock to break and rebound to its original shape, releasing energy.

Answers

5. *See students' pages for annotations.*
6. From the top: fault; epicenter; focus
7. Between B and C; The rocks were deformed in B, but snapped back to their original shape in C which, would have caused an earthquake.

Probing Questions GUIDED Inquiry

Evaluate Remind students that they learned about three different types of faults in the last lesson. **Ask:** How do faults relate to earthquakes? Earthquakes occur when there is movement along a fault. **Prompt:** Think about the direction of motion associated with each type of fault.

Building Reading Skills

Concept Map Encourage students to develop concept maps to organize the information they are learning about earthquakes and their causes.

Optional Online resource: Concept Map support

Learning Alert MISCONCEPTION

Aftershocks A common misconception is that aftershocks do not present the same level of danger as the earthquakes they follow. Seismological evidence has shown that the opposite can be true. Aftershocks can be very powerful. For example, an aftershock of magnitude 6.5 occurred about 3 h after the 7.3 magnitude Landers earthquake of 1992. Aftershocks vary in location and pattern of radiation from the mainshock. As a result, they are very damaging, especially to structures that have already sustained damage.

Unstable Ground

8 Identify As you read, underline the locations where earthquakes occur.

Where do earthquakes happen?

Each year, approximately 500,000 earthquakes are detected worldwide. The map below shows some of these earthquakes. Movement of material and energy in the form of heat in Earth's interior contribute to plate motions that result in earthquakes.

Most earthquakes happen at or near tectonic plate boundaries. Tectonic plate boundaries are areas where Earth's crust experiences a lot of stress. This stress occurs because the tectonic plates are colliding, separating, or grinding past each other horizontally. There are three main types of tectonic plate boundaries: divergent, convergent, and transform. The movement and interactions of the plates causes the crust to break into different types of faults. Earthquakes happen along these faults.

Plate Tectonic Boundaries and Earthquake Locations Worldwide

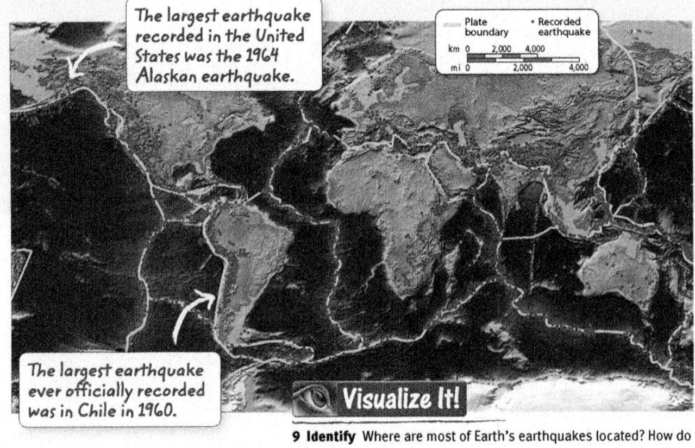

The largest earthquake recorded in the United States was the 1964 Alaskan earthquake.
Plate boundary
Recorded earthquake
km 0 2,000 4,000
mi 0 2,000 4,000
The largest earthquake ever officially recorded was in Chile in 1960.

Visualize It!

9 Identify Where are most of Earth's earthquakes located? How do you know?

10 Correlate In the caption for each diagram, write in the type of fault that is common at each of the types of tectonic plate boundaries.

At Divergent Boundaries

At a divergent boundary, plates pull apart, causing the crust to stretch. Stress that stretches rock and makes rock thinner is called *tension*. Normal faults commonly result when tension pulls rock apart.

Most of the crust at divergent boundaries is thin, so the earthquakes tend to be shallow. Most earthquakes at divergent boundaries are no more than 20 km deep. A mid-ocean ridge is an example of a divergent boundary where earthquakes occur.

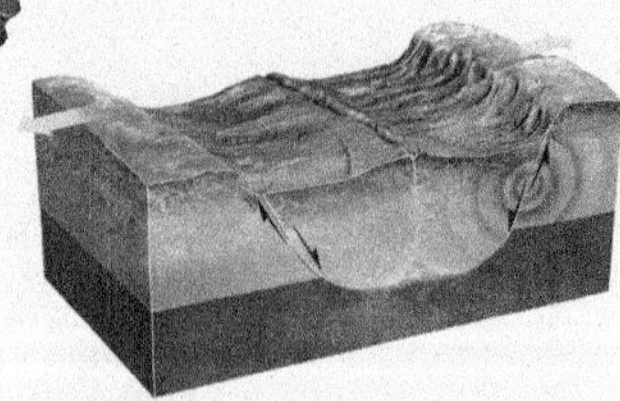

At divergent boundaries, earthquakes are common along ______ faults.

At Convergent Boundaries

Convergent plate boundaries occur when plates collide, causing rock to be squeezed. Stress that shortens or squeezes an object is known as *compression*. Compression causes the formation of reverse faults. Rocks are thrust over one another at reverse faults.

When two plates come together, both plates may crumple up to form mountains. Or one plate can subduct, or sink, underneath the other plate and into the mantle. The earthquakes that happen at convergent boundaries can be very strong. Subduction zone earthquakes occur at depths of up to 700 km.

At convergent boundaries, earthquakes are common along ______ faults.

At Transform Boundaries

A transform boundary is a place where two tectonic plates slide past each other horizontally. Stress that distorts a body by pushing different parts of the body in opposite directions is called *shear stress*. As the plates move, rocks on both sides of the fault are sheared, or broken, as they grind past one another in opposite directions.

Strike-slip faults are common at transform boundaries. Most earthquakes along the faults at transform boundaries are relatively shallow. The earthquakes are generally within the upper 50 km of the crust.

At transform boundaries, earthquakes are common along ______ faults.

Answers

8. *See students' pages for annotations.*
9. at tectonic plate boundaries because most of the earthquakes are along these boundaries
10. normal; reverse; strike–slip

Formative Assessment

Ask: Where do earthquakes happen? Why do they happen? Earthquakes happen at faults. They happen because of the movement of tectonic plates. **Ask:** How do earthquakes and their locations support the theory of plate tectonics? Sample answer: Most earthquakes happen at plate boundaries in response to the motion of the plates.

Interpreting Visuals

Have students look at the images of the three types of plate boundaries along which earthquakes occur. Have them use their hands to model the type of movement that occurs at each type of boundary. Have them relate these motions to the depths at which earthquakes tend to occur at each boundary.

Probing Questions DIRECTED Inquiry

Applying What contributes to the motion of the tectonic plates that cause earthquakes when the plates interact? Sample answer: Plate motion is primarily driven by slab pull, ridge push, and to a much lesser extent, by the convection current in Earth's mantle.

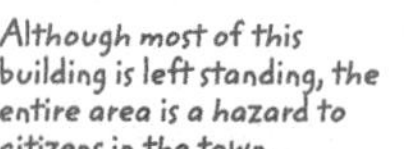

11 Design You are an emergency management professional. You have been assigned to create an earthquake safety brochure for your town. Create a brochure that demonstrates ways people can protect themselves during an earthquake.

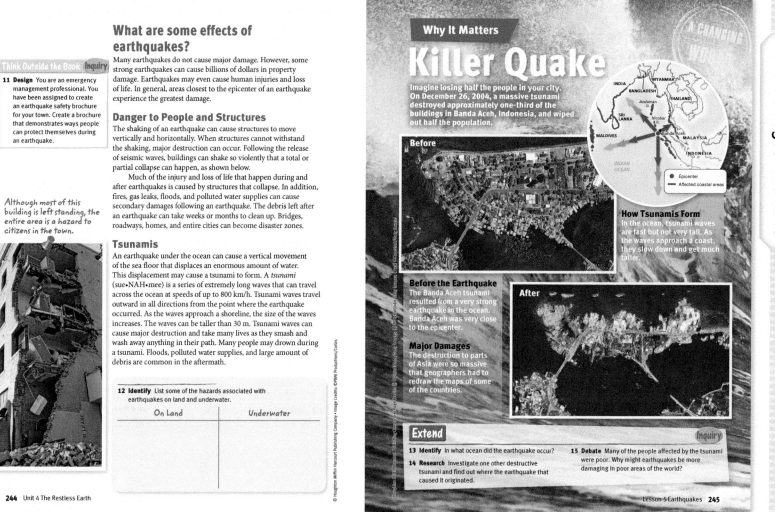

What are some effects of earthquakes?

Many earthquakes do not cause major damage. However, some strong earthquakes can cause billions of dollars in property damage. Earthquakes may even cause human injuries and loss of life. In general, areas closest to the epicenter of an earthquake experience the greatest damage.

Danger to People and Structures

The shaking of an earthquake can cause structures to move vertically and horizontally. When structures cannot withstand the shaking, major destruction can occur. Following the release of seismic waves, buildings can shake so violently that a total or partial collapse can happen, as shown below.

Much of the injury and loss of life that happen during and after earthquakes is caused by structures that collapse. In addition, fires, gas leaks, floods, and polluted water supplies can cause secondary damages following an earthquake. The debris left after an earthquake can take weeks or months to clean up. Bridges, roadways, homes, and entire cities can become disaster zones.

Although most of this building is left standing, the entire area is a hazard to citizens in the town.

Tsunamis

An earthquake under the ocean can cause a vertical movement of the sea floor that displaces an enormous amount of water. This displacement may cause a tsunami to form. A *tsunami* (sue•NAH•mee) is a series of extremely long waves that can travel across the ocean at speeds of up to 800 km/h. Tsunami waves travel outward in all directions from the point where the earthquake occurred. As the waves approach a shoreline, the size of the waves increases. The waves can be taller than 30 m. Tsunami waves can cause major destruction and take many lives as they smash and wash away anything in their path. Many people may drown during a tsunami. Floods, polluted water supplies, and large amount of debris are common in the aftermath.

12 Identify List some of the hazards associated with earthquakes on land and underwater.

On Land	Underwater

Why It Matters

Killer Quake

A CHANGING WORLD

Imagine losing half the people in your city. On December 26, 2004, a massive tsunami destroyed approximately one-third of the buildings in Banda Aceh, Indonesia, and wiped out half the population.

Before

INDIA
MYANMAR
BANGLADESH
THAILAND
Andaman Is.
SRI LANKA
Nicobar Is.
MALDIVES
Banda Aceh
MALAYSIA
INDONESIA
INDIAN OCEAN
Epicenter
Affected coastal areas

How Tsunamis Form
In the ocean, tsunami waves are fast but not very tall. As the waves approach a coast, they slow down and get much taller.

Before the Earthquake
The Banda Aceh tsunami resulted from a very strong earthquake in the ocean. Banda Aceh was very close to the epicenter.

After

Major Damages
The destruction to parts of Asia were so massive that geographers had to redraw the maps of some of the countries.

Extend Inquiry

13 Identify In what ocean did the earthquake occur?

14 Research Investigate one other destructive tsunami and find out where the earthquake that caused it originated.

15 Debate Many of the people affected by the tsunami were poor. Why might earthquakes be more damaging in poor areas of the world?

Student Pages 242–245

Answers

11. Sample answers: Drop, cover, and hold on, preferably under sturdy furniture; stay away from falling objects; have an emergency medical kit.
12. Sample answers: On land: buildings fall down, gas leaks, fires, floods; From the sea: large waves wash away everything in their paths, floods, victims drown
13. Indian Ocean
14. Sample answer: The Sanriku Tsunami on June 15, 1896, caused more than 27,000 deaths. The earthquake was located off the Sanriku coast of Japan in the Pacific Ocean.
15. Sample answer: Many of the buildings were constructed poorly. Many of the people may not have had access to immediate medical treatment.

Learning Alert

Flexible Buildings Point out to students that earthquakes are often more readily perceived by people located on high floors of buildings rather than by those located on lower floors nearer the ground. Explain that this occurs because tall buildings intensify minor tremors. Demonstrate this concept by holding a meter stick upright and shaking it back and forth. Have students observe the difference in the range of motion at the top and the bottom of the meter stick.

Why It Matters

Direct students' attention to the before and after photographs in Why It Matters: Killer Quake. Ask students to find at least two landmarks that appear in both photos. Then ask them to use their observations to identify and describe parts of the area that have been swept away by the tsunami. Sample answer: The bridge in the right lower quadrant was swept away; most of the land in the region between the two bridges is covered by water, with many structures at the upper portion of this region swept away; nearly all of the structures in the top half of the image were swept away. There also seems to be far less land above water now than before the tsunami came through.

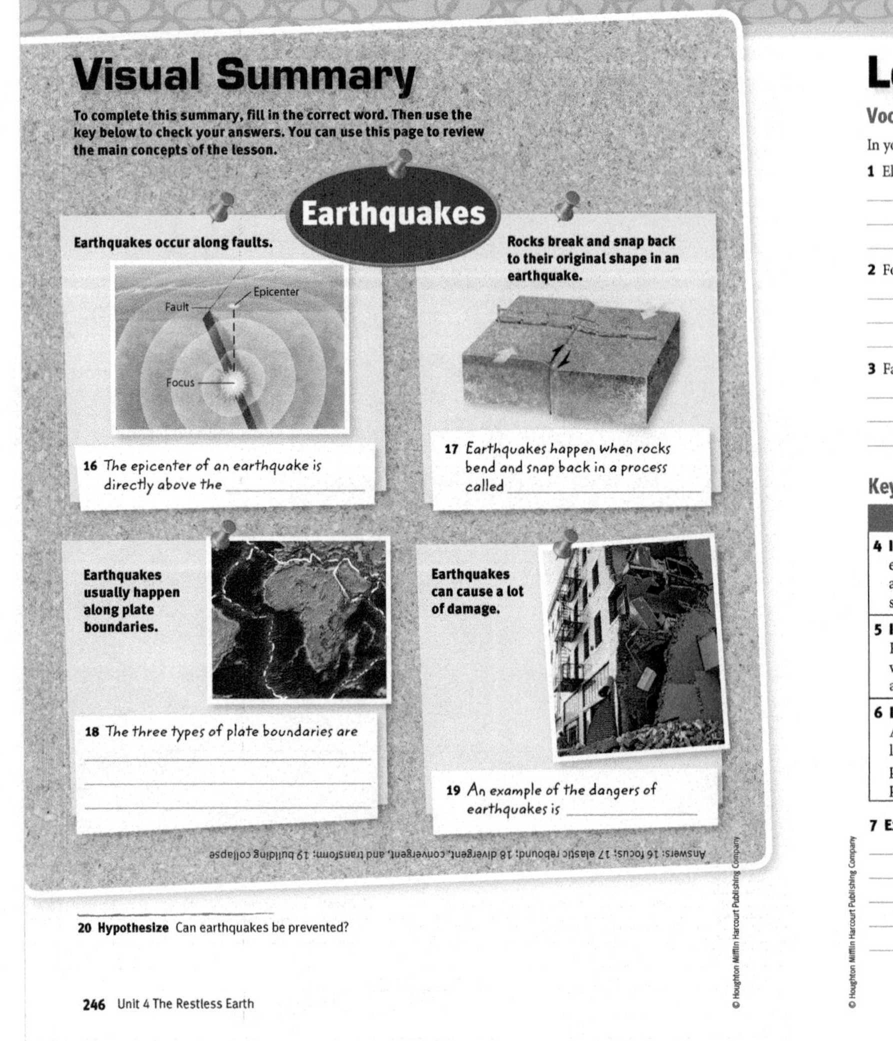

Visual Summary

To complete this summary, fill in the correct word. Then use the key below to check your answers. You can use this page to review the main concepts of the lesson.

Earthquakes

Earthquakes occur along faults.

16 The epicenter of an earthquake is directly above the ____________

Rocks break and snap back to their original shape in an earthquake.

17 Earthquakes happen when rocks bend and snap back in a process called ____________

Earthquakes usually happen along plate boundaries.

18 The three types of plate boundaries are ____________

Earthquakes can cause a lot of damage.

19 An example of the dangers of earthquakes is ____________

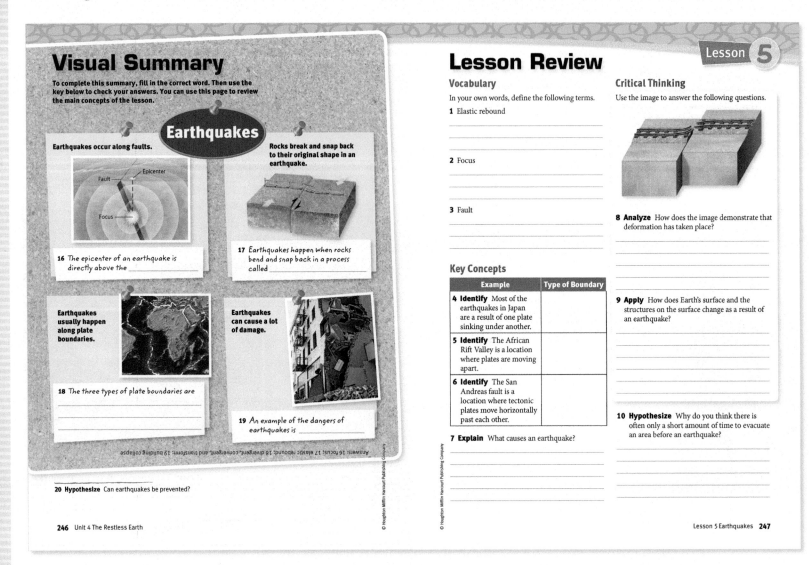

Answers: 16 focus; 17 elastic rebound; 18 divergent, convergent, and transform; 19 building collapse

20 **Hypothesize** Can earthquakes be prevented?

Lesson Review

Lesson 5

Vocabulary

In your own words, define the following terms.

1 Elastic rebound

2 Focus

3 Fault

Key Concepts

Example	Type of Boundary
4 Identify Most of the earthquakes in Japan are a result of one plate sinking under another.	
5 Identify The African Rift Valley is a location where plates are moving apart.	
6 Identify The San Andreas fault is a location where tectonic plates move horizontally past each other.	

7 Explain What causes an earthquake?

Critical Thinking

Use the image to answer the following questions.

8 Analyze How does the image demonstrate that deformation has taken place?

9 Apply How does Earth's surface and the structures on the surface change as a result of an earthquake?

10 Hypothesize Why do you think there is often only a short amount of time to evacuate an area before an earthquake?

Visual Summary Answers

16. focus
17. elastic rebound
18. divergent; convergent; transform
19. building collapse
20. No. Earthquakes are caused by the movement of tectonic plates. Tectonic plate motion cannot be stopped.

Lesson Review Answers

1. Sample answer: the release of the stress that deformed the shape of the rock, which allows the rock to snap back into its original shape
2. Sample answer: the location inside Earth where an earthquake originates
3. Sample answer: a large crack in Earth's crust along which rock on either side move past each other
4. convergent
5. divergent
6. transform
7. The movement of tectonic plates causes stress to build up along a fault. Earthquakes occur when energy in the form of seismic waves is released during elastic rebound.
8. The railroad tracks on either side of the fault have been displaced in opposite directions from each other.
9. Structures can be shaken violently back and forth. Buildings can collapse, giant waves can wash inland, and land can shift over large distances along a fault with enough time.
10. Earthquakes result from a sudden release of energy that has been building up over a long time. It is difficult to accurately calculate the amount of energy stored in rock deep in the crust.

Teacher Notes

Building a Seismometer

Purpose To build a seismometer

Learning Goals

- Explain how scientists measure earthquakes.
- Design, test, and modify a seismometer.

Academic Vocabulary

seismometer, inertia, seismogram, seismologist

Prerequisite Knowledge

- Basic understanding of Earth's layers and plate tectonics
- Familiarity with earthquakes and waves
- Basic understanding of how earthquakes are measured

Materials

large square wooden frame
metal weights
string
fine-point felt-tip pen
long strips or roll of paper
tape
spring
various hooks and hardware

21st Century SKILLS

Theme: Global Awareness

Activities focusing on 21st Century Skills are included for this feature and can be found on the following pages.

These activities focus on the following skills:

- **Creativity and Innovation**
- **ICT (Information, Communications, and Technology) Literacy**
- **Flexibility and Adaptability**

You can learn more about the 21st Century Skills in the front matter of this Teacher's Edition.

Content Refresher

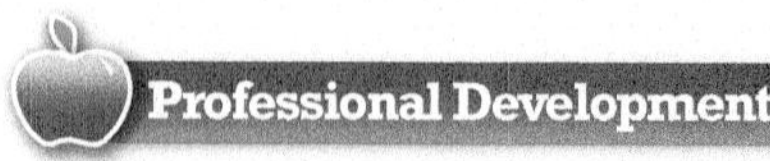

Measuring Earthquakes Scientists measure earthquakes according to their magnitude and intensity. Magnitude measures the energy an earthquake releases at its source. Intensity is a measure of the shaking produced at a specific location by the earthquake.

Magnitude can be measured using the Richter scale and the Moment Magnitude scale. The Moment Magnitude scale is more accurate for larger earthquakes and is what scientists use today. When you read about earthquakes in the news, the earthquake's strength is likely expressed using moment magnitude. The larger the number on the Moment Magnitude scale, the stronger the earthquake. An earthquake's strength on the Moment Magnitude scale is based on three things: the size of the area where the fault moved, the distance the fault moved, and the rigidity of the rocks making up that fault.

The Richter scale may be misleading to people because it is a logarithmic scale. The strength of an earthquake is ten times greater for every whole number increase on the scale. For example, a magnitude-4 earthquake on the Richter scale causes shaking 10 times greater in amplitude than a magnitude-3 earthquake. This is another reason for using the Moment Magnitude scale.

The largest earthquake ever recorded took place in Chile and registered a moment magnitude of 9.5. This earthquake took place in 1960. Five earthquakes of magnitude-9 or higher have occurred since 1900. The most recent earthquake of these five earthquakes occurred in 2011 in Tōhoku, Japan.

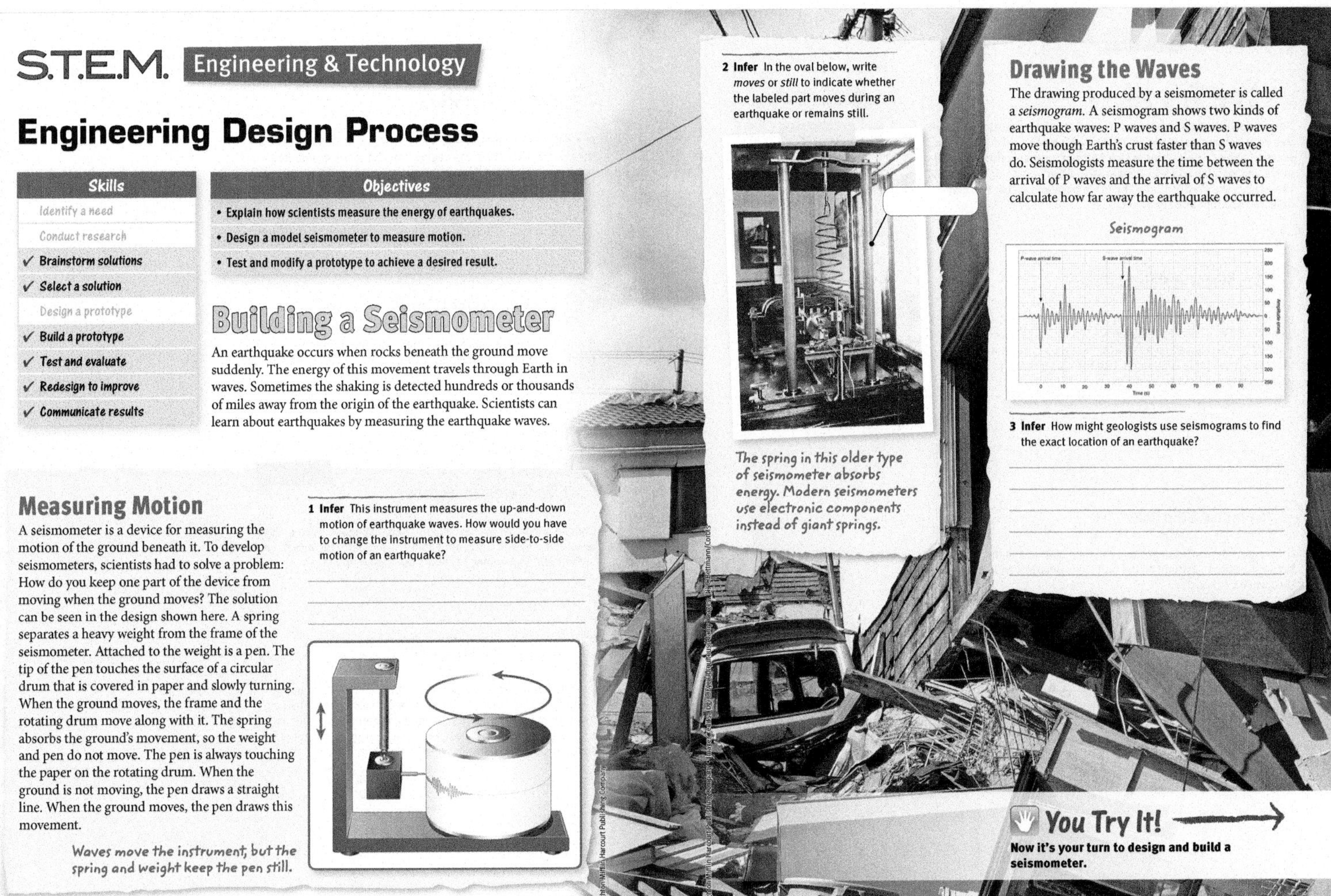

S.T.E.M. Engineering & Technology

Engineering Design Process

Skills
Identify a need
Conduct research
✓ Brainstorm solutions
✓ Select a solution
Design a prototype
✓ Build a prototype
✓ Test and evaluate
✓ Redesign to improve
✓ Communicate results

Objectives

- Explain how scientists measure the energy of earthquakes.
- Design a model seismometer to measure motion.
- Test and modify a prototype to achieve a desired result.

Building a Seismometer

An earthquake occurs when rocks beneath the ground move suddenly. The energy of this movement travels through Earth in waves. Sometimes the shaking is detected hundreds or thousands of miles away from the origin of the earthquake. Scientists can learn about earthquakes by measuring the earthquake waves.

Measuring Motion

A seismometer is a device for measuring the motion of the ground beneath it. To develop seismometers, scientists had to solve a problem: How do you keep one part of the device from moving when the ground moves? The solution can be seen in the design shown here. A spring separates a heavy weight from the frame of the seismometer. Attached to the weight is a pen. The tip of the pen touches the surface of a circular drum that is covered in paper and slowly turning. When the ground moves, the frame and the rotating drum move along with it. The spring absorbs the ground's movement, so the weight and pen do not move. The pen is always touching the paper on the rotating drum. When the ground is not moving, the pen draws a straight line. When the ground moves, the pen draws this movement.

Waves move the instrument, but the spring and weight keep the pen still.

1 Infer This instrument measures the up-and-down motion of earthquake waves. How would you have to change the instrument to measure side-to-side motion of an earthquake?

2 Infer In the oval below, write *moves* or *still* to indicate whether the labeled part moves during an earthquake or remains still.

The spring in this older type of seismometer absorbs energy. Modern seismometers use electronic components instead of giant springs.

Drawing the Waves

The drawing produced by a seismometer is called a *seismogram*. A seismogram shows two kinds of earthquake waves: P waves and S waves. P waves move though Earth's crust faster than S waves do. Seismologists measure the time between the arrival of P waves and the arrival of S waves to calculate how far away the earthquake occurred.

Seismogram

3 Infer How might geologists use seismograms to find the exact location of an earthquake?

You Try It! →

Now it's your turn to design and build a seismometer.

248 Unit 4 The Restless Earth

249

Answers

1. Sample answer: The pen would have to point down and not move with the paper as it moves side to side.
2. moves
3. Sample answer: Geologists could use three or more seismograms and calculate the distance from the seismometers to the source of the quake. If they draw circles on a map around the location of the seismometer with a radius that equals the distance to the earthquake, then the place on the map where all three circles intersect would be the location of the earthquake.

Engineering Design Process

S.T.E.M. Engineering & Technology

You Try It!

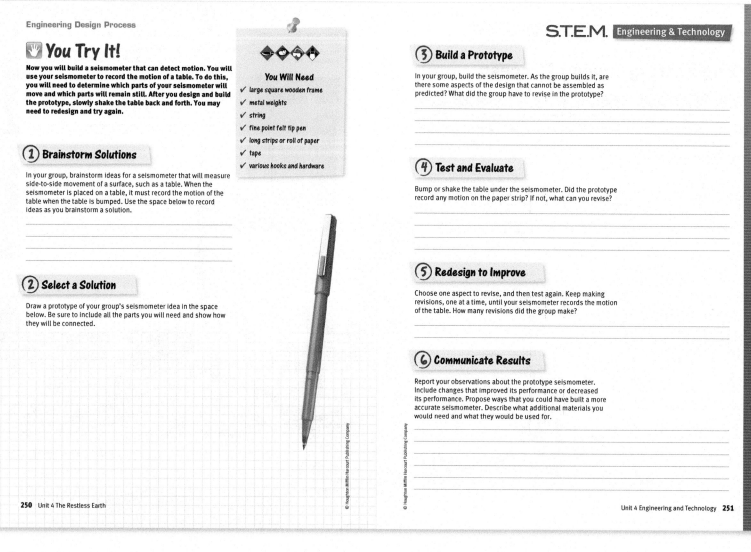

Now you will build a seismometer that can detect motion. You will use your seismometer to record the motion of a table. To do this, you will need to determine which parts of your seismometer will move and which parts will remain still. After you design and build the prototype, slowly shake the table back and forth. You may need to redesign and try again.

You Will Need

- ✓ large square wooden frame
- ✓ metal weights
- ✓ string
- ✓ fine point felt tip pen
- ✓ long strips or roll of paper
- ✓ tape
- ✓ various hooks and hardware

(1) Brainstorm Solutions

In your group, brainstorm ideas for a seismometer that will measure side-to-side movement of a surface, such as a table. When the seismometer is placed on a table, it must record the motion of the table when the table is bumped. Use the space below to record ideas as you brainstorm a solution.

(2) Select a Solution

Draw a prototype of your group's seismometer idea in the space below. Be sure to include all the parts you will need and show how they will be connected.

(3) Build a Prototype

In your group, build the seismometer. As the group builds it, are there some aspects of the design that cannot be assembled as predicted? What did the group have to revise in the prototype?

(4) Test and Evaluate

Bump or shake the table under the seismometer. Did the prototype record any motion on the paper strip? If not, what can you revise?

(5) Redesign to Improve

Choose one aspect to revise, and then test again. Keep making revisions, one at a time, until your seismometer records the motion of the table. How many revisions did the group make?

(6) Communicate Results

Report your observations about the prototype seismometer. Include changes that improved its performance or decreased its performance. Propose ways that you could have built a more accurate seismometer. Describe what additional materials you would need and what they would be used for.

© Houghton Mifflin Harcourt Publishing Company

250 Unit 4 The Restless Earth

Unit 4 Engineering and Technology 251

Answers

1. Answers will vary. Students should create designs in which the pen hangs vertically from a string with the paper on the base or on a roller attached to the base.
2. Student drawing should include a frame that moves with the table, pen assembly that dampens the motion of the pen when the frame moves, and a paper strip that moves with the frame.
3. Answers will vary. Students should report actual results from experiment whether it was successful or not.
4. Answers will vary based on students' designs. Accept all reasonable answers.
5. Answers will vary based on students' designs. Accept all reasonable answers.
6. Answers will vary based on students' designs. Accept all reasonable answers.

21st Century SKILLS

Learning and Innovation Skills

small groups 15 min

Creativity and Innovation After students have designed a working seismometer, have them form groups to brainstorm ideas about how to improve seismometer performance. Invite groups to refine, analyze, and evaluate ideas to maximize creative effort. Encourage students to demonstrate originality and inventiveness and to be open and responsive to new and diverse perspectives. Challenge students to learn from their failures, and to understand that creativity and engineering design are processes of small successes and frequent setbacks.

Information, Media, and Technology Skills

 pairs or small groups  20 min

ICT (Information, Communications, and Technology) Literacy Invite pairs or small groups of students to use the Internet to research more about earthquakes and their effects. Then have students use digital technologies to develop a media presentation that highlights the most interesting information they found. Students should make sure to credit the appropriate sources when they present their findings.

Life and Career Skills

 pairs or small groups  20 min

Flexibility and Adaptability Invite pairs or small groups of students to make a better seismometer using different materials or a different design. Let students assign roles and responsibilities to complete the project. Encourage students to be flexible about their designs, to incorporate feedback from others, and to deal positively with praise or setbacks. Let students negotiate to reach workable solutions that all group members agree on.

Differentiated Instruction

Basic *Seismic Waves*

 individuals 10 min

Invite students to draw a sketch that shows how seismic waves radiate out from the epicenter of an earthquake below ground. Then have students use a globe or ball as a three-dimensional model as they explain to a partner how waves radiate out from an epicenter. How are the two models—the sketch and the three-dimensional model—alike and different? Which model is easier to understand? Encourage students to share their ideas.

Advanced *Seismometers in Space*

 individuals or pairs  20 min

Invite students to design a seismometer that could be used to test for seismic activity on another planet. Remind students that the force of gravity is different on different planets. How would more or less gravity affect how the seismometer is built?

ELL *Modeling Earthquakes*

 individuals or pairs 10 min

Have students use pieces of paper or cardboard to model how tectonic plates move during an earthquake. Challenge students to show a fault and how plates move against each other to cause an earthquake. Encourage students to use these words to describe what happens: *fault, tectonic plate, seismic waves.*

Customize Your Feature

- ☐ **21st Century Skills** Learning and Innovation Skills
- ☐ **21st Century Skills** Information, Media, and Technology Skills
- ☐ **21st Century Skills** Life and Career Skills
- ☐ Basic Seismic Waves
- ☐ Advanced Seismometers in Space
- ☐ ELL Modeling Earthquakes

Measuring Earthquake Waves

Essential Question How are seismic waves used to study earthquakes?

For more detailed information about the topics in this lesson, refer to the Content Refresher in the Unit Opener pages.

Opening Your Lesson

Begin the lesson by assessing students' prerequisite and prior knowledge.

Prerequisite Knowledge

- A general understanding of earthquakes

Accessing Prior Knowledge

Invite students to make a tri-fold FoldNote KWL chart about what they know about earthquakes. Have students put what they know in the first column and what they want to know in the second column. After they have finished the lesson, they can complete the third column with what they learned.

Online resource: Tri-Fold FoldNote support

Customize Your Opening

- ☐ **Accessing Prior Knowledge,** above
- ☐ **Print Path** Engage Your Brain, SE p. 253
- ☐ **Print Path** Active Reading, SE p. 253
- ☐ **Digital Path** Lesson Opener

Key Topics/Learning Goals	Supporting Concepts
The Causes of Earthquakes 1 Describe an earthquake. 2 Compare an earthquake's focus to its epicenter.	• Sudden movements of rock along faults cause earthquakes. Seismic waves are released, causing ground motion. • A focus is where an earthquake begins. An epicenter is directly above the focus and is recorded as the earthquake's location.
Seismic Waves and Their Measurement 1 Explain how energy from an earthquake is released. 2 Describe the properties of body and surface waves. 3 Explain how seismometers and seismograms are used.	• A seismic wave is energy that travels through Earth from an earthquake. • Body waves travel through Earth's interior. Body waves travel faster than surface waves. • Surface waves can be very destructive. • Seismometers measure body and surface waves, and lag time can show how far waves have traveled from the epicenter.
Earthquake Magnitude and Intensity 1 Compare magnitude and intensity. 2 Explain how different scales are used to measure magnitude and intensity.	• Magnitude is a measure of an earthquake's strength. Intensity is a measure of the amount of damage caused. • The Richter scale measures magnitude in whole numbers and fractions. The Moment Magnitude scale estimates energy released. • The Modified Mercalli Intensity scale gauges the observable effects of an earthquake.
Factors Determining the Effects of Earthquakes 1 List factors that determine the effects of an earthquake. 2 Explain how damage relates to earthquake magnitude, geology, distance from the epicenter, and structure type.	• Greater magnitude results in more energy released and greater ground motion. • The farther an area is from the epicenter, the less destructive an earthquake will be. • Solid rock shakes less than loose sediment or wet sediment. • Wood or steel construction and solid foundations help structures survive shaking.

Options for Instruction

Two parallel paths provide coverage of the Essential Questions, with a strong **Inquiry** strand woven into each. Follow the **Print Path,** the **Digital Path,** or your customized combination of print, digital, and inquiry.

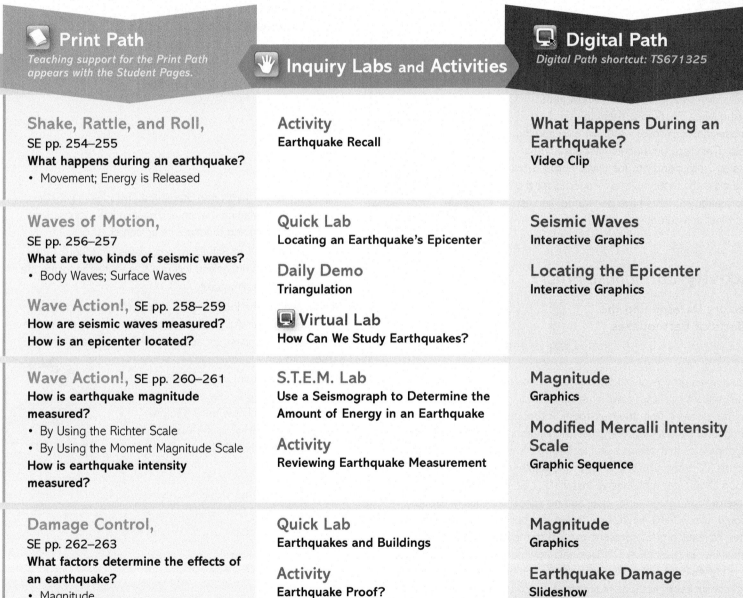

 Print Path *Teaching support for the Print Path appears with the Student Pages.*	 Inquiry Labs and Activities	Digital Path *Digital Path shortcut: TS671325*
Shake, Rattle, and Roll, SE pp. 254–255 **What happens during an earthquake?** • Movement; Energy is Released	**Activity** **Earthquake Recall**	**What Happens During an Earthquake?** **Video Clip**
Waves of Motion, SE pp. 256–257 **What are two kinds of seismic waves?** • Body Waves; Surface Waves **Wave Action!,** SE pp. 258–259 **How are seismic waves measured?** **How is an epicenter located?**	**Quick Lab** **Locating an Earthquake's Epicenter** **Daily Demo** **Triangulation** **Virtual Lab** **How Can We Study Earthquakes?**	**Seismic Waves** **Interactive Graphics** **Locating the Epicenter** **Interactive Graphics**
Wave Action!, SE pp. 260–261 **How is earthquake magnitude measured?** • By Using the Richter Scale • By Using the Moment Magnitude Scale **How is earthquake intensity measured?**	**S.T.E.M. Lab** **Use a Seismograph to Determine the Amount of Energy in an Earthquake** **Activity** **Reviewing Earthquake Measurement**	**Magnitude** **Graphics** **Modified Mercalli Intensity Scale** **Graphic Sequence**
Damage Control, SE pp. 262–263 **What factors determine the effects of an earthquake?** • Magnitude • Local Geology • Distance from the Epicenter • Building Construction	**Quick Lab** **Earthquakes and Buildings** **Activity** **Earthquake Proof?**	**Magnitude** **Graphics** **Earthquake Damage** **Slideshow** **Earthquake Engineering** **Interactive Graphic**

Options for Assessment

See the Evaluate page for options, including Formative Assessment, Summative Assessment, and Unit Review.

Engage and Explore

Activities and Discussion

Activity *Earthquake Recall*

Engage

Introducing Key Topics

 small groups/whole class
 15 min
 **GUIDED** inquiry

At the beginning of the lesson, give students several minutes to brainstorm what they already know about earthquakes. Encourage them to use short phrases and individual words when recording facts. Then record students' responses on a master list to display to the class. Finally, work as a class to create several categories for the information students have generated, and list each fact in a category.

Activity *Earthquake Proof?*

Factors Determining the Effects of Earthquakes

 small groups
 varies
 **INDEPENDENT** inquiry

Direct small groups of students to use various materials to create a small scale model of a town or several buildings. Building materials can be gathered from the classroom or brought in, and can include cardboard, craft sticks, toothpicks, aluminum foil, egg cartons, and anything else that seems suitable. Divide the class into at least three groups. Give one group tape, and give another group glue. The third group should get no adhesive materials at all. If there are more than three groups, assign tape, glue, and no adhesives equally. Groups should take 30–40 minutes to design and build their structures. Then have each group present its town to the class to see if it can withstand an "earthquake." Place each town on a surface, then shake it gently. **Ask:** How did different construction and adhesive materials and construction methods contribute to each town's stability during the "earthquake?" Sample answer: The town that was put together with tape and toothpicks survived well; I think because the materials used were light, and the buildings were not tall.

Labs and Demos

Daily Demo *Triangulation*

Seismic Waves and their Measurement

 whole class
 15 min
 **GUIDED** inquiry

PURPOSE **To demonstrate triangulation**

MATERIALS

- compass
- map
- pencil

1 Display a map of the United States that includes major cities. Tell students to imagine that an earthquake has just occurred and that you are going to locate its epicenter.

2 Point out the cities of San Francisco, Dallas, and Sioux City on the map. Explain that you will use these cities to locate the epicenter of the earthquake.

3 Without sharing the location of the epicenter with students (Albuquerque), carefully draw a circle around each of the three cities, using a compass for accuracy. Make sure each circle passes through Albuquerque.

4 **Analyze Ask:** What is the epicenter of the earthquake? Sample answer: Albuquerque **Ask:** How do you know this? Sample answer: because that is the place on the map where all three circles intersect

 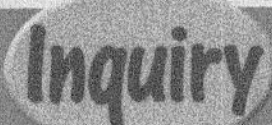

Levels of Inquiry	DIRECTED inquiry	GUIDED inquiry	INDEPENDENT inquiry
	introduces inquiry skills within a structured framework.	develops inquiry skills within a supportive environment	deepens inquiry skills with student-driven questions or procedures.

Quick Lab *Earthquakes and Buildings*

PURPOSE **To investigate how the construction of a building affects its stability during an earthquake**

See the Lab Manual or go Online for planning information.

Quick Lab *Locating an Earthquake's Epicenter*

Seismic Waves and Their Measurement

 pairs
 15 min
 **GUIDED** inquiry

Students read a map and a graph, and use triangulation to locate the epicenter of an earthquake.

PURPOSE **To understand the use of triangulation**

See the Lab Manual or go Online for planning information.

S.T.E.M. Lab *Use a Seismograph to Determine the Amount of Energy in an Earthquake*

Earthquake Magnitude and Intensity

 small groups
 45 min
 **GUIDED/INDEPENDENT** inquiry

Students build a seismograph, model earthquakes, take readings, and develop an earthquake magnitude scale.

PURPOSE **To analyze seismograph readings**

MATERIALS

- block, wood
- brick
- dowel, wood
- eye screws (2)
- marker
- ring stand with clamp
- roll of adding machine paper
- scissors
- string
- tape
- washers (inner diameter large enough to fit over the marker)
- safety goggles

Virtual Lab *How Can We Study Earthquakes?*

Seismic Waves and Their Measurement

 flexible
 45 min
 **GUIDED**

Students read seismographs and use triangulation to determine an earthquake's epicenter

PURPOSE To demonstrate how seismometers can be used to locate epicenters of earthquakes

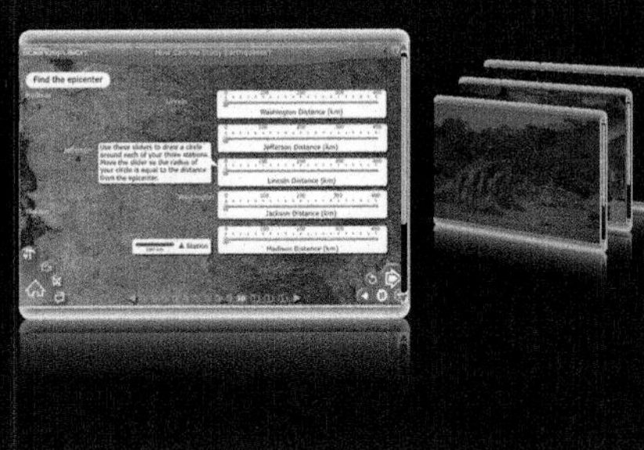

Customize Your Labs

See the Lab Manual for lab datasheets.

Go Online for editable lab datasheets.

Activities and Discussion

- ☐ **Activity** Earthquake Recall
- ☐ **Activity** Earthquake Proof?

Labs and Demos

- ☐ **Daily Demo** Triangulation
- ☐ **Quick Lab** Earthquakes and Buildings
- ☐ **Quick Lab** Locating an Earthquake's Epicenter
- ☐ **S.T.E.M. Lab** Use a Seismograph
- ☐ **Virtual Lab** How Can We Study Earthquakes?

Your Resources

Explain Science Concepts

Key Topics	Print Path	Digital Path
The Causes of Earthquakes	☐ **Shake, Rattle, and Roll,** SE pp. 254–255 • Active Reading (Annotation strategy), #5 • Sequence, #6 • Visualize It!, #7  Seismic waves caused extensive damage to structures during this 1995 earthquake in Japan.	☐ **What Happens During an Earthquake?** See what happens during an earthquake. 
Seismic Waves and Their Measurement	☐ **Waves of Motion,** SE pp. 256–257 • Active Reading (Annotation strategy), #8 • Visualize It!, #9 • Compare, #10 ☐ **Wave Action!,** SE pp. 258–259 • Do the Math, #11 • Visualize It!, #12 • Active Reading, #13 • Think Outside the Book, #14	☐ **Seismic Waves** View how the three kinds of seismic waves travel. ☐ **Locating the Epicenter** Learn how to locate the epicenter of an earthquake using seismograms.
Earthquake Magnitude and Intensity	☐ **Wave Action!,** SE pp. 260–261 • Active Reading (Annotation strategy), #15 • Identify, #16 • Visualize It!, #17	☐ **Magnitude** Explore earthquake magnitude. ☐ **Modified Mercalli Intensity Scale** Explore how the intensity of an earthquake is measured. 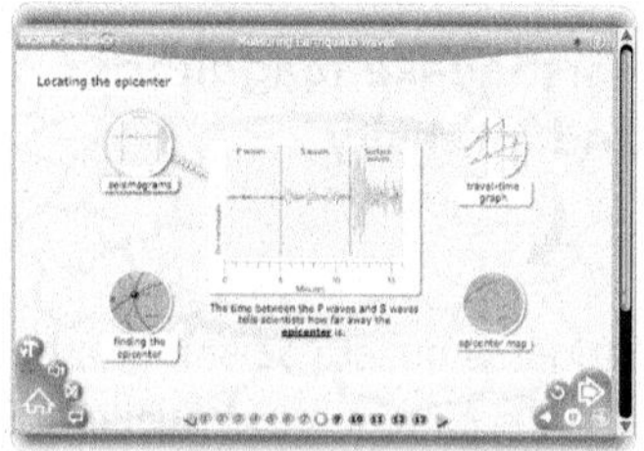
Factors Determining the Effects of Earthquakes	☐ **Damage Control,** SE pp. 262–263 • Apply, #18 • Visualize It!, #19  When ground shaking occurs, the grains lose contact with one another, and the strength of the soil decreases.	☐ **Magnitude** Explore earthquake magnitude. ☐ **Earthquake Damage** Learn the factors involved in determining how much damage an earthquake may cause. ☐ **Earthquake Engineering** See how engineers can design buildings to withstand earthquakes.

Differentiated Instruction

Basic *Wave Summary*

Seismic Waves and Their Measurement

 individuals
 20–30 min

Summarize Have students write a short summary of how seismic waves are measured. Students should include information on seismometers, seismograms, lag time, triangulation, and epicenters. Summaries should be in students' own words. When complete, have each student share their summary with a partner to correct any mistakes or to add or cut information.

Advanced *Earthquake Comparison*

Factors Determining the Effects of Earthquakes

 small groups
varies

Poster Have groups of students work together to research and create a poster comparing the effects of two or three earthquakes of similar magnitude in different parts of the world. Groups should present their research to the class in a brief oral presentation.

ELL *Whose Fault Is It?*

The Causes of Earthquakes

 individuals/whole class
 10 min

Definition Cards Struggling students or students who are English language learners may have difficulty with the scientific context of the word *fault.* Explain that there are two definitions for the word *fault.* Provide students with index cards and access to dictionaries, and guide them as they look up both the common and scientific definitions for *fault.* Have each student write the common definition on one side of the index card and the scientific definition on the other side of the card. To further explain the scientific definition of the word, show students a picture or diagram of a *fault.*

Lesson Vocabulary

focus	**seismic waves**	**magnitude**
epicenter	**seismogram**	**intensity**

Previewing Vocabulary

 whole class
 15 min

Word Origins Give students the following information to aid in their understanding of the vocabulary:

- seismic waves, seismogram: The Greek root *seis-* means "to shake." The suffix *-ic* means "related to." The suffix *-gram* means "written" or "drawn."
- epicenter: One of the meanings of the prefix *epi-* is "close to"; so *epi* + *center* means "close to the center."

Reinforcing Vocabulary

 individuals
 ongoing

Description Wheel To help students remember the vocabulary, have them develop a description wheel for each term and for any other words from the lesson that they have difficulty remembering. Have students write the word in the center circle and then write the definition and details on the spokes.

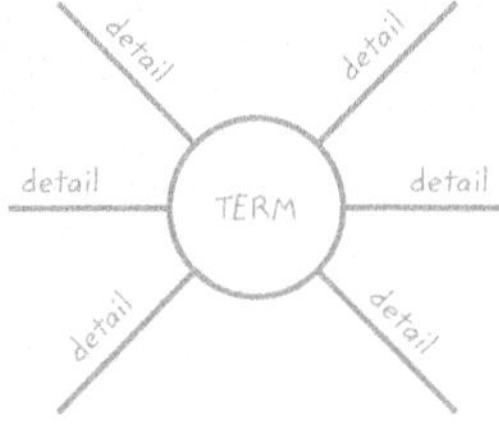

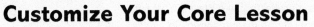

Customize Your Core Lesson

Core Instruction

- ☐ **Print Path** choices
- ☐ **Digital Path** choices

Vocabulary

- ☐ **Previewing Vocabulary** Word Origins
- ☐ **Reinforcing Vocabulary** Description Wheel

Your Resources

Differentiated Instruction

- ☐ **Basic** Wave Summary
- ☐ **Advanced** Earthquake Comparison
- ☐ **ELL** Whose Fault Is It?

Extend Science Concepts

Reinforce and Review

Activity *Reviewing Earthquake Measurements*

Synthesizing Key Topics

 whole class
20 min

Write the following words and phrases on the board:

- seismogram
- lag time
- triangulation
- Richter scale
- Moment Magnitude scale
- Modified Mercalli scale
- focus

Ask for a volunteer to explain or define each term. After the student explains a term, ask if anyone else in the class would like to add anything to that explanation. If there are errors or omissions in students' explanations, address them. Continue with each term until all terms on the list have been reviewed.

Graphic Organizer

Synthesizing Key Topics

 individuals
 20 min

Cluster Diagram Have students create cluster diagrams for the lesson content. The center circle should include the lesson title: Measuring Earthquake Waves. Students should generate as many connecting circles as necessary to include key information and relevant details from the lesson. Once students have completed the activity, have them share their cluster diagrams with a partner to compare content, add missing information, and make corrections to the content.

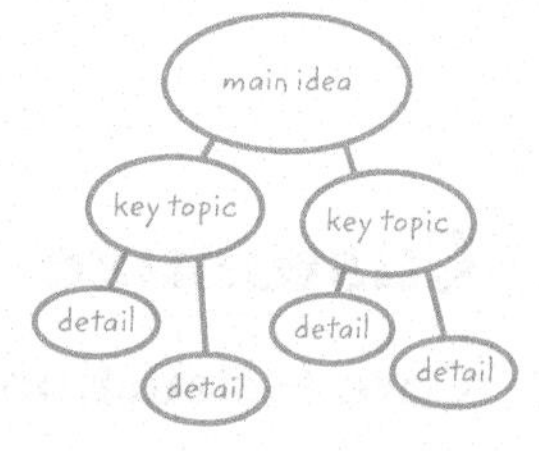

Optional Online resource: Cluster Diagram support

Going Further

Social Studies Connection *Historical Earthquakes*

Synthesizing Key Topics

 individuals
varied

Research and Presentation Encourage students to research a historical earthquake. Provide a list of choices, such as the earthquake that occurred in 1906 in San Francisco, in 1964 in Alaska, in 1976 in Tangshan, China, and in 2004 off the coast of Sumatra, if needed. Have students find out where and when the earthquake took place, where the epicenter was located, the magnitude and intensity of the earthquake, and the effects of the earthquake. Encourage students to use visual aids and photographs. Students can present their research in a written report, in poster form, or in a slide presentation.

Math Connection *Triangulation*

Seismic Waves and Their Measurement

 whole class
10 min

Quick Discussion Tell students that triangulation is based on the work of a mathematician. Willebrord Snell figured out how to use triangulation to survey distance in 1615. We now use triangulation for a variety of applications, including locating an earthquake's epicenter, surveying land, and navigating. Ask students if they can think of other ways triangulation might be used. Tell students that global positioning satellites have replaced some uses of triangulation; discuss with students which uses they think are being replaced and which will not be replaced by GPS.

Customize Your Closing

See the Assessment Guide for quizzes and tests.

Go Online to edit and create quizzes and tests.

Reinforce and Review

- ☐ Activity Earthquake Review
- ☐ Graphic Organizer Cluster Diagram
- ☐ Print Path Visual Summary, SE p. 264
- ☐ Print Path Lesson Review, SE p. 265
- ☐ **Digital Path** Lesson Closer

Evaluate Student Mastery

Formative Assessment

See the teacher support below the Student Pages for additional Formative Assessment questions.

Ask the following questions to assess student mastery of the material. **Ask:** Which type of wave travels through Earth's interior? body waves **Ask:** What are two types of body waves? P waves and S waves **Ask:** What is the difference between P waves and S waves? P waves are faster and move through solids and fluids. S waves are slower and only move through solid rock. **Ask:** What are surface waves? Surface waves travel along Earth's surface, moving it up and down or from side to side. They cause more damage than body waves.

Reteach

Formative assessment may show that students need reinforcement for certain topics. The resources below are recommended for reteaching. If students were introduced to a topic through the Print Path, you can also use the Digital Path to reteach, or vice versa.
Can be assigned to individual students

The Causes of Earthquakes

Activity Earthquake Recall

Seismic Waves and their Measurement

Basic Wave Summary

Earthquake Magnitude and Intensity

S.T.E.M. Lab Use a Seismograph

Virtual Lab How Do We Study Earthquakes?

Factors Determining the Effects of Earthquakes

Quick Lab Earthquakes and Buildings

Activity Earthquake Proof?

Summative Assessment

Alternative Assessment

Research and Reporting

Online resources: student worksheet; optional rubrics

Measuring Earthquake Waves

Climb the Pyramid: ***Research and Reporting***
Pretend you are a news reporter. In order to report on a fictional earthquake, you must develop your understanding of the causes of earthquakes, how they are measured, and their effects. You will execute a short research plan and then write a short newspaper article to report the details of this recent imaginary earthquake.

1. Work on your own.
2. Begin at the bottom of the pyramid. Choose one item from each layer and check your choices.
3. Have your teacher approve your plan.
4. Submit or present your results.

__ Newspaper Article
Write a newspaper article on a recent imaginary earthquake. Include a short background on earthquakes, then describe the earthquake's magnitude, intensity, and damages sustained in the community.

__ Triangulation Map
Review triangulation by researching different triangulation maps of previous earthquakes. Choose one map, and write a short summary describing how the epicenter of the earthquake is identified.

__ Seismogram
Review seismograms by researching several seismograms for past earthquakes. Choose one and write a short description of how lag times are used to determine an earthquake's magnitude.

__ Earthquake Locations
Research areas where earthquakes occur frequently. Write a short explanation of why earthquakes occur more frequently in certain locations.

__ Before and After
Make a picture collage or drawing that depicts the way a city or town looked before and after an earthquake. Cite any sources on the back.

__ Lasting Construction
Research construction materials, methods, and designs that can withstand strong shaking. Write a short recommendation for how to build in earthquake-prone areas.

Going Further

- [ ] Social Studies Connection
- [ ] Math Connection

Formative Assessment

- [ ] Strategies Throughout TE
- [ ] Lesson Review SE

Summative Assessment

- [ ] Alternative Assessment Research and Reporting
- [ ] Lesson Quiz
- [ ] Unit Tests A and B
- [ ] Unit Review SE End-of-Unit

Your Resources

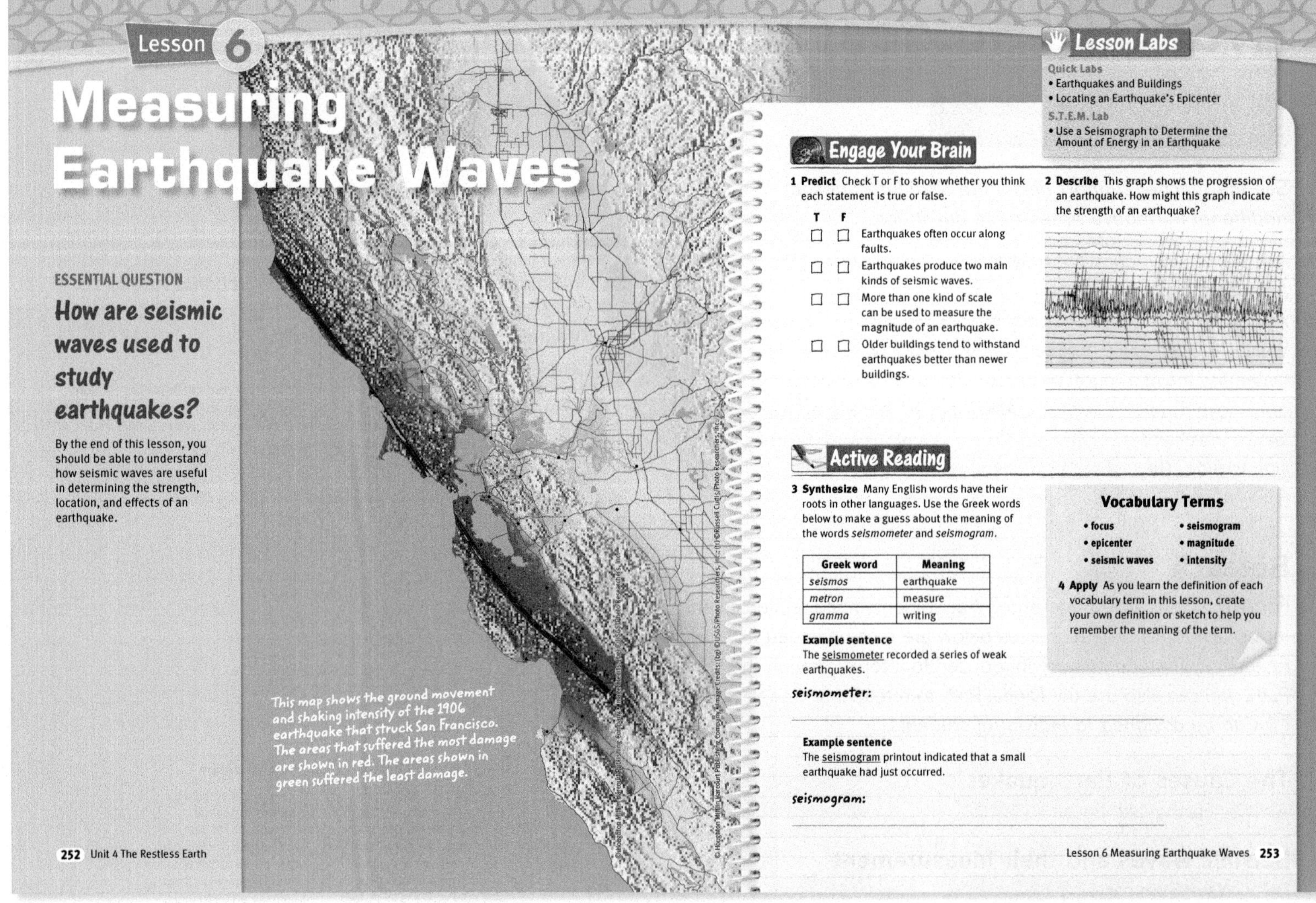

Lesson 6

Measuring Earthquake Waves

ESSENTIAL QUESTION

How are seismic waves used to study earthquakes?

By the end of this lesson, you should be able to understand how seismic waves are useful in determining the strength, location, and effects of an earthquake.

This map shows the ground movement and shaking intensity of the 1906 earthquake that struck San Francisco. The areas that suffered the most damage are shown in red. The areas shown in green suffered the least damage.

252 Unit 4 The Restless Earth

Lesson Labs

Quick Labs
- Earthquakes and Buildings
- Locating an Earthquake's Epicenter

S.T.E.M. Lab
- Use a Seismograph to Determine the Amount of Energy in an Earthquake

Engage Your Brain

1 Predict Check T or F to show whether you think each statement is true or false.

T	F	
☐	☐	Earthquakes often occur along faults.
☐	☐	Earthquakes produce two main kinds of seismic waves.
☐	☐	More than one kind of scale can be used to measure the magnitude of an earthquake.
☐	☐	Older buildings tend to withstand earthquakes better than newer buildings.

2 Describe This graph shows the progression of an earthquake. How might this graph indicate the strength of an earthquake?

Active Reading

3 Synthesize Many English words have their roots in other languages. Use the Greek words below to make a guess about the meaning of the words *seismometer* and *seismogram*.

Greek word	Meaning
seismos	earthquake
metron	measure
gramma	writing

Example sentence
The seismometer recorded a series of weak earthquakes.

seismometer:

Example sentence
The seismogram printout indicated that a small earthquake had just occurred.

seismogram:

Vocabulary Terms
- focus
- epicenter
- seismic waves
- seismogram
- magnitude
- intensity

4 Apply As you learn the definition of each vocabulary term in this lesson, create your own definition or sketch to help you remember the meaning of the term.

Lesson 6 Measuring Earthquake Waves 253

Answers

Answers for 1–3 should represent students' current thoughts, even if incorrect.

1. T; T; T; F
2. Sample answer: The strength is shown by the total length of the waves on the graph.
3. Sample answers: seismometer: an instrument that records earthquake waves; seismogram: a readout produced by a seismometer.
4. Students should define or sketch each vocabulary term in the lesson.

Opening Your Lesson

Review students' answers to items 1 and 2 to assess what students already know about earthquakes.

Prerequisites Students should already have a basic understanding of earthquakes from a previous lesson. This lesson allows students to develop a deeper understanding of earthquakes and how they are measured.

Interpreting Visuals

Identify Students may need support to understand the seismogram. **Ask:** What part of the seismogram shows the most earthquake activity? Sample answer: The middle part of the seismogram shows the most activity. **Ask:** How can you tell? Sample answer: The higher lines in the middle part of the seismogram indicate greater earthquake activity.

Shake, Rattle, and Roll

What happens during an earthquake?

Have you ever felt the ground move under your feet? Many people have. Every day, somewhere in the world, earthquakes happen. An earthquake occurs when blocks of rock move suddenly and release energy. This energy travels through rock as waves.

Movement Takes Place Along a Fault

Earth's lithosphere (LITH•uh•sfir) is the rocky outer layer of Earth that includes the crust. The lithosphere is made up of large plates. These plates pull apart, push together, or move past one another. As plates move, stress on rocks at or near the edges of the plates increases. This stress causes faults to form. A *fault* is a break in a body of rock along which one block moves relative to another. Stress along faults causes the rocks to deform, or change from their original shape. If this stress becomes too great, rocks along a fault will break and move along the fault. Once rocks break, the pieces of broken rock return to an undeformed shape. When rocks along a fault break and move along a fault, energy is released into the surrounding rock in the form of waves. This process is what causes earthquakes.

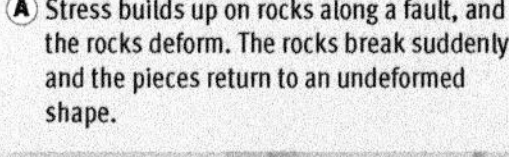

5 Identify As you read, underline the definition of a fault.

Energy Is Released as Seismic Waves

As stress builds up in rocks along a fault, the energy that is stored in the deforming rock increases. When the rock breaks, the rocks on either side of the fault slip past one another and return to an undeformed state. The location along a fault at which the first motion of an earthquake takes place is called the **focus**. The **epicenter** is the point on Earth's surface directly above an earthquake's starting point or focus. A large amount of stored energy is released when rocks along a fault slip. This energy travels away from the focus and through Earth in all directions as seismic (SYZ•mik) waves. **Seismic waves** are vibrations that cause different types of ground motion. The strength of an earthquake is based on the energy that is released as rocks break and return to an undeformed shape.

Energy moves outward from the water drop as ripples on the water.

Visualize It!

7 Compare How are the ripples that are moving through the water in this pond similar to seismic waves that travel through Earth? How are they different?

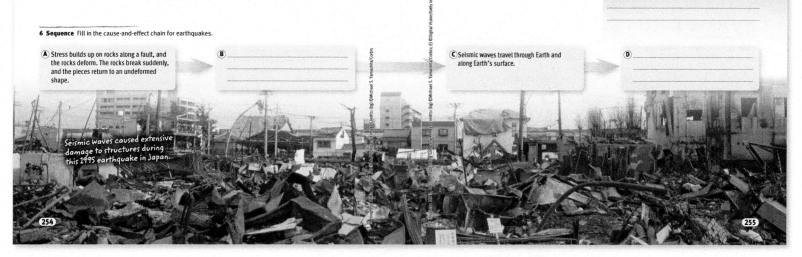

6 Sequence Fill in the cause-and-effect chain for earthquakes.

Ⓐ Stress builds up on rocks along a fault, and the rocks deform. The rocks break suddenly, and the pieces return to an undeformed shape.

Ⓑ

Ⓒ Seismic waves travel through Earth and along Earth's surface.

Ⓓ

Seismic waves caused extensive damage to structures during this 1995 earthquake in Japan.

254 255

Answers

5. *See students' pages for annotations.*
6. B: Energy is released as seismic waves into the surrounding rock. D: An earthquake is felt on Earth's surface as seismic waves cause ground motion.
7. Water waves are caused by energy moving through water just as seismic waves are caused by energy moving through rock. Water waves travel across the surface of the water, whereas seismic waves travel in three dimensions.

Probing Questions GUIDED Inquiry

Applying **Ask:** Why do you think it is important to understand the causes of earthquakes? Sample answers: It may help us predict future earthquakes; it could help connect the causes of earthquakes to the amount of damage done by them; it can help us understand Earth's geology and plate tectonics.

Using Annotations

Text Structure: Main Idea and Details To help students better understand the main idea and details of how energy from earthquakes is released as seismic waves, direct them to look for and circle the word *energy* as they read. Then, direct students to underline details about energy found in the section. Tell students that seismic waves are energy and that paying attention to this word will help them better understand the definition of seismic wave.

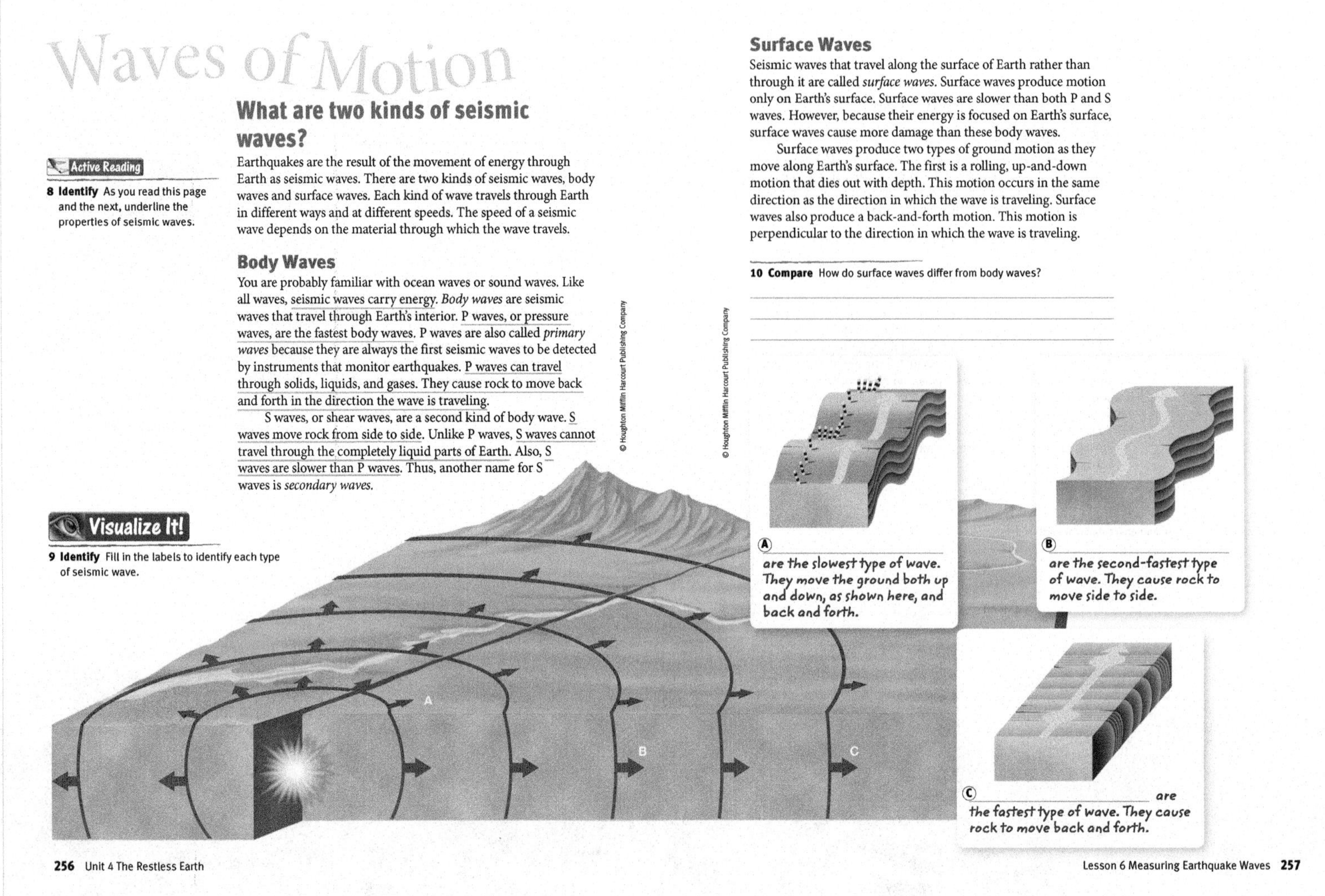

Waves of Motion
What are two kinds of seismic waves?
Active Reading
8 Identify As you read this page and the next, underline the properties of seismic waves.
Earthquakes are the result of the movement of energy through Earth as seismic waves. There are two kinds of seismic waves, body waves and surface waves. Each kind of wave travels through Earth in different ways and at different speeds. The speed of a seismic wave depends on the material through which the wave travels.
Body Waves
You are probably familiar with ocean waves or sound waves. Like all waves, seismic waves carry energy. Body waves are seismic waves that travel through Earth's interior. P waves, or pressure waves, are the fastest body waves. P waves are also called primary waves because they are always the first seismic waves to be detected by instruments that monitor earthquakes. P waves can travel through solids, liquids, and gases. They cause rock to move back and forth in the direction the wave is traveling.
S waves, or shear waves, are a second kind of body wave. S waves move rock from side to side. Unlike P waves, S waves cannot travel through the completely liquid parts of Earth. Also, S waves are slower than P waves. Thus, another name for S waves is secondary waves.
Visualize It!
9 Identify Fill in the labels to identify each type of seismic wave.
Surface Waves
Seismic waves that travel along the surface of Earth rather than through it are called surface waves. Surface waves produce motion only on Earth's surface. Surface waves are slower than both P and S waves. However, because their energy is focused on Earth's surface, surface waves cause more damage than these body waves.
Surface waves produce two types of ground motion as they move along Earth's surface. The first is a rolling, up-and-down motion that dies out with depth. This motion occurs in the same direction as the direction in which the wave is traveling. Surface waves also produce a back-and-forth motion. This motion is perpendicular to the direction in which the wave is traveling.
10 Compare How do surface waves differ from body waves?
A
B
C
A are the slowest type of wave. They move the ground both up and down, as shown here, and back and forth.
B are the second-fastest type of wave. They cause rock to move side to side.
C are the fastest type of wave. They cause rock to move back and forth.
256 Unit 4 The Restless Earth
Lesson 6 Measuring Earthquake Waves 257

Answers

8. *See students' pages for annotations.*
9. A: surface waves; B: S, or secondary waves; C: P, or primary waves
10. Body waves travel through Earth's interior, while surface waves travel along Earth's surface. Body waves travel more rapidly than surface waves do. Surface waves cause more damage than body waves do.

Building Reading Skills

Venn Diagram Direct students to create a Venn diagram to compare and contrast P and S waves. Have students write the similarities between the two types of waves in the overlapping center of the two circles and the differences in each nonoverlapping section. Remind students to label each circle in the diagram as a P wave or an S wave.

Formative Assessment

Ask: How do surface waves cause damage to buildings? Sample answer: Surface waves travel along Earth's surface, moving it up and down and from side to side. When the surface of the ground moves up and down, everything on Earth's surface, including buildings, roads, and living things, moves with it. This movement causes damage to solid structures that have little flexibility, including buildings.

For students who need additional support answering this question, ask them to imagine surface waves moving through Earth's crust in the same way that waves move across the surface of the ocean. Then direct them to imagine how the waves could affect buildings and other infrastructure.

Wave Action!

How are seismic waves measured?

Imagine walls shaking, windows rattling, and glasses and dishes clinking. After only seconds, the vibrating stops. Within minutes, news reports give information about the strength and the location of the earthquake. How could scientists learn this information so quickly? Scientists use instruments called *seismometers* to record the seismic waves generated by earthquakes. Seismometers are located at seismometer stations that are arranged in networks. When seismic waves reach a seismometer, the seismometer produces a seismogram. A **seismogram** is a tracing of earthquake motion. Seismograms also record the arrival times of seismic waves at a seismometer station. Seismograms are plotted on a graph like the one shown below. Scientists use the graph to pinpoint the location of an earthquake's epicenter.

Do the Math You Try It

P waves travel faster than S waves and are the first waves to be recorded at a seismometer station. The difference between the arrival times of P waves and S waves is called *lag time*. Lag time increases as the waves travel farther from their point of origin. Lag time can be used to find the distance to an earthquake's epicenter.

Identify

11 Calculate What are the lag times for each of the locations A, B, and C?

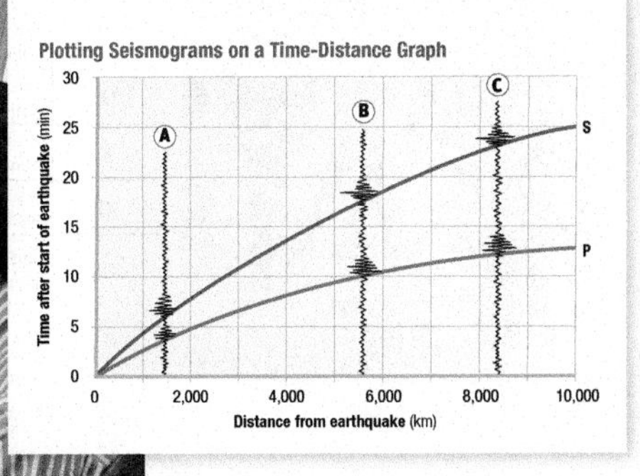

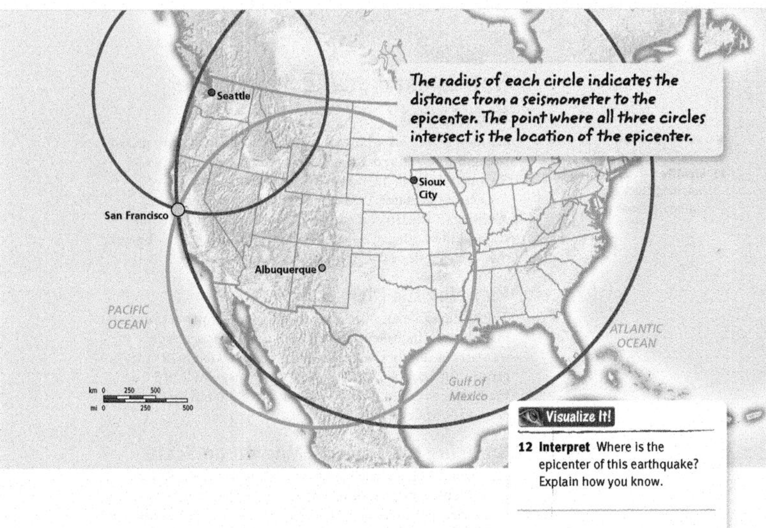

Visualize It!

12 Interpret Where is the epicenter of this earthquake? Explain how you know.

How is an earthquake's epicenter located?

Scientists use the data from seismograms to find an earthquake's epicenter. The S-P time method is an easy way to locate the epicenter of an earthquake. The method is based on the differences in arrival times of P and S waves, called lag time, at different seismometer stations. Lag time tells scientists how far waves have traveled from the epicenter. The epicenter of the earthquake can then be located by drawing circles around at least three seismometer stations on a map, as shown above. The radius of each circle is equal to the distance from that seismometer station to the earthquake's epicenter. The point at which all of the circles intersect is the epicenter. This process is called *triangulation*. Today, computers perform these calculations.

Active Reading **13 Identify** What is the name of the process used to locate an earthquake's epicenter?

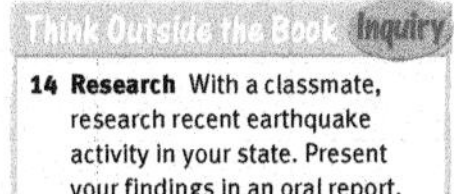

14 Research With a classmate, research recent earthquake activity in your state. Present your findings in an oral report.

Answers

11. A: about 3 minutes; B: about 8 minutes; C: about 11 minutes
12. The epicenter is San Francisco; it is the point where the three circles intersect.
13. triangulation
14. Answers will vary depending on the state in which the student lives. Oral presentations should show an understanding of what causes earthquake activity.

Formative Assessment

Ask: What is lag time? Lag time is the difference between the time when P waves arrive and the time when S waves arrive. **Ask:** What is lag time used to determine? Lag time is used to determine the distance to the epicenter of an earthquake.

Do the Math

Guide students through the process of determining lag time for the arrival of P and S waves at location A. Have students identify the units for each axis on the graph. Make sure they understand that the units on the y-axis (vertical) are minutes and the units on the x-axis are kilometers. Have students trace with their fingers from where the blue line and seismograph A intersect over to the y-axis. **Ask:** How much time elapsed between when the earthquake occurred and when the P waves arrived at location A? about four minutes Next, have students repeat this for the red line. **Ask:** How much time elapsed between when the earthquake occurred and when the S waves arrived at location A? about six minutes **Ask:** What is the lag time for location A? about two minutes Monitor students as they repeat the process for locations B and C. Alternatively, have students work in pairs or small groups to find the lag times for locations B and C.

How is earthquake magnitude measured?

Active Reading

15 Identify As you read, underline how magnitude is related to earthquake strength.

Seismograms can also provide information about an earthquake's strength. The height of the waves on a seismogram indicates the amount of ground motion. Ground motion can be used to calculate **magnitude**, the measure of energy released by an earthquake. The larger the magnitude of an earthquake is, the stronger the earthquake. Seismologists express magnitude by using the Richter scale or the Moment Magnitude scale.

By Using the Richter Scale

The Richter scale measures the ground motion from an earthquake to find the earthquake's strength. Each time the magnitude increases by one unit, the measured ground motion is 10 times greater. For example, an earthquake with a magnitude of 5.0 on the Richter scale produces 10 times as much ground motion as an earthquake with a magnitude of 4.0.

By Using the Moment Magnitude Scale

The Moment Magnitude scale has largely replaced the Richter scale. Moment magnitude measures earthquake strength based on the size of the area of the fault that moves, the average distance that the fault moves, and the rigidity of the rocks in the fault. The Moment Magnitude scale is more accurate for large earthquakes than the Richter scale is. The moment magnitude of an earthquake is expressed by a number. The larger the number is, the stronger the earthquake was. The largest earthquake ever recorded took place in Chile and registered a moment magnitude of 9.5.

16 Identify After the Chilean earthquake in 1960, which has been the strongest earthquake in the last 100 years?

Year	Location	Moment Magnitude
2011	Tōhoku, Japan	9.0
2010	Port-au-Prince, Haiti	7.0
1994	Northridge, California	6.7
1964	Prince William Sound, Alaska	9.2
1960	Southern Chile	9.5

The 1964 earthquake on Kodiak Island, Alaska, measured 9.2 on the Moment Magnitude scale.

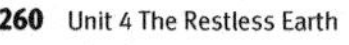

How is earthquake intensity measured?

The effects of an earthquake and how the earthquake is felt by people are known as the earthquake's **intensity**. An earthquake's magnitude is different from its intensity. Magnitude measures how much energy is released by an earthquake. Intensity measures the effects of an earthquake at Earth's surface.

The Modified Mercalli scale is used to describe an earthquake's intensity. The scale ranges from I to XII. Earthquakes that have an intensity value of I are barely noticeable. Earthquakes that have an intensity value of XII cause total destruction. Intensity values vary from place to place and are usually highest near the epicenter of the earthquake.

Visualize It!

17 Infer Describe the damage that you see in the photograph. What Modified Mercalli scale rating would you give this earthquake?

Intensity	Description
I	felt by very few people under especially favorable conditions
II	felt by few people at rest; some suspended items may swing
III	felt by most people indoors; vibrations feel like passing trucks
IV	felt by many people; windows or dishes rattle
V	felt by nearly everyone; some objects are broken or overturned
VI	felt by all people; heavy objects are moved; slight damage to structures
VII	causes slight to moderate damage to buildings; chimneys may topple
VIII	causes considerable damage to ordinary buildings; some partial collapse
IX	causes considerable damage to earthquake-resistant buildings
X	destroys many structures, including foundations; rails are bent
XI	destroys most structures; bridges destroyed; rails are bent
XII	causes total destruction; objects tossed through the air

Not all earthquakes result in catastrophic damage. During this earthquake, only moderate damage occurred.

Answers

15. *See students' pages for annotations.*
16. Prince William Sound, Alaska
17. Sample answer: There is a large opening in the ground. The rating could be a VII because there is slight damage but not enough damage to be rated as VIII. A rating of VIII would include considerable damage to buildings.

Building Reading Skills

Venn Diagram Direct students to compare and contrast the Richter and Moment Magnitude scales using a Venn diagram. Have students list the similarities for the two scales in the overlapping portion of the two circles and the differences between the scales in the nonoverlapping parts of the two circles.

Probing Questions GUIDED Inquiry

Analyzing **Ask:** What are the strengths and weaknesses of measuring an earthquake's intensity using the Modified Mercalli scale? Sample answers: A potential strength is the ability to measure the effects of an earthquake. A potential weakness is that the effects of earthquakes vary depending on the infrastructure and geological features of an area, making this scale conditional rather than empirical.

Tell students to imagine the following scenario: Two earthquakes of the same magnitude affect two different cities—one riverside city with very tall, old buildings made of stone and a modern city built on a rock plateau with smaller, steel buildings. **Ask:** How would these differences affect the perception of the intensity of the earthquakes? Sample answer: A city built on rock with buildings constructed of material that is less likely to crumble will likely experience the earthquake much less intensely than a city built on sediment with buildings made from material that can crumble.

Damage Control

What factors determine the effects of an earthquake?

The effects of an earthquake can vary over a wide area. Four factors determine the effects of an earthquake on a given area. These factors are magnitude, the local geology, the distance from the epicenter, and the type of construction used in an area.

Magnitude

Recall that an earthquake's magnitude is directly related to its strength. Stronger earthquakes cause more ground motion and, thus, cause more damage than weaker earthquakes. As an earthquake's magnitude increases, the intensity of an earthquake is commonly higher.

Local Geology

The amount of damage caused by an earthquake also depends on the material through which seismic waves travel. In general, solid rock is not likely to increase an earthquake's intensity. However, seismic waves can become more dangerous when they travel through loose soils and sediments that are saturated with water. When water-saturated soil or sediment is shaken by seismic waves, the soil and sediment particles become completely surrounded by water. This process, which is shown below, is called *liquefaction*. Liquefaction can intensify ground shaking or cause the ground to settle. Settling can cause structures to tilt or collapse.

18 Apply Why would it be potentially dangerous to build a home or building on loose soil or sediment?

Grains in silty or sandy soils are normally in contact with one another, which gives the soil strength and stiffness.

When ground shaking occurs, the grains lose contact with one another, and the strength of the soil decreases.

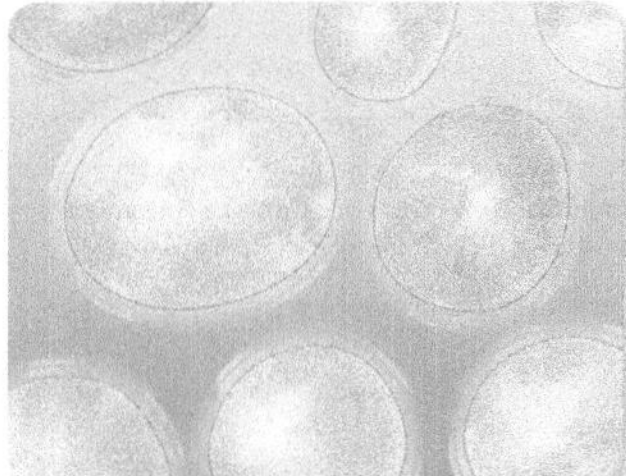

Distance from the Epicenter

Surface waves, which move along Earth's surface, are the most destructive of all seismic waves. The more energy a surface wave carries, the stronger the ground motion will be and the more damage the wave will cause. However, surface waves decrease in size and energy the farther that they travel from the epicenter of an earthquake. Therefore, the farther an area is located from the epicenter, the less damage it will suffer.

Building Construction

The materials with which structures are built also determine the amount of earthquake damage. Flexible structures are more likely to survive strong ground shaking. Structures that are made of brick or concrete are not very flexible and are easily damaged. Wood and steel are more flexible. Taller buildings are more susceptible to damage than shorter buildings. This diagram shows technologies in use that control how much tall buildings sway during earthquakes. Other technologies are designed to prevent seismic waves from moving through buildings.

19 Apply How are mass dampers and active tendon systems similar in the way they protect a building from earthquake damage?

A **mass damper** is a weight placed in the roof of a building. Motion sensors detect building movement during an earthquake and send messages to a computer. The computer then signals controls in the roof to shift the mass damper to counteract the building's movement.

The **active tendon system** works much like the mass damper system in the roof. Sensors notify a computer that the building is moving. Then the computer activates devices to shift a large weight to counteract the movement.

Base isolators act as shock absorbers during an earthquake. They are made of layers of rubber and steel wrapped around a lead core. Base isolators absorb seismic waves and prevent the waves from traveling through the building.

Answers

18. The loose soil or sediment can easily shift during an earthquake, causing the home or building to shift as well and possibly collapse.
19. Both mass dampers and active tendon systems use computers to shift weights that counteract the movement caused by an earthquake.

Building Reading Skills

Idea Wheel Direct students to take notes on the four factors that determine the effects of an earthquake using an Idea Wheel. Have students determine the main idea and write it in the center of the wheel. Then have students take notes on each of the four factors that determine an earthquake's effects in each of the four sections of the Idea Wheel. Students should share and compare the information they included in each section of the wheel with a partner to check their notes.

Optional Online resource: Idea Wheel support

Formative Assessment

Ask: Why does geology affect the amount of damage done by an earthquake? Sample answer: Loose soil that contains a lot of water can liquefy during an earthquake, which can intensify the shaking of the ground and cause much more damage than an earthquake that occurs in an area where the rock is solid. **Ask:** What is magnitude and what impact does it have on an earthquake's effects? Sample answer: Magnitude is a measure of an earthquake's strength. A stronger earthquake will do more damage than a weaker earthquake would to the same area.

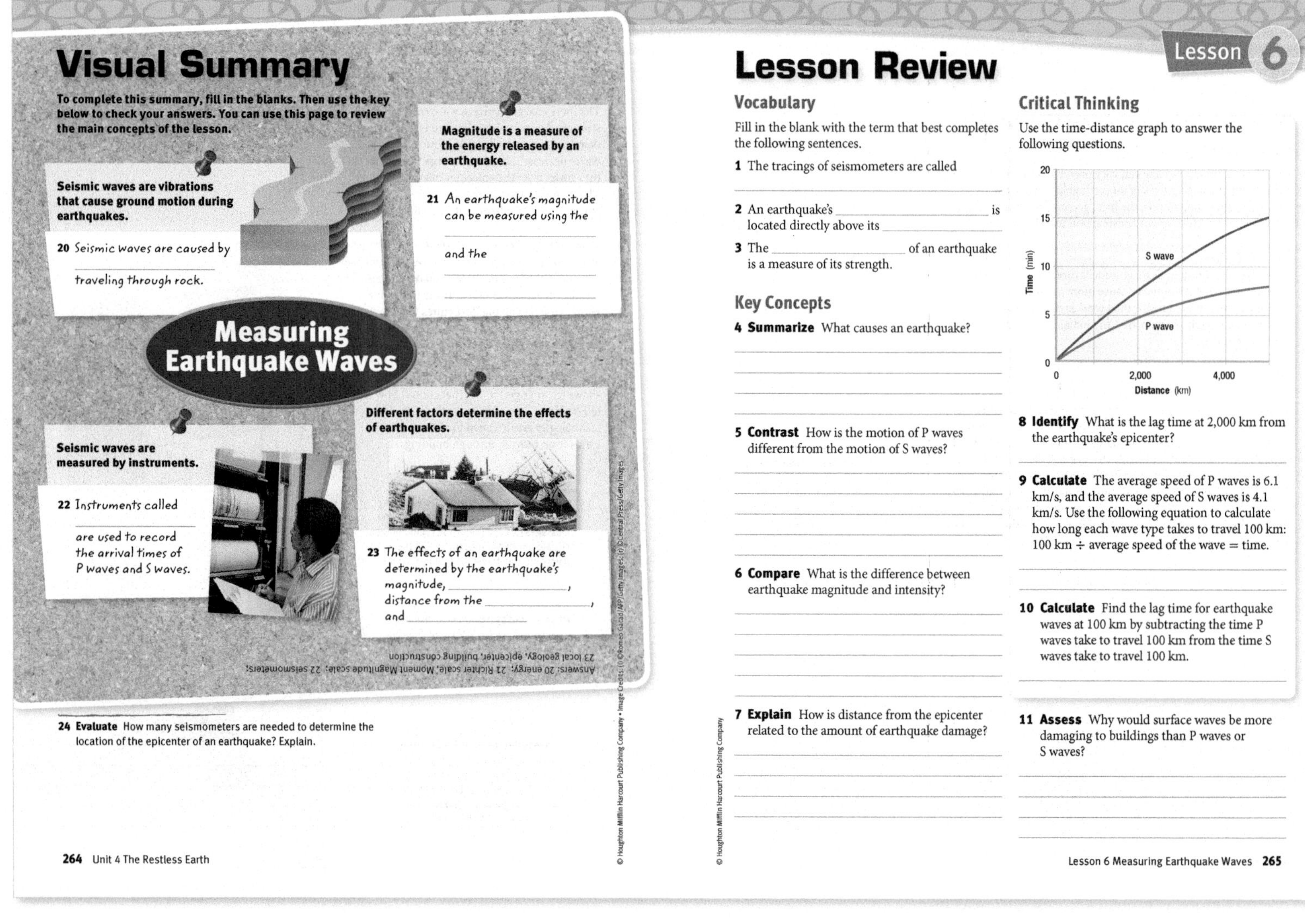

Visual Summary Answers

20. energy
21. Richter scale; Moment Magnitude scale
22. seismometers
23. local geology; epicenter; building construction
24. Three; two seismometer stations can narrow the location of the earthquake to two possible locations. Adding a third enables scientists to determine which of the two locations is correct.

Lesson Review Answers

1. seismograms
2. epicenter; focus
3. magnitude
4. Earthquakes occur when rock along a fault moves or breaks and releases energy as seismic waves.
5. P waves move rock back and forth in the direction in which the wave is traveling, while S waves move rock from side to side, perpendicular to the direction in which the wave is traveling.
6. Magnitude is a measure of energy released, whereas intensity is a measure of the damage caused by an earthquake.
7. The amount of damage caused by an earthquake usually decreases with increasing distance from the epicenter of an earthquake.
8. about 2.5 minutes
9. P wave: about 16.4 s; S wave: about 24.4 s
10. about 8 s
11. Sample answer: Surface waves travel along Earth's surface, causing ground motion that can damage structures on Earth's surface. Thus, they move the ground more than P waves and S waves, which primarily travel through Earth.

Teacher Notes

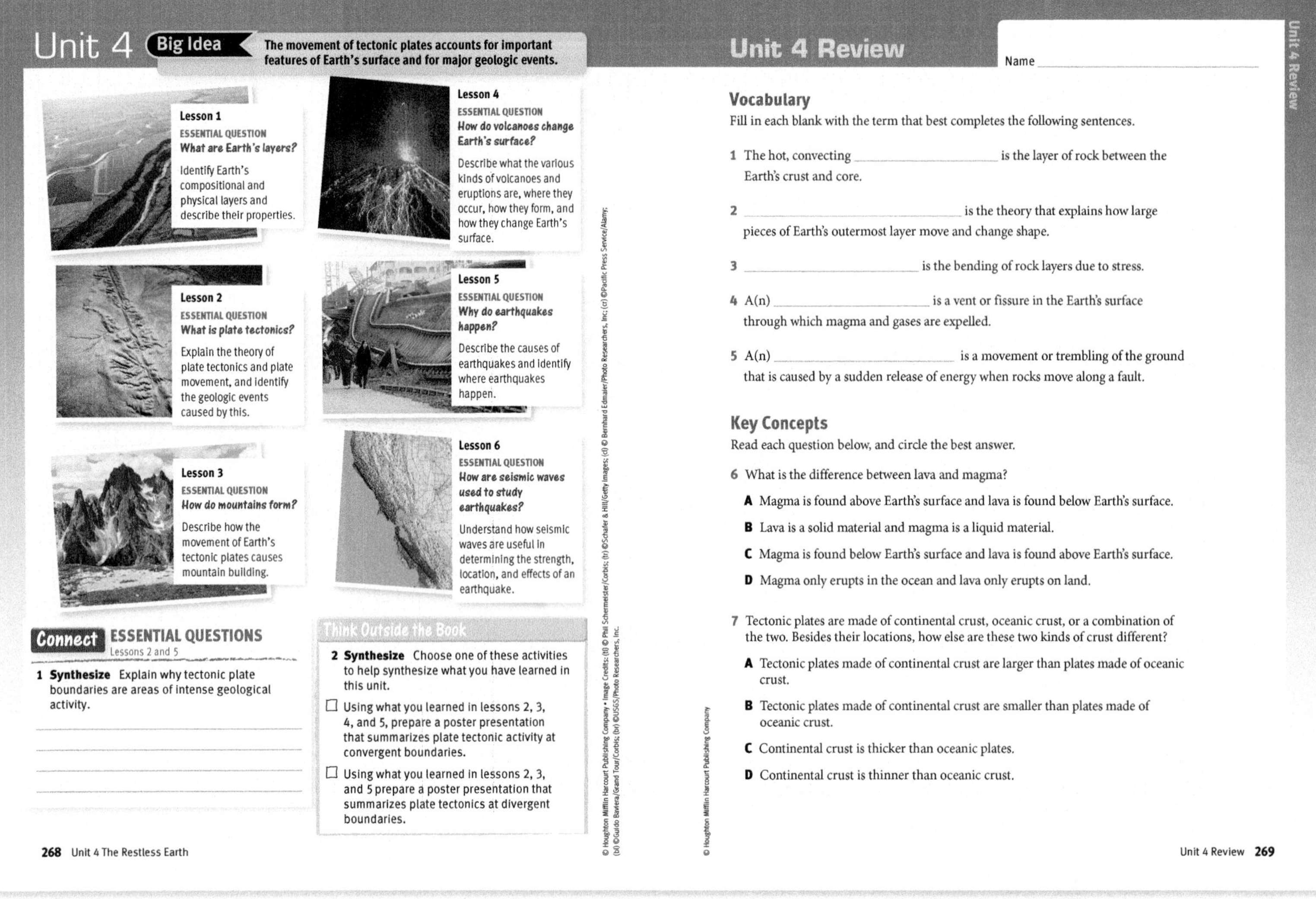

Unit 4 Big Idea The movement of tectonic plates accounts for important features of Earth's surface and for major geologic events.

Lesson 1
ESSENTIAL QUESTION
What are Earth's layers?
Identify Earth's compositional and physical layers and describe their properties.

Lesson 4
ESSENTIAL QUESTION
How do volcanoes change Earth's surface?
Describe what the various kinds of volcanoes and eruptions are, where they occur, how they form, and how they change Earth's surface.

Lesson 2
ESSENTIAL QUESTION
What is plate tectonics?
Explain the theory of plate tectonics and plate movement, and identify the geologic events caused by this.

Lesson 5
ESSENTIAL QUESTION
Why do earthquakes happen?
Describe the causes of earthquakes and identify where earthquakes happen.

Lesson 3
ESSENTIAL QUESTION
How do mountains form?
Describe how the movement of Earth's tectonic plates causes mountain building.

Lesson 6
ESSENTIAL QUESTION
How are seismic waves used to study earthquakes?
Understand how seismic waves are useful in determining the strength, location, and effects of an earthquake.

Connect ESSENTIAL QUESTIONS
Lessons 2 and 5

1 Synthesize Explain why tectonic plate boundaries are areas of intense geological activity.

Think Outside the Book

2 Synthesize Choose one of these activities to help synthesize what you have learned in this unit.

☐ Using what you learned in lessons 2, 3, 4, and 5, prepare a poster presentation that summarizes plate tectonic activity at convergent boundaries.

☐ Using what you learned in lessons 2, 3, and 5 prepare a poster presentation that summarizes plate tectonics at divergent boundaries.

268 Unit 4 The Restless Earth

Unit 4 Review

Name ______

Vocabulary
Fill in each blank with the term that best completes the following sentences.

1 The hot, convecting ______ is the layer of rock between the Earth's crust and core.

2 ______ is the theory that explains how large pieces of Earth's outermost layer move and change shape.

3 ______ is the bending of rock layers due to stress.

4 A(n) ______ is a vent or fissure in the Earth's surface through which magma and gases are expelled.

5 A(n) ______ is a movement or trembling of the ground that is caused by a sudden release of energy when rocks move along a fault.

Key Concepts
Read each question below, and circle the best answer.

6 What is the difference between lava and magma?
A Magma is found above Earth's surface and lava is found below Earth's surface.
B Lava is a solid material and magma is a liquid material.
C Magma is found below Earth's surface and lava is found above Earth's surface.
D Magma only erupts in the ocean and lava only erupts on land.

7 Tectonic plates are made of continental crust, oceanic crust, or a combination of the two. Besides their locations, how else are these two kinds of crust different?
A Tectonic plates made of continental crust are larger than plates made of oceanic crust.
B Tectonic plates made of continental crust are smaller than plates made of oceanic crust.
C Continental crust is thicker than oceanic plates.
D Continental crust is thinner than oceanic crust.

Unit 4 Review 269

Unit Summary Answers

1. At tectonic plate boundaries, Earth's crust is either pushed together, pulled apart, or sheared. This causes earthquakes. It also causes deformation in the form of folds and faults. This forms rift valleys or mountains over time. A tectonic slab melting under another plate can cause volcanism. A rift valley can also allow magma to rise and cause volcanism.
2. Option 1: Posters should include: Two plates traveling toward each other can cause mountain building, volcanism, and earthquakes. Plates collide and rock can be uplifted, forming mountains. One plate may be subducted beneath the other. The plate being subducted can partially melt, causing volcanism.

   Option 2: Posters should include: Two plates move away from each other, creating rift valleys, mid-ocean ridges, and sea-floor spreading. Where plates separate, magma can come up through cracks. It erupts as lava, cools, and forms new oceanic crust. This new crust sits higher than older crust, forming mid-ocean ridges. Faults form, and earthquakes can occur along them.

Unit Review Response to Intervention

A Quick Grading Chart follows the Answers. See the Assessment Guide for more detail about correct and incorrect answer choices. Refer back to the Lesson Planning pages for activities and assignments that can be used as remediation for students who answer questions incorrectly.

Answers

1. mantle The mantle is the middle layer of three layers of the Earth—the core, the crust, and the mantle. (Lesson 1)
2. Plate tectonics Earth's lithosphere is divided into tectonic plates, which move around on top of the convecting asthenosphere. (Lesson 2)
3. Folding Folding is a result of the stress from tectonic forces over a long period of time. (Lesson 2)
4. volcano Volcanoes are vents or fissures on Earth's surface where magma and gases are expelled. (Lesson 4)

Name ____________________

8 In the diagram below, an earthquake is taking place.

Cross Section of Lithosphere during an Earthquake

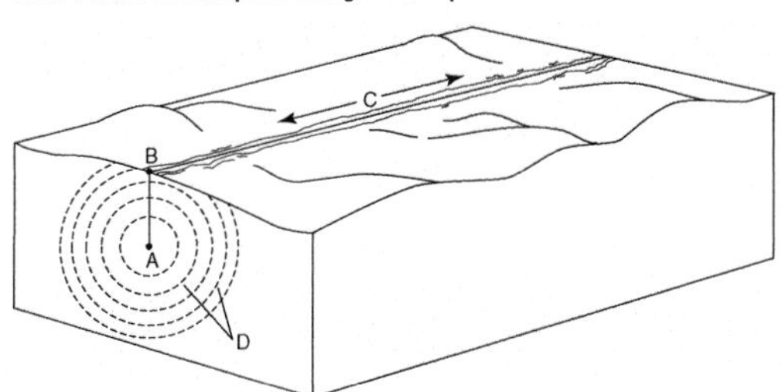

Where is the focus of the earthquake located?

A Point A

B Point B

C along the line labeled C

D along the series of circles labeled D

9 Volcanic eruptions can have many characteristics. They can be slow, fast, calm, explosive, or a combination of these. Which type of eruption is associated with the release of pyroclastic materials?

A a calm eruption

B an explosive eruption

C a fast eruption

D a slow eruption

10 What happens at a divergent tectonic plate boundary?

A Two tectonic plates move horizontally past one another.

B Two tectonic plates pull away from each other, forming a rift valley or mid-ocean ridge.

C Two tectonic plates come together to form one plate.

D Two tectonic plates collide, causing subduction.

11 A major tsunami occurred in the Indian Ocean on December 26, 2004 resulting in the loss of thousands of lives. The tsunami was caused by a major earthquake that originated below the point on the map on the ocean floor. The dashed lines on the map indicate the path of the tsunami's waves.

December 2004 Tsunami

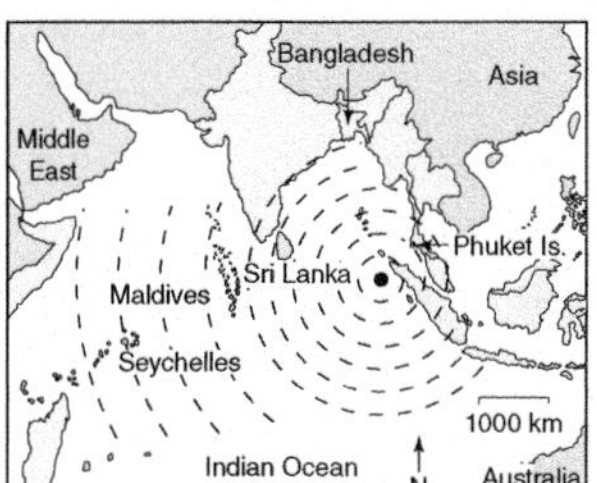

What term refers to the point on the ocean's surface indicated by the dot at the center of the waves?

A fault boundary

B earthquake focus

C earthquake epicenter

D tectonic plate boundary

12 Which of the following is a major difference between Earth's inner core and Earth's outer core?

A The inner core is liquid and the outer core is solid.

B The inner core is solid and the outer core is liquid.

C The inner core is gas and the outer core is solid.

D The inner core is solid and the outer core is gas.

13 Volcanic islands can form over hot spots. The Hawaiian Islands started forming over a hot spot in the Pacific Ocean millions of years ago. What process causes the hot, solid rock to rise through the mantle at these locations?

A condensation

B conduction

C convection

D radiation

Answers *(continued)*

5. earthquake Potential energy builds up along the fault when it is locking; then when the fault slips, the energy is released in the form of an earthquake. (Lesson 5)
6. Answer C is correct because magma is below Earth's surface and lava is above Earth's surface. (Lesson 4)
7. Answer C is correct because continental crust is thicker than oceanic crust. (Lesson 2)
8. Answer A is correct because the focus is the point at which an earthquake originates, which is beneath the surface of Earth and usually along a fault. (Lesson 6)
9. Answer B is correct because an explosive eruption typically releases pyroclastic materials. (Lesson 4)
10. Answer B is correct because plates move away from each other at divergent boundaries and commonly form rift valleys and mid-ocean ridges. (Lesson 2)
11. Answer C is correct because the epicenter is the point on Earth's surface directly above the focus. (Lesson 6)
12. Answer B is correct because the inner core is solid and the outer core is liquid. (Lesson 1)
13. Answer C is correct because convection is the transfer of energy by the movement of matter. (Lesson 4)
14. Answer B is correct because A is the core, B is the mantle, and C is the crust. (Lesson 1)
15. Answer B is correct because these five layers are divided based on physical properties. (Lesson 1)
16. Answer C is correct because the lines marked by J are pointing to a fault line.(Lesson 2)
17. Answer D is correct because there are no plate boundaries inside the continent of Africa along which earthquakes would take place. (Lesson 5)

Name ____________

14 Earth's three compositional layers are the mantle, core, and crust.

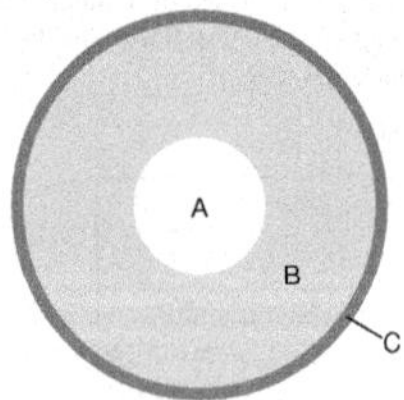

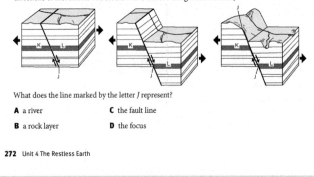

Which statement below is correct?

A A is the crust, B is the core, and C is the mantle.

B A is the core, B is the mantle, and C is the crust.

C A is the inner core, B is the outer core, and C is the mantle.

D A is the core, B is the crust, and C is the mantle.

15 Earth can be divided into five layers: lithosphere, asthenosphere, mesosphere, outer core, and inner core. Which properties are used to make these divisions?

A compositional properties

B physical properties

C chemical properties

D elemental properties

16 This diagram shows the formation of a fault-block mountain. Arrows outside of the blocks show the directions of force. Arrows inside the blocks show the directions of movement. The blocks *K* and *L* move along a line marked *J*.

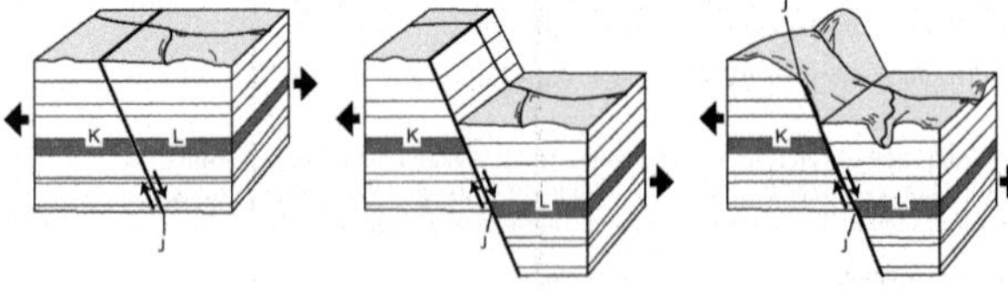

What does the line marked by the letter *J* represent?

A a river

B a rock layer

C the fault line

D the focus

© Houghton Mifflin Harcourt Publishing Company

17 The map below shows the epicenters of some major earthquakes of 2003.

Locations of Major Earthquakes in 2003

Atlantic Ocean

Pacific Ocean

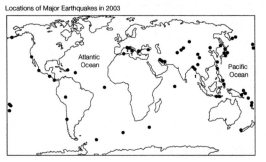

What is the most likely reason that there were no major earthquakes recorded in the interior of the continent of Africa?

A There are no faults in Africa.

B The landmass of Africa is too large to be affected by earthquakes.

C The plate boundary inside Africa is too small to form earthquakes.

D No major plate boundaries cut through the continent of Africa.

Critical Thinking

Answer the following questions in the space provided.

18 Explain how a convergent boundary is different from a transform boundary. Then, name one thing that commonly occurs along both convergent boundaries and transform boundaries.

Answers *(continued)*

18. Key Elements:
    - At a convergent boundary, the tectonic plates move toward each other. Mountain building, volcanism, subduction, and large earthquakes occur at these boundaries. At a transform boundary, the two plates slide past each other. Mountain building and volcanism are uncommon along the boundaries. Earthquakes can occur often along these boundaries.
    - Earthquakes occur along both types. (Lessons 2, 3, 4, and 5)
19. Key Elements:
    - A is the lithosphere, B is the asthenosphere, and C is the mesosphere.
    - The lithosphere is the crust and rigid upper mantle, and it is divided up as tectonic plates that "float" on top of the asthenosphere. The asthenosphere is slow-flowing rock, and the mesosphere is the lower part of the mantle where the rock flows even more slowly. Convection in the mantle is a driving force of the tectonic plates of the lithosphere. (Lessons 1, 2)
20. Key Elements:
    - The Moment Magnitude scale measures earthquake strength based on the size of the area of the fault that moves, the average distance that the fault moves, and the rigidity of the rocks in the fault. The larger the number is, the stronger the earthquake was.
    - The Richter scale measures the ground motion from an earthquake to find the earthquake's strength.
    - Measurements from the Richter scale could be misleading because each time the magnitude increases by one unit, the measured ground motion is 10 times greater. Therefore, a magnitude 2 has 10 times the ground motion as a magnitude 1, and magnitude 3 has 100 times the ground motion of a magnitude 1! You can see how this exponentially increases as you go up the scale. (Lesson 6)

19 The diagram below shows the five physical layers of Earth.

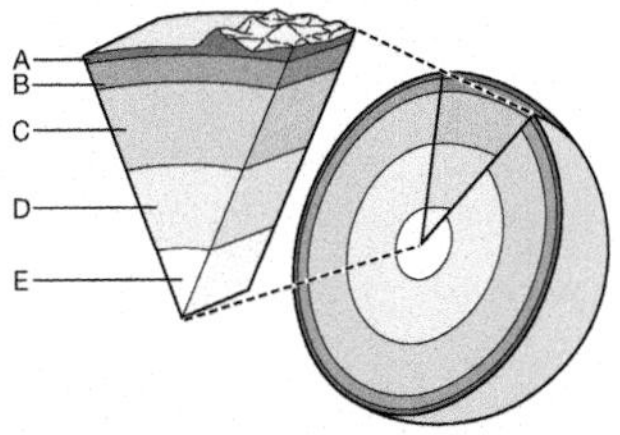

A
B
C
D
E

Identify the physical layers A, B, and C. Describe the relationship between these layers and how it is important to understanding plate tectonics.

20 Explain the difference between the Richter scale and the Moment Magnitude scale. Why might measurements from the Richter Scale be misleading to someone who does not know how it works?

Connect ESSENTIAL QUESTIONS
Lessons 3 and 4

Answer the following question in the space provided.

21 Explain how forces from tectonic plate movement can build these three types of mountains: folded mountains, fault-block mountains, and volcanic mountains.

Answers *(continued)*

21. Key Elements:

- The movement of tectonic plates produces stress that causes rock to deform (strain). Strain can result in folds and/or faults (this depends on many factors not covered). Faults can create fault-block mountains after a very long time of uplift and erosion. Large folds can create folded mountains. When two plates come together at a convergent margin, subduction can cause volcanic activity, resulting in volcanic mountains.
- Fault-block mountains can also form when tension from divergent boundaries causes faults, and the blocks of rock on either side of the fault move up or drop down relative to other blocks.
- Sometimes, volcanic activity beneath Earth's surface forces magma upward toward Earth's surface. The forces associated with upwelling can cause uplift of the crust, and the lava and other material (such as ash and cinder) erupted from the vent can build up into a mountain over time. (Lessons 3, 4)

Quick Grading Chart

Use the chart below for quick test grading. The lesson correlations can help you target reteaching for missed items.

Item	Answer	Cognitive Complexity	Lesson
1.	—	Low	1
2.	—	Low	2
3.	—	Low	2
4.	—	Low	4
5.	—	Low	5
6.	C	Moderate	4
7.	C	Moderate	2
8.	A	Moderate	6
9.	B	Moderate	4
10.	B	Moderate	2
11.	C	Moderate	6
12.	B	Moderate	1
13.	C	Moderate	4
14.	B	Moderate	1
15.	B	Moderate	1
16.	C	Moderate	2
17.	D	Moderate	5
18.	—	Moderate	2, 3, 4, 5
19.	—	Moderate	1, 2
20.	—	Moderate	6
21.	—	Moderate	3, 4

Cognitive Complexity refers to the demand on thinking associated with an item, and may vary with the answer choices, the number of steps required to arrive at an answer, and other factors, but not the ability level of the student.

Teacher Notes

Resources

Student Edition Resources

Teacher Edition Resources

Student Edition

Handbook

References

Mineral Properties

Here are five steps to take in mineral identification:

1 Determine the color of the mineral. Is it light-colored, dark-colored, or a specific color?

2 Determine the luster of the mineral. Is it metallic or non-metallic?

3 Determine the color of any powder left by its streak.

4 Determine the hardness of your mineral. Is it soft, hard, or very hard? Using a glass plate, see if the mineral scratches it.

5 Determine whether your sample has cleavage or any special properties.

TERMS TO KNOW	DEFINITION
adamantine	a non-metallic luster like that of a diamond
cleavage	how a mineral breaks when subject to stress on a particular plane
luster	the state or quality of shining by reflecting light
streak	the color of a mineral when it is powdered
submetallic	between metallic and nonmetallic in luster
vitreous	glass-like type of luster

Silicate Minerals					
Mineral	**Color**	**Luster**	**Streak**	**Hardness**	**Cleavage and Special Properties**
Beryl	deep green, pink, white, bluish green, or yellow	vitreous	white	7.5–8	1 cleavage direction; some varieties fluoresce in ultraviolet light
Chlorite	green	vitreous to pearly	pale green	2–2.5	1 cleavage direction
Garnet	green, red, brown, black	vitreous	white	6.5–7.5	no cleavage
Hornblende	dark green, brown, or black	vitreous	none	5–6	2 cleavage directions
Muscovite	colorless, silvery white, or brown	vitreous or pearly	white	2–2.5	1 cleavage direction
Olivine	olive green, yellow	vitreous	white or none	6.5–7	no cleavage
Orthoclase	colorless, white, pink, or other colors	vitreous	white or none	6	2 cleavage directions
Plagioclase	colorless, white, yellow, pink, green	vitreous	white	6	2 cleavage directions
Quartz	colorless or white; any color when not pure	vitreous or waxy	white or none	7	no cleavage

Nonsilicate Minerals					
Mineral	**Color**	**Luster**	**Streak**	**Hardness**	**Cleavage and Special Properties**
Native Elements					
Copper	copper-red	metallic	copper-red	2.5–3	no cleavage
Diamond	pale yellow or colorless	adamantine	none	10	4 cleavage directions
Graphite	black to gray	submetallic	black	1–2	1 cleavage direction
Carbonates					
Aragonite	colorless, white, or pale yellow	vitreous	white	3.5–4	2 cleavage directions; reacts with hydrochloric acid
Calcite	colorless or white to tan	vitreous	white	3	3 cleavage directions; reacts with weak acid; double refraction
Halides					
Fluorite	light green, yellow, purple, bluish green, or other colors	vitreous	none	4	4 cleavage directions; some varieties fluoresce
Halite	white	vitreous	white	2.0–2.5	3 cleavage directions
Oxides					
Hematite	reddish brown to black	metallic to earthy	dark red to red-brown	5.6–6.5	no cleavage; magnetic when heated
Magnetite	iron-black	metallic	black	5.5–6.5	no cleavage; magnetic
Sulfates					
Anhydrite	colorless, bluish, or violet	vitreous to pearly	white	3–3.5	3 cleavage directions
Gypsum	white, pink, gray, or colorless	vitreous, pearly, or silky	white	2.0	3 cleavage directions
Sulfides					
Galena	lead-gray	metallic	lead-gray to black	2.5–2.8	3 cleavage directions
Pyrite	brassy yellow	metallic	greenish, brownish, or black	6–6.5	no cleavage

© Houghton Mifflin Harcourt Publishing Company

References

Geologic Time Scale

Geologists developed the geologic time scale to represent the 4.6 billion years of Earth's history that have passed since Earth formed. This scale divides Earth's history into blocks of time. The boundaries between these time intervals (shown in millions of years ago or mya in the table below), represent major changes in Earth's history. Some boundaries are defined by mass extinctions, major changes in Earth's surface, and/or major changes in Earth's climate.

Divisions of Time

The divisions of time shown here represent major changes in Earth's surface and when life developed and changed significantly on Earth. As new evidence is found, the boundaries of these divisions may shift. The Phanerozoic eon is divided into three eras. The beginning of each of these eras represents a change in the types of organisms that dominated Earth. And, each era is commonly characterized by the types of organisms that dominated the era. These eras are divided into periods, and periods are divided into epochs.

The four major divisions that encompass the history of life on Earth are Precambrian time, the Paleozoic era, the Mesozoic era, and the Cenozoic era. The largest divisions are eons. **Precambrian time** is made up of the first three eons, over 4 billion years of Earth's history.

The **Paleozoic era** lasted from 542 mya to 251 mya. All major plant groups, except flowering plants, appeared during this era. By the end of the era, reptiles, winged insects, and fishes had also appeared. The largest known mass extinction occurred at the end of this era.

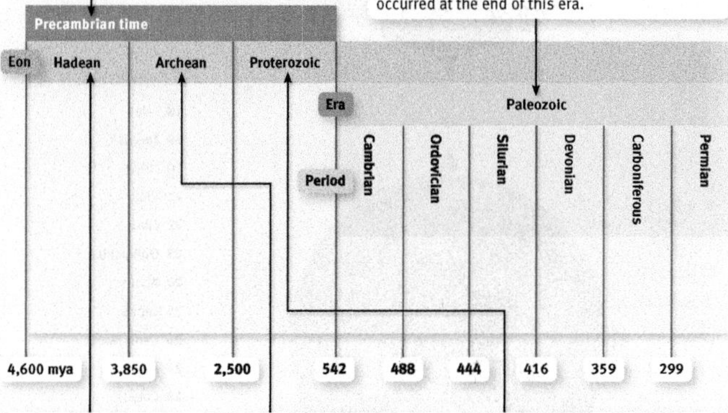

The **Phanerozoic eon** began 542 mya. We live in this eon.

The **Mesozoic era** lasted from 251 mya to 65.5 mya. During this era, many kinds of dinosaurs dominated land, and giant lizards swam in the ocean. The first birds, mammals, and flowering plants also appeared during this time. About two-thirds of all land species went extinct at the end of this era.

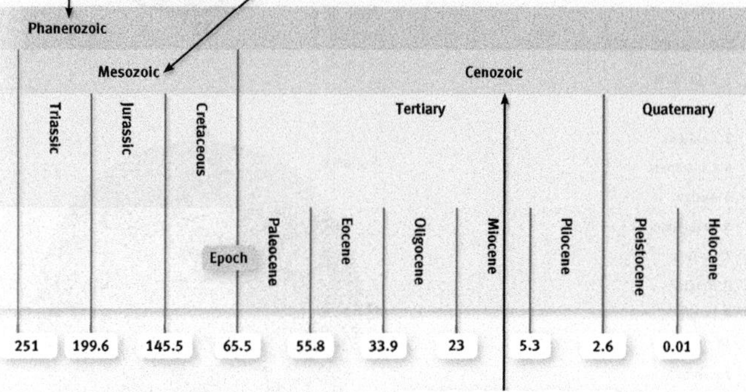

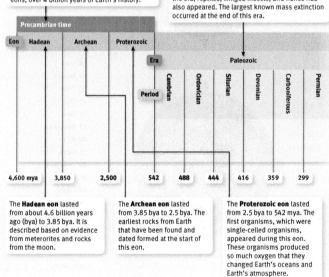

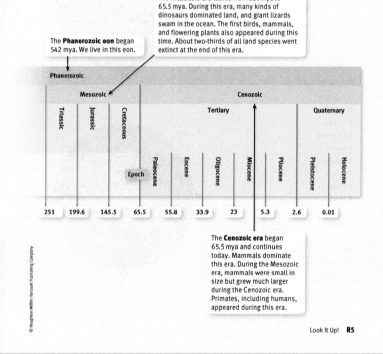

The **Hadean eon** lasted from about 4.6 billion years ago (bya) to 3.85 bya. It is described based on evidence from meteorites and rocks from the moon.

The **Archean eon** lasted from 3.85 bya to 2.5 bya. The earliest rocks from Earth that have been found and dated formed at the start of this eon.

The **Proterozoic eon** lasted from 2.5 bya to 542 mya. The first organisms, which were single-celled organisms, appeared during this eon. These organisms produced so much oxygen that they changed Earth's oceans and Earth's atmosphere.

The **Cenozoic era** began 65.5 mya and continues today. Mammals dominate this era. During the Mesozoic era, mammals were small in size but grew much larger during the Cenozoic era. Primates, including humans, appeared during this era.

Star Charts for the Northern Hemisphere

A star chart is a map of the stars in the night sky. It shows the names and positions of constellations and major stars. Star charts can be used to identify constellations and even to orient yourself using Polaris, the North Star.

Because Earth moves through space, different constellations are visible at different times of the year. The star charts on these pages show the constellations visible during each season in the Northern Hemisphere.

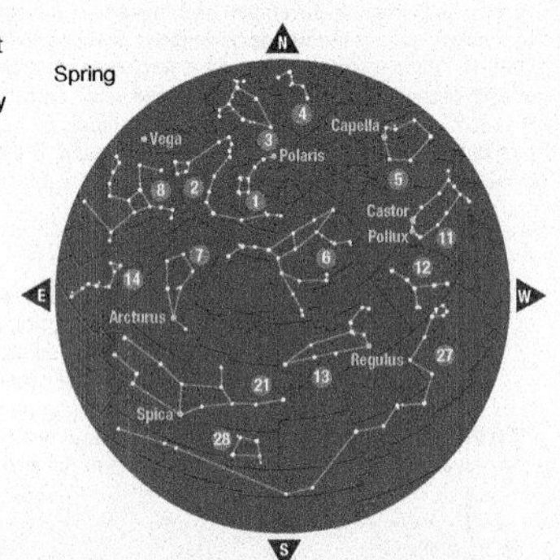
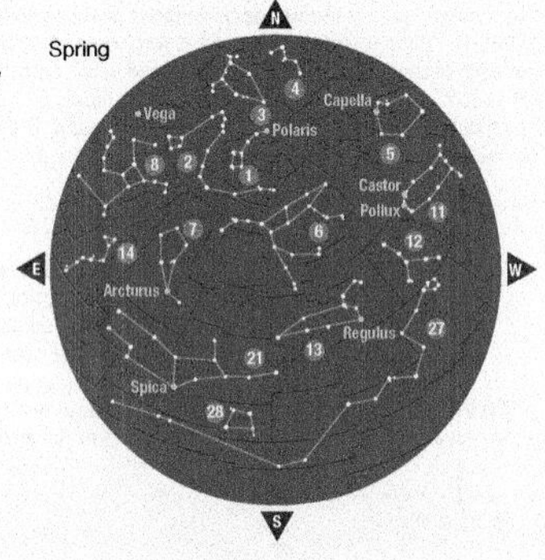

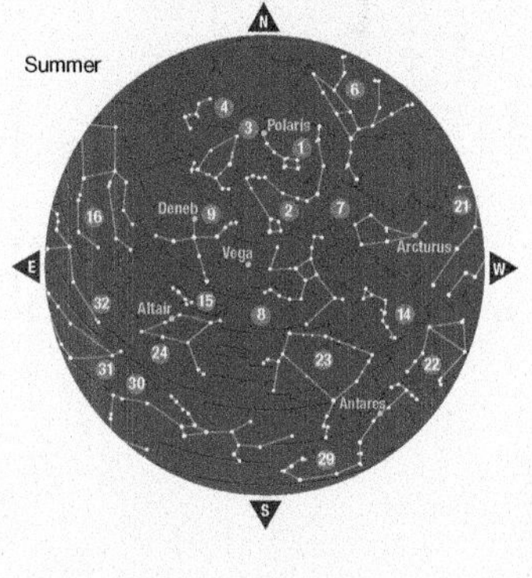

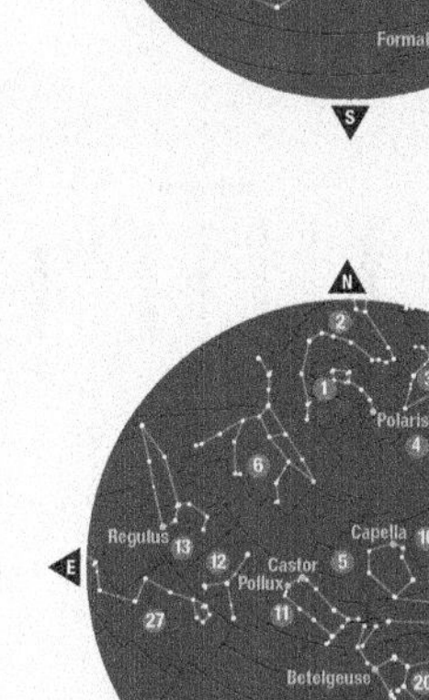

Winter

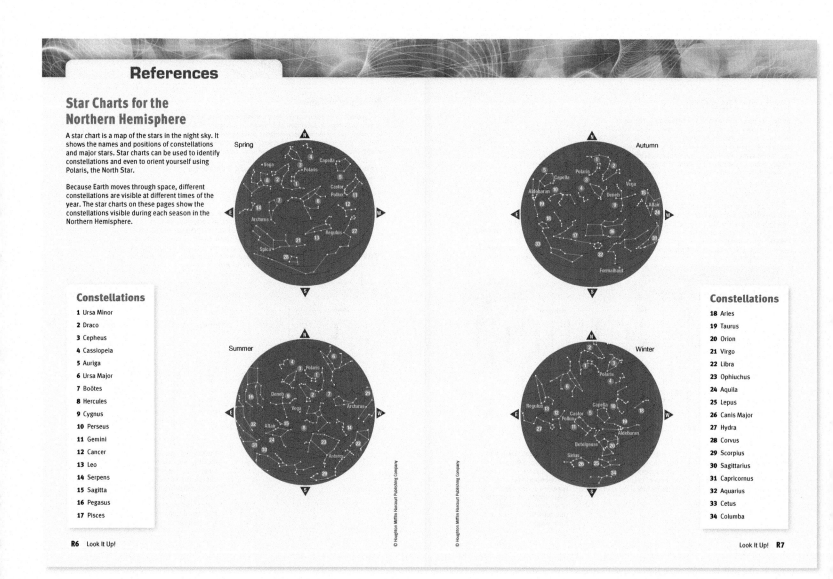

Constellations

1 Ursa Minor
2 Draco
3 Cepheus
4 Cassiopeia
5 Auriga
6 Ursa Major
7 Boötes
8 Hercules
9 Cygnus
10 Perseus
11 Gemini
12 Cancer
13 Leo
14 Serpens
15 Sagitta
16 Pegasus
17 Pisces

Constellations

18 Aries
19 Taurus
20 Orion
21 Virgo
22 Libra
23 Ophiuchus
24 Aquila
25 Lepus
26 Canis Major
27 Hydra
28 Corvus
29 Scorpius
30 Sagittarius
31 Capricornus
32 Aquarius
33 Cetus
34 Columba

References

World Map

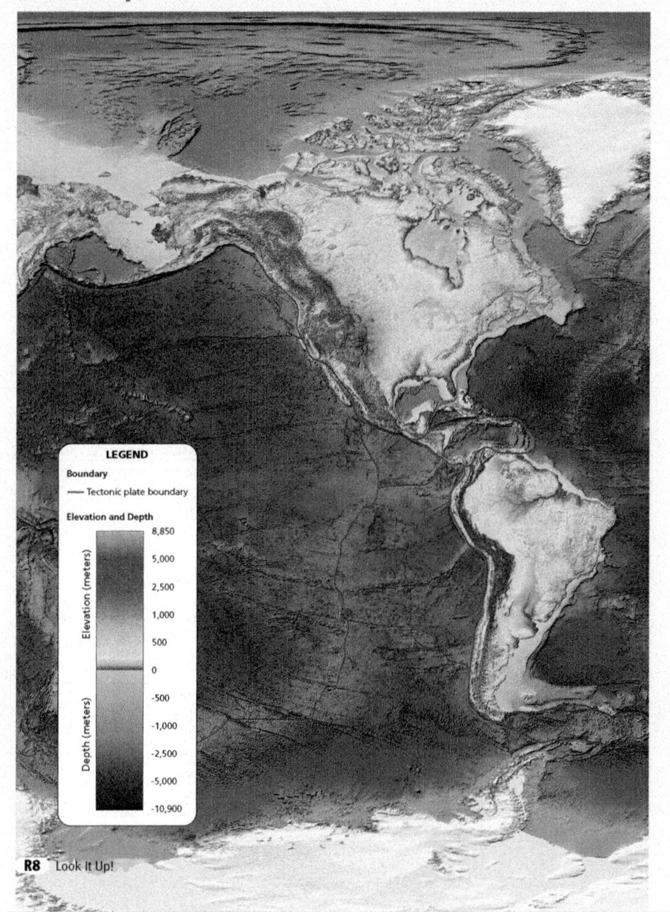

Classification of Living Things

Domains and Kingdoms

All organisms belong to one of three domains: Domain Archaea, Domain Bacteria, or Domain Eukarya. Some of the groups within these domains are shown below. (Remember that genus names are italicized.)

Domain Archaea

The organisms in this domain are single-celled prokaryotes, many of which live in extreme environments.

Archaea		
Group	**Example**	**Characteristics**
Methanogens	*Methanococcus*	produce methane gas; can't live in oxygen
Thermophiles	*Sulpholobus*	require sulphur; can't live in oxygen
Halophiles	*Halococcus*	live in very salty environments; most can live in oxygen

Domain Bacteria

Organisms in this domain are single-celled prokaryotes and are found in almost every environment on Earth.

Bacteria		
Group	**Example**	**Characteristics**
Bacilli	*Escherichia*	rod shaped; some bacilli fix nitrogen; some cause disease
Cocci	*Streptococcus*	spherical shaped; some cause disease; can form spores
Spirilla	*Treponema*	spiral shaped; cause diseases such as syphilis and Lyme disease

Domain Eukarya

Organisms in this domain are single-celled or multicellular eukaryotes.

Kingdom Protista Many protists resemble fungi, plants, or animals, but are smaller and simpler in structure. Most are single celled.

Protists		
Group	**Example**	**Characteristics**
Sarcodines	*Amoeba*	radiolarians; single-celled consumers
Ciliates	*Paramecium*	single-celled consumers
Flagellates	*Trypanosoma*	single-celled parasites
Sporozoans	*Plasmodium*	single-celled parasites
Euglenas	*Euglena*	single celled; photosynthesize
Diatoms	*Pinnularia*	most are single celled; photosynthesize
Dinoflagellates	*Gymnodinium*	single celled; some photosynthesize
Algae	*Volvox*	single celled or multicellular; photosynthesize
Slime molds	*Physarum*	single celled or multicellular; consumers or decomposers
Water molds	powdery mildew	single celled or multicellular; parasites or decomposers

Kingdom Fungi Most fungi are multicellular. Their cells have thick cell walls. Fungi absorb food from their environment.

Fungi		
Group	**Examples**	**Characteristics**
Threadlike fungi	bread mold	spherical; decomposers
Sac fungi	yeast; morels	saclike; parasites and decomposers
Club fungi	mushrooms; rusts; smuts	club shaped; parasites and decomposers
Lichens	British soldier	a partnership between a fungus and an alga

Kingdom Plantae Plants are multicellular and have cell walls made of cellulose. Plants make their own food through photosynthesis. Plants are classified into divisions instead of phyla.

Plants		
Group	**Examples**	**Characteristics**
Bryophytes	mosses; liverworts	no vascular tissue; reproduce by spores
Club mosses	*Lycopodium*; ground pine	grow in wooded areas; reproduce by spores
Horsetails	rushes	grow in wetland areas; reproduce by spores
Ferns	spleenworts; sensitive fern	large leaves called fronds; reproduce by spores
Conifers	pines; spruces; firs	needlelike leaves; reproduce by seeds made in cones
Cycads	*Zamia*	slow growing; reproduce by seeds made in large cones
Gnetophytes	*Welwitschia*	only three living families; reproduce by seeds
Ginkgoes	*Ginkgo*	only one living species; reproduce by seeds
Angiosperms	all flowering plants	reproduce by seeds made in flowers; fruit

Kingdom Animalia Animals are multicellular. Their cells do not have cell walls. Most animals have specialized tissues and complex organ systems. Animals get food by eating other organisms.

Animals		
Group	**Examples**	**Characteristics**
Sponges	glass sponges	no symmetry or specialized tissues; aquatic
Cnidarians	jellyfish; coral	radial symmetry; aquatic
Flatworms	planaria; tapeworms; flukes	bilateral symmetry; organ systems
Roundworms	*Trichina*; hookworms	bilateral symmetry; organ systems
Annelids	earthworms; leeches	bilateral symmetry; organ systems
Mollusks	snails; octopuses	bilateral symmetry; organ systems
Echinoderms	sea stars; sand dollars	radial symmetry; organ systems
Arthropods	insects; spiders; lobsters	bilateral symmetry; organ systems
Chordates	fish; amphibians; reptiles; birds; mammals	bilateral symmetry; complex organ systems

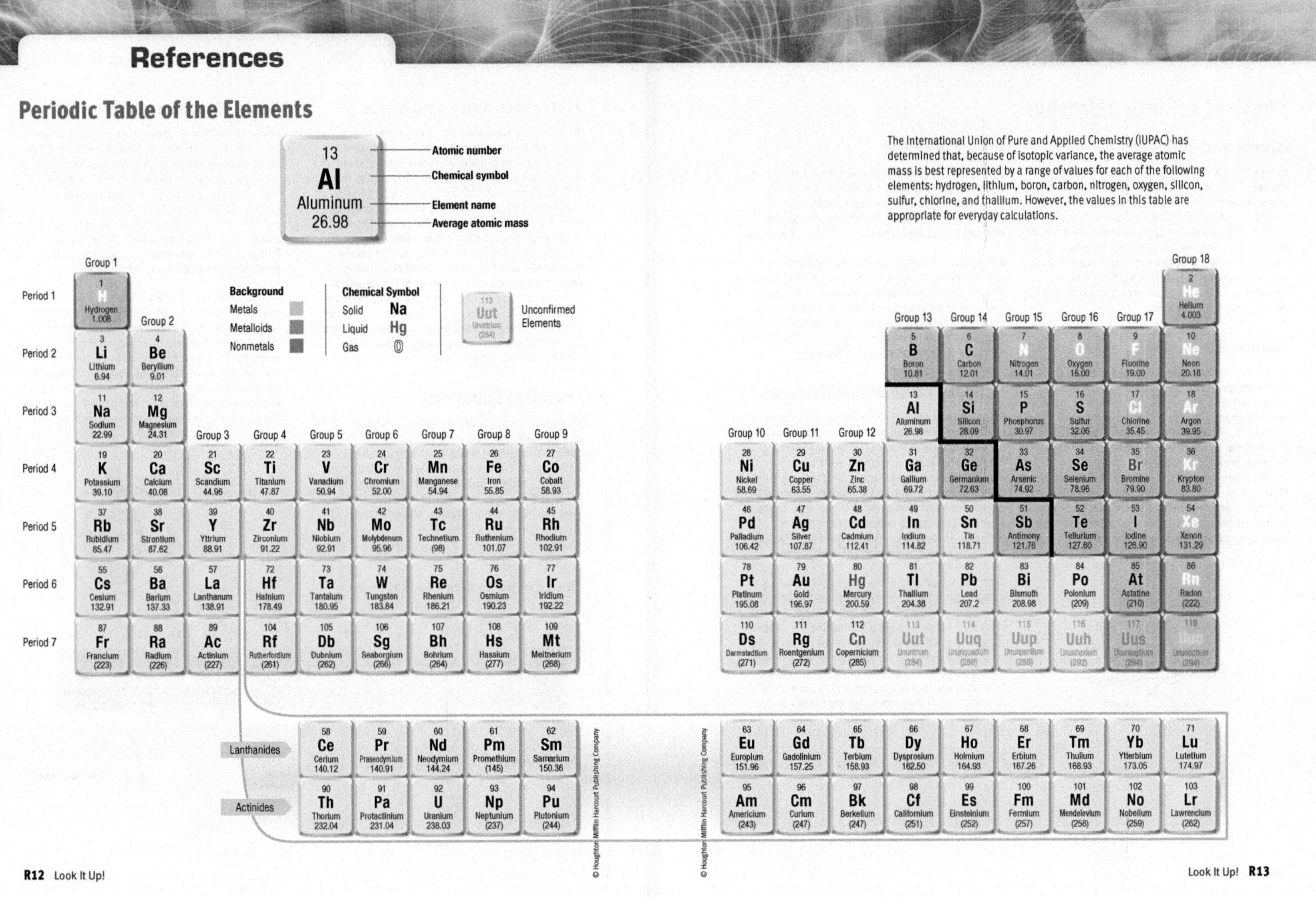

References

Periodic Table of the Elements

Key	
13	Atomic number
Al	Chemical symbol
Aluminum	Element name
26.98	Average atomic mass

Background: Metals, Metalloids, Nonmetals

Chemical Symbol: Solid Na; Liquid Hg; Gas O

113 Uut Ununtrium (284) — Unconfirmed Elements

The International Union of Pure and Applied Chemistry (IUPAC) has determined that, because of isotopic variance, the average atomic mass is best represented by a range of values for each of the following elements: hydrogen, lithium, boron, carbon, nitrogen, oxygen, silicon, sulfur, chlorine, and thallium. However, the values in this table are appropriate for everyday calculations.

	Group 1	Group 2	Group 3	Group 4	Group 5	Group 6	Group 7	Group 8	Group 9	Group 10	Group 11	Group 12	Group 13	Group 14	Group 15	Group 16	Group 17	Group 18
Period 1	1 H Hydrogen 1.008																	2 He Helium 4.003
Period 2	3 Li Lithium 6.94	4 Be Beryllium 9.01											5 B Boron 10.81	6 C Carbon 12.01	7 N Nitrogen 14.01	8 O Oxygen 16.00	9 F Fluorine 19.00	10 Ne Neon 20.18
Period 3	11 Na Sodium 22.99	12 Mg Magnesium 24.31											13 Al Aluminum 26.98	14 Si Silicon 28.09	15 P Phosphorus 30.97	16 S Sulfur 32.06	17 Cl Chlorine 35.45	18 Ar Argon 39.95
Period 4	19 K Potassium 39.10	20 Ca Calcium 40.08	21 Sc Scandium 44.96	22 Ti Titanium 47.87	23 V Vanadium 50.94	24 Cr Chromium 52.00	25 Mn Manganese 54.94	26 Fe Iron 55.85	27 Co Cobalt 58.93	28 Ni Nickel 58.69	29 Cu Copper 63.55	30 Zn Zinc 65.38	31 Ga Gallium 69.72	32 Ge Germanium 72.63	33 As Arsenic 74.92	34 Se Selenium 78.96	35 Br Bromine 79.90	36 Kr Krypton 83.80
Period 5	37 Rb Rubidium 85.47	38 Sr Strontium 87.62	39 Y Yttrium 88.91	40 Zr Zirconium 91.22	41 Nb Niobium 92.91	42 Mo Molybdenum 95.96	43 Tc Technetium (98)	44 Ru Ruthenium 101.07	45 Rh Rhodium 102.91	46 Pd Palladium 106.42	47 Ag Silver 107.87	48 Cd Cadmium 112.41	49 In Indium 114.82	50 Sn Tin 118.71	51 Sb Antimony 121.76	52 Te Tellurium 127.60	53 I Iodine 126.90	54 Xe Xenon 131.29
Period 6	55 Cs Cesium 132.91	56 Ba Barium 137.33	57 La Lanthanum 138.91	72 Hf Hafnium 178.49	73 Ta Tantalum 180.95	74 W Tungsten 183.84	75 Re Rhenium 186.21	76 Os Osmium 190.23	77 Ir Iridium 192.22	78 Pt Platinum 195.08	79 Au Gold 196.97	80 Hg Mercury 200.59	81 Tl Thallium 204.38	82 Pb Lead 207.2	83 Bi Bismuth 208.98	84 Po Polonium (209)	85 At Astatine (210)	86 Rn Radon (222)
Period 7	87 Fr Francium (223)	88 Ra Radium (226)	89 Ac Actinium (227)	104 Rf Rutherfordium (261)	105 Db Dubnium (262)	106 Sg Seaborgium (266)	107 Bh Bohrium (264)	108 Hs Hassium (277)	109 Mt Meitnerium (268)	110 Ds Darmstadtium (271)	111 Rg Roentgenium (272)	112 Cn Copernicium (285)	113 Uut Ununtrium (284)	114 Uuq Ununquadium (289)	115 Uup Ununpentium (288)	116 Uuh Ununhexium (292)	117 Uus Ununseptium (294)	118 Ununoctium (294)

Lanthanides	58 Ce Cerium 140.12	59 Pr Praseodymium 140.91	60 Nd Neodymium 144.24	61 Pm Promethium (145)	62 Sm Samarium 150.36	63 Eu Europium 151.96	64 Gd Gadolinium 157.25	65 Tb Terbium 158.93	66 Dy Dysprosium 162.50	67 Ho Holmium 164.93	68 Er Erbium 167.26	69 Tm Thulium 168.93	70 Yb Ytterbium 173.05	71 Lu Lutetium 174.97
Actinides	90 Th Thorium 232.04	91 Pa Protactinium 231.04	92 U Uranium 238.03	93 Np Neptunium (237)	94 Pu Plutonium (244)	95 Am Americium (243)	96 Cm Curium (247)	97 Bk Berkelium (247)	98 Cf Californium (251)	99 Es Einsteinium (252)	100 Fm Fermium (257)	101 Md Mendelevium (258)	102 No Nobelium (259)	103 Lr Lawrencium (262)

© Houghton Mifflin Harcourt Publishing Company

References

Physical Science Refresher

Atoms and Elements

Every object in the universe is made of matter. **Matter** is anything that takes up space and has mass. All matter is made of atoms. An **atom** is the smallest particle into which an element can be divided and still be the same element. An **element**, in turn, is a substance that cannot be broken down into simpler substances by chemical means. Each element consists of only one kind of atom. An element may be made of many atoms, but they are all the same kind of atom.

Atomic Structure

Atoms are made of smaller particles called **electrons, protons,** and **neutrons.** Electrons have a negative electric charge, protons have a positive charge, and neutrons have no electric charge. Together, protons and neutrons form the **nucleus,** or small dense center, of an atom. Because protons are positively charged and neutrons are neutral, the nucleus has a positive charge. Electrons move within an area around the nucleus called the **electron cloud.** Electrons move so quickly that scientists cannot determine their exact speeds and positions at the same time.

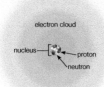

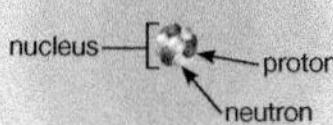

Atomic Number

To help distinguish one element from another, scientists use the atomic numbers of atoms. The **atomic number** is the number of protons in the nucleus of an atom. The atoms of a certain element always have the same number of protons.

When atoms have an equal number of protons and electrons, they are uncharged, or electrically neutral. The atomic number equals the number of electrons in an uncharged atom. The number of neutrons, however, can vary for a given element. Atoms of the same element that have different numbers of neutrons are called **isotopes.**

Periodic Table of the Elements

In the periodic table, each element in the table is in a separate box. And the elements are arranged from left to right in order of increasing atomic number. That is, an uncharged atom of each element has one more electron and one more proton than an uncharged atom of the element to its left. Each horizontal row of the table is called a **period.** Changes in chemical properties of elements across a period correspond to changes in the electron arrangements of their atoms.

Each vertical column of the table is known as a **group.** A group lists elements with similar physical and chemical properties. For this reason, a group is also sometimes called a family. The elements in a group have similar properties because their atoms have the same number of electrons in their outer energy level. For example, the elements helium, neon, argon, krypton, xenon, and radon all have similar properties and are known as the noble gases.

Molecules and Compounds

When two or more elements join chemically, they form a **compound.** A compound is a new substance with properties different from those of the elements that compose it. For example, water, H_2O, is a compound formed when hydrogen (H) and oxygen (O) combine. The smallest complete unit of a compound that has the properties of that compound is called a **molecule.** A chemical formula indicates the elements in a compound. It also indicates the relative number of atoms of each element in the compound. The chemical formula for water is H_2O. So, each water molecule consists of two atoms of hydrogen and one atom of oxygen. The subscript number after the symbol for an element shows how many atoms of that element are in a single molecule of the compound.

Chemical Equations

A chemical reaction occurs when a chemical change takes place. A chemical equation describes a chemical reaction using chemical formulas. The equation indicates the substances that react and the substances that are produced. For example, when carbon and oxygen combine, they can form carbon dioxide, shown in the equation below: $C + O_2 \longrightarrow CO_2$

Acids, Bases, and pH

An **ion** is an atom or group of chemically bonded atoms that has an electric charge because it has lost or gained one or more electrons. When an acid, such as hydrochloric acid, HCl, is mixed with water, it separates into ions. An **acid** is a compound that produces hydrogen ions, H^+, in water. The hydrogen ions then combine with a water molecule to form a hydronium ion, H_3O^+. A **base,** on the other hand, is a substance that produces hydroxide ions, OH^-, in water.

To determine whether a solution is acidic or basic, scientists use pH. The **pH** of a solution is a measure of the hydronium ion concentration in a solution. The pH scale ranges from 0 to 14. Acids have a pH that is less than 7. The lower the number, the more acidic the solution. The middle point, pH = 7, is neutral, neither acidic nor basic. Bases have a pH that is greater than 7. The higher the number is, the more basic the solution.

The pH of Some Common Materials

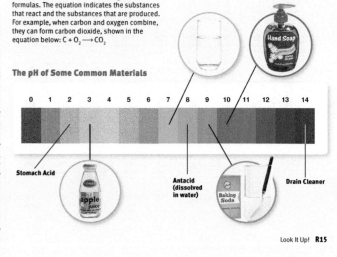

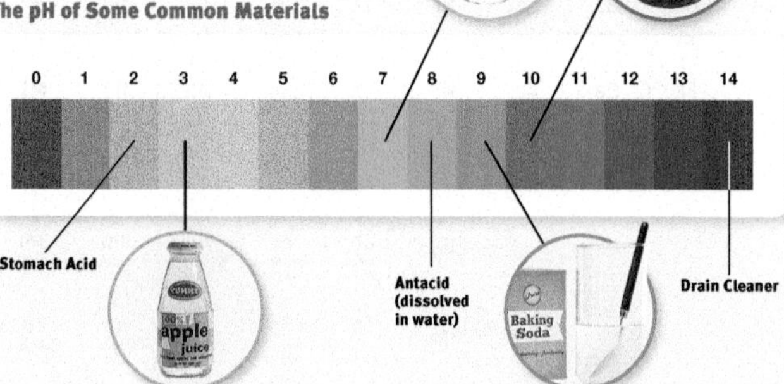

References

Physical Laws and Useful Equations

Law of Conservation of Mass

Mass cannot be created or destroyed during ordinary chemical or physical changes.

The total mass in a closed system is always the same no matter how many physical changes or chemical reactions occur.

Law of Conservation of Energy

Energy can be neither created nor destroyed.

The total amount of energy in a closed system is always the same. Energy can be changed from one form to another, but all of the different forms of energy in a system always add up to the same total amount of energy, no matter how many energy conversions occur.

Law of Universal Gravitation

All objects in the universe attract each other by a force called gravity. The size of the force depends on the masses of the objects and the distance between the objects.

The first part of the law explains why lifting a bowling ball is much harder than lifting a marble. Because the bowling ball has a much larger mass than the marble does, the amount of gravity between Earth and the bowling ball is greater than the amount of gravity between Earth and the marble.

The second part of the law explains why a satellite can remain in orbit around Earth. The satellite is placed at a carefully calculated distance from Earth. This distance is great enough to keep Earth's gravity from pulling the satellite down, yet small enough to keep the satellite from escaping Earth's gravity and wandering off into space.

Newton's Laws of Motion

Newton's first law of motion states that an object at rest remains at rest, and an object in motion remains in motion at constant speed and in a straight line unless acted on by an unbalanced force.

The first part of the law explains why a football will remain on a tee until it is kicked off or until a gust of wind blows it off. The second part of the law explains why a bike rider will continue moving forward after the bike comes to an abrupt stop. Gravity and the friction of the sidewalk will eventually stop the rider.

Newton's second law of motion states that the acceleration of an object depends on the mass of the object and the amount of force applied.

The first part of the law explains why the acceleration of a 4 kg bowling ball will be greater than the acceleration of a 6 kg bowling ball if the same force is applied to both balls. The second part of the law explains why the acceleration of a bowling ball will be greater if a larger force is applied to the bowling ball. The relationship of acceleration (a) to mass (m) and force (F) can be expressed mathematically by the following equation:

$$\text{acceleration} = \frac{\text{force}}{\text{mass}}, \text{ or } a = \frac{F}{m}$$

This equation is often rearranged to read *force* = *mass* × acceleration, or $F = m \times a$

Newton's third law of motion states that whenever one object exerts a force on a second object, the second object exerts an equal and opposite force on the first.

This law explains that a runner is able to move forward because the ground exerts an equal and opposite force on the runner's foot after each step.

Average speed

$$\text{average speed} = \frac{\text{total distance}}{\text{total time}}$$

Example:

A bicycle messenger traveled a distance of 136 km in 8 h. What was the messenger's average speed?

$$\frac{136 \text{ km}}{8 \text{ h}} = 17 \text{ km/h}$$

The messenger's average speed was **17 km/h.**

Average acceleration

$$\text{average acceleration} = \frac{\text{final velocity} - \text{starting velocity}}{\text{time it takes to change velocity}}$$

Example:

Calculate the average acceleration of an Olympic 100 m dash sprinter who reached a velocity of 20 m/s south at the finish line. The race was in a straight line and lasted 10 s.

$$\frac{20 \text{ m/s} - 0 \text{ m/s}}{10 \text{ s}} = 2 \text{ m/s/s}$$

The sprinter's average acceleration was **2 m/s/s south.**

Net force

Forces in the Same Direction

When forces are in the same direction, add the forces together to determine the net force.

Example:

Calculate the net force on a stalled car that is being pushed by two people. One person is pushing with a force of 13 N northwest, and the other person is pushing with a force of 8 N in the same direction.

$$13 \text{ N} + 8 \text{ N} = 21 \text{ N}$$

The net force is **21 N northwest.**

Forces in Opposite Directions

When forces are in opposite directions, subtract the smaller force from the larger force to determine the net force. The net force will be in the direction of the larger force.

Example:

Calculate the net force on a rope that is being pulled on each end. One person is pulling on one end of the rope with a force of 12 N south. Another person is pulling on the opposite end of the rope with a force of 7 N north.

$$12 \text{ N} - 7 \text{ N} = 5 \text{ N}$$

The net force is **5 N south.**

Pressure

Pressure is the force exerted over a given area. The SI unit for pressure is the pascal. Its symbol is Pa.

$$\text{pressure} = \frac{\text{force}}{\text{area}}$$

Example:

Calculate the pressure of the air in a soccer ball if the air exerts a force of 10 N over an area of 0.5 m^2.

$$\text{pressure} = \frac{10\text{N}}{0.5 \text{ m}^2} = \frac{20\text{N}}{\text{m}^2} = 20 \text{ Pa}$$

The pressure of the air inside the soccer ball is **20 Pa.**

A How-To Manual for Active Reading

This book belongs to you, and you are invited to write in it. In fact, the book won't be complete until you do. Sometimes you'll answer a question or follow directions to mark up the text. Other times you'll write down your own thoughts. And when you're done reading and writing in the book, the book will be ready to help you review what you learned and prepare for tests.

Active Reading Annotations

Before you read, you'll often come upon an Active Reading prompt that asks you to underline certain words or number the steps in a process. Here's an example.

12 Identify In this paragraph, number the sequence of sentences that describe replication.

Marking the text this way is called **annotating,** and your marks are called **annotations.** Annotating the text can help you identify important concepts while you read.

There are other ways that you can annotate the text. You can draw an asterisk (*) by vocabulary terms, mark unfamiliar or confusing terms and information with a question mark (?), and mark main ideas with a double underline. And you can even invent your own marks to annotate the text!

Other Annotating Opportunities

Keep your pencil, pen, or highlighter nearby as you read, so you can make a note or highlight an important point at any time. Here are a few ideas to get you started.

- Notice the headings in red and blue. The blue headings are questions that point to the main idea of what you're reading. The red headings are answers to the questions in the blue ones. Together these headings outline the content of the lesson. After reading a lesson, you could write your own answers to the questions.
- Notice the bold-faced words that are highlighted in yellow. They are highlighted so that you can easily find them again on the page where they are defined. As you read or as you review, challenge yourself to write your own sentence using the bold-faced term.
- Make a note in the margin at any time. You might
  - Ask a "What if" question
  - Comment on what you read
  - Make a connection to something you read elsewhere
  - Make a logical conclusion from the text

Use your own language and abbreviations. Invent a code, such as using circles and boxes around words to remind you of their importance or relation to each other. Your annotations will help you remember your questions for class discussions, and when you go back to the lesson later, you may be able to fill in what you didn't understand the first time you read it. Like a scientist in the field or in a lab, you will be recording your questions and observations for analysis later.

Active Reading Questions

After you read, you'll often come upon Active Reading questions that ask you to think about what you've just read. You'll write your answer underneath the question. Here's an example.

Active Reading

8 Describe Where are phosphate groups found in a DNA molecule?

This type of question helps you sum up what you've just read and pull out the most important ideas from the passage. In this case the question asks you to **describe** the structure of a DNA molecule that you have just read about. Other times you may be asked to do such things as **apply** a concept, **compare** two concepts, **summarize** a process, or **identify a cause-and-effect** relationship. You'll be strengthening those critical thinking skills that you'll use often in learning about science.

Reading and Study Skills

Using Graphic Organizers to Take Notes

Graphic organizers help you remember information as you read it for the first time and as you study it later. There are dozens of graphic organizers to choose from, so the first trick is to choose the one that's best suited to your purpose. Following are some graphic organizers to use for different purposes.

To remember lots of information	To relate a central idea to subordinate details	To describe a process	To make a comparison
• Arrange data in a Content Frame • Use Combination Notes to describe a concept in words and pictures	• Show relationships with a Mind Map or a Main Idea Web • Sum up relationships among many things with a Concept Map	• Use a Process Diagram to explain a procedure • Show a chain of events and results in a Cause-and-Effect Chart	• Compare two or more closely related things in a Venn Diagram

Content Frame

1 Make a four-column chart.

2 Fill the first column with categories (e.g., snail, ant, earthworm) and the first row with descriptive information (e.g., group, characteristic, appearance).

3 Fill the chart with details that belong in each row and column.

4 When you finish, you'll have a study aid that helps you compare one category to another.

Invertebrates

NAME	GROUP	CHARACTERISTICS	DRAWING
snail	mollusks	mangle	
ant	arthropods	six legs, exoskeleton	
earthworm	segmented worms	segmented body, circulatory and digestive systems	
heartworm	roundworms	digestive system	
sea star	echinoderms	spiny skin, tube feet	
jellyfish	cnidarians	stinging cells	

Combination Notes

1 Make a two-column chart.

2 Write descriptive words and definitions in the first column.

3 Draw a simple sketch that helps you remember the meaning of the term in the second column.

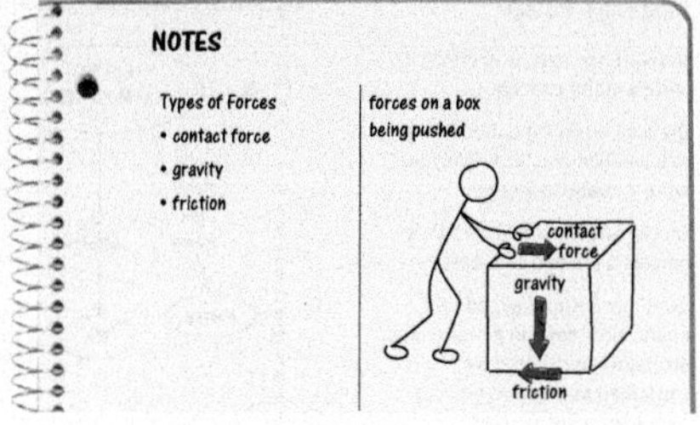

Types of Forces
• contact force

contact force

Mind Map

1 Draw an oval, and inside it write a topic to analyze.

2 Draw two or more arms extending from the oval. Each arm represents a main idea about the topic.

3 Draw lines from the arms on which to write details about each of the main ideas.

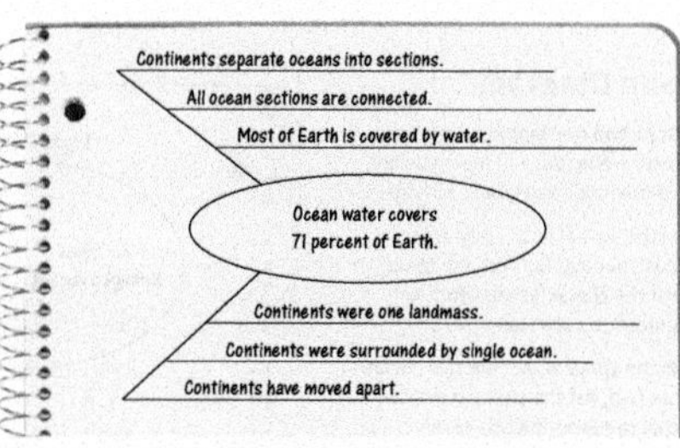

Continents separate oceans into sections.
All ocean sections are connected.
Most of Earth is covered by water.
Ocean water covers 71 percent of Earth.
Continents were one landmass.
Continents were surrounded by single ocean.

Main Idea Web

1 Make a box and write a concept you want to remember inside it.

2 Draw boxes around the central box, and label each one with a category of information about the concept (e.g., definition, formula, descriptive details).

3 Fill in the boxes with relevant details as you read.

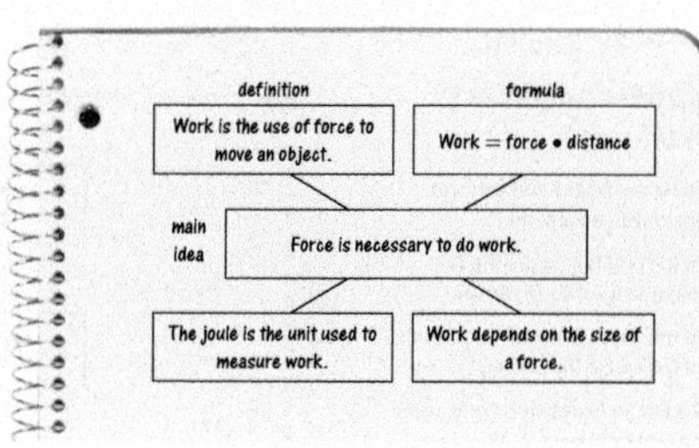

definition
Work is the use of force to move an object.
formula
Work = force • distance
main idea
Force is necessary to do work.
The joule is the unit used to measure work.
Work depends on the size of a force.

Reading and Study Skills

Concept Map

1 Draw a large oval, and inside it write a major concept.
2 Draw an arrow from the concept to a smaller oval, in which you write a related concept.
3 On the arrow, write a verb that connects the two concepts.
4 Continue in this way, adding ovals and arrows in a branching structure, until you have explained as much as you can about the main concept.

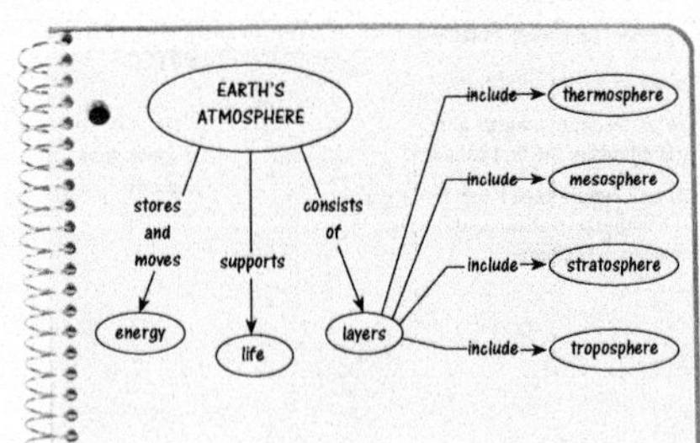

Venn Diagram

1 Draw two overlapping circles or ovals—one for each topic you are comparing—and label each one.
2 In the part of each circle that does not overlap with the other, list the characteristics that are unique to each topic.
3 In the space where the two circles overlap, list the characteristics that the two topics have in common.

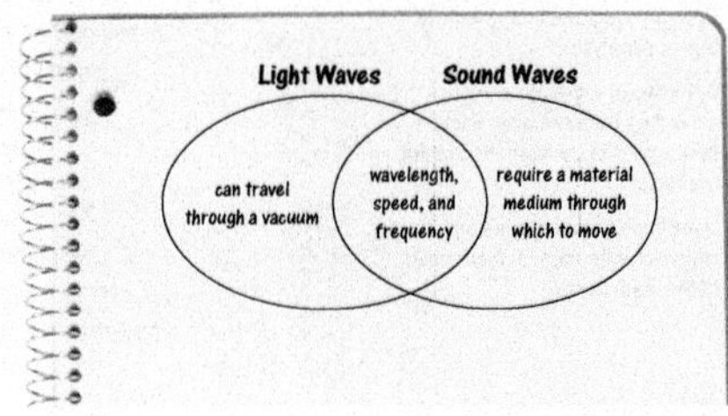

Cause-and-Effect Chart

1 Draw two boxes and connect them with an arrow.
2 In the first box, write the first event in a series (a cause).
3 In the second box, write a result of the cause (the effect).
4 Add more boxes when one event has many effects, or vice versa.

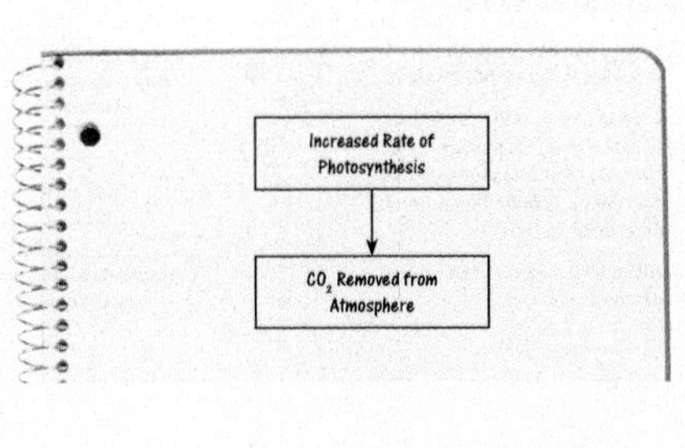

Process Diagram

A process can be a never-ending cycle. As you can see in this technology design process, engineers may backtrack and repeat steps, they may skip steps entirely, or they may repeat the entire process before a useable design is achieved.

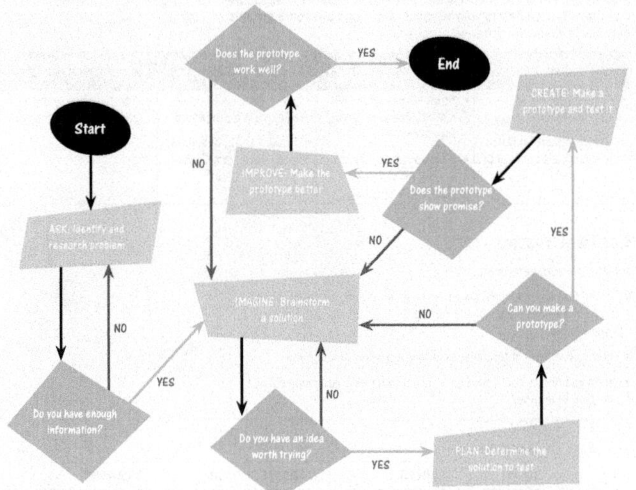

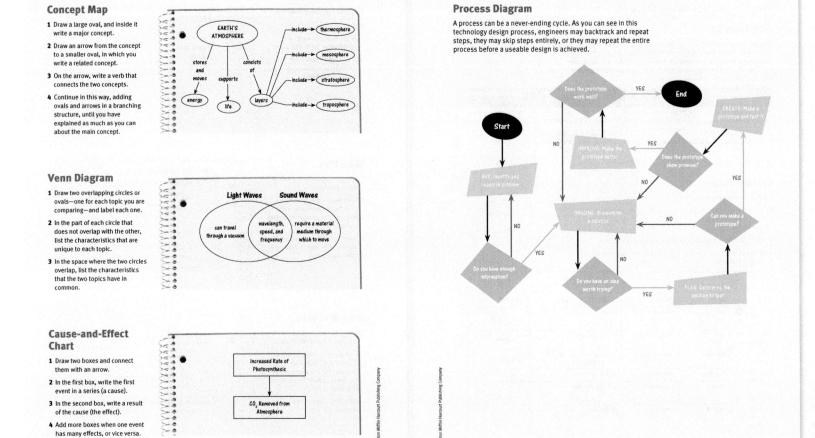

Reading and Study Skills

Using Vocabulary Strategies

Important science terms are highlighted where they are first defined in this book. One way to remember these terms is to take notes and make sketches when you come to them. Use the strategies on this page and the next for this purpose. You will also find a formal definition of each science term in the Glossary at the end of the book.

Description Wheel

1 Draw a small circle.
2 Write a vocabulary term inside the circle.
3 Draw several arms extending from the circle.
4 On the arms, write words and phrases that describe the term.
5 If you choose, add sketches that help you visualize the descriptive details or the concept as a whole.

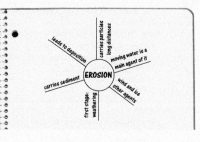

EROSION
leads to deposition
carries particles long distances
moving water is a main agent of it
wind and ice other agents
first stage: weathering
carries sediment

Four Square

1 Draw a small oval and write a vocabulary term inside it.
2 Draw a large rectangle around the oval, and divide the rectangle into four smaller squares.
3 Label the smaller squares with categories of information about the term, such as: definition, characteristics, examples, non-examples, appearance, and root words.
4 Fill the squares with descriptive words and drawings that will help you remember the overall meaning of the term and its essential details.

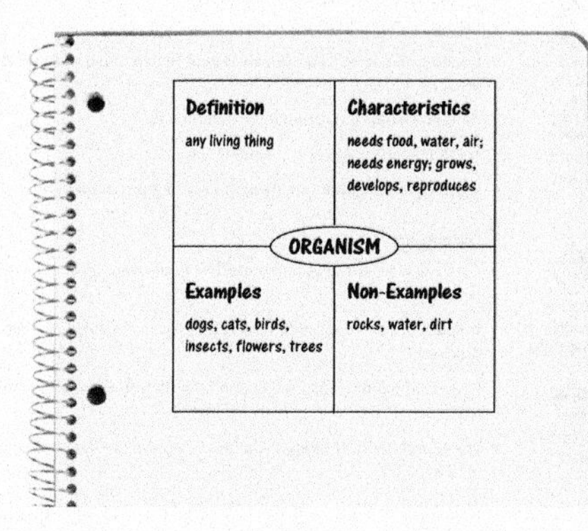

Frame Game

1 Draw a small rectangle, and write a vocabulary term inside it.
2 Draw a larger rectangle around the smaller one. Connect the corners of the larger rectangle to the corners of the smaller one, creating four spaces that frame the word.
3 In each of the four parts of the frame, draw or write details that help define the term. Consider including a definition, essential characteristics, an equation, examples, and a sentence using the term.

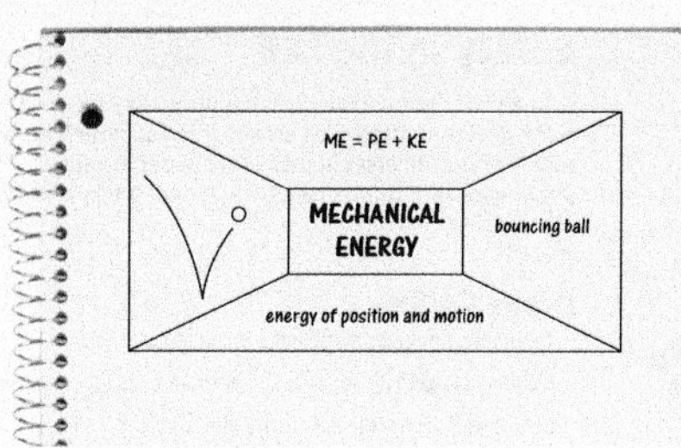

Magnet Word

1 Draw horseshoe magnet, and write a vocabulary term inside it.
2 Add lines that extend from the sides of the magnet.
3 Brainstorm words and phrases that come to mind when you think about the term.
4 On the lines, write the words and phrases that describe something essential about the term.

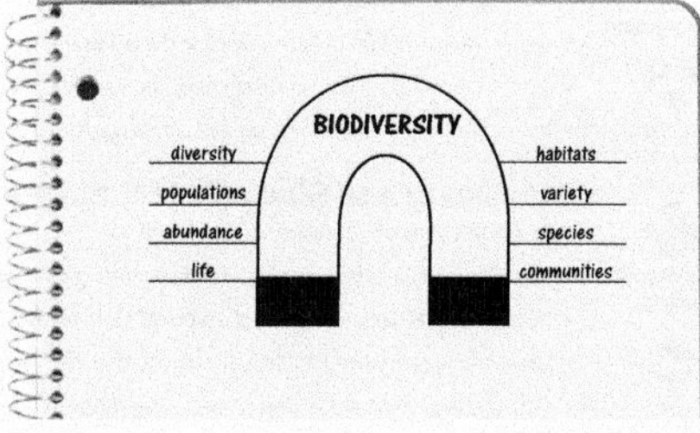

Word Triangle

1 Draw a triangle, and add lines to divide it into three parts.
2 Write a term and its definition in the bottom section of the triangle.
3 In the middle section, write a sentence in which the term is used correctly.
4 In the top section, draw a small picture to illustrate the term.

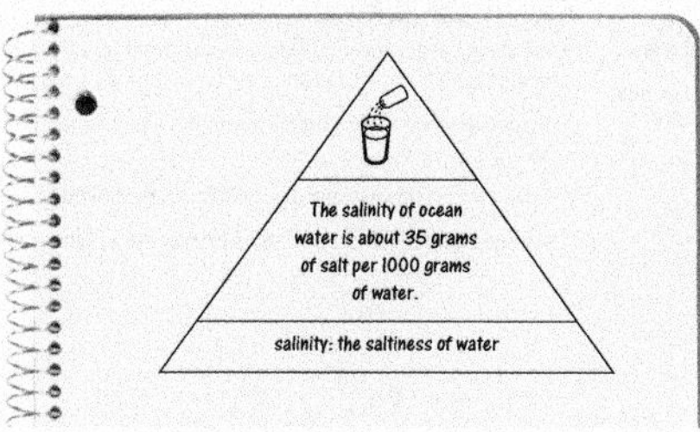

Science Skills

Safety in the Lab

Before you begin work in the laboratory, read these safety rules twice. Before starting a lab activity, read all directions and make sure that you understand them. Do not begin until your teacher has told you to start. If you or another student are injured in any way, tell your teacher immediately.

Dress Code

Eye Protection

- Wear safety goggles at all times in the lab as directed.
- If chemicals get into your eyes, flush your eyes immediately.
- Do not wear contact lenses in the lab.
- Do not look directly at the sun or any intense light source or laser.

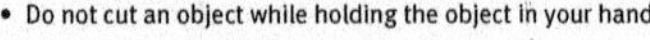

- Do not cut an object while holding the object in your hand.

Hand Protection

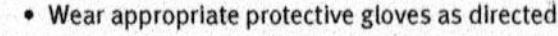

- Wear appropriate protective gloves as directed.

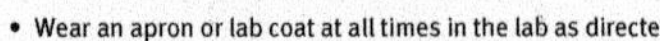

- Wear an apron or lab coat at all times in the lab as directed.

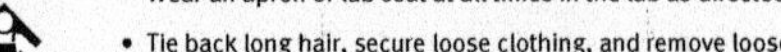

- Tie back long hair, secure loose clothing, and remove loose jewelry.

Clothing Protection

- Do not wear open-toed shoes, sandals, or canvas shoes in the lab.

Glassware and Sharp Object Safety

Glassware Safety

- Do not use chipped or cracked glassware.
- Use heat-resistant glassware for heating or storing hot materials.
- Notify your teacher immediately if a piece of glass breaks.

Sharp Objects Safety

- Use extreme care when handling all sharp and pointed instruments.
- Cut objects on a suitable surface, always in a direction away from your body.

Chemical Safety

Chemical Safety

- If a chemical gets on your skin, on your clothing, or in your eyes, rinse it immediately (shower, faucet or eyewash fountain) and alert your teacher.
- Do not clean up spilled chemicals unless your teacher directs you to do so.
- Do not inhale any gas or vapor unless directed to do so by your teacher.
- Handle materials that emit vapors or gases in a well-ventilated area.

Electrical Safety

Electrical Safety

- Do not use equipment with frayed electrical cords or loose plugs.
- Do not use electrical equipment near water or when clothing or hands are wet.
- Hold the plug housing when you plug in or unplug equipment.

Heating and Fire Safety

Heating Safety

- Be aware of any source of flames, sparks, or heat (such as flames, heating coils, or hot plates) before working with any flammable substances.
- Know the location of lab fire extinguishers and fire-safety blankets.
- Know your school's fire-evacuation routes.
- If your clothing catches on fire, walk to the lab shower to put out the fire.
- Never leave a hot plate unattended while it is turned on or while it is cooling.
- Use tongs or appropriate insulated holders when handling heated objects.
- Allow all equipment to cool before storing it.

Wafting

Plant and Animal Safety

Plant Safety

- Do not eat any part of a plant.
- Do not pick any wild plants unless your teacher instructs you to do so.

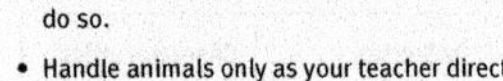

- Handle animals only as your teacher directs.

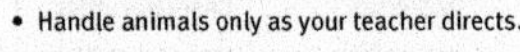

- Treat animals carefully and respectfully.

- Wash your hands thoroughly after handling any plant or animal.

Animal Safety

Cleanup

Proper Waste Disposal

- Clean all work surfaces and protective equipment as directed by your teacher.

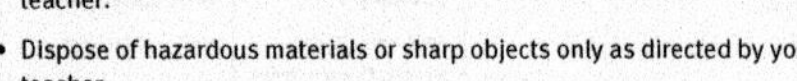

- Dispose of hazardous materials or sharp objects only as directed by your teacher.

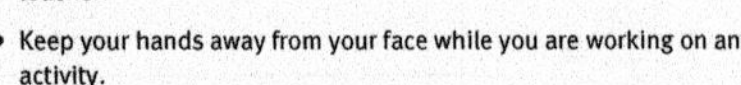

- Keep your hands away from your face while you are working on any activity.

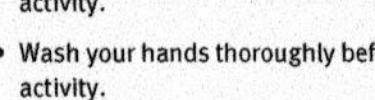

- Wash your hands thoroughly before you leave the lab or after any activity.

Hygienic Care

Science Skills

Designing, Conducting, and Reporting an Experiment

An experiment is an organized procedure to study something under specific conditions. Use the following steps of the scientific method when designing or conducting a controlled experiment.

1 Identify a Research Problem

Every day, you make observations by using your senses to gather information. Careful observations lead to good questions, and good questions can lead you to an experiment. Imagine, for example, that you pass a pond every day on your way to school, and you notice green scum beginning to form on top of it. You wonder what it is and why it seems to be growing. You list your questions, and then you do a little research to find out what is already known. A good place to start a research project is at the library. A library catalog lists all of the resources available to you at that library and often those found elsewhere. Begin your search by using:

- keywords or main topics.
- similar words, or synonyms, of your keyword.

The types of resources that will be helpful to you will depend on the kind of information you are interested in. And, some resources are more reliable for a given topic than others. Some different kinds of useful resources are:

- magazines and journals (or periodicals)—articles on a topic.
- encyclopedias—a good overview of a topic.
- books on specific subjects—details about a topic.
- newspapers—useful for current events.

The Internet can also be a great place to find information. Some of your library's reference materials may even be online. When using the Internet, however, it is especially important to make sure you are using appropriate and reliable sources. Websites of universities and government agencies are usually more accurate and reliable than websites created by individuals or businesses. Decide which sources are relevant and reliable for your topic. If in doubt, check with your teacher.

Take notes as you read through the information in these resources. You will probably come up with many questions and ideas for which you can do more research as needed. Once you feel you have enough information, think about the questions you have on the topic. Then, write down the problem that you want to investigate. Your notes might look like these.

© Houghton Mifflin Harcourt Publishing Company

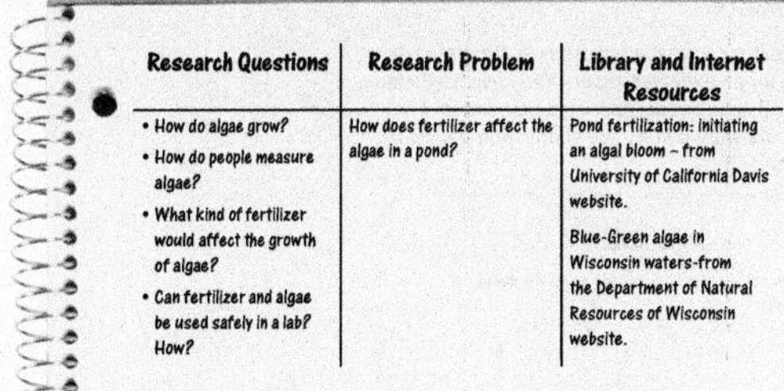

Research Questions	Research Problem	Library and Internet Resources
• How do algae grow? • How do people measure algae? • What kind of fertilizer would affect the growth of algae? • Can fertilizer and algae be used safely in a lab? How?	How does fertilizer affect the algae in a pond?	Pond fertilization: initiating an algal bloom – from University of California Davis website. Blue-Green algae in Wisconsin waters-from the Department of Natural Resources of Wisconsin website.

As you gather information from reliable sources, record details about each source, including author name(s), title, date of publication, and/or web address. Make sure to also note the specific information that you use from each source. Staying organized in this way will be important when you write your report and create a bibliography or works cited list. Recording this information and staying organized will help you credit the appropriate author(s) for the information that you have gathered.

Representing someone else's ideas or work as your own, (without giving the original author credit), is known as plagiarism. Plagiarism can be intentional or unintentional. The best way to make sure that you do not commit plagiarism is to always do your own work and to always give credit to others when you use their words or ideas.

Current scientific research is built on scientific research and discoveries that have happened in the past. This means that scientists are constantly learning from each other and combining ideas to learn more about the natural world through investigation. But, a good scientist always credits the ideas and research that they have gathered from other people to those people. There are more details about crediting sources and creating a bibliography under step 9.

2 Make a Prediction

A prediction is a statement of what you expect will happen in your experiment. Before making a prediction, you need to decide in a general way what you will do in your procedure. You may state your prediction in an if-then format.

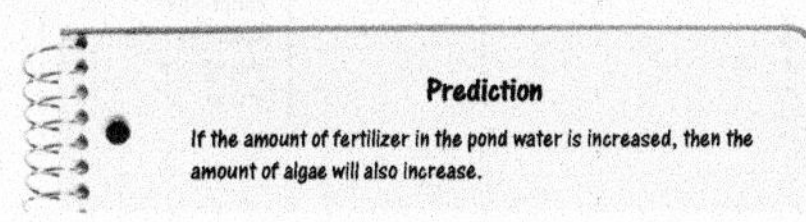

Prediction

If the amount of fertilizer in the pond water is increased, then the amount of algae will also increase.

3 Form a Hypothesis

Many experiments are designed to test a hypothesis. A hypothesis is a tentative explanation for an expected result. You have predicted that additional fertilizer will cause additional algae growth in pond water; your hypothesis should state the connection between fertilizer and algal growth.

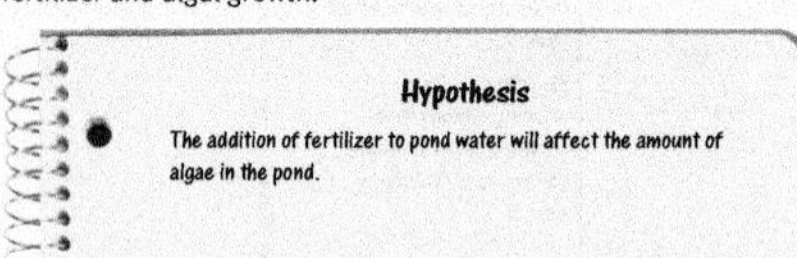

Hypothesis

The addition of fertilizer to pond water will affect the amount of algae in the pond.

4 Identify Variables to Test the Hypothesis

The next step is to design an experiment to test the hypothesis. The experimental results may or may not support the hypothesis. Either way, the information that results from the experiment may be useful for future investigations.

Experimental Group and Control Group

An experiment to determine how two factors are related has a control group and an experimental group. The two groups are the same, except that the investigator changes a single factor in the experimental group and does not change it in the control group.

Experimental Group: two containers of pond water with one drop of fertilizer solution added to each

Control Group: two containers of the same pond water sampled at the same time but with no fertilizer solution added

Variables and Constants

In a controlled experiment, a variable is any factor that can change. Constants are all of the variables that are kept the same in both the experimental group and the control group.

The independent variable is the factor that is manipulated or changed in order to test the effect of the change on another variable. The dependent variable is the factor the investigator measures to gather data about the effect.

Independent Variable	Dependent Variable	Constants
Amount of fertilizer in pond water	Growth of algae in the pond water	• Where and when the pond water is obtained • The type of container used • Light and temperature conditions where the water is stored

5 Write a Procedure

Write each step of your procedure. Start each step with a verb, or action word, and keep the steps short. Your procedure should be clear enough for someone else to use as instructions for repeating your experiment.

Procedure

1. *Use the masking tape and the marker to label the containers with your initials, the date, and the identifiers "Jar 1 with Fertilizer," "Jar 2 with Fertilizer," "Jar 1 without Fertilizer," and "Jar 2 without Fertilizer."*
2. *Put on your gloves. Use the large container to obtain a sample of pond water.*
3. *Divide the water sample equally among the four smaller containers.*
4. *Use the eyedropper to add one drop of fertilizer solution to the two containers labeled, "Jar 1 with Fertilizer," and "Jar 2 with Fertilizer".*
5. *Cover the containers with clear plastic wrap. Use the scissors to punch ten holes in each of the covers.*
6. *Place all four containers on a window ledge. Make sure that they all receive the same amount of light.*
7. *Observe the containers every day for one week.*
8. *Use the ruler to measure the diameter of the largest clump of algae in each container, and record your measurements daily.*

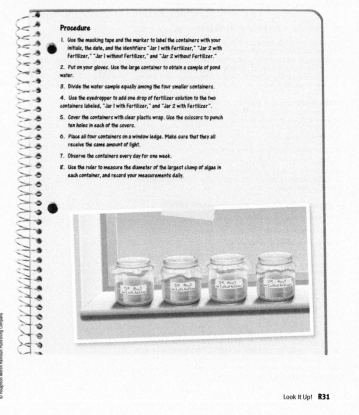

Science Skills

6 Experiment and Collect Data

Once you have all of your materials and your procedure has been approved, you can begin to experiment and collect data. Record both quantitative data (measurements) and qualitative data (observations), as shown below.

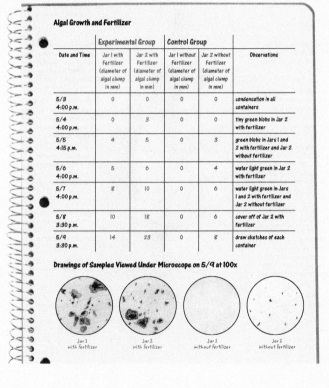

Algal Growth and Fertilizer

	Experimental Group		Control Group		
Date and Time	Jar 1 with Fertilizer (diameter of algal clump in mm)	Jar 2 with Fertilizer (diameter of algal clump in mm)	Jar 1 without Fertilizer (diameter of algal clump in mm)	Jar 2 without Fertilizer (diameter of algal clump in mm)	Observations
5/3 4:00 p.m.	0	0	0	0	condensation in all containers
5/4 4:00 p.m.	0	3	0	0	tiny green blobs in Jar 2 with fertilizer
5/5 4:15 p.m.	4	5	0	3	green blobs in Jars 1 and 2 with fertilizer and Jar 2 without fertilizer
5/6 4:00 p.m.	5	6	0	4	water light green in Jar 2 with fertilizer
5/7 4:00 p.m.	8	10	0	6	water light green in Jars 1 and 2 with fertilizer and Jar 2 without fertilizer
5/8 3:30 p.m.	10	18	0	6	cover off of Jar 2 with fertilizer
5/9 3:30 p.m.	14	23	0	8	drew sketches of each container

Drawings of Samples Viewed Under Microscope on 5/9 at 100x

Jar 1 with fertilizer | Jar 2 with fertilizer | Jar 1 without fertilizer | Jar 2 without fertilizer

7 Analyze Data

After you complete your experiment, you must analyze all of the data you have gathered. Tables, statistics, and graphs are often used in this step to organize and analyze both the qualitative and quantitative data. Sometimes, your qualitative data are best used to help explain the relationships you see in your quantitative data.

Computer graphing software is useful for creating a graph from data that you have collected. Most graphing software can make line graphs, pie charts, or bar graphs from data that has been organized in a spreadsheet. Graphs are useful for understanding relationships in the data and for communicating the results of your experiment.

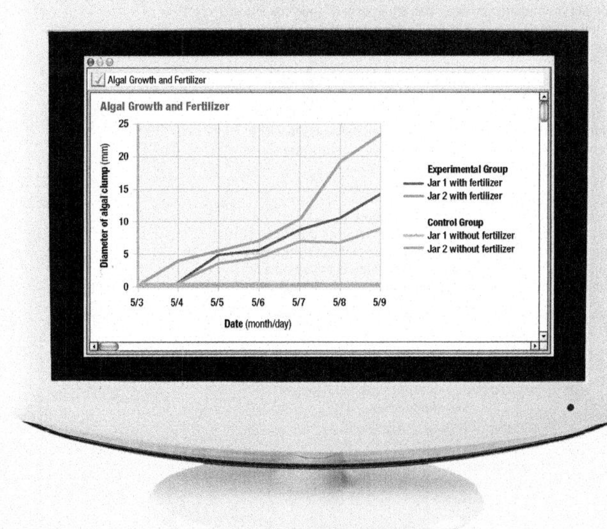

Science Skills

8 Make Conclusions

To draw conclusions from your experiment, first, write your results. Then, compare your results with your hypothesis. Do your results support your hypothesis? What have you learned?

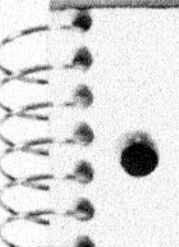

Conclusion

More algae grew in the pond water to which fertilizer had been added than in the pond water to which fertilizer had not been added. My hypothesis was supported. I conclude that it is possible that the growth of algae in ponds can be influenced by the input of fertilizer.

9 Create a Bibliography or Works Cited List

To complete your report, you must also show all of the newspapers, magazines, journals, books, and online sources that you used at every stage of your investigation. Whenever you find useful information about your topic, you should write down the source of that information. Writing down as much information as you can about the subject can help you or someone else find the source again. You should at least record the author's name, the title, the date and where the source was published, and the pages in which the information was found. Then, organize your sources into a list, which you can title Bibliography or Works Cited.

Usually, at least three sources are included in these lists. Sources are listed alphabetically, by the authors' last names. The exact format of a bibliography can vary, depending on the style preferences of your teacher, school, or publisher. Also, books are cited differently than journals or websites. Below is an example of how different kinds of sources may be formatted in a bibliography.

BOOK: Hauschultz, Sara. Freshwater Algae. Brainard, Minnesota: Northwoods Publishing, 2011.

ENCYCLOPEDIA: Lasure, Sedona. "Algae is not all just pond scum." Encyclopedia of Algae. 2009.

JOURNAL: Johnson, Keagan. "Algae as we know it." Sci Journal, vol 64. (September 2010): 201-211.

WEBSITE: Dout, Bill. "Keeping algae scum out of birdbaths." Help Keep Earth Clean. News. January 26, 2011. <www.SaveEarth.org>.

Using a Microscope

Scientists use microscopes to see very small objects that cannot easily be seen with the eye alone. A microscope magnifies the image of an object so that small details may be observed. A microscope that you may use can magnify an object 400 times—the object will appear 400 times larger than its actual size.

Body The body separates the lens in the eyepiece from the objective lenses below.

Nosepiece The nosepiece holds the objective lenses above the stage and rotates so that all lenses may be used.

High-Power Objective Lens This is the largest lens on the nosepiece. It magnifies an image approximately 40 times.

Stage The stage supports the object being viewed.

Diaphragm The diaphragm is used to adjust the amount of light passing through the slide and into an objective lens.

Mirror or Light Source Some microscopes use light that is reflected through the stage by a mirror. Other microscopes have their own light sources.

Eyepiece Objects are viewed through the eyepiece. The eyepiece contains a lens that commonly magnifies an image ten times.

Coarse Adjustment This knob is used to focus the image of an object when it is viewed through the low-power lens.

Fine Adjustment This knob is used to focus the image of an object when it is viewed through the high-power lens.

Low-Power Objective Lens This is the smallest lens on the nosepiece. It magnifies images about 10 times.

Arm The arm supports the body above the stage. Always carry a microscope by the arm and base.

Stage Clip The stage clip holds a slide in place on the stage.

Base The base supports the microscope.

Science Skills

Measuring Accurately

Precision and Accuracy

When you do a scientific investigation, it is important that your methods, observations, and data be both precise and accurate.

Low precision: The darts did not land in a consistent place on the dartboard.

Precision, but not accuracy: The darts landed in a consistent place, but did not hit the bull's eye.

Prescision and accuracy: The darts landed consistently on the bull's eye.

Precision

In science, *precision* is the exactness and consistency of measurements. For example, measurements made with a ruler that has both centimeter and millimeter markings would be more precise than measurements made with a ruler that has only centimeter markings. Another indicator of precision is the care taken to make sure that methods and observations are as exact and consistent as possible. Every time a particular experiment is done, the same procedure should be used. Precision is necessary because experiments are repeated several times and if the procedure changes, the results might change.

Example

Suppose you are measuring temperatures over a two-week period. Your precision will be greater if you measure each temperature at the same place, at the same time of day, and with the same thermometer than if you change any of these factors from one day to the next.

Accuracy

In science, it is possible to be precise but not accurate. *Accuracy* depends on the difference between a measurement and an actual value. The smaller the difference, the more accurate the measurement.

Example

Suppose you look at a stream and estimate that it is about 1 meter wide at a particular place. You decide to check your estimate by measuring the stream with a meter stick, and you determine that the stream is 1.32 meters wide. However, because it is difficult to measure the width of a stream with a meter stick, it turns out that your measurement was not very accurate. The stream is actually 1.14 meters wide. Therefore, even though your estimate of about 1 meter was less precise than your measurement, your estimate was actually more accurate.

Graduated Cylinders

How to Measure the Volume of a Liquid with a Graduated Cylinder

- Be sure that the graduated cylinder is on a flat surface so that your measurement will be accurate.
- When reading the scale on a graduated cylinder, be sure to have your eyes at the level of the surface of the liquid.
- The surface of the liquid will be curved in the graduated cylinder. Read the volume of the liquid at the bottom of the curve, or meniscus (muh-NIHS-kuhs).
- You can use a graduated cylinder to find the volume of a solid object by measuring the increase in a liquid's level after you add the object to the cylinder.

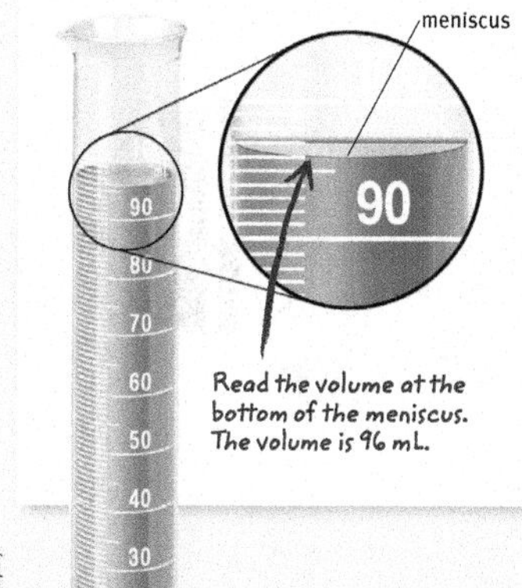

Read the volume at the bottom of the meniscus. The volume is 96 mL.

Metric Rulers

How to Measure the Length of a Leaf with a Metric Ruler

1. Lay a ruler flat on top of the leaf so that the 1-centimeter mark lines up with one end. Make sure the ruler and the leaf do not move between the time you line them up and the time you take the measurement.
2. Look straight down on the ruler so that you can see exactly how the marks line up with the other end of the leaf.
3. Estimate the length by which the leaf extends beyond a marking. For example, the leaf below extends about halfway between the 4.2-centimeter and 4.3-centimeter marks, so the apparent measurement is about 4.25 centimeters.
4. Remember to subtract 1 centimeter from your apparent measurement, since you started at the 1-centimeter mark on the ruler and not at the end. The leaf is about 3.25 centimeters long (4.25 cm − 1 cm = 3.25 cm).

Science Skills

Triple Beam Balance

This balance has a pan and three beams with sliding masses, called riders. At one end of the beams is a pointer that indicates whether the mass on the pan is equal to the masses shown on the beams.

How to Measure the Mass of an Object

1 Make sure the balance is zeroed before measuring the mass of an object. The balance is zeroed if the pointer is at zero when nothing is on the pan and the riders are at their zero points. Use the adjustment knob at the base of the balance to zero it.

2 Place the object to be measured on the pan.

3 Move the riders one notch at a time away from the pan. Begin with the largest rider. If moving the largest rider one notch brings the pointer below zero, begin measuring the mass of the object with the next smaller rider.

4 Change the positions of the riders until they balance the mass on the pan and the pointer is at zero. Then add the readings from the three beams to determine the mass of the object.

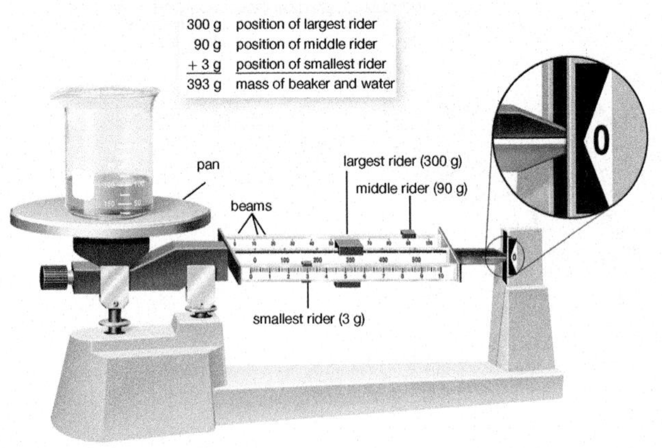

Using the Metric System and SI Units

Scientists use International System (SI) units for measurements of distance, volume, mass, and temperature. The International System is based on powers of ten and the metric system of measurement.

Basic SI Units		
Quantity	**Name**	**Symbol**
length	meter	m
volume	liter	L
mass	gram	g
temperature	kelvin	K

SI Prefixes		
Prefix	**Symbol**	**Power of 10**
kilo-	k	1000
hecto-	h	100
deca-	da	10
deci-	d	0.1 or $\frac{1}{10}$
centi-	c	0.01 or $\frac{1}{100}$
milli-	m	0.001 or $\frac{1}{1000}$

Changing Metric Units

You can change from one unit to another in the metric system by multiplying or dividing by a power of 10.

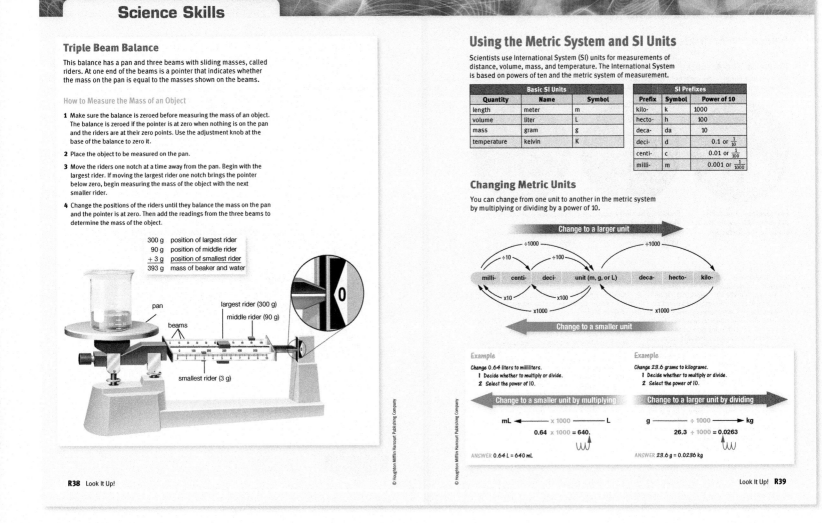

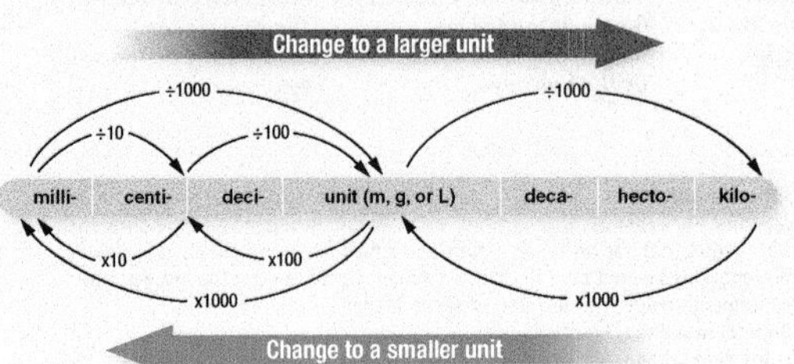

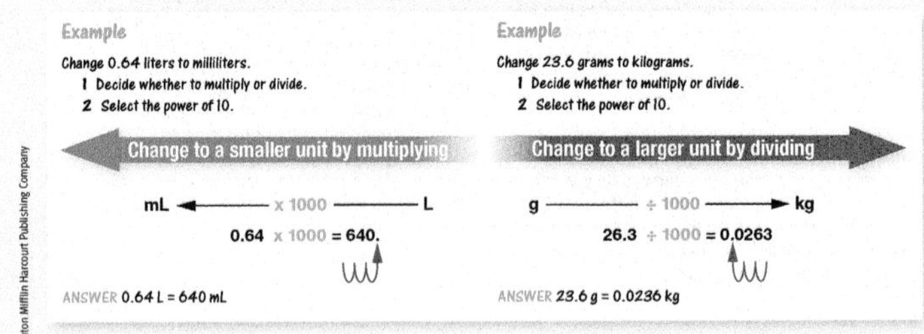

Example
Change 0.64 liters to milliliters.
1 Decide whether to multiply or divide.
2 Select the power of 10.
Change to a smaller unit by multiplying
mL ← x 1000 — L
0.64 x 1000 = 640.
ANSWER 0.64 L = 640 mL
Example
Change 23.6 grams to kilograms.
1 Decide whether to multiply or divide.
2 Select the power of 10.
Change to a larger unit by dividing
g — ÷ 1000 → kg
26.3 ÷ 1000 = 0.0263
ANSWER 23.6 g = 0.0236 kg

Science Skills

Converting Between SI and U.S. Customary Units

Use the chart below when you need to convert between SI units and U.S. customary units.

SI Unit	From SI to U.S. Customary			From U.S. Customary to SI		
Length	**When you know**	**multiply by**	**to find**	**When you know**	**multiply by**	**to find**
kilometer (km) = 1000 m	kilometers	0.62	miles	miles	1.61	kilometers
meter (m) = 100 cm	meters	3.28	feet	feet	0.3048	meters
centimeter (cm) = 10 mm	centimeters	0.39	inches	inches	2.54	centimeters
millimeter (mm) = 0.1 cm	millimeters	0.04	inches	inches	25.4	millimeters
Area	**When you know**	**multiply by**	**to find**	**When you know**	**multiply by**	**to find**
square kilometer (km^2)	square kilometers	0.39	square miles	square miles	2.59	square kilometers
square meter (m^2)	square meters	1.2	square yards	square yards	0.84	square meters
square centimeter (cm^2)	square centimeters	0.155	square inches	square inches	6.45	square centimeters
Volume	**When you know**	**multiply by**	**to find**	**When you know**	**multiply by**	**to find**
liter (L) = 1000 mL	liters	1.06	quarts	quarts	0.95	liters
	liters	0.26	gallons	gallons	3.79	liters
	liters	4.23	cups	cups	0.24	liters
	liters	2.12	pints	pints	0.47	liters
milliliter (mL) = 0.001 L	milliliters	0.20	teaspoons	teaspoons	4.93	milliliters
	milliliters	0.07	tablespoons	tablespoons	14.79	milliliters
	milliliters	0.03	fluid ounces	fluid ounces	29.57	milliliters
Mass	**When you know**	**multiply by**	**to find**	**When you know**	**multiply by**	**to find**
kilogram (kg) = 1000 g	kilograms	2.2	pounds	pounds	0.45	kilograms
gram (g) = 1000 mg	grams	0.035	ounces	ounces	28.35	grams

Temperature Conversions

Even though the kelvin is the SI base unit of temperature, the degree Celsius will be the unit you use most often in your science studies. The formulas below show the relationships between temperatures in degrees Fahrenheit (°F), degrees Celsius (°C), and kelvins (K).

$°C = \frac{5}{9}(°F - 32)$ $°F = \frac{9}{5}°C + 32$ $K = °C + 273$

Examples of Temperature Conversions

Condition	Degrees Celsius	Degrees Fahrenheit
Freezing point of water	0	32
Cool day	10	50
Mild day	20	68
Warm day	30	86
Normal body temperature	37	98.6
Very hot day	40	104
Boiling point of water	100	212

Math Refresher

Performing Calculations

Science requires an understanding of many math concepts. The following pages will help you review some important math skills.

Mean

The mean is the sum of all values in a data set divided by the total number of values in the data set. The mean is also called the *average*.

Example

Find the mean of the following set of numbers: 5, 4, 7, and 8.

Step 1 Find the sum.

$5 + 4 + 7 + 8 = 24$

Step 2 Divide the sum by the number of numbers in your set. Because there are four numbers in this example, divide the sum by 4.

$24 \div 4 = 6$

Answer The average, or mean, is 6.

Median

The median of a data set is the middle value when the values are written in numerical order. If a data set has an even number of values, the median is the mean of the two middle values.

Example

To find the median of a set of measurements, arrange the values in order from least to greatest. The median is the middle value.

13 mm 14 mm 16 mm 21 mm 23 mm

Answer The median is 16 mm.

Mode

The mode of a data set is the value that occurs most often.

Example

To find the mode of a set of measurements, arrange the values in order from least to greatest and determine the value that occurs most often.

13 mm, 14 mm, 14 mm, 16 mm,
21 mm, 23 mm, 25 mm

Answer The mode is 14 mm.

A data set can have more than one mode or no mode. For example, the following data set has modes of 2 mm and 4 mm:

2 mm 2 mm 3 mm 4 mm 4 mm

The data set below has no mode, because no value occurs more often than any other.

2 mm 3 mm 4 mm 5 mm

Math Refresher

Ratios

A **ratio** is a comparison between numbers, and it is usually written as a fraction.

Example

Find the ratio of thermometers to students if you have 36 thermometers and 48 students in your class.

Step 1 Write the ratio.

$$\frac{36 \text{ thermometers}}{48 \text{ students}}$$

Step 2 Simplify the fraction to its simplest form.

$$\frac{36}{48} = \frac{36 \div 12}{48 \div 12} = \frac{3}{4}$$

The ratio of thermometers to students is 3 to 4 or 3:4.

Proportions

A **proportion** is an equation that states that two ratios are equal.

$$\frac{3}{1} = \frac{12}{4}$$

To solve a proportion, you can use cross-multiplication. If you know three of the quantities in a proportion, you can use cross-multiplication to find the fourth.

Example

Imagine that you are making a scale model of the solar system for your science project. The diameter of Jupiter is 11.2 times the diameter of the Earth. If you are using a plastic-foam ball that has a diameter of 2 cm to represent the Earth, what must the diameter of the ball representing Jupiter be?

$$\frac{11.2}{1} = \frac{x}{2 \text{ cm}}$$

Step 1 Cross-multiply.

$$\frac{11.2}{1} = \frac{x}{2}$$

$$11.2 \times 2 = x \times 1$$

Step 2 Multiply.

$$22.4 = x \times 1$$

$$x = 22.4 \text{ cm}$$

You will need to use a ball that has a diameter of 22.4 cm to represent Jupiter.

Rates

A **rate** is a ratio of two values expressed in different units. A unit rate is a rate with a denominator of 1 unit.

Example

A plant grew 6 centimeters in 2 days. The plant's rate of growth was $\frac{6 \text{ cm}}{2 \text{ days}}$. To describe the plant's growth in centimeters per day, write a unit rate.

Divide numerator and denominator by 2:

$$\frac{6 \text{ cm}}{2 \text{ days}} = \frac{6 \text{ cm} \div 2}{2 \text{ days} \div 2}$$

Simplify:

$$= \frac{3 \text{ cm}}{1 \text{ day}}$$

Answer The plant's rate of growth is 3 centimeters per day.

Percent

A **percent** is a ratio of a given number to 100. For example, 85% = 85/100. You can use percent to find part of a whole.

Example

What is 85% of 40?

Step 1 Rewrite the percent as a decimal by moving the decimal point two places to the left.

0.85

Step 2 Multiply the decimal by the number that you are calculating the percentage of.

$$0.85 \times 40 = 34$$

85% of 40 is 34.

Decimals

To **add** or **subtract decimals**, line up the digits vertically so that the decimal points line up. Then, add or subtract the columns from right to left. Carry or borrow numbers as necessary.

Example

Add the following numbers: 3.1415 and 2.96.

Step 1 Line up the digits vertically so that the decimal points line up.

$$\begin{array}{r} 3.1415 \\ +\,2.96 \\ \hline \end{array}$$

Step 2 Add the columns from right to left, and carry when necessary.

$$\begin{array}{r} 3.1415 \\ +\,2.96 \\ \hline 6.1015 \end{array}$$

The sum is 6.1015.

Fractions

A **fraction** is a ratio of two nonzero whole numbers.

Example

Your class has 24 plants. Your teacher instructs you to put 5 plants in a shady spot. What fraction of the plants in your class will you put in a shady spot?

Step 1 In the denominator, write the total number of parts in the whole.

$$\frac{?}{24}$$

Step 2 In the numerator, write the number of parts of the whole that are being considered.

$$\frac{5}{24}$$

So, $\frac{5}{24}$ of the plants will be in the shade.

Math Refresher

Simplifying Fractions

It is usually best to express a fraction in its simplest form. Expressing a fraction in its simplest form is called **simplifying a fraction.**

Example

Simplify the fraction $\frac{30}{45}$ to its simplest form.

Step 1 Find the largest whole number that will divide evenly into both the numerator and denominator. This number is called the greatest common factor (GCF).

Factors of the numerator 30:
1, 2, 3, 5, 6, 10, **15**, 30

Factors of the denominator 45:
1, 3, 5, 9, **15**, 45

Step 2 Divide both the numerator and the denominator by the GCF, which in this case is 15.

$\frac{30}{45} = \frac{30 \div 15}{45 \div 15} = \frac{2}{3}$

Thus, $\frac{30}{45}$ written in its simplest form is $\frac{2}{3}$.

Adding and Subtracting Fractions

To **add** or **subtract fractions** that have the same denominator, simply add or subtract the numerators.

Examples

$\frac{3}{5} + \frac{1}{5} = ?$ and $\frac{3}{4} - \frac{1}{4} = ?$

Step 1 Add or subtract the numerators.
$\frac{3}{5} + \frac{1}{5} = \frac{4}{\ }$ and $\frac{3}{4} - \frac{1}{4} = \frac{2}{\ }$

Step 2 Write in the common denominator, which remains the same.
$\frac{3}{5} + \frac{1}{5} = \frac{4}{5}$ and $\frac{3}{4} - \frac{1}{4} = \frac{2}{4}$

Step 3 If necessary, write the fraction in its simplest form.
$\frac{4}{5}$ cannot be simplified, and $\frac{2}{4} = \frac{1}{2}$.

To **add** or **subtract** fractions that have **different denominators,** first find the least common denominator (LCD).

Examples

$\frac{1}{2} + \frac{1}{6} = ?$ and $\frac{3}{4} - \frac{2}{3} = ?$

Step 1 Write the equivalent fractions that have a common denominator.
$\frac{3}{6} + \frac{1}{6} = ?$ and $\frac{9}{12} - \frac{8}{12} = ?$

Step 2 Add or subtract the fractions.
$\frac{3}{6} + \frac{1}{6} = \frac{4}{6}$ and $\frac{9}{12} - \frac{8}{12} = \frac{1}{12}$

Step 3 If necessary, write the fraction in its simplest form.
$\frac{4}{6} = \frac{2}{3}$, and $\frac{1}{12}$ cannot be simplifed.

Multiplying Fractions

To **multiply fractions,** multiply the numerators and the denominators together, and then simplify the fraction to its simplest form.

Example

$\frac{5}{9} \times \frac{7}{10} = ?$

Step 1 Multiply the numerators and denominators.
$\frac{5}{9} \times \frac{7}{10} = \frac{5 \times 7}{9 \times 10} = \frac{35}{90}$

Step 2 Simplify the fraction.
$\frac{35}{90} = \frac{35 \div 5}{90 \div 5} = \frac{7}{18}$

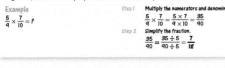

Dividing Fractions

To **divide fractions,** first rewrite the divisor (the number you divide by) upside down. This number is called the reciprocal of the divisor. Then multiply and simplify if necessary.

Example

$\frac{5}{8} \div \frac{3}{2} = ?$

Step 1 Rewrite the divisor as its reciprocal.
$\frac{3}{2} \rightarrow \frac{2}{3}$

Step 2 Multiply the fractions.
$\frac{5}{8} \times \frac{2}{3} = \frac{5 \times 2}{8 \times 3} = \frac{10}{24}$

Step 3 Simplify the fraction.
$\frac{10}{24} = \frac{10 \div 2}{24 \div 2} = \frac{5}{12}$

Using Significant Figures

The **significant figures** in a decimal are the digits that are warranted by the accuracy of a measuring device.

When you perform a calculation with measurements, the number of significant figures to include in the result depends in part on the number of significant figures in the measurements. When you multiply or divide measurements, your answer should have only as many significant figures as the measurement with the fewest significant figures.

Examples

Using a balance and a graduated cylinder filled with water, you determined that a marble has a mass of 8.0 grams and a volume of 3.5 cubic centimeters. To calculate the density of the marble, divide the mass by the volume.

Write the formula for density: Density $= \frac{\text{mass}}{\text{volume}}$

Substitute measurements: $= \frac{8.0\ \text{g}}{3.5\ \text{cm}^3}$

Use a calculator to divide: $\approx 2.285714286\ \text{g/cm}^3$

Answer Because the mass and the volume have two significant figures each, give the density to two significant figures. The marble has a density of 2.3 grams per cubic centimeter.

Using Scientific Notation

Scientific notation is a shorthand way to write very large or very small numbers. For example, 73,500,000,000,000,000,000,000 kg is the mass of the moon. In scientific notation, it is 7.35×10^{22} kg. A value written as a number between 1 and 10, times a power of 10, is in scientific notation.

Examples

You can convert from standard form to scientific notation.

Standard Form	Scientific Notation
720,000 5 decimal places left	7.2×10^5 Exponent is 5.
0.000291 4 decimal places right	2.91×10^{-4} Exponent is –4.

You can convert from scientific notation to standard form.

Scientific Notation	Standard Form
4.63×10^7 Exponent is 7.	46,300,000 7 decimal places right
1.08×10^{-6} Exponent is –6.	0.00000108 6 decimal places left

Math Refresher

Making and Interpreting Graphs

Circle Graph

A circle graph, or pie chart, shows how each group of data relates to all of the data. Each part of the circle represents a category of the data. The entire circle represents all of the data. For example, a biologist studying a hardwood forest in Wisconsin found that there were five different types of trees. The data table at right summarizes the biologist's findings.

Wisconsin Hardwood Trees	
Type of tree	**Number found**
Oak	600
Maple	750
Beech	300
Birch	1,200
Hickory	150
Total	3,000

How to Make a Circle Graph

1 To make a circle graph of these data, first find the percentage of each type of tree. Divide the number of trees of each type by the total number of trees, and multiply by 100%.

$$\frac{600 \text{ oak}}{3{,}000 \text{ trees}} \times 100\% = 20\%$$

$$\frac{750 \text{ maple}}{3{,}000 \text{ trees}} \times 100\% = 25\%$$

$$\frac{300 \text{ beech}}{3{,}000 \text{ trees}} \times 100\% = 10\%$$

$$\frac{1{,}200 \text{ birch}}{3{,}000 \text{ trees}} \times 100\% = 40\%$$

$$\frac{150 \text{ hickory}}{3{,}000 \text{ trees}} \times 100\% = 5\%$$

A Community of Wisconsin Hardwood Trees

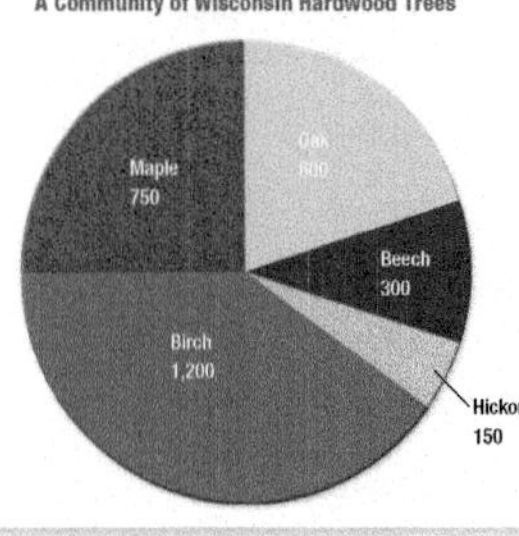

2 Now, determine the size of the wedges that make up the graph. Multiply each percentage by 360°. Remember that a circle contains 360°.

$20\% \times 360° = 72°$ $25\% \times 360° = 90°$

$10\% \times 360° = 36°$ $40\% \times 360° = 144°$

$5\% \times 360° = 18°$

3 Check that the sum of the percentages is 100 and the sum of the degrees is 360.

$20\% + 25\% + 10\% + 40\% + 5\% = 100\%$

$72° + 90° + 36° + 144° + 18° = 360°$

4 Use a compass to draw a circle and mark the center of the circle.

5 Then, use a protractor to draw angles of 72°, 90°, 36°, 144°, and 18° in the circle.

6 Finally, label each part of the graph, and choose an appropriate title.

Line Graphs

Line graphs are most often used to demonstrate continuous change. For example, Mr. Smith's students analyzed the population records for their hometown, Appleton, between 1910 and 2010. Examine the data at right.

Because the year and the population change, they are the variables. The population is determined by, or dependent on, the year. Therefore, the population is called the **dependent variable,** and the year is called the **independent variable.** Each year and its population make a **data pair.** To prepare a line graph, you must first organize data pairs into a table like the one at right.

Population of Appleton, 1910–2010	
Year	**Population**
1910	1,800
1930	2,500
1950	3,200
1970	3,900
1990	4,600
2010	5,300

How to Make a Line Graph

1 Place the independent variable along the horizontal (x) axis. Place the dependent variable along the vertical (y) axis.

2 Label the x-axis "Year" and the y-axis "Population." Look at your greatest and least values for the population. For the y-axis, determine a scale that will provide enough space to show these values. You must use the same scale for the entire length of the axis. Next, find an appropriate scale for the x-axis.

3 Choose reasonable starting points for each axis.

4 Plot the data pairs as accurately as possible.

5 Choose a title that accurately represents the data.

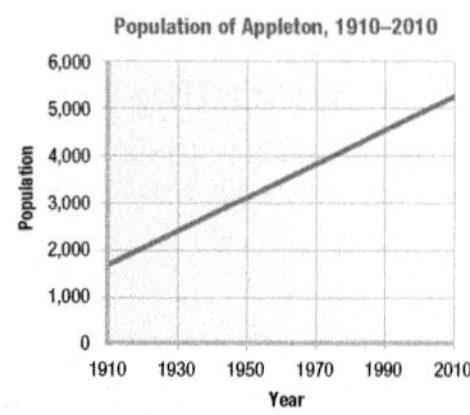

How to Determine Slope

Slope is the ratio of the change in the y-value to the change in the x-value, or "rise over run."

1 Choose two points on the line graph. For example, the population of Appleton in 2010 was 5,300 people. Therefore, you can define point A as (2010, 5,300). In 1910, the population was 1,800 people. You can define point B as (1910, 1,800).

2 Find the change in the y-value.
(y at point A) − (y at point B) =
5,300 people − 1,800 people =
3,500 people

3 Find the change in the x-value.
(x at point A) − (x at point B) =
2010 − 1910 = 100 years

4 Calculate the slope of the graph by dividing the change in y by the change in x.

$$slope = \frac{change\ in\ y}{change\ in\ x}$$

$$slope = \frac{3{,}500 \text{ people}}{100 \text{ years}}$$

$slope = 35$ people per year

In this example, the population in Appleton increased by a fixed amount each year. The graph of these data is a straight line. Therefore, the relationship is **linear.** When the graph of a set of data is not a straight line, the relationship is **nonlinear.**

Math Refresher

Bar Graphs

Bar graphs can be used to demonstrate change that is not continuous. These graphs can be used to indicate trends when the data cover a long period of time. A meteorologist gathered the precipitation data shown here for Summerville for April 1–15 and used a bar graph to represent the data.

Precipitation in Summerville, April 1–15			
Date	Precipitation (cm)	Date	Precipitation (cm)
April 1	0.5	April 9	0.25
April 2	1.25	April 10	0.0
April 3	0.0	April 11	1.0
April 4	0.0	April 12	0.0
April 5	0.0	April 13	0.25
April 6	0.0	April 14	0.0
April 7	0.0	April 15	6.50
April 8	1.75		

How to Make a Bar Graph

1 Use an appropriate scale and a reasonable starting point for each axis.

2 Label the axes, and plot the data.

3 Choose a title that accurately represents the data.

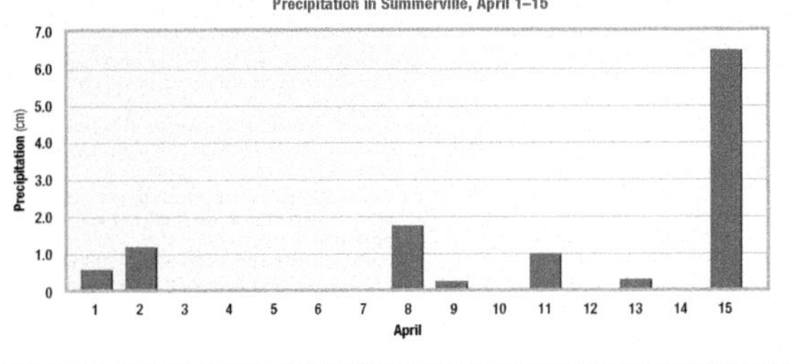

Glossary

Pronunciation Key			
Sound	Symbol	Example	Respelling
ă	a	pat	PAT
ā	ay	pay	PAY
âr	air	care	KAIR
ä	ah	father	FAH•ther
är	ar	argue	AR•gyoo
ch	ch	chase	CHAYS
ĕ	e	pet	PET
ĕ (at end of a syllable)	eh	settee lessee	seh•TEE leh•SEE
ĕr	ehr	merry	MEHR•ee
ē	ee	beach	BEECH
g	g	gas	GAS
ĭ	i	pit	PIT
ĭ (at end of a syllable)	ih	guitar	gih•TAR
ī	y eye (only for a complete syllable)	pie island	PY EYE•luhnd
îr	ir	hear	HIR
j	j	germ	JERM
k	k	kick	KIK
ng	ng	thing	THING
ngk	ngk	bank	BANGK

Sound	Symbol	Example	Respelling
ŏ	ah	bottle	BAHT'l
ō	oh	toe	TOH
ô	aw	caught	KAWT
ôr	ohr	roar	ROHR
oi	oy	noisy	NOYZ•ee
o͝o	u	book	BUK
o͞o	oo	boot	BOOT
ou	ow	pound	POWND
s	s	center	SEN•ter
sh	sh	cache	CASH
ŭ	uh	flood	FLUHD
ûr	er	bird	BERD
z	z	xylophone	ZY•luh•fohn
z	z	bags	BAGZ
zh	zh	decision	dih•SIZH•uhn
ə	uh	around broken focus	uh•ROWND BROH•kuhn FOH•kuhs
ər	er	winner	WIN•er
th	th	thin they	THIN THAY
w	w	one	WUHN
wh	hw	whether	HWETH•er

Student Edition

Glossary

A

abrasion (uh·BRAY·zhuhn) the process by which rock is reduced in size by the scraping action of other rocks driven by water, wind, and gravity (23)
abrasión proceso por el cual se reduce el tamaño de las rocas debido al efecto de desgaste de otras rocas arrastradas por el agua, el viento o la gravedad

absolute dating (AB·suh·loot DAYT·ing) any method of measuring the age of an event or object in years (108)
datación absoluta cualquier método que sirve para determinar la edad de un suceso u objeto en años

acid precipitation (AS·id prih·sip·ih·TAY·shuhn) rain, sleet, or snow that contains a high concentration of acids (24)
precipitación ácida lluvia, aguanieve o nieve que contiene una alta concentración de ácidos

alluvial fan (uh·LOO·vee·uhl FAN) a fan-shaped mass of material deposited by a stream when the slope of the land decreases sharply (33)
abanico aluvial masa en forma de abanico de materiales depositados por un arroyo cuando la pendiente del terreno disminuye bruscamente

asthenosphere (as·THEN·uh·sfir) the soft layer of the mantle on which the tectonic plates move (196)
astenosfera la capa blanda del manto sobre la que se mueven las placas tectónicas

atmosphere (AT·muh·sfir) a mixture of gases that surrounds a planet, moon, or other celestial body (10)
atmósfera una mezcla de gases que rodea un planeta, una luna, u otras cuerpos celestes

atom (AT·uhm) the smallest unit of an element that maintains the properties of that element (142)
átomo la unidad más pequeña de un elemento que conserva las propiedades de ese elemento

B

barrier island (BAIR·ee·er EYE·luhnd) a long ridge of sand or narrow island that lies parallel to the shore (38)
isla barrera un largo arrecife de arena o una isla angosta ubicada paralela a la costa

beach (BEECH) an area of the shoreline that is made up of deposited sediment (38)
playa un área de la costa que está formada por sedimento depositado

biosphere (BY·uh·sfir) the part of Earth where life exists; includes all of the living organisms on Earth (11)
biosfera la parte de la Tierra donde existe la vida; comprende todos los seres vivos de la Tierra

C

chemical weathering (KEM·ih·kuhl WETH·er·ing) the chemical breakdown and decomposition of rocks by natural processes in the environment (24)
desgaste químico la descomposición química que sufren las rocas por procesos naturales del entorno

cleavage (KLEE·vij) in geology, the tendency of a mineral to split along specific planes of weakness to form smooth, flat surfaces (149)
exfoliación en geología, la tendencia de un mineral a agrietarse a lo largo de planos débiles específicos y formar superficies lisas y planas

climate (KLY·mit) the weather conditions in an area over a long period of time (88)
clima las condiciones del tiempo en un área durante un largo período de tiempo

composition (kahm·puh·ZISH·uhn) the chemical makeup of a rock; describes either the minerals or other materials in the rock (172)
composición la constitución química de una roca; describe los minerales u otros materiales presentes en ella

compound (KAHM·pownd) a substance made up of atoms of two or more different elements joined by chemical bonds (142)
compuesto una sustancia formada por átomos de dos o más elementos diferentes unidos por enlaces químicos

compression (kuhm·PRESH·uhn) stress that occurs when forces act to squeeze an object (221)
compresión estrés que se produce cuando distintas fuerzas actúan para estrechar un objeto

convection (kuhn·VEK·shuhn) the movement of matter due to differences in density; the transfer of energy due to the movement of matter (195, 210)
convección el movimiento de la materia debido a diferencias en la densidad; la transferencia de energía debido al movimiento de la materia

convergent boundary (kuhn·VER·juhnt BOWN·duh·ree) the boundary between tectonic plates that are colliding (208)
límite convergente el límite entre placas tectónicas que chocan

core (KOHR) the central part of Earth below the mantle (195)
núcleo la parte central de la Tierra, debajo del manto

© Houghton Mifflin Harcourt Publishing Company

creep (KREEP) the slow downhill movement of weathered rock material (52)
arrastre el movimiento lento y descendente de materiales rocosos desgastados

crust (KRUHST) the thin and solid outermost layer of Earth above the mantle (195)
corteza la capa externa, delgada y sólida de la Tierra, que se encuentra sobre el manto

cryosphere (KRY·oh·sfir) those portions of Earth's surface where water occurs in a solid form (9)
criosfera partes de la superficie de la Tierra donde el agua se encuentra en estado sólido

crystal (KRIS·tuhl) a solid whose atoms, ions, or molecules are arranged in a regular, repeating pattern (143)
cristal un sólido cuyos átomos, iones o moléculas están ordenados en un patrón regular y repetitivo

D

deformation (dee·fohr·MAY·shuhn) the bending, tilting, and breaking of Earth's crust; the change in the shape of rock in response to stress (218, 241)
deformación el proceso de doblar, inclinar y romper la corteza de la Tierra; el cambio en la forma de una roca en respuesta a la tensión

delta (DEL·tuh) a mass of material deposited in a triangular or fan shape at the mouth of a river or stream (33)
delta un depósito de materiales en forma de triángulo o abanico ubicado en la desembocadura de un río

deposition (dep·uh·ZISH·uhn) the process in which material is laid down (30, 157)
sublimación inversa el proceso por medio del cual un material se deposita

divergent boundary (dy·VER·juhnt BOWN·duh·ree) the boundary between two tectonic plates that are moving away from each other (209)
límite divergente el límite entre dos placas tectónicas que se están separando una de la otra

dune (DOON) a mound of wind-deposited sand that moves as a result of the action of wind (47)
duna un montículo de arena depositada por el viento que se mueve como resultado de la acción de éste

E

Earth system (ERTH SIS·tuhm) all of the nonliving things, living things, and processes that make up the planet Earth, including the solid Earth, the hydrosphere, the atmosphere, and the biosphere (6)
sistema terrestre todos los seres vivos y no vivos y los procesos que componen el planeta Tierra, incluidas la Tierra sólida, la hidrosfera, la atmósfera y la biosfera

earthquake (ERTH·kwayk) a movement or trembling of the ground that is caused by a sudden release of energy when rocks along a fault move (240)
terremoto un movimiento o temblor del suelo causado por una liberación súbita de energía que se produce cuando las rocas ubicadas a lo largo de una falla se mueven

elastic rebound (ee·LAS·tik REE·bownd) the sudden return of elastically deformed rock to its undeformed shape (241)
rebote elástico ocurre cuando una roca deformada elásticamente vuelve súbitamente a su forma no deformada

element (EL·uh·muhnt) a substance that cannot be separated or broken down into simpler substances by chemical means (142)
elemento una sustancia que no se puede separar o descomponer en sustancias más simples por medio de métodos químicos

energy budget (EN·er·jee BUHJ·it) the net flow of energy into and out of a system (14)
balance energético el flujo neto de energía que entra y sale de un sistema

epicenter (EP·ih·sen·ter) the point on Earth's surface directly above an earthquake's starting point, or focus (240, 255)
epicentro el punto de la superficie de la Tierra que queda justo arriba del punto de inicio, o foco, de un terremoto

erosion (ee·ROH·zhuhn) the process by which wind, water, ice, or gravity transports soil and sediment from one location to another (30, 157)
erosión el proceso por medio del cual el viento, el agua, el hielo o la gravedad transporta tierra y sedimentos de un lugar a otro

F

fault (FAWLT) a break in a body of rock along which one block moves relative to another (220, 241)
falla una grieta en un cuerpo rocoso a lo largo de la cual un bloque se mueve respecto de otro

floodplain (FLUHD·playn) an area along a river that forms from sediments deposited when the river overflows its banks (33)
llanura de inundación un área a lo largo de un río formada por sedimentos que se depositan cuando el río se desborda

focus (FOH·kuhs) the location within Earth along a fault at which the first motion of an earthquake occurs (240, 255)
foco el lugar dentro de la Tierra a lo largo de una falla donde ocurre el primer movimiento de un terremoto

folding (FOHLD·ing) the bending of rock layers due to stress (219)
plegamiento fenómeno que ocurre cuando las capas de roca se doblan debido a la compresión

fossil (FAHS·uhl) the trace or remains of an organism that lived long ago, most commonly preserved in sedimentary rock (81, 100)
fósil los indicios o los restos de un organismo que vivió hace mucho tiempo, comúnmente preservados en las rocas sedimentarias

G

geologic column (jee·uh·LAHJ·ik KAHL·uhm) an ordered arrangement of rock layers that is based on the relative ages of the rocks and in which the oldest rocks are at the bottom (101)
columna geológica un arreglo ordenado de capas de rocas que se basa en la edad relativa de las rocas y en el cual las rocas más antiguas están al fondo

geologic time scale (jee·uh·LAHJ·ik TYM SKAYL) the standard method used to divide Earth's long natural history into manageable parts (122)
escala de tiempo geológico el método estándar que se usa para dividir la larga historia natural de la Tierra en partes razonables

geology (jee·AHL·uh·jee) the scientific study of the origin, history, and structure of Earth and the processes that shape Earth (120)
geología el estudio científico del origen, la historia y la estructura del planeta Tierra y los procesos que le dan forma

geosphere (JEE·oh·sfir) the mostly solid, rocky part of Earth; extends from the center of the core to the surface of the crust (7)
geosfera la capa de la Tierra que es principalmente sólida y rocosa; se extiende desde el centro del núcleo hasta la superficie de la corteza terrestre

glacial drift (GLAY·shuhl DRIFT) the rock material carried and deposited by glaciers (48)
deriva glacial el material rocoso que es transportado y depositado por los glaciares

glacier (GLAY·sher) a large mass of ice that exists year-round and moves over land (48)
glaciar una masa grande de hielo que existe durante todo el año y se mueve sobre la tierra

groundwater (GROWND·waw·ter) the water that is beneath Earth's surface (34)
agua subterránea el agua que está debajo de la superficie de la Tierra

H

half-life (HAF·lyf) the time required for half of a sample of a radioactive isotope to break down by radioactive decay to form a daughter isotope (108)
vida media el tiempo que se requiere para que la mitad de una muestra de un isótopo radiactivo se descomponga por desintegración radiactiva y forme un isótopo hijo

hot spot (HAHT SPAHT) a volcanically active area of Earth's surface, commonly far from a tectonic plate boundary (234)
mancha caliente un área volcánicamente activa de la superficie de la Tierra que comúnmente se encuentra lejos de un límite entre placas tectónicas

humus (HYOO·muhs) dark, organic material formed in soil from the decayed remains of plants and animals (59)
humus material orgánico obscuro que se forma en la tierra a partir de restos de plantas y animales en descomposición

hydrosphere (HY·druh·sfir) the portion of Earth that is water (8)
hidrosfera la porción de la Tierra que es agua

I–K

ice core (EYES KOHR) a long cylinder of ice obtained from drilling through ice caps or ice sheets; used to study past climates (89)
testigo de hielo un cilindro largo de hielo que se obtiene al perforar campos de hielo o capas de hielo continentales; se usa para estudiar los climas del pasado

igneous rock (IG·nee·uhs RAHK) rock that forms when magma cools and solidifies (158)
roca ígnea una roca que se forma cuando el magma se enfría y se solidifica

intensity (in·TEN·sih·tee) in Earth science, the amount of damage caused by an earthquake (261)
intensidad en las ciencias de la Tierra, la cantidad de daño causado por un terremoto

L

landslide (LAND·slyd) the sudden movement of rock and soil down a slope (53)
derrumbamiento el movimiento súbito hacia abajo de rocas y suelo por una pendiente

lava (LAH·vuh) magma that flows onto Earth's surface; the rock that forms when lava cools and solidifies (228)
lava magma que fluye a la superficie terrestre; la roca que se forma cuando la lava se enfría y se solidifica

lithosphere (LITH·uh·sfir) the solid, outer layer of Earth that consists of the crust and the rigid upper part of the mantle (196)
litosfera la capa externa y sólida de la Tierra que está formada por la corteza y la parte superior y rígida del manto

loess (LUHS) fine-grained sediments of quartz, feldspar, hornblende, mica, and clay deposited by the wind (47)
loess sedimentos de grano fino de cuarzo, feldespato, horneblenda, mica y arcilla depositados por el viento

luster (LUHS·ter) the way in which a mineral reflects light (149)
brillo la forma en que un mineral refleja la luz

M–N

magma (MAG·muh) the molten or partially molten rock material containing trapped gases produced under Earth's surface (228)
magma el material rocoso total o parcialmente fundido que contiene gases atrapados que se producen debajo de la superficie terrestre

magnitude (MAG·nih·tood) a measure of the strength of an earthquake (260)
magnitud una medida de la intensidad de un terremoto

mantle (MAN·tl) the layer of rock between Earth's crust and core (195)
manto la capa de roca que se encuentra entre la corteza terrestre y el núcleo

matter (MAT·er) anything that has mass and takes up space (142)
materia cualquier cosa que tiene masa y ocupa un lugar en el espacio

mesosphere (MEZ·uh·sfir) the strong, lower part of the mantle between the asthenosphere and the outer core (196)
mesosfera la parte fuerte e inferior del manto que se encuentra entre la astenosfera y el núcleo externo

metamorphic rock (met·uh·MOHR·fik RAHK) a rock that forms from other rocks as a result of intense heat, pressure, or chemical processes (158)
roca metamórfica una roca que se forma a partir de otras rocas como resultado de calor intenso, presión o procesos químicos

mineral (MIN·er·uhl) a natural, usually inorganic solid that has a characteristic chemical composition and an orderly internal structure (142)
mineral un sólido natural, normalmente inorgánico, que tiene una composición química característica y una estructura interna ordenada

mudflow (MUHD·floh) the flow of a mass of mud or rock and soil mixed with a large amount of water (53)
flujo de lodo el flujo de una masa de lodo o roca y suelo mezclados con una gran cantidad de agua

oxidation (ahk·sih·DAY·shuhn) a chemical reaction in which a material combines with oxygen to form new material; in geology, oxidation is a form of chemical weathering (24)
oxidación una reacción química en la que un material se combina con oxígeno para formar un material nuevo; en geología, la oxidación es una forma de desgaste químico

P–Q

Pangaea (pan·JEE·uh) the supercontinent that formed 300 million years ago and that began to break up 200 million years ago (203)
Pangea el supercontinente que se formó hace 300 millones de años y que comenzó a separarse hace 200 millones de años

physical weathering (FIZ·ih·kuhl WETH·er·ing) the mechanical breakdown of rocks into smaller pieces that is caused by natural processes and that does not change the chemical composition of the rock material (20)
desgaste físico el rompimiento mecánico de una roca en pedazos más pequeños que ocurre por procesos naturales y que no modifica la composición química del material rocoso

plate tectonics (PLAYT tek·TAHN·iks) the theory that explains how large pieces of Earth's outermost layer, called tectonic plates, move and change shape (206)
tectónica de placas la teoría que explica cómo se mueven y cambian de forma las placas tectónicas, que son grandes porciones de la capa más externa de la Tierra

R

radioactive decay (ray·dee·oh·AK·tiv dee·KAY) the process in which a radioactive isotope tends to break down into a stable isotope of the same element or another element (108)
desintegración radiactiva el proceso por medio del cual un isótopo radiactivo tiende a desintegrarse y formar un isótopo estable del mismo elemento o de otro elemento

radiometric dating (ray·dee·oh·MET·rik DAYT·ing) a method of determining the absolute age of an object by comparing the relative percentages of a radioactive (parent) isotope and a stable (daughter) isotope (109)
datación radiométrica un método para determinar la edad absoluta de un objeto comparando los porcentajes relativos de un isótopo radiactivo (precursor) y un isótopo estable (hijo)

relative dating (REL·uh·tiv DAYT·ing) any method of determining whether an event or object is older or younger than other events or objects (94)
datación relativa cualquier método que se utiliza para determinar si un acontecimiento u objeto es más viejo o más joven que otros acontecimientos u objetos

rift zone (RIFT ZOHN) an area of deep cracks that forms between two tectonic plates that are pulling away from each other (162)
zona de rift un área de grietas profundas que se forma entre dos placas tectónicas que se están alejando una de la otra

rock (RAHK) a naturally occurring solid mixture of one or more minerals or organic matter (172)
roca una mezcla sólida de uno o más minerales o de materia orgánica que se produce de forma natural

rock cycle (RAHK SY·kuhl) the series of processes in which rock forms, changes from one type to another, is broken down or melted, and forms again by geologic processes (160)
ciclo de las rocas la serie de procesos por medio de los cuales una roca se forma, cambia de un tipo a otro, se destruye o funde y se forma nuevamente por procesos geológicos

rockfall (RAHK·fawl) the rapid mass movement of rock down a steep slope or cliff (53)
desprendimiento de rocas el movimiento rápido y masivo de rocas por una pendiente empinada o un precipicio

S

sandbar (SAND·bar) a low ridge of sand deposited along the shore of a lake or sea (38)
barra de arena un arrecife bajo de arena depositado a lo largo de la orilla de un lago o del mar

sea-floor spreading (SEE·flohr SPRED·ing) the process by which new oceanic lithosphere (sea floor) forms when magma rises to Earth's surface at mid-ocean ridges and solidifies, as older, existing sea floor moves away from the ridge (204)
expansión del suelo marino el proceso por medio del cual se forma nueva litósfera oceánica (suelo marino) cuando el magma sube a la superficie de la Tierra en las dorsales oceánicas y se solidifica, a medida que el antiguo suelo marino existente se aleja de la dorsal oceánica

sedimentary rock (sed·uh·MEN·tuh·ree RAHK) a rock that forms from compressed or cemented layers of sediment (158)
roca sedimentaria una roca que se forma a partir de capas comprimidas o cementadas de sedimento

seismic wave (SYZ·mik WAYV) a wave of energy that travels through Earth and away from an earthquake in all directions (255)
onda sísmica una onda de energía que viaja a través de la Tierra y se aleja de un terremoto en todas direcciones

seismogram (SYZ·muh·gram) a tracing of earthquake motion that is recorded by a seismograph (258)
sismograma una traza del movimiento de un terremoto registrada por un sismógrafo

shear stress (SHIR STRES) stress that occurs when forces act in parallel but opposite directions, pushing parts of a solid in opposite directions (220)
tensión de corte el estrés que se produce cuando dos fuerzas actúan en direcciones paralelas pero opuestas, lo que empuja las partes de un sólido en direcciones opuestas

shoreline (SHOHR·lyn) the boundary between land and a body of water (35)
orilla el límite entre la tierra y una masa de agua

soil (SOYL) a loose mixture of rock fragments, organic material, water, and air that can support the growth of vegetation (58)
suelo una mezcla suelta de fragmentos de roca, material orgánico, agua y aire en la que puede crecer vegetación

soil horizon (SOYL huh·RY·zuhn) each layer of soil within a soil profile (61)
horizonte del suelo una de las capas en que se divide el perfil del suelo; tiene características bien definidas, es relativamente uniforme y se encuentra casi paralela a la superficie terrestre

soil profile (SOYL PROH·fyl) a vertical section of soil that shows the layers, or horizons (61)
perfil del suelo una sección vertical de suelo que muestra las capas u horizontes

streak (STREEK) the color of a mineral in powdered form (148)
veta el color de un mineral en forma de polvo

subsidence (suhb·SYD·ns) the sinking of regions of Earth's crust to lower elevations (162)
hundimiento del terreno el hundimiento de regiones de la corteza terrestre a elevaciones más bajas

superposition (soo·per·puh·ZISH·uhn) a principle that states that younger rocks lie above older rocks if the layers have not been disturbed (95)
superposición un principio que establece que las rocas más jóvenes se encontrarán sobre las rocas más viejas si las capas no han sido alteradas

T

tectonic plate (tek·TAHN·ik PLAYT) a block of lithosphere that consists of the crust and the rigid, outermost part of the mantle (206, 231)
placa tectónica un bloque de litosfera formado por la corteza y la parte rígida y más externa del manto

tectonic plate boundary (tek·TAHN·ik PLAYT BOWN·duh·ree) the edge between two or more plates, classified as divergent, convergent, or transform by the movement taking place between the plates (241)
límite de placa tectónica el borde entre dos o más placas clasificado como divergente, convergente o transformante por el movimiento que se produce entre las placas

tension (TEN·shuhn) stress that occurs when forces act to stretch an object (221)
tensión estrés que se produce cuando distintas fuerzas actúan para estirar un objeto

texture (TEKS·cher) the quality of a rock that is based on the sizes, shapes, and positions of the rock's grains (173)
textura la cualidad de una roca que se basa en el tamaño, la forma y la posición de los granos que la forman

trace fossil (TRAYS FAHS·uhl) a fossilized structure, such as a footprint or a coprolite, that formed in sedimentary rock by animal activity on or within soft sediment (83)
fósil traza una estructura fosilizada, como una huella o un coprolito, que se formó en una roca sedimentaria por la actividad de un animal sobre sedimento blando o dentro de éste

transform boundary (TRANS·fohrm BOWN·duh·ree) the boundary between tectonic plates that are sliding past each other horizontally (209)
límite de transformación el límite entre placas tectónicas que se están deslizando horizontalmente una sobre otra

U

unconformity (uhn·kuhn·FOHR·mih·tee) a break in the geologic record created when rock layers are eroded or when sediment is not deposited for a long period of time (97)
disconformidad una ruptura en el registro geológico, creada cuando las capas de roca se erosionan o cuando el sedimento no se deposita durante un largo período de tiempo

uniformitarianism (yoo·nuh·fohr·mih·TAIR·ee·uh·niz·uhm) a principle that geologic processes that occurred in the past can be explained by current geologic processes (80)
uniformitarianismo un principio que establece que es posible explicar los procesos geológicos que ocurrieron en el pasado en función de los procesos geológicos actuales

uplift (UHP·lift) the rising of regions of Earth's crust to higher elevations (162)
levantamiento la elevación de regiones de la corteza terrestre a elevaciones más altas

vent (VENT) an opening at the surface of Earth through which volcanic material passes (228)
chimenea una abertura en la superficie de la Tierra a través de la cual pasa material volcánico

volcano (vahl·KAY·noh) a vent or fissure in Earth's surface through which magma and gases are expelled (228)
volcán una chimenea o fisura en la superficie de la Tierra a través de la cual se expulsan magma y gases

W-Z

weathering (WETH·er·ing) the natural process by which atmospheric and environmental agents, such as wind, rain, and temperature changes, disintegrate and decompose rocks (20, 157)
meteorización el proceso natural por medio del cual los agentes atmosféricos o ambientales, como el viento, la lluvia y los cambios de temperatura, desintegran y descomponen las rocas

State STANDARDS FOR ENGLISH LANGUAGE ARTS

Correlations

This table shows correlations to the *Reading Standards for Literacy in Science and Technical Subjects* for grades 6–8.

Go online at thinkcentral.com for correlations of all *ScienceFusion* Modules to Common Core State Standards for Mathematics and to the rest of the *Common Core State Standards for English Language Arts*.

Grade 6–8 Standard Code	Citations for Module K "Introduction to Science and Technology"
READING STANDARDS FOR LITERACY IN SCIENCE AND TECHNICAL SUBJECTS	
Key Ideas and Details	
RST.6–8.1 Cite specific textual evidence to support analysis of science and technical texts.	*Student Edition* pp. 25, 75, 113 *Teacher Edition* pp. 98, 117
RST.6–8.2 Determine the central ideas or conclusions of a text; provide an accurate summary of the text distinct from prior knowledge or opinions.	*Student Edition* pp. 25, 32, 60, 75, 113, 132, 137, 149, 157, 163, 171, 189 *Teacher Edition* pp. 17, 21, 22, 35, 51, 61, 62, 98, 106, 117, 128, 130, 161, 178, 179, 206, 213, 237, 240. Also use "Synthesizing Key Topics" items in the Extend Science Concepts sections of the Teacher Edition.
RST.6–8.3 Follow precisely a multistep procedure when carrying out experiments, taking measurements, or performing technical tasks.	*Student Edition* pp. 83, 90–91 *Teacher Edition* p. 94 *Other* Use the Lab Manual, Project-Based Assessments, Video-Based Projects, and the Virtual Labs.
Craft and Structure	
RST.6–8.4 Determine the meaning of symbols, key terms, and other domain-specific words and phrases as they are used in a specific scientific or technical context relevant to *grades 6–8 texts and topics.*	*Student Edition* pp. 5, 17, 31, 43, 63, 64, 77, 93, 115, 131, 141, 153, 169, 181 *Teacher Edition* p. 111. Also use "Previewing Vocabulary" and "Reinforcing Vocabulary" items in the Explain Science Concepts sections of the Teacher Edition.

Grade 6–8 Standard Code (continued)	Citations for Module K "Introduction to Science and Technology"
RST.6–8.5 Analyze the structure an author uses to organize a text, including how the major sections contribute to the whole and to an understanding of the topic.	*Student Edition* p. 75 *Teacher Edition* pp. 51, 128, 213, 237, 240
RST.6–8.6 Analyze the author's purpose in providing an explanation, describing a procedure, or discussing an experiment in a text.	*Student Edition* pp. 25, 75 *Teacher Edition* pp. 14, 47, 98
Integration of Knowledge and Ideas	
RST.6–8.7 Integrate quantitative or technical information expressed in words in a text with a version of that information expressed visually (e.g., in a flowchart, diagram, model, graph, or table).	*Student Edition* pp. 3, 35, 54, 66–67, 81, 122–123, 144, 147, 158, 159 *Teacher Edition* pp. 21, 40, 53, 54, 123, 194, 201, 206, 208, 224, 237, 240. Also use the "Graphic Organizer" items in the Teacher Edition. *Other* Use the lessons in the Digital Path.
RST.6–8.8 Distinguish among facts, reasoned judgment based on research findings, and speculation in a text.	*Student Edition* pp. 13, 25, 74–75, 113 *Teacher Edition* pp. 14, 17, 98
RST.6–8.9 Compare and contrast the information gained from experiments, simulations, video, or multimedia sources with that gained from reading a text on the same topic.	*Student Edition* pp. 113, 137, 163 *Teacher Edition* pp. 40, 79, 117 *Other* Use the Lab Manual, Project-Based Assessments, Video-Based Projects, and the lessons in the Digital Path.
Range of Reading and Level of Text Complexity	
RST.6–8.10 By the end of grade 8, read and comprehend science/technical texts in the grades 6–8 text complexity band independently and proficiently.	*Student Edition* pp. 3, 22, 75, 90, 113, 132, 137, 149, 157, 163, 171, 189. Also use all lessons in the Student Edition. *Teacher Edition* pp. 47, 48, 61, 62, 117

Science Trade Books

Bibliography

This bibliography is a compilation of trade books that can supplement the materials covered in *ScienceFusion* Grades 6–8. Many of the books are recommendations of the National Science Teachers Association (NSTA) and the Children's Book Council (CBC) as outstanding science trade books for children. These books were selected because they meet the following rigorous criteria: they are of literary quality and contain substantial science content; the theories and facts are clearly distinguished; they are free of gender, ethnic, and socioeconomic bias; and they contain clear, accurate, up-to-date information. Several selections are award-winning titles, or their authors have received awards.

As with all materials you share with your class, we suggest you review the books first to ensure their appropriateness. While titles are current at time of publication, they may go out of print without notice.

Grades 6–8

Acids and Bases (Material Matters/ Express Edition) by Carol Baldwin (Heinemann-Raintree, 2005) focuses on the properties of acids and bases with photographs and facts.

Acids and Bases by Eurona Earl Tilley (Chelsea House, 2008) provides a thorough, basic understanding of acid and base chemistry, including such topics as naming compounds, writing formulas, and physical and chemical properties.

Across the Wide Ocean: The Why, How, and Where of Navigation for Humans and Animals at Sea by Karen Romano Young (Greenwillow, 2007) focuses on navigational tools, maps, and charts that researchers and explorers use to learn more about oceanography. AWARD-WINNING AUTHOR

Adventures in Sound with Max Axiom, Super Scientist (Graphic Science Series) by Emily Sohn (Capstone, 2007) provides information about sound through a fun graphic novel.

Air: A Resource Our World Depends on (Managing Our Resources) by Ian Graham (Heinemann-Raintree, 2005) examines this valuable natural resource and answers questions such as "How much does Earth's air weigh?" and "Why do plants need wind?"

The Alkaline Earth Metals: Beryllium, Magnesium, Calcium, Strontium, Barium, Radium (Understanding the Elements of the Periodic Table) by Bridget Heos (Rosen Central, 2009) describes the characteristics of these metals, including their similar physical and molecular properties.

All About Light and Sound (Mission: Science) by Connie Jankowski (Compass Point, 2010) focuses on the importance of light and sound and how without them we could not survive.

Alternative Energy: Beyond Fossil Fuels by Dana Meachen Rau (Compass Point, 2010) discusses the ways that water, wind, and sun provide a promising solution to our energy crisis and encourages readers to help the planet by conserving energy. AWARD-WINNING AUTHOR

Amazing Biome Projects You Can Build Yourself (Build it Yourself Series) by Donna Latham (Nomad, 2009) provides an overview of eight terrestrial biomes, including characteristics about climate, soil, animals, and plants.

Archaea: Salt-Lovers, Methane-Makers, Thermophiles, and Other Archaeans (A Class of Their Own) by David M. Barker (Crabtree, 2010) provides interesting facts about different types of archaeans.

The Art of Construction: Projects and Principles for Beginning Engineers and Architects by Mario Salvadori (Chicago Review, 2000) explains how tents, houses, stadiums, and bridges are built, and how to build models of such structures using materials found around the house. AWARD-WINNING AUTHOR

Astronomy: Out of This World! by Simon Basher and Dan Green (Kingfisher, 2009) takes readers on a journey of the universe and provides information about the planets, stars, galaxies, telescopes, space missions, and discoveries.

At the Sea Floor Café: Odd Ocean Critter Poems by Leslie Bulion (Peachtree, 2011) provides poetry to educate students about how ocean creatures search for food, capture prey, protect their young, and trick their predators.

Battery Science: Make Widgets That Work and Gadgets That Go by Doug Stillinger (Klutz, 2003) offers an array of activities and gadgets to get students excited about electricity.

The Biggest Explosions in the Universe by Sara Howard (BookSurge, 2009) tells the story of stars in our universe through fun text and captivating photographs.

Biology: Life as We Know It! by Simon Basher and Dan Green (Kingfisher, 2008) offers information about all aspects of life from the animals and plants to the minuscule cells, proteins, and DNA that bring them to life.

Birds of a Feather by Jane Yolen (Boyds Mills Press, 2011) offers facts and information about birds through fun poetry and beautiful photographs. AWARD-WINNING AUTHOR

Blackout!: Electricity and Circuits (Fusion) by Anna Claybourne (Heinemann-Raintree, 2005) provides an array of facts about electricity and how we rely on it for so many things in everyday life. AWARD-WINNING AUTHOR

Cell Division and Genetics by Robert Snedden (Heinemann, 2007) explains various aspects of cells and the living world, including what happens when cells divide and how characteristics are passed on from one generation to another. AWARD-WINNING AUTHOR

Chemistry: Getting a Big Reaction by Dan Green and Simon Basher (Kingfisher, 2010) acts as a guide about the chemical "characters" that fizz, react, and combine to make up everything around us.

Cool Stuff Exploded by Chris Woodford (Dorling Kindersley, 2008) focuses on today's technological marvels and tomorrow's jaw-dropping devices. OUTSTANDING SCIENCE TRADE BOOK

Disaster Deferred: How New Science Is Changing Our View of Earthquake Hazards in the Midwest by Seth Stein (Columbia University, 2010) discusses technological innovations that make earthquake prediction possible.

The Diversity of Species (Timeline: Life on Earth) by Michael Bright (Heinemann, 2008) explains how and why things on Earth have genetic and physical differences and how they have had and continue to have an impact on Earth.

Drip! Drop!: How Water Gets to Your Tap by Barbara Seuling (Holiday House, 2000) introduces students to JoJo and her dog, Willy, who explain the water cycle and introduce fun experiments about filtration, evaporation, and condensation. AWARD-WINNING AUTHOR

Eat Fresh Food: Awesome Recipes for Teen Chefs by Rozanne Gold (Bloomsbury, 2009) includes more than 80 recipes and places a strong emphasis on fresh foods throughout the book.

Eco-Tracking: On the Trail of Habitat Change (Worlds of Wonder) by Daniel Shaw (University of New Mexico, 2010) recounts success stories of young people involved in citizen science efforts and encourages others to join in to preserve nature's ecosystems.

Electric Mischief: Battery-Powered Gadgets Kids Can Build by Alan Bartholomew (Kids Can Press, 2002) offers a variety of fun projects that include making battery connections and switches and building gadgets such as electric dice and a bumper car.

Electricity (Why It Works) by Anna Claybourne (QED Publishing, 2008) provides information about electricity in an easy-to-follow manner. AWARD-WINNING AUTHOR

Electricity and Magnetism (Usborne Understand Science) by Peter Adamczyk (Usborne, 2008) explains the basics about electricity and magnetism, including information about static electricity, electric circuits, and electromagnetism.

Energy Transfers (Energy Essentials) by Nigel Saunders and Steven Chapman (Raintree, 2005) explains the different types of energy, how they can change, and how different forms of energy help us in our everyday lives.

The Everything Machine by Matt Novak (Roaring Brook, 2009) tells the silly story of a machine that does everything for a group of people until they wake up one day and discover that the machine has stopped working. AWARD-WINNING AUTHOR

Experiments with Plants and Other Living Things by Trevor Cook (PowerKids, 2009) provides fun, hands-on experiments to teach students about flowers, plants, and biology.

Exploring the Oceans: Seafloor by John Woodward (Heinemann, 2004) takes readers on a virtual tour through the bottom part of the ocean, highlighting the plants and animals that thrive in this environment.

Extreme Structures: Mega Constructions of the 21st Century (Science Frontiers) by David Jefferis (Crabtree, 2006) takes a look at how some of the coolest buildings in the world were built and what other kinds of structures are being planned for the future. AWARD-WINNING AUTHOR

Fascinating Science Projects: Electricity and Magnetism by Bobbi Searle (Aladdin, 2002) teaches the concepts of electricity and magnetism through dozens of projects and experiments and color illustrations.

Fizz, Bubble and Flash!: Element Explorations and Atom Adventures for Hands-on Science Fun! by Anita Brandolini, Ph.D. (Williamson, 2003) introduces chemistry to students in a nonintimidating way and focuses on the elements and the periodic table. PARENTS' CHOICE

Floods: Hazards of Surface and Groundwater Systems (The Hazardous Earth) by Timothy M. Kusky (Facts on File, 2008) explores the processes that control the development and flow in river and stream systems and when these processes become dangerous.

Fossils (Geology Rocks!) by Rebecca Faulkner (Raintree, 2008) educates students about rock formation and the processes and characteristics of rocks and fossils.

Friends: True Stories of Extraordinary Animal Friendships by Catherine Thimmesh (Houghton Mifflin Harcourt, 2011) depicts true stories of unlikely animal friendships, including a wild polar bear and a sled dog as well as a camel and a Vietnamese pig. AWARD-WINNING AUTHOR

The Frog Scientist (Scientists in the Field) by Pamela S. Turner (Houghton Mifflin Harcourt, 2009) follows a scientist and his protégés as they research the effects of atrazine-contaminated water on vulnerable amphibians. BOOKLIST EDITORS' CHOICE

From Steam Engines to Nuclear Fusion: Discovering Energy (Chain Reactions) by Carol Ballard (Heinemann-Raintree, 2007) tells the fascinating story of energy, from the heat produced by a simple fire to the extraordinary power contained in an atom.

Fully Charged (Everyday Science) by Steve Parker (Heinemann-Raintree, 2005) explains how electricity is generated, harnessed, and used and also the difference between electricity, including static electricity, and electronics. AWARD-WINNING AUTHOR

Galileo for Kids: His Life and Ideas by Richard Panchyk (Chicago Review, 2005) includes experiments that demonstrate scientific principles developed by the astronomer Galileo.

Genes and DNA by Richard Walker (Kingfisher, 2003) offers an abundance of information about characteristics of genes, gene function, DNA technology, and genetic engineering, as well as other fascinating topics. NSTA TRADE BOOK; OUTSTANDING SCIENCE TRADE BOOK

Hands-on Science Series: Simple Machines by Steven Souza and Joseph Shortell (Walch, 2001) investigates the concepts of work, force, power, efficiency, and mechanical advantage.

How Animals Work by David Burnie (Dorling Kindersley, 2010) provides vivid photographs and intriguing text to describe various animals and their characteristics, diets, and families. AWARD-WINNING AUTHOR

How Does an Earthquake Become a Tsunami? (How Does it Happen?) by Linda Tagliaferro (Heinemann-Raintree, 2009) describes the changes in water, waves, and tides that occur between an earthquake and a tsunami. AWARD-WINNING AUTHOR

How the Future Began: Machines by Clive Gifford (Kingfisher, 1999) acts as a guide to historical and current developments in the field of machinery, including mass production, computers, robots, microengineering, and communications technology. AWARD-WINNING AUTHOR

How Scientists Work (Simply Science) by Natalie M. Rosinsky (Compass Point, 2003) discusses the scientific method, equipment, and procedures and also describes how scientists compile information and answer questions.

How to Clean a Hippopotamus: A Look at Unusual Animal Partnerships by Steve Jenkins and Robin Page (Houghton Mifflin Harcourt, 2010) explores animal symbiosis with fun illustrations and a close-up, step-by-step view of some of nature's most fascinating animal partnerships. ALA NOTABLE BOOK

Human Spaceflight (Frontiers in Space) by Joseph A. Angelo (Facts on File, 2007) examines the history of space exploration and the evolution of space technology from the dawn of the space age to the present time.

The Hydrosphere: Agent of Change by Gregory L. Vogt, Ed.D. (Twenty-First Century, 2006) discusses the impact this 20-mile-thick sphere has had on the surface of the planet and the processes that go on there, including the ability of Earth to sustain life. AWARD-WINNING AUTHOR

In Rivers, Lakes, and Ponds (Under the Microscope) by Sabrina Crewe (Chelsea Clubhouse, 2010) educates readers about the microscopic critters that live in these various bodies of water.

A Kid's Guide to Climate Change and Global Warming: How to Take Action! by Cathryn Berger Kaye, M.A. (Free Spirit, 2009) encourages students to learn about the climate changes happening around the world and to get involved to help save our planet.

Lasers (Lucent Library of Science and Technology) by Don Nardo (Lucent, 2003) discusses the scientific discovery and development of lasers—high-intensity light—and their use in our daily lives. AWARD-WINNING AUTHOR

Leonardo's Horse by Jean Fritz (Putnam, 2001) tells the story of Leonardo da Vinci—the curious and inquisitive artist, engineer, and astronomer—who created a detailed horse sculpture for the city of Milan. ALA NOTABLE BOOK; NOTABLE SOCIAL STUDIES TRADE BOOK; NOTABLE CHILDREN'S BOOK IN THE LANGUAGE ARTS

Light: From Sun to Bulbs by Christopher Cooper (Heinemann, 2003) invites students to investigate the dazzling world of physical science and light through fun experiments. AWARD-WINNING AUTHOR

Magnetism and Electromagnets (Sci-Hi: Physical Science) by Eve Hartman (Raintree, 2008) offers colorful illustrations, photographs, quizzes, charts, graphs, and text to teach students about magnetism.

Making Good Choices About Nonrenewable Resources (Green Matters) by Paula Johanson (Rosen Central, 2009) focuses on the different types of nonrenewable natural resources, alternative resources, conservation, and making positive consumer choices.

Making Waves: Sound (Everyday Science) by Steve Parker (Heinemann-Raintree, 2005) describes what sound is, how it is formed and used, and properties associated with sound, such as pitch, speed, and volume. AWARD-WINNING AUTHOR

The Manatee Scientists: Saving Vulnerable Species (Scientists in the Field Series) by Peter Lourie (Houghton Mifflin Harcourt, 2011) discusses three species of manatees and the importance of preserving these mammals. AWARD-WINNING AUTHOR

The Man Who Named the Clouds by Julie Hannah and Joan Holub (Albert Whitman, 2006) tells the story of 18th-century English meteorologist Luke Howard and also discusses the ten classifications of clouds.

Medicine in the News (Science News Flash) by Brian R. Shmaefsky, Ph.D. (Chelsea House, 2007) focuses on medical advancements that are in the news today and the innovative tools that are used for diagnosis and treatment.

Metals and Metalloids (Periodic Table of the Elements) by Monica Halka, Ph.D., and Brian Nordstrom, Ed.D. (Facts on File, 2010), offers information about the physics, chemistry, geology, and biology of metals and metalloids.

Meteorology: Ferguson's Careers in Focus by Ferguson (Ferguson, 2011) profiles 18 different careers pertaining to the science of the atmosphere and its phenomena.

The Microscope (Great Medical Discoveries) by Adam Woog (Lucent, 2003) recounts how the microscope has had an impact on the history of medicine.

Microscopes and Telescopes: Great Inventions by Rebecca Stefoff (Marshall Cavendish Benchmark, 2007) describes the origin, history, development, and societal impact of the telescope and microscope. OUTSTANDING SCIENCE TRADE BOOK

Mighty Animal Cells by Rebecca L. Johnson (Millbrook, 2007) takes readers on a journey to discover how people and animals grow from just one single cell. AWARD-WINNING AUTHOR

Moon (Eyewitness Books) by Jacqueline Mitton (Dorling Kindersley, 2009) offers information about our planet's mysterious nearest neighbor, from the moon's waterless seas and massive craters to its effect on Earth's ocean tides and its role in solar eclipses. AWARD-WINNING AUTHOR

MP3 Players (Let's Explore Technology Communications) by Jeanne Sturm (Rourke, 2010) discusses the technological advances in music in our society.

Nanotechnologist (Cool Science Careers) by Ann Heinrichs (Cherry Lake, 2009) provides information about nanotechnologists—scientists who work with materials on a subatomic or atomic level.

Ocean: An Illustrated Atlas by Sylvia A. Earle (National Geographic, 2008) provides an overview on the ocean as a whole, each of the major ocean basins, and the future of the oceans. AWARD-WINNING AUTHOR

Oceans (Insiders) by Beverly McMillan and John A. Musick (Simon & Schuster, 2007) takes readers on a 3-D journey of the aquatic universe—exploring the formation of waves and tsunamis as well as the plant and animal species that live beneath the ocean's surface.

Organic Chemistry and Biochemistry (Facts at Your Fingertips) by Graham Bateman (Brown Bear, 2011) provides diagrams, experiments, and testing aids to teach students the basics about organic chemistry and biochemistry.

An Overcrowded World?: Our Impact on the Planet (21st Century Debates) by Rob Bowden (Heinemann, 2002) investigates how and why the world's population is growing so fast, the effects of this growth on wildlife and habitats, and the pressure on resources, and suggests ways of controlling growth.

The Pebble in My Pocket: A History of Our Earth by Meredith Hooper (Viking, 1996) follows the course of a pebble, beginning 480 million years ago, through a fiery volcano and primordial forest and along the icy bottom of a glacier and how it looks today as the result of its journey. AWARD-WINNING AUTHOR

The Periodic Table: Elements with Style! by Simon Basher and Adrian Dingle (Kingfisher, 2007) offers information about the different elements that make up the periodic table and their features and characteristics.

Phenomena: Secrets of the Senses by Donna M. Jackson (Little, Brown, 2008) focuses on the senses and how to interpret them and discusses ways that technology is changing how we experience the world around us. AWARD-WINNING AUTHOR

Pioneers of Light and Sound (Mission: Science) by Connie Jankowski (Compass Point, 2010) focuses on various scientists and their accomplishments and achievements.

Planet Animal: Saving Earth's Disappearing Animals by B. Taylor (Barron's, 2009) focuses on the planet's most endangered animals, their relationships to the environment, and steps that are being taken to try to save these animals from extinction.

Plant and Animal Science Fair Projects (Biology Science Projects Using the Scientific Method) by Yael Calhoun (Enslow, 2010) provides an array of experiments about plants and animals and describes the importance of the scientific method, forming a hypothesis, and recording data for any given project.

Plant Secrets: Plant Life Processes by Anna Claybourne (Heinemann-Raintree, 2005) includes informative text, vivid photographs, and detailed charts about characteristics of various plants. AWARD-WINNING AUTHOR

Polar Regions: Human Impacts (Our Fragile Planet) by Dana Desonie (Chelsea House, 2008) focuses on pollutants and global warming in the Arctic and Antarctic and future dangers that will occur if our planet continues on its current path.

Potato Clocks and Solar Cars: Renewable and Non-renewable Energy by Elizabeth Raum (Raintree, 2007) explores various topics, including alternative energy sources, fossil fuels, and sustainable energy.

The Power of Pressure (How Things Work) by Andrew Dunn (Thomson Learning, 1993) explains how water pressure and air work and how they are used in machines.

Protists and Fungi (Discovery Channel School Science) by Katie King and Jacqueline A. Ball (Gareth Stevens, 2003) focuses on the appearance, behavior, and characteristics of various protists and fungi, using examples of algae, mold, and mushrooms.

Protozoans, Algae and Other Protists by Steve Parker (Compass Point, 2010) introduces readers to the parts, life cycles, and reproduction of various types of protists, from microscopic protozoans to seaweedlike algae, and some of the harmful effects protists have on humans. AWARD-WINNING AUTHOR

Sally Ride: The First American Woman in Space by Tom Riddolls (Crabtree, 2010) focuses on the growth and impact of Sally Ride Science—an educational program founded by the astronaut to encourage girls to pursue hobbies and careers in science.

Science and Technology in 20th Century American Life by Christopher Cumo (Greenwood, 2008) takes readers on a history of technology from agricultural implements through modern computers, telecommunications, and skateboards.

Sedimentary Rock (Geology Rocks!) by Rebecca Faulkner (Raintree, 2008) educates students about rock formation and the processes and characteristics of sedimentary rock.

Shaping the Earth by Dorothy Hinshaw Patent (Clarion/Houghton Mifflin, 2000) combines vivid photographs with informative text to explain the forces that have created the geological features on Earth's surface. AWARD-WINNING AUTHOR

Silent Spring by Rachel Carson (Houghton Mifflin, 2002) celebrates marine biologist and environmental activist Rachel Carson's contribution to Earth through an array of essays.

Skywalkers: Mohawk Ironworkers Build the City by David Weitzman (Flash Point, 2010) focuses on the ironworkers who constructed bridges and skyscrapers in New York and Canada. AWARD-WINNING AUTHOR

Sustaining Earth's Energy Resources (Environment at Risk) by Ann Heinrichs (Marshall Cavendish, 2010) offers information on Earth's sources of nonrenewable and renewable energy, how they are used, and their disadvantages and benefits.

Team Moon: How 400,000 People Landed Apollo 11 on the Moon by Catherine Thimmesh (Houghton Mifflin, 2006) tells the story of the first moon landing and celebrates the dedication, ingenuity, and perseverance of the people who made this event happen. ALA NOTABLE BOOK; ORBIS PICTUS HONOR; NOTABLE CHILDREN'S BOOK IN THE LANGUAGE ARTS; ALA BEST BOOK FOR YOUNG ADULTS; GOLDEN KITE HONOR

The Top of the World: Climbing Mount Everest by Steve Jenkins (Houghton Mifflin, 1999) describes the conditions and terrain of Mount Everest, attempts that have been made to scale this peak, and information about the equipment and techniques of mountain climbing. ALA NOTABLE BOOK; SLJ BEST BOOK; BOSTON GLOBE–HORN BOOK AWARD; ORBIS PICTUS HONOR

Transmission of Power by Fluid Pressure: Air and Water by William Donaldson (Nabu, 2010) describes the transmission of fluid pressure as it pertains to the elements of air and water in the world of motion, forces, and energy.

Tsunami: The True Story of an April Fools' Day Disaster by Gail Langer Karwoski (Darby Creek, 2006) offers a variety of viewpoints about the wave that struck Hawaii in 1946. NOTABLE SOCIAL STUDIES TRADE BOOK

Vapor, Rain, and Snow: The Science of Clouds and Precipitation (Weatherwise) by Paul Fleisher (Lerner, 2010) answers an array of questions about water, such as "How does a cloud form?" and "Why do ice cubes shrink in the freezer?" AWARD-WINNING AUTHOR

Water Supplies in Crisis (Planet in Crisis) by Russ Parker (Rosen Central, 2009) describes a world where safe drinking water is not readily available, polluted water brings disease, and lakes are disappearing.

Weird Meat-Eating Plants (Bizarre Science) by Nathan Aaseng (Enslow, 2011) provides information about a variety of carnivorous plants, reversing the food chain's usual order. AWARD-WINNING AUTHOR

What Are Igneous Rocks? (Let's Rock!) by Molly Aloian (Crabtree, 2010) explains how granite, basalt, lava, silica, and quartz are formed after hot molten rock cools.

What's Living Inside Your Body? by Andrew Solway (Heinemann, 2004) offers information about an array of viruses, germs, and parasites that thrive inside the human body.

Why Should I Bother to Keep Fit? (What's Happening?) by Kate Knighton and Susan Meredith (Usborne, 2009) motivates students to get fit and stay fit.

The World of Microbes: Bacteria, Viruses, and Other Microorganisms (Understanding Genetics) by Janey Levy (Rosen Classroom, 2010) describes the world of microbes, a history of microbiology, and the characteristics of both harmful and beneficial bacteria.

Written in Bone: Buried Lives of Jamestown and Colonial Maryland by Sally M. Walker (Carolrhoda, 2009) describes the way that scientists used forensic anthropology to investigate colonial-era graves near Jamestown, Virginia. ALA NOTABLE BOOK; OUTSTANDING SCIENCE TRADE BOOK; NOTABLE SOCIAL STUDIES TRADE BOOK

You Blink Twelve Times a Minute and Other Freaky Facts About the Human Body by Barbara Seuling (Picture Window, 2009) provides fun and unusual facts about various ailments, medical marvels, and body parts and their functions. AWARD-WINNING AUTHOR

Correction to

ScienceSaurus

ScienceSaurus, ***A Student Handbook,*** is a "mini-encyclopedia" that students can use to find out more about unit topics. It contains numerous resources including concise content summaries, an almanac, many tables, charts, and graphs, history of science, and a glossary. ***ScienceSaurus*** is available from Houghton Mifflin Harcourt..

ScienceFusion Page References	Topics	*ScienceFusion* Grades 6-8
Scientific Investigation, pp. 1–19		
	Scientific Inquiry	Mod K, Unit 1, Lessons 1-3
		Mod K, Unit 2, Lessons 1, 3
	Designing Your Own Investigations	Mod K, Unit 1, Lessons 2, 4
Working in the Lab, pp. 20–72		
	Laboratory Safety	Mod K, Unit 2, Lesson 2
	Glassware and Microscopes	Mod K, Unit 2, Lesson 2
	Measurement	Mod K, Unit 2, Lesson 2
Life Science, pp. 73–164		
	Structure of Life	Mod A, Unit 1, Lessons 1-3
		Mod A, Unit 2, Lessons 1, 3
	Human Biology	Mod C, Unit 1, Lessons 1-6
		Mod C, Unit 2, Lesson 1
	Physiology and Behavior	Mod A, Unit 1, Lesson 5
		Mod B, Unit 2, Lessons 3-6
	Genes and Heredity	Mod A, Unit 2, Lessons 2-6
	Change and Diversity of Life	Mod B, Unit 1, Lessons 2-4

ScienceFusion Page References	Topics	*ScienceFusion* Grades 6-8
Life Science, pp. 73–164 (continued)		
	Ecosystems	Mod D, Unit 1, Lessons 1-4
		Mod D, Unit 2, Lessons 1-4
		Mod D, Unit 2, Lesson 5
	Classification	Mod B, Unit 1, Lesson 5
		Mod B, Unit 2, Lessons 3, 5
Earth Science, pp. 165–248		
	Geology	Mod E, Unit 4, Lesson 1
		Mod E, Unit 3, Lessons 1-3
		Mod E, Unit 4, Lessons 2-5
		Mod E, Unit 1, Lessons 2-4
		Mod E, Unit 2, Lessons 1-4
		Mod E, Unit 1, Lessons 3, 5
	Oceanography	Mod F, Unit 1, Lesson 1
		Mod F, Unit 2, Lessons 1, 3
	Meteorology	Mod F, Unit 3, Lesson 1
		Mod F, Unit 1, Lesson 2
		Mod F, Unit 4, Lesson 1, 2, 3, 6
	Astronomy	Mod G, Unit 3, Lessons 1-3
		Mod G, Unit 2, Lessons 2-6
		Mod G, Unit 1, Lessons 1-3
Physical Science, pp. 249–321		
	Matter	Mod H, Unit 1, Lessons 1-6
		Mod H, Unit 3, Lessons 1-4
		Mod H Unit 4, Lessons 1-3
		Mod H, Unit 5, Lessons 1-3

ScienceFusion Page References	Topics	*ScienceFusion* Grades 6-8
Physical Science, pp. 249–321 (continued)		
	Forces and Motion	Mod I, Unit 1, Lessons 1-5
		Mod I, Unit 2, Lessons 1-3
	Energy	Mod H, Unit 2, Lessons 1-4
		Mod I, Unit 3, Lessons 1-5
		Mod J, Unit 1, Lessons 1, 2
		Mod J, Unit 2, Lessons 1, 2
		Mod J, Unit 3, Lessons 1-4
Natural Resources and the Environment, pp. 322–353		
	Earth's Natural Resources	Mod D, Unit 3, Lessons 2-5
	Resource Conservation	Mod D, Unit 3, Lesson 5
	Solid Waste and Pollution	Mod D, Unit 4, Lessons 1-4 Mod F, Unit 4, Lesson 7
Science, Technology, and Society, pp. 354–373		
	Science and Technology	Mod A, Unit 2, Lesson 7
		Mod G, Unit 4, Lesson 2
		Mod I, Unit 3, Lesson 6
		Mod J, Unit 2, Lesson 3
		Mod J, Unit 3, Lesson 5
	Science and Society	Mod K, Unit 1, Lesson 4
		Mod K, Unit 3, Lesson 6

ScienceFusion Page References	Topics	*ScienceFusion* Grades 6-8
Almanac, pp. 374–438		
	Scientific Numbers	May be used with all units.
	Using Data Tables and Graphs	Mod K, Unit 2, Lesson 1
	Solving Math Problems in Science	May be used with all units.
	Classroom and Research Skills	May be used with all units.
	Test-Taking Skills	May be used with all units.
	References	May be used with all units.
Yellow Pages, pp. 439–524		
	History of Science Timeline	See People in Science features.
	Famous Scientists	See People in Science features.
	Greek and Latin Word Roots	Glossary
	Glossary of Scientific Terms	Glossary

Index

Key:

Teacher Edition page numbers follow the Student Edition page numbers and are printed in blue type.
Student Edition page numbers for highlighted definitions are printed in **boldface** type.
Student Edition page numbers for illustrations, maps, and charts are printed in *italics*.

Example:

Student Edition Pages | **Teacher Edition Pages**

atom, *352*, 352–355, 364–372, **367;** 355, 395, 397, 401, 443, 445

C

Key:

Teacher Edition page numbers follow the Student Edition page numbers and are printed in blue type.
Student Edition page numbers for highlighted definitions are printed in **boldface** type.
Student Edition page numbers for illustrations, maps, and charts are printed in *italics*.

Key:

Teacher Edition page numbers follow the Student Edition page numbers and are printed in blue type.
Student Edition page numbers for highlighted definitions are printed in **boldface** type.
Student Edition page numbers for illustrations, maps, and charts are printed in *italics*.

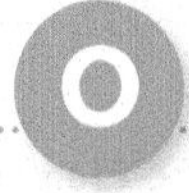

Key:

Teacher Edition page numbers follow the Student Edition page numbers and are printed in blue type.
Student Edition page numbers for highlighted definitions are printed in **boldface** type.
Student Edition page numbers for illustrations, maps, and charts are printed in *italics*.

Key:

Teacher Edition page numbers follow the Student Edition page numbers and are printed in blue type.
Student Edition page numbers for highlighted definitions are printed in **boldface** type.
Student Edition page numbers for illustrations, maps, and charts are printed in *italics*.